The Conceptual Mind

The Conceptual Mind

New Directions in the Study of Concepts

edited by Eric Margolis and Stephen Laurence

The MIT Press
Cambridge, Massachusetts
London, England

MIT Press books may be purchased at special quantity discounts for business or sales promotional use. For information, please email special_sales@mitpress.mit.edu.

This book was set in ITC Stone Serif Std 9/13pt by Toppan Best-set Premedia Limited, Hong Kong. Printed and bound in the United States of America.

Library of Congress Cataloging-in-Publication Data

The conceptual mind : new directions in the study of concepts / edited by Eric Margolis and Stephen Laurence.
      pages cm
Includes bibliographical references and index.
ISBN 978-0-262-02863-9 (hardcover : alk. paper)
1. Concepts. 2. Philosophy of mind. 3. Knowledge, Theory of. I. Margolis, Eric, 1968– II. Laurence, Stephen.
BD418.3.C64 2015
121'.4—dc23
2014034214

10 9 8 7 6 5 4 3 2 1

Contents

Contributors

Aurore Avarguès-Weber, Research Centre for Animal Cognition, CNRS–Université de Toulouse

Eef Ameel, Faculty of Psychology and Educational Sciences, University of Leuven

Megan Bang, College of Education, University of Washington

H. Clark Barrett, Department of Anthropology and Center for Behavior, Evolution, and Culture, UCLA

Pascal Boyer, Department of Anthropology and Department of Psychology, Washington University in St. Louis

Elisabeth Camp, Department of Philosophy, Rutgers University

Susan Carey, Department of Psychology, Harvard University

Daniel Casasanto, Department of Psychology, University of Chicago

Nicola S. Clayton, Department of Psychology, University of Cambridge

Dorothy L. Cheney, Department of Biology, University of Pennsylvania

Vyvyan Evans, School of Linguistics & English Language, Bangor University

Jerry A. Fodor, Department of Philosophy and Rutgers Center for Cognitive Science, Rutgers University

Silvia P. Gennari, Department of Psychology, University of York

Tobias Gerstenberg, Department of Brain and Cognitive Sciences, MIT

Martin Giurfa, Research Centre for Animal Cognition, CNRS–Université de Toulouse

Noah D. Goodman, Department of Psychology, Stanford University

J. Kiley Hamlin, Department of Psychology, University of British Columbia

James A. Hampton, Department of Psychology, City University London

Mutsumi Imai, Department of Environmental Information, Keio University at Shonan Fujisawa

Charles W. Kalish, Department of Educational Psychology, University of Wisconsin

Frank C. Keil, Department of Psychology, Yale University

Jonathan F. Kominsky, Department of Psychology, Yale University

Stephen Laurence, Department of Philosophy and Heng Centre for Cognitive Studies, University of Sheffield

Gary Lupyan, Department of Psychology, University of Wisconsin

Edouard Machery, Department of History and Philosophy of Science, University of Pittsburgh

Bradford Z. Mahon, Department of Brain and Cognitive Sciences, Department of Neurosurgery, University of Rochester

Asifa Majid, Center for Language Studies and Donders Institute for Language, Cognition, and Behaviour, Radboud University Nijmegen, and Max Planck Institute for Psycholinguistics

Barbara C. Malt, Department of Psychology, Lehigh University

Eric Margolis, Department of Philosophy, University of British Columbia

Douglas Medin, Department of Psychology, Northwestern University

Nancy J. Nersessian, School of Interactive Computing, Georgia Institute of Technology and Department of Psychology, Harvard University

bethany ojalehto, Department of Psychology, Northwestern University

Anna Papafragou, Department of Psychological and Brain Sciences and Department of Linguistics and Cognitive Science, University of Delaware

Joshua M. Plotnik, Department of Psychology, University of Cambridge

Noburo Saji, Department of Child Psychology, Kamakura Women's University

Robert M. Seyfarth, Department of Psychology, University of Pennsylvania

Joshua B. Tenenbaum, Department of Brain and Cognitive Sciences, MIT

Sandra Waxman, Department of Psychology, Northwestern University

Daniel A. Weiskopf, Department of Philosophy, Georgia State University

Anna Wierzbicka, School of Literature, Languages, and Linguistics, Australian National University

Preface

Fifteen years have passed since the publication of *Concepts: Core Readings*, our previous volume with MIT Press, and much has happened in the study of concepts since then. The main lines of inquiry from *Concepts: Core Readings* have been investigated in much greater depth, leading to many exciting findings and theoretical developments. New lines of inquiry have also blossomed, with researchers from an ever-broader range of disciplines making important contributions that deserve wider attention. The aim of *The Conceptual Mind: New Directions in the Study of Concepts* is to take stock of these developments and, more importantly, to look to the future.

Although *The Conceptual Mind* represents some of the best recent work on concepts, it isn't a collection of survey papers of the kind that are found in handbooks and other reference works. Rather, our intent has been to bring together a diverse group of leading theorists who work on concepts and have them write about an aspect of their current views, with special emphasis on their latest work and what they take to be the big ideas that should guide future research over the next decade. For this reason, we view *The Conceptual Mind* as more of a companion to *Concepts: Core Readings* than a replacement. The earlier volume includes many of the modern classics in the study of concepts and elucidates the way in which contemporary theories emerge from an interplay of philosophical and scientific lines of inquiry. It also identifies the major positions that have been taken regarding the structure of concepts, and addresses the advantages and challenges that each of these face. *The Conceptual Mind*, in contrast, is devoted to the state of the art as it looks now, in 2015. Given how much the study of concepts has opened up in recent years, it covers a more extensive range of topics and approaches than its predecessor. For convenience, we have organized the volume around ten major themes:

Concepts and Animals
Concepts and the Brain
Concepts and Evolution
Concepts and Perception

Concepts and Language
Concepts across Cultures
Concept Acquisition and Conceptual Change
Concepts and Normativity
Concepts in Context
Concepts and Conceptual Individuation

Readers who are interested in a particular area of research may use these headings to find what they are looking for but should note that the placement of a chapter in a given section is more a matter of emphasis than a principled distinction, as most chapters touch on more than one of these themes.

We would like to thank all the contributors to this volume for their goodwill, their patience, and their thought-provoking suggestions regarding where the study of concepts is heading. Thanks also to Philip Laughlin and the excellent editorial team at MIT Press for their support and for their help with this project.

Notational Convention

In this volume, small caps are used as the standard notation for specific concepts (e.g., ANIMAL for a concept that refers to animals).

I Concepts and Animals

1 Conceptual Learning by Miniature Brains

Aurore Avarguès-Weber and Martin Giurfa

1.1 Introduction

Concepts are considered "the glue that holds our mental life together … in that they tie our past experiences together to our present interactions with the world" (Murphy 2002). They act as a cornerstone of human cognition and underlie analogy, language, and mathematical abilities, among others (Lamberts and Shanks 1997). For instance, humans and nonhuman primates learn conceptual relationships such as SAME, DIFFERENT, LARGER THAN, BETTER THAN, and so on. In all cases, the relationships have to be encoded by the brain independently of the physical nature of the objects linked by the relation (Zentall, Galizio, and Critchfield 2002).

Consequently, concepts are associated with high levels of cognitive sophistication and are not, therefore, expected in an insect brain. Yet, recent works have shown that the miniature brain of honeybees can rapidly learn conceptual relationships between visual stimuli (Avarguès-Weber et al. 2012; Avarguès-Weber, Dyer, and Giurfa 2011; Chittka and Geiger 1995; Dacke and Srinivasan 2008; Giurfa et al. 2001; Gross et al. 2009; Zhang et al. 2005). These results challenge the traditional view attributing supremacy to larger brains when it comes to elaborating conceptual knowledge, and they have, therefore, wide implications for understanding how brains can form abstract conceptual relations in the absence of language. We address the following questions in this chapter: (1) Which kind of evidence have we gathered for conceptual learning in bees? (2) What do bees gain from this cognitive capacity? Is it just an epiphenomenon inculcated by training procedures conceived by experimenters, or is it really adaptive and applied in an ecological context? (3) Which neurobiological mechanisms may be underpinning this kind of problem solving in a computationally restricted bee brain?

Before answering these questions, we start by presenting the honeybee and highlight aspects of its behavior that have made this insect a suitable model for cognitive research.

1.2   The Honeybee *Apis mellifera*: A Model for the Study of Simple and Higher-Order Forms of Associative Learning

Insects have historically fascinated biologists because they offer the possibility of studying sophisticated behaviors (Avarguès-Weber, Deisig, and Giurfa 2011; Chittka and Niven 2009) and simultaneously accessing the neural bases of such behaviors (Busto, Cervantes-Sandoval, and Davis 2010; Davis 2005; Giurfa 2007; Menzel 1999). The fact that insects possess miniature nervous systems with a reduced number of neurons is an advantage when the goal is the identification of networks or specific neurons that mediate the production of behavior. Although neural circuits underlying behavior are simple in appearance, they in fact exhibit an exquisite architecture (Strausfeld 2012).

Among insects, the honeybee has emerged as a powerful model for the study of associative learning (Avarguès-Weber, Mota, and Giurfa 2012; Giurfa 2007; Menzel and Giurfa 1999; Srinivasan 2010). Several reasons justify this choice, which started with the first pioneering works of Karl von Frisch (1914). In a natural context and despite their small size, honeybees exhibit an extremely rich behavioral repertoire (von Frisch 1967). Their lifestyle is social and relies on a complex division of labor achieved by reproductive (queen and drones) and nonreproductive individuals (workers) (Winston 1987). Aged workers forage for food (nectar and/or pollen), which they bring back to the colony. In these activities, a bee forager travels over distances of several kilometers and visits hundreds of flowers in quick and efficient succession. It also collects resin or water, or roams for information-gathering purposes. Sensory capacities and motor performances are highly developed (Galizia, Eisenhardt, and Giurfa 2011). Bees see the world in color (Avarguès-Weber, Mota, and Giurfa 2012; Menzel and Backhaus 1991), discriminate shapes and patterns (Srinivasan 1994), and resolve movements with a high temporal resolution (Srinivasan, Poteser, and Kral 1999). Their olfactory sense is able to distinguish a large range of odors (Guerrieri et al. 2005; Vareschi 1971), and only taste perception seems to be limited (de Brito Sanchez 2011; Robertson and Wanner 2006).

In a natural context, bees learn and memorize the local cues characterizing the places of interest, which are essentially the hive and the food sources (Menzel 1985; Menzel, Greggers, and Hammer 1993). In the case of food sources, learning and memory are the very basis of floral constancy, a behavior exhibited by foragers that consists in exploiting a unique floral species as long as it offers profitable nectar or pollen reward (Chittka, Thomsen, and Waser 1999; Grant 1951). Learning and memorizing the sensory cues of the exploited flower through their association with nectar or pollen reward is what allows a bee forager to track a particular species in the field. When flower profitability diminishes, bees switch to a different species, thus showing the capacity to extinguish previously learned associations.

Honeybees communicate information about important locations around the hive through ritualized body movements, called the "waggle dance," which transmit information about distance to and direction toward an attractive food source or nest site (von Frisch 1967). Hive bees recruited by the waggle dance decode from the speed of dance movement the distance to the food source and from the angle of the waggling phase relative to gravity the flight direction relative to the sun. In this context, learning about food sources is also possible within the hive as recruited bees learn to associate the odor of nectar brought by a dancer with the nectar that it regurgitates and passes them through trophallactic (mouth-to-mouth) contacts (Farina, Gruter, and Diaz 2005; Gil and De Marco 2005).

The complexity and richness of the honeybee's life is therefore appealing in terms of the opportunities it offers for the study of learning and memory. Such an appeal would be useless, however, if these phenomena would not be amenable to controlled laboratory conditions. Several protocols have been developed to allow experimental access in terms of controlled training and testing conditions, thus underlining the remarkable plasticity of this insect, which can learn even under restrictive (in terms of movement, for instance) or stressful (in terms of the aversive reinforcement experienced) conditions (Giurfa 2007; Giurfa and Sandoz 2012).

Here we will focus on visual learning protocols in which free-flying honeybees are trained to choose visual targets paired with sucrose solution as the equivalent of nectar reward. Experiments on concept learning in bees have all used this training procedure.

1.3   Visual Learning in Free-Flying Honeybees

Free-flying honeybees can be conditioned to visual stimuli such as colors, shapes and patterns, depth and motion contrast, among others (Giurfa and Menzel 1997; Lehrer 1997; Srinivasan 1994; von Frisch 1914; Wehner 1981). In such a protocol, each bee is individually marked by means of a color spot on the thorax or the abdomen so that individual performances can be recorded. The marked bee is generally displaced by the experimenter toward the training and test place, where it is rewarded with sucrose solution to promote its regular return (figure 1.1). Such pretraining is performed without presenting the training stimuli in order to avoid uncontrolled learning. When the bee starts visiting the experimental place actively (i.e., without being displaced by the experimenter), the training stimuli are presented and the choice of the appropriate visual target reinforced with sucrose solution. Bees are trained and tested individually to achieve a precise control of the experience of each subject. It is also important to control the distance at which a choice is made because orientation and choice are mediated by different visual cues at different distances or angles subtended by the target (Giurfa and Menzel 1997).

In this protocol, it is possible to gather hundreds of decisions in a relatively short time. A motivated bee will perform dozens of visits to the feeding site in a day, returning from the hive every 5 to 10 minutes, approximately. Several behaviors can be used

Figure 1.1
An individually marked free-flying honeybee collecting sucrose solution on a concentric-disc pattern.

to quantify the bees' choices in these experiments. Touches (i.e., the flights toward a target that end with a contact of the bee's antennae or legs with the stimulus surface) and landings on a given stimulus are usually recorded to this end. The associations built in these contexts can be operant, classical, or both, that is, they may link visual stimuli (conditioned stimulus, CS) and reward (unconditioned stimulus, US), the response of the animal (e.g., landing) and the US, or both. The experimental framework is nevertheless mainly operant because the bee's behavior is the determinant for whether the sucrose reinforcement is obtained.

1.4   Conceptual Learning in Honeybees

Recent work has shown that the miniature brain of bees can rapidly learn conceptual relationships between visual stimuli. Concept learning is particularly interesting for the study of a supposedly limited brain because it relies on relations between objects

(Zentall, Galizio, and Critchfield 2002; Zentall et al. 2008) and requires transfer of a rule independently of the physical nature of the stimuli considered (colors, shape, size, etc.) (Murphy 2002, 2010). Solving conceptual problems poses, therefore, a problem for simplistic views depicting bees, and insects in general, as rather rigid machines devoid of plasticity.

Various recent reports have indicated that honeybees learn conceptual rules of different sorts. These include SAMENESS/DIFFERENCE (Giurfa et al. 2001), ABOVE/BELOW (Avarguès-Weber, Dyer, and Giurfa 2011), and the mastering of two rules simultaneously, ABOVE/BELOW (or RIGHT/LEFT) and DIFFERENT FROM (Avarguès-Weber et al. 2012). Similarly, recent reports on "numerosity" in bees suggest a capacity to extract information about number irrespective of the physical features of the objects counted (Chittka and Geiger 1995; Dacke and Srinivasan 2008; Gross et al. 2009).

1.4.1 Sameness/Difference Concepts

The learning of the concepts of SAMENESS and DIFFERENCE was demonstrated through the protocols of delayed matching to sample (DMTS) and delayed nonmatching to sample (DNMTS), respectively (Giurfa et al. 2001). In these protocols an animal is presented a nonreinforced sample and has afterwards to choose among two or more stimuli, one of which corresponds to the sample previously shown. If trained in a DMTS, the animal has to choose the stimulus matching the sample to obtain a positive reinforcement; if trained in a DNMTS, it has to choose the opposite to the sample to obtain the reinforcement.

Honeybees were trained to enter a Y-maze to collect sucrose solution on one of the arms of the maze (figure 1.2a, plate 1); the position of the reward changed randomly between the arms of the maze from visit to visit. In a first experiment, individually marked bees were trained following a DMTS protocol to determine if they were capable of learning a concept of SAMENESS. Bees were presented with a changing nonrewarded sample (i.e., one of two different color discs—"color group"—or one of two different black-and-white gratings, vertical or horizontal—"pattern group") at the entrance of a maze (figure 1.2b, plate 1). The bee was rewarded only if it chose the stimulus identical to the sample once within the maze. Bees trained with colors and presented in transfer tests with black-and-white gratings that they had not experienced before solved the problem and chose the grating identical to the sample at the entrance of the maze. Similarly, bees trained with the gratings and tested with colors in transfer tests also solved the problem and chose the novel color corresponding to that of the sample grating at the maze entrance (figure 1.2c, plate 1). Transfer was not limited to different types of visual stimuli (pattern vs. color), but could also operate between drastically different sensory modalities, such as olfaction and vision (Giurfa et al. 2001). Bees also mastered a DNMTS task, thus showing that they learn a rule of DIFFERENCE between stimuli as well (Giurfa et al. 2001).

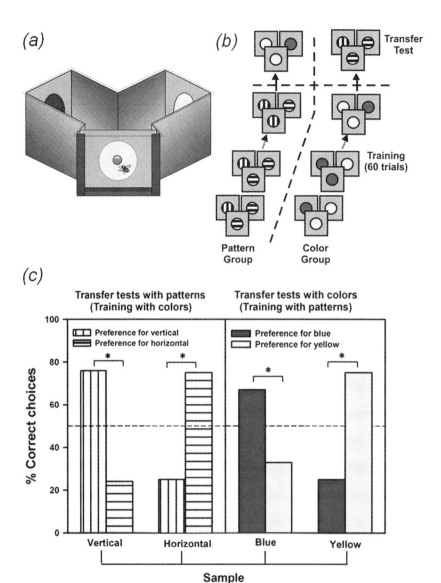

Figure 1.2 (plate 1)

SAMENESS learning in honeybees (Giurfa et al. 2001). (a) Y-maze used to train bees in a delayed matching-to-sample task. Bees had to enter the maze to collect sugar solution on one of the back walls. A sample was shown at the maze entrance before bees accessed the arms of the maze. (b) Training protocol. A group of bees were trained during sixty trials with black-and-white vertical and horizontal gratings (pattern group); another group was trained with colors, blue and yellow (color group). After training, both groups were subjected to a transfer test with novel stimuli (patterns for bees trained with colors, colors for bees trained with patterns). (c) Performance of the pattern group and the color group in the transfer tests with novel stimuli. Both groups chose the novel stimulus corresponding to the sample although they had no experience with such test stimuli. *: p < 0.05.

These results were the first to document that bees learn rules relating stimuli in their environment. The results were later verified in experiments showing that bees categorize visual images based on general features common to these images (Zhang et al. 2004) and in a study showing that the working memory underlying the solving of the DMTS task lasts for approximately five seconds (Zhang et al. 2005), a period that coincides with the duration of other visual and olfactory short-term memories characterized in simpler forms of associative learning in honeybees (Menzel 1999).

1.4.2 Numerosity

The ability to abstract information about number has always been at the core of animal cognition studies (Davis and Perusse 1988). The broader question underlying this research is whether animals encode information about number when they are presented with stimuli that are variable in other respects (Gallistel and Gelman 2000). Several studies have shown that animals, including rats, lions, and various species of primates, have an approximate sense of number (referred to as "numerosity"). Are insects also endowed with this capacity?

A pioneer study on honeybee navigation suggested that bees are capable of counting when passing successive landmarks en route to the goal and that this numerical information may be used to decide when to land on a feeding place (Chittka and Geiger 1995). Bees were trained to fly along a 300-meter transect, along which were four identical tents equally spaced, to reach an artificial feeder placed between the third and fourth tents. After training, the spacing between tents was increased, thus creating a potential conflict: either the bees relied on the exact distance previously flown, in which case they should land between the second and third tents, or they relied on the number of tents passed en route to the goal, in which case they should land after the third tent as during training but now increasing considerably the distance flown. Most but not all (78%; 80 of 103 bees) of the bees landed at the correct distance; a significant percentage (22%; 23 of 103) chose to fly more than 100 meters farther and landed after passing the correct number of three tents. The intensive training along the route may have favored attending to the real distance rather than to the number of tents passed; yet, for some bees, the latter criterion mediated their decision to land. The performance of these bees was taken as evidence for "proto-counting" because it met basic criteria in most definitions of true counting, except the fundamental transfer experiment showing that the numerical performance was independent of the kind of objects used as landmarks to indicate the way to the goal (Chittka and Geiger 1995). The performance of bees was not, in any event, a case of serial recognition of different landmarks, that is, a succession of different snapshots defining a route, because the tents passed en route to the goal were all identical; the only way bees could decide where to land was, therefore, through a form of counting applied to the tents.

More recently, two new works have explored this ability in honeybees. In one of them (Dacke and Srinivasan 2008), bees were trained to fly into a tunnel to find a food reward after a given number of landmarks (e.g., yellow stripes on the walls and floor of the tunnel), thus reproducing in a reduced scale the rationale of the previous tent experiment. Yet here, the shape, size, and positions of the landmarks were changed in the different testing conditions to avoid confounding factors. Bees showed a stronger preference to land after the correct number of landmarks in nonrewarded tests irrespective of the distance flown within the tunnel, and even in conditions in which the landmarks were perceptually distinguishable from those used during the training. This capacity was visible up to four landmarks passed en route to the goal but not farther, thus indicating a limit in the bees' counting capacity (Dacke and Srinivasan 2008). These results showed that honeybees are capable of counting in a navigational context and that such counting operates sequentially, incrementing progressively the number of landmarks retained.

In the other recent work, honeybees had to fly into a Y-maze and choose the stimulus containing the same number of items as a sample presented at the entrance of the maze, following a delayed matching-to-sample protocol (Gross et al. 2009). Bees were trained to match sample images of two or three visual stimuli, and they learned to choose a stimulus with two elements if this was the cue shown at the entrance of the maze, or a stimulus with three elements if this was the cue present at the maze entrance (figure 1.3a, plate 2).

In these experiments, training was performed with groups of twenty bees instead of individuals, and bees were rewarded for correct decisions during the tests, thus introducing undesired additional training on stimuli for which bees should remain naïve. Although arguments were provided to justify these procedures, the confounding factors complicate the interpretation of the results. Yet, besides these experimental caveats, results seem to clearly show a sense of numerosity in bees, as insects correctly matched the sample of three or of two elements presented at the entrance of the maze (Gross et al. 2009). Correct matching was independent of the physical features of the stimuli presented in the test as choice of two versus three and could be transferred to stimuli differing in color, shape, and configuration or orientation (figure 1.3, plate 2). Low-level cues such as cumulated area, edge length, and illusionary shape similarity formed by the elements did not mediate the bees' choice of two versus three. Interestingly, although bees were able to match a sample with three elements versus an unknown stimulus presenting four elements, they were unable to match a sample with four elements per se, even when presented against a competing stimulus with three elements. Experiments in which higher numbers were shown also resulted in unsuccessful performances, thus revealing that three was the numerosity limit exhibited by the bees in the delayed matching-to-sample task (Gross et al. 2009).

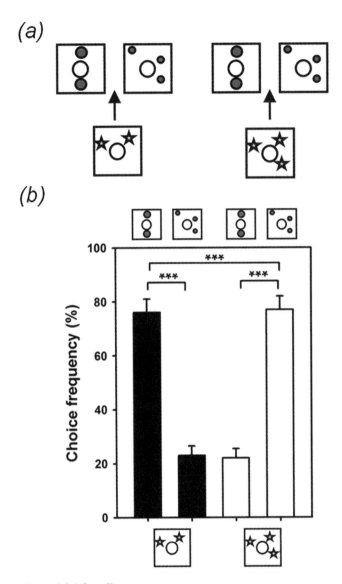

Figure 1.3 (plate 2)

Numerosity in honeybees (Gross et al. 2009). (a) Training protocol performed in a Y-maze (see figure 1.2a). Bees were trained in a delayed matching-to-sample task to match stimuli containing two or three elements. The sample with two or three elements was shown at the maze entrance before bees accessed the arms of the maze. The bees had to choose the arm containing the stimulus composed of the same number of elements as the sample to obtain sucrose reward. The appearance of the elements and their spatial positions differed between the sample and the target (one example shown) so that bees had to focus on number and not on other perceptual cues to solve the task. (b) In transfer tests, the bees were able to match the stimuli according to the number of their composing elements, if numbers didn't exceed four. ***: $p < 0.001$.

1.4.3 ABOVE/BELOW Concepts

For many animals that must operate in complex natural environments, spatial concepts such as RIGHT, LEFT, ABOVE, and BELOW are of crucial importance to generate appropriate relational displacements and orientation in their environment. A recent work studied whether honeybees learn an ABOVE/BELOW relationship between visual stimuli and transfer it to novel stimuli that are perceptually different from those used during the training (Avarguès-Weber, Dyer, and Giurfa 2011). Bees were trained to fly into a Y-maze and choose visual stimuli presented above or below a horizontal bar. Training followed a differential conditioning procedure in which one spatial relation (e.g., target above bar) was associated with sucrose solution, while the other relation (e.g., target below bar) was associated with quinine solution. One group of bees was rewarded on the *target above bar* relation, while another group was rewarded on the *target below bar* relation. After completing the training, bees were subjected to a nonrewarded transfer test, in which a novel target stimulus (not used during the training) was presented above or below the bar. Despite the novelty of the test situation, which preserved the spatial relationship to the bar as the single criterion predicting the presence of sucrose reward, bees responded appropriately: if trained for the above relationship, they chose the novel stimulus above the bar, and if trained for the below relationship, they chose the novel stimulus below the bar (Avarguès-Weber, Dyer, and Giurfa 2011).

Yet, because all stimuli used during the training always appeared in the same region of the visual field (e.g., upper field for bees trained to *above* and lower field for bees trained to *below*), an alternative interpretation could posit that instead of learning a conceptual relationship, bees simply relied on the statistical distributions of image differences. A series of snapshots acquired during training would determine an average stimulus, which would be spatially distinct between the *above* and the *below* training. Furthermore, if bees relied on a simple cue like the center of gravity of the patterns (Ernst and Heisenberg 1999), which would be associated with reward, the problem becomes elemental.

Both interpretations can account for the results of the experiment described above, thus questioning a cognitive interpretation based on concept learning. Yet, they are ruled out by a second experiment in which instead of using a salient horizontal bar as referent, two stimuli positioned one above the other were used so that one acted as the target and the other as the referent (figure 1.4a). Both stimuli could be well discriminated by the bees. The target varied from trial to trial in order to promote the extraction of an abstract ABOVE/BELOW relationship (Avarguès-Weber, Dyer, and Giurfa 2011) (figure 1.4a). As before, one group of bees was trained to select the *target above referent* relationship (*above* group) and another group the *target below referent* relationship (*below* group). Bees rapidly learned to master their respective relationship, and when subjected to a first transfer test in which a novel stimulus was introduced as target, they preferred the spatial relationship for which they were trained (figure 1.4b).

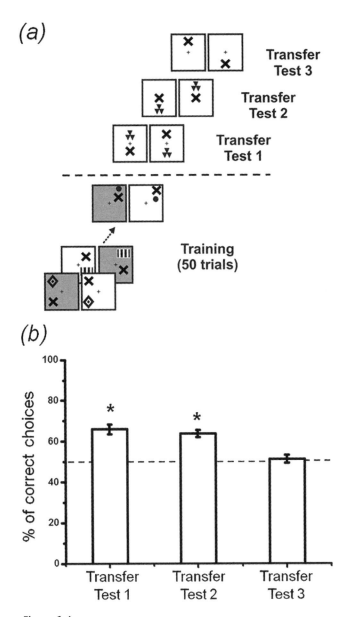

Figure 1.4

ABOVE/BELOW learning in honeybees (Avarguès-Weber, Dyer, and Giurfa 2011). (a) Training protocol. A group of bees were trained during fifty trials to fly into a Y-maze to choose black patterns on
a white background. Patterns were a variable target disposed above or below a constant referent.
Half of the bees were rewarded on the "target above referent" relation, whereas the other half was
rewarded on the "target below referent" relation. The referent pattern was either the disc or the
cross depending on the group of bees trained. In the example shown, the referent is the cross, and
the relationship rewarded during training, indicated in pink, is ABOVE ("above the cross"). After
training, bees were subjected to three types of transfer tests with novel stimuli. (b) Performance
in the transfer tests. Bees learned the concept of ABOVE/BELOW and transferred it to novel stimuli,
fulfilling the learned relationship (Transfer Test 1). Transfer tests 2 and 3 showed that neither the
spatial location of the referent on the background nor the center of gravity of stimuli was used as
a discrimination cue to resolve the task. *: $p < 0.05$

A second transfer test was performed to verify that bees used the relative position of both target and referent and not just the fact that in most cases, the referent appeared in the upper or lower visual field of the *below* or the *above* group, respectively. In this second transfer test, the referent was located in the middle of the background for both the rewarded and the nonrewarded stimulus so that it could not help the bees choose between them (figure 1.4a). In this case, bees still appropriately chose the stimulus pair presenting the spatial relationship for which they were trained (figure 1.4b).

Even more important was a third transfer test in which only the referent was presented in the upper or the lower part of the background (figure 1.4a) to determine whether its absolute position was an orientation cue used by the bees, instead of its position relative to the target, which was now absent. Had the bees relied on the center of gravity of stimuli or the statistical distribution of images, they should choose again correctly despite the absence of the target; if, however, the relationship between target and referent had mediated the bees' choices, then performance should collapse. This is exactly what happened, and choice in this test was random (figure 1.4b), thus showing that bees did indeed learn a spatial relationship between two stimuli, a target and a referent (Avarguès-Weber, Dyer, and Giurfa 2011).

1.4.4   Mastering Two Concepts Simultaneously

Processing several concepts simultaneously presupposes an even higher level of cognitive sophistication than dealing with one concept at a time. In a recent work (Avarguès-Weber et al. 2012), honeybees were shown to rapidly master two abstract concepts simultaneously, one based on spatial relationships (ABOVE/BELOW and RIGHT/LEFT), and another based on the perception of DIFFERENCE (figure 1.5, plate 3).

Bees were trained to discriminate visual stimuli composed of two images linked by a specific spatial relationship (either ABOVE/BELOW or RIGHT/LEFT depending on bees). To obtain the sucrose reward, the bees had to choose the appropriate spatial relationship, irrespective of the images defining the relationship. Importantly, the two images composing a stimulus were always different (figure 1.5a, plate 3). After training, subsequent tests showed that bees learned the rule based on the spatial relation, so that they transferred their choice to novel images never seen before if these subtended the appropriate relationship (figure 1.5b, plate 3). Moreover, they also extracted from the training the fact that the two images were different so that they preferred the appropriate relationship defined by two different images to the same relationship defined by two identical images (figure 1.5, plate 3). Notably, if the inappropriate relationship was presented, in one case defined by two different images and in the other by two identical images, bees preferred the stimulus with the two different images where, at least, the rule of difference was preserved. Finally, in a conflictive situation in which the bees had to choose between the appropriate spatial relationship defined by identical images and the inappropriate relationship defined by different images, the bees demonstrated no preference (figure 1.5, plate 3). These three tests showed that bees were able to master simultaneously two different concepts: the ABOVE/BELOW, RIGHT/LEFT concept and the DIFFERENCE concept. They assigned them the same weight in their decision-making process so that their choice was guided by the presence of both or at least one of the concepts. As a consequence, performance collapsed in the conflictive situation.

As in the previous study (Avarguès-Weber, Dyer, and Giurfa 2011), a series of internal within-subject controls and simulation algorithms allowed researchers to exclude confounding low-level cues, such as the global center of gravity, the global orientation of the stimuli, or the retinotopic similarity between the rewarded stimuli. These results thus demonstrated that the miniature brains of bees can extract at least two different concepts from a set of complex pictures and combine them in a rule for subsequent choices (Avarguès-Weber et al. 2012).

1.5 An Ecological Scenario for Conceptual Learning in Bees

The problems solved by bees in conceptual problems reveal an impressive capacity to detect relational rules between visual targets in their environment. Are these capacities adaptive and applied in an ecological context, or are they epiphenomena inculcated by training protocols? Although a definitive answer to this question is so far elusive, we can discuss possible scenarios in which conceptual relationships could be extracted and used to improve behavioral efficiency.

Among such possible scenarios, one emerges as a potential context for conceptual learning in the case of honeybees: the navigation scenario (Chittka and Jensen 2011). Honeybees are central-place foragers, that is, their foraging trips start and end at the same fixed point in space: the hive. In their foraging bouts, bees may fly several kilometers and follow straight or complex routes to and back from the food source (Menzel et al. 1996; Menzel and Giurfa 2006; Menzel et al. 2012). Although bees use sky-based information as a navigation compass, prominent landmarks and landscape information also define routes and determine navigation strategies (Chittka, Geiger, and Kunze 1995; Collett 1996; Collett and Zeil 1998; Dacke and Srinivasan 2008). In this context, mastering spatial relationships to build generic representations around the hive or the food source may be particularly useful. Extracting relationships such as ABOVE/BELOW, SAME/DIFFERENT, or TO THE RIGHT/LEFT OF may help stabilize routes in a changing environment and insulate bees against potential disorientation induced by seasonal changes in the aspect of landmarks.

Counting could be useful in navigation tasks where the number of landmarks encountered during a foraging trip or near the hive may contribute to efficient orientation of free-flying bees (Chittka, Geiger, and Kunze 1995; Dacke and Srinivasan 2008). Furthermore, it could also improve foraging through evaluation of food source profitability (e.g., number of flowers within a patch) or facilitate social learning (see above)

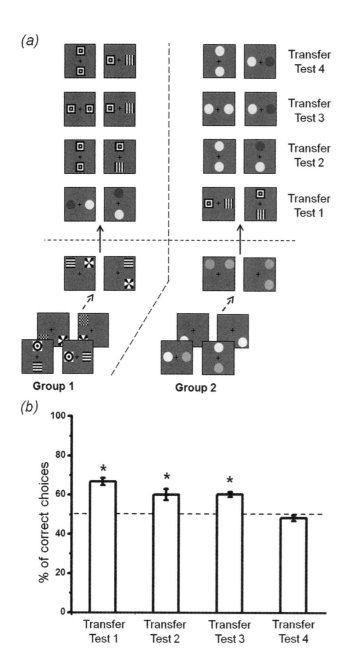

Figure 1.5 (plate 3)
Simultaneous mastering of two concepts in honeybees (Avarguès-Weber et al. 2012). Bees learned to use two concepts simultaneously: ABOVE/BELOW (or RIGHT/LEFT) and DIFFERENCE. (a) Bees were trained with sucrose reward in a Y-maze to choose the stimulus presenting two different patterns (Group 1) or two different colored discs (Group 2) in an above/below (or right/left) relationship depending on the group of bees. Appearances and relative position of the patterns varied from trial to trial. (b) After a thirty training trials, bees succeeded in transferring the spatial relation rule to unknown stimuli presenting the appropriate spatial relationship. Bees of Group 1 trained with patterns transferred their choice to colored discs arranged in the proper spatial relationship, and bees of Group 2 trained with colored discs transferred their choice to patterns arranged in the proper spatial relationship. Additional tests (transfer tests 2 to 4) demonstrated that bees additionally learned that the patterns linked by the spatial relation had to be different. Bees used both rules simultaneously in transfer tests. *: $p < 0.05$.

by mediating foraging decisions according to the number of bees already present on a patch of flowers (Gross et al. 2009).

This hypothesis allows predicting that not only honeybees, but also other insects that share the capacity to navigate in a complex and structured environment and to return constantly to the nest as a fixed point in space should be able to learn conceptual relationships between visual targets. This hypothesis would, nevertheless, exclude central-place foragers that perform their foraging in an unstructured environment (such as the Sahara Desert in the case of *Cataglyphis bicolor* ants; see Wehner [2003] for review), where the possibility of relating landmarks through conceptual relationships is rather reduced. For these insects, sky-compass-based information can provide the essential toolkit to navigate efficiently. Similarly, central-place foragers with reduced foraging activities (i.e., with scarce foraging bouts per unit time) are not necessarily expected to have evolved conceptualization capacities, as their opportunities to extract spatial relationships between objects in their environment, even if structured, would be limited.

1.6   Neurobiological Mechanisms Underlying Conceptual Learning in Bees

Neural correlates of rules have been reported in the prefrontal cortex of both monkeys and rodents (Miller et al. 2003; Wallis, Anderson, and Miller 2001; White and Wise 1999). In the dorsolateral, ventrolateral, and orbitofrontal prefrontal cortex of monkeys, electrophysiological recordings showed the presence of neurons exhibiting greater activity during "SAMENESS" trials (DMTS) as well as neurons showing greater activity during "DIFFERENCE" trials (DNMTS), regardless of which visual sample was used (Wallis, Anderson, and Miller 2001). In the case of insects, with no prefrontal cortex, the critical question is which neural architecture could mediate this performance.

While human brains have an average volume of 1,450 cm^3 and comprise 100 billion neurons, a bee brain has a volume of 1 mm^3 and comprises fewer than 1 million neurons. Yet higher-order associative structures allowing the combination of information pertaining to different sensory modalities, and presenting a multimodal output consistent with generalization across modalities, exist in the bee brain. Mushroom bodies (MBs) occupy one-third of the bee brain and are candidates for mediating conceptual learning (figure 1.6, plate 4).

In the honeybee, each MB consists of approximately 170,000 tightly packed parallel neurons, the Kenyon cells. The bee mushroom bodies receive compartmentalized multisensory input (olfactory, visual, mechanosensory, gustatory) (Ehmer and Gronenberg 2002; Mobbs 1982; Strausfeld 2002), and their extrinsic neurons, such as the Pe1 neuron, respond to a variety of stimuli, including sucrose, odors, mechanosensory stimuli, and visual stimuli (Grünewald 1999; Homberg and Erber 1979; Rybak and Menzel 1998) (figure 1.6, plate 4). This multimodal convergence is consistent with a capacity for integrating sensory information across various modalities and MB subcompartments and suits the MBs for higher-order multimodal computations, particularly for relational associations.

Like the prefrontal cortex of primates (Barbey and Patterson 2011), MBs are also associated with reinforcement systems and display an intrinsic relationship with memory systems. Octopaminergic neurons, such as the VUMmx1 neuron (ventral unpaired median neuron of the maxillary neuromere 1), which serves the function of a reward system, converge with the regions of olfactory input of the MBs. Also, dopaminergic neurons, which act as a punishment system (Vergoz et al. 2007), converge

Figure 1.6 (plate 4)
Three-dimensional reconstruction of a honeybee brain. (a) The mushroom bodies, which are multimodal structures receiving segregated visual, olfactory, mechanosensory, and gustatory afferences, are shown in red. (b) Three-dimensional reconstruction of a mushroom body in frontal view (vmb). Two calyces, a lateral (l) and a medial one (m), fuse in a single peduncle. Each calyx is subdivided into three main regions, the lip, the collar (col) and the basal ring (br). (c) Scheme of a mushroom body (delimited by dashed straight lines), showing segregated multisensory input at the level of the calyx and integrated multimodal output at the level of the vertical (α) lobe. The somata of the Kenyon cells (KC), which integrate the mushroom body, are located in the calyx bowl. The dendrites of the KC form the calyx, which is subdivided into three main regions, the lip, receiving olfactory afferences; the collar, receiving mainly visual but also mechanosensory and gustatory afferences; and the basal ring, receiving olfactory, mechanosensory, and gustatory afferences (Mobbs 1982; Schröter and Menzel 2003; Strausfeld 2002). The axons of the KC subdivide and form the vertical (α) and the medial (β) lobe. An extrinsic, multimodal peduncle neuron, the Pe1 neuron (Mauelshagen 1993; Okada et al. 2007; Rybak and Menzel 1998), is shown, whose dendrites arborize across the vertical lobe; its axon projects to the lateral horn (delimited by a dashed circle).

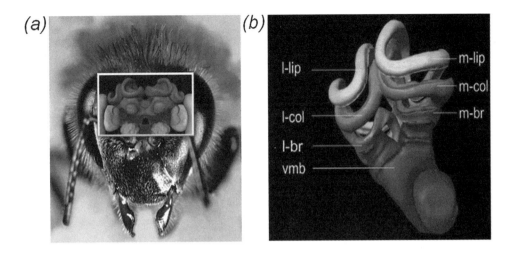

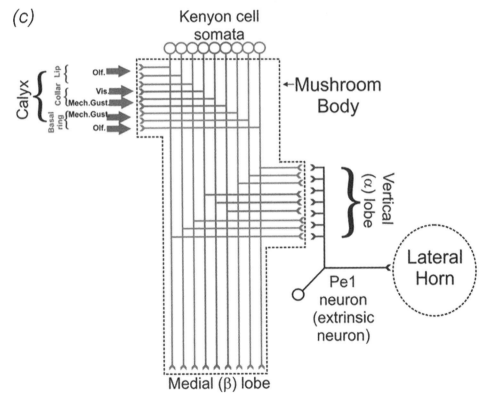

with specific regions of the MBs (Tedjakumala 2014). Finally, MBs have been historically characterized as a substrate for associative memories, in particular of long-term
memories (Erber, Masuhr, and Menzel 1980; Menzel, Erber, and Masuhr 1974; Menzel
and Müller 1996).

All in all, the question of whether MBs are the insect pendant of the primate prefrontal cortex is not relevant even if studies on the prefrontal cortex may be inspirational to
guide research on mushroom body function and vice versa. The critical question is to
determine whether and how mushroom body architecture is crucial to mediate concept
learning and which neural requisites are important to extract relational rules. From this
perspective, experiments addressing, through specific mushroom body blocking and
activation, whether or not these structures are necessary and sufficient for concept
learning, are of fundamental importance and still need to be performed.

1.7   Concept Learning in Bees: A Philosophical Perspective

We have seen that honeybees may behave as if they were guided by different kinds of
concepts inculcated by specific training procedures, that such concepts admit a plausible ecological scenario, and that neural structures exist in the bee brain that could
support concept learning. From the point of view of an empirical biologist, behavior,
ecology, and neurobiology converge to favor the argument that the miniature brain
of bees, despite an apparent reduced computational power (at least in terms of the
number of neurons), is capable of elaborating conceptual knowledge.

Yet, a fundamental philosophical question one may ask is, in what sense do honeybees have concepts? In other words, is the nature of concepts elaborated by bees
comparable to those available in humans? To what extent does the proposition that
we have been using all along this chapter—honeybees solve discrimination problems
using concepts—track what bees really use to master such discriminations? Is it for
instance possible that the term *concept* is anchored to us, humans, in a way that it is
not anchored to a bee?

The questions are important but difficult to answer because they refer to the recurrent problem of accessing the contents of an animal's mind (here, an insect's mind).
Although we may not be able to ascribe in a straightforward way a conceptual content to a bee's mind, we can nevertheless assume that there exists a content that can
be correctly ascribed to describe efficiently the multiple discriminations reviewed in
this chapter. Because bees choose on the basis of relationships between stimuli, that
such relations may bind variable objects whose physical nature becomes irrelevant
during the problem to be solved, and that bees transfer their choice to novel situations
never seen before if the learned relationships can be detected, a content revolving
around simple discrimination learning has to be ruled out. Such discrimination learning would be stimulus specific and would preclude the kind of transfer observed in the

experiments reviewed here. It thus seems safe to assume that the proposition "bees may use concepts to solve discrimination problems" is safe and tracks what bees do, irrespective of the nature of their conceptual knowledge.

This conclusion may create the idea that concepts are, at the end, not so elaborated and would not represent, contrary to what we tend to believe (Murphy 2002), a higher-order form of mental representation. This argument may be valid but has some caveats: Do we claim that concepts are lower-form representations just because bees possess them? In other words, if bees solve conceptual discriminations, does it have necessarily to be on the basis of "simple" and even "primitive" representations? It is sometimes assumed that "simple" and "miniature" nervous systems like those of insects implement cognitive faculties by radically different mechanisms compared with vertebrates, rather relying on innate routines and elemental forms of associative learning. However, constructing a great division between simple and advanced nervous systems will lead us astray, because the basic logical structure of the processes underlying spontaneity, decision making, planning, and communication are similar in many respects in big and small brains (Chittka and Niven 2009; Menzel and Giurfa 2001).

What may be more or less demanding for the small brain of an insect is also not obvious. For example, will it be more difficult to follow a navigation strategy based on route following or on using a cognitive map? Is it easier to store many sequential images defining a long route or to extract a concept connecting these images? Are neural processes derived from behavioristic learning theory less demanding than those derived from cognitive concepts? The answer at this stage is that we simply do not know, and that the only way to find out is to search for neural mechanisms within a broader conceptual frame.

1.8   Conclusion

Concept learning, described originally as a higher-order form of learning and considered a cornerstone of human cognition (Lamberts and Shanks 1997), is a capacity that can be ascribed to honeybees based on a rich dataset spanning different forms of conceptual problem solving. Several forms of conceptual learning have been demonstrated so far in these insects, and further studies could add new forms to the list of concepts that bees can master. The fact that only these insects have been shown to solve learning sets leading to concept formation does not make honeybees a cognitive exception among insects. Other insect species sharing essential traits such as central-place navigation in structured environments, associated learning and memory skills, and highly frequent foraging activities may perhaps be capable of comparable performances.

In the experiments reviewed in this chapter, the performance of the bees at the beginning of the different learning sets was always random in terms of choosing or not the rewarded solution versus the nonrewarded alternative. This fact underlines, therefore, that bees did not show any preexisting bias facilitating (or impeding) the formation of a concept. In all cases, bees learned to solve the discriminations by acquiring a particular concept, thus revealing not only a high degree of behavioral plasticity, but also that concepts are incorporated via learning. Whether bees possess, in addition, innate concepts is difficult to determine. Innate predispositions for sensory cues such as colors exist in bees and other pollinators and favor first encounters with flowers in the initial foraging trips (Giurfa et al. 1995). But whether concept extraction is facilitated to favor efficient navigation performances remains unknown.

The case of honeybees reveals that minimal neural architectures are capable of extracting the regularities underlying concept formation. In the absence of a prefrontal cortex, structures in the bee brain that are simpler in terms of their number of neurons, but not necessarily in terms of their functional principles, can support conceptual knowledge. The essential task is therefore to identify and characterize the circuits that mediate concept learning in the bee brain. Such an endeavor is possible, because reversible and targeted blocking of neural transmission in specific areas of the bee brain is an available technical tool (Devaud et al. 2007). Coupling this procedure with protocols inducing concept formation should enable determining the circuits that are necessary and sufficient for achieving this task. If the honeybee has reaffirmed its model status for learning studies through behavioral experiments demonstrating concept learning, it can also play a significant role in unraveling the neural bases of this capacity.

Acknowledgments

This work was supported by the Institut Universitaire de France, the French Research Council (CNRS), and the University Paul Sabatier.

References

Avarguès-Weber, A., N. Deisig, and M. Giurfa. 2011. Visual cognition in social insects. *Annual Review of Entomology* 56:423–443.

Avarguès-Weber, A., A. G. Dyer, M. Combe, and M. Giurfa. 2012. Simultaneous mastering of two abstract concepts with a miniature brain. *Proceedings of the National Academy of Sciences of the United States of America* 109:7481–7486.

Avarguès-Weber, A., A. G. Dyer, and M. Giurfa. 2011. Conceptualization of above and below relationships by an insect. *Proceedings. Biological Sciences* 278:898–905.

Avarguès-Weber, A., T. Mota, and M. Giurfa. 2012. New vistas on honey bee vision. *Apidologie* 43:244–268.

Barbey, A. K., and R. Patterson. 2011. Architecture of explanatory inference in the human pre-frontal cortex. *Frontiers in Psychology* 2:162.

Busto, G. U., I. Cervantes-Sandoval, and R. L. Davis. 2010. Olfactory learning in *Drosophila*. *Physiology (Bethesda, MD)* 25:338–346.

Chittka, L., and K. Geiger. 1995. Can honey bees count landmarks? *Animal Behaviour* 49:159–164.

Chittka, L., K. Geiger, and J. A. N. Kunze. 1995. The influences of landmarks on distance estimation of honey bees. *Animal Behaviour* 50:23–31.

Chittka, L., and K. Jensen. 2011. Animal cognition: Concepts from apes to bees. *Current Biology* 21:R116–R119.

Chittka, L., and J. Niven. 2009. Are bigger brains better? *Current Biology* 19:R995–R1008.

Chittka, L., J. D. Thomson, and N. M. Waser. 1999. Flower constancy, insect psychology, and plant evolution. *Naturwissenschaften* 86:361–377.

Collett, T. S. 1996. Insect navigation *en route* to the goal: Multiple strategies for the use of landmarks. *Journal of Experimental Biology* 199:227–235.

Collett, T. S., and J. Zeil. 1998. Places and landmarks: An arthropod perspective. In *Spatial Representation in Animals*, ed. S. Healy, 18–53. Oxford: Oxford University Press.

Dacke, M., and M. V. Srinivasan. 2008. Evidence for counting in insects. *Animal Cognition* 11:683–689.

Davis, R. L. 2005. Olfactory memory formation in *Drosophila*: From molecular to systems neuroscience. *Annual Review of Neuroscience* 28:275–302.

Davis, H., and R. Perusse. 1988. Numerical competence in animals: Definition issues, current evidence, and a new research agenda. *Behavioral and Brain Sciences* 114:561–615.

de Brito Sanchez, M. G. 2011. Taste perception in honey bees. *Chemical Senses* 36:675–692.

Devaud, J. M., A. Blunk, J. Podufall, M. Giurfa, and B. Grünewald. 2007. Using local anaesthetics to block neuronal activity and map specific learning tasks to the mushroom bodies of an insect brain. *European Journal of Neuroscience* 26:3193–3206.

Ehmer, B., and W. Gronenberg. 2002. Segregation of visual input to the mushroom bodies in the honeybee (*Apis mellifera*). *Journal of Comparative Neurology* 451:362–373.

Erber, J., T. Masuhr, and R. Menzel. 1980. Localization of short-term memory in the brain of the bee, *Apis mellifera*. *Physiological Entomology* 5:343–358.

Ernst, R., and M. Heisenberg. 1999. The memory template in *Drosophila* pattern vision at the flight simulator. *Vision Research* 39:3920–3933.

Farina, W. M., C. Gruter, and P. C. Diaz. 2005. Social learning of floral odours inside the honeybee hive. *Proceedings. Biological Sciences* 272:1923–1928.

Galizia, C., D. Eisenhardt, and M. Giurfa. 2011. *Honeybee Neurobiology and Behavior: A Tribute to Randolf Menzel*. Berlin: Springer.

Gallistel, C. R., and R. Gelman. 2000. Non-verbal numerical cognition: From the reals to integers. *Trends in Cognitive Sciences* 7:307–314.

Gil, M., and R. J. De Marco. 2005. Olfactory learning by means of trophallaxis in *Apis mellifera*. *Journal of Experimental Biology* 208:671–680.

Giurfa, M. 2007. Behavioral and neural analysis of associative learning in the honeybee: A taste from the magic well. *Journal of Comparative Physiology. A, Neuroethology, Sensory, Neural, and Behavioral Physiology* 193:801–824.

Giurfa, M., and R. Menzel. 1997. Insect visual perception: Complex abilities of simple nervous systems. *Current Opinion in Neurobiology* 7:505–513.

Giurfa, M., J. A. Núñez, L. Chittka, and R. Menzel. 1995. Colour preferences of flower-naive honeybees. *Journal of Comparative Physiology. A, Neuroethology, Sensory, Neural, and Behavioral Physiology* 177:247–259.

Giurfa, M., and J. C. Sandoz. 2012. Invertebrate learning and memory: Fifty years of olfactory conditioning of the proboscis extension response in honeybees. *Learning & Memory (Cold Spring Harbor, NY)* 19:54–66.

Giurfa, M., S. Zhang, A. Jenett, R. Menzel, and M. V. Srinivasan. 2001. The concepts of "sameness" and "difference" in an insect. *Nature* 410:930–933.

Grant, V. 1951. The fertilization of flowers. *Scientific American* 12:1–6.

Gross, H. J., M. Pahl, A. Si, H. Zhu, J. Tautz, and S. Zhang. 2009. Number-based visual generalisation in the honeybee. *PLoS ONE* 4:e4263.

Grünewald, B. 1999. Physiological properties and response modulations of mushroom body feedback neurons during olfactory learning in the honeybee *Apis mellifera*. *Journal of Comparative Physiology. A, Neuroethology, Sensory, Neural, and Behavioral Physiology* 185:565–576.

Guerrieri, F., M. Schubert, J. C. Sandoz, and M. Giurfa. 2005. Perceptual and neural olfactory similarity in honeybees. *PLoS Biology* 3:e60.

Homberg, U., and J. Erber. 1979. Response characteristics and identification of extrinsic mushroom body neurons of the bee. *Zeitschrift für Naturforschung* 34:612–615.

Lamberts, K., and D. Shanks. 1997. *Knowledge, Concepts, and Categories*. Cambridge, MA: MIT Press.

Lehrer, M. 1997. Honeybees' visual spatial orientation at the feeding site. In *Detection and Communication in Arthropods*, ed. M. Lehrer, 115–144. Basel: Birkhäuser.

Mauelshagen, J. 1993. Neural correlates of olfactory learning paradigms in an identified neuron in the honeybee brain. *Journal of Neurophysiology* 69:609–625.

Menzel, R. 1985. Learning in honey bees in an ecological and behavioral context. In *Experimental Behavioral Ecology and Sociobiology*, ed. B. Hölldobler and M. Lindauer, 55–74. Stuttgart: Gustav Fischer Verlag.

Menzel, R. 1999. Memory dynamics in the honeybee. *Journal of Comparative Physiology. A, Neuroethology, Sensory, Neural, and Behavioral Physiology* 185:323–340.

Menzel, R., and W. Backhaus. 1991. *Colour vision in insects*. London: MacMillan Press.

Menzel, R., J. Erber, and T. Masuhr. 1974. Learning and memory in the honeybee. In *Experimental Analysis of Insect Behaviour*, ed. L. Barton-Browne, 195–217. Berlin: Springer.

Menzel, R., K. Geiger, L. Chittka, J. Joerges, J. Kunze, and U. Muller. 1996. The knowledge base of bee navigation. *Journal of Experimental Biology* 199:141–146.

Menzel, R., and M. Giurfa. 1999. Cognition by a mini brain. *Nature* 400:718–719.

Menzel, R., and M. Giurfa. 2001. Cognitive architecture of a mini-brain: the honeybee. *Trends in Cognitive Sciences* 5:62–71.

Menzel, R., and M. Giurfa. 2006. Dimensions of cognition in an insect, the honeybee. *Behavioral and Cognitive Neuroscience Reviews* 5:24–40.

Menzel, R., U. Greggers, and M. Hammer. 1993. Functional organization of appetitive learning and memory in a generalist pollinator, the honey bee. In *Insect Learning: Ecology and Evolutionary Perspectives*, ed. D. R. Papaj and A. C. Lewis, 79–125. New York: Chapman and Hall.

Menzel, R., K. Lehmann, G. Manz, J. Fuchs, M. Koblofsky, and U. Greggers. 2012. Vector integration and novel shortcutting in honeybee navigation. *Apidologie* 43:229–243.

Menzel, R., and U. Müller. 1996. Learning and memory in honeybees: From behavior to neural substrates. *Annual Review of Neuroscience* 19:379–404.

Miller, E. K., A. Nieder, D. J. Freedman, and J. D. Wallis. 2003. Neural correlates of categories and concepts. *Current Opinion in Neurobiology* 13:198–203.

Mobbs, P. G. 1982. The brain of the honeybee *Apis mellifera* I. The connections and spatial organization of the mushroom bodies. *Philosophical Transactions of the Royal Society of London. Series B, Biological Sciences* 298:309–354.

Murphy, G. L. 2002. *The Big Book of Concepts*. Cambridge, MA: MIT Press.

Murphy, G. L. 2010. What are categories and concepts? In *The Making of Human Concepts*, ed. D. Mareschal, P. C. Quinn, and S. E. G. Lea, 11–28. Oxford: Oxford University Press.

Okada, R., J. Rybak, G. Manz, and R. Menzel. 2007. Learning-related plasticity in PE1 and other mushroom body-extrinsic neurons in the honeybee brain. *Journal of Neuroscience* 27: 11736–11747.

Robertson, H. M., and K. W. Wanner. 2006. The chemoreceptor superfamily in the honey bee, *Apis mellifera*: Expansion of the odorant, but not gustatory, receptor family. *Genome Research* 16:1395–1403.

Rybak, J., and R. Menzel. 1998. Integrative properties of the Pe1-neuron, a unique mushroom body output neuron. *Learning & Memory (Cold Spring Harbor, NY)* 5:133–145.

Schröter, U., and R. Menzel. 2003. A new ascending sensory tract to the calyces of the honeybee mushroom body, the subesophageal-calycal tract. *Journal of Comparative Neurology* 465:168–178.

Srinivasan, M. V. 1994. Pattern recognition in the honeybee: Recent progress. *Journal of Insect Physiology* 40 (3): 183–194.

Srinivasan, M. V. 2010. Honey bees as a model for vision, perception, and cognition. *Annual Review of Entomology* 55:267–284.

Srinivasan, M. V., M. Poteser, and K. Kral. 1999. Motion detection in insect orientation and navigation. *Vision Research* 39:2749–2766.

Strausfeld, N. J. 2002. Organization of the honey bee mushroom body: Representation of the calyx within the vertical and gamma lobes. *Journal of Comparative Neurology* 450:4–33.

Strausfeld, N. J. 2012. *Arthropod Brains: Evolution, Functional Elegance, and Historical Significance.* Cambridge, MA: Belknap Press.

Tedjakumala, R. 2014. *The role of dopamine network and signalling in aversive network in honey bee.* Ph.D. Thesis. University Toulouse 3, France.

Vareschi, E. 1971. Duftunterscheidung bei der Honigbiene—Einzelzell-Ableitungen und Verhaltensreaktionen. *Zeitschrift fur Vergleichende Physiologie* 75:143–173.

Vergoz, V., E. Roussel, J. C. Sandoz, and M. Giurfa. 2007. Aversive learning in honeybees revealed by the olfactory conditioning of the sting extension reflex. *PLoS ONE* 2:e288.

von Frisch, K. 1914. Der Farbensinn und Formensinn der Biene. *Zoologische Jahrbucher. Abteilung fur Allgemeine Zoologie und Physiologie der Tiere* 35:1–188.

von Frisch, K. 1967. *The Dance Language and Orientation of Bees.* Cambridge, MA: Belknap Press.

Wallis, J. D., K. C. Anderson, and E. K. Miller. 2001. Single neurons in prefrontal cortex encode abstract rules. *Nature* 411:953–956.

Wehner, R. 1981. Spatial vision in arthropods. In *Handbook of Sensory Physiology VIc,* ed. H. J. Autrum, 287–616. Berlin: Springer.

Wehner, R. 2003. Desert ant navigation: How miniature brains solve complex tasks. *Journal of Comparative Physiology. A, Neuroethology, Sensory, Neural, and Behavioral Physiology* 189:579–588.

White, I. M., and S. P. Wise. 1999. Rule-dependent neuronal activity in the prefrontal cortex. *Experimental Brain Research* 126:315–335.

Winston, M. L. 1987. *The Biology of the Honey Bee.* Cambridge, MA: Harvard University Press.

Zentall, T. R., M. Galizio, and T. S. Critchfield. 2002. Categorization, concept learning, and behavior analysis: An introduction. *Journal of the Experimental Analysis of Behavior* 78:237–248.

Zentall, T. R., E. A. Wasserman, O. F. Lazareva, R. K. R. Thompson, and M. J. Rattermann. 2008. Concept learning in animals. *Comparative Cognition and Behavior Reviews* 3:13–45.

Zhang, S., F. Bock, A. Si, J. Tautz, and M. V. Srinivasan. 2005. Visual working memory in decision making by honey bees. *Proceedings of the National Academy of Sciences of the United States of America* 102:5250–5255.

Zhang, S. W., M. V. Srinivasan, H. Zhu, and J. Wong. 2004. Grouping of visual objects by honeybees. *Journal of Experimental Biology* 207:3289–3298.

2 Convergent Cognitive Evolution across Animal Taxa: Comparisons of Chimpanzees, Corvids, and Elephants

Joshua M. Plotnik and Nicola S. Clayton

2.1 Introduction

The study of intelligence has, for several decades, focused on the primate lineage. This focus is based on an assumption that the most recent common ancestor of humans and other nonhuman primates was subjected to environmental pressures requiring behavioral flexibility. More recently, however, there has been increased interest in the study of other, nonprimate groups with seemingly similar cognitive complexity. Due to the distance between these species' evolutionary lineages, these animals, which include elephants (Byrne, Bates, and Moss 2009), dolphins (Marino 2002), and corvids and parrots (Emery and Clayton 2004), must have evolved intelligence independently. So called convergent cognitive evolution is an exciting new area of research that aims to bridge the gap between humans and other animals in the evolution of physical and social complexity. In general, the term "convergent cognitive evolution" implies that certain measures of intelligence—among others, problem solving, perspective taking, cooperation, and causal reasoning—may have evolved independently in evolutionarily distant species that are subjected to similar selection pressures (e.g., de Waal 1996; Emery and Clayton 2004; Marino 2002; Shettleworth 2010).

Convergent evolution explains the emergence of similar adaptations that evolve independently in a number of different organisms under similar environmental pressures (Keeton and Gould 1986). Convergence is supported by empirical evidence for similar behavioral or anatomical traits present in a group of species, but absent in their common ancestor. The forelimbs of birds, bats and flying insects, for instance, all evolved into functional wings even though their common ancestor did not share this trait (Seed, Emery, and Clayton 2009). The common ancestor of mammals and cephalopods had simple, photoreceptive vision but not the similar, complex camera-like eye found in its descendants (Conway Morris 2005). This suggests that convergent evolution may shape similar, optimal adaptations (both behavioral and anatomical) in remarkably dissimilar species. The reason for these separate yet parallel evolutionary trajectories is most likely similar social and ecological pressures on animals living in similar environments. Intelligence then, for example, most likely evolved in constantly changing environments in which an animal's behavior would need to be able to adapt rather quickly to change. Greater behavioral flexibility and the capacity for the development of abstract knowledge would then not necessarily be unique to primates.

Thus, what makes the study of convergent cognitive evolution so exciting is its departure from traditional animal models for intelligence (specifically nonhuman primates) as well as the notion that it allows psychologists to test hypotheses about the evolution of intelligence across unrelated animal taxa. We endeavor then to test hypotheses on the complexity of both physical (or technical) and social cognition in animals such as chimpanzees, corvids and elephants, for instance, by focusing on the differences and similarities in environmental constraints to which they have been subjected. Within the past twenty years, a growing body of empirical evidence has emerged to support these animals' reputation for intelligence.

In this chapter, we briefly illustrate how the field of comparative cognition is changing in light of this evidence, and use chimpanzees, elephants, and corvids as examples to illustrate how specific animal families may have evolved similar cognitive capabilities over hundreds of millions of years of evolutionary separation. This convergence does not preclude them from developing different anatomical or behavioral traits depending on the environments in which they lived, hence bird wings, chimpanzee arms, and elephant trunks. These species are remarkably different in size and shape, but here we discuss their cognitive similarities and how such analogous intelligence may have evolved across distant taxa. Specifically, we provide selected evidence for convergent cognitive evolution to illustrate the importance of continued attention to this field, and to a more comprehensive approach to understanding how the environment in which animals live and how specific, selective forces that have shaped flexibility in their behavior have contributed to the evolution of their intelligence.

2.2   The How and Why of Intelligence: Physical and Social Cognition Explained?

If apes, corvids, and elephants evolved specific, complex cognitive mechanisms for technological and social behavior, what characteristics of their environment may have been influential in driving convergence?

2.1.1   Physical
One area of focus suggests that brain size relative to body size—often considered a measure of intelligence (e.g., Jerison 1973)—is influenced by what, where and how animals forage (Seed, Emery, and Clayton 2009). Primates, for instance, reliant on fruiting plants that (a) ripen only at certain times of year, and (b) occur in only certain, predictable areas, may have evolved intelligence specifically to locate and remember food location and edibility (Milton 1981). Corvids are known for their

caching abilities, and their ability to remember what, where, and when they have cached food (e.g., Clayton and Dickinson 1998, 1999) as well as who was watching (e.g., Dally, Emery, and Clayton 2006). Elephants are known for returning to specific food and water sources (Foley, Pettorelli, and Foley 2008; Sukumar 2003) along or off their migration routes after periods of extreme droughts. These environmental challenges, which must require more than basic spatiotemporal abilities, may have shaped the evolution of intelligence.

Although finding food is one thing, actually acquiring it is another. Foraging techniques and the use of tools are among the more prominent focal areas for understanding how a need for a physical understanding of one's environment shaped the evolution of intelligence in animals. Byrne (1996, 2004) argued that advanced cognition has been driven by the complexity of primate foraging and the multilevel use of tools—as seen, for example, in gorillas (*Gorilla gorilla*), which must navigate plant defenses to eat nettle leaves (Byrne 1996), and in wild chimpanzee (*Pan troglodytes*) nut cracking and termite fishing (Boesch and Boesch-Achermann 2000; Whiten et al. 1999). Although tool use is more common in the animal kingdom than once believed, this level of complexity of tool use is reserved for only a select few species. Corvids are well known for their tool use in the wild, and one species of crow also crafts its own tools—New Caledonian crows (*Corvus moneduloides*) manufacture stepped-cut tools from leaves and hook tools from sticks or other substrates to fish for food (Hunt 1996). In captivity, some corvids are known to use tools even when traditionally they do not in the wild (e.g., rooks [*Corvus frugilegus*]—Bird and Emery 2009a, 2009b; Eurasian jays [*Garrulus glandarius*]—Cheke, Bird, and Clayton 2011).

Mendes, Hanus, and Call (2007) argued that great ape tool use is unmatched in the animal kingdom, as corvids and other animal tool use is potentially less flexible and complex. Seed, Emery, and Clayton (2009) argue that these species-level differences could be need rather than capacity based. The corvid beak is, for many food-retrieval applications, just as good as a primate-made tool or hand, and the corvid's overall size compared with that of the ape makes the use of some tools impractical or impossible (Seed, Emery and Clayton, 2009). Elephants (African—*Loxodonta* genus, Asian—*Elephas maximus*) are not well known for their tool use (but see tree branch modification for fly swatting—Hart et al. 2001), although this is possibly because they have a built-in tool (their trunk) that is unmatched in primates or birds. The elephant trunk has no bones and at least forty thousand muscles, so the elephant may use its trunk in ways a primate might use a manufactured tool. In addition, while the small body of a corvid may prohibit it from using some tools practically, the large body size of an elephant may make the use of some tools redundant. Elephants routinely use their body weight to crush fruits or knock down trees to obtain food, thus making artificial tools unnecessary. Although tool use might not be a precursor for the evolution of complex cognition, its existence in certain species may be a measurable expression of technological intelligence useful for categorizing how flexibility in behavior allows animals to selectively manipulate their environments.

2.1.2 Social

Animals engage in three general categories of social behavior within their environments that have most certainly shaped variability in cognition (Seed, Emery and Clayton 2009). Competing with others to strategically maximize one's own fitness ("competition"—e.g., Humphrey 1976; Byrne and Whiten 1997), working together with others for mutual gain ("cooperation"—Dugatkin 1997; de Waal 1996, 2008; Emery et al. 2007), and learning from conspecifics ("social learning"—Galef and Laland 2005) represent categories of behavior that require flexibility and thus may have influenced complex cognitive development in animals. There is evidence, to varying degrees, for all three behavioral categories in corvids (Seed, Emery, and Clayton 2009) and elephants (Poole 1996; Sukumar 2003), but here we focus on cooperation as an example because it is the only one we have empirical, laboratory-based evidence for in both taxa. Cooperation is relatively common in the animal kingdom, but how it is expressed across species varies markedly (Dugatkin 1997).

Living in groups provides animals with an opportunity to increase their fitness through cooperative efforts, an increase that would be largely unobtainable through individual action. Cooperative hunting or predator defense is relevant here, but so is targeted helping (assisting others in immediate need of help, for instance—de Waal 1996, 2008). The difficulty in differentiating between the cognitive pressures on similar cooperative behavior across species—that is, how the intelligence of cooperative-breeding birds or hunting lions compares to fission-fusion elephant families or wild chimpanzee groups—makes studying them in a laboratory setting all the more important (Seed, Emery, and Clayton 2009). Socially complex animals that may (a) compete for food and sexual resources via alliance and coalition formation (e.g., Harcourt and de Waal 1992) and (b) cooperate with specific partners and sometimes switch partners based on changes in dominance or environment make interesting test subjects for intelligence. The dynamics of their social relationships may in fact suggest that more complex cognitive mechanisms underlie their day-to-day decision making. For example, socially monogamous birds that sustain long-term partnerships may end these relationships if mating attempts fail (Mock and Fujioka 1990), suggesting they choose to remain with partners based on the success of the cooperative partnership. Emery and colleagues (2007) found that paired rooks regularly coordinate their behavior, and Seed, Clayton, and Emery (2007) found that individuals affiliate with their partners after the latter have been in a conflict. Seed, Emery, and Clayton (2009) argue that this, with the result that the birds do not reconcile with other, aggressive parties, suggests that corvids—a largely monogamous bird family—form strong social bonds with their partners but do not form socially important relationships with others. In addition, a recent study by Ostojić and colleagues (2013) showed that corvids select food to share based on their partners' current food preference and their previous meals. The authors demonstrated that this result was due neither to the subjects' own food desires nor reading their partners' behavior toward the food, suggesting the birds may be able to attribute desire to others.

This behavior, mainly focused on a single partner, differs sharply from that of chimpanzees, for instance, which regularly both reconcile with others they compete with and console those with which they are affiliated (for a review, see Aureli and de Waal 2000), an alternative social mechanism that seems to mitigate the fluctuation in social relationship quality. Elephants live in largely related, matriarchal family groups in which conflict is relatively rare (Payne 2003; Poole 1996; Plotnik and de Waal 2014). Unlike in chimpanzee groups, changes in hierarchy are uncommon because family groups consist of younger offspring (both male and female), and adult females ("sisters"), led usually by one of the oldest (Douglas-Hamilton and Douglas-Hamilton 1975; Payne 2003; Poole 1996). Thus, although social cohesion is important in elephants (e.g., Douglas-Hamilton and Douglas-Hamilton 1975; Plotnik and de Waal 2014), the need to choose important partners (and keep track of potential competition) may not be. Although corvids live in largely monogamous pairings and elephants live in largely related, closely bonded family groups, this difference does not preclude either from possessing social intelligence. Although the need for careful calculation in partner choice may underlie the complexity of ape social intelligence, it may be less important in monogamous corvids and female-family-centric elephants. Perhaps social complexity in these species is instead driven by the physical challenges they face in their environment, and the way in which these challenges may require coordinated efforts by or toward partners. At the end of this chapter, we discuss some of the empirical evidence for this idea, which suggests that although partner choice is important for determining the likelihood of success in a cooperative interaction, an ability to learn about or understand how cooperative, joint action works may be just as relevant.

Intelligence in animals is grounded in theories on physical and social cognition, but the study of it is reliant on controlled laboratory experiments that assess an animal's capacity for behavioral flexibility in a novel context. Although work on chimpanzee cognition is decades old (for a review before 2000, see Tomasello and Call 1997; for a discussion of more recent studies, see Seed and Tomasello 2010), a focus on convergence in cognitive abilities across species is relatively new, and thus the growth in abundance of studies on corvids and elephants is recent (Emery and Clayton 2004; Byrne, Bates, and Moss 2009). Here, we briefly review some areas of physical and social cognition research across chimpanzees, corvids, and elephants to show that the study of convergent cognitive evolution is a growing field bent on understanding how commonalities in the environmental constraints facing evolutionarily distant species drive similarities in intelligence.

2.3   Comparing Cognition across Taxa: Technical Intelligence

The technical intelligence hypothesis argues that the cognitive complexity of certain animals, specifically apes, has been shaped by the need for behavioral flexibility in foraging techniques because of difficulties in extracting or processing food (e.g., Byrne 1997). These techniques require some sort of innovation on the part of the animal to successfully manipulate a difficult environment.

2.3.1   Tool Use and Causal Reasoning

Until van Lawick-Goodall (1968) demonstrated that chimpanzees use physical objects other than their own body parts to extend their normal physical reach (adapted from the well-known definitions of tool use provided by Beck 1980; Jones and Kamil 1973), tool use was considered a human-specific trait. Although many animal species—both vertebrate and invertebrate—in fact use tools (Beck 1980; Emery and Clayton 2009b), the daily use of tools for foraging is relatively rare (for reviews, see Tomasello and Call 1997; van Horik, Clayton, and Emery 2012), and only chimpanzees, orangutans (*Pongo* genus), and crows are known to use, manipulate, and manufacture tools regularly in the wild (e.g., Fox, Sitompul, and Van Schaik 1999; Hunt 1996; Hunt and Gray 2004; McGrew 1992). The proximate mechanisms underlying tool use, however, are far less well defined (Povinelli 2000). As tool-use repertoire differs among species (e.g., elephants using sticks to scratch or fly-switch—Chevalier-Skolnikoff and Liska 1993; Hart et al. 2001; dolphins (*Tursiops truncatus*) using sponges as foraging tools—Krützen et al. 2005; Smolker et al. 2010; or octopuses (*Amphioctopus marginatus*) using self-assembled coconut-shell halves as shelter—Finn, Tregenza, and Norman 2009), so does the cognition underlying it (Emery and Clayton 2009b; Povinelli 2000). Chimpanzees are generally regarded as the best users of tools other than humans,[1] but there are some exciting examples of complex tool use in corvids as well (for a review, see Emery and Clayton 2009b). New Caledonian crows are known for manipulating leaves to make serrated probes, and both crows and rooks create and manipulate tools specific to food-retrieval tasks (Bird and Emery 2009a, 2009b; Hunt 1996; Hunt and Gray 2004; Weir, Chappell, and Kacelnik 2002), as well as choose specific tools based on their size and length to solve specific problems (i.e., retrieve hidden food—Bird and Emery 2009a; Chappell and Kacelnik 2002, 2004). The complexity of the manufacture of such tools suggests that an animal may know its end goal before it starts to create a tool from fresh material, but how much cognition is required to manufacture even the

1. For example, for work on cultural transmission of tool use, see Whiten et al. (1999) and Whiten, Horner, and de Waal (2005); for variation in tool use and manufacture across wild populations (including ant dipping, nut cracking, and termite fishing), see the review in Boesch and Tomasello (1998); and for the production of multiple tools for different purposes in the same activity, see Sanz and Morgan (2007).

most remarkable tools in nonhuman animals is yet unknown (van Horik, Clayton, and Emery 2012).

Many of these attempts to investigate the correlation between complex physical cognition and tool use have occurred in the laboratory (Emery and Clayton 2009b). Although few species regularly make tools in the wild, there is substantial innovation (and behavioral flexibility) in other, non-tool-using animals. Rooks (Bird and Emery 2009b), Eurasian jays (Cheke, Bird, and Clayton 2011), and orangutans (Mendes, Hanus, and Call 2007) solved an Aesop's fable-based problem by obtaining food within a tube using a tool. The birds, when faced with a tube containing water, used stones to raise the water level (and thus the food), while the orangutans spit water into the tube—the tube was dry—to raise the food to an obtainable level. Another testing paradigm, the trap-tube task, generally requires an animal to insert a tool (or in the case of non-tool-using animals, use a tool already part of the apparatus) to retrieve a food reward by avoiding a trap when it is functional, or ignoring it when it is nonfunctional (Emery and Clayton 2009b). If an animal is able to solve one version of the trap task and then transfer its success to modifications (i.e., slight variations in trap functionality or the relevance of specific characteristics of the traps) of the same task, this suggests rather complex physical intelligence. For instance, Seed and colleagues (2006) showed that rooks could solve different variations of the trap-tube task by (a) avoiding traps that had solid bases and were thus functional, and (b) ignoring (i.e., pulling food over) traps that had a solid top or no top or bottom at all and were thus nonfunctional. One rook was also successful when presented with novel tube configurations, which may suggest a more complex, causal understanding. Although rooks, crows (Taylor et al. 2009), and chimpanzees (Seed et al. 2009) show some success on these tasks, additional studies are needed to investigate further how well animals understand the ways in which tools work. From a theoretical perspective, these studies suggest that the presence of tool use in the wild is not the only predictor of overall physical intelligence. Although tool use was once seen as a benchmark indicator of cognitive complexity, demonstrations of physical cognition in non-tool-using species suggest that its evolution in animals may be independent of specific behavioral traits (Emery and Clayton 2009b). Instead, intelligent animals may demonstrate the capacity for "cognitive" and "behavioral" flexibility, which allows them to solve novel and unique problems with which they otherwise might not have prior or extensive experience (Byrne 1995; Roth and Dicke 2005). This is an important point; as we previously discussed, tool-use demonstrations in the wild may only occur in those species with a limited natural ability to manipulate their physical environment. Although a recent study showed that an elephant used insightful problem solving in a task requiring him to stand on a box to retrieve food (Foerder et al. 2011), there is little evidence to date of elephants using complex tools in captivity or the wild. But, as the technical intelligence hypothesis suggests, tools should only be created and manipulated by those species that require them for extracting food from their environments. Elephants are large animals with an extremely flexible built-in tool (their trunk), which suggests that the evolution of complex cognition in some species may be a result of a combination of specific physical and social needs. Whereas chimpanzee and corvid intelligence may have evolved as a result of both technical and social environmental pressures, other species like elephants may have evolved complex cognition more as a result of the latter.

2.4   Comparing Cognition across Taxa: Social Intelligence

Although an animal's physical environment may affect its behavioral repertoire, and more importantly, its cognitive range, this may not be sufficient to explain the variability of intelligence within and across species. Instead, it has been suggested that the complexity of animals' social relationships—specifically their need and ability to differentiate between individuals, and to cooperate, deceive, and compete with others—was an important factor in the evolution of intelligence, particularly in primates (Byrne and Whiten 1997; Humphrey 1976). Although this "social intelligence" hypothesis, and variations of it, has evolved over the past several decades to include a more comprehensive approach to understanding intelligence (e.g., including both comparative and neuroscience approaches—see Emery et al. [2007] for a review), it has received widespread support from those studying the evolution of intelligence in primates, and fits well with recent evidence for complex cognition in nonprimates living in diverse social systems.

2.4.1   Perspective Taking

The ability of animals to exploit or manipulate their social relationships is well documented in primates (de Waal 1982, 1996), but similar social complexity has also been observed in cetaceans (Marino 2002), corvids (Emery et al. 2007), and elephants (de Silva, Ranjeewa, and Kryazhimskiy 2011; Payne 2003; Plotnik and de Waal 2014; Poole 1996). Much of this manipulation is probably due to food competition in the wild or a need to solve problems cooperatively as well as the ability of certain individuals to monopolize preferred or specific food resources (Boesch and Boesch 1989; Mitani and Watts 2001). In primate social hierarchies, there are significant fitness advantages for individuals that are able to monopolize such food resources, in terms of access to mates and the stability of formed alliances (Gomes and Boesch 2009; Harcourt and de Waal 1992). Thus, it makes sense that cognitive abilities would have evolved to give animals an opportunity to manipulate their social environment to gain access to such resources, particularly in situations where competition is especially relevant for fitness benefits (de Waal 1982; Dugatkin 1997). Hare and colleagues (2000), for example, showed that when subordinate and dominant chimpanzees were paired in a visual task in which the subordinate chimpanzee could see two pieces of food while the dominant could see only one, the subordinate individual went for the food invisible to the dominant individual. This finding was supported by subsequent tests in which the behavior of either the subordinate (they were released first to control for potential confounds of dominant gaze or behavior—Hare et al. 2000), or the dominant (by replacing informed with uninformed dominants or giving the dominant more information about the hidden food's location—Hare, Call, and Tomasello 2001) was manipulated. Other examples of great ape perspective taking have focused on an ape's ability to understand what humans can see and know (Hare et al. 2002; Shillito et al. 2005). Together, these results suggest that apes may recognize what others see and know and adjust their behavior accordingly. There is the possibility, however, that potentially more parsimonious explanations for the chimpanzees' behavior exist, specifically that changes in their behavior are due to the chimpanzees' ability to read partner behavior rather than an understanding of partner mental states (Emery and Clayton 2009a; Karin-D'Arcy and Povinelli 2002; Povinelli and Vonk 2004).

Corvids are interesting models for studying perspective taking because of their well-known food-caching strategies, which include hiding food items for future retrieval in various locations and over varying lengths of time (de Kort and Clayton 2006; Vander Wall 1990). The flexibility in caching strategies within and across species makes it a useful behavior for assessing complex cognition (Grodzinski and Clayton 2010). Spatial memory underlies these birds' ability to find caches (Clayton 1998; Shettleworth 2002) and to remember what caches have already been removed when returning to retrieve those still present (Clayton and Dickinson 1999). The ability to experimentally manipulate and observe caching behavior has made for some exciting new areas of research in corvid cognition (for a review, see Emery and Clayton 2004). From a temporal perspective (i.e., perspectives on time), corvids have been shown to possess episodic-like memory (often referred to as the retrospective component of mental time travel) in their storage and retrieval of caches, specifically that they can remember what food they stored, when and where (Clayton and Dickinson 1998; Clayton, Yu, and Dickinson 2001), and who was watching when they cached (Dally, Emery, and Clayton 2006), and an ability for anticipating what they will need in the future when deciding on their caching strategies (e.g., Correia, Dickinson, and Clayton 2007; Raby et al. 2007; Cheke and Clayton 2012). This complex memory for food storage gives corvids an advantage not only in temporal perspective taking but also in social perspective taking. It has been suggested that this concept of perspective taking may have evolved as an adaptation against cache theft (Bugnyar and Heinrich 2005; Emery and Clayton 2001)—allowing these birds to change the location and timing of their caches based on whether or not conspecifics are present to observe. Indeed, it has been argued that such perspective taking led to the evolution of increasingly complex cache theft and cache-protection tactics via a ratchet mechanism akin to a co-evolutionary arms race (Emery, Dally, and Clayton 2004; Shaw and Clayton 2012). Corvids are well known for their sociality and their ability to find and pilfer conspecific cache stores (Bugnyar and Kotrschal 2002; Bugnyar and Heinrich 2006; Shaw and Clayton 2012; Watanabe and Clayton 2007). The potential victims of such pilfering have been shown to hide food in hard-to-see locations (Bugnyar and Kotrschal 2002; Dally, Emery, and Clayton 2004, 2005), and to move caches from locations seen by previous observers (Emery and Clayton 2001, 2004, 2008). Perhaps even stronger evidence comes from the finding that the birds only move caches if they have been observed and, importantly, only if they have stolen another bird's caches before (Emery and Clayton 2001). Taken together, this body of evidence suggests the corvids' behavior may be a result of mental attribution or recognition of the other's point of view (Dally, Emery, and Clayton 2010).

Corvids may also tactically deceive other individuals by manipulating cache locations and by sham caching (going through the motions without actually hiding food— Heinrich 1999) or changing their pilfering behavior in the presence of conspecifics (Bugnyar and Heinrich 2005, 2006). Anecdotal and some experimental evidence for tactical deception also exists for primates (e.g., Hare, Call, and Tomasello 2006; Whiten and Byrne 1988), but it is surprisingly limited. In addition, emphasis on anecdotal evidence to infer cognition is problematic (Bates and Byrne 2007; Byrne and Bates 2011; Whiten and Byrne 1988).

At this point, evidence for perspective taking in animals such as elephants and dolphins is largely anecdotal, due to difficulties in testing these species in controlled settings. It is important, though, to provide these examples as a starting point for future experiments. Examples of potential perspective taking in elephants include plugging and covering small water sources to prevent others from finding them (Shoshani 1992), and targeted helping directed toward others in need, including lifting or coordinating the rescue of injured or trapped conspecifics (e.g., Moss 1988, 73; Payne 1998, 64). Similar examples of helping distressed conspecifics exist for dolphins as well (Caldwell and Caldwell 1966, 766; Siebenaler and Caldwell 1956, 126), specifically in cases when an incapacitated individual needs assistance reaching the water's surface to breathe. These observations suggest that elephants and dolphins would make interesting candidates for empirical perspective-taking studies that distinguish between simple behavior reading and the more complex, representative understanding of what a conspecific knows, needs, or can see as a mechanism for maximizing the benefits of decision making (de Waal 1996, 2009).

Interestingly, these species' considerable behavioral flexibility, a common theme throughout this chapter, would allow them to form core concepts that could be applied to both the physical and the social world. Perspective taking and transitive inference are two prime examples of such concepts. Transitive inference, for instance, can be applied to the physical world (e.g., understanding that if A is bigger than B and B is bigger than C, then A must also be bigger than C). The same conceptual knowledge can also be applied to the social world in making the inference that A must be dominant over C. Similarly, perspective taking can be applied to the physical world by understanding that one's view of the world changes over time, and in the social world by understanding that another individual may have a different perspective from one's own. In this way, mental time travel and theory of mind can be seen as engaging the same conceptual understanding.

2.4.2 Cue Following

Another area of research focuses on conspecific or interspecies behavioral cue following, and the information animals use to make decisions. Theoretically, an animal's ability to follow conspecific cues would have important implications for decision making based on what others see and know, and thus may have similar cognitive underpinnings as perspective taking.

Emery and coauthors (1997) showed that rhesus monkeys (*Macaca mulatta*) follow the gaze of conspecifics, and others have shown that corvids and apes both follow the gazes of humans and move their own location to get a better look at where a human is looking (Bräuer, Call, and Tomasello 2005; Bugnyar, Stowe, and Heinrich 2004; Schloegl, Kotrschal, and Bugnyar 2007; see Davidson et al. 2014 for a review of gaze following research). An often-used paradigm for assessing how animals follow social cues is the object-choice task. A subject animal is allowed to choose one of two objects (usually cups or buckets) under or behind which is hidden food or a target item (Call 2004; Hare and Tomasello 1999; Miklósi and Soproni 2006). Often, these studies involve a human experimenter who provides a limited visual cue—pointing, orienting, or gazing—to the food or item's hidden location. Such studies have been conducted on the great apes (chimpanzees—Bräuer et al. 2006; Hare et al. 2002; Itakura et al. 1999; Itakura and Tanaka 1998; Mulcahy and Call 2009; Povinelli et al. 1997; orangutans—Call and Tomasello 1994; Itakura and Tanaka 1998; and gorillas—Peignot and Anderson 1999), but interestingly, these studies have produced mixed results, with many suggesting that nonhuman primates (also see monkeys—Itakura and Anderson 1996; Neiworth et al. 2002; Vick and Anderson 2000) differ within and across species on their success in this task. Surprisingly, many nonprimate species have been tested on similar visual object-choice tasks and have done well by following the human-provided social cue to find hidden food (e.g., domestic dogs, *Canis familiaris*—Agnetta, Hare, and Tomasello 2000; Hare and Tomasello 1999, 2005; Miklósi, Topal, and Csanyi 1998; African gray parrots, *Psittacus erithacus*—Giret, Miklósi, Kreutzer, and Bovet 2009; domestic goats, *Capra hircus*—Kaminski et al. 2005; horses, *Equus caballus*—Maros, Gacsi, and Miklósi 2008; Proops, Walton, and McComb 2010; dingoes, *Canis dingo*—Smith and Litchfield 2010; South African fur seals—*Arctocephalus pusillus*—Scheumann and Call 2004; jackdaws, *Corvus monedula*—von Bayern and Emery 2009; Clark's nutcrackers, *Nucifraga columbiana*—Tornick et al. 2011; and African elephants, *Loxodonta africana*—Smet and Byrne 2013, but see Plotnik et al. 2013 for negative results in Asian elephants, *Elephas maximus*). Hare and colleagues (2002) showed that domesticated dogs but not hand-reared wolves could use these same cues and argued that this discrepancy between species that could and could not follow human-provided social cues was most likely due to the process of domestication, which drove the artificial selection for the ability to follow human social cues. An animal's ability to follow social cues in conspecifics or humans, or the lack thereof, may not be a direct sign of intelligence but suggests that it is important first to identify the social, behavioral cues different species use before attempting to assess how these species employ complex cognition in decision-making processes.

2.4.3   Cooperation

Behavioral flexibility is often an indicator of higher-level cognition that is perhaps necessary for social relationships driven by changing partner roles and fluctuating levels of cooperation and competition (de Waal 1996; Emery and Clayton 2004). The ultimate mechanisms underlying cooperation have been well-studied (Axelrod and Hamilton 1981; Dugatkin 1997; Trivers 1971), but the proximate, cognitive mechanisms have not. Empirical investigations of how animals "think" about cooperation generally look at animals' reactions to their partners' behavior (Noë 2006). The ultimate mechanisms underlying cooperation—for example, kin selection (altruistic behavior directed toward genetic relatives—Hamilton 1964), byproduct mutualism (behavior, individually selfish, that provides immediate benefits to others—Brown 1983), and reciprocal altruism (benefits obtained through the exchange of altruistic acts over time—Trivers 1971)— vary across the animal kingdom; cooperation is not rare, but much of the proximate mechanisms underlying it are most likely innately programmed and not cognitively complex (de Waal 1996).

Crawford (1937) presented a landmark study on chimpanzees that served as the basis for most future experimental research on cooperation in animals. Two chimpanzees needed to pull two ropes attached to an out-of-reach box to retrieve food placed on top of it; the box was too heavy for a single individual's effort, and thus a coordinated effort by both chimpanzees was needed to pull in the box. The chimpanzees did not immediately coordinate their pulling efforts, but after some teaching and reinforcement, they learned to cooperate without human cuing. The chimpanzees nonetheless needed to learn to coordinate their pulling on the task to successfully and consistently obtain food. Primatologists have often debated the cognitive complexity underlying cooperative behavior (for example, see Boesch 1994 and Stanford et al. 1994 for a discussion of chimpanzee hunting behavior). However, in the empirical study of cooperation in a controlled laboratory environment, the focus is on the capacity of animals to maintain cooperative behavior without cuing from an experimenter, even if initially, some of the behavioral mechanisms were learned during the task (Hirata and Fuwa 2007; Melis, Hare, and Tomasello 2006). In experiments, the difference between test and control variables often allows for the testing of whether animal performance is due to random chance or a recognition (or understanding) of how a task works; in cooperation, this might mean the difference between an animal cooperating by chance or by demonstrating an understanding of partnership and coordination (Mendres and de Waal 2000). Incidentally, this fundamental mantra of experimental psychology is one of the most difficult aspects of designing experiments focused on comparing cognition across species. If we cannot ask animals what they are thinking directly, we must design controls and specific conditions within an experiment to attempt to assess cognition empirically.

More than fifty years after Crawford (1937), Chalmeau (1994) and Chalmeau and Gallo (1996) tested whether two chimpanzees could simultaneously pull a handle to obtain food. Although dominance was an important factor (the dominant male obtained most of the food), his attention to his partner during the task increased with time, which may indicate his understanding of the need for a partner (Hirata and Fuwa 2007). Mendres and de Waal (2000) used a bar-pull apparatus (similar to Crawford's rope-pull task in that the bars were attached to a sliding tray) to demonstrate that capuchin monkeys (*Cebus apella*) could learn about the need for partner collaboration in a cooperation task, although Chalmeau, Visalberghi, and Gallo (1997) and Visalberghi, Quarantotti, and Tranchida (2000) suggested that the monkeys only cooperated when their random pulling occurred at the same time. Melis, Hare, and Tomasello (2006) adopted a procedure designed by Hirata and Fuwa (2007—described below) and found that chimpanzees not only knew they needed a partner to successfully retrieve food (one chimpanzee had to release another into the experiment room by pulling a door pin, and only did so when a partner was needed), but also chose more effective partners when a choice was available.

Hirata and Fuwa's (2007) apparatus was a simple task similar to Crawford's (1937) rope pull in that two individuals needed to pull two ropes to retrieve an out-of-reach food reward. The former's apparatus, however, did not rely on the weight of a box being too much for a single individual's effort; instead, the two ropes were actually two ends of the same rope, threaded through and around the out-of-reach food trays. Thus,, if one rope end was pulled without the other, the entire rope would become unthreaded and the food unobtainable. This modification made it easier to test whether the resulting cooperation (i.e., when the food was successfully obtained by two pulling chimpanzees) was due to random chance or to an understanding of the task. Hirata and Fuwa (2007) first trained the chimpanzees to pull both ends together without the help of a partner. When they were then allowed to try to pull each rope end individually (and cooperatively) with a partner, they failed. After varying the lengths of available rope so that shorter rope ends required faster coordination than longer ones (because one chimpanzee's pulling before the arrival of the partner would mean faster failure), the chimpanzees gradually learned to coordinate their efforts. Chimpanzees regularly looked toward their partners before pulling, and when paired with human partners, actually recruited or solicited them for cooperation. The chimpanzees became highly successful even when the available rope end was short and they had to wait for their partner before pulling. This finding suggests that chimpanzees can learn how to cooperate in a task requiring behavioral flexibility, and to coordinate their behavior when necessary.

Similar studies on nonprimates, although few in number thus far, have produced varying results. In a task similar to Hirata and Fuwa (2007), rooks pulled the two rope ends when they arrived together (Scheid and Noë 2010; Seed, Clayton, and Emery 2008). However, although there was evidence the rooks synchronized their actions in order to solve the task, they failed to wait for a partner's arrival if they arrived separately, suggesting a possible lack of understanding about the need for a partner (Seed, Clayton, and Emery 2008). In studies on hyenas (*Crocuta crocuta*—Drea and Carter 2009) and capuchin monkeys (Mendres and de Waal 2000) that used similar cooperative pulling apparatuses, the subjects seemed to recognize that a partner's presence was important for obtaining food, but their successful cooperation did not necessarily indicate or require an understanding that their partner's participation in the task mattered. Chimpanzees, however, seemed to have an understanding of both (Hare et al. 2007; Hirata and Fuwa 2007; Melis, Hare, and Tomasello 2006). Plotnik and colleagues (2011) tested Asian elephants and found that they pulled cooperatively and waited to pull if

Figure 2.1
Multiple viewpoints (from the ground—1; a bird's eye view—2; from the side—3) of the elephant cooperation apparatus, from Plotnik et al. (2011). In test and control trials, two elephants walked down two separate roped-off lanes (represented as dashed lines in views 1 and 2). Both ends of the same rope needed to be pulled concurrently by both elephants to successfully move the table, and thus coordinated cooperation was needed to obtain the food rewards. Drawings by Frans B. M. de Waal and republished with permission.

their partner arrived later (figure 2.1). In an additional condition, the elephants inhibited pulling if the partner lacked rope access, and retreated when the partner failed to pull. Various elephant pairs also exhibited different successful strategies, including one elephant who learned that standing on the rope while the partner did all the pulling was as successful a strategy as simultaneous coordinated pulling. Although these results are not conclusive in predicting the cognition needed for such collaboration, elephants perhaps also understood something about the role their partners played in the cooperative task. Some species, including elephants, may possess cooperative abilities that rival those of the apes (Plotnik et al. 2011), although various aspects of proximate-level cooperation remain to be tested.

2.5   Conclusion

2.5.1   Problems Facing Experimenters: How Animals "View" Their World

Although we have provided specific examples for chimpanzees, corvids, and elephants, this does not preclude other animals from demonstrating convergent cognitive evolution. The obvious behavioral and physiological differences that exist in evolutionarily distinct species, however, present an important concern for experimental psychologists—how can one draw comparisons between species when the ecological validity of certain paradigms differs dramatically for distant taxa? We may first look to similarities in behavior across species before trying to draw psychological comparisons (Emery and Clayton 2009a, 2009b; Stevens and Hauser 2004), but even this may suggest unfair contrasts.

Some of the most classical experiments in comparative cognition, for instance, specifically those focused on nonhuman primates, present animals with a problem to solve. The aforementioned object-choice task in visual cue reading, the trap-tube task in causal reasoning and tool use, and the rope-pulling task in cooperation experiments all require the subject animal to visualize the presented problem or task in order to solve it. If vision is necessary for even the most basic problem-solving tasks, this may present a problem for animals that have enhanced nonvisual, or multimodal sensory perception, including elephants (Byrne, Bates, and Moss 2009), dolphins and other cetaceans (Marino 2002), and even pigs (*Sus scrofa domesticus*—Croney et al. 2003; Held et al. 2001, 2002). Primates overwhelmingly solve problems in their environment by processing visual information (Hare et al. 2000; Hare et al. 2001; Tomasello and Call 1997), although primate vocal communication certainly affects social decision making (Cheney and Seyfarth 1992; Snowdon, Brown, and Petersen 1983). The same goes for corvids (Balda, Pepperberg, and Kamil 1998; Emery and Clayton 2004; Seed et al. 2006), but not elephants, which may rely more heavily on olfactory information in navigating their physical environment and acoustic information in their social world (Bates et al. 2007; Bates et al. 2008; Langbauer 2000; McComb et al. 2000; McComb et al. 2002; Payne 2003). Elephants present an interesting conundrum in that they are a highly social, cognitively complex species with a visual capacity that seems to be inferior to their olfactory and acoustic senses (Fowler and Mikota 2006; Plotnik et al. 2014; Sukumar 2003). Although they have done well on both mirror self-recognition (Plotnik, de Waal, and Reiss 2006) and cooperation (Plotnik et al. 2011) tasks, more complex physical cognition paradigms may be very difficult for elephants if they are only given sufficient visual information to investigate them (Plotnik et al. 2013). Thus, presenting subjects with cognitive tasks that require the processing of visual information may bias the results in favor of a negative outcome if visual information processing—especially in natural, physical or social cognition scenarios—is ecologically invalid for the test species.

If the study of convergent cognitive evolution is to proceed across several evolutionary taxa, greater attention will need to be given to the design of experiments that can be manipulated for and then compared across species with different ecological or sensory adaptations.

2.5.2   Final Remarks

The study of convergent cognitive evolution, or the emergence of comparable cognitive complexity in evolutionarily distant species, is an exciting new area of research that encourages collaboration among primatologists, psychologists, and biologists, and lends important credence to the idea that humans are not alone as physically and socially intelligent beings. In this chapter, we have briefly outlined some of the evidence for physical and social understanding in nonhuman animals, and how the use of behavioral flexibility allows them to apply core concepts such as perspective taking to both the social and the physical world. This evidence strongly supports the argument that understanding the evolution of human intelligence requires a broader viewpoint than that drawn by traditional psychology alone. If we are to look beyond the primate lineages to find those other nonhuman animals truly capable of being cognitive beings, we must both assess the environmental pressures that would have driven intelligence and find empirical ways to test hypotheses about their physical and social cognition that allow for constructive, accurate comparisons of animal behavior.

References

Agnetta, B., B. Hare, and M. Tomasello. 2000. Cues to food locations that domestic dogs (*Canis familiaris*) of different ages do and do not use. *Animal Cognition* 3:107–112.

Aureli, F., and F. B. M. de Waal, eds. 2000. *Natural Conflict Resolution*. Berkeley: University of California Press.

Axelrod, R., and W. D. Hamilton. 1981. The evolution of cooperation. *Science* 211:1390–1396.

Balda, R. P., I. M. Pepperberg, and A. C. Kamil. 1998. *Animal Cognition in Nature: The Convergence of Psychology and Biology in Laboratory and Field*. San Diego: Academic Press.

Bates, L. A., and R. W. Byrne. 2007. Creative or created: Using anecdotes to investigate animal cognition. *Methods (San Diego, Calif.)* 42:12–21.

Bates, L. A., K. N. Sayialel, N. W. Njiraini, C. J. Moss, J. H. Poole, and R. W. Byrne. 2007. Elephants classify human ethnic groups by odor and garment color. *Current Biology* 17 (22): 1938–1942.

Bates, L. A., K. N. Sayialel, N. W. Njiraini, J. H. Poole, C. J. Moss, and R. W. Byrne. 2008. African elephants have expectations about the locations of out-of-sight family members. *Biology Letters* 4 (1): 34–36.

Beck, B. B. 1980. *Animal Tool Behaviour*. New York: Garland.

Bird, C. D., and N. J. Emery. 2009a. Insightful problem solving and creative tool modification by captive nontool-using rooks. *Proceedings of the National Academy of Sciences of the United States of America* 106:10370–10375.

Bird, C. D., and N. J. Emery. 2009b. Rooks use stones to raise the water level to reach a floating worm. *Current Biology* 19:1410–1414.

Boesch, C. 1994. Cooperative hunting in wild chimpanzees. *Animal Behaviour* 48:653–667.

Boesch, C., and H. Boesch. 1989. Hunting behavior of wild chimpanzees in the Tai National Park. *American Journal of Physical Anthropology* 78:547–573.

Boesch, C., and H. Boesch-Achermann. 2000. *The Chimpanzees of the Tai Forest*. Oxford: Oxford University Press.

Boesch, C., and M. Tomasello. 1998. Chimpanzee and human cultures. *Current Anthropology* 39:591–614.

Bräuer, J., J. Call, and M. Tomasello. 2005. All great ape species follow gaze to distant locations and around barriers. *Journal of Comparative Psychology* 119 (2): 145–154.

Bräuer, J., J. Kaminski, J. Riedel, J. Call, and M. Tomasello. 2006. Making inferences about the location of hidden food: Social dog, causal ape. *Journal of Comparative Psychology* 120 (1): 38–47.

Brown, J. L. 1983. Cooperation: A biologist's dilemma. *Advances in the Study of Behavior* 13: 1–37.

Bugnyar, T., and B. Heinrich. 2005. Ravens, *Corvus corax*, differentiate between knowledgeable and ignorant competitors. *Proceedings of the Royal Society, B: Biological Sciences* 272:1641–1646.

Bugnyar, T., and B. Heinrich. 2006. Pilfering ravens, *Corvus corax*, adjust their behaviour to social context and identity of competitors. *Animal Cognition* 9:369–376.

Bugnyar, T., and K. Kotrschal. 2002. Observational learning and the raiding of food caches in ravens (*Corvus corax*): Is it "tactical" deception? *Animal Behaviour* 64:185–195.

Bugnyar, T., M. Stowe, and B. Heinrich. 2004. Ravens, *Corvus corax*, follow gaze direction of humans around obstacles. *Proceedings of the Royal Society, B: Biological Sciences* 271:1331–1336.

Byrne, R. W. 1995. *The Thinking Ape: Evolutionary Origins of Intelligence*. Oxford: Oxford University Press.

Byrne, R. W. 1996. The misunderstood ape: Cognitive skills of the gorilla. In *Reaching Into Thought: The Minds of the Great Apes*, ed. A. E. Russon, K. A. Bard, and S. T. Parker, 113–130. Cambridge: Cambridge University Press.

Byrne, R. W. 1997. The technical intelligence hypothesis: An additional evolutionary stimulus to intelligence? In *Machiavellian Intelligence II. Extensions and Evaluations*, ed. A. Whiten and R. W. Byrne, 289–311. Cambridge: Cambridge University Press.

Byrne, R. W. 2004. The manual skills and cognition that lie behind hominid tool use. In *The Evolution of Thought: Evolutionary Origins of Great Ape Intelligence*, ed. A. E. Russon and D. R. Begun, 31–44. Cambridge: Cambridge University Press.

Byrne, R. W., and L. A. Bates. 2011. Cognition in the wild: Exploring animal minds with observational evidence. *Biology Letters* 7 (4): 619–622.

Byrne, R. W., L. A. Bates, and C. J. Moss. 2009. Elephant cognition in primate perspective. *Comparative Cognition and Behavior Reviews* 4:1–15.

Byrne, R. W., and A. Whiten. 1997. Machiavellian intelligence. In *Machiavellian Intelligence II. Extensions and Evaluations*, ed. A. Whiten and R. W. Byrne, 1–23. Cambridge: Cambridge University Press.

Caldwell, M. C., and D. K. Caldwell. 1966. Epimeletic (care-giving) behavior in Cetacea. In *Whales, Dolphins and Porpoises*, ed. K. S. Norris, 755–789. Berkeley: University of California Press.

Call, J. 2004. Inferences about the location of food in the great apes (*Pan paniscus, Pan troglodytes, Gorilla gorilla,* and *Pongo pygmaeus*). *Journal of Comparative Psychology* 118 (2): 232–241.

Call, J., and M. Tomasello. 1994. Production and Comprehension of Referential Pointing by Orangutans (Pongo-Pygmaeus). *Journal of Comparative Psychology* 108 (4): 307–317.

Chalmeau, R. 1994. Do chimpanzees cooperate in a learning task? *Primates* 35:385–392.

Chalmeau, R., and A. Gallo. 1996. What chimpanzees (*Pan troglodytes*) learn in a cooperative task. *Primates* 37:39–47.

Chalmeau, R., E. Visalberghi, and A. Gallo. 1997. Capuchin monkeys (*Cebus apella*) fail to understand a cooperative task. *Animal Behaviour* 54:1215–1225.

Chappell, J., and A. Kacelnik. 2002. Tool selectivity in a non-primate, the New Caledonian crow (*Corvus moneduloides*). *Animal Cognition* 5:71–78.

Chappell, J., and A. Kacelnik. 2004. Selection of tool diameter by New Caledonian crows (*Corvus moneduloides*). *Animal Cognition* 7:121–127.

Cheke, L. G., C. D. Bird, and N. S. Clayton. 2011. Tool-use and instrumental learning in the Eurasian jay (*Garrulus glandarius*). *Animal Cognition* 14:441–455.

Cheke, L. G., and N. S. Clayton. 2012. Eurasian jays (*Garrulus glandarius*) overcome their current desires to anticipate two distinct future needs and plan for them appropriately. *Biology Letters* 8:171–175.

Cheney, D. L., and R. M. Seyfarth. 1992. *How Monkeys See the World: Inside the Mind of Another Species*. Chicago: University of Chicago Press.

Chevalier-Skolnikoff, S., and J. Liska. 1993. Tool use by wild and captive elephants. *Animal Behaviour* 46:209–219.

Clayton, N. S. 1998. Memory and the hippocampus in food-storing birds: A comparative approach. *Neuropharmacology* 37:441–452.

Clayton, N. S., and A. Dickinson. 1998. Episodic-like memory during cache recovery by scrub jays. *Nature* 395:272–274.

Clayton, N. S., and A. Dickinson. 1999. Scrub jays (*Aphelocoma coerulescens*) remember the relative time of caching as well as the location and content of their caches. *Journal of Comparative Psychology* 113:403–416.

Clayton, N. S., K. S. Yu, and A. Dickinson. 2001. Scrub jays (*Aphelocoma coerulescens*) form integrated memories of the multiple features of caching episodes. *Journal of Experimental Psychology: Animal Behavior Processes* 27:17–29.

Conway Morris, S. 2005. *Life's Solution: Inevitable Humans in a Lonely Universe*. Cambridge: Cambridge University Press.

Correia, S. P. C., A. Dickinson, and N. S. Clayton. 2007. Western scrub-jays anticipate future needs independently of their current motivational state. *Current Biology* 17:856–861.

Crawford, M. P. 1937. The cooperative solving of problems by young chimpanzees. *Comparative Psychology Monographs* 14:1–88.

Croney, C. C., K. M. Adams, C. G. Washington, and W. R. Stricklin. 2003. A note on visual, olfactory and spatial cue use in foraging behavior of pigs: Indirectly assessing cognitive abilities. *Applied Animal Behaviour Science* 83:303–308.

Dally, J. M., N. J. Emery, and N. S. Clayton. 2004. Cache protection strategies by western scrub-jays (*Aphelocoma californica*): Hiding food in the shade. *Proceedings of the Royal Society, B: Biological Sciences* 271 (supplement 6): S387–S390.

Dally, J. M., N. J. Emery, and N. S. Clayton. 2005. Cache protection strategies by western scrub-jays (*Aphelocoma californica*): Implications for social cognition. *Animal Behaviour* 70:1251–1263.

Dally, J. M., N. J. Emery, and N. S. Clayton. 2006. Food-caching western scrub-jays keep track of who was watching when. *Science* 312:1662–1665.

Dally, J. M., N. J. Emery, and N. S. Clayton. 2010. Avian theory of mind and counter espionage by food-caching western scrub-jays (*Aphelocoma californica*). *European Journal of Developmental Psychology* 7:17–37.

Davidson, G. L., S. Butler, E. Fernández-Juricic, A. Thornton, and N. S. Clayton. 2014. Gaze sensitivity: Function and mechanisms from sensory and cognitive perspectives. *Animal Behaviour* 87:3–15.

de Kort, S. R., and N. S. Clayton. 2006. An evolutionary perspective on caching by corvids. *Proceedings: Biological Sciences* 273:417–423.

de Silva, S., A. D. Ranjeewa, and S. Kryazhimskiy. 2011. The dynamics of social networks among female Asian elephants. *BioMed Central Ecology* 11:17.

de Waal, F. B. M. 1982. *Chimpanzee Politics*. London: Jonathan Cape.

de Waal, F. B. M. 1996. *Good Natured: The Origins of Right and Wrong in Humans and Other Animals*. Cambridge: Harvard University Press.

de Waal, F. B. M. 2008. Putting the altruism back into altruism: The evolution of empathy. *Annual Review of Psychology* 59:279–300.

de Waal, F. B. M. 2009. *The Age of Empathy: Nature's Lessons for a Kinder Society*. New York: Crown.

Douglas-Hamilton, I., and O. Douglas-Hamilton. 1975. *Among the Elephants*. New York: Viking.

Drea, C. M., and A. N. Carter. 2009. Cooperative problem solving in a social carnivore. *Animal Behaviour* 78:967–977.

Dugatkin, L. A. 1997. *Cooperation Among Animals: An Evolutionary Perspective*. Oxford: Oxford University Press.

Emery, N. J., and N. S. Clayton. 2001. Effects of experience and social context on prospective caching strategies by scrub jays. *Nature* 414:443–446.

Emery, N. J., and N. S. Clayton. 2004. The mentality of crows: Convergent evolution of intelligence in corvids and apes. *Science* 306:1903–1907.

Emery, N. J., and N. S. Clayton. 2008. How to build a scrub-jay that reads minds. In *Origins of the Social Mind: Evolutionary and Developmental Views*, ed. S. Itakura and K. Fujita, 65–97. Tokyo: Springer Japan.

Emery, N. J., and N. S. Clayton. 2009a. Comparative social cognition. *Annual Review of Psychology* 60:87–113.

Emery, N. J., and N. S. Clayton. 2009b. Tool use and physical cognition in birds and mammals. *Current Opinion in Neurobiology* 19:27–33.

Emery, N. J., J. Dally, and N. S. Clayton. 2004. Western scrub-jays (*Aphelocoma californica*) use cognitive strategies to protect their caches from thieving conspecifics. *Animal Cognition* 7: 37–43.

Emery, N. J., E. N. Lorincz, D. I. Perrett, M. W. Oram, and C. I. Baker. 1997. Gaze following and joint attention in rhesus monkeys (*Macaca mulatta*). *Journal of Comparative Psychology* 111:286–293.

Emery, N. J., A. M. Seed, A. M. P. von Bayern, and N. S. Clayton. 2007. Cognitive adaptations of social bonding in birds. *Philosophical Transactions of the Royal Society of London: Series B, Biological Sciences* 362:489–505.

Finn, J. K., T. Tregenza, and M. D. Norman. 2009. Defensive tool use in a coconut-carrying octopus. *Current Biology* 19:R1069–R1070.

Foerder, P., M. Galloway, T. Barthel, D. E. Moore, and D. Reiss. 2011. Insightful problem solving in an Asian elephant. *PLoS ONE* 6:e23251.

Foley, C., N. Pettorelli, and L. Foley. 2008. Severe drought and calf survival in elephants. *Biology Letters* 4:541–544.

Fowler, M. E., and S. K. Mikota. 2006. *Biology, Medicine, and Surgery of Elephants*. Oxford: Blackwell.

Fox, E. A., A. F. Sitompul, and C. P. Van Schaik. 1999. Intelligent tool use in wild Sumatran orangutans. In *The Mentalities of Gorillas and Orangutans: Comparative Perspectives*, ed. S. T. Parker, R. W. Mitchell, and H. L. Miles, 99–116. Cambridge: Cambridge University Press.

Galef, G. G., and K. N. Laland. 2005. Social learning in animals: Empirical studies and theoretical models. *Bioscience* 55:489–499.

Giret, N., A. Miklósi, M. Kreutzer, and D. Bovet. 2009. Use of experimenter-given cues by African gray parrots (*Psittacus erithacus*). *Animal Cognition* 12 (1): 1–10.

Gomes, C. M., and C. Boesch. 2009. Wild chimpanzees exchange meat for sex on a long-term basis. *PLoS ONE* 4 (4): e5116.

Grodzinski, U., and N. S. Clayton. 2010. Problems faced by food-caching corvids and the evolution of cognitive solutions. *Philosophical Transactions of the Royal Society of London: Series B, Biological Sciences* 365:977–987.

Hamilton, W. D. 1964. The genetical evolution of social behaviour I. *Journal of Theoretical Biology* 7:1–16.

Harcourt, A. H., and F. B. M. de Waal. 1992. *Coalitions and Alliances in Humans and Other Animals*. Oxford: Oxford University Press.

Hare, B., M. Brown, C. Williamson, and M. Tomasello. 2002. The domestication of social cognition in dogs. *Science* 298 (5598): 1634–1636.

Hare, B., J. Call, B. Agnetta, and M. Tomasello. 2000. Chimpanzees know what conspecifics do and do not see. *Animal Behaviour* 59:771–785.

Hare, B., J. Call, and M. Tomasello. 2001. Do chimpanzees know what conspecifics know? *Animal Behaviour* 61 (1): 139–151.

Hare, B., J. Call, and M. Tomasello. 2006. Chimpanzees deceive a human competitor by hiding. *Cognition* 101:495–514.

Hare, B., A. P. Melis, V. Woods, S. Hastings, and R. Wrangham. 2007. Tolerance allows bonobos to outperform chimpanzees on a cooperative task. *Current Biology* 17 (7): 619–623.

Hare, B., and M. Tomasello. 1999. Domestic dogs (*Canis familiaris*) use human and conspecific social cues to locate hidden food. *Journal of Comparative Psychology* 113 (2): 173–177.

Hare, B., and M. Tomasello. 2005. Human-like social skills in dogs? *Trends in Cognitive Sciences* 9 (9): 439–444.

Hart, B. L., L. A. Hart, M. McCoy, and C. R. Sarath. 2001. Cognitive behaviour in Asian elephants: Use and modification of branches for fly switching. *Animal Behaviour* 62 (5): 839–847.

Heinrich, B. 1999. *Mind of the Raven*. New York: HarperCollins.

Held, S., M. Mendl, C. Devereux, and R. W. Byrne. 2001. Behaviour of domestic pigs in a visual perspective taking task. *Behaviour* 138:1337–1354.

Held, S., M. Mendl, K. Laughlin, and R. W. Byrne. 2002. Cognition studies with pigs: Livestock cognition and its implication for production. *Journal of Animal Science* 80:E10–E17.

Hirata, S., and K. Fuwa. 2007. Chimpanzees (*Pan troglodytes*) learn to act with other individuals in a cooperative task. *Primates* 48 (1): 13–21.

Humphrey, N. K. 1976. The social function of intellect. In *Growing Points in Ethology*, ed. G. Bateson and R. A. Hinde, 303–317. Cambridge, MA: Cambridge University Press.

Hunt, G. R. 1996. Manufacture and use of hook-tools by New Caledonian crows. *Nature* 379:249–251.

Hunt, G. R., and R. D. Gray. 2004. The crafting of hook tools by wild New Caledonian crows. *Biology Letters* 271 (S3): S88–S90.

Itakura, S., B. Agnetta, B. Hare, and M. Tomasello. 1999. Chimpanzee use of human and conspecific social cues to locate hidden food. *Developmental Science* 2 (4): 448–456.

Itakura, S., and J. R. Anderson. 1996. Learning to use experimenter-given cues during an object-choice task by a capuchin monkey. *Cahiers De Psychologie Cognitive-Current Psychology of Cognition* 15 (1): 103–112.

Itakura, S., and M. Tanaka. 1998. Use of experimenter-given cues during object-choice tasks by chimpanzees (*Pan troglodytes*), an orangutan (*Pongo pygmaeus*), and human infants (*Homo sapiens*). *Journal of Comparative Psychology* 112 (2): 119–126.

Jerison, H. J. 1973. *Evolution of the Brain and Intelligence*. New York: Academic Press.

Jones, T. B., and A. C. Kamil. 1973. Tool-making and tool-using in the northern blue jay. *Science* 180:1076–1078.

Kaminski, J., J. Riedel, J. Call, and M. Tomasello. 2005. Domestic goats, *Capra hircus*, follow gaze direction and use social cues in an object choice task. *Animal Behaviour* 69:11–18.

Karin-D'Arcy, M. R., and D. J. Povinelli. 2002. Do chimpanzees know what each other see? A closer look. *International Journal of Comparative Psychology* 15:21–54.

Keeton, W. T., and J. L. Gould. 1986. *Biological Science*. 4th ed. New York: Norton.

Krützen, M., J. Mann, M. R. Heithaus, R. C. Connor, L. Bejder, and W. B. Sherwin. 2005. Cultural transmission of tool use in bottlenose dolphins. *Proceedings of the National Academy of Sciences of the United States of America* 102:8939–8943.

Langbauer, W. R. 2000. Elephant communication. *Zoo Biology* 19:425–445.

Marino, L. 2002. Convergence of complex cognitive abilities in cetaceans and primates. *Brain, Behavior and Evolution* 59:21–32.

Maros, K., M. Gacsi, and A. Miklósi. 2008. Comprehension of human pointing gestures in horses (*Equus caballus*). *Animal Cognition* 11 (3): 457–466.

McComb, K., C. Moss, S. Sayialel, and L. Baker. 2000. Unusually extensive networks of vocal recognition in African elephants. *Animal Behaviour* 59 (6): 1103–1109.

McComb, K., D. Reby, L. Baker, C. Moss, and S. Sayialel. 2002. Long-distance communication of acoustic cues to social identity in African elephants. *Animal Behaviour* 65:317–329.

McGrew, W. C. 1992. *Chimpanzee Material Culture: Implications for Human Evolution*. Cambridge: Cambridge University Press.

Melis, A. P., B. Hare, and M. Tomasello. 2006. Chimpanzees recruit the best collaborators. *Science* 311:1297–1300.

Mendes, N., D. Hanus, and J. Call. 2007. Raising the level: Orangutans use water as a tool. *Biology Letters* 3 (5): 453–455.

Mendres, K. A., and F. B. M. de Waal. 2000. Capuchins do cooperate: The advantage of an intuitive task. *Animal Behaviour* 60:523–529.

Miklósi, A., and K. Soproni. 2006. A comparative analysis of animals' understanding of the human pointing gesture. *Animal Cognition* 9 (2): 81–93.

Miklósi, A., J. Topal, and V. Csanyi. 1998. Use of experimenter-given cues in dogs. *Animal Cognition* 1:113–121.

Milton, K. 1981. Distribution patterns of tropical plant foods as an evolutionary stimulus to primate mental development. *American Anthropologist* 83:534–548.

Mitani, J. C., and D. P. Watts. 2001. Why do chimpanzees hunt and share meat? *Animal Behaviour* 61:915–924.

Mock, D. W., and M. Fujioka. 1990. Monogamy and long-term pair bonding in vertebrates. *Trends in Ecology & Evolution* 5:39–43.

Moss, C. 1988. *Elephant Memories: Thirteen Years in the Life of an Elephant Family*. New York: Fawcett Columbine.

Mulcahy, N. J., and J. Call. 2009. The performance of bonobos (*Pan paniscus*), chimpanzees (*Pan troglodytes*), and orangutans (*Pongo pygmaeus*) in two versions of an object-choice task. *Journal of Comparative Psychology* 123 (3): 304–309.

Neiworth, J. J., M. A. Burman, B. M. Basile, and M. T. Lickteig. 2002. Use of experimenter-given cues in visual co-orienting and in an object-choice task by a new world monkey species, cotton top tamarins (*Saguinus oedipus*). *Journal of Comparative Psychology* 116 (1): 3–11.

Noë, R. 2006. Cooperation experiments: Coordination through communication versus acting apart together. *Animal Behaviour* 71:1–18.

Ostojić, L., R. C. Shaw, L. G. Cheke, and N. S. Clayton. 2013. Evidence suggesting that desire-state attribution may govern food sharing in Eurasian jays. *Proceedings of the National Academy of Sciences of the United States of America* 110(10): 4123–4128.

Payne, K. 1998. *Silent Thunder: In the Presence of Elephants*. New York: Simon & Schuster.

Payne, K. 2003. Sources of social complexity in the three elephant species. In *Animal Social Complexity: Intelligence, Culture, and Individualized Societies*, ed. F. B. M. de Waal and P. L. Tyack, 57–85. Cambridge, MA: Harvard University Press.

Peignot, P., and J. R. Anderson. 1999. Use of experimenter-given manual and facial cues by gorillas (*Gorilla gorilla*) in an object-choice task. *Journal of Comparative Psychology* 113 (3): 253–260.

Plotnik, J. M., and F. B. M. de Waal. 2014. Asian elephants (*Elephas maximus*) reassure others in distress. *PeerJ* 2:e278.

Plotnik, J. M., F. B. M. de Waal, and D. Reiss. 2006. Self-recognition in an Asian elephant. *Proceedings of the National Academy of Sciences of the United States of America* 103:17053–17057.

Plotnik, J. M., R. Lair, W. Suphachoksahakun, and F. B. M. de Waal. 2011. Elephants know when they need a helping trunk in a cooperative task. *Proceedings of the National Academy of Sciences of the United States of America* 108 (12): 5116–5121.

Plotnik, J. M., J. J. Pokorny, T. Keratimanochaya, C. Webb, H. F. Beronja, A. Hennessey, J. Hill, et al. 2013. Visual cues given by humans are not sufficient for Asian elephants (*Elephas maximus*) to find hidden food. *PLoS ONE* 8 (4): e61174.

Plotnik, J. M., R. C. Shaw, D. L. Brubaker, L. N. Tiller, and N. S. Clayton. 2014. Thinking with their trunks: Elephants use smell but not sound to locate food and exclude nonrewarding alternatives. *Animal Behaviour* 88:91–98.

Poole, J. H. 1996. *Coming of Age with Elephants*. New York: Hyperion.

Povinelli, D. J. 2000. *Folk Physics for Apes*. New York: Oxford University Press.

Povinelli, D. J., J. E. Reaux, D. T. Bierschwale, A. D. Allain, and B. B. Simon. 1997. Exploitation of pointing as a referential gesture in young children, but not adolescent chimpanzees. *Cognitive Development* 12 (4): 327–365.

Povinelli, D. J., and J. Vonk. 2004. We don't need a microscope to explore the chimpanzees' mind. *Mind & Language* 19:1–28.

Proops, L., M. Walton, and K. McComb. 2010. The use of human-given cues by domestic horses, *Equus caballus*, during an object choice task. *Animal Behaviour* 79 (6): 1205–1209.

Raby, C. R., D. M. Alexis, A. Dickinson, and N. S. Clayton. 2007. Planning for the future by western scrub-jays. *Nature* 445:919–921.

Roth, G., and U. Dicke. 2005. Evolution of the brain and intelligence. *Trends in Cognitive Sciences* 9:250–257.

Sanz, C. M., and D. B. Morgan. 2007. Chimpanzee tool technology in the Goualougo Triangle, Republic of Congo. *Journal of Human Evolution* 52:420–433.

Scheid, C., and R. Noë. 2010. The performance of rooks in a cooperative task depends on their temperament. *Animal Cognition* 13:545–553.

Scheumann, M., and J. Call. 2004. The use of experimenter-given cues by South African fur seals (*Arctocephalus pusillus*). *Animal Cognition* 7 (4): 224–230.

Schloegl, C., K. Kotrschal, and T. Bugnyar. 2007. Gaze following in common ravens, *Corvus corax*: Ontogeny and habituation. *Animal Behaviour* 74:769–778.

Seed, A. M., J. Call, N. J. Emery, and N. S. Clayton. 2009. Chimpanzees solve the trap problem when the confound of tool-use is removed. *Journal of Experimental Psychology: Animal Behavior Processes* 35:23–34.

Seed, A. M., N. S. Clayton, and N. J. Emery. 2007. Third-party postconflict affiliation in rooks, *Corvus frugilegus*. *Current Biology* 17:152–158.

Seed, A. M., N. S. Clayton, and N. J. Emery. 2008. Cooperative problem solving in rooks (*Corvus frugilegus*). *Proceedings of the Royal Society, B: Biological Sciences* 275:1421–1429.

Seed, A. M., N. J. Emery, and N. S. Clayton. 2009. Intelligence in corvids and apes: A case of convergent evolution? *Ethology* 115:401–420.

Seed, A. M., S. Tebbich, N. J. Emery, and N. S. Clayton. 2006. Investigating physical cognition in rooks, *Corvus frugilegus*. *Current Biology* 16 (7): 697–701.

Seed, A. M., and M. Tomasello. 2010. Primate cognition. *Trends in Cognitive Sciences* 2:407–419.

Shaw, R. C., and N. S. Clayton. 2012. Eurasian jays (*Garrulus glandarius*) flexibly switch caching and pilfering tactics in response to social context. *Animal Behaviour* 84:1191–1200.

Shettleworth, S. J. 2002. Spatial behavior, food storing, and the modular mind. In *The Cognitive Animal: Empirical and Theoretical Perspectives on Animal Cognition*, ed. M. Bekoff, C. Allen, and G. M. Burghardt, 123–128. Cambridge: MIT Press.

Shettleworth, S. J. 2010. *Cognition, Evolution and Behaviour*. New York: Oxford University Press.

Shillito, D. J., R. W. Shumaker, G. G. Gallup, and B. B. Beck. 2005. Understanding visual barriers: Evidence for level 1 perspective taking in an orangutan, *Pongo pygmaeus*. *Animal Behaviour* 69:679–687.

Shoshani, J., ed. 1992. *Elephants: Majestic Creatures of the Wild*. Emmaus, PA: Rodale Press.

Siebenaler, J. B., and D. K. Caldwell. 1956. Cooperation among adult dolphins. *Journal of Mammalogy* 37:126–128.

Smet, A. F., and R. W. Byrne. 2013. African elephants can use human pointing cues to find hidden food. *Current Biology* 23 (20): 2033–2037.

Smith, B. P., and C. A. Litchfield. 2010. Dingoes (*Canis dingo*) can use human social cues to locate hidden food. *Animal Cognition* 13 (2): 367–376.

Smolker, R., A. Richard, R. C. Connor, J. Mann, and P. Berggren. 2010. Sponge carrying by dolphins (Delphinidae, *Tursiops* sp.): A foraging specialization involving tool use? *Ethology* 103:454–465.

Snowdon, C. T., C. H. Brown, and M. R. Petersen, eds. 1983. *Primate Communication*. Cambridge: Cambridge University Press.

Stanford, C. B., J. Wallis, E. Mpongo, and J. Goodall. 1994. Hunting decisions in wild chimpanzees. *Behaviour* 131:1–20.

Stevens, J. R., and M. D. Hauser. 2004. Why be nice? Psychological constraints on the evolution of cooperation. *Trends in Cognitive Sciences* 8 (2): 60–65.

Sukumar, R. 2003. *The Living Elephants: Evolutionary Ecology, Behaviour, and Conservation*. Oxford: Oxford University Press.

Taylor, A. H., G. R. Hunt, F. S. Medina, and R. D. Gray. 2009. Do New Caledonian crows solve physical problems through causal reasoning? *Proceedings of the Royal Society, B: Biological Sciences* 276:247–254.

Tomasello, M., and J. Call. 1997. *Primate Cognition*. Oxford: Oxford University Press.

Tornick, J. K., B. M. Gibson, D. Kispert, and M. Wilkinson. 2011. Clark's nutcrackers (*Nucifraga columbiana*) use gestures to identify the location of hidden food. *Animal Cognition* 14 (1): 117–125.

Trivers, R. L. 1971. The evolution of reciprocal altruism. *Quarterly Review of Biology* 46:35–57.

van Horik, J., N. S. Clayton, and N. J. Emery. 2012. Convergent evolution of cognition in corvids, apes and other animals. In *The Oxford Handbook of Comparative Evolutionary Psychology*, ed. J. Vonk and T. K. Shackelford, 80–101. Oxford: Oxford University Press.

van Lawick-Goodall, J. 1968. The behaviour of free-living chimpanzees in the Gombe Stream Reserve. *Animal Behaviour Monographs* 1:161–311.

Vander Wall, S. B. 1990. *Food Hoarding in Animals*. Chicago: University of Chicago Press.

Vick, S. J., and J. R. Anderson. 2000. Learning and limits of use of eye gaze by capuchin monkeys (*Cebus apella*) in an object-choice task. *Journal of Comparative Psychology* 114 (2): 200–207.

Visalberghi, E., B. P. Quarantotti, and F. Tranchida. 2000. Solving a cooperation task without taking into account the partner's behavior: The case of capuchin monkeys (*Cebus apella*). *Journal of Comparative Psychology* 114:297–301.

von Bayern, A. M. P., and N. J. Emery. 2009. Jackdaws respond to human attentional states and communicative cues in different contexts. *Current Biology* 19 (7): 602–606.

Watanabe, S., and N. S. Clayton. 2007. Observational visuospatial encoding of the cache locations of others by western scrub-jays (*Aphelocoma californica*). *Journal of Ethology* 25:271–279.

Weir, A. A. S., J. Chappell, and A. Kacelnik. 2002. Shaping of hooks in New Caledonian crows. *Science* 297:981.

Whiten, A., and R. W. Byrne. 1988. Tactical deception in primates. *Behavioral and Brain Sciences* 11:233–244.

Whiten, A., J. Goodall, W. C. McGrew, T. Nishida, V. Reynolds, Y. Sugiyama, and C. Boesch. 1999. Cultures in chimpanzees. *Nature* 399:682–685.

Whiten, A., V. Horner, and F. B. M. de Waal. 2005. Conformity to cultural norms of tool use in chimpanzees. *Nature* 437:737–740.

3 The Evolution of Concepts about Agents: Or, What Do Animals Recognize When They Recognize an Individual?

Robert M. Seyfarth and Dorothy L. Cheney

3.1 Introduction

We now know that the mind of a human infant is neither a blank slate nor, in William James's words, "one great blooming, buzzing confusion" (1890, 462). Instead, infants are born with what Carey (2010, 2011) has called a set of "innate, representational primitives" (2011, 113) that guide infants' learning and their expectations of how objects are likely to behave. Three *core systems* of knowledge have been suggested, each specialized for representing and reasoning about entities of different kinds (Carey and Spelke 1996). One core system deals with the causal and spatial relations among objects, another concerns number, and a third deals with agents. Here, we focus on core systems of knowledge about agents—their goals, attentional states, and the causal mechanisms that underlie their behavior.

The prevalence in human infants of a core system of knowledge about agents suggests that at some point in our evolutionary history, a predisposition to recognize certain entities in the world as capable of self-generated motion, with goals and the motivation to achieve them (Carey 2011; Frith and Frith 2012), gave some individuals a fitness advantage over others. In modern humans, the advantages to be gained from this style of thinking are obvious. How might it have benefited our nonhuman, prelinguistic ancestors?

Old World monkeys live in societies where survival and reproduction depend on social skills. To succeed, an individual must be able to predict the behavior of others, and to do this she must understand their social relationships. Here we propose that the demands of social life have favored individuals who can recognize other animals' social attributes and treat these properties as inextricable parts of an individual's identity. To illustrate our argument, we focus on female baboons and their recognition of other individuals' dominance rank and kinship.

Rank and kinship, we suggest, are examples of social concepts—baboons' representational primitives. Recognizing these attributes in others, however, poses a problem because there are no overt, physical markers of a female's social position. Instead, animals acquire this knowledge by observing other individuals' social interactions and learning the statistical regularities associated with them. Knowledge of other animals' rank and kinship, among their other attributes, permits baboons to predict how those animals are likely to behave when interacting with other group members. We can see in the social cognition of baboons the evolutionary origins of our theory of mind, our concepts about agents, and our inclination to classify other individuals in part according to both their social relationships and the intentions we attribute to them.

3.2   Individual Recognition

Individual recognition is widespread in animals (Tibbetts and Dale 2007). Many species have specialized brain cells that respond particularly strongly to faces (Tsao et al. 2006; Leopold and Rhodes 2010), voices (Petkov et al. 2008), and familiar speakers (Belin and Zattore 2003). Although such recognition has most often been documented in the auditory mode through playback experiments (e.g., Cheney and Seyfarth 1980; Rendall, Rodman, and Emond 1996), subjects in these experiments often seem to be engaged in more complex cross-modal or even multimodal processing. A baboon who looks toward the source of the sound when she hears her offspring's call (Cheney and Seyfarth 2007) acts as if the sound has created an expectation of what she will see if she looks in that direction.

The first evidence that animals might integrate multiple cues to form a representation of an individual came from work by Johnston and Bullock (2001) on hamsters. Golden hamsters have at least five different odors that are individually distinctive. In a typical experiment, a male familiar with females A and B was exposed (and became habituated to) the vaginal secretions of female A. He was then tested with either A's or B's flank secretions. Males tested with A's flank secretions showed little response (across-odor habituation); however, males tested with B's flank secretions responded strongly. The authors concluded that "when a male was habituated to one odor he was also becoming habituated to the integrated representation of that individual" (Johnston and Peng 2008, 122) and was therefore not surprised to encounter a different odor from the same animal. Hamsters, they suggested, have an integrated, multiodor memory of other individuals. Recent experiments indicate that direct physical contact with an individual—not just exposure to its odors—is necessary for such memories to develop (Johnston and Peng 2008).

But what about the representation of individuals across sensory modalities? Dogs (Adachi, Kuwahata, and Fujita 2007) and squirrel monkeys (Adachi and Fujita 2007) associate the faces and voices of their caretakers, rhesus macaques spontaneously match the faces and voices of familiar conspecifics and familiar humans (Adachi and Hampton 2011; Sliwa et al. 2011; Ghazanfar et al. 2005), and both horses and crows associate the vocalizations of a familiar group member with the sight of that individual

(Proops, McComb, and Reby 2009; Kondo, Izawa, and Watanabe 2012). Humans, of course, routinely integrate the perception of faces and voices to form the rich, multi-modal concept of a person (Campanella and Belin 2007).

Supporting these behavioral observations, neurophysiological data reveal extensive connections between auditory and visual areas in mammalian brains (Cappe and Barone 2005), particularly between those areas involved in the recognition of voices and faces among rhesus macaques (Ghazanfar and Logothetis 2003; Ghazanfar et al. 2005; Sliwa et al. 2011) and humans (von Kriegstein et al. 2005; Blank, Anwander, and von Kreigstein 2011). These links between face- and voice-recognition areas provide further evidence, in both monkeys and humans, for a "cross-modal, cognitive representation" of individual identity (Sliwa et al. 2011, 1735).

3.3   Other Social Classifications

Many animals not only recognize individuals but also classify them into groups, organizing them according to their close social bonds, linear dominance ranks, and transient sexual relations. Baboons (*Papio hamadryas* spp.) provide some good examples.

Baboons live throughout Africa in groups of 50 to 150 individuals. Males and females have very different life histories. Males emigrate to other groups at around eight to ten years of age. Females, in contrast, remain in their natal group throughout their lives, maintaining close bonds with their matrilineal kin through frequent grooming, mutual support in coalitions, tolerance at feeding sites, and interactions with each other's infants (Cheney and Seyfarth 2007; Silk et al. 2010a). Adult females can also be ranked in a stable, linear dominance hierarchy that determines priority of access to resources. From birth, daughters acquire ranks similar to those of their mothers. As a result, the stable core of a baboon group consists of a hierarchy of matrilines, in which all members of, say, matriline B outrank or are outranked by all members of matrilines C and A, respectively. Rank relations are generally stable over time, with few reversals occurring either within or between families. When reversals do occur, however, their consequences differ significantly depending on who is involved. For example, if the third-ranking female in matriline B (B_3) rises in rank above her second-ranking sister (B_2), the reversal affects only these individuals; the B family's rank relative to other families remains unchanged. However, a rank reversal between females from different matrilines (for example, C_1 rising in rank above B_3) usually causes all members of matriline C to rise above all members of matriline B (Cheney and Seyfarth 1990, 2007). The ranked, matrilineal society of baboons is typical of many Old World monkeys.

Among baboon females, the ability to form stable, enduring social bonds can increase individuals' reproductive success. At two long-term study sites in Kenya and Botswana, females had highly differentiated relationships with other females in their group. Some pairs—usually but not always matrilineal kin—interacted often, maintaining close bonds that lasted for many years, while others interacted infrequently. Those with the most stable, enduring relationships had higher offspring survival (Silk, Alberts, and Altmann 2003, Silk et al. 2009) and lived longer (Silk et al. 2010b) than females with weaker relationships. High dominance rank also had a significant effect on longevity but was a less powerful predictor than relationship quality.

Baboons, then, are born into a social world that is filled with statistical regularities: animals interact in highly predictable ways. Natural selection has favored individuals who can recognize these patterns, because knowing about other animals' relationships is both the best way to predict their behavior and essential to forming the kind of stable, enduring bonds that lead to high reproductive success. Field experiments have shown that, by the time she is an adult, a female baboon recognizes the close bonds among matrilineal kin (Cheney and Seyfarth 1999; see also below) and the linear rank relations both among females (Cheney, Seyfarth, and Silk 1995) and among males (Kitchen, Cheney, and Seyfarth 2005). When females hear the vocalizations of a juvenile involved in an aggressive interaction, they respond by looking at the juvenile's mother (Cheney and Seyfarth 1999; see also Cheney and Seyfarth 1980). Similarly, when baboons hear a sequence of aggressive and submissive calls that mimic a higher-ranking animal threatening a lower-ranking animal, they respond only briefly. If the calls of the participants are reversed, however, subjects respond significantly more strongly, as if the apparent rank reversal violates their expectations (Cheney, Seyfarth, and Silk 1995; a control sequence ruled out the possibility that the violating sequence evoked a stronger response simply because it was rare).

To test whether subjects classify females simultaneously according to both matrilineal kinship and dominance rank, Bergman and colleagues (2003) played sequences of calls mimicking within- and between-matriline rank reversals to subjects in matched trials. In one trial, subjects heard an apparent rank reversal involving two members of the same matriline: for example, female B_3 giving threat-grunts and female B_2 screaming. In another trial, the same subject heard an apparent rank reversal involving the members of two different matrilines: for example, female C_1 giving threat-grunts and female B_3 screaming. As a control, subjects heard a fight sequence that was consistent with the female dominance hierarchy. To control for the rank distance separating the subject and the individual whose calls were being played, each subject heard a rank reversal (either within or between family) that involved the matriline one step above her own (cf. Penn, Holyoak, and Povinelli 2008). Within this constraint, the rank distance separating apparent opponents within and between families was systematically varied.

Listeners responded with apparent surprise to sequences of calls that appeared to violate the existing dominance hierarchy. Moreover, between-family rank reversals elicited a consistently stronger response than did within-family rank reversals (Bergman et al. 2003). Subjects acted as if they classified individuals simultaneously according to both kinship and rank. The classification of individuals simultaneously according to these two criteria has also been documented in Japanese macaques (Schino, Tiddi, and Polizzi di Sorrentino 2006).

These results are difficult to explain without assuming that, when one baboon hears another vocalize, the listener encodes information not just about the caller's identity but also about her dominance rank and family membership, among many other attributes. This encoding is immediate and occurs automatically: just as we cannot hear a word without thinking about its meaning, a baboon cannot hear a vocalization without thinking about the animal who is calling, what she looks like, and her rank and family membership. These features are an inextricable part of the caller's identity, bound together in much the same way that auditory and visual cues are bound together in a cross-modal cognitive percept. Individual recognition thus constitutes a form of *object perception* (e.g., Bregman 1990; Miller and Cohen 2010), in which a variety of disparate stimuli are linked together to form a coherent object. As a result, perception of one of the object's attributes (for example, her voice) creates a rich variety of expectations in the perceiver's mind of—for instance—what she will see when she looks toward the sound, whom the caller is likely to dominate, and who is likely to support her in an aggressive interaction. Individual recognition, then, is more than just the recognition of an individual. It includes the recognition of that individual's place in society.

3.4 Social Concepts

What mechanisms underlie animals' knowledge of the relations that exist among others? One hypothesis argues that memory and classical conditioning are entirely sufficient to explain primates' social knowledge. As they mature, baboons observe behaviors that link individuals in predictable ways. These associations, stored in memory, allow an observer to predict how others are likely to interact. According to this view, the baboons' knowledge should not be described as conceptual because, in contrast to the case among humans, we have no independent evidence for the existence of such concepts. Baboons' social knowledge is therefore best explained by relatively simple hypotheses based on learned associations and prodigious memory (e.g., Schusterman and Kastak 1998).

Explanations based on memory and associative learning are powerful and appealing under simplified laboratory conditions, but they strain credulity when applied to behavior in nature, where animals confront more complex sets of stimuli. A young baboon, for example, must learn thousands of dyadic (and tens of thousands of triadic) relations in order to predict other animals' behavior. The magnitude of the

problem makes one wonder whether simple associations, even coupled with prodigious memory, are equal to the task (Seyfarth and Cheney 2001). Faced with the
problem of memorizing a huge, ever-changing dataset, humans (Mandler 1967) and
rats (Macuda and Roberts 1995) are predisposed to search for a higher-order rule that
makes the task easier. Why should other animals be any different?

In fact, several results suggest that, even if it begins with relatively simple Pavlov-
ian associations, primates' social knowledge is rapidly organized into units of thought
that resemble our concepts (Dasser 1988). Consider, for example, the speed of animals'
reactions to events. When a baboon hears a sequence of vocalizations that violates the
dominance hierarchy, she responds within seconds (Cheney and Seyfarth 2007). When
a macaque or capuchin monkey involved in a fight tries to recruit an ally, she seems to
know almost immediately which individuals would be the most effective partners (Silk
1999; Perry, Barrett, and Manson 2004; Schino, Tiddi, and Polizzi di Sorrentino 2006).
The speed of these reactions suggests that animals are not searching through a massive, unstructured database of simple, dyadic associations but have instead organized
their knowledge about individuals into categories, including what we call dominance
hierarchies and matrilineal (family) groups.

These categories share many features with human concepts. For example, they
cannot be reduced to any one, or even a few, perceptual attributes. High-ranking females
are not older or larger than low-ranking females, nor do they live in larger kin groups.
Males change dominance ranks often. Family members do not always look alike, sound
alike, or share any other physical features that make them easy to tell apart. None of
this variation, however, affects other animals' classifications: a three-legged member of
family B is still a member of family B.

Nor is the classification of individuals into family groups based on different types
or rates of interaction. The members of high-ranking families are not necessarily more
aggressive than others, nor do they feed in different areas, forage together, or groom
or play more often. In fact, grooming within families can be highly variable (Silk et al.
2010a), yet this has no effect on other animals' perception of who belongs in which
family.

Social categories, moreover, persist despite changes in their composition. Among
baboons, for instance, the recognition of a linear, transitive hierarchy persists despite
demographic changes in the individuals who occupy each rank. Linear, transitive rank
orders and matrilineal kin groups thus qualify as concepts because, in the mind of a
baboon, their existence is independent of the individuals that compose them.

Finally, the classification of individuals is a cognitive operation that affects behavior.
When a listener hears vocalizations from two individuals interacting elsewhere, her
response depends not just on the animals' identities but also on their ranks and family
membership (Bergman et al. 2003). Such data support the view that social concepts are
units of thought with causal power: they determine how individuals behave.

3.5 Concepts, Expectations, and the Attribution of Motives to Others

If the formation of social concepts is adaptive, however, individuals confront a problem because, as already noted, the entities that make up these concepts are heterogeneous. We propose that, faced with this dilemma, natural selection has favored those individuals who analyze social interactions according to causal relations between behaviors, and who categorize others at least in part according to their perceived intentions. Here are some experiments that lead us to these conclusions.

3.5.1 Rank Reversal and the Violation of Expectation

The rank reversal experiments described above (Cheney, Seyfarth, and Silk 1995; Bergman et al. 2003; Kitchen, Cheney, and Seyfarth 2005) all relied on the violation-of-expectation method: the listener responded more strongly to "D_2 threatens and B_1 screams" than to "B_1 threatens and D_2 screams" because the former sequence violated the listener's expectations about how these individuals ought to behave toward each other. But this logic holds only if the listener assumes both that B_1's scream *was caused by* D_2's threat-grunt, and that D_2's threat-grunt indicates an aggressive intent toward B_1. Without this assumption of causality, there would be no violation of expectation.

Rank reversal experiments also suggest that listeners attribute intentions and motives toward others: D_2 has aggressive intentions toward B_1, and this attribution of intent, combined with knowledge of D_2's and B_1's relative ranks, causes the strong response. By contrast, an alternative, simpler explanation makes no reference to a theory of mind: D_2's threat-grunts simply indicate impending or probable aggressive behavior toward B_1. In sections 3.5.2–3.5.4, we describe experiments designed to test between these two hypotheses. In section 3.5.5, we review some of the relevant neurophysiological data.

3.5.2 Judging the "Directedness" of a Vocalization

Primates are constantly required to make judgments about other animals' intentions. This demand is particularly striking in the context of vocal communication, when listeners must make inferences about the intended recipient of another animal's calls. Primate groups are noisy, tumultuous societies, and an individual could not manage her social interactions if she assumed that every vocalization she heard was directed at her. Of course, listeners can often draw inferences about the intended target of a vocalization from the direction of the caller's gaze; however, such cues are not always available. Even in the absence of visual signals, monkeys are able to make such inferences based on their knowledge of a signaler's identity and the nature of recent interactions.

In one study, for example, subjects heard an aggressive threat-grunt from an individual shortly after they had either exchanged aggression or groomed with that individual. Subjects who heard a female's threat-grunt shortly after grooming with her ignored the call: that is, they acted as if they assumed that the female was threatening another individual. But subjects who heard the same call after receiving aggression responded strongly: they acted as if they assumed that the call was directed at them and signaled further aggression (Engh et al. 2006). This result could not be explained by a simple contingency judgment, since the prior event—the vocalization—was the same in each case. Nor could results be explained by assuming that any prior interaction with individual X "primed" subjects to expect further interaction with X, because prior aggression and prior grooming affected the subjects' responses to the vocalization in different ways. Finally, the effects of prior behavior were specific to the subject's former partner: hearing the partner's threat-grunt did not affect the subject's behavior toward other, previously uninvolved individuals. The simplest explanation would seem to be that female baboons make inferences about the target of a vocalization even in the absence of visual cues, and that the nature of prior interactions creates an expectation on the part of the subject—an expectation that is based on the attribution of intentions to another. After a fight, the subject assumes that her rival has aggressive intentions toward her; after grooming, she draws the opposite conclusion (Cheney and Seyfarth 2007).

3.5.3 Judging the Intent to Reconcile

Tests of *reconciliatory* grunting in baboons provide further suggestion that listeners' responses to vocalizations depend not only on the identity of the caller but also on their assessment of the caller's motives and the intended target of the call. In many species of primates, aggressors will occasionally "reconcile" with their victims by extending a friendly gesture toward them shortly after the fight. Among baboons, reconciliation most commonly occurs in the form of a grunt. Grunts are signals of benign intent; they lower the probability of subsequent aggression and facilitate friendly interactions (Cheney, Seyfarth, and Silk 1995; Silk, Cheney, and Seyfarth 1996). In one playback experiment, a female baboon that had recently been threatened heard within minutes either the grunt of her aggressor or the grunt of another dominant female unrelated to her aggressor. After hearing her former aggressor's grunt, the female was more likely to approach her aggressor and to tolerate her aggressor's approach than after hearing the grunt of the other, uninvolved dominant female. She acted as if she attributed friendly motives to the aggressor, and therefore treated the call as a reconciliatory signal that renewed aggression was unlikely (Cheney and Seyfarth 1997).

   In a subsequent experiment, victims were played the grunt of a close relative of their aggressor. In this case, too, they treated the grunt as a signal of reconciliation, responding as they would have if the aggressor herself had grunted: they were more likely to approach the aggressor or the reconciling relative and more likely to tolerate either individual's approach. By contrast, females who heard the grunt of a dominant female unrelated to the original aggressor showed no such response. Here again, subjects acted as if they assumed that the grunt by the aggressor's relative was directed at them as a signal of benign intent, and they accepted this grunt as a proxy of reconciliation with their opponent. In other words, they acted as if they attributed some kind of shared intention to the aggressor and her relative—one that they did not attribute to the unrelated female who vocalized in the control condition (Wittig, Crockford, Wikberg, et al. 2007). The alternative, behaviorist explanation based solely on learned contingencies seems increasingly unlikely. If, after receiving aggression from B_1, subjects respond as if they expect further aggression from B_1 (Engh et al. 2006), but after receiving aggression from B_1 and hearing a grunt from B_2, subjects respond as if they expect no further aggression from B_1 (Wittig, Crockford, Wikberg, et al. 2007), the difference cannot be based on B_1's prior reconciliatory behavior because B_1 has not reconciled. The difference can only be explained if we assume that subjects have different expectations—or ascribe different motives—to B_1.

3.5.4   Judging the Intention of Alliance Partners

Finally, in a test of *vocal alliances* among baboons, a subject who had recently been threatened by a more dominant female heard either the aggressive threat-grunt of a close relative of her opponent or the threat-grunt of a female belonging to a different matriline. Subjects responded more strongly in the first condition, avoiding both the signaler, the original antagonist, and other members of her family for a significantly longer time than in the control condition (Wittig, Crockford, Seyfarth, et al. 2007). Once again, subjects changed their behavior toward another individual based on an interaction not with the individual herself but with one of the individual's close kin. Subjects acted as if they attributed some kind of shared intention to closely related individuals—a motivation that they did not attribute to others who belonged to different matrilines.

3.5.5   The Attribution of Motives

When deciding "Who, me?" upon hearing a vocalization, baboons must take into account the identity of the signaler (who is it?), the type of call given (friendly or aggressive?), the nature of their prior interactions with the signaler (were they aggressive, friendly, or neutral?), and the correlation between past interactions and future ones (does a recent grooming interaction lower or increase the likelihood of aggression?). Learned contingencies doubtless play a role in these assessments. But because listeners' responses depend on simultaneous consideration of all these factors, it seems likely that these assessments are also based at least in part on inferences about other individuals' motives and intentions.

Neurobiological research supports this hypothesis. In both monkeys and humans, the perception of gaze direction and goal-directed behavior appear to activate the same areas of the brain, including the superior temporal sulcus (STS) and the amygdala. The STS is particularly sensitive to the orientation of another individual's eyes (Jellema et al. 2000; Emery and Perrett 2000). Mutual gaze evokes greater activity in the STS than does averted gaze, suggesting that the STS facilitates the processing of social information (Pelphrey, Viola, and McCarthy 2004). In both monkeys and humans, STS also responds to goal-directed actions and perceptions. Cells in monkeys' STS show particularly increased activity to goal-directed hand movement when the actor they are observing is gazing at his or her hand (Jellema et al. 2000; Lorincz et al. 2005). It therefore seems possible that STS may be involved in representing what others see and what their actions and intentions are (Gallagher and Frith 2003). Similarly, in both monkeys and humans. the amygdala responds strongly to social stimuli, particularly aversive ones. It also seems to be important for processing information about gaze direction (Adolphs, Russell, and Tranel 1999; Kawashima et al. 1999; Fine, Lumsden, and Blair 2001; Santos, Flombaum, and Phillips 2006).

Other areas of monkeys' brains seem to be sensitive to the intentions that underlie behavior. As in humans, *mirror* neurons in the inferior parietal lobule (IPL) of monkeys' brains are activated both when a monkey performs a specific action and when it observes someone else performing that action. Furthermore, neurons that code for specific acts, such as grasping, seem to be context dependent. Some mirror neurons in monkeys respond more when they grasp a piece of food to eat it than when they grasp the same food to place it into a container. This same context dependence is preserved when monkeys observe *another* individual performing these actions. Significantly, many neurons begin to fire *before* the other individual actually performs a specific action—that is, before grasping to eat as opposed to grasping to place. Thus, it seems possible that these neurons encode not only the specific motor act but also the actor's intentions (Fogassi et al. 2005; see also Nakahara and Miyashita 2005; Rizzolatti and Craighero 2004; Rizzolatti and Buccino 2005). These results are perhaps not surprising, given the benefits of being able to predict what others are going to do.

Furthermore, like the behavioral evidence for cross-modal visual-auditory recognition, the behavioral evidence for the simultaneous recognition of identity and motives receives support from the neurophysiological literature. In humans, one region of the fusiform gyrus, the fusiform face area (FFA), is more engaged by human faces than by any other visual stimulus (Kanwisher, McDermott, and Chun 1997; Kanwisher 2000). While the FFA was originally thought to be activated only by faces, however, some recent studies have shown that this activation depends on other factors, including the attribution of motives to the stimuli involved. Healthy adults showed heightened FFA activation when they were asked to observe three geometric figures engaged in "movements intended to suggest a sense of personal agency" and "interactions that were meant to be easily interpreted as social" (Schultz et al. 2003, 417). Subjects were then asked to state when the "interaction" was friendly or not. Activation of the FFA was therefore not restricted to faces but limited instead to those stimuli that had an animate, social character. The authors conclude that the fusiform gyrus and FFA encode information not only about facial identity but also about the "semantic attributes of people because of repeated perceptual experiences with faces that occur during social interactions" (Schultz et al. 2003, 423). Making much the same argument as we have here, the authors speculate that "the nature of the information stored in the FG might … [include] anything that would be helpful in defining faces. … There would be a measure of efficiency from this arrangement … that is, having representations and computations of more abstract attributes of people interdigitated with front-end perceptual processes about physical attributes" (Schultz et al. 2003, 423–424). Farah and Heberlein (2010) review evidence that the human brain contains a dedicated system for representing "the appearance, actions, and thoughts of people" that is innate, autonomous, and functions with a great deal of automaticity. This is just what we would expect to find if natural selection had acted strongly throughout primate evolution to favor a brain and perceptual system that innately, simultaneously, and automatically merged information about an individual's identity and motives.

In all the baboon experiments just mentioned, baboons that heard a vocalization rapidly assessed the type of vocalization and the identity of the caller, and integrated this information with their memory of recent events and their knowledge of the relationships among all the individuals involved. Based on these data, they appeared to attribute motives to the participants and to judge the motives of different individuals to be similar or different. When dealing with individuals perceived to share motives (typically matrilineal kin), they responded in particular ways; when dealing with individuals perceived not to share motives (usually unrelated animals), they reacted differently. If the call was aggressive and came from a relative of an individual with whom the listener had just fought, the call appeared to create in the listener's mind the expectation of an alliance directed against her, because the opponent and the caller, being members of the same kin group, were assumed to have similar motivations and were expected to act in concert. The listener therefore moved away. By contrast, if the call was aggressive and came from an individual who was unrelated to the previous opponent, it created no such expectation, because most alliances occur within families. Females therefore behaved as if they assumed that the call was directed at someone else.

3.6   Summary

For millions of years our ancestors lived in highly social groups where they saw, heard, and interacted with the same individuals over extended periods. Under these conditions, another animal's identity becomes inseparable from its social position and its intentions toward others. As a result, natural selection seems to have favored among baboons and other primates a perceptual system in which the recognition of an individual activates a rich cognitive network of information—about how the individual looks and sounds, its dominance rank, its family membership, and its motivation to behave toward specific others in particular ways. Individual recognition thus constitutes a form of object perception, in which many different stimuli are bound together to create a single coherent object—the individual—who behaves in predictable ways toward other objects or individuals. In baboons, the predictable ways are defined in part by the rules of close bonds among matrilineal kin and a linear dominance hierarchy. The object perception of others has been shaped by natural selection to be automatic, effortless, and accurate—if it were not, the individual could not succeed in its social environment.

To achieve these goals, natural selection has favored in baboons a mind that organizes data on individuals according to concepts—in the baboons' case, concepts that we humans label with names like *matrilineal family* and *linear dominance rank order*. The baboons have no such names, but they do have the concepts. Not explicit concepts, of course—we have no evidence that baboons can attach labels to different social relations, or that they are consciously aware of kin categories or their own knowledge of them—but implicit knowledge about which animals go together, how they are likely to interact, and the extent to which their motives are shared. Young children exhibit implicit knowledge when they learn and remember facts but cannot explain how they came to know them. When three-year-old children, for example, were shown the contents of a drawer, they could easily recount the drawer's contents at a later date, but they could not explain how they acquired this knowledge—they explained that they "just knew," or that they had always known what was in the drawer (reviewed in Nelson 2005). Children's knowledge at this age, like that of the baboons', is implicit, not explicit, but no less effective for all that.

3.7   Implications

3.7.1   For Research on Theory of Mind

There is at present some controversy over the extent of a theory of mind in animals. Much of the debate focuses on whether apes can attribute knowledge or false beliefs to others (Call and Tomasello 2008). There are, however, many more rudimentary ways in which animals might attribute a mental state to another, and some of these attributions may be considerably more widespread in the animal kingdom.

Baboons and other monkeys do not seem able to attribute knowledge or beliefs to each other (Cheney and Seyfarth 2007). They do, however, seem to attribute motives and intentions, as illustrated by the many experiments reviewed here. Indeed, there is growing evidence that many animal species routinely attend to other individuals' visual attention and intentions (e.g., Flombaum and Santos 2005; Bugnyar and Heinrich 2005; Burkhart et al. 2012; MacLean and Hare 2012), and even distinguish deliberate acts from accidental ones (e.g., Buttleman et al. 2007). Like young children

(Repacholi and Gopnik 1997), monkeys appear to attribute likes, dislikes, and intentions to others despite their failure to appreciate more complex mental states.

3.7.2 For Research on the Perception of Group Membership

Among social psychologists. there is considerable interest in the ways in which humans classify others into groups, because such classifications may lead to stereotypes, prejudice, and conflict (e.g., Brewer 1999; Spelke and Kinzler 2007; Fiske 2010). What are the origins of this tendency? It has been known for years that birds (Brooks and Falls 1975), primates (Cheney and Seyfarth 1982; Cheney 1987), and many other species recognize individuals outside their own group and associate them with particular areas. Conflict between groups, sometimes lethal, is well documented among hyenas (Smith et al. 2010), lions (Mosser and Packer 2009), and chimpanzees (Mitani, Watts, and Amsler 2010). Mahajan and coauthors (2011) add to this literature by showing that semi-free-ranging rhesus monkeys associated a novel object with a specific social group and appeared to attach a positive valence to members of their own group but a negative valence to members of a neighboring group. These distinctions between the members of one's own versus the members of another group could, however, be based on familiarity versus unfamiliarity, rates of interaction, or association with a particular range or territory.

The experiments reviewed here indicate that classification of others into distinct social units is ubiquitous in the everyday life of baboons, and indeed is essential for the formation of social bonds, offspring survival, and longevity. This classification occurs among individuals who live in the same group, range over the same area, see each other every day, and interact with each other often. Perhaps most important for those interested in comparison with humans, a baboon's classification of others seems to be based at least in part on the intentions she attributes to them—specifically, how she expects them to behave toward her and toward each other.

3.7.3 For Neurophysiological Studies of Primate Cognition

We have argued that a variety of information is bound together in the perception of primate vocalizations: information about the caller's identity, appearance, social relationships, and behavioral intentions. This view is consistent with the hypothesis that object knowledge—in both monkeys and humans—"may be represented in multiple cortical areas that store information about different object attributes, such as form … and motion" (Chao and Martin 2000, 478; see also Mahon and Caramazza 2009; Coutanche and Thompson-Schill 2013). If this hypothesis proves correct, and if similar mechanisms underlie the recognition of objects and individuals, then it should be possible to identify areas in the brain that are specialized not only for the identification of familiar voices, faces, and their integration but also for the identification of appropriate social interactions or, conversely, the detection of interactions that violate the social order. The recent paper by Kumaran, Melo, and Emrah (2012) represents a first step in this direction.

Acknowledgments

Research on baboons was supported by the National Science Foundation, the National Institutes of Health, the Leakey Foundation, the National Geographic Society, and the University of Pennsylvania. We thank Yale Cohen and Marc Coutanche for comments.

References

Adachi, I., and K. Fujita. 2007. Cross-modal representation of human caretakers in squirrel monkeys. *Behavioural Processes* 74:27–32.

Adachi, I., and R. Hampton. 2011. Rhesus monkeys see who they hear: Spontaneous cross-modal memory for familiar conspecifics. *PLoS ONE* 6:e23345.

Adachi, I., H. Kuwahata, and K. Fujita. 2007. Dogs recall their owner's face upon hearing the owner's voice. *Animal Cognition* 10:17–21.

Adolphs, R., J. A. Russell, and D. Tranel. 1999. A role for the human amygdala in recognizing emotional arousal from unpleasant stimuli. *Psychological Science* 10:167–171.

Belin, P., and R. J. Zattore. 2003. Adaptation to speaker's voice in right anterior temporal lobe. *Neuroreport* 14:2105–2109.

Bergman, T., J. C. Beehner, D. L. Cheney, and R. M. Seyfarth. 2003. Hierarchical classification by rank and kinship in baboons. *Science* 302:1234–1236.

Blank, H., A. Anwander, and K. von Kreigstein. 2011. Direct structural connections between voice- and face-recognition areas. *Journal of Neuroscience* 31:12906–12915.

Bregman, A. S. 1990. *Auditory Scene Analysis*. Cambridge, MA: MIT Press.

Brewer, M. B. 1999. The psychology of prejudice: Ingroup love or outgroup hate? *Journal of Social Issues* 55:429–444.

Brooks, R. J., and J. B. Falls. 1975. Individual recognition by song in white-throated sparrows. III. Song features used in individual recognition. *Canadian Journal of Zoology* 53:1749–1761.

Bugnyar, T., and B. Heinrich. 2005. Ravens, *Corvus corax*, differentiate between knowledgeable and ignorant competitors. *Proceedings: Biological Sciences* 272:1641–1646.

Burkhart, J., A. Kupferberg, S. Glasauer, and C. van Schaik. 2012. Even simple forms of social learning rely on intention attribution in marmoset monkeys (*Callithrix jacchus*). *Journal of Comparative Psychology* 126:129–138.

Buttleman, D., M. Carpenter, J. Call, and M. Tomasello. 2007. Enculturated chimpanzees imitate rationally. *Developmental Science* 10:F31–F38.

Call, J., and M. Tomasello. 2008. Does the chimpanzee have a theory of mind? 30 years later. *Trends in Cognitive Sciences* 12:187–192.

Campanella, S., and P. Belin. 2007. Integrating face and voice in person perception. *Trends in Cognitive Sciences* 11:535–543.

Cappe, C., and P. Barone. 2005. Heteromodal connections supporting multisensory integration at low levels of cortical processing in the monkey. *European Journal of Neuroscience* 22: 2886–2902.

Carey, S. 2010. *The Origin of Concepts*. New York: Oxford University Press.

Carey, S. 2011. The origin of concepts: A précis. *Behavioral and Brain Sciences* 34:116–137.

Carey, S., and E. Spelke. 1996. Science and core knowledge. *Philosophy of Science* 63:515–533.

Chao, L., and A. Martin. 2000. Representation of manipulable man-made objects in the dorsal stream. *NeuroImage* 12:478–484.

Cheney, D. L. 1987. Interactions and relationships between groups. In *Primate Societies*, ed. B. B. Smuts, D. L. Cheney, R. M. Seyfarth, R. W. Wrangham, and T. T. Struhsaker, 267–281. Chicago: University of Chicago Press.

Cheney, D. L., and R. M. Seyfarth. 1980. Vocal recognition in free-ranging vervet monkeys. *Animal Behaviour* 28:362–367.

Cheney, D. L., and R. M. Seyfarth. 1982. Recognition of individuals within and between groups of free-ranging vervet monkeys. *American Zoologist* 22:519–529.

Cheney, D. L., and R. M. Seyfarth. 1990. *How Monkeys See the World*. Chicago: University of Chicago Press.

Cheney, D. L., and R. M. Seyfarth. 1997. Reconciliatory grunts by dominant female baboons influence victims' behaviour. *Animal Behaviour* 54:409–418.

Cheney, D. L., and R. M. Seyfarth. 1999. Recognition of other individuals' social relationships by female baboons. *Animal Behaviour* 58:67–75.

Cheney, D. L., and R. M. Seyfarth. 2007. *Baboon Metaphysics*. Chicago: University of Chicago Press.

Cheney, D. L., R. M. Seyfarth, and J. B. Silk. 1995. The responses of female baboons to anomalous social interactions: Evidence for causal reasoning? *Journal of Comparative Psychology* 109: 134–141.

Coutanche, M., and S. Thompson-Schill. 2013. Informational connectivity: Identifying the co-emergence of multi-voxel patterns across the brain. *Frontiers in Neuroscience* 7 (15): 1–14.

Dasser, V. 1988. A social concept in Java monkeys. *Animal Behaviour* 36:225–230.

Emery, N. J., and D. I. Perrett. 2000. How can studies of the monkey brain help us understand "theory of mind" and autism in humans? In *Understanding Other Minds: Perspectives from Develop-*

mental Cognitive Neuroscience, 2nd ed., ed. S. Baron-Cohen, H. Tager-Flusberg, and D. Cohen, 279–301. Oxford: Oxford University Press.

Engh, A. L., R. R. Hoffmeier, D. L. Cheney, and R. M. Seyfarth. 2006. Who, me? Can baboons infer the target of a vocalization? *Animal Behaviour* 71:381–387.

Farah, M., and A. Heberlein. 2010. Personhood: An illusion rooted in brain function? In *Neuroethics*, ed. M. Farah, 321–338. Cambridge, MA: MIT Press.

Fine, C., J. Lumsden, and J. R. Blair. 2001. Dissociation between "theory of mind" and executive functions in a patient with early left amygdala damage. *Brain* 124:287–298.

Fiske, S. T. 2010. *Social Beings: Core Motives in Social Psychology.* 2nd ed. New York: Wiley.

Flombaum, J. I., and L. R. Santos. 2005. Rhesus monkeys attribute perceptions to others. *Current Biology* 15:447–452.

Fogassi, L., P. F. Ferrari, B. Gesierich, S. Rozzi, F. Chersi, and G. Rizzolatti. 2005. Parietal lobe: From action organization to intention understanding. *Science* 308:662–667.

Frith, C. D., and U. Frith. 2012. Mechanisms of social cognition. *Annual Review of Psychology* 63:287–313.

Gallagher, H. L., and C. D. Frith. 2003. Functional imaging of "theory of mind." *Trends in Cognitive Sciences* 7:77–83.

Ghazanfar, A., and N. Logothetis. 2003. Facial expressions linked to monkey calls. *Nature* 423:937–938.

Ghazanfar, A., J. X. Maier, K. L. Hoffman, and N. Logothetis. 2005. Multisensory integration of dynamic faces and voices in rhesus monkey auditory cortex. *Journal of Neuroscience* 25: 5004–5012.

James, W. 1890. *Principles of Psychology.* London: MacMillan.

Jellema, T., C. I. Baker, B. Wicker, and D. I. Perrett. 2000. Neural representation for the perception of the intentionality of actions. *Brain and Cognition* 44:280–302.

Johnston, R. E., and T. A. Bullock. 2001. Individual recognition by use of odors in golden hamsters: The nature of individual representation. *Animal Behaviour* 61:545–557.

Johnston, R. E., and A. Peng. 2008. Memory for individuals: Hamsters (*Mesocricetus auratus*) require contact to develop multi-component representations (concepts) of others. *Journal of Comparative Psychology* 122:121–131.

Kanwisher, N. 2000. Domain specificity in face perception. *Nature Neuroscience* 3:759–763.

Kanwisher, N., J. McDermott, and M. M. Chun. 1997. The fusiform face area: A module in human extrastriate cortex specialized for face perception. *Journal of Neuroscience* 17:4302–4311.

Kawashima, S., M. Sugiura, T. Kato, A. Nakamura, K. Hatano, K. Ito, H. Fukuda, S. Kojima, and K. Nakamura. 1999. The human amygdala plays an important role in gaze monitoring: A PET study. *Brain* 122:779–783.

Kitchen, D. M., D. L. Cheney, and R. M. Seyfarth. 2005. Male chacma baboons (*Papio hamadryas ursinus*) discriminate loud call contests between rivals of different relative ranks. *Animal Cognition* 8:1–6.

Kondo, N., E. Izawa, and S. Watanabe. 2012. Crows cross-modally recognize group members but not non-group members. *Proceedings: Biological Sciences* 279:1937–1942.

Kumaran, D., H. W. Melo, and D. Emrah. 2012. The emergence and representation of knowledge about social and nonsocial hierarchies. *Neuron* 76:653–666.

Leopold, D. A., and G. Rhodes. 2010. A comparative view of face perception. *Journal of Comparative Psychology* 124:233–251.

Lorincz, E. N., T. Jellema, J.-C. Gómez, N. Barraclough, D. Xiao, and D. I. Perrett. 2005. Do monkeys understand actions and minds of others? Studies of single cells and eye movements. In *From Monkey Brain to Human Brain*, ed. S. Dehaene, J.-R. Duhamel, M. D. Hauser, and G. Rizzolatti, 189–210. Cambridge, MA: MIT Press.

MacLean, E. L., and B. Hare. 2012. Bonobos and chimpanzees infer the target of another's attention. *Animal Behaviour* 83:345–353.

Macuda, T., and W. A. Roberts. 1995. Further evidence for hierarchical chunking in rat spatial memory. *Journal of Experimental Psychology: Animal Behavior Processes* 21:20–32.

Mahajan, N., M. A. Martinez, N. L. Gutierrez, G. Diesendruk, M. R. Banaji, and L. Santos. 2011. The evolution of intergroup bias: Perceptions and attitudes in rhesus macaques. *Journal of Personality and Social Psychology* 100:387–405.

Mahon, B. Z., and A. Caramazza. 2009. Concepts and categories: A cognitive neuropsychological perspective. *Annual Review of Psychology* 6:27–51.

Mandler, G. 1967. Organization and memory. In *The Psychology of Learning and Motivation: Advances in Research and Theory*, ed. K. W. Spence and J. T. Spence, 327–372. San Diego: Academic Press.

Miller, C. T., and Y. Cohen. 2010. Vocalizations as auditory objects: Behavior and neurophysiology. In *Primate Neuroethology*, ed. M. Platt and A. A. Ghazanfar, 236–254. Oxford: Oxford University Press.

Mitani, J., D. Watts, and S. Amsler. 2010. Lethal aggression leads to territorial expansion in wild chimpanzees. *Current Biology* 20:R507–R508.

Mosser, A., and C. Packer. 2009. Group territoriality and the benefits of sociality in the African lion, *Pathera leo*. *Animal Behaviour* 78:359–370.

Nakahara, K., and T. Miyashita. 2005. Understanding intentions: Through the looking glass. *Science* 308:6444–6445.

Nelson, K. 2005. Emerging levels of consciousness in early human development. In *The Missing Link in Cognition: Origins of Self-Reflecting Consciousness*, ed. H. S. Terrace and J. Metcalf, 116–141. New York: Oxford University Press.

Pelphrey, K. A., R. J. Viola, and G. McCarthy. 2004. When strangers pass: Processing of mutual and averted social gaze in the superior temporal sulcus. *Psychological Science* 15:598–603.

Penn, D., K. Holyoak, and D. Povinelli. 2008. Darwin's mistake: Explaining the discontinuity between human and nonhuman minds. *Behavioral and Brain Sciences* 31:109–178.

Perry, S., H. C. Barrett, and J. Manson. 2004. White-faced capuchin monkeys show triadic awareness in their choice of allies. *Animal Behaviour* 67:165–170.

Petkov, C. I., C. Kayser, T. Steudel, K. Whittingstall, M. Augath, and N. K. Logothetis. 2008. A voice region in the monkey brain. *Nature Neuroscience* 11:367–374.

Proops, L., K. McComb, and D. Reby. 2009. Cross-modal individual recognition in domestic horses (*Equus caballus*). *Proceedings of the National Academy of Sciences of the United States of America* 106:947–951.

Rendall, D., P. S. Rodman, and R. E. Emond. 1996. Vocal recognition of individuals and kin in free-ranging rhesus monkeys. *Animal Behaviour* 51:1007–1015.

Repacholi, B., and A. Gopnik. 1997. Early reasoning about desires: Evidence from 14- and 18-month olds. *Developmental Psychology* 33:12–21.

Rizzolatti, G., and G. Buccino. 2005. The mirror neuron system and its role in imitation and language. In *From Monkey Brain to Human Brain*, ed. S. Dehaene, J.-R. Duhamel, M. D. Hauser, and G. Rizzolatti, 189–210. Cambridge, MA: MIT Press.

Rizzolatti, G., and L. Craighero. 2004. The mirror-neuron system. *Annual Review of Neuroscience* 27:169–192.

Santos, L. R., J. I. Flombaum, and W. Phillips. 2006. The evolution of human mindreading: How non-human primates can inform social cognitive neuroscience. In *Evolutionary Cognitive Neuroscience*, ed. S. M. Platek, J. P. Keenan, and T. K. Shackelford, 433–456. Cambridge, MA: MIT Press.

Schino, G., B. Tiddi, and E. Polizzi di Sorrentino. 2006. Simultaneous classification by rank and kinship in Japanese macaques. *Animal Behaviour* 71:1069–1074.

Schultz, R. T., D. J. Grelotti, A. Klin, J. Kleinman, C. Van der Gaag, R. Marois, and P. Skudlarski. 2003. The role of the fusiform face area in social cognition: Implications for the pathobiology of autism. *Philosophical Transactions of the Royal Society of London: Series B, Biological Sciences* 358:415–427.

Schusterman, R. J., and D. A. Kastak. 1998. Functional equivalence in a California sea lion: Relevance to animal social and communicative interactions. *Animal Behaviour* 55:1087–1095.

Seyfarth, R. M., and D. L. Cheney. 2001. Cognitive strategies and the representation of social relationships by monkeys. In *Evolutionary Psychology and Motivation, Nebraska Symposium on Motivation*, vol. 48, ed. J. A. French, A. C. Kamil, and D. W. Leger, 145–178. Lincoln: University of Nebraska Press.

Silk, J. B. 1999. Male bonnet macaques use information about third-party rank relationships to recruit allies. *Animal Behaviour* 58:45–51.

Silk, J. B., S. Alberts, and J. Altmann. 2003. Social bonds of female baboons enhance infant survival. *Science* 302:1331–1334.

Silk, J. B., J. C. Beehner, T. Bergman, C. Crockford, A. Engh, L. Moscovice, R. Wittig, R. M. Seyfarth, and D. L. Cheney. 2010a. Female chacma baboons form strong, equitable, and enduring social bonds. *Behavioral Ecology and Sociobiology* 64:1733–1747.

Silk, J. B., J. C. Beehner, T. Bergman, C. Crockford, A. Engh, L. Moscovice, R. Wittig, R. M. Seyfarth, and D. L. Cheney. 2010b. Strong and consistent social bonds enhance the longevity of female baboons. *Current Biology* 20:1359–1361.

Silk, J. B., J. C. Beehner, T. Bergman, C. Crockford, R. M. Wittig, A. L. Engh, R. M. Seyfarth, and D. L. Cheney. 2009. The benefits of social capital: Close bonds among female baboons enhance offspring survival. *Proceedings: Biological Sciences* 276:3099–3104.

Silk, J. B., D. L. Cheney, and R. M. Seyfarth. 1996. The form and function of post-conflict interactions between female baboons. *Animal Behaviour* 52:259–268.

Sliwa, J., J. R. Duhamel, O. Pascalis, and S. Wirth. 2011. Spontaneous voice-face identity matching by rhesus monkeys for familiar conspecifics and humans. *Proceedings of the National Academy of Sciences of the United States of America* 108:1735–1740.

Smith, J. E., R. VanHorn, K. S. Powning, A. R. Cole, K. E. Graham, S. K. Memenis, and K. Holekamp. 2010. Evolutionary forces favoring intragroup coalitions among spotted hyenas and other animals. *Behavioral Ecology* 21:284–303.

Spelke, E., and K. Kinzler. 2007. Core knowledge. *Developmental Science* 10:89–96.

Tibbetts, E. A., and J. Dale. 2007. Individual recognition: It is good to be different. *Trends in Ecology & Evolution* 22:529–537.

Tsao, G. Y., W. A. Friewald, R. B. Tootell, and M. S. Livingston. 2006. A cortical region consisting entirely of face-selective cells. *Science* 311:670–674.

von Kriegstein, K., A. Kleinschmidt, P. Sterzer, and A. L. Giraud. 2005. Interaction of face and voice areas during speaker recognition. *Journal of Cognitive Neuroscience* 17:367–376.

Wittig, R. M., C. Crockford, R. M. Seyfarth, and D. L. Cheney. 2007. Vocal alliances in chacma baboons, *Papio hamadryas ursinus*. *Behavioral Ecology and Sociobiology* 61:899–909.

Wittig, R. M., C. Crockford, E. Wikberg, R. M. Seyfarth, and D. L. Cheney. 2007. Kin-mediated reconciliation substitutes for direct reconciliation in baboons. *Proceedings: Biological Sciences* 274:1109–1115.

II Concepts and the Brain

4 Missed Connections: A Connectivity-Constrained Account of the Representation and Organization of Object Concepts

Bradford Z. Mahon

4.1 Introduction

One of the most exciting open issues in the cognitive and brain sciences is how conceptual knowledge is represented and organized in the brain. A recent proliferation of methods that allow cognition to be studied in vivo in healthy subjects has accelerated our understanding of how the brain processes conceptual knowledge. Two broad goals can be framed for the empirical study of concepts: a scientific goal and a clinical goal.

The scientific goal is to develop a model of how concepts are organized and represented, at both the cognitive and neural levels. Such a model would specify the format of conceptual information and the processing dynamics that govern how that information is retrieved according to current task demands. For instance, the types of information that are prioritized are different if one looks at a cup with the intention of taking a drink from it, versus with the intention of identifying it as being "my cup," versus checking whether it is empty. A model would specify how the same visual input in all such situations is "routed" through sensorimotor and conceptual systems. This would involve specifying what information is necessary for the task, versus relevant but not necessary, versus activated but entirely ancillary, as well as the order in which information is retrieved. Such a model would specify how conceptual knowledge interfaces with other cognitive systems, such as planning and executive function, linguistic processing, as well as how it interfaces with sensorimotor input and output systems. Finally, such a model would also specify not only the structure and processing dynamics of the conceptual system at a cognitive level, but how that system is organized and distributed in the brain.

The clinically oriented goal can be separated into prognostic and treatment-oriented components. On the basis of a working model of how concepts are organized and represented, a prognostic clinical goal is, for instance, to develop accurate means for determining expected outcomes after acute brain injury, or the trajectory of loss of conceptual information in the context of progressive degenerative diseases such as Alzheimer's disease or semantic dementia. Another clinically oriented goal is to use a working model of conceptual organization to help guide neurosurgical planning of the location and extent of cortical resections. Finally, we would want to use our understanding of how concepts are organized and represented in the brain to guide rehabilitation of lost function, where rehabilitation can include existing cognitive-behavioral therapy and prospective approaches that may seek to actually repair or replace damaged tissue.

To date, the study of concepts in the brain has generally focused on analyses of the factors that modulate processing local to a particular region of the conceptual system—for instance, the *visual* factors that modulate visual object recognition, or the *motor* factors that modulate object-directed action. This local, bottom-up, approach has been inherited from well-established traditions in neurophysiology and psychophysics, where it has been enormously productive for mapping psychophysical continua in primary sensory systems. Here I argue, however, that the same approach will not yield equally useful insights for understanding the principles that determine the organization and representation of conceptual knowledge. The reason is that unlike the peripheral sensory systems, the patterns of neural responses that reflect conceptual processing are only partially driven by the physical input—they are also driven by how the stimulus is interpreted, and that interpretation does not occur in a single, isolated region. Thus, a critical step for developing a model of conceptual organization and representation is to articulate how multiple sources of information are integrated in real time and how concepts interface with other cognitive and sensorimotor systems. This means that to move forward, as a field, the connectivity of the conceptual system with language, executive, sensory, motor, and other systems must become the new "unit of analysis." Connectivity is not just wiring; the connections are not passive conduits through which information is passed. The connectivity of the system constrains the order in which information is accessed and can be weighted, and that weighting of information is a central aspect of the computations that form conceptual processing.

The current state of the field, summarized below, is characterized by a somewhat more static notion of concepts and has developed largely by setting issues of connectivity aside. As will be seen, a tremendous amount of progress has been made in recent decades. But the depth of our understanding of both old and new theoretical questions will quickly reach asymptote without a shift in emphasis toward understanding the role played by connectivity. In keeping with the theme of this volume, this chapter is my attempt to shoot an azimuth of where we are headed as a field; I do this by outlining a theoretical framework that places connectivity at the center of what needs to be understood.

4.2 Overview of the Hypothesis Space

A distinction can be drawn between hypotheses about concept organization and hypotheses about concept representation. Hypotheses about how concepts are organized in the brain are typically concerned with the causes of an observed physical distribution of conceptual information in different regions of cortex and the reasons the conceptual system is observed to fractionate along the lines that it does under conditions of brain damage. Hypotheses about how concepts are represented are concerned with the representational format of conceptual information. For instance, a representational issue is whether conceptual knowledge is represented in a modality-specific format (visual, motor) or in an abstract format. As might be expected, the distinction between representation and organization is blurred by theories that make claims about, or have implications for, both the organization and the representation of concepts. Nevertheless, it is useful to draw a distinction between organization and representation, principally because there exists an asymmetry in the types of confirmatory empirical evidence that have been marshaled in support of theories that focus on representation versus theories that focus on organization.

The literature review below is fast and loose, and heavily curated; it is entirely in the service of motivating a shift in perspective toward studying the connectivity of the conceptual system. It also makes little attempt to be ecumenical and is guided by a theoretical framework that has been developed over the past ten years with Alfonso Caramazza (Caramazza and Mahon 2003, 2006; Mahon and Caramazza 2003, 2005, 2008, 2009, 2011). An array of excellent reviews from other theoretical perspectives that discuss a broader range of findings can be found in Barsalou (1999); Binder and Desai (2011); Borgo and Shallice (2003); Chatterjee (2010); Cree and MacRae (2003); Gallese and Lakoff (2005); Glenberg, Sato, and Cattaneo (2008); Grill-Spector and Malach (2004); Hart et al. (2007); Humphreys and Forde (2001); Johnson-Frey (2004); Kemmerer et al. (2012); Kemmerer (forthcoming); Kiefer and Pulvermüller (2012); Laws (2005); Lewis (2006); Martin (2007); Op de Beeck, Haushofer, and Kanwisher (2008); Patterson, Nestor, and Rogers (2007); Pülvermuller (2005); Sartori and Lombardi (2004); Simmons and Barsalou (2003); Thompson-Schill (2003); Tyler and Moss (2001); Vinson et al. (2003).

The scope of the argument to follow is restricted to the representation and organization of object concepts. This leaves most of conceptual space unaccounted for, including concepts expressed as nouns that do not have physical referents (e.g., DREAM, GOAL, PIETY, etc.), as well as concepts that apply to actions, abstract verbs, and many other types of concepts, such as numbers, theory of mind, moral concepts, and logical concepts and reasoning (among other domains as well). The restricted scope of the review helps to gain a solid, if limited, footing on the theoretical issues pertaining to the organization and representation of object concepts. A complete theory would presumably have within its scope all domains of conceptual processing; whether it will be possible to develop such an account is an empirical and methodological challenge that we face as a field.

4.3 Associative Evidence and Theories of the Representation of Concepts

A widely discussed theoretical framework about the representation of conceptual knowledge is the "embodied cognition hypothesis." The central idea of this framework, applied to concepts, is that sensorimotor representations are reactivated or "simulated" in the course of conceptual analysis, and that sensorimotor activation is a necessary and intermediary step in the computation of meaning (see Allport 1985 for an early formulation of this view). The strong (and arguably most interesting) form of this view is that there is no representational distinction between conceptual information and sensorimotor information: retrieving concepts consists of simulation or reactivation of sensorimotor information that is/was activated, either when we initially acquired the concept or when we interact with instantiations of that concept. Because this is the central claim of the hypothesis, the theory is committed to the view that conceptual retrieval involves the retrieval of stored sensorimotor information. These sensorimotor "memories" are sensory or motor in their format, and therefore they are assumed to be "token-based" representations, or representations of actual instances of sensory or motor experiences. Another way to think about such theories is that they are a type of exemplar-based model of semantic memory, where the exemplars consist of sensorimotor information and are in a sensory or motor format.

An important type of evidence argued to support the embodied cognition hypothesis consists of demonstrations that motor processes are automatically engaged when participants perform conceptual and perceptual tasks that do not require, on a logical analysis of the task, overt activation of the motor system. Such motor activation has been observed in functional neuroimaging, neurophysiological recordings in nonhuman primates and in humans, EEG, behavior, transcranial magnetic stimulation (TMS), and kinematic analyses (for empirical reviews and theoretical discussions, see, e.g., Barsalou et al. 2003; Boulenger et al. 2006; Gallese and Lakoff 2005; Martin 2007; Pulvermüller 2005; Rizzolatti and Craighero 2004). For instance, Hauk and colleagues (2004) found overlap in the regions of the motor cortex that were activated for both physical actions and words that describe actions (e.g., *kick*). Foot-related action words like *kick* activated dorsal parts of the motor cortex while hand-related action words like *pick* activated more lateral and ventral parts of the motor cortex, following the known pattern of somatotopy. As another example, Glenberg, Sato, and Cattaneo (2008) found that when participants moved hundreds of beans from a container near them to a container farther away, they were slower to judge sentences as sensible that described action events in which objects were moved away from the body. Glenberg and colleagues argued that fatiguing the motor system selectively interfered with the comprehension of sentences whose meaning implied a directionality congruent with the direction of the prior bean movements.

Recent interest in the embodiment of concepts parallels recent interest in motor theories of perception. The original motor theory of speech perception (Liberman et al. 1967; Liberman and Mattingly 1985) stated that speech recognition was fundamentally a process of recognizing the motor actions (tongue/articulatory movements) of the speaker and not one of recognizing the auditory perceptual information per se. Thus, speech recognition consisted of simulating the motor output programs that would be necessary to produce the sounds being recognized. The motor theory of speech perception, and more recently, the motor theory of action recognition, have enjoyed a renaissance because of the discovery of so-called mirror neurons: neurons in premotor and other motor-relevant structures in macaques that fire both when the monkey performs an action and when it observes another individual (human, monkey) performing an action (e.g., di Pellegrino et al. 1992; Gallese et al. 1996). Mirror neurons are thought to provide the empirical substrate for a reformulated motor theory of action perception, and thus provide independent evidence for the notion that processing in one system (perception) is in part constituted by (i.e., involves as a necessary and intermediary step) processing in the motor system (for critical discussion, see Binder and Desai 2011; Chatterjee 2010; Dinstein et al. 2008; Hickok 2009, 2010; Hickok et al. 2008; Hickok et al. 2011; Lingnau, Gesierich, and Caramazza 2009; Mahon and Caramazza 2005, 2008; Stasenko, Garcea, and Mahon, 2013).

The critical issue is whether demonstrations that the motor system is activated during perceptual or conceptual analysis indicate, as presumed by the embodied cognition hypothesis and the motor theory of action recognition, that motor information plays a constitutive (i.e., necessary) role in perceptual or conceptual analysis. The alternative is that activation spreads from perceptual or conceptual levels of processing through to motor processes. There are different ways in which such an alternative could be formulated. For instance, it could be argued, in the context of motor activation during perception, that the dynamics of the sensorimotor systems are such that activation propagates to the motor system only after the stimulus has been recognized as such. Alternatively, it could be argued that activation cascades forward to the motor system from input levels of processing *prior* to completion of processing at those input levels. The broader point is that a range of alternative accounts can be formulated to explain why the motor system is activated during perception (for discussion, see Mahon and Caramazza 2008; Stasenko, Garcea, and Mahon, 2013).

By analogy, there is evidence that the phonology of words that are never overtly produced, but that are semantically related to actually produced words, is activated in the course of speech production (e.g., Costa, Caramazza, and Sebastián-Gallés 2000;

Peterson and Savoy 1998). It has never been argued, however, that such observations sanction the inference that the activated phonological information constitutes, even in part, the semantics of the unproduced words. Rather, the debate concerns the dynamics of information flow within the speech production system, and whether it is cascaded activation or serial and discrete. The relationship between evidence and theory exactly mirrors the relationship between observations of motor activation during perceptual or conceptual processing, and the embodied cognition hypothesis. Thus the implication is that the representational inferences that have been argued to support the embodied cognition hypothesis are, at best, premature, and the available evidence is, at best, (only) consistent with the embodied cognition hypothesis.

4.4   Patient Evidence and the Embodied Cognition Hypothesis

Recent work with brain-damaged patients highlighted cases where conceptual and motor abilities are seen to be impaired together—that is, theoretically interesting associations of impairments. For instance, Pazzaglia, Pizzamiglio, and colleagues (2008) observed that patients with buccofacial apraxia (impairments producing sounds related to facial and mouth structures, e.g., whistling or slurping a straw) had greater difficulty recognizing mouth action sounds compared with hand action sounds, whereas patients with limb apraxia (difficulties performing skilled actions like pounding a hammer) had greater difficulty recognizing limb action sounds compared with mouth action sounds (see Mahon 2008 for discussion; see also Pazzaglia, Pizzamiglio, et al. 2008). Buxbaum and colleagues (2005) found an association at the group level in the ability of patients to imitate certain types of actions and their ability to recognize actions (see Negri et al. 2007 for replication, extension, and critical discussion). Boulenger and colleagues (2008) combined a masked priming paradigm with a lexical decision task to study semantic priming effects in a nondemented group of Parkinson's patients (n = 10) who were either off or on dopaminergic treatment. It is known that Parkinson's patients show relative inactivation of motor cortices when they are off, compared with when they are on, dopaminergic treatment. The authors found that the magnitude of the masked priming was modulated according to whether the patients were on or off their medication, and importantly, this modulation was present only for action word targets and not for concrete nouns. Another recent and rich example is the study by Bonner and Grossman (2012), who found that patients with logopenic variant of primary progressive aphasia, a variant that leads to cortical atrophy first around Hershel's gyrus, were impaired for knowledge about the typical sounds that objects make.

However, there is also dissociative patient evidence indicating that action production can be impaired while action recognition is spared, both in the domain of hand actions (Negri et al. 2007; Rumiati et al. 2001; Rapcsak et al. 1995; for reviews, see Mahon and Caramazza 2005, 2008) and in the domain of speech perception (Hickok et al. 2011; Rogalsky et al. 2011; for reviews, see Hickok 2009, 2010; Stasenko, Garcea, and Mahon, 2013; Toni et al. 2008). For instance, patients with apraxia of object use are not necessarily impaired for naming the same objects or retrieving function knowledge about those objects (e.g., Buxbaum, Veramonti, and Schwartz 2000; Buxbaum and Saffran 2002; Ochipa, Rothi, and Heilman 1989; Rapcsak et al. 1995; for review, see Mahon and Caramazza 2005).

The existence of *dissociative* evidence is problematic for the claim that motor information forms a necessary component of conceptual or perceptual processing. The dissociative patient evidence is sufficient to reject strong forms of the embodied concept hypothesis and strong forms of the motor theory of action perception (for discussion, see Garcea and Mahon 2012; Mahon and Caramazza 2005, 2008; Stasenko, Garcea, and Mahon, 2013; Hickok 2010; Chatterjee 2010). This conclusion carries with it the burden of explaining (1) why the motor system is activated during (perceptual and conceptual) tasks that do not, on a logical analysis of what is involved in those tasks, necessitate overt activation of motor information, and (2) why the above-described associative patient evidence is observed (e.g., Buxbaum, Kyle, and Menon 2005; Bonner and Grossman 2012; Pazzaglia, Pizzamiglio, et al. 2008, Pazzaglia, Smania, et al 2008). One possibility is that activation spreads from perceptual or conceptual levels of representation to the motor system. In the context of the embodied cognition hypothesis, the question arises as to what function such activation might serve. The associative patient evidence suggests that such activation is not irrelevant or ancillary but that it may play some, as yet unspecified, function. I return to these issues below.

The broader point is that the core issue that must be elucidated concerns how information is exchanged among sensory, motor, and conceptual systems. What we are missing, as a field, is a theory of the dynamics of activation spread between perceptual or conceptual processes and the motor system. Only in the context of a specific theory of the dynamics of sensorimotor and conceptual processing can strong inferences about the representational format of concepts be derived from observations that the motor system is automatically activated during perceptual or conceptual tasks.

4.5   Dissociative Evidence and Theories of the Organization of Concepts

One of the most intriguing of neuropsychological phenomena are category-specific semantic deficits. Category-specific semantic deficits are impairments to conceptual knowledge that differentially, or selectively, affect information from one semantic category. Figure 4.1A (plate 5) shows the picture-naming performance from some well-studied patients and represents the full range of semantic categories that can be differentially or selectively impaired in patients with category-specific semantic deficits. The categories of category-specific semantic deficits are living animate (animals), living inanimate (fruits/vegetables), conspecifics, and tools (for an exhaustive review of the empirical literature through 2001, see Capitani et al. 2003).

A. Picture naming performance by category

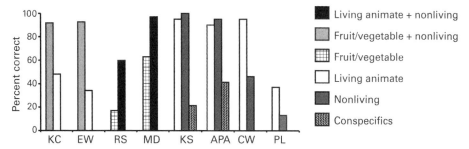

B. Semantic probe questions by category and modality

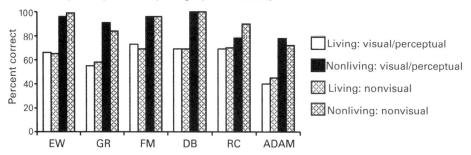

Figure 4.1 (plate 5)
Patients with category-specific semantic deficits may be differentially, or even selectively, impaired for knowledge of animals, plants, conspecifics, or artifacts. The knowledge impairment cannot be explained in terms of a differential impairment to a sensory or motor-based modality of information. While discussion and debate continues as to whether noncategorical dimensions of organization may lead to category-specific brain organization, there is consensus that the phenomenon itself is *categorical*. (A) Picture-naming performance of patients studied with materials that were carefully balanced to equate various continuous dimensions across categories (e.g., frequency, familiarity, visual complexity). The four major patterns of category-specific semantic deficits are represented. (B) Semantic attribute question performance for six representative patients with differential impairments for living animate. As shown across the patients, impairments for a category are associated with impairments for all types of knowledge about items from that category. Figure reproduced from Mahon and Caramazza (2011), with permission.

Category-specific semantic deficits have been particularly fertile ground for the development and evaluation of hypotheses about how conceptual information is organized. The general question that these theories seek to answer is, How is knowledge organized in the normal system such that damage can lead to impairments that respect semantic category distinctions? Current theories can be separated into *reductionist* and *nonreductionist* approaches; reductionist theories do not posit semantic category as an organizing principle in the mind/brain, while nonreductionist theories do posit semantic category as an organizing principle. Within reductionist theories, a further distinction can be made between *eliminativist reductionist* and *non-eliminativist reductionist*, with eliminativist approaches denying any principles of neural organization whatsoever, and non-eliminativist making clear positive proposals about neural organization (but not appealing to semantic category or domain as an organizing principle).

4.5.1 Eliminativist Reductionist Theories

It was recognized early on in the study of category-specific semantic deficits that the impairments in some patients could be explained because items from different semantic categories tended to differ along certain variables, such as lexical frequency, concept familiarity, or the visual complexity of the images that were used to establish the presence of impairments. Thus, if items were sampled without attention to those variables, then some categories within the neuropsychological tests might be "easier" than other categories, thus leading to spurious category dissociations (see Funnell and Sheridan 1992; for recent discussion and for extensive normative work, see Barbarotto et al. 2002; Cree and MacRae 2003). More recently, Sartori, Lombardi, and colleagues (Mechelli et al. 2006; Sartori and Lombardi 2004; Sartori, Lombardi, and Mattiuzzi 2005) developed a measure termed *semantic relevance*, which is a nonlinear combination of the frequency with which particular features are produced for an item and the distinctiveness of that feature across all concepts in the database. In addition, the issue of whether items from some categories are more visually complex than others can be expressed as a cognitive issue and not merely an issue about the stimuli over which patients are tested. It may be argued that the structure of the world, and our representation of that structure, is such that the visual knowledge of one category is more "tightly packed" or "crowded" than other categories. Arguments differ as to which categories have representations that are more densely packed, but proposals agree that a higher density of representations renders them more susceptible to impairment (e.g., Humphreys and Forde 2001; Laws 2005).[1]

---

1. It should be noted, however, that it is not obvious that higher density (i.e., higher within-category similarity) should lead to greater susceptibility to impairment, as, for instance, Tyler, Moss, and colleagues (Tyler et al. 2000; Tyler and Moss 2001) argued in a somewhat different context that high correlations among shared features confer resistance to damage (but see Devlin et al. 2002).

In summary, a number of dimensions may vary across semantic categories that are represented at both conceptual and nonconceptual levels of processing (e.g., lexical frequency, concept familiarity, visual/structural similarity). The critical test of such accounts, as accounts of the existence of the phenomenon of category-specific deficits, is (1) whether category dissociations remain when items are carefully matched across categories (for discussion, see Capitani et al. 2003), and (2) whether double dissociations can be observed over the same materials across patients (e.g., Caramazza and Hillis 1991). Because both (1) and (2) have been answered in the affirmative, we can conclude that category-specific semantic deficits are not spurious, that is, cannot be reduced to such uncontrolled dimensions. This conclusion rules out the broad class of eliminativist reductionist theories (for evidence and arguments, see Caramazza and Mahon 2003; Mahon and Caramazza 2009).

4.5.2 Non-eliminativist Reductionist Theories

The modern study of concepts in the brain was inaugurated by the empirical and theoretical work of Warrington, McCarthy, and Shallice (Warrington and McCarthy 1983, 1987; Warrington and Shallice 1984). In a series of papers, they documented the first well-described cases of category-specific semantic deficits and proposed the most influential theory that is still widely discussed today: the sensory/functional theory.

The sensory/functional theory makes two assumptions:

1. First, the semantic system is organized by modality or type of information. The original distinction drawn was between visual-perceptual and functional-associative systems (see Lhermitte and Beauvois 1973 for earlier work on this assumption). More recently, Crutch and Warrington (2003; see also Cree and MacRae 2003; Vigliocco et al. 2004) proposed that the semantic system may be more finely structured by modality or type of information. For instance, *visual-perceptual* can be further fractionated into color, form, and surface properties (Cree and MacRae 2003; Crutch and Warrington 2003).

2. Second, the ability to recognize items from different semantic categories differentially depends on different modalities or types of information. For instance, the ability to recognize and identify animals, it was argued, differentially depends on visual-perceptual information, while the ability to recognize tools and other man-made artifacts differentially depends on functional-associative knowledge. The comprehensive semantic feature norming work of Cree and MacRae (2003; see also Vigliocco et al. 2004) is largely directed at this second assumption. Cree and MacRae asked healthy subjects to produce features of common objects, and the resulting features were taxonimized into nine *knowledge types* that could have plausible neural bases. The authors then used clustering methods to argue that some knowledge types were more important or salient for some semantic categories.

The two core assumptions of the sensory/functional theory together explain category-specific semantic deficits as arising from damage to a modality or type of knowledge on which successful identification of items from the impaired category differentially depends. For this reason, the theory is non-eliminativist (it makes a strong and positive claim about neural organization) but is reductionist with respect to semantic categories (as it posits the relevant underlying organizational principle is modality rather than category).

It is important to note that the sensory/functional theory is not committed to a particular view about the format of conceptual representations—that is, the sensory/functional theory could, or could not, be formulated as an embodied cognition hypothesis. The hypothesis that semantic information can be distinguished by modality or type could be proposed as a claim about the *content* of semantic information and not its format (for discussion, see Caramazza et al. 1990). This is a point that is often obscured in the literature, where the sensory/functional theory is assumed to be a claim about the format of conceptual knowledge and thus run together with embodied proposals. However, one can accept a strong representational distinction between concepts and sensorimotor processes (i.e., conceptual information is dissociable from sensorimotor processes), and still argue that modality or type of information is the principle dimension along which concepts are organized. In fact, this was the original proposal by Warrington and her collaborators. Subsequent developments of the theory (e.g., Martin, Ungerleider, and Haxby 2000) have argued for more nuanced positions, for instance, that object concepts are stored adjacent to the sensory and motor systems that were active when the concept was acquired. Even the (so-called) sensory/motor theory of Martin and collaborators (see also Martin 2007), however, is not committed to the view that the format of conceptual representations is strictly sensorimotor. Still other hypotheses argue for somewhat stronger marriages between the sensory/functional theory and embodied views of concepts (see, for instance, Simmons and Barsalou 2003).

A number of arguments have been raised against the sensory/functional theory. On the one hand, the evidence marshaled in support of the assumption that different categories differentially rely on different types or modalities of knowledge for their recognition has been questioned on methodological grounds (e.g., Caramazza and Shelton 1998). More recent investigations (e.g., Cree and MacRae 2003) largely overcame the methodological limitations that attended earlier studies. The findings of the more recent and sophisticated normative studies, however, are not obviously relevant to the key assumption that different types of knowledge are differentially important for distinguishing *within* categories. For instance, Cree and MacRae showed that different types of knowledge are important for distinguishing among different categories, or one category from other categories. In one finding, the authors showed that color is important for distinguishing fruits and vegetables from other categories, while biological motion was important for distinguishing animals from other categories. Patients with category-specific semantic deficits, however, have difficulties distinguishing not between categories but *within* categories. Thus, it is not obvious that there is in fact evidence for the assumption that different types or modalities of information are differentially important for distinguishing among items *within* categories.

Another argument against the sensory/functional theory, and perhaps the most damaging argument, is that patients with category-specific semantic deficits do not present with differential impairments for the modality or type of knowledge on which the impaired category (putatively) depends (see figure 4.1B, plate 5). In other words, patients with disproportionate impairments for animals do not have a corresponding disproportionate impairment for visual-perceptual knowledge. Similarly, patients with disproportionate impairments for visual-perceptual knowledge do not necessarily have a disproportionate impairment for animals. Such dissociations between the category specificity of the deficit and the modality specificity of the deficit are the norm, rather than the exception (see Capitani et al. 2003).

4.5.3 Nonreductionist Theories

According to the nonreductionist view, category-specific semantic deficits arise because the damage affects a brain region or network of brain regions that is devoted to a particular semantic domain of knowledge. The *domains* for which there are specialized systems are limited to those that could have had an evolutionarily significant history (living animate, living inanimate, conspecifics, and tools). This hypothesis was initially articulated in the context of category-specific semantic impairments by Caramazza and Shelton (1998; see also, e.g., Capitani et al. 2003; Farah and Rabinowitz 2003; Samson and Pillon 2003). Subsequent formulations of the domain-specific hypothesis (Caramazza and Mahon 2003, 2006; Mahon and Caramazza 2009, 2011) have emphasized that the semantic system is also organized by modality or type of information. In other words, there may be two orthogonal dimensions of organizations, perhaps hierarchically structured: domain and modality. I return to this issue below.

In summary, the picture that emerges from the last several decades of work on category-specific semantic deficits is as follows: (1) Category-specific semantic deficits survive stringent control of stimulus variables and are observed to doubly dissociate across patients tested with the same set of materials. These facts rule out, broadly speaking, theories that posit that the phenomenon arises because a dimension (e.g., visual complexity, relevance) is correlated with a semantic category distinction. (2) Category-specific semantic deficits affect all types of knowledge that have been tested, indicating that a deficit to a particular modality or type of knowledge cannot explain the existence of the phenomenon (figure 4.1B, plate 5). In this context, we (e.g., Caramazza and Mahon 2003; Mahon and Caramazza 2009) have concluded that semantic domain is an organizing principle of conceptual knowledge of objects, and that the most attractive model (for other reasons, see below) has at least two orthogonal dimensions of organization: semantic domain and modality or type of information.

4.6   Functional MRI Evidence for the Constraints That Shape Object Knowledge in the Brain

4.6.1   Ventral and Dorsal Object-Processing Streams

An important development in cognitive neuroscience that has paralleled the articulation of theories of semantic organization is the discovery of multiple channels of visual processing (Goodale and Milner 1992; Ungerleider and Mishkin 1982). It is now known that cortical visual processing bifurcates into two independent but interconnected streams (for discussion of how best to characterize the two streams, see Pisella et al. 2006; Schenk 2006; see also Merigan and Maunsell 1993). The ventral object-processing stream projects from V1 through the ventral occipital and temporal cortices, terminating in anterior regions of the temporal lobe, and subserves visual object identification. The dorsal object-processing stream projects from V1 through the dorsal occipital cortex to the posterior parietal cortex, and subserves object-directed action and spatial analysis for the purpose of object-directed grasping. The *two visual systems* hypothesis was initially formulated on the basis of neuropsychological evidence, in which ventral lesions led to impairments for perception and identification of object attributes but spared action toward the same objects, while dorsal lesions led to action impairments that spared perception (e.g., Goodale et al. 1991; Pisella et al. 2000; Ungerleider and Mishkin 1982). There has since been an enormous amount of imaging work confirming the distinction between ventral and dorsal object-processing streams (e.g., Binkofski et al. 1998; Culham et al. 2003; Mahon et al. 2007; Shmuelof and Zohary 2005).

4.6.2   Category Specificity in the Ventral Object-Processing Stream

There is a vibrant literature studying category specificity in humans using functional magnetic resonance imaging (fMRI). The most widely studied categories in high level visual regions, and the categories for which specific regions of the brain exhibit differential blood oxygen level dependent (BOLD) responses are faces, animals, body parts, tools, places, and words (for reviews, see Bookheimer 2002; Gerlach 2007; Grill-Spector and Malach 2004; Martin 2007; Op de Beeck, Haushofer, and Kanwisher 2008; Thompson-Schill 2003). On the ventral surface of the temporo-occipital cortex, in the ventral object-processing stream, there is a consistent topography by semantic category across individuals. For instance, viewing tools leads to differential BOLD contrast in the left medial fusiform gyrus, while viewing animate living things (animals and faces) leads to differential BOLD contrast in the lateral fusiform gyrus (Chao, Haxby, and Martin 1999; Kanwisher, McDermott, and Chun 1997; for earlier work, see Allison et al. 1994). The region of the lateral fusiform gyrus that exhibits larger responses to faces compared with a range of other categories (Downing et al. 2006) has been named the fusiform face area (FFA). The face area tends to be lateralized (or biased) toward the right hemisphere, while often in the homologous region of the left hemisphere, selectivity for printed words is observed (for review, see Dehaene et al. 2005; for modeling work and discussion of this asymmetry, see Plaut and Behrmann 2011). Place stimuli, such as houses or scenes, differentially drive BOLD responses in a more anterior and medial location in the ventral stream adjacent to the hippocampus, called the parahippocampal gyrus (the region called the parahippocampal place area, or PPA; Epstein and Kanwisher 1998; see also Bar and Aminoff 2003). Finally, there are also articulated category effects in lateral occipital cortex (Weiner et al. 2010), and category specificity in those lateral occipital regions has been dissociated using TMS (Pitcher et al. 2009).

The organization by semantic category in the ventral object-processing stream described above is largely invariant to the task and stimuli used in the experiment (e.g., linguistic, image, auditory), although the responses are strongly modulated by task and attention (Chao et al. 1999; Kanwisher and Downing 1998). In other words, what determines the location of category-specific responses is the category (i.e., content) of the stimulus and not its format. Category-specific responses in the ventral stream are also generally invariant to stimulus manipulations such as orientation, size, and contrast (Avidan et al. 2002; Levy et al. 2001; see figure 4.2, plate 6, for some examples of category specificity in the ventral stream). Importantly, what seems to matter for driving category-specific responses in the ventral stream is not so much the physical stimulus, but the interpretation that is applied to a stimulus. For instance, simple geometric shapes that *move* in either an animate or mechanical way, drive neural activity in the tool-specific and animal-specific brain networks, respectively (e.g., Martin and Weisberg 2003).

There is general agreement that the format of information represented in temporo-occipital regions exhibiting category-specific responses is something like high-level *visual* representations. Damage to the fusiform gyrus or lingual gyrus is known to produce various types of visual agnosia, including color agnosia, and sometimes alexia when the damage is restricted to the left hemisphere (Miceli et al. 2001; Stasenko et al., 2014) or prosopagnosia when damage involves the right hemisphere. Similarly, damage to lateral occipital cortex can lead to profound visual-form agnosia, as in the very well-studied patient DF (Goodale et al. 1991).

4.6.3 Category Specificity in the Dorsal Object-Processing Stream

Tools, compared with a range of baseline stimuli, differentially drive BOLD contrast in the left posterior middle temporal gyrus, left parietal cortex, and left premotor cortex (figure 4.2, plate 6). The left middle temporal region that exhibits differential BOLD responses when viewing manipulable objects (e.g., Martin et al. 1996; Thompson-Schill et al. 1999; for a review, see Devlin et al. 2002) plays an important role in processing the semantics of actions (e.g., Kable, Lease-Spellmeyer, and Chatterjee 2002; Kemmerer et al. 2008; Martin et al. 1995) as well as mechanical (i.e., unarticulated)

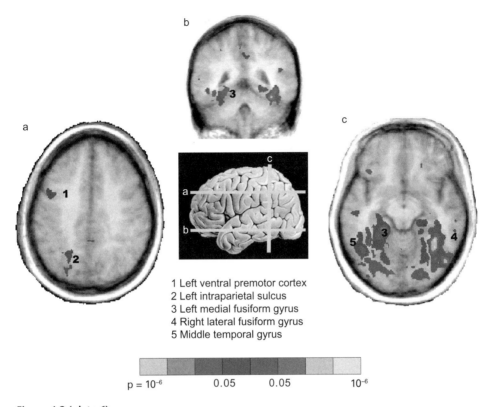

1 Left ventral premotor cortex
2 Left intraparietal sulcus
3 Left medial fusiform gyrus
4 Right lateral fusiform gyrus
5 Middle temporal gyrus

p = 10^{-6} 0.05   0.05 10^{-6}

Figure 4.2 (plate 6)
Category-specific patterns of BOLD response in the healthy brain. This figure shows in red a
network of regions that are differentially activated for living animate things, and in blue, a
network of regions that are differentially activated for nonliving things (Data from Chao et al
2002; figure reproduced from Martin and Chao, 2001, with permission).

motion (Beauchamp et al. 2002, 2003; Martin and Weisberg 2003; Wheatley, Milleville,
and Martin 2007).

Regions of bilateral dorsal occipital cortex, posterior parietal cortex, through to the
anterior intraparietal sulcus, are automatically activated when participants observe
manipulable objects (e.g., Chao and Martin 2000; Fang and He 2005). Dorsal occipital
and posterior parietal regions are important for determining volumetric and spatial
information about objects relevant to pointing, while the anterior intraparietal sulcus
is thought to be important for hand preshaping for object prehension (Binkofski et al.
1998; Culham et al. 2003; Frey et al. 2005). Optic ataxia, an impairment in reaching
or grasping objects, is classically associated with lesions to posterior and superior parietal structures (e.g., Pisella et al. 2000). Optic ataxia is not necessarily associated with

difficulties in manipulating objects according to their function (as optic ataxia patients may be able to manipulate the objects once they are in hand).

Viewing or naming tools also differentially activates the left inferior parietal lobule (e.g., Mahon et al. 2007; Rumiati et al. 2004), a region that is important for representing complex object-associated manipulations. This region is also activated when congenitally blind individuals think about tools, indicating that visual experience with objects is not necessary for the specificity to emerge (Mahon, Schwarzbach, and Caramazza 2010). Damage to the left inferior parietal lobule is classically associated with apraxia of object use (Rothi, Ochipa, and Heilman 1991; Rushworth, Krams, and Passingham 1997; Johnson-Frey 2004; see also discussion above in the context of the embodied cognition hypothesis).

4.6.4 Implications of the Imaging Evidence

The power of the functional MRI approach to studying category specificity is that it provides a window into *all* regions that are involved in processing information about different categories, regardless of whether involvement of those regions is necessary. Several different accounts of the causes of category-specific neural responses in humans have been suggested. Most of those accounts are directed at understanding the causes of category specificity in the ventral stream (Grill-Spector and Malach 2004; Haxby et al. 2001; Martin 2007; Mahon et al. 2007; Mechelli et al. 2006; Rogers et al. 2005). It is generally agreed that differential BOLD responses for tools in dorsal stream regions are driven by automatic extraction of motor-relevant information (e.g., Martin 2007; see discussion above in the context of the embodied cognition hypothesis).

Our own view of the causes of category specificity in the ventral stream is that it emerges because different regions of the ventral stream are innately connected with other regions of the brain that process nonvisual information about the same categories (for discussion of this connectivity-constrained account of category specificity, see Mahon et al. 2007, 2009; Mahon and Caramazza 2009, 2011). The core aspect of this proposal is that connectivity is what is innate and what drives domain specificity. In other words, the domain specificity of a given region is not driven (only) by organizational principles expressed over information local to that region, but by the broader network architecture in which that region is embedded (Mahon and Caramazza 2011). Thus, for instance, the regions that exhibit specificity for tools (medial fusiform gyrus) do so because that region has (by hypothesis) privileged connectivity with motor-relevant structures that are involved in actually manipulating objects (Mahon et al 2007). Thus, the high-level visual representations for tools occupy those regions of the visual system that are already connected with other regions of the brain that process motor-relevant information about tools. Similarly, the argument would be that faces are represented in regions of high-level visual cortex that have privileged connectivity to regions of the brain that process affective information. By hypothesis, regions of the lateral occipital cortex that differentially respond to images of the hands will express privileged connectivity to somatomotor areas that also represent the hands (Bracci et al. 2012). This kind of a *connectivity-constrained account* (Riesenhuber 2007) can explain why there would be specialization for printed words, a class of stimuli for which there can be no plausible evolutionary history (see Martin 2006). In other words, the fact that there is specialization for printed words in the same way that there is specialization for categories that could have evolutionarily significant histories (faces, tools, places, etc.), suggests that what is innate is not the content of the category, but rather a basic scaffolding of connectivity between high-level visual regions and other parts of the brain. Because those other parts of the brain will have their own biases toward specifics functions, innately specified connectivity would be sufficient to drive specialization by semantic category in high-level visual regions. In the case of the visual word-form area in the ventral object-processing stream, the prediction is made that it will exhibit privileged connectivity to left hemisphere language regions (see also Plaut and Behrmann 2011; for data from the domain of faces, see Thomas et al. 2009).

Several recently reported lines of evidence support the view that semantic domain innately constrains the organization of object knowledge, and that connectivity is the substrate for domain specificity. There are three strands of this evidence.

1. *There are deep similarities between monkeys and humans in the "semantic space" of object representations in the ventral stream.* An expectation of the view that innate constraints shape category specificity in the ventral stream is that such specificity, at least for some categories, will also be found in nonhuman primates. It is well known, using neurophysiological recordings, that preferences for natural object stimuli exist in the inferior temporal (IT) cortex of monkeys (e.g., Kiani et al. 2007; Tanaka et al. 1991), comparable to observations with similar methods in awake human subjects (Kreiman, Koch, and Fried 2000). More recently, functional imaging with macaques (Tsao et al. 2006) and chimpanzees (Parr et al. 2009) suggests that at least for the category of faces, clusters of face-preferring voxels can be found in the temporal cortex in monkeys, comparable to what is observed in humans. Such common patterns of neural organization for some classes of items in monkeys and humans could, of course, be entirely driven by dimensions of visual similarity, which are known to modulate responses in the IT cortex (Op de Beeck, Wagemans, and Vogels 2001). Even when serious attempts have been made to explain such responses in terms of dimensions of visual similarity, however, taxonomic structure emerges over and above the contribution of known visual dimensions. For instance, Kriegeskorte and colleagues (2008) used multivoxel pattern analysis to compare the similarity structure of a large array of different body, face, animal, plant, and artifact stimuli in the monkey IT cortex and the human temporo-occipital cortex. The similarity among the stimuli was measured in terms of the similarity in patterns of brain responses they elicited, separately on the basis of the neurophysiological data

(monkeys, Kiani et al. 2007) and fMRI data (humans). The similarity structure that emerged revealed a tight taxonomic structure common to monkeys and humans (see figure 4.3, plate 7). Importantly, that similarity structure was not present in early visual cortex and could not be reproduced from computational models of low-level visual processing (see Kriegeskorte et al. 2008 for details and discussion).

2. *There is an innate component to face recognition.* Two recent reports highlight greater neural or functional similarity between monozygotic twin pairs than between dizygotic twin pairs (for discussion, see Park, Newman, and Polk 2009; Zhu et al. 2010). The strength of these studies is that experiential contributions are held constant across the two types of twin pairs. In an fMRI study, Polk and colleagues (2007) studied the similarity between twin pairs in the distribution of responses to faces, houses, pseudowords, and chairs in the ventral stream. The authors found that face and place-related responses within face and place-selective regions, respectively, were significantly more similar for monozygotic than for dizygotic twins. In another study, Wilmer and colleagues (2010) studied the face recognition and memory abilities in monozygotic and dizygotic twin pairs (using some of the tests developed by Duchaine and Nakayama 2006). Wilmer and colleagues found that the correlation in performance on the face-recognition task for monozygotic twins was more than double that for dizygotic twins. This difference was not present for control tasks of verbal and visual memory, indicating selectivity in the genetic contribution to facial recognition abilities (see also Zhu et al. 2010).

3. *Category-specific neural organization does not require visual experience.* Recent findings indicate that visual experience is not necessary for the same, or similar, patterns of category specificity to be present in the ventral stream. In an early positron emission tomography study, Büchel and colleagues (1998) showed that congenitally blind subjects show activation for words (presented in Braille) in the same region of the ventral stream as sighted individuals (presented visually; see also Reich et al. 2011). Pietrini and colleagues (2004) used multivoxel pattern analysis to show that the pattern of activation over voxels in the ventral stream was more consistent across different exemplars within a category than exemplars across categories. More recently, we have shown that the same medial-to-lateral bias in category preferences on the ventral surface of the temporo-occipital cortex that is present in sighted individuals is present in congenitally blind subjects (Mahon et al. 2009). Specifically, in congenitally blind participants, nonliving things, compared to animals, elicited stronger activation in medial regions of the ventral stream (see figure 4.4, plate 8).

Although these studies on category specificity in blind individuals represent only a first-pass analysis of the role of visual experience in driving category specificity in the ventral stream, they indicate that visual experience is not necessary for category specificity to emerge in the ventral stream. Although this is not incompatible with

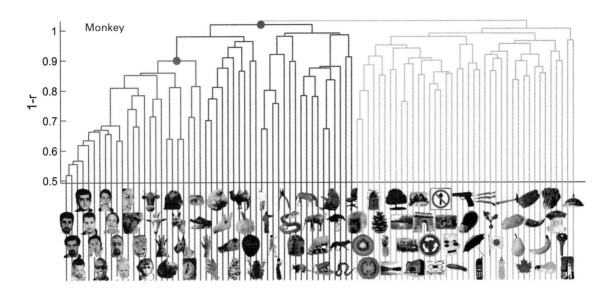

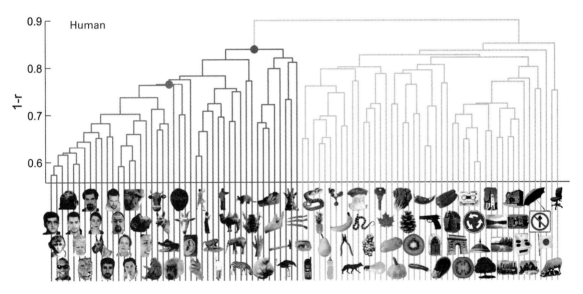

Figure 4.3 (plate 7)

Dendrograms showing similarity of response patterns across visual stimuli in monkey inferior temporal (IT) cortex and human ventral temporal cortex. Kriegeskorte and colleagues (2008) analyzed neurophysiological data from monkey IT cortex and human fMRI data when participants (monkeys, humans) were viewing numerous stimuli from many different categories. The similarity of the neural responses across the stimuli was analyzed separately for monkeys and humans. The figures, reproduced from Kriegeskorte and colleagues (2008, figure 4.4) use hierarchical clustering to describe the similarity space of the stimuli. The fascinating aspect of these data is that they show, with entirely independent analysis pipelines, that high-level visual cortex in monkeys and humans represents largely the same similarity space for visual stimuli. Figure reproduced with permission, from Kriegeskorte and colleagues (2008).

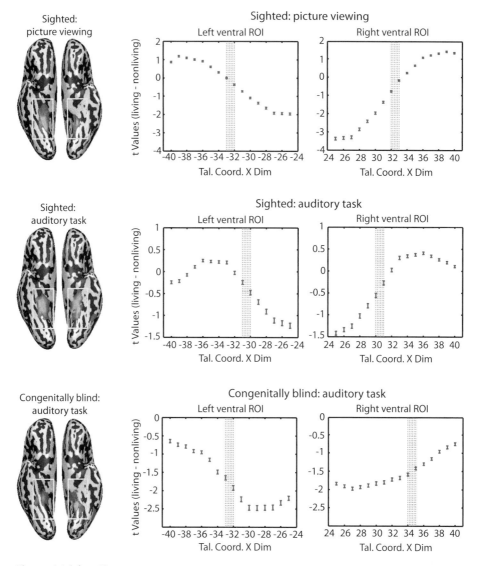

Figure 4.4 (plate 8)

Category-specific organization does not require visual experience. Congenitally blind and sighted participants were presented with spoken words of living things (animals) and nonliving things (tools, nonmanipulable objects) and were asked to make size judgments about the referents of the words. The sighted participants were also shown pictures corresponding to the same stimuli in a separate scan. For sighted participants viewing pictures, the known finding was replicated that nonliving things such as tools and large nonmanipulable objects lead to differential neural responses in medial aspects of ventral temporo-occipital cortex. This pattern of differential BOLD responses for nonliving things in medial aspects of ventral temporo-occipital cortex was also observed in congenitally blind participants and sighted participants performing the size judgment task over auditory stimuli. These data indicate that the medial-to-lateral bias in the distribution of category-specific responses does not depend on visual experience. For details of the study, see Mahon and colleagues (2009). Figure reproduced from Mahon and colleagues (2009) with permission.

the view that visual experience has an important role to play in shaping the organization of high-level visual areas in sighted individuals, it does point to an organizational constraint that cannot be reduced, in its entirety, to visual experience. The hypothesis that we have advanced (Mahon and Caramazza 2011), and which I believe the functional imaging data from blind individuals support, is that endogenously specified connectivity is the basic organizational constraint, or scaffolding, within which experience-dependent organizational principles operate. Furthermore, and by hypothesis, that endogenously specified connectivity will have a granularity that matches the domains for which neural specificity has been described in the ventral object-processing pathway.

4.7 Current and New Directions

Based on the brief overview of existing theories and evidence summarized above, several conclusions can be extrapolated, which I pull together here. I also try to frame what I believe are the issues that will drive research as the field moves forward, and beyond the issues with which it has been occupied over the last several decades. My approach to these prospective suggestions is to outline forward-leaning conclusions that indicate new questions. The broad and overarching suggestion is that there will be a common answer to the set of questions that are outlined. In short form, that answer is that the only way to gain a deeper understanding of the informational content, the organization of that content, and the dynamics of the conceptual system and its interface with other systems will be through research that unpacks the structure and function of connectivity.

4.7.1 Empirical Generalization I: Category-Specific Phenomena Cannot Be Dissolved

As described above, very rich phenomena of category specificity in the human brain were initially discovered by Warrington and her collaborators in brain-damaged patients in the eighties, and with functional imaging in humans by Martin, Allison, McCarthy, Kanwisher, and others in the nineties. Since those initial discoveries, much of the research on category specificity in the human brain has been concerned with characterizing the boundaries of the phenomena. In the context of patients with category-specific semantic deficits, emphasis has been placed on whether categories vary along continuous dimensions, such as familiarity, lexical frequency, structural or visual complexity, distinctiveness of their critical features, relevance (and so on). The common theoretical supposition behind those approaches is that category-specific deficits arise as a result of difficulties with one (or multiple) dimensions that are correlated with a semantic category boundary. In the context of category-specific responses in the ventral object-processing stream, there has been an emphasis on understanding the visual dimensions that putatively drive an organization by category in the ventral stream. The common theoretical assumption is that category specificity in the ventral stream arises through a type of experience-dependent *coagulative* process by which dimensions of organization native to the visual system combine in either linear or nonlinear ways to result in a "lumpy" organization by category.

Because of the common theoretical suppositions that have driven research on category specificity in the brain, much experimental work has focused on parametrically manipulating a dimension of interest and studying how category-specific phenomena are modulated as a function of that dimension. This approach has been enormously important for describing the boundaries of category-specific phenomena. But perhaps the most important outcome of all this research is that we still have category-specific phenomena that need explanation. In other words, a dimension could have been discovered that when *controlled* or parametrically varied would have "absorbed" the category effects into the dimension. That has not been the case—we are left with the conclusion that category-specific phenomena are insoluble into the continuous dimensions that have been identified to vary by category. Although there is still much ongoing work that will flesh out the details of this conclusion, my prospective suggestions presuppose that this conclusion will endure. This then frames anew an old question:

Question I: What neural and cognitive constraints drive an organization of object knowledge by semantic category in the human brain?

4.7.2 Empirical Generalization II: Important Aspects of Conceptual Processing Are Not Embodied

Research on the putative *embodiment* of concepts and the role of the motor system in supporting perceptual analysis of actions has focused on demonstrations that the motor system is activated across a range of situations that would not seem to necessitate motor activation. There are multiple ways in which motor activation during conceptual and perceptual analysis can be interpreted, ranging from the view that motor activation constitutes a necessary and intermediary step in conceptual and perceptual analysis, to the claim that motor activation is entirely ancillary to, and irrelevant for, conceptual and perceptual analysis. The fact that multiple patient studies have reported associations between motor impairments and conceptual or perceptual impairments would seem to rule out the view that motor activation is entirely irrelevant for conceptual and perceptual analysis. On the other hand, dissociative patient studies demonstrating that motor abilities can be compromised while sparing conceptual or perceptual abilities rule out the view that motor activation is necessary or constitutive of conceptual or perceptual analysis.

I think that the situation here is analogous to asking whether the function of a car engine is *embodied* in the movement of the car—it depends on what you mean. If the car is in gear, then there will be a direct mapping of turns of the tires on the road to revolutions of the crank in the engine. But the car can be put in neutral, in which case the engine can turn independently of the wheels. In fact, it is precisely this property that makes gears (i.e., the transmission) such a useful interface between the engine and the tires—gears are what give a car the flexibility to start at a dead stop and go to maximal speed using a single engine. Thus, asking why motor activation attends conceptual processing is like asking why the wheels turn when the engine turns—the answer is because the car is in gear and the engine is connected with the wheels via the transmission. The answer is the same if you ask why the engine turns if you push a car that is in gear (i.e., jump starting; see, e.g., Glenberg, Sato, and Cattaneo 2008).

A counterpoint to this analogy is that cars would not be of any use if they did not move—that is, a car that only sat in neutral would not really "be" a car. So there is a priority placed on being in gear, but at the same time, there is not a one-to-one relationship between the output of the motor while in gear and the turning of the tires—the force given off by the engine must be interpreted into a format that can be implemented into turns of the wheels. Likewise, conceptual processing, with no interface with the world, would not be particularly useful. But this objection somewhat misplaces the original question: the theoretical issue at stake concerns the format of conceptual processing, and whether it is dissociable from sensory and motor knowledge. And in that regard, the analogy is robust, in that even though the utility of cars is expressed when the engine is engaged with the wheels, turns of the engine and turns of the wheels are dissociable (cf. being in neutral). So although it may make sense at one level to think of the function of an engine as being "embodied" in the movement of the car—that is, at the level of understanding a particular *state* the car can be in—the more basic point is that the function of the engine does not depend, in any constitutive, logical, or necessary way, on the wheels.

Imagine that our state of knowledge of the function of cars was what it is with regard to the human brain, and one observed that turns of the engine were related to turns of the tires. One might then reasonably ask, à la embodied cognition, whether the engine and the tires were really one and the same process. This is where I would suggest we are with respect to understanding the relationship between sensorimotor activation and conceptual processing. But once one discovered the behavior of the car when it was in neutral, then the question would logically shift to asking how the engine was *connected* to the tires. Similarly, I believe that the key issue we face as a field with respect to issues of embodiment does not have to do with demonstrating *that* cognition can behave in a way that indicates it can be synchronous with, or sensitive to, sensorimotor processing; the key open issue concerns how to understand the structure and dynamics of the interface between concepts and the sensorimotor systems.

Question II: If motor processes are not necessary for conceptual or perceptual processes, then why are they automatically engaged during conceptual and perceptual processing?

4.7.3 A Consilience for Questions I and II

The suggestion of this chapter is that Questions I and II have a common answer, as yet unspecified in its details, but which in broad strokes consists of a theory of connectivity among sensorimotor and conceptual representations. The strategy within the field has been to divide and then reconnect. In that context, it is generally understood that connectivity does not itself constitute information—the information is *represented* in the local regions that are connected, and the connections are something like passive conduits that pass bundles of information from region to region. The suggestion here is that connectivity is itself a computation that underlies conceptual analysis. This would require that we consider the performance of the entire network of regions as a unit of analysis, and regard the information represented by the function of the whole network as (at least at one level) a *unit of analysis*.

According to the task in which participants are engaged, stimuli will be analyzed by the same network in different ways, and information distributed throughout the network will be combined in different orders, with different weights, and to different ends. As an example, consider how the dorsal and ventral visual pathways interact when you reach out to pick up a hammer in order to simply move it over six inches versus picking it up with the intention of using it to hammer a nail. When you pick it up to move it, the grasp point on the object need only be calibrated such that the object is picked up efficiently (i.e., at its center of mass) and such that the grasp does not preclude, either because of the arrangement of other objects in the world or for biomechanical constraints, the (planned or intended) final position of the hammer once it is put down. When you pick up a hammer in order to use it, however, you *explicitly* do not pick it up at its center of mass, precisely to capitalize on the lever-like properties of hammer manipulation that allow the function of the object to be realized. The systems that recognize the object as such, and interface with systems that represent the behavioral intentions, are dissociable from the visuo-motor analysis that actually gets the hand from its starting position to its grip point on the object. Thus, while the same set of regions may be activated both when picking up a hammer to move it and when picking up a hammer to use it, the role that the different types of knowledge we have about hammers play in shaping the overall behavior is very different. What distinguishes the two situations is not therefore the types of information that are accessed (at some point in the action) but the order in which those different types of information are accessed and the weight that the different types of information are given in shaping the overall behavior (for discussion, see Mahon and Wu, forthcoming). Such dynamic reordering and reweighting of information must be mediated by connectivity, because the different types of information are known to be represented by dissociable brain regions.

Decisions that are made by our cognitive systems about how to act on the world (e.g., what to attend to, how to shape the hand to grasp an object, *that* an object should be grasped) are not made in isolation: such decisions are made in concert with information that is computed about the world, including the current state of our body, as well as our behavioral goals and internal states, by widely distributed and dissociable neurocognitive systems. Perception is not just for its own sake; perception always occurs in the context of a behavioral goal, whether that goal is to take a drink of coffee or simply to look at or inspect the mug. The suggestion here is that the structure and dynamics of the conceptual system can be understood as a result of the varied pressures made on the conceptual system in the service of different behavioral goals, or tasks, and the consequent need to integrate qualitatively different types of information. Those pressures can be understood along multiple time scales, including phylogenetic, ontogenetic, and online-processing time scales.

The structure of neurocognitive information models is typically constrained by an analysis of what information is necessary to complete a given task. However, more than what is "strictly necessary" to perform a task, conceptual processing is also sensitive to information that is available but may not be (strictly speaking) necessary to perform the task. This notion of the *availability* of multiple types of information that could bear on a given cognitive decision is what we have referred to as *cognitive promiscuity* (for discussion, see Mahon and Caramazza 2008). Cognitive promiscuity, implemented through the dynamics of information exchange among sensory, motor, and conceptual representations, is the foothold for understanding why the motor system is activated during conceptual and perceptual analysis. Cognitive promiscuity is also responsible, by hypothesis, for the need to integrate high-level visual analysis with motor-relevant computations about manipulable objects, or computations about the affective quality of facial expressions with visual information about faces, or phonology with representations of printed words; thus, cognitive promiscuity is the umbrella property that motivates why connectivity between regions of the ventral stream and other regions of the brain would drive specialization by semantic category in the ventral stream. Understanding the constraints that shape the organization of the conceptual system then becomes a project of unpacking the dynamics of cognitive promiscuity.

4.7.4 One Answer for a Distributed Question

It is a well-established fact that conceptual information is widely distributed in the brain, in the sense that different aspects, or parts, of a concept are represented in dissociable brain systems. For instance, for the concept HAMMER, knowledge about its typical visual appearance and structure, knowledge about the sounds created when hammering, knowledge about the function of hammers, and knowledge about how to actually use hammers are all represented in dissociable brain systems. To date, the general approach in the field has been to dissect out the components of concepts, sometimes referred to as the features of the concept, and describe the principles (cognitive and neural) that affect the representation and organization of each individual part. But that would be like treating leg pain with only an understanding of the function and physiology of the leg, and no understanding of how compression of spinal nerve fibers might (remotely) cause leg pain. In order to understand the constraints that shape specificity over one type of information (e.g., visual) in one part of the brain for a given category of items, it is critical to understand how the visual information about that class of items is integrated with nonvisual information about the same category represented by other brain regions.

Although functional imaging or anatomical studies of white matter tractography might seem to be the most obvious means for understanding connectivity in humans, they are by no means the only approach. In particular, many rich empirical phenomena have been taken as motivation for hypotheses about the format of conceptual representations (i.e., that they are embodied) that may be better understood as phenomena that result from the connectivity of the system. For instance, as noted above, making repetitive arm movements, such as moving beans from a close to a far container, can lead to slower responses for judging the grammaticality of sentences that describe actions away from the body (Glenberg, Sato, and Cattaneo 2008). This has been taken to mean that the understanding of the sentence "You passed the salt to your friend'" involves, as a constitutive part, motor simulation. An alternative explanation is that understanding that sentence occurs without intervening access to motor information, but that the state of the motor system is not irrelevant for understanding the sentence. In other words, the decision mechanism that oversees the grammaticality judgment may be sensitive to information that is not part of the grammaticality judgment, but that being available cannot be ignored, and it therefore affects response time. Thus, rather than asking whether the format of lexical semantic representations is motoric, it may be more productive to ask about the nature of the decision mechanism involved in making judgments about sentences, and the types of information to which that decision mechanism is sensitive.

Another class of data that could be brought to bear on understanding the cognitive promiscuity of the conceptual system are the patterns of association and dissociation of function observed in brain-damaged patients. Findings from brain damaged patients are generally emphasized in the measure to which different types of information dissociate from one another. Such dissociations are critical for drawing inferences about the functional independence of different types of knowledge. However, of particular importance for informing a theory of connectivity may be associations of impairments. Price, Friston, and colleagues (Friston and Price 2011; Price and Friston 2002; Price et al. 2001) have explored what they refer to as *dynamic diaschisis*. Dynamic diaschisis is the idea that damage to one region of the brain can alter, and potentially impair, the function of anatomically remote but functionally interconnected regions. For instance, consider the fact that all types of knowledge (visual-perceptual and functional-associative) are impaired for the damaged categories in patients with category-specific deficits (figure 4.1B, plate 5). Such patterns of associated impairments are ambiguous between the brain damage actually destroying tissue that is critical for representing the different types of knowledge (either the same region or neighboring regions) and the damage propagating at a functional level through dynamic diaschisis.

Concepts, as they are deployed in the service of behavior, are more than the sum of their parts. As functionally unified representations, they allow the flexible recombination of information based on inferences that go beyond the dissociable pieces of information that form the concept. Connectivity, as the basis for the functional integrity of concepts, lies at the heart of how concepts are both distributed and functionally unified. Thus, my argument here has been that characterizing connectivity at a cognitive and neural level is not just an incremental step that will finally allow us to understand how the different parts of the system are wired together and how information is communicated among regions. Connectivity is an information-bearing property of the system that must be understood on its own terms. Furthermore, I would suggest that connectivity is the key to unlocking the reason why there is neural specificity for different categories in the first place, and why the motor system is engaged in many tasks that we know can be completed without motor information.

Acknowledgments

I would like to thank Eric Margolis and Stephen Laurence, as well as Alena Stasenko, Frank Garcea, and Jessica Cantlon, for their comments on an earlier version of this manuscript. I would like to thank Alfonso Caramazza for the many years of discussion on these issues. I am grateful to Alex Martin and Niko Kriegeskorte for providing the graphics in figures 4.2 and 4.3 (plates 6 and 7), respectively. Preparation of this manuscript was supported in part by NIH grant R21 NS076176.

References

Allison, T., G. McCarthy, A. Nobre, A. Puce, and A. Belger. 1994. Human extrastriate visual cortex and the perception of faces, words, numbers and colors. *Cerebral Cortex* 4:544–554.

Allport, D. A. 1985. Distributed memory, modular subsystems and dysphasia. In *Current Perspectives in Dysphasia*, ed. S. K. Newman and R. Epstein, 207–244. New York: Churchill Livingstone.

Avidan, G., R. Hasson, T. Hendler, E. Zohary, and R. Malach. 2002. Analysis of the neuronal selectivity underlying low fMRI signals. *Current Biology* 12:964–972.

Bar, M., and E. Aminoff. 2003. Cortical analysis of visual context. *Neuron* 38:347–358.

Barbarotto, R., M. Laiacona, V. Macchi, and E. Capitani. 2002. Picture-reality decisions, semantic categories and gender: A new set of pictures, with norms and an experimental study. *Neuropsychologia* 40:1637–1653.

Barsalou, L. W. 1999. Perceptual symbol systems. *Behavioral and Brain Sciences* 22:637–660.

Barsalou, L. W., W. K. Simmons, A. K. Barbey, and C. D. Wilson. 2003. Grounding conceptual knowledge in modality-specific subsystems. *Trends in Cognitive Sciences* 7:84–91.

Beauchamp, M. S., K. E. Lee, J. V. Haxby, and A. Martin. 2002. Parallel visual motion processing streams for manipulable objects and human movements. *Neuron* 34:149–159.

Beauchamp, M. S., K. E. Lee, J. V. Haxby, and A. Martin. 2003. Differential response to real and point-light displays of moving humans and manipulable objects. *Journal of Cognitive Neuroscience* 15:991–1001.

Binder, J. R., and R. H. Desai. 2011. The neurobiology of semantic memory. *Trends in Cognitive Sciences* 15:527–536.

Binkofski, F., C. Dohle, S. Posse, K. M. Stephan, H. Hefter, R. J. Seitz, and H. J. Freund. 1998. Human anterior intraparietal area subserves prehension: A combined lesion and functional MRI activation study. *Neurology* 50:1253–1259.

Bonner, M. F., and M. Grossman. 2012. Gray matter density of auditory association cortex relates to knowledge of sound concepts in primary progressive aphasia. *Journal of Neuroscience* 32: 7986–7991.

Bookheimer, S. Y. 2002. Functional MRI of language: New approaches to understanding the cortical organization of semantic processing. *Annual Review of Neuroscience* 25:151–188.

Borgo, F., and T. Shallice. 2003. Category specificity and feature knowledge: Evidence from new sensory-quality categories. *Cognitive Neuropsychology* 20:327–353.

Boulenger, V., L. Mechtouff, S. Thobois, E. Broussolle, M. Jeannerod, and T. A. Nazir. 2008. Word processing in Parkinson's disease is impaired for action verbs but not concrete nouns. *Neuropsychologia* 46:743–756.

Boulenger, V., A. C. Roy, Y. Paulignan, V. Deprez, M. Jeannerod, and T. A. Nazir. 2006. Cross-talk between language processes and overt motor behavior in the first 200 ms of processing. *Journal of Cognitive Neuroscience* 18:1607–1615.

Bracci, S., C. Cavina-Pratesi, M. Ietswaart, A. Caramazza, and M. V. Peelen. 2012. Closely overlapping responses to tools and hands in left lateral occipitotemporal cortex. *Journal of Neurophysiology* 107:1443–1456.

Büchel, C., C. Price, and K. Friston. 1998. A multimodal language region in the ventral visual pathway. *Nature* 394:274–277.

Buxbaum, L. J., K. M. Kyle, and R. Menon. 2005. On beyond mirror neurons: Internal representations subserving imitation and recognition of skilled object-related actions in humans. *Cognitive Brain Research* 25:226–239.

Buxbaum, L. J., and E. M. Saffran. 2002. Knowledge of object manipulation and object function: Dissociations in apraxic and non apraxic subjects. *Brain and Language* 82:179–199.

Buxbaum, L. J., T. Veramonti, and M. F. Schwartz. 2000. Function and manipulation tool knowledge in apraxia: Knowing "what for" but not "how." *Neurocase* 6:83–97.

Capitani, E., M. Laiacona, B. Mahon, and A. Caramazza. 2003. What are the facts of category-specific disorders? A critical review of the clinical evidence. *Cognitive Neuropsychology* 20:213–261.

Caramazza, A., and A. E. Hillis. 1991. Lexical organization of nouns and verbs in the brain. *Nature* 349:788–790.

Caramazza, A., A. E. Hillis, B. C. Rapp, and C. Romani. 1990. The multiple semantics hypothesis: Multiple confusions? *Cognitive Neuropsychology* 7:161–189.

Caramazza, A., and B. Z. Mahon. 2003. The organization of conceptual knowledge: The evidence from category-specific semantic deficits. *Trends in Cognitive Sciences* 7:354–361.

Caramazza, A., and B. Z. Mahon. 2006. The organization of conceptual knowledge in the brain: The future's past and some future direction. *Cognitive Neuropsychology* 23:13–38.

Caramazza, A., and J. R. Shelton. 1998. Domain specific knowledge systems in the brain: The animate-inanimate distinction. *Journal of Cognitive Neuroscience* 10:1–34.

Chao, L. L., J. V. Haxby, and A. Martin. 1999. Attribute-based neural substrates in temporal cortex for perceiving and knowing about objects. *Nature Neuroscience* 2:913–919.

Chao, L. L., and A. Martin. 2000. Representation of manipulable manmade objects in the dorsal stream. *NeuroImage* 12:478–484.

Chatterjee, A. 2010. Disembodying cognition. *Language and Cognition* 2:79–116.

Costa, A., A. Caramazza, and N. Sebastián-Gallés. 2000. The cognate facilitation effect: Implications for models of lexical access. *Journal of Experimental Psychology: Learning, Memory, and Cognition* 26:1283–1296.

Cree, G. S., and K. MacRae. 2003. Analyzing the factors underlying the structure and computation of meaning of chipmunk, cherry, chisel, cheese, and cello (and many other such concrete nouns). *Journal of Experimental Psychology: General* 132:163–201.

Crutch, S. J., and E. K. Warrington. 2003. The selective impairment of fruit and vegetable knowledge: A multiple processing channels account of fine-grain category specificity. *Cognitive Neuropsychology* 20:355–372.

Culham, J. C., S. L. Danckert, J. F. X. DeSouza, J. S. Gati, R. S. Menon, and M. A. Goodale. 2003. Visually guided grasping produces fMRI activation in dorsal but not ventral stream brain areas. *Experimental Brain Research* 153:180–189.

Dehaene, S., L. Cohen, M. Sigman, and F. Vinckier. 2005. The neural code for written words: A proposal. *Trends in Cognitive Sciences* 9:335–341.

Devlin, J. T., R. P. Russell, M. H. Davis, C. J. Price, H. E. Moss, M. J. Fadili, and L. K. Tyler. 2002. Is there an anatomical basis for category-specificity? Semantic memory studies in PET and fMRI. *Neuropsychologia* 40:54–75.

Dinstein, I., C. Thomas, M. Behrmann, and D. J. Heeger. 2008. A mirror up to nature. *Current Biology* 18:R13–R18.

di Pellegrino, G., L. Fadiga, L. Fogassi, V. Gallese, and G. Rizzolatti. 1992. Understanding motor events: A neurophysiology study. *Experimental Brain Research* 91:176–180.

Downing, P. E., A. W. Chan, M. V. Peelen, C. M. Dodds, and N. Kanwisher. 2006. Domain specificity in visual cortex. *Cerebral Cortex* 16:1453–1461.

Duchaine, B., and K. Nakayama. 2006. The Cambridge face memory test: Results for neurologically intact individuals and an investigation of its validity using inverted face stimuli and prosopagnosic participants. *Neuropsychologia* 44:576–585.

Epstein, R., and N. Kanwisher. 1998. A cortical representation of the local visual environment. *Nature* 392:598–601.

Fang, F., and S. He. 2005. Cortical responses to invisible objects in the human dorsal and ventral pathways. *Nature Neuroscience* 8:1380–1385.

Farah, M. J., and C. Rabinowitz. 2003. Genetic and environmental influences on the organization of semantic memory in the brain: Is "living things" an innate category? *Cognitive Neuropsychology* 20:401–408.

Frey, S. H., D. Vinton, R. Newman-Norlund, and S. T. Grafton. 2005. Cortical topography of human anterior intraparietal cortex active during visually-guided grasping. *Cognitive Brain Research* 23:397–405.

Friston, K. J., and C. J. Price. 2011. Modules and brain mapping. *Cognitive Neuropsychology* 28:241–250.

Funnell, E., and J. Sheridan. 1992. Categories of knowledge? Unfamiliar aspects of living and nonliving things. *Cognitive Neuropsychology* 9:135–153.

Gallese, V., L. Fadiga, L. Fogassi, and G. Rizzolatti. 1996. Action recognition in the premotor cortex. *Brain* 119:593–609.

Gallese, V., and G. Lakoff. 2005. The brain's concepts: The role of the sensory-motor system in conceptual knowledge. *Cognitive Neuropsychology* 22:455–479.

Garcea, F. E., and B. Z. Mahon. 2012. What is in a tool concept? Dissociating manipulation knowledge from function knowledge. *Memory & Cognition* 40:1303–1313.

Gerlach, C. 2007. A review of functional imaging studies on category specificity. *Journal of Cognitive Neuroscience* 19:296–314.

Glenberg, A. M., M. Sato, and L. Cattaneo. 2008. Use-induced motor plasticity affects the processing of abstract and concrete language. *Current Biology* 18:R1–R2.

Goodale, M. A., and A. D. Milner. 1992. Separate visual pathways for perception and action. *Trends in Neurosciences* 15:20–25.

Goodale, M. A., A. D. Milner, L. S. Jakobsen, and D. P. Carey. 1991. A neurological dissociation between perceiving objects and grasping them. *Nature* 349:154–156.

Grill-Spector, K., and R. Malach. 2004. The human visual cortex. *Annual Review of Neuroscience* 27:649–677.

Hart, J., Jr., R. Anand, S. Zoccoli, M. Maguire, J. Gamino, G. Tillman, R. King, and M. A. Kraut. 2007. Neural substrates of semantic memory. *Journal of the International Neuropsychological Society* 13:865–880.

Hauk, O., I. Johnsrude, and F. Pulvermüller. 2004. Somatotopic representation of action words in human motor and premotor cortex. *Neuron* 41:301–307.

Haxby, J. V., M. I. Gobbini, M. L. Furey, A. Ishai, J. L. Schouten, and P. Pietrini. 2001. Distributed and overlapping representations of faces and objects in ventral temporal cortex. *Science* 293:2425–2430.

Hickok, G. 2009. Eight problems for the mirror neuron theory of action understanding in monkeys and humans. *Journal of Cognitive Neuroscience* 21:1229–1243.

Hickok, G. 2010. The role of mirror neurons in speech perception and action word semantics. *Language and Cognitive Processes* 25:749–776.

Hickok, G., M. Costanzo, R. Capasso, and G. Miceli. 2011. The role of Broca's area in speech perception: Evidence from aphasia revisited. *Brain and Language* 119:214–220.

Hickok, G., K. Okada, W. Barr, J. Pa, C. Rogalsky, K. Donnelly, L. Barde, and A. Grant. 2008. Bilateral capacity for speech sound processing in auditory comprehension: Evidence from Wada procedures. *Brain and Language* 107:179–184.

Humphreys, G. W., and E. M. E. Forde. 2001. Hierarchies, similarity, and interactivity in object recognition: "Category-specific" neuropsychological deficits. *Behavioral and Brain Sciences* 24:453–475.

Johnson-Frey, S. H. 2004. The neural bases of complex tool use in humans. *Trends in Cognitive Sciences* 8:71–78.

Kable, J. W., J. Lease-Spellmeyer, and A. Chatterjee. 2002. Neural substrates of action event knowledge. *Journal of Cognitive Neuroscience* 14:795–805.

Kanwisher, N., and P. Downing. 1998. Separating the wheat from the chaff. *Science* 252:57–58.

Kanwisher, N., J. McDermott, and M. M. Chun. 1997. The fusiform face area: A module in human extrastriate cortex specialized for face perception. *Journal of Neuroscience* 17:4302–4311.

Kemmerer, D. Forthcoming. *The Cognitive Neuroscience of Language: An Introduction.* New York: Psychology Press.

Kemmerer, D., J. Gonzalez Castillo, T. Talavage, S. Patterson, and C. Wiley. 2008. Neuroanatomical distribution of five semantic components of verbs: Evidence from fMRI. *Brain and Language* 107:16–43.

Kemmerer, D., D. Rudrauf, K. Manzel, and D. Tranel. 2012. Behavioral patterns and lesion sites associated with impaired processing of lexical and conceptual knowledge of actions. *Cortex* 48:826–848.

Kiani, R., H. Esteky, K. Mirpour, and K. Tanaka. 2007. Object category structure in response patterns of neuronal population in monkey inferior temporal cortex. *Journal of Neurophysiology* 97:4296–4309.

Kiefer, M., and F. Pulvermüller. 2012. Conceptual representations in mind and brain: Theoretical developments, current evidence and future directions. *Cortex* 48:805–825.

Kreiman, G., C. Koch, and I. Fried. 2000. Category-specific visual responses of single neurons in the human medial temporal lobe. *Nature Neuroscience* 3:946–953.

Kriegeskorte, N., M. Mur, D. A. Ruff, R. Kiani, J. Bodurka, H. Esteky, K. Tanaka, and P. A. Bandettini. 2008. Matching categorical object representations in inferior temporal cortex of man and monkey. *Neuron* 60:1126–1141.

Laws, K. 2005. "Illusions of normality": A methodological critique of category-specific naming. *Cortex* 41:842–851.

Levy, I., U. Hasson, G. Avidan, T. Hendler, and R. Malach. 2001. Center-periphery organization of human object areas. *Nature Neuroscience* 4:533–539.

Lewis, J. 2006. Cortical networks related to human use of tools. *Neuroscientist* 12:211–231.

Lhermitte, F., and M.-F. Beauvois. 1973. A visual speech disconnection syndrome: Report of a case with optic aphasia, agnosic alexia and color agnosia. *Brain* 96:695–714.

Liberman, A. M., F. S. Cooper, D. P. Shankweiler, and M. Studdert-Kennedy. 1967. Perception of the speech code. *Psychological Review* 74:431–461.

Liberman, A. M., and I. G. Mattingly. 1985. The motor theory of speech perception revised. *Cognition* 21:1–36.

Lingnau, A., B. Gesierich, and A. Caramazza. 2009. Asymmetric fMRI adaptation reveals no evidence for mirror neurons in humans. *Proceedings of the National Academy of Sciences of the United States of America* 106:9925–9930.

Mahon, B. Z. 2008. Action recognition: Is it a motor process? *Current Biology* 18:R1068–R1069.

Mahon, B. Z., S. Anzellotti, J. Schwarzbach, M. Zampini, and A. Caramazza. 2009. Category-specific organization in the human brain does not require visual experience. *Neuron* 63:397–405.

Mahon, B. Z., and A. Caramazza. 2003. Constraining questions about the organization and representation of conceptual knowledge. *Cognitive Neuropsychology* 20:433–450.

Mahon, B. Z., and A. Caramazza. 2005. The orchestration of the sensory-motor system: Clues from neuropsychology. *Cognitive Neuropsychology* 22:480–494.

Mahon, B. Z., and A. Caramazza. 2008. A critical look at the embodied cognition hypothesis and a new proposal for grounding conceptual content. *Journal of Physiology, Paris* 102:59–70.

Mahon, B. Z., and A. Caramazza. 2009. Concepts and categories: A cognitive neuropsychological perspective. *Annual Review of Psychology* 60:27–51.

Mahon, B. Z., and A. Caramazza. 2011. What drives the organization of object knowledge in the brain? *Trends in Cognitive Sciences* 15:97–103.

Mahon, B. Z., S. Milleville, G. A. L. Negri, R. I. Rumiati, A. Caramazza, and A. Martin. 2007. Action-related properties of objects shape object representations in the ventral stream. *Neuron* 55:507–520.

Mahon, B. Z., J. Schwarzbach, and A. Caramazza. 2010. The representation of tools in left parietal cortex independent of visual experience. *Psychological Science* 21:764–771.

Mahon, B. Z., and W. Wu. Forthcoming. Does conceptual analysis penetrate the dorsal visual pathway? To appear in *Cognitive Penetration*, ed. J. Zeimbekis and A. Raftopoulos.

Martin, A. 2006. Shades of Dejerine—Forging a causal link between the visual word form area and reading. *Neuron* 50:173–190.

Martin, A. 2007. The representation of object concepts in the brain. *Annual Review of Psychology* 58:25–45.

Martin, A., and L. L. Chao. 2001. Semantic memory and the brain: Structure and processes. *Current Opinion in Neurobiology* 11:194–201.

Martin, A., J. V. Haxby, F. M. Lalonde, C. L. Wiggs, and L. G. Ungerleider. 1995. Discrete cortical regions associated with knowledge of color and knowledge of action. *Science* 270:102–105.

Martin, A., L. G. Ungerleider, and J. V. Haxby. 2000. Category specificity and the brain: The sensory/motor model of semantic representations of objects. In *The New Cognitive Neurosciences*. 2nd ed., ed. M. S. Gazzaniga, 1023–1036. Cambridge, MA: MIT Press.

Martin, A., and J. Weisberg. 2003. Neural foundations for understanding social and mechanical concepts. *Cognitive Neuropsychology* 20:575–587.

Martin, A., C. L. Wiggs, L. G. Ungerleider, and J. V. Haxby. 1996. Neural correlates of category-specific knowledge. *Nature* 379:649–652.

Mechelli, A., G. Sartori, P. Orlandi, and C. J. Price. 2006. Semantic relevance explains category effects in medial fusiform gyri. *NeuroImage* 15:992–1002.

Merigan, W. H., and J. H. Maunsell. 1993. How parallel are the primate visual pathways? *Annual Review of Neuroscience* 16:369–402.

Miceli, G., E. Fouch, R. Capasso, J. R. Shelton, F. Tamaiuolo, and A. Caramazza. 2001. The dissociation of color from form and function knowledge. *Nature Neuroscience* 4:662–667.

Negri, G. A. L., R. I. Rumiati, A. Zadini, M. Ukmar, B. Z. Mahon, and A. Caramazza. 2007. What is the role of motor simulation in action and object recognition? Evidence from apraxia. *Cognitive Neuropsychology* 24:795–816.

Ochipa, C., L. J. G. Rothi, and K. M. Heilman. 1989. Ideational apraxia: A deficit in tool selection and use. *Annals of Neurology* 25:190–193.

Op de Beeck, H. P., J. Haushofer, and N. G. Kanwisher. 2008. Interpreting fMRI data: Maps, modules, and dimensions. *Nature Reviews: Neuroscience* 9:123–135.

Op de Beeck, H., J. Wagemans, and R. Vogels. 2001. Inferotemporal neurons represent low-dimensional configurations of parameterized shapes. *Nature Neuroscience* 4:1244–1252.

Park, J., L. I. Newman, and T. A. Polk. 2009. Face processing: The interplay of nature and nurture. *Neuroscientist* 15:445–449.

Parr, L. A., E. Hecht, S. K. Barks, T. M. Preuss, and J. R. Votaw. 2009. Face processing in the chimpanzee brain. *Current Biology* 19:50–53.

Patterson, K., P. J. Nestor, and T. T. Rogers. 2007. Where do you know what you know? The representation of semantic knowledge in the human brain. *Nature Reviews: Neuroscience* 8: 976–988.

Pazzaglia, M., L. Pizzamiglio, E. Pes, and S. M. Aglioti. 2008. The sound of actions in apraxia. *Current Biology* 18:1766–1772.

Pazzaglia, M., N. Smania, E. Corato, and S. M. Aglioti. 2008. Neural underpinnings of gesture discrimination in patients with limb apraxia. *Journal of Neuroscience* 28:3030–3040.

Peterson, R. P., and P. Savoy. 1998. Lexical selection and phonological encoding during language production: Evidence for cascading processing. *Journal of Experimental Psychology: Learning, Memory, and Cognition* 24:539–557.

Pietrini, P., M. L. Furey, E. Ricciardi, M. I. Gobbini, W. H. Wu, L. Cohen, M. Guazzelli, and J. V. Haxby. 2004. Beyond sensory images: Object-based representation in the human ventral pathway. *Proceedings of the National Academy of Sciences of the United States of America* 101:5658–5663.

Pisella, L., B. F. Binkofski, K. Lasek, I. Toni, and Y. Rossetti. 2006. No double-dissociation between optic ataxia and visual agnosia: Multiple substreams for multiple visuo-manual integrations. *Neuropsychologia* 44:2734–2748.

Pisella, L., H. Gréa, C. Tilikete, A. Vighetto, M. Desmurget, G. Rode, D. Boisson, and Y. Rossetti. 2000. An "automatic pilot" for the hand in human posterior parietal cortex: Toward reinterpreting optic ataxia. *Nature Neuroscience* 3:729–736.

Pitcher, D., L. Charles, J. T. Devlin, V. Walsh, and B. Duchaine. 2009. Triple dissociation of faces, bodies, and objects in extrastriate cortex. *Current Biology* 19:319–324.

Plaut, D. C., and M. Behrmann. 2011. Complementary neural representations for faces and words: A computational perspective. *Cognitive Neuropsychology* 28:251–275.

Polk, T. A., J. Park, M. R. Smith, and D. C. Park. 2007. Nature versus nurture in ventral visual cortex: A functional magnetic resonance imaging study of twins. *Journal of Neuroscience* 27: 13921–13925.

Price, C. J., and K. J. Friston. 2002. Degeneracy and cognitive anatomy. *Trends in Cognitive Sciences* 6:416–421.

Price, C. J., E. A. Warburton, C. J. Moore, R. S. Frackowiak, and K. J. Friston. 2001. Dynamic diaschisis: Anatomically remote and context-sensitive human brain lesions. *Journal of Cognitive Neuroscience* 13:419–429.

Pulvermüller, F. 2005. Brain mechanisms linking language and action. *Nature Reviews: Neuroscience* 6:576–582.

Rapcsak, S. Z., C. Ochipa, K. C. Anderson, and H. Poizner. 1995. Progressive Ideomotor apraxia: Evidence for a selective impairment of the action production system. *Brain and Cognition* 27: 213–236.

Reich, L., M. Szwed, L. Cohen, and A. Amedi. 2011. A ventral visual stream reading center independent of visual experience. *Current Biology* 21:363–368.

Riesenhuber, M. 2007. Appearance isn't everything: News on object representation in cortex. *Neuron* 55:341–344.

Rizzolatti, G., and L. Craighero. 2004. The mirror-neuron system. *Annual Review of Neuroscience* 27:169–192.

Rogalsky, C., T. Love, D. Driscoll, S. W. Anderson, and G. Hickok. 2011. Are mirror neurons the basis of speech perception? Evidence from five cases with damage to the purported human mirror system. *Neurocase* 17:178–187.

Rogers, T. T., J. Hocking, A. Mechilli, K. Patterson, and C. Price. 2005. Fusiform activation to animals is driven by the process, not the stimulus. *Journal of Cognitive Neuroscience* 17: 434–445.

Rothi, L. J. G., C. Ochipa, and K. Heilman. 1991. A cognitive neuropsychological model of limb praxis. *Cognitive Neuropsychology* 8:443–458.

Rumiati, R. I., P. H. Weiss, T. Shallice, G. Ottoboni, J. Noth, L. Zilles, and G. R. Fink. 2004. Neural basis of pantomiming the use of visually presented objects. *NeuroImage* 21:1224–1231.

Rumiati, R. I., S. Zanini, L. Vorano, and T. Shallice. 2001. A form of ideational apraxia as a selective deficit of contention scheduling. *Cognitive Neuropsychology* 18:617–642.

Rushworth, M. F., M. Krams, and R. E. Passingham. 1997. The attentional role of the left parietal cortex: The distinct lateralization and localization of motor attention in the human brain. *Journal of Cognitive Neuroscience* 13:698–710.

Samson, D., and A. Pillon. 2003. A case of impaired knowledge for fruit and vegetables. *Cognitive Neuropsychology* 20:373–400.

Sartori, G., and L. Lombardi. 2004. Semantic relevance and semantic disorders. *Journal of Cognitive Neuroscience* 16:439–452.

Sartori, G., L. Lombardi, and L. Mattiuzzi. 2005. Semantic relevance best predicts normal and abnormal name retrieval. *Neuropsychologia* 43:754–770.

Schenk, T. 2006. An allocentric rather than perceptual deficit in patient DF. *Nature Neuroscience* 9:1369–1370.

Shmuelof, L., and E. Zohary. 2005. Dissociation between ventral and dorsal fMRI activation during object action recognition. *Neuron* 47:457–470.

Simmons, W. K., and L. W. Barsalou. 2003. The similarity-in-topography principle: Reconciling theories of conceptual deficits. *Cognitive Neuropsychology* 20:451–486.

Stasenko, A., F. E. Garcea, M. Dombovy, and B. Z. Mahon. 2014. When concepts lose their color: A case of selective loss of knowledge of object color. *Cortex 58:* 217-238.

Stasenko, A., F. E. Garcea, and B. Z. Mahon. 2013. What happens to the motor theory of perception when the motor theory is damaged? *Language and Cognition. 5:* 225-238

Tanaka, K., H. Saito, Y. Fukada, and M. Moriya. 1991. Coding visual images of objects in the inferotemporal cortex of the macaque monkey. *Journal of Neurophysiology* 66:170–189.

Thomas, C., G. Avidan, K. Humphreys, K. J. Jung, F. Gao, and M. Behrmann. 2009. Reduced structural connectivity in ventral visual cortex in congenital prosopagnosia. *Nature Neuroscience* 12:29–31.

Thompson-Schill, S. L. 2003. Neuroimaging studies of semantic memory: Inferring "how" from "where." *Neuropsychologia* 41:280–292.

Thompson-Schill, S. L., G. K. Aguirre, M. D'Esposito, and M. J. Farah. 1999. A neural basis for category and modality specificity of semantic knowledge. *Neuropsychology* 37:671–676.

Toni, I., F. P. de Lange, M. L. Noordzij, and P. Hagoort. 2008. Language beyond action. *Journal of Physiology, Paris* 102:71–79.

Tsao, D. Y., W. A. Freiwald, R. B. H. Tootell, and M. S. Livingstone. 2006. A cortical region consisting entirely of face-selective cells. *Science* 311:669–674.

Tyler, L. K., H. E. Moss, M. R. Durrant-Peatfield, and J. P. Levy. 2000. Conceptual structure and the structure of concepts: A distributed account of category-specific deficits. *Brain and Language* 75:195–231.

Tyler, L. K., and H. E. Moss. 2001. Towards a distributed account of conceptual knowledge. *Trends in Cognitive Sciences* 5:244–252.

Ungerleider, L. G., and M. Mishkin. 1982. Two cortical visual systems. In *Analysis of Visual Behavior*, ed. D. J. Ingle, M. A. Goodale, and R. J. W. Mansfield, 549–586. Cambridge, MA: MIT Press.

Vigliocco, G., D. P. Vinson, W. Lewis, and M. F. Garrett. 2004. Representing the meanings of object and action words: The featural and unitary semantic space hypothesis. *Cognitive Psychology* 48:422–488.

Vinson, D. P., G. Vigliocco, S. Cappa, and S. Siri. 2003. The breakdown of semantic knowledge: Insights from a statistical model of meaning representation. *Brain and Language* 86:347–365.

Warrington, E. K., and R. A. McCarthy. 1983. Category specific access dysphasia. *Brain* 106:859–878.

Warrington, E. K., and R. A. McCarthy. 1987. Categories of knowledge: Further fractionations and an attempted integration. *Brain* 110:1273–1296.

Warrington, E. K., and T. Shallice. 1984. Category specific semantic impairments. *Brain* 107:829–854.

Weiner, K. S., R. Sayres, J. Vinberg, and K. Grill-Spector. 2010. fMRI-Adaptation and category selectivity in human ventral temporal cortex: Regional differences across time scales. *Journal of Neurophysiology* 103:3349–3365.

Wheatley, T., S. C. Milleville, and A. Martin. 2007. Understanding animate agents: Distinct roles for the social network and mirror system. *Psychological Science* 18:469–474.

Wilmer, J. B., L. Germine, C. F. Chabris, G. Chatterjee, M. Williams, E. Loken, K. Nakayama, and B. Duchaine. 2010. Human face recognition ability is specific and highly heritable. *Proceedings of the National Academy of Sciences of the United States of America* 16:5238–5241.

Zhu, Q., Y. Song, S. Hu, X. Li, M. Tian, Z. Zhen, Q. Dong, N. Kanwisher, and J. Liu. 2010. Heritability of the specific cognitive ability of face perception. *Current Biology* 20:137–142.

5 Concept Nativism and Neural Plasticity

Stephen Laurence and Eric Margolis

5.1 Introduction[1]

One of the most important recent developments in the study of concepts has been the resurgence of interest in nativist accounts of the human conceptual system. However, many theorists suppose that a key feature of neural organization—the brain's plasticity—undermines the nativist approach to concept acquisition. In this chapter, we argue that although this view of the matter has an initial air of plausibility, it gets things exactly backward. Not only does the brain's plasticity fail to undermine concept nativism, but a detailed examination of the neurological evidence actually provides powerful support *for* concept nativism, giving rise to what we call the *argument from neural wiring*. The brain is most definitely an organ that is altered by experience, but as we will see, the ways in which it is altered support a nativist perspective on cognitive architecture.

5.2 The Contemporary Empiricism-Nativism Debate

Nativist views of concepts trace back to Plato, Descartes, Leibniz, and other philosophers who theorized about the existence of innate ideas. Partly for this reason, nativism about the conceptual system is sometimes characterized simply as the view that there *are* innate ideas or concepts, and empiricism as the view that the mind is initially a blank slate in that it has no innate structure whatsoever. However, this way of distinguishing empiricism from nativism is ill-advised.

First, to characterize empiricism as the view that the mind begins with no innate structure would have the unfortunate consequence of there not really being any empiricists. It has long been recognized by all parties to the empiricism-nativism debate that a mind without any innate structure—a truly blank slate—wouldn't be capable of learning. There has to be *something* that accounts for why human beings come to know

1. This article was fully collaborative; the order of the authors' names is arbitrary.

anything at all about the world around them. As Quine once noted, even "the behaviorist is knowingly and cheerfully up to his neck in innate mechanisms" (Quine 1969, 95–96).[2] Second, although it is true that nativists are more likely than empiricists to embrace innate concepts in addition to other types of innate psychological structures, focusing exclusively on whether concepts are innate doesn't do justice to mainstream views of the conceptual system. Empiricists may accept some innate concepts, and nativists may hold that what matters is not innate concepts per se, but rather the existence of a rich innate basis for acquiring concepts.

For these reasons, we think it best to characterize concept nativism directly in terms of what is at stake in the disagreement between empiricists and nativists. For contemporary theorists in philosophy and cognitive science, the disagreement revolves around the character of the innate psychological structures that underlie concept acquisition.

According to empiricist approaches, there are few if any innate concepts, and concept acquisition is, by and large, governed by a small number of innate general-purpose cognitive systems being repeatedly engaged. Sometimes this point is put by saying that empiricists claim that concepts are largely acquired on the basis of experience and hence that the conceptual system is predominantly a product of learning. But the crucial fact here isn't that empiricists place a lot of weight on learning. (As we'll see in a moment, nativists do too.) Rather, what is characteristic of empiricism in the empiricism-nativism debate is its *distinctively empiricist approach to learning*. The empiricist view is that concept learning overwhelmingly traces back to general-purpose cognitive systems and that these provide the psychological underpinning for the many varied concepts that humans come to possess. For example, on a typical empiricist view, concepts related to agency and concepts related to number are both the product of the same kind of psychological processes embedded in the same general-purpose concept-acquisition systems. The reason agency representations form in the one case and numerical representations in the other is simply a reflection of the differing experiences of the learner resulting in the different input to these systems.

The nativist approach, in contrast, holds that innate concepts and/or innate special-purpose cognitive systems (of varying degrees of specialization) play a key role in conceptual development, alongside general-purpose cognitive systems. So what is characteristic of nativism in the empiricism-nativism debate is its *distinctively nativist*

2. Some contemporary theorists who undoubtedly fall on the empiricist side of the empiricism-nativism divide have rejected the label *empiricism* because of its association with the view that the mind lacks innate structure. For example, in a discussion relating work in neuroscience to theories of conceptual development, Steven Quartz remarks, "I have avoided using the term empiricism, instead stating the strategy in terms of not being strongly innate. My reason for this lies in the common identification of empiricism with *Tabula Rasa* learning" (Quartz 2003, 34). Since we take there to be a substantive issue at stake between theorists like Quartz and concept nativists, a better characterization of empiricism is clearly needed.

approach to concept acquisition, crucially involving a substantial number of innate concepts, numerous innate special-purpose systems involved in concept acquisition, or, most likely, some combination of the two. A nativist view is perfectly at home with the claim that representations of agency might depend on psychological processes that reflect the operation of innate agency-specific concept-acquisition systems, while representations of number depend on separate, innate number-specific concept-acquisition systems. The reason agency representations form in the one case and numerical representations in the other would then be due as much to the fact that they are governed by different innate special-purpose acquisition systems as to the differing input to these systems.

As frameworks for explaining concept acquisition, both nativism and empiricism come in differing strengths. A strong form of empiricism would claim that there are no innate concepts whatsoever and that concept acquisition depends exclusively on a small number of general-purpose psychological systems. Jesse Prinz defends a view along these lines, holding that concepts "are all learned, not innate" (Prinz 2005, 679). After arguing against what he takes to be the main proposals for special-purpose innate concept-acquisition systems, he summarizes his discussion by noting, "I do not believe that any of these domains is innate. That is to say, I do not think we have innate domain-specific knowledge that contributes to structuring our concepts" (Prinz 2005, 688).

A weaker empiricist view might admit that there are a limited number of special-purpose cognitive mechanisms that constrain how the conceptual system develops in certain isolated cases, particularly cases supporting basic biological needs, but apart from these few minor exceptions, concept acquisition is governed solely by general-purpose cognitive systems. Rogers and McClelland (2004) defend such a view. After arguing that a general-purpose connectionist model can explain how adult semantic memory is organized, they suggest that there may be a handful of instances of prepared learning, including, for example, a tendency to withdraw from strong stimuli and to respond favorably to the taste of fat and sugar. Nonetheless, Rogers and McClelland state that they are "reluctant ... to accept that, in general, human semantic cognition is prepared in this way," arguing instead that "domain-general mechanisms can discover the sorts of domain-specific principles that are evident in the behavior of young children" (Rogers and McClelland 2004, 369).

Nativist views also come in differing strengths. In fact, arguably one of the main reasons concept nativism has had so few adherents is because of its association with one of the most audacious nativist positions ever defended—Jerry Fodor's radical concept nativism (Fodor 1975, 1981). According to this view, nearly all concepts corresponding to individual words in natural languages are innate, including the likes of LINGUINI, CARBURETOR, BEATNIK, and QUARK. Notice that it isn't just the sheer volume of innate concepts that makes this view so outrageous—the thousands and thousands of concepts corresponding to actual and potential natural language words—but also the fact that most of these concepts are clearly newcomers in human history, dependent on specific historical, cultural, and technological conditions for their appearance. Fodor once tried to explain how it might be that so many innate concepts could be sitting around unused for much of human history only to suddenly become active. His suggestion was that they get "triggered" by innately specified environmental conditions whose occurrence might depend on highly contingent prior events. But this really is a singularly implausible maneuver on his part, and Fodor's view has found few if any advocates even among nativists.[3] Fodor's radical concept nativism is not just an outlier position within the empiricism-nativism debate, it is also an outlier position on the *nativist* side.[4]

What would a more reasonable concept nativist position look like? First, while denying that all or virtually all concepts are innate, it would nonetheless embrace the existence of a substantial number of innate concepts, including concepts that pick out abstract categories. Second, it would embrace a variety of innate special-purpose acquisition systems that are geared to particular conceptual domains. And third, it would also embrace concepts acquired via relatively general-purpose innate acquisition systems—indeed, any tenable form of concept nativism will acknowledge that a great deal of the conceptual system is acquired, at least in part, by such general-purpose systems.

Which concepts and special-purpose acquisition systems should a nativist say are innate? Ultimately, of course, this is an empirical question; there is no specific list that a concept nativist must be committed to. In our view, though, likely contenders include concepts and innate special-purpose systems associated with the representation of objects, physical causation, distance, movement, space, time, geometry, agency, goals, perception, emotions, thought, biological kinds, life stages, disease, tools, predators, prey, food, danger, sex, kinship, group membership, dominance, status, norms, morality, logic, and number. Note, however, that this isn't to advocate the grossly implausible claim that *all* concepts related to these domains are innate or acquired via innate special-purpose systems. For example, any sensible form of concept nativism would reject the idea that PASTA and BONBON are innate but might nonetheless accept that there is an innate special-purpose acquisition system, or set of systems, that is involved in the conceptualization of food. Likewise, concept nativists needn't suppose that the concepts for advanced mathematics are innate but may well maintain that there are innate numerical representations of one kind or another.

3. Chomsky (1991) flirted with Fodor's radical concept nativism, but even Fodor himself has now rejected the view (Fodor 1998, 2008).
4. See, for example, Laurence and Margolis (2002) and Pinker (2007) for highly critical assessments of Fodor's radical concept nativism that are nonetheless quite congenial to nativism in general.

Earlier we noted that it would be wrong to suppose that only empiricists hold that concepts are learned. We can now see why. This is because nativism isn't confined to postulating innate concepts. Rather, a big part of concept nativism is its appeal to innate special-purpose systems of acquisition, and these systems are often best understood as learning systems. For instance, an innate special-purpose system for food might support the learning of which items in the environment are to be eaten and which are to be avoided, guiding food preferences and food-seeking behavior. Or an innate special-purpose system for faces might support the learning of concepts of individuals. These hypothesized systems are very much in the business of learning about the world, according to the nativist. They are just specialized for learning particular information in a way that is highly constrained by the nature of the learning system.

To a large extent, then, the difference between nativism and empiricism isn't *whether* learning is central to human concept acquisition but rather their differing views of *how* learning works. While empiricists take learning to be almost exclusively mediated by innate general-purpose learning systems, nativists maintain that general-purpose learning systems, though real and important, are not sufficient, and also postulate numerous innate special-purpose learning systems, holding that they are central to conceptual development, to categorization, and to other concept-involving higher-level cognitive processes.

It is also worth emphasizing that nativists don't deny the existence of relatively domain-general concept acquisition, although nativists are likely to see even domain-general acquisition as typically relying on special-purpose systems or constraints of one kind or another. For example, socially mediated learning undoubtedly facilitates the acquisition of a wide range of concepts, including concepts that are peculiar to a learner's culture. But on a nativist view, this learning is likely to be mediated by innate systems for acquiring cultural norms (Sripada and Stich 2006), by innate systems that are responsive to pedagogical cues (Csibra and Gergely 2011), and by innate biases governing cultural transmission, including biases regarding who to imitate (Boyd and Richerson 1985).

In the rest of the chapter, we take up the question of how the facts related to neural structure and function bear on the evaluation of concept nativism, but before we do that, we should briefly comment on the status of the argument we offer for concept nativism—the argument from neural wiring—and how it fits into the larger case for the nativist framework. This argument is intended as a nondemonstrative argument that takes the form of an inference to the best explanation. And so we maintain that the argument provides strong—though defeasible—support for concept nativism. We take it that the status of concept nativism turns entirely on nondemonstrative arguments of this kind. Empiricists sometimes write as though empiricism is the default position and that nothing short of an incontestable proof for concept nativism should move us away from this default (see, e.g., Prinz 2005, 2012). However, this outlook is misplaced.

Given that empiricists and nativists disagree about what is clearly a factual question about the structure of the mind, both sides are equally in need of evidence and argument to establish their view and must equally make the case that the balance of empirical considerations stands in their favor. Proofs have no more place here than they do in other disputes about the workings of the mind. Any nondemonstrative argument for concept nativism will also need to be considered in light of the other empirical arguments that bear on the empiricism-nativism debate. Although we don't have the space in this chapter to examine other arguments, we believe that there are important arguments for concept nativism drawing on evidence from developmental psychology, animal psychology, evolutionary psychology, anthropology, and other fields, that these arguments are mutually reinforcing, and that it is this total package that makes concept nativism such an attractive view.[5] Fortunately, though, the argument from neural wiring offers considerable support for concept nativism even taken in isolation. So while we don't want to give the impression that concept nativism stands or falls with this one argument, we do think the argument from neural wiring constitutes a solid reason for favoring concept nativism all the same.

5.3 Plasticity as a Challenge to Nativism

As we noted above, plasticity is often seen as providing an argument against nativism, not for it. We will begin, then, with the considerations that are generally thought to show that neural plasticity poses a serious challenge to concept nativism.

Plasticity has become a catchall term for the many ways in which neural organization and function change in response to an animal's experience and action, as well as to traumas to its brain and body. A standard example that is often used to illustrate the general idea is the reorganization of the sensory map of the hand in the brain in response to an injury or to changes in the way the hand is used. The normal arrangement in the somatosensory cortex is for adjacent groups of cells to correspond to adjacent regions of the body—for example, neurons that respond to the index finger reside close to neurons that respond to the middle finger. What happens if the nerve fibers connecting a finger to the spinal cord are severed? One might expect the cortical area that previously responded to that finger to atrophy, but this is not what happens. Instead, this cortical area is taken over by the adjacent finger(s), changing the function of that cortical area so that it responds to the adjacent finger(s). Likewise, even if one of two adjacent fingers is simply used more or happens to receive a greater amount of stimulation, some of the neurons that were originally responsive to the less active or less stimulated finger become responsive to the more stimulated finger. As one major

---

5. For detailed discussion of a broad range of arguments for concept nativism and their interrelations, see Laurence and Margolis (unpublished ms.).

textbook summarizes the matter, "This functional plasticity suggests that the adult cortex is a dynamic place where changes can still happen. Such phenomena demonstrate a remarkable plasticity" (Gazzaniga, Irvy, and Mangun 2009, 102).

Neural plasticity doesn't stop with potential changes to the boundaries of somatosensory representations. Even more interesting are instances in which cortical circuits deprived of their usual sensory input come to be recruited by a differing sensory modality. An important example of this type of reorganization can be found in early-blind Braille readers. When tested on *tactile* discrimination tasks, they show increased activation in the *visual* cortex compared to sighted subjects, who show deactivation in this area (Sadato et al. 1996).[6] Studies using repetitive transcranial magnetic stimulation (rTMS) further confirm the role of the visual cortex in the blind. This technique employs a magnetic pulse to disrupt neural activity in a targeted region of the brain. When rTMS is used to disrupt neural activity in the occipital (visual) cortex, blind subjects have difficulty identifying Braille and embossed roman letters, whereas there is no effect on sighted subjects engaged in comparable tactile discrimination tasks (Cohen et al. 1997).

Perhaps the most celebrated instance of neural plasticity comes from a study with ferrets in which ferrets' brains were surgically rewired shortly after birth (Sharma, Angelucci, and Sur 2000; von Melchner, Pallas, and Sur 2000). Retinal projections were rerouted so that the neural signals that would normally go to the primary visual cortex were fed to the primary auditory cortex via the auditory thalamus. When the ferrets were tested as adults, not only did the auditory cortex in those with rewired brains come to exhibit patterns of activity that are characteristic of the visual cortex (e.g., it contained groups of cells that responded differentially to stimulus orientation), but the ferrets were able to approach objects that could only be detected by sight. The take-home message, according to one of the original research reports announcing these results, is that "the pattern of early sensory activation can instruct the functional architecture of cortex to a significant extent" (Sharma, Angelucci, and Sur 2000, 846).

There is, of course, a question of how much of the brain exhibits this level of plasticity. Is plasticity unique to sensory-perceptual systems? One reason to think it isn't is that there are cases in which children recover from focal damage to cortical areas involved in language. Amazingly, there are even cases of children who come to develop near-normal linguistic abilities after undergoing a hemispherectomy, in which one cerebral hemisphere is disabled or entirely removed (Curtiss and Schaeffer 2005; Curtiss and de Bode 2003). One child (known as EB) who underwent a left

6. Early-blind subjects include those who are blind from birth as well as those who developed blindness early in life. In the study by Sadato and colleagues, this includes children who were blind before the age of seven, while in some of the other studies we cite below, the cutoff point for being considered an early-blind subject is at significantly earlier ages.

hemispherectomy at two and a half years old managed to recover much of his language skills two years later.[7] When tested at age fourteen, his language was found to be normal in most respects, with all his linguistic functions now residing solely in his right hemisphere (Danelli et al. 2013).

There may also be general theoretical reasons to suppose that the parts of the brain that are involved in higher cognitive processes are plastic and hence can take on any number of differing functions. Buller and Hardcastle (2000) argue that this is extremely likely given that dedicated brain circuits per se don't exist even for "our most basic [i.e., sensory] processes" (313). In general, they claim, "the dedication of a brain system to a particular task domain is subject to change as the inputs to that brain system change" (313). The reason there is the appearance of isolable and stable neural structures is that "plastic human brains have encountered recurrent environmental demands throughout history" (317). Elman et al. (1996) express a similar view. After reviewing the evidence regarding brain plasticity in animals and humans, they conclude that there may be some "primitive innate representations in the midbrain, … but the cortex appears to be an organ of plasticity, a self-organizing and experience-sensitive network of representations that emerge progressively across the course of development" (315).

It is worth noting that singling out the cortex isn't uncommon among empiricists who place a lot of weight on brain plasticity. Quartz (2003), for example, disagrees with Elman and colleagues about subcortical structures, maintaining instead that innate neural systems are the norm in most animals. But he agrees that a significant level of plasticity is a peculiar feature of the human cortex, pointing, in particular, to the example of how the occipital cortex functions differently in blind Braille readers than in sighted control subjects (as in the work by Sadato et al. 1996 described above). According to Quartz, "The sharp contrast between cortical and subcortical structures suggests that the evolution of cortex may represent the evolution of a new acquisition strategy" (Quartz 2003, 36).

In sum, there is a lot to be said for the view that the brain exhibits a great deal of plasticity in terms of its functional structure. It also isn't difficult to see why this fact is often thought to favor empiricist approaches to conceptual development. Widespread and significant instances of neural plasticity suggests an inherent openness to the functions that any cortical area can take on. If this is right, then the brain's concept acquisition capacities needn't be innately constrained toward any particular outcome. Instead, cortical circuits might simply form as required to accommodate a learner's needs given whatever contingent sensory input has been received and the wiring that has been previously established. Buller and Hardcastle (2000) capture this picture in suggesting that neural plasticity goes hand in hand with the idea of a content-neutral

---

7. In right-handed individuals, like EB before his surgery, language is usually controlled by structures in the left hemisphere.

capacity for addressing information-processing tasks. As they put it, "Our ancestors may have encountered diverse problems, but the brain evolved a *general solution* to those problems" (317; italics added).

5.4 The Argument from Neural Wiring

We have seen that the phenomenon of neural plasticity appears to constitute a major objection to concept nativism. The more equipotential the brain, the less plausible it is that there are innate special-purpose acquisition systems. And examples like the ones reviewed in the last section do seem to point in the direction of a highly equipotential brain with a functional organization that fits naturally with an empiricist approach to cognitive and conceptual development. However, appearances are misleading. In this section, we argue that not only do the facts pertaining to neural plasticity fail to discredit concept nativism, but a careful look at the relevant neurological evidence strongly favors the nativist approach. What we are calling the *argument from neural wiring* is an argument for nativism that draws on a broad range of neurological evidence showing that neural plasticity is highly constrained in ways that are best explained within a nativist framework.

5.4.1 Plasticity Revisited

We begin with some observations about a few of the striking examples from the last section. It is instructive to see that even in these instances, which are often thought to make nativist views look hopeless, the changes that the brain undergoes aren't as flexible and open-ended as they first appear.

Consider the finding that language can be recovered after the loss of the cortical areas that normally support linguistic processing, even with the loss of as much as half of the cortex. We saw this with EB, who had his left cerebral hemisphere removed when he was just two years old and yet grew up to have near-normal language abilities. In his daily life, he doesn't exhibit any noticeable signs of language impairment. Clinical assessments have also found his language to be near normal (compared to age-matched controls), with below average performance in only a few tests (e.g., in reading, he had difficulty with homophones and words that have been borrowed from other languages). These minor difficulties only highlight how strong his core linguistic abilities are. EB is a particularly interesting case study among hemispherectomy patients because the pathology he suffered didn't involve epilepsy and was localized in one hemisphere, leaving the other hemisphere intact and healthy. The pathologies that lead to hemispherectomy aren't usually so localized; generally there is damage to both hemispheres.

At first glance, then, this may suggest that EB offers a clear-cut illustration of how the plasticity of the brain stands in opposition to a nativist theory of development. EB's right hemisphere took on cognitive functions that are usually located elsewhere in the brain—a massive relocation of the neural circuitry for language (and for much else). But functional magnetic imaging (fMRI) shows that the areas in his right hemisphere supporting his linguistic abilities aren't scattered in unpredictable ways, as one might expect if his recovery were based on the powers of a truly equipotential brain. Rather, EB's language areas are homologs of the left hemisphere areas activated in linguistic tasks in healthy control subjects.[8] Danelli et al. (2013) performed an in-depth fMRI analysis of language production versus comprehension, automatic versus controlled language processes, and auditory versus visual processing, finding that "the overall neurofunctional architecture of EB's right hemispheric language system mirrors a left-like linguistic neural blueprint" (225). This result points to a highly constrained neural organization that illustrates an important general principle: the brain's two hemispheres incorporate a large measure of potential redundancy of function that can be exploited at certain stages of development. This is a form of plasticity, to be sure, but not a kind that favors empiricism.

What about the ferrets? Certainly this at least illustrates true equipotentiality? After all, their rewired brains led to the auditory cortex developing features of the visual cortex, and even to the ferrets being able to respond to visual stimuli relying on processing that could only occur in their auditory cortex. Surprisingly, even this case fails to provide a strong argument against nativist theories of conceptual and cognitive development.

For one thing, generalizing from one relatively small area of the auditory cortex to the rest of the brain is a huge leap (Pinker 2002). Even if it turns out that this portion of the auditory cortex and its downstream perceptual processing is highly malleable in a way that reflects a given input modality, it doesn't follow that the processing for higher cognitive functions can be handled by arbitrary cortical areas. Higher cognitive processes may well involve dedicated brain areas even if sensory processes do not.

---

8. Contrary findings in clinical and neuroimaging studies have led to a controversy about whether there are language-specific neural circuits—circuits that are specialized for and selectively activated by language processing. On the one hand, clinical studies have found sharp dissociations between linguistic and nonlinguistic deficits, suggesting the existence of language-specific areas of the brain. But on the other hand, neuroimaging studies with neurotypical subjects have failed to show processing regions exclusively devoted to language processing. The problem with the neuroimaging work that fed this controversy, however, is that the selection of the brain regions for examination didn't take into account individual differences in neuroanatomy. Once the classic language areas are singled out in a way that is sensitive to these differences, fMRI studies reveal the existence of neural regions selectively activated by linguistic processes to the exclusion of other cognitive processes (such as mental arithmetic and general working memory) in accordance with the clinical data (Fedorenko, Behr, and Kanwisher 2011).

In the previous section, we encountered an argument by Buller and Hardcastle suggesting the opposite conclusion. Their claim was that sensory processes are among the most "basic" in the cortex, and consequently, that if there are no dedicated brain areas for these processes, then it is even less likely that there would be dedicated areas for higher cognitive processes. However, a lot is being packed into the idea of a so-called basic psychological process in this argument. It may be true that, when the brain receives external environmental stimulation, sensory processes are typically activated earlier than higher cognitive processes. However, this isn't enough to get Buller and Hardcastle's argument off the ground. What they need is for sensory processes to be more fundamental than higher cognitive processes in ontogeny—for the development of the neural systems for cognitive processes to depend on the prior development of, and input from, the neural systems for sensory processes. But this claim would be question-begging in the present context. Whether there is such a dependence is partly what empiricists and nativists disagree about when the debate turns to the wiring of the brain.

Moreover, the point about the danger of an overgeneralization isn't just about the divide between sensation and cognition. It also applies to the internal structure of perceptual systems as well. The effect of the rewiring experiments was that the primary auditory cortex in a ferret with a rewired brain was able to process information from the retina that normally would have been processed by the primary visual cortex, and consequently came to take on some of the features that are characteristic of the primary visual cortex. The primary visual cortex is connected to a large number of distinct brain regions that support further specific types of visual processing, including computations responsible for downstream representations of location, direction of motion, speed, shape, and so on. If the redirected sensory input in the ferrets had led to the development of all this downstream structure in the auditory cortex, that would amount to exactly the sort equipotentiality of cortical areas that empiricists could use against nativists. But, in fact, none of this downstream structure was reproduced. The overall wiring of the ferrets' auditory cortex was largely unchanged (Majewska and Sur 2006).

This situation—in which the primary auditory cortex in some sense allowed the ferrets to "see" despite the fact that downstream auditory areas weren't significantly altered—leads to a puzzle. *How is it that the primary auditory cortex can process and make any use of visual information?* Interestingly, Sur, the team leader in the ferret study, has answered that "the animals with visual inputs induced into the auditory pathway provide a different window on some of the same operations that should occur normally in auditory thalamus and cortex" (Sur 1988, 45; quoted in Pinker 2002, 96). In other words, the processing that is supposed to be handled by these different sensory areas is somewhat similar. Pinker expands on this idea by noting that there are general high-level likenesses between the computations that might be expected to take place in hearing and vision, as sound-makers with different pitches may be treated like objects in different locations, and sharp changes in pitch may be treated like motions in space

(Bregman and Pinker 1978). If this is right, then even though the rewiring experiments show that the auditory cortex can be recruited for a certain amount of visual processing, this is because the auditory cortex and the visual cortex overlap in the types of computations they naturally support. Far from being a model case of the environment instructing an equipotential cortex, Sur and colleagues's rewiring experiments illustrate the way in which cortical structure and function remain largely unchanged even in the extreme case of input coming from a different sensory system.

5.4.2 Constrained Plasticity in Neural Structural Organization

So far, our response to the appeal to plasticity as an argument against concept nativism has been to show that some of the flagship examples of plasticity don't really amount to the sort of flexibility of neural organization that would tell against the nativist approach to cognitive and conceptual development. We now turn to evidence related to the wiring of the brain that directly supports the nativist perspective. The general form of our argument is to point to aspects of neural, cognitive, and conceptual development that exhibit *constrained plasticity*—development that is not open-endedly plastic, but instead is highly constrained in ways that suggest important innate biases, predispositions, and limits on neural structure and function. We begin, in this section, by briefly presenting some evidence indicating that neural structural organization is not primarily driven by environmental input or feedback configuring the brain.

In a landmark investigation, Verhage et al. (2000) examined neurological development in a group of mutant (or *knockout*) mice whose brains (as a result of the genetic mutation) were unable to release any neurotransmitters and thus were deprived of all synaptic transmission.[9] Accordingly, these mice would have had no experience-driven neural development whatsoever. Verhage and colleagues compared these mice to control littermates and found that up until birth, their brains were remarkably similar.[10] As these researchers explain:

Despite the general, complete, and permanent loss of synaptic transmission in the knockout mice, their brains were assembled correctly (Fig. 3). Neuronal proliferation, migration, and differentiation into specific brain areas were unaffected. At E12 [embryonic day 12], brains from null mutant and control littermates were morphologically indistinguishable (Fig. 3, A and B). … At birth, late-forming brain areas such as the neocortex appeared identical in null mutant and control littermates, including a distinctive segregation of neurons into cortical layers (Fig. 3, C and D). Furthermore, fiber pathways were targeted correctly in null mutants … (Fig. 3, G and H). (Verhage et al. 2000, 866; figure references are to figure 3 in the original article, reproduced here as figure 5.1, plate 9.)

9. Specifically, Verhage and colleagues suppressed the expression of the munc18-1 gene in the mutants.
10. After birth, of course, the mutant mice died. Without functioning synaptic communication, the brain can't support even the most basic life functions, such as breathing.

Control   Null   Control   Null

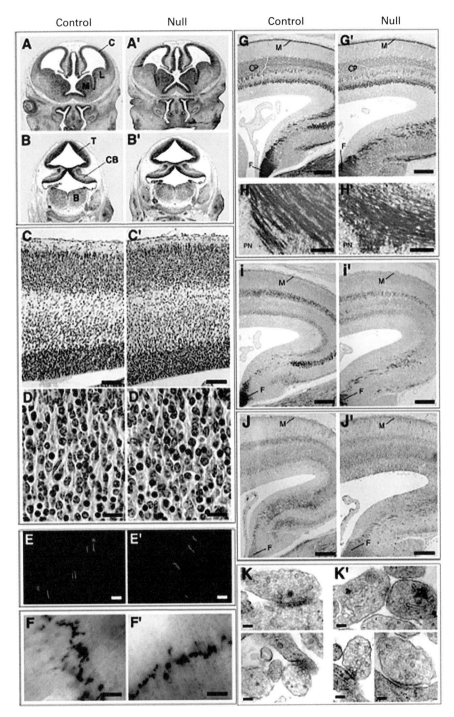

Figure 5.1 (plate 9)
Neurological development in mutant mice that were genetically engineered to eliminate synaptic transmission (null) and in normal control mice (control). (From Verhage et al. 2000. Used with permission.)

This degree of similarity shows that many features of even the fine-grained structure of the brain can develop without any sensory input or feedback. Experience-driven neural activity may play more of a role in fine-tuning and maintaining this layout than in establishing the overall organization itself (Marcus 2004). None of this is to say that the brain isn't plastic to some degree.[11] But it underscores the fact that neural development isn't open-endedly plastic.

5.4.3 Constrained Plasticity in Functional Organization

Constrained plasticity isn't confined to neural structural organization. It also extends to the functional specificity associated with particular cortical areas. This is especially apparent in instances of congenital and early sensory deficits, such as blindness, in which the specific cognitive function of the affected cortical area is preserved. Preserved function in these cases argues for constrained plasticity because it shows that the information processing associated with the region isn't dictated by the sensory information it receives.

Viewed in a certain light, congenital sensory deficits are essentially rewiring experiments. Cortical areas that usually process sensory information from an impaired modality (e.g., subareas of the visual cortex in the congenitally blind) end up taking input from another sensory modality, an organization (or reorganization) known as *cross-modal plasticity*. An empiricist who supposes that the cortex has a high degree of equipotentiality should predict that the resulting functions of these cortical areas would differ from the normal case, reflecting the difference in the input. But recent work with congenitally blind subjects shows that, contrary to this prediction, what typically happens is that downstream components of the visual cortex and related brain areas have the same functional specificity in the congenitally blind as in sighted individuals.

Consider, for example, the representation of the spatial location of objects in the visual cortex. In one study, Renier et al. (2010) presented early-blind subjects with auditory stimuli that varied in terms of sound type (different piano chords) and spatial location.[12] Using fMRI, their brain activity was measured during two behavioral conditions, an identification condition (in which they had to determine whether sequentially presented stimuli were of the same sound type) and a location condition (in which they had to determine whether they had the same location). Renier and colleagues found that the anterior part of the right middle occipital gyrus (MOG)—a

11. Notice that it shouldn't be controversial that the brain is plastic in the minimal sense that changes to the brain occur as people learn, think, and experience the world. This is simply a requirement of any broadly materialist theory of the mind.

12. In this experiment, the early-blind subjects were either blind from birth or by the second year of life, without ever having had normal vision or, at the time of testing, memories of visual experience.

part of the visual cortex associated with the representation of visual spatial location in sighted subjects—was differentially active for the auditory spatial localization task relative to the auditory identification task. The researchers also ran an analogous tactile task with the same subjects. In this case, their fingertips were given different types of stimulation (for the identification task), or there was stimulation to different fingers (for the spatial location task). Once again, fMRI data revealed that the right anterior MOG was differentially active for the spatial localization task relative to the identification task.[13] The upshot of this study is that, while the MOG is clearly plastic—in the early blind it comes to subserve auditory and tactile spatial localization abilities that it does not subserve in sighted individuals—the plasticity it exhibits is a form of constrained plasticity. The MOG continues to carry out the function of spatial localization in the early blind, just with different types of sensory input.

Further fMRI studies have revealed the same pattern of constrained plasticity in other neural regions with associated spatial functions. For example, Lingnau et al. (2014) examined the activity in the posterior parietal cortex (PPC), which is involved in the representation of space for purposes of guiding action. The PPC normally takes its sensory input primarily from vision and exhibits a pronounced gradient—with posterior subregions recruited more heavily for (visual) guidance of reaching and grasping, and anterior subregions more for planning and execution of motor action. Using a proprioceptively guided reaching task, however, Lingnau and colleagues were able to show that the same pattern of functional differentiation occurs in congenitally blind subjects. The researchers compared the brain activity of congenitally blind subjects and blindfolded sighted subjects performing one of two actions on an object (touching with fingertips vs. grasping with their whole hand) in a specified location (chosen from five possible locations). In this case, the principle of constrained plasticity predicts that sighted and blind subjects would have similar activation in the anterior portions of the PPC (since all subjects would be equally engaged in the planning and execution of motor action), but that there would be significantly greater activation in the posterior portions of the PPC in the blind (since in the blind, the PPC would be accommodated to *nonvisual* sources of information regarding spatial location). This is exactly what Lingnau and colleagues found, leading them to conclude that "neural plasticity acts within a relatively rigid framework of predetermined functional specialization" (Lingnau et al. 2014, 547).

One of the major features of the visual cortex is the functional division corresponding to two broad networks of interrelated neural regions. The ventral visual stream (the *what pathway*) represents object properties, and is involved in object recognition;

13. Blindfolded sighted control subjects doing these auditory and tactile tasks did not show the same activation of the MOG. However, MOG activation in sighted subjects did occur in a comparable visual task.

the dorsal visual stream (the *where pathway*) represents object location and the spatial relations between objects, and is involved in object-directed action. The results from Renier et al. (2010) and Lingnau et al. (2014) that we have been reviewing indicate that the dorsal visual stream continues to exist in early-blind and congenitally blind subjects and that its component subregions engage in the same functional processing for object location despite profound changes in sensory input (auditory or proprioceptive vs. visual).

Further studies of the dorsal visual stream fill out this picture by showing that it's not just the representation of spatial location that is preserved. For example, Wolbers, Zahorik, and Giudice (2011) examined activity in the dorsal occipitotemporal cortex in congenitally blind adults, focusing on a region of interest encompassing the hMT+ complex, which normally represents the direction of visual motion. To determine whether this region retains the same function when deprived of its usual (visual) input, an fMRI scan was taken while congenitally blind subjects heard leftward and rightward broadband noise signals, as well as static control stimuli. Wolbers and colleagues found that the region of interest was specifically involved in motion detection in congenitally blind subjects even though the sensory input in this case was auditory, not visual.[14] Once again, we have an impressive instance of plasticity (the fact that the dorsal visual pathway is co-opted for auditory processing), but the plasticity is constrained, preserving the normal functional specificity of a dorsal pathway subregion.

Constrained plasticity has been found in the ventral visual pathway as well. For example, Striem-Amit et al. (2012) trained congenitally blind subjects and sighted controls to use a sensory substitution device, which transforms visual information from a head-mounted camera into auditory information so that soundscapes can be used to detect visual stimuli. Blind and (blindfolded) sighted subjects had up to an hour and a half of training on the device before being tested on simple geometric shapes in different locations. Upon hearing the prompt "shape," they had to judge whether the stimulus was circular or angular; upon hearing "location," they had to judge whether it was on the left or the right side. fMRI data showed that both the blind and the sighted

14. Currently, far more studies are directed to visual impairments than to other sensory impairments, but there is evidence that the same overall pattern holds when the impairment is to cortical areas that usually draw on nonvisual input. For example, work with deaf cats has shown that just as the visual cortex can process auditory or tactile stimuli in the congenitally blind, the auditory cortex can process visual stimuli in the congenitally deaf. Lomber, Meredith, and Kral (2010) examined congenitally deaf cats, which possess enhanced visual location abilities. By temporarily deactivating differing portions of the auditory cortex (using surgically implanted cooling loops), these researchers were able to determine that the cortical area responsible for this enhancement is the posterior auditory field, a region involved in the localization of *acoustic* stimuli in hearing cats.

groups exhibited differential activation for location versus shape, with activation for shape in the inferior temporal cortex (in the ventral visual stream), and activation for location in the precuneus and middle temporal sulcus/gyrus (in the dorsal visual stream). What's more, in blind subjects, there was increased activation for shape information in the ventral visual stream (in ventral Brodmann area 19), suggesting that prior use of the ventral visual stream for auditory stimuli enhanced this function. Thus it would appear that the large-scale functional architecture of the visual cortex—the division of labor between the dorsal and ventral streams—develops in much the same way, and with the same functions being performed in various subregions of these streams, with or without visual experience.

These and related studies showing preserved functional specificity in the visual cortex support what is known as the *metamodal hypothesis* regarding the brain's functional organization (Pascual-Leone and Hamilton 2001). According to this hypothesis, much of the brain is composed of distinct computational systems whose functions are established independently of their sensory input. These systems are capable of processing sensory information from differing modalities but settle on a given modality when the input it provides is the best fit for the computations carried out—thus giving the appearance of modal specificity. On this view, it is a misnomer to speak of the "visual cortex," the "auditory cortex," and so forth. Rather, each of these broad areas is composed of neural systems that engage in computations that create a preference for a given modality, but the computations performed aren't inherently about visual or auditory content, so when the preferred input is unavailable, the brain switches to the next best fit. As our discussion above suggests, there is now a considerable amount of evidence in support of the metamodal hypothesis. For our purposes, though, what matters is the implication for nativism. Notice that to the extent that the brain is organized in this way, we have grounds to suppose that the functional specificity associated with particular regions of the brain is innate. The reason the hMT+ computes direction of motion, for example, can't be because this is required by its visual input; it performs the same function in the complete absence of visual input in the congenitally blind. Rather, the most plausible explanation of its functional specificity is that this brain region is innately organized for computing direction of motion, and this results in it selecting visual input when visual input is available because visual input is optimal for the computations it performs.

Some of the examples of innate neural systems we have been reviewing may not seem especially conceptual. However, whether they involve conceptual representations or not, they do at least contribute to the formation and processing of representations that undoubtedly are—for example, concepts of movement, location, and spatial relations—and thereby count as part of the arrangement of special-purpose systems that explains concept acquisition for nativists. In any case, other work speaks more directly to the neural basis of conceptual-level representations.

For example, Mahon et al. (2009) examined the ventral visual stream's representation of living versus nonliving kinds. It is well known that the ventral visual stream exhibits neural specialization for these differing categories, with the representation of artifacts (e.g., tools and nonmanipulable objects) in medial regions and the representation of living animate things (e.g., animals and faces) in lateral regions. A common assumption in neuropsychology is that this medial-to-lateral organization stems from the differing visual features associated with these categories, which are claimed to lead to differing types of visual experiences with exemplars from these categories (e.g., Rogers et al. 2005). One way to test this supposition is to compare sighted and congenitally blind subjects using a common task that would be expected to generate ventral visual stream activation in sighted subjects. This is exactly what Mahon and colleagues did, asking sighted and congenitally blind subjects to make size judgments upon hearing words for artifacts and animals. In both blind and sighted subjects, the same medial-to-lateral organization was found. Now, if representations of living and nonliving kinds were organized as they are in the ventral visual stream of sighted subjects because of a response to some measure of visual similarity, it would be deeply surprising to find the same fine-grained functional differentiation along the medial-to-lateral axis among the congenitally blind. As these researchers note, the data suggest instead "that the organization of the ventral stream innately anticipates the different types of computations that must be carried out over objects from different conceptual domains" (Mahon et al. 2009, 403).

It is certainly noteworthy that the organization of high-level representations in the visual cortex is retained notwithstanding the complete lack of visual input. But just as important are instances of higher cognitive *amodal* neural systems retaining their functional specificity despite a lack of visual input. After all, these systems still depend on sensory information, so the information they draw on will differ in dramatic ways when visual information is not available. Consider, for example, the effect of blindness on the development of ordinary mentalizing abilities, which include the ability to attribute mental states to others and to oneself, and the ability to reason about mental states and their role in behavior. Blind individuals lack access to many of the perceptual cues that are typically associated with these abilities, such as others' facial expressions, direction of gaze, and body posture. Blind individuals also can't rely on first-person experience to understand other people's visual perception of events. Despite these radical differences, however, the location of the neural substrates for mentalizing in early-blind individuals (including congenitally blind individuals) is the same as for sighted individuals (Bedny, Pascual-Leone, and Saxe 2009). Notice how unexpected this is on the assumption that mentalizing is acquired largely on the basis of general-purpose processes that are especially sensitive to perceptual cues. Why would the same cortical areas end up with the same peculiar functions given such grossly different access to the evidence for mental activity? In contrast, this constancy in function is naturally explained on the hypothesis that these cortical areas and the functions they realize are determined independently of perceptual input, reflecting a psychological capacity that is, to a significant extent, innate.[15]

In sum, there is considerable evidence for preserved functional specificity of neural areas even when an early sensory deficit promotes cross-modal plasticity. If the cortex were an equipotential network, the brain ought to undergo an immense functional reorganization in cases of congenital and early blindness. But that's not what happens at all. We've seen the preservation of the fine-grained functional structure in what is usually thought of as a visual-motor area, in areas that represent spatial properties (such as location and direction of motion), in the large-scale functional differentiation between the ventral and dorsal visual streams, in the functional specificity within the ventral stream (which includes different areas for representing artifacts and living kinds), and in amodal neural centers (e.g., areas associated with mentalizing) that rely heavily on sensory input. Taken together these and related studies constitute a diverse and compelling body of evidence for constrained plasticity.[16]

15. Bedny, Pascual-Leone, and Saxe (2009) offer a qualification to these conclusions, citing work that suggests that an understanding of false belief develops at a later age in blind individuals than in sighted individuals, perhaps as late as eight years old (e.g., Peterson, Peterson, and Webb 2000). However, this work is based on what has come to be called *elicited-response* false-belief tasks (where children are asked direct questions regarding the mental states of others), rather than *spontaneous-response* false-belief tasks (where children display their knowledge of others' mental states in their spontaneous responses to false beliefs in others) (Baillargeon, Scott, and He 2010). Since sighted children have been shown to pass spontaneous-response tasks at much younger ages than elicited-response tasks (Onishi and Baillargeon 2005; Surian, Caldi, and Sperber 2007; Luo 2011; Kovács, Téglás, and Endress 2010), it would be very interesting and revealing to determine if blind infants can pass nonvisual, nonverbal spontaneous-response false-belief tasks at a comparable age to sighted infants. As far as we know, though, all spontaneous-response false-belief tasks that have been run on infants to date have been visually-based tasks, so new tasks would need to be designed to test this possibility.

16. Another case of preserved functional specificity in the face of sensory deficits can be found in an area of the visual cortex that is involved in word and letter recognition in reading. The neural region subserving this ability is in fact remarkably stable across individuals and languages. Meta-analyses of numerous studies show that "the same region of the left lateral occipitotemporal sulcus always is activated, to within a few millimeters, whenever literate humans read" (Dehaene and Cohen 2011, 256). This case is particularly interesting in light of the fact that reading is such a recent cultural invention; there couldn't be a biological adaptation for reading per se. Rather, the most plausible explanation of this functional specificity—a broadly nativist explanation—is that the abstract categorization of words and letters is always subserved by this neural region because it has an innate computational structure and functional connectivity that makes it uniquely well suited to playing this role, and that the cultural practice of reading has been altered in history to better accommodate the peculiarities of the computational processes that it did evolve for (Dehaene 2009). Similar considerations address the neural plasticity in blind Braille readers.

5.4.4   Constrained Plasticity in Cognitive and Conceptual Impairments

We turn now to a second type of case that argues in favor of the innate functional specificity of particular brain regions: cognitive and conceptual impairments due to focal brain damage and genetic anomalies. Such impairments argue for constrained plasticity because they show that the brain is unable to compensate for certain difficulties despite ample opportunity for neural reorganization and exposure to relevant features of the environment.

Neurological disorders typically don't affect a single functional system in isolation but rather involve a variety of co-occurring deficits. For example, a stroke may result in damage to functionally distinct yet physiologically neighboring brain areas that are equally dependent on the impeded blood flow. Nonetheless, cognitive deficits are sometimes quite specific. For example, prosopagnosia, a deficit in the ability to recognize faces, may be accompanied by other forms of agnosia but can also occur as a selective deficit in which the impairment is peculiar to faces. In this case, individuals may be unable to recognize altered versions of faces yet have no difficulty in recognizing comparably altered complex objects that aren't faces (Busigny, Graf, et al. 2010; Busigny, Joubert, et al. 2010; see also Rezlescu et al. 2014). This sort of specificity regarding a representational deficit can persist despite many years of exposure to relevant stimuli and a strong vested interest in the subject domain. Individuals who suffer from prosopagnosia, for example, will often have as much difficulty recognizing faces of familiar and emotionally significant people in their lives (parents, children, partners) as they have with strangers. In addition, *category-specific deficits* in semantic memory (memory related to general knowledge) aren't tied to any particular type of task or a given modality (Capitani et al. 2003). A selective deficit for the category of living kinds, for instance, may show up equally in an inability to recognize animals in a picture-naming task and in purely verbal queries about the features of different animals.

The specificity of a category-specific deficit might be explained in a number of different ways. We consider two broad classes of explanation regarding deficits in semantic memory, focusing on the well-studied example of category-specific deficits in the representation of living kinds—for example, patients with significant impairments for animals (elephant, duck, etc.) in contrast with artifacts (pen, key, etc.). The standard empiricist explanation of such cases holds that semantic memory isn't organized in terms of a categorical distinction between the living and the nonliving (or animal vs. artifact), but instead is organized in terms of the properties that exemplars of particular categories possess. Different types of properties are taken to figure more prominently in the representation of categories of living versus nonliving kinds. For instance, on one influential account, visual properties are taken to be more prominent for living kinds, and functional properties for nonliving kinds. If this account were correct, then focal damage to the neural substrate for the representation of visual properties would disproportionately affect living kinds, while damage to the representation of functional properties would disproportionately affect nonliving kinds (Warrington and McCarthy 1983; Farah and McClelland 1991). The nativist approach, in contrast, maintains that semantic memory *is* organized in terms of a categorical distinction between living and nonliving kinds, and that in general there are innately dedicated neural circuits related to a number of fundamental category types with particular evolutionary significance, such as animals, tools, faces, and food (Caramazza and Shelton 1998; Mahon and Caramazza 2009).

As our interest is in the empiricism-nativism debate, a particularly important type of case to consider in evaluating these two different types of explanations is one in which a category-specific deficit results from neural damage or from a genetic disorder that affects early development. Farah and Rabinowitz (2003) documented the case of Adam, who sustained brain damage when he was just one day old. At age sixteen, Adam was tested for his knowledge of living and nonliving kinds, and a significant difference between the two was found. Adam had a severe impairment for knowledge regarding living kinds (responding to testing at chance levels), yet his performance was normal or near normal regarding nonliving kinds. His difficulty with living kinds was also comprehensive in that it affected visual and nonvisual properties alike, while his knowledge of nonliving kinds (both visual and nonvisual) was spared. Consequently, Adam's psychological profile conflicts with the empiricist explanation of category-specific deficits in terms of selective damage to the representation of a given type of property (in this case, to visual properties).

What's more, Adam's case speaks directly to the limitations on neural plasticity in cognitive development. Even though the neural damage occurred very early in development, and Adam had years of experience in infancy and childhood in which other aspects of his psychological development proceeded normally, his brain wasn't able to compensate for the damage it had sustained. As Farah and Rabinowitz put it:

... phrased in terms of Adam's surviving brain tissue, despite its adequacy for acquiring semantic memory about nonliving things, it could not take over the function of semantic memory for living things. This implies that prior to any experience with living and nonliving things, we are destined to represent our knowledge of living and nonliving things with distinct neural substrates. This in turn implies that the distinction between living and nonliving things, and the anatomical localization of knowledge of living things, are specified in the human genome. (408)

In a related study, Farah et al. (2000) examined a different specific representational deficit in the same subject, namely, Adam's difficulty with faces. At the age of sixteen, Adam had the classic profile of prosopagnosia—lesions in the occipitotemporal cortex (bilaterally), with a severe impairment in the ability to recognize faces relative to good, though not perfect, object-recognition abilities.[17] As with the living/nonliving

17. "In everyday life he is unable to recognise faces, whereas his object recognition ability is fully adequate for activities of daily living" (Farah et al. 2000, 122).

distinction, this uneven cognitive profile raises the question of why other neural tissue was unable to compensate for the damaged neural tissue—a striking lack of plasticity—especially given the obvious importance of face recognition in daily life.

Now, there are a number of possible explanations for why the representation of faces might be impaired, just as there are different possible explanations for the selective impairment to the representation of living (or nonliving) kinds. Duchaine et al. (2006) addressed this issue by examining another patient, Edward, who suffered from developmental prosopagnosia. In this study, the researchers took advantage of the opportunity to test on a single subject all of the alternatives to the nativist domain-specific explanation that have appeared in the face-perception literature. Among the empiricist explanations Duchaine and colleagues looked into were the possibilities that Edward suffered from a general difficulty regarding the representation of individuals within a category, a general difficulty with holistic processing, a general difficulty with configural processing (i.e., representing the spacing between features), and a general difficulty in acquiring expertise for object categories. For example, the configural-processing explanation was evaluated by having Edward make same-different judgments for photographs of faces and houses that had been digitally altered. The distance between the eyes or windows was changed, or these features themselves were replaced with similar features in the same relative spacing. In this case, Edward's performance was normal for detecting changes to houses, but three standard deviations below the mean for detecting commensurate changes to faces. Likewise, the expertise hypothesis was evaluated using corresponding face- and body-matching tests, in which the goal was to identify which of two rotated faces or headless bodies matched a target. Here, too, Edward had great difficulty with faces, but his performance with bodies was normal—in fact, he scored in the high end of the normal range for body recognition. These and the results from Duchaine and colleagues' other tests indicate that Edward's difficulty was genuinely face specific, and consequently that there are face-specific developmental mechanisms that may be selectively impaired.

Edward's impairment (unlike Adam's) was most likely the result of a genetic anomaly.[18] Though not all genetic disorders that result in representational deficits are as focused as prosopagnosia—most result in uneven but predictable profiles of spared conceptual abilities and impairments—they can still provide an excellent source of

18. Face-recognition ability is highly heritable. Polk et al. (2007) compared the patterns of neural activity to faces and other stimuli in monozygotic and dizygotic siblings and found that the activity was significantly more similar for monozygotic siblings for faces and places, but not for pseudowords or chairs. Likewise, Wilmer et al. (2010) tested monozygotic and dizygotic twins on a face-memory task and several control tasks for nonface memory. They found that "genetic differences can account for most of the stable variation in face recognition ability in healthy adults" and that this is specific to faces (Wilmer et al. 2010, 5239).

evidence regarding the limits on the brain's plasticity. For example, individuals with Williams syndrome, a rare genetic disorder (Schubert 2009), show severe deficits in certain types of reorientation tasks that rely on geometric representation[19] but relatively spared face-recognition abilities (Lakusta, Dessalegn, and Landau 2010; Bellugi et al. 2000), and they have intact biological motion representation despite other types of motion representation deficits (Jordan et al. 2002; Reiss et al. 2005).

One particularly well-studied and illuminating case is the impairment to mentalizing abilities found in individuals with autism spectrum disorder (ASD).[20] In a classic early investigation, Baron-Cohen, Leslie, and Frith (1985) examined three groups of children on a false-belief task—clinically normal preschool children, children with Down syndrome, and high-functioning children with ASD. In their false-belief task (known as the *Sally-Anne task*), subjects witness a protagonist (Sally) place a marble in her basket, which is then moved (by Anne) to a box while Sally is away from the scene. When Sally returns, subjects are asked where she will look for her marble. Baron-Cohen, Leslie, and Frith found that clinically normal children and Down syndrome children both answered correctly, saying that she will look in the basket (where Sally should falsely think that it is), while children with ASD overwhelmingly gave the incorrect response, saying that she will look in the box (where it actually is). Subsequent work by Leslie and Thaiss (1992) showed that this failure is specific to the understanding of belief and is not part of a general difficulty with understanding representation. Leslie and Thaiss compared clinically normal preschool children with high-functioning children with ASD—this time using both false-belief tasks and structurally similar tasks with photographs and maps. (In a false-photograph task, for example, a Polaroid photo is taken of an object in one location, and the object is moved before the photo is developed. Then the question asked is where the object will be in the photograph.) Leslie and Thaiss found that children with ASD who failed false-belief tasks were able to pass false-photograph or false-map tasks. By contrast, children who didn't have ASD found the false-photograph and false-map tasks more difficult than the false-belief task.

More recent work has found that children with ASD not only have difficulties with elicited-response false-belief tasks (in which they are explicitly asked to respond to a false-belief scenario), but are also unable to anticipate an actor's actions when presented with evidence of the actor's false belief in a spontaneous-response task

19. In a typical reorientation task, subjects in a rectangular room are shown the hiding place for an object and are gently spun around until they become disoriented. They are then asked to locate the object, which requires using the geometry of the room to become reoriented.

20. Heritability studies indicate a strong genetic component in ASD, but it appears that there are numerous different genetic anomalies that give rise to the characteristic impairments in ASD (see, e.g., Huguet, Ey, and Bourgeron 2013).

(Senju et al. 2010). This is not due to a general inability to understand action, as they correctly predict an agent's actions when the agent doesn't have a false belief and are able to correctly attribute goals to an agent even when the agent fails to achieve his or her goal (Carpenter, Pennington, and Rogers 2001). Further, this sort of impairment persists into adulthood. Senju et al. (2009) found that adults with ASD who can correctly answer explicit questions about what an agent with false beliefs will do nonetheless fail to spontaneously anticipate that an agent will act the same way in a live situation. This suggests that they are solving elicited-response tasks using consciously formulated rules that substitute for an intuitive understanding of the source of action. Other work suggests a similar conclusion. Ordinarily people modulate their behavior when they are observed because of the potential effect on their social reputation (e.g., giving more money to a charity in the presence of others than when alone). In contrast, high-functioning adults with ASD don't modulate their behavior in this way (Izuma et al. 2011). Likewise, ordinarily people take into account the absence of negative intentions when formulating a moral judgment pertaining to someone who accidentally causes a negative outcome. Here, too, high-functioning adults with ASD behave differently, treating cases with and without negative intentions equally (Moran et al. 2011).[21] Thus, a convergence of evidence suggests that ASD is associated with a selective representational impairment, one that affects the formation and use of certain mental state concepts but not other concepts of comparable difficulty.

5.4.5   Summary and the Future

We began this section by reexamining the argument against nativist views of concepts that appeals to considerations having to do with neural plasticity and showed that this argument isn't so compelling after all. We then presented a range of different types of evidence for the opposing nativist hypothesis of constrained plasticity:

1. *Evidence from preserved neural structural organization in the absence of relevant environmental input* This was seen in the genetically altered mice, whose brains developed the same structural organization as their normal littermates even though the genetic manipulations disrupted all synaptic transmission, eliminating any possibility for sensory information or feedback to affect development.

2. *Evidence from preserved neural functional specificity despite early sensory deprivation* This was seen, for example, in the preservation of the large-scale functional organization of the visual system in the congenitally blind (the division of labor inherent to the ventral and dorsal visual streams), and in cases where the functional and representational

---

21. The right temporo-parietal junction (rTPJ), which is known to be a critical mentalizing brain area (Koster-Hale and Saxe 2013), is particularly involved in modulating moral judgments according to whether a harm is accidental or intentional (Buckholtz et al. 2008; Young and Saxe 2009). Interestingly, the normal spatially distinct responses within the rTPJ for accidental versus intentional harms is absent in adults with ASD (Koster-Hale et al. 2013).

specificity of particular neural subregions remains the same even though the input is no longer visual (e.g., the assignment of the same neural region to the abstract representation of living kinds).

3. *Evidence from conceptual and cognitive deficits resulting from early focal neurological trauma* In this case, we saw that the brain's plasticity is unable to compensate for such deficits despite ample opportunity for neural reorganization and exposure to relevant features of the environment (e.g., Adam's inability to represent faces or living kinds in adulthood).

4. *Evidence from conceptual and cognitive deficits resulting from genetic anomalies* The brain's plasticity is also unable to compensate for deficits resulting from developmental genetic anomalies (e.g., spatial deficits associated with Williams syndrome and mentalizing deficits associated with autism), despite ample opportunity for neural reorganization and exposure to relevant features of the environment.

We conclude that the neural plasticity of the brain takes the form of *constrained* plasticity—development that is not open-endedly plastic, but instead is highly constrained in ways that suggest important innate biases, predispositions, and limits on structure and function.[22]

We want to reiterate, however, that the case for concept nativism doesn't stand entirely with the argument from neural wiring. Although what has been discovered about the details of neural structure and function strongly supports the nativist viewpoint, equally important are the findings in such fields as animal psychology, developmental psychology, evolutionary psychology, linguistics, and cross-cultural studies. Moreover, the connection between work in these (and other) areas of cognitive science and the argument from neural wiring is a relatively unexplored and potentially rich source of insight about the origins of human concepts. For this reason, we suggest that an exciting and important direction for future work on concepts is to revisit the argument from neural wiring with the aim of looking for a far more extensive body of innate systems of representation, guided by nativist hypotheses that are independently motivated in these other areas of cognitive science.

5.5 Conclusion

Concept nativism holds that a significant number of concepts are either innate or acquired via innate special-purpose acquisition systems. Concept nativism isn't opposed to learning; rather, it offers a distinctive perspective on learning, one that is

22. This list of different types of evidence for the hypothesis of constrained plasticity is not intended to be exhaustive. Though space considerations prohibit an exploration of additional types of evidence, two that are worth mentioning are (1) evidence from twin studies (see, e.g., footnote 18 above) and (2) evidence for parallel neurological structures subserving the same functions across species (see, e.g., Kriegeskorte et al. 2008).

grounded in the idea that much learning takes place only because the mind is innately structured to extract specific types of information from the world and to process this information in particular ways. Concept nativism tells us that we shouldn't assume there is a single general-purpose acquisition mechanism that accounts for the origin of our concepts for animals, artifacts, mental states, individual people, and so on. These and other content domains may well depend on distinct special-purpose innate acquisition systems that are geared toward specific types of content.

The case for concept nativism takes the form of an inference to the best explanation that draws on evidence from a range of disciplines. What we have shown here is that one of the major objections to nativism—its alleged neurological implausibility in the face of neural plasticity—is unfounded. Neural plasticity isn't as flexible and open-ended as nativism's critics have supposed. On the contrary, the plasticity of the brain is highly constrained in a way that argues *for* concept nativism. The brain is not comprised of an equipotential network that is sculpted into differentiated functional units through sensory experience. Rather, the brain is innately differentiated into a complex arrangement of distinct neural systems specialized for processing specific types of information, exactly as concept nativism predicts.

Acknowledgments

We would like to thank Brad Mahon and Gerado Viera for their comments on an earlier draft. Thanks also to Canada's Social Sciences and Humanities Research Council and the UK's Arts and Humanities Research Council for supporting this research.

References

Baillargeon, R., R. M. Scott, and Z. He. 2010. False-belief understanding in infants. *Trends in Cognitive Sciences* 14 (3): 110–118.

Baron-Cohen, S., A. M. Leslie, and U. Frith. 1985. Does the autistic child have a "theory of mind"? *Cognition* 21 (1): 37–46.

Bedny, M., A. Pascual-Leone, and R. R. Saxe. 2009. Growing up blind does not change the neural bases of theory of mind. *Proceedings of the National Academy of Sciences of the United States of America* 106 (27): 11312–11317.

Bellugi, U., L. Lichtenberger, W. Jones, Z. Lai, and M. St. George. 2000. I. The neurocognitive profile of Williams syndrome: A complex pattern of strengths and weaknesses. *Journal of Cognitive Neuroscience* 12 (supplement 1): 7–29.

Boyd, R., and P. Richerson. 1985. *Culture and the Evolutionary Process*. Chicago: University of Chicago Press.

Bregman, A. S., and S. Pinker. 1978. Auditory streaming and the building of timbre. *Canadian Journal of Psychology* 32 (1): 19–31.

Buckholtz, J. W., C. L. Asplund, P. E. Dux, D. H. Zald, J. C. Gore, O. D. Jones, and R. Marois. 2008. The neural correlates of third-party punishment. *Neuron* 60 (5): 930–940.

Buller, D. J., and V. Hardcastle. 2000. Evolutionary psychology, meet developmental neurobiology: Against promiscuous modularity. *Brain and Mind* 1 (3): 307–325.

Busigny, T., M. Graf, E. N. Mayer, and B. Rossion. 2010. Acquired prosopagnosia as a face-specific disorder: Ruling out the general visual similarity account. *Neuropsychologia* 48 (7): 2051–2067.

Busigny, T., S. Joubert, O. Felician, M. Ceccaldi, and B. Rossion. 2010. Holistic perception of the individual face is specific and necessary: Evidence from an extensive case study of acquired prosopagnosia. *Neuropsychologia* 48 (14): 4057–4092.

Capitani, E., M. Laiacona, B. Z. Mahon, and A. Caramazza. 2003. What are the facts of category-specific deficits? A critical review of the clinical evidence. *Cognitive Neuropsychology* 20:213–261.

Caramazza, A., and J. R. Shelton. 1998. Domain-specific knowledge systems in the brain: The animate-inanimate distinction. *Journal of Cognitive Neuroscience* 10:1–34.

Carpenter, M., B. F. Pennington, and S. J. Rogers. 2001. Understanding of others' intentions in children with autism. *Journal of Autism and Developmental Disorders* 31 (6): 589–599.

Chomsky, N. 1991. Linguistics and cognitive science: Problems and mysteries. In *The Chomskyan Turn*, ed. A. Kasher, 26–53. Oxford: Blackwell.

Cohen, L. G., P. Celnik, A. Pascual-Leone, B. Corwell, L. Faiz, J. Dambrosia, M. Honda, et al. 1997. Functional relevance of cross-modal plasticity in blind humans. *Nature* 389 (6647): 180–183.

Csibra, G., and G. Gergely. 2011. Natural pedagogy as evolutionary adaptation. *Philosophical Transactions of the Royal Society of London: Series B, Biological Sciences* 366:1149–1157.

Curtiss, S., and S. de Bode. 2003. How normal is grammatical development in the right hemisphere following hemispherectomy? The root infinitive stage and beyond. *Brain and Language* 86 (2): 193–206.

Curtiss, S., and J. Schaeffer. 2005. Syntactic development in children with hemispherectomy: The I-, D-, and C-systems. *Brain and Language* 94 (2): 147–166.

Danelli, L., G. Cossu, M. Berlingeri, G. Bottini, M. Sberna, and E. Paulesu. 2013. Is a lone right hemisphere enough? Neurolinguistic architecture in a case with a very early left hemispherectomy. *Neurocase* 19 (3): 209–231.

Dehaene, S. 2009. *Reading in the Brain*. New York: Viking.

Dehaene, S., and L. Cohen. 2011. The unique role of the visual word form area in reading. *Trends in Cognitive Sciences* 15 (6): 254–262.

Duchaine, B. C., G. Yovel, E. J. Butterworth, and K. Nakayama. 2006. Prosopagnosia as an impairment to face-specific mechanisms: Elimination of the alternative hypotheses in a developmental case. *Cognitive Neuropsychology* 23 (5): 714–747.

Elman, J. L., E. A. Bates, M. H. Johnson, A. Karmiloff-Smith, D. Parisi, and K. Plunkett. 1996. *Rethinking Innateness: A Connectionist Perspective on Development.* Cambridge, MA: MIT Press.

Farah, M. J., and J. L. McClelland. 1991. A computational model of semantic memory impairment: Modality specificity and emergent category specificity. *Journal of Experimental Psychology: General* 120 (4): 339–357.

Farah, M. J., and C. Rabinowitz. 2003. Genetic and environmental influences on the organisation of semantic memory in the brain: Is "living things" an innate category? *Cognitive Neuropsychology* 20 (3–6): 401–408.

Farah, M. J., C. Rabinowitz, G. E. Quinn, and G. T. Liu. 2000. Early commitment of neural substrates for face recognition. *Cognitive Neuropsychology* 17 (1–3): 117–123.

Fedorenko, E., M. K. Behr, and N. Kanwisher. 2011. Functional specificity for high-level linguistic processing in the human brain. *Proceedings of the National Academy of Sciences of the United States of America* 108 (39): 16428–16433.

Fodor, J. A. 1975. *The Language of Thought.* Tomas Y. Crowell.

Fodor, J. A. 1981. The present status of the innateness controversy. In *Representations: Philosophical Essays on the Foundations of Cognitive Science.* Cambridge, MA: MIT Press.

Fodor, J. 1998. *Concepts: Where Cognitive Science Went Wrong.* Oxford: Oxford University Press.

Fodor, J. A. 2008. *LOT2: The Language of Thought Revisited.* Oxford: Oxford University Press.

Gazzaniga, M. S., R. B. Irvy, and G. R. Mangun. 2009. *Cognitive Neuroscience: The Biology of the Mind.* 3rd ed. New York: Norton.

Huguet, G., E. Ey, and T. Bourgeron. 2013. The genetic landscapes of autism spectrum disorders. *Annual Review of Genomics and Human Genetics* 14 (1): 191–213.

Izuma, K., K. Matsumoto, C. F. Camerer, and R. Adolphs. 2011. Insensitivity to social reputation in autism. *Proceedings of the National Academy of Sciences of the United States of America* 108 (42): 17302–17307.

Jordan, H., J. E. Reiss, J. E. Hoffman, and B. Landau. 2002. Intact perception of biological motion in the face of profound spatial deficits: Williams syndrome. *Psychological Science* 13 (2): 162–167.

Koster-Hale, J., and R. Saxe. 2013. Functional neuroimaging of theory of mind. In *Understanding Other Minds*, 3rd ed., ed. S. Baron-Cohen, M. Lombardo, and H. Tager-Flusberg, 132–163. Oxford University Press.

Koster-Hale, J., R. Saxe, J. Dungan, and L. L. Young. 2013. Decoding moral judgments from neural representations of intentions. *Proceedings of the National Academy of Sciences of the United States of America* 110 (14): 5648–5653.

Kovács, Á. M., E. Téglás, and A. D. Endress. 2010. The social sense: Susceptibility to others' beliefs in human infants and adults. *Science* 330 (6012): 1830–1834.

Kriegeskorte, N., M. Mur, D. A. Ruff, R. Kiani, J. Bodurka, H. Esteky, K. Tanaka, and P. A. Bandettini. 2008. Matching categorical object representations in inferior temporal cortex of man and monkey. *Neuron* 60 (6): 1126–1141.

Lakusta, L., B. Dessalegn, and B. Landau. 2010. Impaired geometric reorientation caused by genetic defect. *Proceedings of the National Academy of Sciences of the United States of America* 107 (7): 2813–2817.

Laurence, S., and E. Margolis. 2002. Radical concept nativism. *Cognition* 86: 25–55.

Laurence, S., and E. Margolis. Unpublished ms. *Building Blocks of Thought.*

Leslie, A. M., and L. Thaiss. 1992. Domain specificity in conceptual development: Neuropsychological evidence from autism. *Cognition* 43 (3): 225–251.

Lingnau, A., L. Strnad, C. He, S. Fabbri, Z. Han, Y. Bi, and A. Caramazza. 2014. Cross-modal plasticity preserves functional specialization in posterior parietal cortex. *Cerebral Cortex* 24:541–549.

Lomber, S. G., M. A. Meredith, and A. Kral. 2010. Cross-modal plasticity in specific auditory cortices underlies visual compensations in the deaf. *Nature Neuroscience* 13 (11): 1421–1427.

Luo, Y. 2011. Do 10-month-old infants understand others' false beliefs? *Cognition* 121 (3): 289–298.

Mahon, B. Z., S. Anzellotti, J. Schwarzbach, M. Zampini, and A. Caramazza. 2009. Category-specific organization in the human brain does not require visual experience. *Neuron* 63 (3): 397–405.

Mahon, B. Z., and A. Caramazza. 2009. Concepts and categories: A cognitive neuropsychological perspective. *Annual Review of Psychology* 60 (1): 27–51.

Majewska, A. K., and M. Sur. 2006. Plasticity and specificity of cortical processing networks. *Trends in Neurosciences* 29 (6): 323–329.

Marcus, G. 2004. *The Birth of the Mind: How a Tiny Number of Genes Creates the Complexities of Human Thought.* New York: Basic Books.

Moran, J. M., L. L. Young, R. Saxe, S. M. Lee, D. O'Young, P. L. Mavros, and J. D. Gabrieli. 2011. Impaired theory of mind for moral judgment in high-functioning autism. *Proceedings of the National Academy of Sciences of the United States of America* 108 (7): 2688–2692.

Onishi, K. H., and R. Baillargeon. 2005. Do 15-month-old infants understand false beliefs? *Science* 308:255–258.

Pascual-Leone, A., and R. Hamilton. 2001. The metamodal organization of the brain. *Progress in Brain Research* 134:427–445.

Peterson, C. C., J. L. Peterson, and J. Webb. 2000. Factors influencing the development of a theory of mind in blind children. *British Journal of Developmental Psychology* 18 (3): 431–447.

Pinker, S. 2002. *The Blank Slate: The Modern Denial of Human Nature*. New York: Penguin.

Pinker, S. 2007. *The Stuff of Thought*. New York: Viking.

Polk, T. A., J. Park, M. R. Smith, and D. C. Park. 2007. Nature versus nurture in ventral visual cortex: A functional magnetic resonance imaging study of twins. *Journal of Neuroscience* 27: 13921–13925.

Prinz, J. 2005. The return of concept empiricism. In *Handbook of Categorization in Cognitive Science*, ed. H. Cohen and C. Lefebvre, 679–695. Amsterdam; Boston: Elsevier Science.

Prinz, J. 2012. *Beyond Human Nature: How Culture and Experience Shapes Our Lives*. London: Allen Lane.

Quartz, S. R. 2003. Innateness and the brain. *Biology and Philosophy* 18 (1): 13–40.

Quine, W. V. O. 1969. Linguistics and philosophy. In *Language and Philosophy: A Symposium*, ed. S. Hook, 95–98. New York: NYU Press.

Reiss, J. E., J. E. Hoffman, and B. Landau. 2005. Motion processing specialization in Williams syndrome. *Vision Research* 45 (27): 3379–3390.

Renier, L. A., I. Anurova, A. G. De Volder, S. Carlson, J. VanMeter, and J. P. Rauschecker. 2010. Preserved functional specialization for spatial processing in the middle occipital gyrus of the early blind. *Neuron* 68 (1): 138–148.

Rezlescu, C., J. J. S. Barton, D. Pitcher, and B. Duchaine. 2014. Normal acquisition of expertise with greebles in two cases of acquired prosopagnosia. *Proceedings of the National Academy of Sciences* 111 (14): 5123–5128.

Rogers, T. T., J. Hocking, A. Mechelli, K. Patterson, and C. Price. 2005. Fusiform activation to animals is driven by the process, not the stimulus. *Journal of Cognitive Neuroscience* 17 (3): 434–445.

Rogers, T. T., and J. L. McClelland. 2004. *Semantic Cognition: A Parallel Distributed Processing Approach*. Cambridge, MA: MIT Press.

Sadato, N., A. Pascual-Leone, J. Grafman, V. Ibañez, M. P. Deiber, G. Dold, and M. Hallett. 1996. Activation of the primary visual cortex by Braille reading in blind subjects. *Nature* 380: 526–528.

Schubert, C. 2009. The genomic basis of the Williams-Beuren syndrome. *Cellular and Molecular Life Sciences* 66 (7): 1178–1197.

Senju, A., V. Southgate, Y. Miura, T. Matsui, T. Hasegawa, Y. Tojo, H. Osanai, and G. Csibra. 2010. Absence of spontaneous action anticipation by false belief attribution in children with autism spectrum disorder. *Development and Psychopathology* 22 (2): 353.

Senju, A., V. Southgate, S. White, and U. Frith. 2009. Mindblind eyes: An absence of spontaneous theory of mind in Asperger syndrome. *Science* 325 (5942): 883–885.

Sharma, J., A. Angelucci, and M. Sur. 2000. Induction of visual orientation modules in auditory cortex. *Nature* 404 (6780): 841–847.

Sripada, C. S., and S. Stich. 2006. A framework for the psychology of norms. In *The Innate Mind: Culture and Cognition*, ed. P. Caruthers, S. Laurence, and S. Stich, 280–301. Oxford: Oxford University Press.

Striem-Amit, E., O. Dakwar, L. Reich, and A. Amedi. 2012. The large-scale organization of "visual" streams emerges without visual experience. *Cerebral Cortex* 22 (7): 1698–1709.

Sur, M. 1988. Visual plasticity in the auditory pathway: Visual inputs induced into auditory thalamus and cortex illustrate principles of adaptive organization in sensory systems. In *Dynamic Interactions in Neural Networks: Models and Data*, ed. M. A. Arbib and S.-i. Amari, 35–51. New York: Springer-Verlag.

Surian, L., S. Caldi, and D. Sperber. 2007. Attribution of beliefs by 13-month-old infants. *Psychological Science* 18 (7): 580–586.

Verhage, M., A. S. Maia, J. J. Plomp, A. B. Brussaard, J. H. Heeroma, H. Vermeer, R. F. Toonen, et al. 2000. Synaptic assembly of the brain in the absence of neurotransmitter secretion. *Science* 287 (5454): 864–869.

von Melchner, L., S. L. Pallas, and M. Sur. 2000. Visual behaviour mediated by retinal projections directed to the auditory pathway. *Nature* 404:871–876.

Warrington, E. K., and R. A. McCarthy. 1983. Category specific access dysphasia. *Brain* 106:859–878.

Wilmer, J. B., L. Germine, C. F. Chabris, G. Chatterjee, M. Williams, E. Loken, K. Nakayama, and B. Duchaine. 2010. Human face recognition ability is specific and highly heritable. *Proceedings of the National Academy of Sciences of the United States of America* 107 (11): 5238–5241.

Wolbers, T., P. Zahorik, and N. A. Giudice. 2011. Decoding the direction of auditory motion in blind humans. *NeuroImage* 56 (2): 681–687.

Young, L., and R. Saxe. 2009. Innocent intentions: A correlation between forgiveness for accidental harm and neural activity. *Neuropsychologia* 47 (10): 2065–2072.

III   Concepts and Evolution

6 The Evolution of Conceptual Design

H. Clark Barrett

6.1 Introduction

The repertoire of concepts that a typical human adult possesses is immense. Depending on how you count them (a matter of debate), any of us easily has thousands of concepts, and probably more like hundreds of thousands, or millions. There are concepts that all of us probably share at least in some way, such as the concepts PERSON, FOOD, MOTHER, WATER, and EYE. These concepts are not necessarily carbon-copy identical in everyone who possesses them; an ophthalmologist's concept EYE, for example, may differ substantially from that of a nonexpert. Moreover, there may be substantial diversity across individuals, cultures, times, and places in the concepts we possess. Among the Shuar of Ecuador, many adults possess the concept ARUTAM, a spirit capable of bestowing power on individuals under the hallucinatory effects of MAIKUA, a plant in the nightshade family. Academic biologists possess concepts like INTRON, CLADE, and ORTHOLOG. And our minds are populated by a vast diversity of idiosyncratic concepts of people, places, events, objects, and practices, from BLACK SABBATH to BUNDT CAKE.

How are we to make sense of this? The concept CONCEPT, of course, is prescientific in origin, and as such, there is no particular reason to expect it to pick out anything real in the world, anything like a natural kind. Indeed, some have argued that the concept CONCEPT is sufficiently muddled as to be not worth keeping (Machery 2009). But as it happens, many scholars continue to use the concept CONCEPT in a scientific context—particularly in philosophy, psychology, and neuroscience (Barsalou 1999, 2005; Caramazza and Mahon 2003; Laurence and Margolis 1999; Carey 2009). If we want a scientific theory of concepts, then, we will have to ask what concepts are, what they do, how we come to have them, and why. And, given that humans are living organisms shaped by the evolutionary process, these are fundamentally biological questions. From an evolutionary point of view, why do organisms have concepts, what role do they play in survival and reproduction, and how does natural selection shape the brain machinery that causes us to have the conceptual repertoires that we, or any species for that matter, come to possess?

One popular approach to understanding concepts from a biological point of view is to start with innateness. Innateness has many definitions in the literature but generally refers to concepts or aspects of concepts that are not acquired via psychological processes such as learning (Carey 2009; Samuels 2002; Spelke and Kinzler 2009). Although innate concepts need not be present at birth, they are usually regarded as remaining fixed or unchanging once they develop, and as developing the same way in everyone, except for cases of developmental disorder or brain damage. Concepts that are acquired or that change over the lifespan as a result of learning or other processes of feedback from the environment or experience are therefore not regarded as innate—or at least, not the altered forms they take after learning has occurred. The innateness approach to concepts, then, attempts to ask what kernels of unlearned knowledge are present in infancy that both continue through adulthood—often called core knowledge—and that allow new concepts to be acquired (Carey 2009; Gopnik and Meltzoff 1997).

Without denying the importance of the so-called starting state in infancy (or more properly, in the zygote), here I would like to start from somewhere else: the developed conceptual phenotype. From a biological point of view, the phenotype is what matters for fitness. This is because it is the phenotype that interacts with the world in the service of survival and reproduction. What I mean by phenotype, in this case, is the array of concepts that humans actually possess and deploy at a given point in their lifespan—whether innate or learned—that make a difference in life, death, and reproduction at that moment. Thus, rather than focusing exclusively on the moment of birth or the first year of infancy—or even on just those aspects of conceptual structure that are identical across all individuals in adulthood—it is worth looking at the full scope and diversity of concepts that humans come to possess, and to ask how this array of concepts comes about because of natural selection acting on the developmental systems that build our conceptual repertoires, both the parts that are universal and the parts that vary. Importantly, this involves thinking about developed conceptual phenotypes as targets of selection: outcomes that natural selection has acted on, thereby shaping the developmental systems that build them (Barrett 2006, 2007, 2015). As a consequence, these developmental systems themselves have designs. The resulting developmental designs are likely to be more complex than simply innate starting states plus general-purpose learning rules, because it is the developmental outcomes, not just the beginnings, that they have been selected to produce. Over evolutionary time this leads to processes akin to guided learning toward designed targets: the full palette of our mature conceptual repertoires, both universal and idiosyncratic.

This is what I will call the *conceptual design* approach. Here I am using the term *design* in its evolutionary sense, as in the evolved design of wings, lungs, the immune system, stereoscopic vision, and the evolved developmental systems that build them (Carroll, Grenier, and Weatherbee 2005). The central premise of this approach is that concepts and the psychological machinery that builds them have been designed, or shaped, by the evolutionary process to carry out certain functions; they exist to help us navigate and act in the world in the service of survival and reproduction, or fitness. By taking an adaptationist, or engineering, approach to conceptual design—akin to the approach taken by functional morphologists who study the design of animal limbs, jaws, lungs, and other organs—we can ask, How do we expect natural selection to shape the developmental machinery that allows us to acquire concepts, even concepts that have a substantial or entirely learned component? Innateness may well be important for thinking about such systems, but equally important will be thinking about the design of developmental outcomes: conceptual phenotypes. Because these phenotypes determine fitness—whether learned or innate—natural selection will shape whatever heritable developmental resources influence their design.

In this chapter I make a case for the conceptual design approach and its potential for an evolutionary theory of concepts. To begin, I consider the question of what concepts are, or what we want the term *concept* to mean, in an evolutionary sense. Next, I present the conceptual design approach and the theoretical commitments it entails. The bulk of the chapter then unpacks how this approach can be used to build theories of conceptual architecture and the developmental machinery that shapes it, using specific examples to illustrate the approach and focusing in particular on architecture organized around conceptual types. Finally, I consider the implications of the conceptual design perspective for understanding our ability to acquire evolutionarily novel concepts. My aim is to show how focusing on evolved design can orient the study of concepts toward new directions that are consistent with the evolutionary developmental or evo-devo turn in contemporary biology.

6.2   What Do We Want the Term *Concept* to Mean?

For a technical term to be of use, it is important for it to have a clear and unambiguous referent. In the case of the concept CONCEPT, this has been a problem. Like many concepts in the cognitive sciences, it has both folk and technical meanings (Stich 1983). As a result, there is not general agreement on what the concept CONCEPT means, from a technical point of view, and diverse theories of concepts exist (see Laurence and Margolis 1999; Machery 2009; Murphy 2002).

My intention here is neither to reject nor endorse any particular theory of what concepts are, but rather, to begin with a working definition of concepts that is broad enough to capture the range of possibilities for what concepts might be, while also being specific enough to target those functions that most theorists generally hold concepts to play in mental activity. In addition, our notion of concepts must be biologically grounded, allowing us to ask what functions concepts play in the life of organisms, and therefore, how evolutionary processes shape them. This, in turn, implies two things we'd like in our theory of concepts. First, it should be broad enough to include the concepts and conceptual machinery of nonhuman animals.[1] Second, it should be a functionalist notion of concepts—that is, a notion of concepts as information structures that play a causal role in mental activity and behavior and not, for example, a notion of concepts as *abstracta* that exist outside the mind (Margolis and Laurence 2007).

Among the many functions, or roles, that concepts are held to play in mental life, one can subsume most of them into two general classes of function, which I will call *generalization* and *inference* (Murphy 2002).[2] By *generalization* I am referring to the grouping, or categorization, function of concepts: the concept cow, for example, lumps together all cows for the purpose of conceptual analysis (this implies additional, subsidiary functions, such as an identification function: group members must be identified as group members in order to group them). By *inference* I am referring to the many informationally productive, or generative, things that can be done by grouping things together conceptually. For example, one frequently discussed kind of inference enabled by concepts is inductive inference, which occurs when I apply knowledge learned from past encounters with cows to a new encounter with a particular cow that I have never encountered before; for example, guessing that a newly encountered cow is able to moo, even though I have not yet observed it doing so. Concepts also enable learning, and in particular, learning that is inferential. For example, if I observe a squirrel making a predator alarm call and did not previously know that squirrels could make such calls, I may now generalize this observation to all squirrels. I've thus learned something about squirrels in general from observing a particular squirrel. Arguably, this would not be possible—or at least, the learning process would be a different one— if I did not have the concept squirrel (see chapter 22).

For those familiar with the large literature on concepts, this reduction of conceptual functions to two basic types might seem excessively simplistic.[3] However, it satisfies

---

1. This is not meant to preclude the possibility that humans can have *types* of concepts that other animals can't or don't have. Indeed, this is almost certainly true, and the type-based analysis that I will be developing here allows for the possibility of conceptual types that are unique to taxa. However, this approach does rule out the position, favored by some, that concepts are unique to humans (e.g., that they are intrinsically language based). Although that might be a defensible approach, it would restrict evolutionary analysis to a much smaller set of phenomena than entertained here and would, among other things, preclude a comparative approach to the evolution of concepts and conceptual design.

2. Technically, everything referred to below is a form of inference. These can be regarded as subtypes that are often distinguished in the literature.

3. For example, it leaves out some frequently discussed functions of concepts, such as the role they play in linguistic reference and communication. We will not preclude the possibility that concepts may play additional roles, but functions that apply only to some subset of concepts (e.g., lexicalized ones) should not be considered necessary features of concepts in general.

our basic objectives of capturing much if not most of what concepts are invoked to explain in the psychological literature, while being sufficiently general as to not pre-judge exactly how concepts might be instantiated or organized in animal minds, or how they are distributed across species. Indeed, we would like those kinds of details to *emerge* from an evolutionary theory of concepts, rather than being built into it. The precise nature of the generalization and inference roles that particular concepts play is, therefore, just what we want to explore from an evolutionary point of view.

A variety of basic questions are raised by an evolutionary perspective on concepts. Perhaps the most basic are these two: Why do we have concepts at all, and why do we have the ones that we do? To the extent that concepts and the mental machinery that produces them are adaptations—the products of natural selection—the answers will have to do with the precise nature of the functions that concepts play, which will entail investigating the basic functions of generalization and inference in further detail. First, however, let's consider some specific examples of concepts, to get an idea of the scope of the phenomena at hand.

The literature on concepts tends to focus on some well-worn examples. Perhaps the most common are concepts of animal taxa, which include species concepts, such as TIGER, and higher-level taxa, such as BIRD. Other common examples are FRUIT, VEGETABLE, FURNITURE, and GAME—concepts whose properties call into question the *classical* view of concepts as based on definitions, or sets of necessary and sufficient features (Rosch 1999; Smith and Medin 1981). There are also so-called natural kind concepts, which include animal taxa like TIGER as well as naturally occurring categories of object or sub-stance, such as WATER and GOLD (Keil 1992). Then there are concepts of individuals, such as individual people (e.g., SHAKESPEARE, ALBERT EINSTEIN) and individual objects (THE MORNING STAR, THE MOON, THE SPHINX). Already, this grab bag of concepts spans a broad range and has spurred many debates about the nature of concepts. Perhaps most importantly, it raises the question of whether concepts come in *kinds* or *types*. For example, are con-cepts of natural kinds, like TIGER and GOLD, different from concepts of artifact kinds, like FURNITURE? Are concepts of individuals, like SHAKESPEARE, different from concepts of groups of things, like FRUIT? And what is the inventory of types of concepts the mind contains, or can contain? The list above, for example, focuses heavily on physical objects and substances (BIRD, VEGETABLE, GOLD), but clearly we can have non-object-based concepts as well, such as our concepts JUSTICE, ANGER, and INTEGRAL.

How are concepts shared—or not—across species? Many basic concepts, such as concepts of objects, causation, and agency, could very well be shared across species (Barsalou 2005; Carey 2009). Some concepts clearly only humans have, or can have—INTEGRAL, for example, or perhaps the concept FALSE BELIEF (Call and Tomasello 2008). And concepts that are shared, at some level, might be different in the details. Although rats appear to have an elementary understanding of causation, it's not necessarily identical to ours (Blaisdell et al. 2006). Tigers could and probably do have a concept of tigers, which could share some features with our concept TIGER but presumably has others that ours doesn't. For example, the TIGER concept of tigers might include elements of smell, or behavioral signals, that most human tokens of the concept TIGER don't have. Within species, perhaps especially in humans, there are likely to be individual differences in the content of concepts, with biologists, tiger hunters, and four-year-old children having TIGER concepts that probably overlap in some ways and differ in others. And it's likely that other animals have concepts that we don't—for example, concepts used by animals that navigate by the stars or magnetic fields.

A theory of conceptual design will need to be able to account for the repertoire of concepts that species are able to acquire, as well as how these come to be distributed with and across taxa via evolutionary processes of descent with modification. It will also need to be able to account for the particulars of specific conceptual types, such as the distinction between natural and artifact kinds—if, of course, these prove to be legitimately different conceptual types in the human repertoire. And finally, it will need to be able to account for things such as the creation and transmission of evolutionarily novel concepts, such as INTEGRAL and QUARK, in species (notably us) that are able to generate such novelties.

6.3   The Conceptual Design Approach

Natural selection shapes traits because of their effects on survival and reproduction (fitness). Therefore, natural selection shapes concepts and the developmental machinery that acquires them only (1) to the extent that concepts and conceptual machinery are parts of organisms' phenotypes and (2) to the extent that they play a role in helping organisms survive and reproduce. Consideration (1) rules out the idea of concepts as *abstracta*—we can only be considering concepts as they are actually instantiated in neural tissue (whatever that instantiation might be). Consideration (2) suggests that the criteria determining which conceptual abilities persist over evolutionary time must be rooted in fitness and not some other currency such as truth value. This does not mean that truth value cannot play a role in the evolution of concepts, but it does mean that truth values that do not affect fitness are evolutionarily neutral and thus not available to the designing force of natural selection. It also means that aspects of concepts that are *not* true can be retained, if they have a positive effect on fitness. For example, it is conceivable that concepts serving a fitness-promoting social role, such as some religious concepts and social norms, might be favored by natural selection even if certain aspects of their content are false.

However, the considerations above do *not* mean that we should leap straight from fitness to concepts themselves. Natural selection shapes the developmental machinery that allows us to acquire concepts but is not necessarily responsible for the details of every conceptual *token* we possess, any more than natural selection acting on the visual system is responsible for every detail of the specific visual representation of the

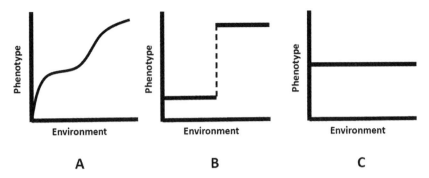

Figure 6.1
Reaction norms represent mapping functions between developmental environments and phenotypic outcomes (horizontal and vertical axes represent values of environmental and phenotypic parameters, respectively). (A) A reaction norm in which phenotypic outcomes are a continuous, smooth function of environmental state. (B) A step function in which the phenotype takes on one of two discrete values depending on environment. (C) A canalized reaction norm: only one phenotype develops, regardless of environment.

computer monitor I'm currently looking at. The machinery of conceptual development evolved because the concepts it enabled our ancestors to acquire proved useful, but it may also enable the acquisition of useless, or even fitness-detrimental, concepts (Tooby and Cosmides 1990). Importantly, however, it is only by thinking about how natural selection shaped the design of this machinery that we can build proper theories of the conceptual repertoires that we are able to develop, even evolutionarily novel ones. This idea—that evolution shapes developmental systems, which in turn build the conceptual phenotype that each of us comes to possess as adults—is the key to the conceptual design approach (Barrett 2006, 2007).

Concept-building machinery can be seen as instantiating developmental input-output functions, mapping between developmental inputs and phenotypic outcomes. In biology these are known as *reaction norms* (Barrett 2012, 2015; Schlichting and Pigliucci 1998) (see figure 6.1). Innate concepts are examples of flat (or canalized) reaction norms, in which the same phenotype develops in everyone regardless of developmental circumstance (barring extreme cases such as developmental disability).[4] Domain-general learning rules can be thought of as reaction norms in which the scope of phenotypic traits affected is very broad. But many other kinds of reaction norms are possible as well.

To develop theories of the reaction norms that build conceptual phenotypes, we must start by considering what functions concepts play, and therefore what form,

---

4. There is debate about whether canalization is equivalent to innateness as conceptualized by most psychologists (Ariew 1996; Griffiths and Machery 2008). The point here is that developmental universality can be seen as an example of a flat reaction norm.

or design, they can be expected to take. Ultimately, only by the signature that concepts leave in behavior, and therefore in survival and reproduction, can natural selection shape them. The roles that concepts play in the mental pathways that lead to behavioral decisions can be diverse and complex, however, involving the interplay of many systems, including perception, learning, inference, judgment, decision making, and motor control. Moreover, not all concepts or conceptual types need play the same or similar roles in each of these systems, meaning that different conceptual types may have very different design features.

Below I propose a tentative list of conceptual functions that can serve as a starting point for thinking about conceptual design features. First, however, let me start with an example of a conceptual type that can serve as a springboard for this discussion: FOOD.

There may be an overarching general concept FOOD that animals possess, but most animals, including humans, are presumably also able to develop concepts of specific foods. In the terminology I will be using here, *types* and *tokens* are relative terms referring to higher and lower levels in a hierarchy, respectively. Thus, food concepts can be thought of as a type of concept (without, for the moment, prejudging the issue of whether there has been selection for machinery specifically designed to acquire this conceptual type). Within the general type, we can acquire specific tokens: FRUIT, VEGETABLE, and MEAT might be tokens of food concepts nested within the general type of FOOD. And there may be tokens nested within these as well: for example, APPLE and ORANGE as tokens of the type FRUIT. Notice that this type/token terminology is relative and does not necessarily privilege one level of the hierarchy as being *the* type. Some scholars have suggested that there is a *basic* level in the conceptual hierarchy that is most privileged or salient for the purposes of learning and inference (e.g., Rosch 1999). This may indeed prove to be the case for some conceptual systems. Rather than assuming it, we will leave this possibility open as one potential design feature that (some) conceptual systems might possess.

Why do organisms have food concepts? Recall the two basic functions that I mentioned above, generalization and inference. Let us assume for the moment that squirrels have a concept NUT, that hummingbirds have a concept NECTAR, and that bears have a concept BERRY.[5] What good do these concepts do for these animals? In terms of

---

5. One could argue, again, that these animals do not have these "concepts" but have only behavioral reactions to certain stimuli. From the functionalist perspective I'm adopting here, I'm not considering this option to be distinct from the proposal that squirrels have a concept NUT, if squirrels generalize in some way across instances of the category of nuts (generalization), and if they show common patterns of learning, inference, and behavior toward members of the category (inference). Some accounts might want more for NUT to count as a concept, and indeed, some species may have additional conceptual functions regarding nuts than squirrels do (e.g., a word for nuts, the ability to talk about them). Here, we will just consider these to be additional possible features or functions of concepts, which a given species might or might not have.

generalization, these concepts allow the animal to group objects (in this case) together for the purposes of learning, inference, decision making, and behavior. This grouping function can only work if there is an identification process—in this case perceptual, though not necessarily for all concepts—that allows the squirrel, for example, to recognize an individual nut as a nut. In most cases, the identification mechanism(s) must be updatable by experience; for example, the squirrel might learn via tasting that a new, perhaps perceptually distinct item has nutlike properties of taste and nutrition and should be grouped with other nuts.

Once an item has been identified as a nut, this allows various conceptual resources associated with nuts to be accessed—what we might call *activating* the concept NUT (the nut is recognized as a nut, tagging the percept with the mental symbol for nuts). Whether all the information associated with nuts should be regarded as *part* of the concept is a question, perhaps semantic. For now we'll entertain that concepts might be complex, consisting of interacting information stores in the brain that might, in some cases, be differentially activated in different circumstances (for example, not everything that is part of your concept GEORGE WASHINGTON might be activated when you see his face on a dollar bill, but we could still consider various facts that don't come immediately to mind as part of your GEORGE WASHINGTON concept).

The various inferential or informationally generative processes that occur when the squirrel's NUT concept is activated could be diverse. Let us use this example to develop an initial list of possible conceptual functions, keeping in mind that this list might not be exhaustive, and that different concepts might exhibit different combinations of functions.

Learning The concept NUT could play a role in learning in several ways. Learned information about nuts, such as their nutritional values, where to find them, and how to handle them once encountered, could be stored as part of the NUT concept, to be activated upon future encounters with nuts. Older information about nuts could also be modified, that is, refinement of perceptual identification criteria upon encounter with nutlike objects that are not nuts. Conceptual knowledge about nuts could also play a role in learning about things related to nuts—for example, if we observe a raccoon eating nuts, we might update our knowledge of raccoons to include a taste for nuts.

Inductive prediction Having a concept NUT allows knowledge learned from prior encounters with nuts to be applied to new encounters. For example, if a newly encountered exemplar satisfies the criteria for being identified as a nut, the squirrel might assume this new object is safe and even desirable to eat.

Reasoning Here I mean *reasoning* in the broadest sense to include various ways of combining representations via rules to lead to new inferences. A squirrel that had object constancy, for example, might infer that a nut that rolls into a hole still exists out of sight (Baillargeon 1994; Carey 2009). This might prompt the squirrel to begin digging to find the nut that it can no longer see. In humans, of course, concepts play a role in many reasoning processes that probably do not exist in other animals.

Decision making Concepts would not exist if not for their role in decision making. For example, knowledge of how nuts are distributed in the environment, and where they can be found, can play a role in the squirrel's foraging decisions. In optimal foraging theory, information about the nutritional value of food items is combined with representations of their distribution in the environment—how many, for example, are likely to be encountered in a resource patch such as a tree—to shape animals' decisions about whether to continue foraging in the same patch or to switch patches (Charnov 1976; Smith 1983).

Action Ultimately, decisions must manifest in action to have an effect on fitness. Concepts can also play a role in how actions are executed. For example, knowledge of how to access the nut inside of a nutshell can play a role in the squirrel's choice of actions to open the nut. Indeed, some concepts may be stored partly in the form of motor representations, or have action representations associated with them (Barsalou 1999). In the case of some kinds of objects, such as human-made tools, action representations may be a key and possibly necessary part of the concept (Johnson-Frey 2004).

Communication One way in which concepts can play a role in communication is if they are lexicalized, or in some way expressed symbolically through gestures or calls. For example, many animals have specialized alarm calls that alert others to the presence of predators, presumably by activating concept of a predator in others' heads (Cheney and Seyfarth 2007). More generally, signaling systems can entail activation of concepts in the minds of others, such as mental state concepts related to aggression or mating, or social role concepts like OPPONENT or TERRITORY OWNER.

Other interfaces Internal to the mind, concepts or conceptual symbols can also allow different inferential systems to communicate with each other. Some scholars, for example, propose that language serves as a medium for conceptual reasoning (Boroditsky 2001; Lakoff and Johnson 1980). It also seems likely that conceptual systems must be able to interface with physiological systems such as, in the case of food, the appetitive system (Jackendoff 1996). Being hungry makes us think about food and therefore activates food concepts, putting us in motion to begin looking for actual tokens of food in the world. This is presumably part of how the decision-making and action functions of food concepts are instantiated, but it is important to note that conceptual systems cannot exist in isolation from other body systems. They must interact or interface with them to be of any use, and this in turn implies that there must be design features that allow them to do so.

Again, this list of conceptual functions is not meant to be exhaustive. Other conceptual functions can and surely do exist, and starting from a concept other than food might generate a different list. However, we are now in a position to begin thinking about how to develop hypotheses about the design of systems that populate the mind with concepts.

6.4   Representational Formats

Let us start again with food concepts, expanding later to different domains. Empirically, we know that humans and other animals are able to acquire food concepts, and we know something about what these concepts are like and what they do. The next step is to begin formalizing the design features of food concepts in the language of computational psychology, and then to think about how evolution shapes the developmental systems that build them.

Computational theories of mind formalize mental processes as computational functions operating over information structures, or representations (Marr 1982; Pylyshyn 1984). Although these computational functions, or mechanisms, must be instantiated neurally, they could in principle take just about any computational form or input-output relationship and include not just processes of inference and decision making but also processes of learning and updating (Griffiths et al. 2010). Similarly, the representations on which they operate are taken to be symbolic in the general sense that they encode information, but many forms of representation are possible (e.g., representations may be distributed across different neural structures). Thus, such theories are intended to be descriptive at the computational level in Marr's (1982) sense, without foreclosing multiple possibilities for how the computational mechanisms and representations might be instantiated neurally.

Where do concepts fit into such a scheme? Some approaches to concepts take them to be forms of mental symbols and, therefore, representations on which computational procedures operate (e.g., Pylyshyn 1984). It's possible, however, that some aspects of what we might take to be conceptual knowledge are instantiated in the computational input-output functions themselves. For example, mechanisms predicting the location of objects that have moved out of sight might embody, in their computational procedures, principles of object behavior, such as rigidity, elasticity, and responses to gravity and friction (Baillargeon 1994; Carey 2009). Thus, in keeping with a broad-picture view of concepts that allows them to be complex information structures with interacting parts, we'll allow the possibility that conceptual knowledge can be distributed across systems of representations and the mechanisms that operate on them.

The design stance is particularly useful for thinking about the complementary design features of evolved computational processes and the individual representations they operate on. Among other things, it doesn't partition innateness or learning purely into one component or the other. Instead, we expect developmental systems to build representations and computational mechanisms such that they interact in functionally fitness-enhancing ways, and learning and other types of plasticity are tools that can be used to do so. It is here that the notion of a reaction norm, with open parameters, or slots that are variable yet formatted according to certain principles, becomes particularly useful.

What computational format might food concepts take, and how might the features of individual food representations be designed to interact with the computational properties of the brain processes that handle them? Imagine, for example, that I observe a doughnut. This tokens an object representation in my visual system, and in my visual working memory in particular. This representation, in the format that the visual system uses, is then fed into various object recognition procedures, which, based on the perceptual cues represented (shape, texture, color, and perhaps contextual information such as my location in a doughnut shop), identify the object as a doughnut, thereby activating my concept DOUGHNUT: a representation of a doughnut *as* a doughnut is tokened. A semantic tag (or its functional equivalent) is attached to the object representation, such that my conceptual knowledge of doughnuts can be brought to bear in guiding my inferences and decisions vis-à-vis the doughnut (for more on tags, see Barrett 2005a, 2015).

Should we regard this particular object representation as a token of my *concept* DOUGHNUT? Perhaps not. It is a token of a doughnut representation, to be sure, but we've allowed that the information that is part of a concept writ large may be widely distributed. It might include, for example, motor routines for grasping doughnuts, recipes for doughnuts, propositional knowledge of the history of doughnut making, episodes of consumption of particularly memorable doughnuts, and the like. This might be a disturbingly wide scope for DOUGHNUT to some, but there is no reason to foreclose the possibility that conceptual systems orchestrate many cognitive resources.[6]

A useful question for thinking about conceptual design is, What features of food concepts and their tokened representations are necessary, or at least *typical*, for them to be able to interact appropriately with the computational systems that are designed to use them? Of course, there might be many, and tokened representations might be designed to interact with *many* systems. For example, the doughnut representation must have whatever features are necessary for it to be handled by the object-representation system, and for it to be fed into motor-planning systems that guide my

---

6. An *atomic* view of concepts would regard *only* the mental symbol or tag for *doughnut* to be the concept DOUGHNUT, and all the knowledge and content I'm describing here would be external to the concept itself (e.g., Fodor 1998). One could formulate such a theory in evolutionary terms, limiting the function of concepts merely to this symbolic function in the language of thought. On the present account, this is *one* function of concepts, but there is no principled reason not to include other functional aspects of conceptual systems as part of an evolutionary theory of conceptual design.

hand to the appropriate place when I reach for the doughnut, such as information about the location of the object in space.

Of course, representations of object locations are not specific to food objects. This demonstrates that a given token may in fact be a member of multiple representational types (just as a token trout is also a token fish, vertebrate, animal, and object). What computational properties might be specific to the doughnut representation as a representation of food *as* food?

An obvious one is nutritional value. There is debate over exactly how nutritional value is represented by animal food-representation systems—calories? protein? fat? vitamins? separate represented values, or a composite value?—as well as what decision rules have evolved to guide animals' decision making with respect to food (Smith 1983). It is not in doubt, however, that *some* kind of representation of nutritional value is a necessary component of food concepts in order for animals to make decisions about what to eat. And other represented values are almost certainly necessary for a food decision-making system to work; for example, representations of where the food type is located or likely to be found, cues to its likely presence (e.g., smell), and other properties such as difficulty of processing or extracting the resource once found (think about, for example, how you'd decide whether it's worth it to try to get honey out of a beehive when encountered) (Charnov 1976; Smith 1983). These, then, are among the minimal or typical representational requirements for a token of a food concept.

What this means is that we would expect tokens of food concepts that develop in adults to have a set of typical, or perhaps required, design features, which in this case take the form of representational *parameters,* or *slots* that must be filled (Boyer 2002). For example, food concepts might possess a *caloric value* slot (figure 6.2).[7] Although it's an open question just what information the brain stores about the nutritional value of foods, for food concepts to play their fitness-relevant role in eating decisions, there must be nutritional value *parameters*, such as caloric content, that are either present or waiting to be filled in each token of food concepts that we possess. Similarly, there must be another parameter or slot for taste, smell, appearance, and probably more.[8]

Beyond design features of representations themselves, there are the design features of computational systems that take those representations as inputs. Representational formats must be designed to interface with the computational processes that use them, and vice versa. If food concepts and their tokens have nutritional value slots, systems

7. One could imagine impoverished or incomplete food concepts in which no nutritional value was represented, but presumably this means an empty slot in the token of the concept. Empty slots might mean the conceptual token cannot be used for certain kinds of decision making about food.

8. In Boyer's (2002) terms, these are slots in conceptual *templates*. The way I am using conceptual *types* here is analogous to conceptual templates.

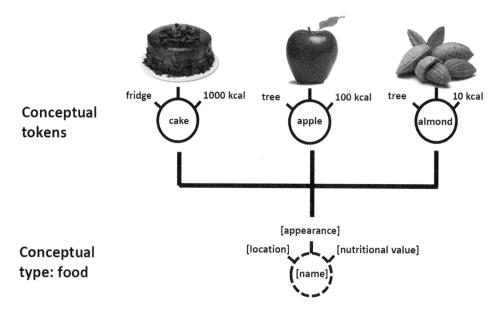

Conceptual tokens

Conceptual type: food

Figure 6.2
Example of a conceptual type (food) instantiated in multiple conceptual tokens. Individual parameters are open in the type (square brackets) and specified in the tokens by environmental input, via developmental reaction norms.

for evaluating and making decisions about food must be designed to expect information in those slots and have computational procedures that use the information in principled ways. For example, decision rules in optimal foraging theory take representations of food density in a patch, coupled with representations of the nutritional value of each item, as inputs and deliver decisions about how long to forage in the patch, using a specific computational rule (Charnov 1976). Similarly, systems for learning about food must be designed to systematically update the class-level representation of a particular food type—such as doughnuts—as a function of experiences with individual tokens of the type, amassed over time; for example, such systems could instantiate Bayesian updating algorithms (Tenenbaum, Griffiths, and Kemp 2006). But for such learning procedures to work, they would need specific priors about the parameters in question—for example, how much to update the summary representation of doughnut nutrition as a function of eating a specific doughnut. And there must be other designed interfaces as well, as in the interface that allows us to inform others that a doughnut is present when we visually observe a doughnut—an interface between perceptual, conceptual, and linguistic systems (Jackendoff 1996).

What is the taxonomy of conceptual types that minds possess or can possess, and how can we answer questions about the grain of domain specificity of the types

(Atkinson and Wheeler 2004; Barrett 2009)? In other words, how might we know if there is conceptual machinery *specific* to foods and food concepts, or if this machinery is just a token of some more general type, with no dedicated evolved machinery for foods per se? For example, what if there is just a single, domain-general concept-formation system, capable of representing any of the property types that a given species' conceptual capacities can represent?

This is of course possible, and a combination of theory and empirics is necessary to answer the question. We'll return to the question of domain taxonomy below, but first consider two points. First, it is a feature of taxonomies that generality at one level doesn't necessarily preclude greater specificity at another level. For example, our concept OBJECT and the conceptual resources for thinking about objects may be both quite broad (in terms of the scope of objects that can be conceptualized) and evolutionarily specialized (e.g., there may exist evolved systems specifically *for* representing and thinking about objects; Carey 2009). But this does not preclude the possibility of additional, specialized systems for specific *categories* of objects such as foods, faces, or artifacts (Boyer 2002; Kanwisher 2010). In other words, it's possible if not likely that objects and foods are not *separate* domains but either nested or partially overlapping ones. Our taxonomy of conceptual types will need to consider this kind of possibility.

Second, the idea of designed *interfaces* between conceptual and other systems suggests that one all-purpose conceptual system might not do the trick. It's likely, for example, that food concepts have specialized and ancient interfaces with systems such as appetite and digestion, required to extract nutritional information and to adjust motivations for food seeking as a function of nutritional state. A general-purpose conceptual system would need to reengineer the links between food concepts, food learning, and these bodily systems each generation—possible, but perhaps less plausible than a designed interface, suggesting at least some domain specificity in food concepts.

Other categories of concept, on the other hand, might require different representational formats and designed interfaces of their own, ones that are distinct from or only partially overlap with food. We've already seen the case of objects, whose conceptual machinery needs to interact in principled ways with visual and motor systems, and which pose a different (though again, partly overlapping) set of representational demands. As an additional example, consider the set of concepts used in mentalistic reasoning or theory of mind, such as the concept BELIEF. The format of belief representations is presumably quite different from the format of food representations, with non-overlapping conceptual slots. For example, belief representations represent something like attitudes toward states of affairs in the world (Leslie 1994). This entails informational slots that are clearly not present in food representations. Foods are not represented as having attitudes or standing in referential relationships to states of affairs. Moreover, the slots and parameters of belief representations are presumably designed to interface with an inferential apparatus designed to predict and retrodict the behavior of other agents on the basis of their represented beliefs—a kind of causal reasoning that is distinct from decision making about food in several ways (foods, for example, are not conceptualized as intentional agents whose external behavior is caused by inner representational states).

Although these considerations aren't enough to settle the issue of whether there are separate domains or subdomains for food and mental-state concepts, it suggests the kinds of functional-specificity considerations we'll need in order to develop properly testable theories of conceptual types. Let us now turn to the issue of developmental systems, and then return to the issue of conceptual repertoires.

6.5   Developmental Systems

Above I introduced the biological concept of a reaction norm (figure 6.1). In biology, this is typically viewed as a mapping function between some environmental parameter space and a phenotypic parameter space, for a given genotype (Schlichting and Pigliucci 1998). This concept can be broadened so that the phenotypic parameter space includes mental phenotypes, such as representations and computational procedures for operating on them (Barrett 2012, 2015). The environment, in turn, can be expanded to include various aspects of an organism's informational environment, including, in the case of humans, our cultural and linguistic environments, as well as social cues such as gestures, facial expressions, and the like.

In this framework, the developmental systems that build conceptual machinery, including conceptual tokens, are reaction norms shaped by selection as a function of the fitness value of the conceptual phenotypes they produce. Just as in the computational theory of mind, these reaction norms are descriptions of developmental systems at the computational level, leaving open various possibilities for how they might be instantiated at the developmental hardware level (i.e., genes, epigenetic machinery, and other developmental resources). One can imagine several kinds of environment-to-phenotype mapping functions these reaction norms might instantiate.

Most obviously, there must exist reaction norms that fill the open informational parameters of evolved representational types and computational procedures. The input-output rules of reaction norms determine how environmental experience is used to populate these open parameter spaces. In biology it is typical to represent these graphically as one-to-one functions, or curves, where each value of some environmental parameter is mapped to a value of the phenotypic parameter; an example might be the function that maps amount of childhood nutrition to adult height, for a given genotype. In psychology, it is relatively straightforward to imagine various learning rules or algorithms instantiating environment-to-phenotype mapping functions. In the behaviorist tradition, for example, the reinforcement schedule would provide the input, and the developed behavioral phenotype would be the output, with conditioning laws as the reaction norm (Gottlieb 2006). In a Bayesian framework, algorithms specify a computational pathway from informational inputs to representational outputs—including, in recent models, conceptual structures—given the appropriate set of priors (including, perhaps, innate priors; Tenenbaum, Griffiths, and Kemp 2006).

In principle, any kind of mapping function could be instantiated as a reaction norm—provided, of course, that a variant of the appropriate developmental system becomes available for natural selection to act on. This might include not just curvelike reaction norms that map from a one-dimensional environmental parameter (e.g., average experienced caloric value of a food item) to a one-dimensional representational parameter (represented nutritional value of the food), but other more complex types of function as well. One can imagine a reaction norm that maps experience with a given lexical item being used referentially, for example, *cow*, to an adult phenotype in which the word *cow* activates the concept COW. Arguably, this is a reaction norm that has been shaped by natural selection—but if so, it is a complex one that could not easily be represented on a graph mapping one linear dimension (environment) onto another (phenotype). Instead, the input and output spaces are of high dimensionality. Similarly, Chomsky's notion of a language-acquisition device could be seen as instantiating a complex reaction norm that maps the set of experienced linguistic utterances to a developing conceptual structure of the language's grammar (Chomsky 1965). Our task in describing concept-building systems is to properly describe the underlying reaction norms in computational terms, and to theorize how they are shaped by selection.

One way of thinking about reaction norms is as *spawners* of phenotypes: they populate the mind with its complement of mechanisms and representations (Barrett 2012, 2015). It is easy to imagine developmental reaction norms spawning individual tokens of concepts and other representations; for example, my concept ELECTRON was brought into being in my brain, from nothing, by some (presumably quite complicated) pathway of developmental procedures. And the design approach suggests that we may also think of mental mechanisms themselves as being spawned during development by procedures using some combination of innate structure plus experience.

Innateness can be accounted for in reaction norm models. For example, aspects of phenotype that develop the same way in everyone, regardless of environment, are flat, or canalized (Ariew 1996; though again, canalization and innateness might not be identical on some definitions; Griffiths and Machery 2008). Adding a temporal dimension to the graph would capture at what age such canalized features develop. But importantly, flatness might be a property of some *dimensions* or aspects of a reaction norm, but not others. For example, all my object concepts, from APPLE to ZEBRA, might have some elements in common, and we could conceptualize this as a dimension of the object-concept phenotype along which the reaction norm is flat. But clearly, my concepts APPLE and ZEBRA also differ in many ways (e.g., represented shape and color; one represented as a food, the other as an intentional agent; etc.). These would be nonflat dimensions of the concept-spawning reaction norm: parameters that are filled using some combination of developmental rules and environmental inputs.

Crucially, some aspects of reaction norms that appear flat across the range of environments humans experience might *not* be flat if a child were raised outside that environmental range. For example, some aspects of the concept GRAVITY, including rules for predicting how objects will fall or not fall depending on how they are supported, might develop the same in all children (Baillargeon 1994). If what we mean by innateness is a flat reaction norm across the environmental range in question, then these aspects of the concept GRAVITY might appear to be innate, if they develop similarly in most children. However, even flat reaction norms do not imply that learning can't be, or isn't, involved in their construction. Indeed, it could well be that children everywhere need the appropriate experience to properly develop concepts such as GRAVITY, SOLIDITY, COLLISION, and the like—but that all children on earth get the same relevant experience (Baillargeon 1994; Barrett 2006). It is an open question whether a child raised in space would develop the same concept of gravity as a child raised on earth.

What rules or computational procedures do reaction norms use to fill the open parameters of conceptual phenotypes? Again, the possibilities are many, constrained only by what kind of developmental machinery can be built out of genes, neurons, and other biological building blocks (Gallistel and King 2009). However, the design approach can be used to generate hypotheses about the minimal set of features a given reaction norm must have—a logic akin to Chomsky's learnability approach to specifying the minimal parameters of a language-acquisition device (Chomsky 1965; Pinker 1989). For example, the process of *fast mapping* of lexical terms to concepts (Heibeck and Markman 1987), in which children learn to map a word to a meaning in a single trial, suggests, at minimum, a reaction norm that (1) spawns an auditory representation of the newly heard word in long-term memory and (2) associates it with a concept. The reaction norm may well have other computational properties, but it must *at least* have these. Similarly, creation of a new animal concept must entail spawning of a new conceptual token and filling at least some of the slots required for identification, for example, some minimal information about what the animal looks like (Barrett and Broesch 2012). Other conceptual types, such as artifacts, might require additional minimal information to spawn a new concept—for example, information about function might be necessary to spawn a new concept of an object as a tool (Kemler Nelson et al. 2003). In each case, the shape of the relevant reaction norm will depend on the nature of the conceptual phenotype it was designed to spawn, with some being quite general and others more specific.

A final point about spawning is that it is presumably a normal part of the function of conceptual reaction norms to spawn *novel tokens* of conceptual types. Humans undoubtedly do not have an innate concept CAKE, and yet, the concept CAKE is probably a perfectly normal exemplar of both an object concept and a food concept. Similarly, SCHADENFREUDE is perhaps not an innate mental-state concept (though it could be). Yet the spawning of the concept SCHADENFREUDE given the appropriate experiential inputs is presumably not outside the normal envelope of the mental-state concept-spawning reaction norm. The token itself might be evolutionarily novel, but in each case, the ability to spawn tokens of this type is *not* novel.

This is an important possibility that is often overlooked in discussions of the ability of evolved systems to handle evolutionary novelty, because many scholars would hold that the ability to acquire the concept CAKE—which is surely an evolutionarily novel token—must be handled by so-called general purpose machinery (e.g., Chiappe and MacDonald 2005). On the account here, the developmental machinery might in fact be specialized, and spawning novel tokens could be exactly what the machinery was designed to do. Systems for face recognition, for example, are probably evolutionarily specialized (Kanwisher 2010), and yet every *specific* face that we see, every token, is evolutionarily unique. Of course, this means that the interesting questions have to do with what kinds of evolved conceptual *types* there are—and, relatedly, whether we have any concepts that are *not* tokens, albeit novel ones, of evolved types. We now turn to the question of conceptual types and their taxonomies.

6.6 Conceptual Types

On the theory outlined here, conceptual types are delineated by reaction norms: a conceptual type exists when there is a reaction norm designed by natural selection to produce tokens of that type. Importantly, conceptual types can be hierarchically organized. Just as muscle cells are a type, and striated and smooth muscle cells are subtypes within it, one can imagine the possibility of subtypes of concepts within, for example, an overarching category of object concepts, as well as crosscutting types (Barrett 2012).[9] In the limit, there may be reaction norms designed to produce a single token of a concept; Konrad Lorenz's geese, for example, might have had just a single concept MOTHER, attached to only one token in the world, by design.

If reaction norms are designed to produce tokens of conceptual types, then they are, by definition, adaptations (i.e., designed by selection). As for any adaptations, the *grain* of the adaptation—how broad or narrow its function or domain is—depends on facts of both descent (evolutionary history) and modification (selection pressure). For example, it's possible to imagine a species with only a single concept-formation mechanism

9. What I mean by *crosscutting* is that some subtypes of a type might have elements or properties that extend outside the domain of the type in which they are nested. Food concepts, for example, link to nonspatial representational systems having to do with appetite, hunger, and bodily state.

because no variants of that mechanism ever appeared for selection to act on (a fact of evolutionary history). If and when variants appear, whether there will be selection for two distinct mechanisms—as opposed to the new variant failing to be selected for, and disappearing—depends on whether there is selection for two, as opposed to one, mechanism. This will depend on facts about what the reaction norms do, and the relative costs and benefits of two versus one—considerations related to the notion of functional incompatibility, or whether subdividing a function results in higher fitness than maintaining a single functional design (e.g., Hughes 1994; Sherry and Schachter 1987).

How, then, do we go about determining the catalog of conceptual types that a species, such as humans, possesses? Clearly it's ultimately an empirical matter, and there do exist proposals about the array of conceptual types. For example, Carey (2009) proposes that humans possess several *core* concepts or conceptual systems (OBJECT, NUMBER, AGENT, CAUSE), as well as domain-general learning mechanisms, including Quinian bootstrapping, which together produce all the conceptual tokens that adult humans come to possess. Although this is a cogent proposal with substantial evidence to support it, there are other possibilities.

For example, it is possible that objects, number, agency, and causality represent aspects or dimensions of reaction norms—perhaps even flat, or canalized, dimensions—which build tokens of these concepts that, while uniform along these dimensions, may be variable along others. Humans could possess multiple kinds of object concept, as reviewed above, with different parametric slots in addition to the core ones (e.g., a horse is an object that is both a natural kind and an agent; a bench is an object with neither of those properties). And there might be multiple kinds of agents, again defined by properties additional to the core ones. This is not necessarily contradictory to Carey's proposal in some ways, but could diverge in others. For example, it's possible that there is no *token* of the general abstract concept OBJECT or CAUSE that is innate. Moreover, it's possible that learning is required to construct the developed versions of any of these concepts, and it's possible that at least some of the learning involves mechanisms specific to the conceptual type, rather than being purely domain general.

It's also possible, if not probable, that the minds of humans and other animals contain conceptual types in addition to the ones Carey proposes. Foods are one type that I have discussed at length. Foods are certainly represented as objects (and some may be a special kind of object, sometimes known as a *stuff* or substance, which can have different physical dynamics than other kinds of object; Prasada, Ferenz, and Haskell 2002). But as reviewed above, they almost certainly entail additional specialized developmental machinery, probably evolutionarily ancient, that not all objects share (this is what I mean by crosscutting as opposed to entirely hierarchical concepts). Other likely evolved conceptual types, probably ancient in mammals, include kinship (and perhaps particular kin types such as PARENT and OFFSPRING), territory, taxa (CONSPECIFIC,

HETEROSPECIFIC) and biological roles: PREDATOR, PREY, and MATE (Barrett 2005b). Clearly these are *related* to concepts of objects and agency, but it is not clear that they can be subsumed within these core systems or simply emerge from the properties of those systems without additional evolved machinery. And humans may have unique conceptual types, such as concepts of tools, social norms, and moral principles, that again *could* potentially emerge simply from these other core systems (i.e., without additional selection), or could alternately be supported by machinery specifically evolved to generate those types. A priori preference won't tell you which it is; you need empirical tests.

How do we know whether any proposed taxonomy of conceptual types is the correct one? At present, the empirical study of concepts is poorly suited to adjudicating between models. As elsewhere in psychology, mutually inconsistent theories of concepts and conceptual structure are able to coexist in the literature for long periods. Potentially, new methods such as model comparison hold promise. For example, statistical model-comparison techniques allow comparison of models with different levels of specificity or generality by controlling for the ability of models with more free parameters to better fit data (Burnham and Anderson 2002). In principle, this could allow a model with four conceptual types to be compared with a model that has more, by seeing which better fits the data in tasks such as categorization and learning tasks. Kemp and Tenenbaum use hierarchical Bayesian models to evaluate whether empirically measured patterns of inductive inference are more consistent with a hierarchical or nonhierarchical conceptual structure, a powerful statistical tool for uncovering the existence of multiple conceptual types (Kemp and Tenenbaum 2008; Tenenbaum, Griffiths, and Kemp 2011).

My goal here is not to engage in empirical evaluation of any particular proposal of conceptual taxonomy, but rather, to offer a new theoretical framework for thinking about conceptual types and conceptual design. In my view, it seems likely that the mind contains a larger taxonomy of conceptual types, some evolutionarily ancient and some recent, than is generally recognized in the literature. Part of this lack of recognition may be due to the focus on innateness, since many designed conceptual types may exist only as (partly) learned tokens. Another part may be due to the tendency of psychologists to focus on humans, without considering the large scope of concepts that humans may share with other animals, as well as the unique concepts that humans are able to form that must, on evolutionary grounds, require human-specific adaptations to form (otherwise, other species would be able to do so).

Yet another part of the reason for the relatively impoverished view of conceptual types that exists in the literature may be due to how domains are typically conceptualized: as mutually exclusive rather than potentially overlapping and combinatorial. On the view proposed here, it's possible that conceptual tokens may in fact exist in multiple domains at once, meaning that different aspects of these conceptual tokens are assembled by different reaction norms. If this is the case, then some seemingly opposed domain-general and domain-specific accounts of concept formation and acquisition might be simultaneously true. For example, concepts might be formed by Bayesian learning procedures, *and* there may be specific parameters for specific conceptual types. If true, the space of possible conceptual types might represent not mutually exclusive domain sets, but rather an intersection of the sets of conceptual types made possible by the brain's diverse reaction norms.

Finally, this raises a point about the phylogenetic distribution of conceptual types across taxa. If conceptual types evolve through processes of descent with modification, then there are likely to be some conceptual types that are both ancient and widely shared—albeit modified in particular lineages, just as gene families and phenotypic traits, like limbs, can be widespread but modified in different descendant lineages. Conceptual types such as objects, food, animals, mates, kinship, and causation could be ancient and widely distributed. Reaction norms for constructing conceptual types— even very general ones such as Bayesian updating procedures or statistical learning— could similarly be ancient and serve as building blocks to be mixed and matched in the development of particular tokens. But this is not necessarily to say that, for example, our concepts of animal taxa are in every way the *same* as those of other species. As mentioned above, tigers almost certainly have a concept TIGER, and though the machinery that builds that concept may be evolutionarily homologous to ours (i.e., descended from a common ancestor), there is no reason that our concepts of tigers can't be different—and perhaps richer—through interaction with developmental machinery that tigers don't possess. For example, our TIGER concepts can include the lexical tag *tiger* and propositionally stored information from scientific biology on the nature of tigers that is not present in tigers' own concept of their species.

In other words, processes of descent with modification of concept-building reaction norms imply that concepts come in versions that may exhibit evolutionary similarities and differences across taxa. And some species might possess whole classes of concepts, descended from more ancient conceptual types, that others don't possess. If true, our capacity to form certain kinds of taxonomically unique concepts, such as the concepts used in mathematics and biology, might have appeared not entirely de novo, but rather via modification of evolutionarily older conceptual machinery in the lineage leading to us.

6.7   Novelty, Flexibility, and Culture

Humans are clearly able to form *new* concepts: concepts that presumably were not formed in our evolutionary past (and in some cases still might not be formed in all humans). For example, until recently nobody had the concept MOBILE PHONE. Now, it's questionable whether there is anyone who doesn't. There doesn't seem to be anything terribly odd or unusual about a concept of mobile phones; many cultures, for example, have concepts of objects that can cause things at a distance. But are there concepts that challenge the view that every token concept we can form is a token of some evolutionarily older type? Carey (2009) gives as examples the concepts ELECTRON, CANCER, INFINITY, and GALAXY. How are we to account for these?

A widely held solution to the problem of novelty is the existence of domain-general learning abilities that have not been selected for any particular phenotypic outcome. However, the fact that concepts like CAKE and MOBILE PHONE don't seem particularly outside the envelope of normal human concepts should give us pause, because these certainly *are* evolutionarily novel conceptual tokens. Although cake presumably didn't exist in human ancestral environments, the concept CAKE seems to be a fairly ordinary case of a human-made food prepared from (in theory) naturally available ingredients: a food-artifact hybrid. Similarly, mobile phones are evolutionarily novel, but the concept MOBILE PHONE is of an object, an artifact, with the interesting causal property of being able to transmit the voice over a distance. It's not hard to imagine this concept being assembled from conceptual resources present long before mobile phones existed (objects, artifacts, causation-at-a-distance, which is a normal feature of communication). Thus, the capacity to generate phenotypic novelty does not *necessarily* require domain-general mechanisms, or imply that novel conceptual tokens can't be tokens of evolutionarily non-novel types.

Are concepts such as ELECTRON and INFINITY outside the scope of this model? Not necessarily. Even on accounts such as Carey's, which depends on domain-general learning, these concepts are assembled at least in part via modifications of innate concepts. Most people, for example, conceptualize electrons as objects (at least when first learned), and infinity is a concept arrived at by imagining the limitless extension of a counting process, which on Carey's account makes use of innate resources. On the account here, the ELECTRON concept would be (potentially) a learned token of an OBJECT concept. It would have some interesting and unusual properties, such as extremely small size—but there is no reason to think that property is unrepresentable as a value of an evolved parameter for object concepts, that is, size (note that contemporary physics considers electrons to be point particles with zero size, and those who fully understand the concept may genuinely be able to grasp this; but it is plausible that for most learners the initial concept is a token of the concept OBJECT, and even physicists may recruit conceptual machinery for thinking about objects when thinking about electrons).

Are there evolutionarily *unrepresentable* parameters, parameters that require, in Carey's terms, construction of entirely new conceptual resources? It's possible, but it depends on what one means by this language. For example, it's clearly the case that whatever evolved conceptual resources we have, including our evolved reaction norms, make *possible* the development of a concept such as INFINITY (arguably, as Carey suggests, a linguistically represented concept grounded in a statement about recursion that is, itself, not represented any more deeply). But a different question is whether genuinely new representational *formats,* ones that have not been selected for, are required to form concepts such as ELECTRON and INFINITY. Whatever is at stake here lies in hypotheses about what the representational formats required are, and what the preexisting repertoire of possible formats is. My suspicion is that most if not all novel concepts make use of previously available representational formats—a form of neural reuse (Anderson, 2010, Barrett, 2012; Dehaene, 2009)—but this is an open question that cannot be resolved in the absence of more specific theories of conceptual types.

This idea of novel tokens of evolutionarily preexisting conceptual types does not mean that humans don't have evolutionarily unique conceptual capacities. It just means that these have been selected for and therefore have functions and design features. For example, as Carey and others argue, spoken language probably makes possible the formation, transmission, acquisition, and representation of concepts that other species can't acquire. Many mathematical concepts, for example, may be dependent on language and make use of its unique ability to combine linguistically encoded symbols using explicit rules in a generative manner (INFINITY would be an example). Also extremely important in humans are processes of cultural transmission (including language) and, of perhaps even greater importance, cultural evolution, which allows the accumulation of conceptual complexity in areas such as mathematics and science (Richerson and Boyd 2005).

If this perspective is correct, then we should not be thinking about two channels of concept acquisition, the innate channel (for evolutionarily old concepts) and the domain-general linguistic and cultural channel (for evolutionarily novel concepts). Instead we should be asking how older conceptual reaction norms interact with newer mechanisms and processes, including language and cultural evolution. Indeed, if spoken language and cumulative cultural evolution are unique to humans, then these skills evolved from their very beginning against a developmental background of existing conceptual reaction norms. We should therefore be asking how these new capacities evolved to exploit the older ones, as much as the other way around. Part of this will involve the study of designed interfaces between older and newer systems. For example, how does our ability to talk and propositionally reason about food—new— develop on top of a much older conceptual apparatus for developing food concepts and linking them to bodily systems?

A useful case study for this is work investigating how written words—a paradigm case of culturally evolved symbolic artifacts—are represented and processed in the brain (Cohen and Dehaene 2004; Dehaene 2009). In a nutshell, it appears that exposure to written language in childhood causes the spawning of an evolutionarily novel token of an object-recognition module, an evolutionarily old type, in the brain's visual cortex. This module shares common features across readers of all the world's languages but is absent in nonreaders—just as one would expect from a contingent, yet functionally specialized, reaction norm (Dehaene 2009). Interestingly, Changizi and colleagues have found evidence that processes of cultural evolution have shaped the world's written characters to make them more easily processed by the brain's object-recognition procedures, suggesting that the properties of object-recognition modules act as a selective filter in the process of cultural evolution of writing systems (Changizi et al. 2006).

One can argue about whether this system instantiates anything conceptual, but it serves as a kind of model for how evolved conceptual reaction norms might interact with processes of cultural evolution of concepts. Just as the brain's ability to discriminate objects acts as a selective filter on the evolution of characters, the brain's ability to acquire concepts can (and presumably must) act as a filter on cultural evolution——a point made in *epidemiological* or *cultural attractor* accounts of cultural transmission (Boyer 2002; Sperber 1996). This is not to say that it filters along *every* parameter of cultural possibility space; but it certainly filters some (if we were unable to acquire a concept, how could it be transmitted?). And this filtering process undoubtedly occurs in many other ways as well—for example, the evolution of tools is shaped by the possibilities of human bodies to use them.

In the brain, then, we might expect a host of evolutionarily novel concepts, and for our repertoire of concepts to be changing all the time—especially as the speed of cultural change accelerates. But this should not be regarded as a process independent of evolved conceptual machinery. Instead, the interesting questions for future research lie in uncovering the parameter space of human conceptual repertoires, and asking how these interact with processes such as cultural evolution.

6.8 Conclusion: Toward Understanding Normal Human Conceptual Diversity

One of the primary virtues of a conceptual design approach is that it does not view the diversity and richness of adult conceptual repertoires as emerging from mere happenstance, solely the product of identical innate starting states meeting a haphazardly patterned world. There is likely to be a reason, for example, that hunters growing up in foraging societies come to possess an elaborate conceptual understanding of animal behavior and biology—and the proposal that this results from combining a few innate conceptual primitives like CAUSE and AGENT, along with general-purpose learning rules, might well be too impoverished to explain it (Liebenberg 1990). Instead, the fleshed-out tokens present in the minds of adults, such as the richly detailed information stored under a Shuar adult's concept JAGUAR or TAPIR, could be the normal type of developmental outcome that selection has shaped developmental systems to build—even if the richness of these concepts is undetectable at birth or early childhood (Boyer 2002; Barrett 2005b). If so, then we will need to resist the simple equation of what is present in infancy with what natural selection builds, and confront the richness of adult concepts as what needs to be explained (without forgetting, of course, that infancy is a crucial step in this process).

How do we do this, empirically? Because the picture of mental development implied by a conceptual design view is substantially more complex than a small number of innate concepts plus learning, the task is not a simple one. However, I will conclude by offering a few suggestions for steps that can be taken in the direction that the conceptual design perspective implies.

A first, monumentally difficult step in this literature would be agreement on terminology. If the study of concepts is to achieve consilience with work in neuroscience, genetics, development, and comparative biology, then it is of crucial importance that we (eventually) agree on what the technical concept CONCEPT is meant to pick out in the mind. Machery (2009), seeking to formalize such a consensus, despairs at the possibility of ever doing so, and to some extent I share his pessimism. However, I suggest that the hierarchical view of mental structure that I have presented here and elsewhere (Barrett 2012, 2015) provides a way of naturalizing concepts without essentializing them. What I mean by this is that like other biological concepts that pick out putative *natural kinds*—or at least kinds that biologists make use of in their daily work, without referential gridlock—a biological theory of concepts can be situated within a view of biological traits as evolving via descent with modification, as constituted of smaller parts or features embedded within larger networks of parts or features, and to some degree as fuzzy in their boundaries. On this view we can treat conceptual systems as just that—systems—in the biological and physical sense. As part of this view, we can use the language of types and tokens, without privileging any level of the hierarchy as *the* conceptual level: my momentary tokening of an individual doughnut representation could be spoken of as a concept, as well as my general concept DOUGHNUT and the higher-level types or categories such as FOOD and OBJECT in which DOUGHNUT is embedded.

A second, crucial step is the empirical documentation of conceptual diversity and richness across individual humans, across human societies, and across species— necessary for a proper evolutionary, comparative perspective on the evolution of concepts. To a large degree, of course, this is already under way: it's what much of psychology, anthropology, neuroscience, and behavioral biology already do. What is lacking, however, is a common framework in which to fit these data together, bringing them to bear on testable theories of conceptual design. What is needed is some way of standardizing data from different cultures, stages in development, and species. In neuroscience and genetics, promising steps are being taken toward standardized data formats through the construction of formal *ontologies*: standardized classifications of brain structures (Price and Friston 2005), genes (Ashburner et al. 2000), and the links between them (Bilder, Sabb, Cannon, et al. 2009). In the case of cognitive ontologies used in brain mapping, these are explicitly about *phenomics*: establishing standardized classifications of cognitive phenotypes in developed brains, and linking behavioral, brain mapping, and genetic data (Bilder, Sabb, Parker, et al. 2009). Some such form of standardization of conceptual knowledge, across individuals, species, and developmental stages, would greatly assist the construction of biologically accurate reaction norms of cognitive development. In addition, a move away from null hypothesis testing and toward model comparison—testing theories against each other, rather than against often implausible nulls—will greatly increase our ability to compare the predictive power of alternative theories, statistically controlling for their relative complexity (Burnham and Anderson 2002).

In order to do this, of course, we'll need actual theories: computationally specified models of the developmental reaction norms that produce conceptual phenotypes. Perhaps the most fully fleshed out of such theories to date are Bayesian models of conceptual development, because these specify, in principle, the complete developmental trajectory from infancy to adulthood given some set of environmental inputs (Kemp and Tenenbaum 2008 Tenenbaum, Griffiths, and Kemp 2006; Tenenbaum et al. 2011). However, even these existing models are almost certainly too simple by orders of magnitude, to the extent that they leave out factors like content specificity, brain architecture, and interactions between the brain's specialized subsystems during development. Models that actually specify a developmental curve of any kind, though, are a step in the right direction. Eventually, these must be situated in a phylogenetic context, to account for descent with modification of human conceptual structures, as well as in the context of developmental gene expression and neural development. At present, there is an enormous gap between the psychological literature on concepts and conceptual development, and the biologically based literatures on brain organization and development—though this gap is beginning to close (e.g., Amodio and Frith 2006; Saxe, Carey, and Kanwisher 2004).

Finally, in keeping with the above, our theories of human conceptual development will need to merge with contemporary evo-devo views of how biological structures evolve and develop (Carroll, Grenier, and Weatherbee 2005). While human conceptual development is often treated as a sui generis phenomenon, frequently starting from philosophical considerations, clearly whatever conceptual capacities we have must have evolved through descent with modification from ancestral structures. Descent with modification leads to, among other things, nested hierarchies of traits: the diverse and functionally differentiated structures of human brains, for example, developed through evolutionary differentiation from a smaller number of ancestral structures. This means that structures such as the cortex are hierarchically organized, with some features shared in common and others functionally divergent (Allman 2000; Barrett, 2012; Krubitzer and Huffman 2000). Because conceptual structure is produced by brain structure, the same is likely true of our conceptual repertoires and the developmental machinery that builds them: the richness of modern-day human conceptual repertoires likely evolved through descent with modification from simpler, ancestral conceptual repertoires. Thus, the conceptual palette of our lineage likely bifurcated and proliferated over evolutionary time, both prior to and after our split from chimpanzees, to become more rich and diverse. But, just like our limbs, livers, and frontal lobes, every concept we possess is likely to retain traces of the ancestral pathway of descent with modification it followed. With sufficient care, we can use these facts about the historical nature of the evolutionary process to build more fine-grained and biologically accurate models of human conceptual development.

As an example of the insight such a hierarchical view might add, consider debates about the evolution of theory of mind, or mindreading, and the array of mental-state concepts, such as BELIEF, DESIRE, and KNOWLEDGE, that are thought to underpin this ability (Nichols and Stich 2003). On some accounts, this is an entirely unique human phenomenon that arose de novo in the human lineage, with no evolutionary continuity with other taxa (Penn and Povinelli 2007). However, this seems unlikely: although there may be many unique *aspects* of human mindreading, it seems likely that human mindreading, like all aspects of human cognition, evolved through descent with modification from ancestral cognitive abilities and is therefore likely to have homologs in other species—including at least some homologous concepts. Comparative research suggests that this is the case, with other species able to interpret cues of communicative intent, such as mating and aggression, and to track indices of mental states such as knowledge. This suggests that there is likely to be some homology in the underlying mechanisms, and in the representations—including concepts—they employ (Call and Tomasello 2008; Hare et al. 2002; Clayton, Dally, and Emery 2007). On the view presented here, this does not require that a chimpanzee's concept of knowledge or desire need be *identical* to ours; but the hypothesis that they are evolutionarily related, or homologous, is likely to shed light on the evolution and development of the brain mechanisms underlying mindreading in our species and theirs.

What is perhaps surprising, given the long history of research and theorizing about the human conceptual repertoire, is how much remains unknown about it. Arguably this results partly from insisting that the story of human conceptual development be a relatively simple one, accounted for by a small number of conceptual building blocks interacting with a complex world. Here I have proposed a new approach, the conceptual design approach, which starts with the functional roles that concepts play in our developed conceptual repertoires and asks how the developmental resources that build these repertoires are shaped by the evolutionary process. Although this is a novel approach and therefore untested, it has the potential to offer new ways of merging the study of concepts with work in neuroscience, brain evolution, and development. By allowing for the possibility that the mind's conceptual repertoire may be built by a diverse family of mechanisms with many possible designs and evolutionary histories, we may discover that the mind's complexity is richer than previously thought—and that it is rich by design.

References

Allman, J. M. 2000. *Evolving Brains*. New York: Scientific American Library.

Amodio, D. M., and C. D. Frith. 2006. Meeting of minds: The medial frontal cortex and social cognition. *Nature Reviews: Neuroscience* 7 (4): 268–277.

Anderson, M. L. (2010). Neural reuse: A fundamental organizational principle of the brain. *Behavioral and Brain Sciences*, *33*, 245–266.

Ariew, A. 1996. Innateness and canalization. *Philosophy of Science* 63:19–27.

Ashburner, M., C. A. Ball, J. A. Blake, D. Botstein, H. Butler,J. M. Cherry, et al. 2000. Gene ontology: Tool for the unification of biology. *Nature Genetics* 25 (1): 25–29.

Atkinson, A. P., and M. Wheeler. 2004. The grain of domains: The evolutionary-psychological case against domain-general cognition. *Mind & Language* 19 (2): 147–176.

Baillargeon, R. 1994. How do infants learn about the physical world? *Current Directions in Psychological Science* 3 (5): 133–140.

Barrett, H. C. 2005a. Enzymatic computation and cognitive modularity. *Mind & Language* 20 (3): 259–287.

Barrett, H. C. 2005b. Adaptations to predators and prey. In *The Handbook of Evolutionary Psychology,* ed. D. M. Buss, 200–223. New York: Wiley.

Barrett, H. C. 2006. Modularity and design reincarnation. In *The Innate Mind: Culture and Cognition,* ed. P. Carruthers, S. Laurence, and S. Stich, 199–217. New York: Oxford University Press.

Barrett, H. C. 2007. Development as the target of evolution: A computational approach to developmental systems. In *The Evolution of Mind: Fundamental Questions and Controversies,* ed. S. Gangestad and J. Simpson, 186–192. New York: Guilford.

Barrett, H. C. 2009. Where there is an adaptation, there is a domain: The form-function fit in information processing. In *Foundations in Evolutionary Cognitive Neuroscience,* ed. S. M. Platek and T. K. Shackelford, 97–116. Cambridge: Cambridge University Press.

Barrett, H. C. 2012. A hierarchical model of the evolution of human brain specializations. *Proceedings of the National Academy of Sciences of the United States of America* 109:10733–10740.

Barrett, H.C. 2015. *The Shape of Thought: How Mental Adaptations Evolve*. New York: Oxford University Press.

Barrett, H. C., and J. Broesch. 2012. Prepared social learning about dangerous animals in children. *Evolution and Human Behavior* 33 (5): 499–508.

Barsalou, L. W. 1999. Perceptual symbol systems. *Behavioral and Brain Sciences* 22 (4): 577–660.

Barsalou, L. W. 2005. Continuity of the conceptual system across species. *Trends in Cognitive Sciences* 9 (7): 309–311.

Bilder, R. M., F. W. Sabb, T. D. Cannon, E. D. London, J. D. Jentsch, D. S. Parker, et al. 2009. Phenomics: The systematic study of phenotypes on a genome-wide scale. *Neuroscience* 164 (1): 30–42.

Bilder, R. M., F. W. Sabb, D. S. Parker, D. Kalar, W. W. Chu, J. Fox, et al. 2009. Cognitive ontologies for neuropsychiatric phenomics research. *Cognitive Neuropsychiatry* 14 (4–5): 419–450.

Blaisdell, A. P., K. Sawa, K. J. Leising, and M. R. Waldmann. 2006. Causal reasoning in rats. *Science* 311 (5763): 1020–1022.

Boroditsky, L. 2001. Does language shape thought? Mandarin and English speakers' conceptions of time. *Cognitive Psychology* 43 (1): 1–22.

Boyer, P. 2002. *Religion Explained*. New York: Basic Books.

Burnham, K. P., and D. R. Anderson. 2002. *Model Selection and Multi-Model Inference: A Practical Information-Theoretic Approach*. New York: Springer.

Call, J., and M. Tomasello. 2008. Does the chimpanzee have a theory of mind? 30 years later. *Trends in Cognitive Sciences* 12 (5): 187–192.

Caramazza, A., and B. Z. Mahon. 2003. The organization of conceptual knowledge: The evidence from category-specific semantic deficits. *Trends in Cognitive Sciences* 7 (8): 354–361.

Carey, S. 2009. *The Origin of Concepts*. New York: Oxford University Press.

Carroll, S. B., J. K. Grenier, and S. D. Weatherbee. 2005. *From DNA to Diversity: Molecular Genetics and the Evolution of Animal Design*. 2nd ed. Oxford: Blackwell.

Changizi, M. A., Q. Zhang, H. Ye, and S. Shimojo. 2006. The structures of letters and symbols throughout human history are selected to match those found in objects in natural scenes. *American Naturalist* 167 (5): E117–E139.

Charnov, E. L. 1976. Optimal foraging, the marginal value theorem. *Theoretical Population Biology* 9 (2): 129–136.

Cheney, D. L., and R. M. Seyfarth. 2007. *Baboon Metaphysics: The Evolution of a Social Mind*. Chicago: University of Chicago Press.

Chiappe, D., and K. MacDonald. 2005. The evolution of domain-general mechanisms in intelligence and learning. *Journal of General Psychology* 132 (1): 5–40.

Chomsky, N. 1965. *Aspects of the Theory of Syntax*. Cambridge, MA: MIT Press.

Clayton, N. S., J. M. Dally, and N. J. Emery. 2007. Social cognition by food-caching corvids: The western scrub-jay as a natural psychologist. *Philosophical Transactions of the Royal Society of London: Series B, Biological Sciences* 362 (1480): 507–522.

Cohen, L., and S. Dehaene. 2004. Specialization within the ventral stream: The case for the visual word form area. *NeuroImage* 22 (1): 466–476.

Dehaene, S. 2009. *Reading in the Brain: The Science and Evolution of a Human Invention*. New York: Viking.

Fodor, J. A. 1998. *Concepts: Where Cognitive Science Went Wrong*. New York: Oxford University Press.

Gallistel, C. R., and A. P. King. 2009. *Memory and the Computational Brain: Why Cognitive Science Will Transform Neuroscience*. New York: Wiley-Blackwell.

Gopnik, A., and A. Meltzoff. 1997. *Words, Thoughts, and Theories*. Cambridge, MA: MIT Press.

Gottlieb, G. 2006. Probabilistic epigenesis. *Developmental Science* 10 (1): 1–11.

Griffiths, P. E., and E. Machery. 2008. Innateness, canalization, and 'biologicizing the mind'. *Philosophical Psychology*, 21(3): 397–414.

Griffiths, T. L., N. Chater, C. Kemp, A. Perfors, and J. B. Tenenbaum. 2010. Probabilistic models of cognition: Exploring representations and inductive biases. *Trends in Cognitive Sciences* 14 (8): 357–364.

Hare, B., M. Brown, C. Williamson, and M. Tomasello. 2002. The domestication of social cognition in dogs. *Science* 298 (5598): 1634–1636.

Heibeck, T. H., and E. M. Markman. 1987. Word learning in children: An examination of fast mapping. *Child Development* 58 (4): 1021–1034.

Hughes, A. L. 1994. The evolution of functionally novel proteins after gene duplication. *Proceedings of the Royal Society of London: Series B, Biological Sciences* 256 (1346): 119–124.

Jackendoff, R. 1996. The architecture of the linguistic-spatial interface. In *Language and Space,* ed. P. Bloom, M. A. Peterson, L. Nadel, and M. F. Garrett, 1–30. Cambridge, MA: MIT Press.

Johnson-Frey, S. H. 2004. The neural bases of complex tool use in humans. *Trends in Cognitive Sciences* 8 (2): 71–78.

Kanwisher, N. 2010. Functional specificity in the human brain: A window into the functional architecture of the mind. *Proceedings of the National Academy of Sciences of the United States of America* 107 (25): 11163–11170.

Keil, F. C. 1992. *Concepts, Kinds, and Cognitive Development*. Cambridge, MA: MIT Press.

Kemler Nelson, D. G., R. Russell, N. Duke, and K. Jones. 2003. Two-year-olds will name artifacts by their functions. *Child Development* 71 (5): 1271–1288.

Kemp, C., and J. B. Tenenbaum. 2008. The discovery of structural form. *Proceedings of the National Academy of Sciences of the United States of America* 105 (31): 10687–10692.

Krubitzer, L., and K. J. Huffman. 2000. A realization of the neocortex in mammals: Genetic and epigenetic contributions to the phenotype. *Brain, Behavior and Evolution* 55 (6): 322–335.

Lakoff, G., and M. Johnson. 1980. *Metaphors We Live By*. Chicago: University of Chicago Press.

Laurence, S., and E. Margolis. 1999. Concepts and cognitive science. In *Concepts: Core Readings,* ed. E. Margolis and S. Laurence, 3–81. Cambridge, MA: MIT Press.

Leslie, A. M. 1994. Pretending and believing: Issues in the theory of ToMM. *Cognition* 50 (1): 211–238.

Liebenberg, L. 1990. *The Art of Tracking: The Origin of Science*. Claremont, South Africa: D. Philip.

Machery, E. 2009. *Doing Without Concepts*. New York: Oxford University Press.

Margolis, E., and S. Laurence. 2007. The ontology of concepts—abstract objects or mental representations? *Noûs* 41 (4): 561–593.

Marr, D. 1982. *Vision: A Computational Investigation into the Human Representation and Processing Of Visual Information*. New York: Henry Holt.

Murphy, G. L. 2002. *The Big Book of Concepts*. Cambridge, MA: MIT Press.

Nichols, S., and S. Stich. 2003. *Mindreading*. New York: Oxford University Press.

Penn, D. C., and D. J. Povinelli. 2007. On the lack of evidence that non-human animals possess anything remotely resembling a "theory of mind." *Philosophical Transactions of the Royal Society of London: Series B, Biological Sciences* 362 (1480): 731–744.

Pinker, S. 1989. *Learnability and Cognition: The Acquisition of Argument Structure*. Cambridge, MA: MIT Press.

Prasada, S., K. Ferenz, and T. Haskell. 2002. Conceiving of entities as objects and as stuff. *Cognition* 83 (2): 141–165.

Price, C. J., and K. J. Friston. 2005. Functional ontologies for cognition: The systematic definition of structure and function. *Cognitive Neuropsychology* 22 (3–4): 262–275.

Pylyshyn, Z. W. 1984. *Computation and Cognition*. Cambridge, MA: MIT Press.

Richerson, P., and R. Boyd. 2005. *Not by Genes Alone: How Culture Transformed Human Evolution*. Chicago: University of Chicago Press.

Rosch, E. 1999. Principles of categorization. In *Concepts: Core Readings,* ed. E. Margolis and S. Laurence, 189–206. Cambridge, MA: MIT Press.

Samuels, R. 2002. Nativism in cognitive science. *Mind & Language* 17 (3): 233–265.

Saxe, R., S. Carey, and N. Kanwisher. 2004. Understanding other minds: Linking developmental psychology and functional neuroimaging. *Annual Review of Psychology* 55:87–124.

Schlichting, C. D., and M. Pigliucci. 1998. *Phenotypic Evolution: A Reaction Norm Perspective*. New York: Sinauer Associates.

Sherry, D. F., and D. L. Schacter. 1987. The evolution of multiple memory systems. *Psychological Review* 94 (4): 439–454.

Smith, E. A. 1983. Anthropological applications of optimal foraging theory: A critical review. *Current Anthropology* 24 (5): 625–651.

Smith, E. E., and D. L. Medin. 1981. *Categories and Concepts*. Cambridge, MA: Harvard University Press.

Spelke, E., and K. Kinzler. 2009. Innateness, learning, and rationality. *Child Development Perspectives* 3 (2): 96–98.

Sperber, D. 1996. *Explaining Culture: A Naturalistic Approach*. Oxford: Blackwell.

Stich, S. P. 1983. *From Folk Psychology to Cognitive Science: The Case against Belief*. Cambridge, MA: MIT Press.

Tenenbaum, J. B., T. L. Griffiths, and C. Kemp. 2006. Theory-based Bayesian models of inductive learning and reasoning. *Trends in Cognitive Sciences* 10 (7): 309–318.

Tenenbaum, J. B., C. Kemp, T. L. Griffiths, and N. D. Goodman. 2011. How to grow a mind: Statistics, structure, and abstraction. *Science* 331 (6022): 1279–1285.

Tooby, J., and L. Cosmides. 1990. The past explains the present: Emotional adaptations and the structure of ancestral environments. *Ethology and Sociobiology* 11 (4): 375–424.

7 How Natural Selection Shapes Conceptual Structure: Human Intuitions and Concepts of Ownership

Pascal Boyer

7.1 Mapping Concepts from World, Language, ... and Evolution

How do we map the inventory of human concepts? Here I propose that a precise description of selective pressures on species-specific cognitive systems is the best source of empirical hypotheses about conceptual repertoires, and I illustrate this in the case of *ownership* concepts. The hypotheses presented here stem from a naturalistic agenda, in which concepts like other mental phenomena are construed as functional properties of cognitive systems (Jackendoff 1983; Margolis and Laurence 2007; Millikan 1998). The example of ownership illustrates how a highly specific selective context can predict and explain equally specific aspects of human concepts. This account also suggests more general though tentative lessons, to do with what general computational properties, if any, should be expected from concepts; whether categorization is crucial to concept structure; and what role concepts play in linguistic reference.

The evolutionary perspective stands in contrast to two other possible ways of proceeding. One is a form of realism that is often implicit in psychological research on conceptual knowledge, and is often combined with the discipline's unreflective empiricism (Carey 2009, 27ff.). This perspective assumes that we can infer a cognitive system's conceptual repertoire from our knowledge of the world that system is embedded in. After all, the argument goes, to survive, complex organisms must entertain beliefs that at least roughly match the way the world is. This makes it likely that many organisms' systems of concepts "carve nature at the joints," to use the common phrase. So the fact that there are actually different kinds of things in the world makes it likely that concepts reflect those distinct categories. For instance, plants and animals are substantially different, so any animal with a complex cognitive system would probably have general concepts for plants and animals.

However, nature does not actually have "joints" that would all be equally relevant to organisms from different species. For instance, it is unlikely that dogs have a fully general concept ANIMAL, because they do not interact with all animals on the basis of a single set of expectations and motivations. One would expect that dogs probably have at least the following distinct concepts: HUMAN, DOG, PREY, because each of these kinds of agents activates a distinct suite of cognitive systems. Being domesticated by humans, dogs interact with them based on cognitive resources that are not used for dealing with other dogs or with prey. But other systems in the dog's mind, for example, mating systems, are uniquely activated by other dogs and not by any other living thing.

A second standard approach is to try to infer a conceptual repertoire from natural language, taking concepts to be stable information structures that correspond to lexical units. This linguistic perspective has dominated general research on concepts, so I will not dwell on its essential tenets and many achievements. I should just point to some of its limitations. First, as Sperber and Wilson point out, though it is clear that human minds contain *as many* concepts as lexical items (barring genuine synonyms), it is quite plausible that they have *vastly more* concepts (Sperber and Wilson 1998, 275), even if we limit ourselves to propositionally encoded information. Second, humans have a large number of ineffable concepts, like modality-encoded information, that organize information in a stable way yet cannot be expressed linguistically (Barsalou et al. 2003). Third, the linguistic turn suggests a radical hiatus between human and other-animal cognition, which ignores behavioral homologies and plausible phylogenetic continuity between species.

Here I will outline and illustrate a third approach in mapping the conceptual landscape, one that starts from selective pressures over evolutionary history, and formulates hypotheses about optimal and feasible cognitive structures that would respond to these pressures in fitness-enhancing ways. Considering selective pressures on organisms provides a lot of information about what their concepts may be like and therefore many rich hypotheses about cognitive architecture that we can test (Tooby, Cosmides, and Barrett 2005). Indeed, one point of this article is to suggest that such evolutionary task analysis provides *much* more information than we would first imagine, and therefore should be used as an important source for an evolutionary account of concepts.

7.2   Ownership as a Conceptual Domain

Ownership is central to human social interaction. Among the culturally universal aspects of ownership are the fact that (a) all known human languages can express, through grammatical or lexical means or both, the special connection between specific agents and particular things, either material (natural objects, artifacts, territories) or abstract (songs, stories, knowledge); (b) there is a principled distinction between mere possession and ownership; (c) ownership is associated with specific emotions and motivations; (d) the acquisition of ownership notions and norms occurs very early and effortlessly, along highly similar developmental lines (Brown 1991; Heine 1997). By contrast, norms of ownership and property rights differ from one place or time to another in terms both of scope (who can own things and what things can be owned) and of implications (what one may do with specific types of property) (Hann 1998).

So how do we approach the conceptual underpinnings of these linguistic, mental, and social phenomena? The first method to concepts mentioned above, from actual kinds to constraints on concepts, is obviously not available here. There is no physical fact of the matter that corresponds to ownership. Whether an agent is the owner of a thing or not is the consequence, not of physical properties of agent and thing, but of shared mental representations between the agent and third parties. The second method, from lexicon and syntax to concepts, provides suggestive but ambiguous information. Ownership is part of a much broader domain of possession relations that includes kin, body parts, and other non-accidental appendages, as it were, of an agent. Possession can be conveyed by attributive means (e.g., "her blue eyes," "Jane's blue eyes") or predicative means ("she has blue eyes") (Heine 1997, 25ff.; Rudmin 1994). The linguistic evidence suggests that possession constructions, and a fortiori specific ownership constructions, are derived from nonpossession semantic structures (Heine 1997, 224), for example, from spatial schemas. For instance, OWN(AGENT, THING) can be seen as a special version of a BE NEXT TO(AGENT, THING) concept, and GIVE(AGENT$_1$, AGENT$_2$, THING) is analogous to MOVE(AGENT$_1$, AGENT$_2$, THING), and so on (Jackendoff 1983). These models also illustrate why semantic structures are only of limited value if we want to elucidate conceptual organization. Mappings, such as from spatial relations to ownership, occur in natural languages because they are intuitively appropriate—which is the case because of specific underlying assumptions about ownership, that are precisely what we want to describe.

Surprisingly, there was until recently very little systematic research on the psychology of ownership—on the intuitions and explicit thoughts engaged when people make claims about who owns what or how property can be transferred (Friedman 2010). Most of the relevant recent evidence comes from developmental psychology. Children have clear and specific intuitions about ownership and, of course, very strong motivations associated with those intuitions. Claims that a particular object is *mine* appear very early in young children's verbal communication, and children engage in frequent disputes over ownership. Although ownership is invisible, children readily infer it from verbal information to the effect that a particular object is *theirs* or *belongs to* another person, and they adjust their behavior accordingly, from thirty-six months (Eisenberg-Berg, Haake, and Bartlett 1981; Ross and Conant 1992), or even from twenty-four months (Blake, Ganea, and Harris 2012). What conceptual structures underpin this competence?

Children's *explicit* statements about ownership are not altogether consistent, and are sometimes downright odd. Children, for instance, agree that some objects can be owned, like artifacts or natural objects extracted from the environment, but they are less certain about abstract ideas. More surprising, four year-olds state that sleeping people cannot "own" objects (Noles and Keil 2011). This may suggest that whatever ownership concepts have developed at that point, they are only weakly connected to the lexical items *own* or *belong*.

In contrast with these generic notions, even very young children have definite *intuitions* about the specific events that create or transfer ownership. In the absence of verbal information, children rely on a first possessor heuristic—whoever used or handled the object first is presumed to be the owner (Blake and Harris 2009; Friedman and Neary 2008). First possessors usually win conflicts over toys at age three, but not at age one (Bakeman and Brownlee 1982). Children's intuitions also imply that effort invested in some object results in ownership. Preschoolers, for instance, judge that an agent A's block of clay belongs to B if B sculpted it, but not if B merely handled it without changing its shape (Kanngiesser, Gjersoe, and Hood 2010). These and other studies show that from thirty-six months or earlier, children are familiar with the exclusion aspect of ownership. They also have stable intuitions regarding transfers of ownership, if these are made sufficiently explicit (Friedman and Neary 2008; Kim and Kalish 2009).

We find a similar contrast between explicit conceptions and intuitions in adults. In response to questionnaires, for instance, adults readily assert that persons cannot be owned (before being reminded of the history of slavery). Like children, they state that specific information can be owned, but not generic knowledge, although they cannot elaborate on the distinction (Noles and Keil 2011). Indeed, questions about what *kinds* of objects can or cannot be owned always trigger vague or inconsistent answers—because it is not clear in what sense ownership could be restricted to any particular ontological domain (Friedman 2010). But adults like children have reliable intuitions about use and possession, for example, they use a first possessor heuristic to determine ownership (Friedman et al. 2011), as do many legal systems the world over— as the saying goes, "possession is 90 percent of the law." This is not absolute, though. Friedman and colleagues demonstrated that intuitions about use and possession are largely dependent on cues concerning the *history* of the object, that is, who made it and how, or who extracted it from natural nonowned resources, what transfers took place, how much effort was involved, and so forth (Friedman et al. 2011). Also, adults' intuitions are sensitive to cues that make one agent responsible for the object being around, or being available, or having a utility, and responsibility here depends on an appreciation of the agent's intentions when he or she displaced or modified the object (Palamar, Le, and Friedman 2012).

The psychological evidence, however, does not by itself explain *why* ownership is construed in this way, why people's intuitions are only imperfectly tracked by their explicit concepts, and why facts about an object's history modulate people's intuitions. To address these questions, one must consider the adaptive functions of these conceptual structures.

7.3   Possession and Ownership (I): Intuitions and Motivations

An evolutionary approach implies that cognitive systems constitute evolved responses to recurrent challenges facing organisms in their evolutionary environments. In the case at hand, I propose (along with others; see, e.g., DeScioli and Wilson 2011) that ownership as a conceptual domain is part of our responses to the fundamental challenge of reaching a measure of coordination that optimizes the extraction of resources.

7.3.1   Ownership Intuitions as an Evolved Coordination Strategy

Humans like other organisms from highly social species can extract resources from their environments better if they avoid a Hobbesian war of all against all, in which the acquisition and use of resources are extremely costly, as every item must be extracted from the environment under the threat of fights with, and potential theft by, conspecifics. That may be why this alleged "state of nature" is not actually very natural. Organisms from many species manage to avoid its pitfalls through coordination, that is, a broad class of strategies in which most organisms abide by some norm of resource extraction—for instance, that the first agent to occupy a territory will keep it, while others will try to find another place (Maynard Smith 1982). Having such norms greatly reduces the costs of resource extraction, thereby increasing each organism's fitness (Johnsson, Nöbbelin, and Bohlin 1999). (Note that adopting coordination strategies in this perspective is a matter of genetic fitness, not group survival—it does not matter if the strategy benefits groups or not). The pressure for coordination norms is especially acute in humans, who are more dependent than any other species on interaction with conspecifics to acquire resources from their environment, and have evolved the required capacities for sophisticated coordination in such endeavors as warfare, hunting, co-parenting, and many others (Dubreuil 2010; Gat 2006; Hrdy 2009).

The term *resource* should be taken in the broadest sense, as any part of the environment, interaction with which can increase the organism's fitness. This includes food, shelter, mates, and potential allies. Now many of the resources extracted are rival goods, such that one agent's enjoyment of the resource diminishes other agents' potential use. Many of these rival goods are also potentially excludable, such that an agent can to some extent bar another agent from access to a particular resource.

Trade and gift giving impose additional evolutionary pressures on ownership cognition. Trade appeared early in human evolution—indeed it may be one of the evolutionary innovations that mark the advent of modern human societies, as well as providing a significant boost to creativity and human innovation (Ridley 2010). As for gift giving, it is a universal feature of human societies. Social relations are created or cemented by gifts. Because of the selective pressures for appropriate understanding of trade and gift giving, human intuitions of ownership should not be immutably linked to an object's history. There should be some possibility for A's ownership of x to be transferred to some other agent. Note, however, that this creates a series of coordination problems. First, if A transfers x to B, the extent to which A is not the owner of x should be construed in the same way by both parties. Second, A and B should have some means of knowing at precisely what point B owns x. Finally, third parties should also receive the information such that they adjust their behaviors accordingly.

The proposal here is that intuitions and motivations concerning who uses what resources constitute such a coordination tool for humans—and evolved from less efficient coordination strategies in the course of human evolution. In this perspective, the complex of intuitions and motivations generally called *ownership* are the outcome of largely tacit computations concerning the relative costs and benefits of using, guarding, or poaching resources, as well as collaborating with others in these diverse courses of action.

7.3.2   The Contents of Possession-Related Intuitions

Ownership, like other aspects of social interaction, is a domain for which normal human beings have specific, largely automatic *intuitions*, that is, mental representations of a particular state of affairs, or motivations to act toward particular states, without a clear or accessible representation of the processes that lead to these intuitions. In the same way as depth perception requires largely unconscious principles to organize visual information, ownership-relevant information in the environment can be processed outside conscious access to yield specific intuitions. Imagine the following scene: Robinson picks up some shells and seaweed on the beach and assembles them as a bracelet that he puts down. Friday handles the bracelet. The scene triggers in most third parties some intuitive representations to the effect that "this is Robinson's bracelet," "this is *not* Friday's bracelet."

The intuitions we consider here are all about some specific agent using some specific resource. Faced with some resource, the organism A has a choice among courses of action that we can label TAKE, NOT-TAKE, DEFEND, or RELINQUISH, each with its associated costs and benefits. Faced with two agents A and B, one of whom is using a resource, there is a choice of actions for C, dependent on the interaction between A and B. If A takes from B, there is a choice among DO NOTHING, HELP TAKE, HELP GUARD, and so on. (Although this seems to invite infinite regress, there may be no selective pressure for any such coordination beyond triadic interaction, as will be discussed presently.) These are the strategic choices. What is the content of the intuitions about these choices?

Our hypothesis here is that, faced with such situations, organisms are equipped with a domain-specific system that takes as input certain cues, as well as some background information, to produce definite intuitions and motivations toward TAKE(x), GUARD(x), HELP TAKE(x), HELP GUARD(x), and so forth.

These intuitions and motivations are principled. The domain-specific system involved is such that in response to specific patterns of situations, it produces predictable intuitions and motivations that guide the organism's behavior. The organization of these intuitions instantiates strategic conventions, that is, evolutionarily stable strategies. They help organisms save energy by avoiding fights for resources and expend that energy on seeking alternative resources.

Note that the intuitions and motivations of different agents are, of course, not always matched. That is, coordination may break down and encounters lead to a number of fights. This may happen because the cues processed by two organisms are different (e.g., an organism actually is the first occupant of a territory, but an intruder failed to perceive that). This may also happen because the potential rewards of fights in some cases outstrip the motivation for strategic withdrawal. That would be the case, for example, if your friend knows that your lottery ticket is a winning one.

7.3.3   Computational Properties of Ownership Intuitions

Note the following important points about the mental representations involved:

This is all intuitive. All the mental content I have described so far comes in the form of *intuitions*, that is, mental content that is *not* the product of deliberate ratiocination; nor is it necessarily explicit. What makes it intuitive is that some representations and motivations, for example, "Don't take berries from this bush!" or "Attack anyone who tries to use this tool!" are entertained without any representation of the processes that led to them. This should be emphasized because intuitions in this sense are contrasted below with reflective mental content.

Intuitions and motivations are outputs of the same systems. The mental representations described here come as a package, in which a description of a state of affairs and a drive to make a certain state of affairs real are intertwined. A particular situation triggers a mental representation that is both description (e.g., Individual A is using object *x*) and motivation (e.g., take *x* away from A!).

Intuitions are domain specific. So far, we have considered common features in all such intuition systems, regardless of their domain of operation. That is why this description is bound to remain extremely abstract. To go further in the description of these cognitive processes, we may need to consider specific domains of such resources, such as mating, foraging, hunting, or tool making. Different domains of behavior, in a highly social species, result in different challenges in terms of access to resources and exclusion of other agents, such that it is unlikely that an optimal system would just realize one single set of principles for them all.

Computations explain norms (not the other way around). One might want to object that the model proposed does not so far capture the normative aspects of ownership. In describing ownership psychology, most attempts at either evolutionary or historical construction start from a rich notion of norms applied to possession and use. Indeed, this may seem the most natural starting point. After all, a concept of ownership should make sense of cases in which someone *is* but *should not* be in possession of an object, and even young children grasp the point. One goal of the present research program, however, is precisely to elucidate the various computational processes leading to, for example, a strong motivation to have the thief restitute stolen goods to their previous possessors, or to a specific feeling of frustration when people take away what we made without compensation. These (and many other) specific emotions and intentions underpin what we call ownership *norms,* but calling them that does not in any sense illuminate the processes involved. The deontic intuition is precisely what we should explain. Instead of assuming, for example, that representations about how a resource was extracted feeds into an ownership norm, I choose here to consider how cues about history (e.g., an agent A extracted object *x* from nature, or agent A invested work into *x*, etc.) directly trigger motivations and intuitions to the effect that A keeps *x*, that one is not motivated to try to appropriate *x*, that others may want to defend A against such exploitation, and so on, which are motivating, predictable, and shared—the features of what we call *norms.*

7.4   Coordination Proposal (II): Explicit Beliefs and Norms

Beyond intuitive representations, people in some circumstances also entertain *reflective representations* of ownership-relevant information. These are explicit, generally verbalized series of representations that explicate, amplify, concatenate, or comment on intuitions. To reprise our example, these would be explicit representations like "It is R's bracelet because R made it," "It is not F's bracelet as R did not give it to F," or "It is not Y's necklace because X only lent it to Y." Note that one does not require the explicit reflections to entertain the intuitions. Young children, for instance, will share some of the intuitions mentioned above without being able to articulate their rationale. This distinction between intuitions and reflections is similar to that between *intuitive* and *reflective beliefs* (Sperber 1997), *aliefs* and *beliefs* (Gendler 2008), or *architectural beliefs* and *metarepresentations* (Cosmides and Tooby 2000).

7.4.1   Why Bother with Explicit Representations?

Why have explicit, universally lexicalized concepts as a complement to (and loosely associated with) specific intuitions? The requirements for extensive coordination among humans make this development, if not inevitable, at least very likely in most human groups. This is because coordination requires compatible motivations, but also shared information. It requires that, once agent X has extracted resource R, most third parties that were not present during resource acquisition adopt the same noninterference strategy as the parties present. In other words, it requires some signal that sums up what can be inferred from the history of acquisition, and it triggers relevant motivations in other agents. This requirement is, of course, not unique to humans. For instance, many animals need to signal that they are "owners" of a particular territory rather than passersby, which they usually convey by specific signals. Humans accomplish that in the species-specific manner that matches their much greater requirements for coordination, through verbal communication of the connection between agent and thing possessed.

Explicit beliefs about ownership do not easily track the subtle contextual cues that modify our intuitions. Consider the familiar case of jokes. Most people would assume that a joke is not something you can "own." So telling a joke you heard is not taken as an instance of plagiarizing, of stealing anyone's property. But the intuition can change. On our way to a fancy dinner, you tell me a great joke that you hope will dazzle the crowd. But as we sit down at the table, I tell that precise joke. Now it seems that in a sense I did take something that was "yours." Even clearer, of course, is the case of a comedian who uses a colleague's material—that is definitely stealing. Why do our intuitions change with the context, given that the actions are similar? An easy (and wrong) answer is that the actions are not similar, because in the case of the comedian (vs. ordinary conversations), a joke is "intellectual property." But that is question begging— we readily assign that label to comedian's jokes precisely because we have intuitions, for example, that they have a special entitlement to getting benefits from their material, that we should approve them when they exclude others from using it, and so on. From the instant a joke is something that can accrue utility, like social prestige, and is rival (you cannot tell the joke to the same people), the intuitive system triggers a clear reaction, while the reflective *ownership* concept would have much difficulty explaining why such contextual circumstances make all the difference. Obviously, it is *possible* to refine our concept of ownership to accommodate such contextual cues. But that is not required. As long as people share intuitions and have some confidence that they do, the strategic norms are in place and transaction costs are diminished.

Given that coordination is made more efficient by explicit concepts and words, what explains the discrepancy noted above, between these explicit understandings and our intuitions? Note that the discrepancy is not specific to the domain of ownership. Indeed, one can observe a similar phenomenon in most cognitive domains handled by both intuitions and deliberate, explicit reflections, as described by *dual process* models (see, e.g., Evans 2003). The fact that explicit representations do not always track intuitions is mostly due to computational differences in the two kinds of systems described in such dual-process models.

Intuitions are delivered by nonconscious integration of many different types of cues, each of which triggers inferences that are then weighted for relevance and trigger specific intuitive content, as well as motivational states. That much is common to many domain-specific inferential systems. In the case at hand, the relevant cues include information about whether the resource is rival (which is itself the outcome of previous computation, based on semantic knowledge but also on episodes or inferences from episodes), information about the history of the connection between an agent and a thing, information about other agents' past interaction with the same thing, and much more besides that. Because the cues are many, and because their inferential potential is often modulated by the values of other cues, they do not lend themselves to the kind of inference typical of explicit, reflective systems. Explicit systems are constrained by the limits of working memory and imagery buffers, which is why they cannot in general represent complex webs of contingencies between multiple aspects of a situation. Explicit thoughts on ownership provide general representations that, to some rough extent, track the usual results of intuitive processes concerning possession and ownership, in the forms of general principles about ownership, for example, "what is owned by X cannot be used by Y," "a gift of R from X to Y entails that X does not own R any longer," and so on.

7.4.2 How Do We Extend the Scope of Ownership Concepts?

Human representations of ownership are not exhausted by intuitions and the kind of explanatory, comment-like reflections described above. In fact, in many human groups, people have put together formal codes of ownership, including legal systems, that extend the scope of intuitive and reflective representations. Most important, these formal systems apply ownership concepts to domains of social interaction for which there are no evolved predispositions. For instance, humans have evolved intuitions about territories and their use. If you occupy a territory, you can exclude others from resources found in that space. But modern legal norms make the exploitation of mineral resources and the use of airspace possible and efficient, by creating specific limited property rights, by creating such notions as royalties and refunds for negative externalities, and so forth. Indeed, modern legal scholarship tends to deny that there is such a thing as ownership in the abstract, which is replaced with the notion of *bundled,* highly specific rights, such as the right to occupy land but not sell it, or the right to sell property but not to damage it, and so forth. (Merrill and Smith 2001). By building these nonintuitive notions, legal systems can extend ownership to domains such as ideas, tunes, and designs, for which our common reflective notion of ownership is defective.

7.5 Implications of the Evolutionary Perspective

A naturalistic evolutionary perspective on mental content diverges in important ways from standard assumptions about concepts. For a long time, theoretical debates about the structure of concepts focused on categorization, notably on prototypicality effects, the role of perceptual imagery, and artificial intelligence models of knowledge representation (see, e.g., Gelman and Medin 1993; Medin, Goldstone, and Gentner 1993; Medin and Wattenmaker 1987; Murphy 2002). Empirical evidence persuaded psychologists to move away from seeing concepts as lists of properties (the so-called classical view), to recognizing that they include prototypes or exemplars, and finally to construing them as encapsulated theories about kinds of objects (Medin and Wattenmaker

1987). These debates have now lost much of their intensity, perhaps because of a realization that the world of mental concepts is far more extensive than previously envisaged, and that representational formats are far more diverse. Depending on the domain, category structure is best described by one format or another, but none of them applies across many different domains (Machery 2009). Moreover, a large part of our conceptual menagerie includes ineffable, modality-specific information that does not easily lend itself to a unified nonmodal code (Barsalou 1993, 1999). These findings converge to suggest that there is simply no possibility of (or need for) a general theory of concepts, if this means a series of general strictures on the representational format of all or most concepts (Machery 2009).

But cognitive and evolutionary considerations may allow us to go further, explaining why concepts come in diverse formats and why these are appropriate to specific conceptual domains. As a starting point, an evolutionary perspective may introduce important corrections to standard assumptions about concepts, to do with (a) the connections between intuitive and reflective representations, (b) the connection between concepts and valuation, and (c) the contribution of concepts to meaning and reference.

7.5.1 Intuitions and Reflections

Concepts as described here include both intuitive components, whose inferential background is not available to conscious inspection, and reflective components, which explicate, enlarge, modify, or otherwise elaborate on intuitions. Consider the example of OWNERSHIP. This is involved in a large spectrum of situations, all the way from simple tactical conflict avoidance (e.g., when three-year-olds tacitly abide by the first possession principle), to large-scale coordination (as when people elaborate property rights for a community). In the first case, the selective pressure is for efficient strategic norms, which require that roughly similar cues trigger roughly similar intuitions and motivations in conspecifics. In the case of large-scale interaction, the complexities of coordination make explicit verbalized rules an efficient addition to intuitions.

This interaction of intuitive and reflective components is familiar in many cognitive domains and usually described as an example of *dual-process* systems (Evans 2003; Hassin, Uleman, and Bargh 2005). From a selective viewpoint, one would expect pressure toward fast, rough-and-ready systems in some domains and slower, integrative systems in other domains. However, again based on these functional considerations, one would certainly not expect the mind to comprise two general-purpose systems that support gut-feeling and reasoning-driven decision making respectively, as is sometimes argued in the dual-process literature (Kahneman 2003). That is because decision making itself, rather than being a unified, all-purpose mental faculty, is fragmented in myriad distinct domain-specific capacities, with their distinct input formats, databases, and computational rules (Barrett and Kurzban 2012).

7.5.2   Concepts and Valuation

As standard research on concepts focused on categorization, it left aside aspects of concepts formation and use that are just as crucial, and especially salient from an evolutionary viewpoint. Concepts, like other cognitive structures, are there to direct behavior efficiently in the context of specific selective pressures. So concepts should be such that they result in appropriate motivations, in the different valuation of distinct courses of actions (Tooby, Cosmides, and Barrett 2005). This is clear in the case of ownership. Indeed, two distinct situations may be construed as cases of ownership versus mere possession, as a result of salient differences in the motivations triggered. For instance, having created an artifact gives us a greater motivation to defend our possession of the artifact than if we had just found it, and this difference in motivation is what creates the intuition that the artifact "belongs" to us. It seems contrived and artificial to distinguish categorization from motivation in this case.

The same may apply to many other concepts. As Tooby and colleagues point out, valuation is ubiquitous in the representation of situations, such that a division between categorization and motivation makes little biological sense (Tooby, Cosmides, and Barrett 2005). Indeed, one may argue that the separation between conceptual functions understood as pure categorization (describing which objects go together) and motivation understood as a separate process of decision making may be a hangover from the classical faculty psychology description of *volition*. To take a simple example, the cognitive system that makes a male chimp notice a female's genital swelling, rather than treat it as visual noise, is the very same system that triggers sexual arousal in the male and prompts courtship behaviors. Or, to return to the dog's ontology as mentioned in introduction, the systems that notice differences between *humans* and *other animate beings* are the same systems that motivate highly specific behaviors toward humans. The point is that valuation is not some external factor that is added to categorization. Valuation generates categories by motivating different behaviors toward different objects (Tooby, Cosmides, and Barrett 2005).

7.5.3   Concepts and Reference: Deflationary Implications

To the extent that philosophers consider mental content to contain structured bundles of information, they generally assume that these conceptual bundles should be such that they can support reference (Block 1987; Rey 1983). There is no space here to discuss accounts of reference and their connections to various hypotheses about mental content. In fact, a normative notion of reference perhaps has no place at all in a naturalized account of cognition, as some philosophers have argued (Davidson 1984; Quine 1960). But it may be of help briefly to signal how a naturalistic evolutionary framework diverges from common normative expectations about concepts.

A possible objection to an evolutionary perspective is that concepts construed in relation to evolutionary pressures denote not genuine kinds in the world, but broader equivalence classes of phenomena with similar effects on a lineage of organisms. For instance, in this view, it is difficult to say that cows have a concept GRASS, when in fact all they seem to have is the concept GREEN, GRASSLIKE LOOKING, SMELLING AND TASTING STUFF, which fails to pick out all grass and only grass. This objection is not really compelling, however, for two reasons. First, a failure to pick out genuine natural kinds in the world is only a problem if one assumes that the point of concepts is to provide organisms with scientifically accurate or metaphysically coherent accounts of the world. By contrast, once we consider concepts as information structures that help organisms survive and reproduce, metaphysically imperfect concepts can be seen as perfectly fine tools. In this perspective, cows and other ruminants have managed rather well so far with GREEN, GRASSLIKE LOOKING, SMELLING AND TASTING STUFF mostly because, on average and over eons of evolutionary history, there were not many nongrass objects in their environment that matched this "flawed" concept. Second, most of our mental concepts track kinds of things that are not proper categories in any case. Even so-called natural kinds are generally not actual classes (Millikan 2005, 106ff). Natural organisms come in different species and genera, that is, *not* in classes but in populations that merge with other populations as one goes back in time and that diverge into distinct species as time passes (Mayr 1996). So there is no distinct class of objects in the world that GRASS or TIGER could normatively refer to. From a naturalist standpoint, then, concepts can do their functional work without "metaphysical correctness."

In functional terms, once we abandon normative metaphysical requirements, concepts are best described as a set of specialized computational *skills* (Millikan 1998), with specific triggers, a specific set of rules for operations, and a range of typical outputs, for example, a modification of that information, the recruitment of specific information from memory, a specific motivation or emotional reaction, and so on. The case of OWNERSHIP illustrates this. The range of mental representations associated with possession and use do not converge on a set of criteria, such that a particular agent could be said to *grasp* the concepts OWN or BELONG while another one does not. There are shared intuitions (e.g., about first possession), external cues that influence these intuitions (e.g., the way a resource was extracted from an environment), as well as reflective thoughts on the intuitions (e.g., about what in general determines ownership and what it implies). The connections between actual situations and the activation of all these representations is a matter of *greater or lesser* success in tracking relevant agent-environment interactions.

More generally, what evolved organisms need are not information bundles that connect to the way the world is, but information bundles that track the way the world affects fitness, which is a property not of the world outside the organism, but of the combination between that world and species-specific adaptations. Taking this into account may allow us to make sense of properties of human concepts that would otherwise remain puzzling and provides a way of mapping human concepts that is based not on a priori philosophical requirements, but on biological matters of fact.

References

Bakeman, R., and J. Brownlee. 1982. Social rules governing object conflicts in toddlers and pre-schoolers. In *Peer Relations*, ed. K. H. Rubin and H. S. Ross, 99–111. Hillsdale, NJ: Erlbaum.

Barrett, H. C., and R. Kurzban. 2012. What are the functions of System 2 modules? A reply to Chiappe and Gardner. *Theory & Psychology* 22 (5): 683–688.

Barsalou, L. W. 1993. Flexibility, structure, and linguistic vagary in concepts: Manifestations of a compositional system of perceptual symbols. In *Theories of Memory*, ed. A. F. Collins, S. E. Gathercole, M. A. Conway, and P. E. Morris, 29–101. Hillsdale, NJ: Erlbaum.

Barsalou, L. W. 1999. Perceptual symbol systems. *Behavioral and Brain Sciences* 22 (4): 577–660.

Barsalou, L. W., W. K. Simmons, A. K. Barbey, and C. D. Wilson. 2003. Grounding conceptual knowledge in modality-specific systems. *Trends in Cognitive Sciences* 7 (2): 84–91.

Blake, P. R., P. A. Ganea, and P. L. Harris. 2012. Possession is not always the law: With age, pre-schoolers increasingly use verbal information to identify who owns what. *Journal of Experimental Child Psychology* 113 (2): 259–272.

Blake, P. R., and P. L. Harris. 2009. Children's understanding of ownership transfers. *Cognitive Development* 24 (2): 133–145.

Block, N. 1987. Advertisement for a semantics for psychology. *Midwest Studies in Philosophy* 10 (1): 615–678.

Brown, D. E. 1991. *Human Universals*. New York: McGraw Hill.

Carey, S. 2009. *The Origin of Concepts*. New York: Oxford University Press.

Cosmides, L., and J. Tooby. 2000. Consider the source: The evolution of adaptations for decoupling and metarepresentation. In *Metarepresentations: A Multidisciplinary Perspective*, ed. D. Sperber, 53–115. New York: Oxford University Press.

Davidson, D. 1984. *Inquiries into Truth and Interpretation*. New York: Clarendon Press.

DeScioli, P., and B. J. Wilson. 2011. The territorial foundations of human property. *Evolution and Human Behavior* 32 (5): 297–304.

Dubreuil, B. 2010. Paleolithic public goods games: Why human culture and cooperation did not evolve in one step. *Biology and Philosophy* 25 (1): 53–73.

Eisenberg-Berg, N., R. J. Haake, and K. Bartlett. 1981. The effects of possession and ownership on the sharing and proprietary behaviors of preschool children. *Merrill-Palmer Quarterly* 27 (1): 61–68.

Evans, J. S. B. T. 2003. In two minds: Dual-process accounts of reasoning. *Trends in Cognitive Sciences* 7 (10): 454–459.

Friedman, O. 2010. Necessary for possession: How people reason about the acquisition of ownership. *Personality and Social Psychology Bulletin* 36 (9): 1161–1169.

Friedman, O., and K. R. Neary. 2008. Determining who owns what: Do children infer ownership from first possession? *Cognition* 107 (3): 829–849.

Friedman, O., K. R. Neary, M. A. Defeyter, and S. L. Malcolm. 2011. Ownership and object history. In *Origins of Ownership of Property: New Directions for Child and Adolescent Development*, vol. 132, ed. H. H. Ross and O. Friedman, 79–90. New York: Wiley.

Gat, A. 2006. *War in Human Civilization*. New York: Oxford University Press.

Gelman, S. A., and D. L. Medin. 1993. What's so essential about essentialism? A different perspective on the interaction of perception, language, and conceptual knowledge. *Cognitive Development* 8 (2): 157–167.

Gendler, T. S. 2008. Alief in action (and reaction). *Mind & Language* 23 (5): 552–585.

Hann, C. M. 1998. *Property Relations: Renewing the Anthropological Tradition*. New York: Cambridge University Press.

Hassin, R. R., J. S. Uleman, and J. A. Bargh, eds. 2005. *The New Unconscious*. Oxford: Oxford University Press.

Heine, B. 1997. *Possession: Cognitive Sources, Forces and Grammaticalization*. Cambridge: Cambridge University Press.

Hrdy, S. B. 2009. *Mothers and Others: The Evolutionary Origins of Mutual Understanding*. Cambridge, MA: Belknap Press.

Jackendoff, R. 1983. *Semantics and Cognition*. Cambridge, MA: MIT Press.

Johnsson, J. I., F. Nöbbelin, and T. Bohlin. 1999. Territorial competition among wild brown trout fry: Effects of ownership and body size. *Journal of Fish Biology* 54 (2): 469–472.

Kahneman, D. 2003. A perspective on judgment and choice: Mapping bounded rationality. *American Psychologist* 58 (9): 697–720.

Kanngiesser, P., N. Gjersoe, and B. M. Hood. 2010. The effect of creative labor on property-ownership transfer by preschool children and adults. *Psychological Science* 21 (9): 1236–1241.

Kim, S., and C. W. Kalish. 2009. Children's ascriptions of property rights with changes of ownership. *Cognitive Development* 24 (3): 322–336.

Machery, E. 2009. *Doing Without Concepts*. New York: Oxford University Press.

Margolis, E., and S. Laurence. 2007. The ontology of concepts—abstract objects or mental representations? *Noûs* 41 (4): 561–593.

Maynard Smith, J. 1982. *Evolution and the Theory of Games*. Cambridge: Cambridge University Press.

Mayr, E. 1996. What is a species, and what is not. *Philosophy of Science* 63 (2): 262.

Medin, D. L., R. L. Goldstone, and D. Gentner. 1993. Respects for similarity. *Psychological Review* 100:254–278.

Medin, D. L., and W. D. Wattenmaker. 1987. Category cohesiveness, theories and cognitive archaeology. In *Concepts and Conceptual Development*, ed. U. Neisser, 25–62. Cambridge: Cambridge University Press.

Merrill, T. W., and H. E. Smith. 2001. What happened to property in law and economics? *Yale Law Journal* 111 (2): 357–398.

Millikan, R. G. 1998. A common structure for concepts of individuals, stuffs and real kinds: More mama, more milk, more mouse. *Behavioral and Brain Sciences* 21:55–100.

Millikan, R. G. 2005. *Language: A Biological Model*. New York: Oxford University Press.

Murphy, G. L. 2002. *The Big Book of Concepts*. Cambridge, MA: MIT Press.

Noles, N. S., and F. Keil. 2011. Exploring ownership in a developmental context. In *Origins of Ownership of Property: New Directions for Child and Adolescent Development*, vol. 132, ed. H. H. Ross and O. Friedman, 91–103. New York: Wiley.

Palamar, M., D. T. Le, and O. Friedman. 2012. Acquiring ownership and the attribution of responsibility. *Cognition* 124 (2): 201–208.

Quine, W. V. O. 1960. *Word and Object*. Cambridge, MA: MIT Press.

Rey, G. 1983. Concepts and stereotypes. *Cognition* 15 (1–3): 237–262.

Ridley, M. 2010. *The Rational Optimist: How Prosperity Evolves*. 1st U.S. ed. New York: Harper.

Ross, H. S., and C. L. Conant. 1992. The social structure of early conflict: Interaction, relationships, and alliances. In *Conflict in Child and Adolescent Development*, ed. C. U. Shantz and W. W. Hartup, 153–185. New York: Cambridge University Press.

Rudmin, F. W. 1994. Cross-cultural psycholinguistic field research: Verbs of ownership and possession. *Journal of Cross-Cultural Psychology* 25 (1): 114–132.

Sperber, D. 1997. Intuitive and reflective beliefs. *Mind & Language* 12 (1): 17.

Sperber, D., and D. Wilson. 1998. The mapping between the mental and the public lexicon. In *Thought and Language*, ed. P. Carruthers and J. Boucher, 184–200. Cambridge: Cambridge University Press.

Tooby, J., L. Cosmides, and H. C. Barrett. 2005. Resolving the debate on innate ideas: Learnability constraints and the evolved interpenetration of motivational and conceptual functions. In *The Innate Mind: Structure and Contents*, ed. P. Carruthers, S. Laurence, and S. Stich, 305–337. New York: Oxford University Press.

IV Concepts and Perception

8   Burge on Perception

Jerry A. Fodor

8.1   Introduction

Tyler Burge has written a long,[1] disputatious, and sometimes difficult book about cognition, with special emphasis on the relation between perception and conceptualization (Burge 2010). Among its many other virtues, it is a serious work of scholarship. People like me, who only rarely can manage to get their references to stay put, will be awed by its fifty-odd pages of bibliography, which cites not just the usual standards in the philosophy of mind and the philosophy of language, but also such exotica as, for example: "development in young infants' reasoning about the occlusion of objects," "exoskeletal sensors for walking," and a lot of other books and papers drawn from the professional literature of psychology and related sciences. It is a contention of Burge's that an embarrassing number of the theses that philosophers of mind have held to be true a priori turn out, in light of the empirical findings, not to be true at all. (Burge's favorite examples are about what, in light of their lack of language, animals and prelinguistic infants can and can't perceive.) Burge is surely right to consider that a scandal. In the old days, philosophers thought that they could arrive at conceptual truths by performing conceptual analyses; so it is perhaps understandable that, when they got around to the philosophy of mind, they ignored empirical findings and did their stuff from armchairs. But then Quine pointed out that successful conceptual analyses have been remarkably thin on the ground, and that nobody seems to be able to say just what a conceptual analysis is. The prospects for an analytic theory of perception now seem about as promising as the prospects for an analytic theory of continental drift; and much the same can be said of the prospects for analytic theories of believing, thinking, remembering, and other cognitive states and processes.

I think that Burge's methodological observations about how philosophical research on perception and cognition should be conducted are patently correct; this paper will

---

1. *Origins of Objectivity* is approximately twenty times longer than the reference copy of *Winnie-the-Pooh* that I keep on my desk to use in emergencies; and it contains many, many fewer jokes.

take them for granted. My primary concern will be the question: "Given that theories of perception/cognition² must be responsible both to empirical findings and to reasonable demands for conceptual coherence, conservatism, and the like, *what theory of perception—or, at a minimum, what* kind *of theory of perception—should we endorse?*" Burge's book repeatedly asks philosophers, psychologists, linguists, ethologists, and anybody else who is prepared to lend a hand, *what is required of a creature, and of its environment, such that the one should be able to perceive the other* "objectively"?³ I think this is indeed a sort of question that we should all be asking and that those are the sorts of people of whom we should ask it. But I'll argue that Burge gets the answer wrong—interestingly wrong, but wrong all the same.

This chapter comes in sections. Section 8.2 is an overview of (what I take to be) the dialectical landscape. This is necessary because Burge's way of carving things up cuts across a distinction that I take to be essential: *perception* versus *perception as*.

8.2   Overview

So what, according to Burge, does one discover if one addresses theories of perception with due attention to the available empirical results? Primarily that philosophers have overintellectualized their accounts of how perception works (and, perhaps, their accounts of how thought does). In particular, Burge thinks that philosophers have done so by holding:

(i) perception typically requires conceptualizing the percept, so what one can perceive depends on which concepts one has;

and

(ii) which concepts one has depends on which beliefs one holds.⁴

This, however, is where exegesis gets sticky. As far as I can tell, Burge thinks that he thinks that (i) and (ii) are both false. I think, however, that his position with respect to

2. To conserve backslashes, I'll use *theory of perception* as short for "theory of perception or of other aspects of cognition" except when I think it matters which of the disjuncts is being discussed. I assume (untendentiously, I hope) that perception is a branch of cognition, hence that the science of perception is a branch of cognitive science. Much of this chapter is about which branch of cognitive science it is and how that part differs from some of the others.
3. To see a thing "objectively" is, at very least, *not* to see it as having properties that it doesn't have. On Burge's view, several features of perception are explained by their being conducive to perceptual objectivity so construed. Burge holds that perceptual constancies are paradigms of these.
4. This sort of view of the semantic content of concepts is often called *internalism,* or *individualism.* Burge uses both terms, as shall I in what follows.

(i) is, in fact, equivocal and that the equivocation matters a lot to what he says about related issues. By contrast, his rejection of (ii) is entirely clear: it is the core of what Burge calls "anti-Individualism." I'll start with (i).

I want to remind you of the traditional distinction between seeing a thing *that is an F* and seeing a thing (whether or not it is an F) *as an F.* Both seeing and *seeing as* can, of course, be instances of objective perception. Burge is perfectly aware of the see/see as distinction, but he seems not to think it bears much weight. In fact, he sometimes uses the two expressions more or less interchangeably. That, in my view, is a Very Bad Mistake; and I think that Burge's treatment of the relation between perception and conceptualization depends on his making it.

An example: A revealing passage on page 244 is germane.[5] Burge is arguing (rightly, I believe) that in the paradigm cases, the object of *sensation* is the same as the object of *perception*: What we sense, like what we see, is a cat lurking in the bushes (not a glimpse, or a "sense datum," or an array of shapes, colors, textures … and so forth as internalists have often supposed). Burge remarks: "… one can immediately and fully apprehend something as a body. … It is not evident that it takes extra time, beyond the moment of viewing, to see a body, or to see something as a body." This sounds to me like a confusion of two claims: On the one hand, there's the (as Wittgenstein might have put it) "grammatical" observation that, if there really is a cat in the bushes, then seeing it and sensing it may be the very same event. (They come apart, however, if there *isn't* a cat.) On the other hand, there's the question whether seeing a cat *as* a cat "takes longer" than (merely) seeing a cat. Only the second question bears on the issue whether inferential (hence conceptual) processes mediate seeing. *Just* seeing a cat may require *some* conceptualization, but it surely doesn't require exercising (or even *having*) the concept CAT. Consider the case where, though what you see is in fact a cat, what you see it *as* is an old shoe. "See" is transparent to substitution of identicals. We typically see things as *things;* but that doesn't settle whether we typically see them *as* something else first, as individualists have traditionally supposed.

Just what I think has gone wrong is a longish story, but a rough approximation fits in a nutshell: on the one hand, there is *no perceiving* without *perceiving as*; and, on the other hand, there is no *perceiving as* without conceptualization; and, on the third hand, there is no conceptualization without concepts. That is what's *right* about (i) and the traditions in the philosophy of mind and in the psychology of perception that endorse it. What's *wrong* with that tradition is its forever wanting to infer from "perceiving requires conceptualization" (because it requires perceiving as, and perceiving as is a species of conceptualization) to "perception must be subject to *epistemic* constraints." The link between the premise (which is true) and the conclusion (which isn't) is the idea that there are typically epistemic constraints on *concept possession*, an idea that

5. All page references are to Burge (2010).

I take to be false root and branch. Accordingly, the path of virtue is to concede that perceiving requires conceptualizing, hence that (contrary to Burge) a viable theory of perception presupposes a viable theory of concept possession. What should be denied to the last ditch, however, is that a viable theory of concept possession requires epistemological foundations. Summary so far: Burge accuses conceptualists[6] of having overintellectualized the psychology of perception. But conceptualism is okay; seeing something at all requires seeing it as something-or-other.

Burge is right to say, as he repeatedly does, that having the concept F does not require knowing "what it is for something to be an F"; or "how to tell whether something is an F"; or "what it's like to see an F" (still less "what it's like to *be* an F"); or "what the criteria for F-ness" are; or "what belongs to the F stereotype"; and so on through many other epistemological theses about the conditions for concept possession that philosophers and psychologists have championed from time to time. Thus, a conceptualist might consistently hold both that conceptual content supervenes (not on what one believes but) on mind-world causal connections, *and* that perception requires conceptualization. Which is to say that conceptualism and anti-individualism can both be true. That is, after all, unsurprising since individualism is about the metaphysics of conceptual content, not about the role of concepts in perceptual (or other) psychological processes. Theories of mind can thus contrive to have the best of both worlds, but only at a price: they are required to bear in mind that *perceiving* requires *perceiving as* and that perceiving as requires conceptualization. But, because he holds that perception *doesn't* imply conceptualization, Burge can't do so. That's the short form of the line of argument I will pursue; details to follow.

Seeing something as an F requires seeing it as an *F*; by contrast, just seeing an F does not since you can perfectly well see an F by seeing it as a G. For convenience of exposition, philosophers like to say this sort of thing in the formal mode (thus inviting the vulgar complaint that philosophy consists of quibbles about words): "perceives an F that is G" is transparent at the G position, but "perceives an F as G" is opaque at the G position. If you see a dog, and the dog you see is brown, then it follows that you see a brown dog. That's so whether or not you notice that the dog is brown, indeed,

---

6. By stipulation, a conceptualist is someone who holds that perception requires conceptualization of the percept. On the conceptualist view, *seeing* a thing is rather like *thinking about* the thing: both require the application of concepts to their objects. Conceptualists hold that "no concepts, no thoughts" and "no concepts, no percepts" are both true: seeing something and seeing something as F requires having the concept F. What's wrong with the tradition Burge opposes isn't that it overintellectualizes *perceiving*; it's that it epistemologizes *concept possession*. It's essential to distinguish between theories about the role of concepts in perceiving and theories of concept possession. I'm going to argue that the conditions for concept possession are, in general, *not epistemic*.

whether or not you notice that it is a dog. By contrast, to see a thing *as* a brown dog is to see it as brown and as a dog; that is so whether or not it is, in fact, either. To see a red geranium as a brown dog is to see a red geranium as brown and as a dog, even though it is neither the one nor the other. This feature of "see as" (and other opaque contexts) really is puzzling; there simply is no rug under which it can be swept. In the case imagined, all there is in the world is you and a red geranium that you see, so *how does the brown dog come in*?

The immensely plausible answer is that it comes in via the concepts deployed in the seeing as. A cat may look at a queen and, in favorable conditions, may even see one. But, though I hold cats in great esteem, I doubt that a cat can see a queen *as* a queen. The reason it can't is, surely, that doing so requires having the concept QUEEN, which cats do not. At one point Burge remarks that a science of vision will need to "take perceptual states as *representational* [sic] in a psychologically distinctive sense" (Burge 2010, 347). Quite so. But in *what* psychologically distinctive sense? Answer: taking a perceptual state as representational requires a distinction between *what is perceived* and *what it is perceived as*; and "see as" is an opaque context; and seeing something as F requires deploying the concept F. Compare zoology; that a thing is a cat does *not* raise the question "what it is a cat *as*?"

So then: On the one hand, no cat that lacks the concept QUEEN can see a queen as such. But, on the other hand, a cat can't see a queen without seeing her as something-or-other. All that being so, a cat can't see anything at all if it has no concepts at all. *Cats without concepts are blind.* (Didn't Kant say something of that sort some while ago?)

I don't know what Burge would say about that; as I remarked, he seems not to make much of the "see"/"see as" distinction. But it is no help in sorting this out that Burge regularly uses versions of the locution "perception of *x as of* an F" both for perceiving an x that is F and for perceiving an x as F, thereby eliding the distinction between them. So, for example, when Burge is discussing the way that perceptual constancies militate in favor of the objectivity of perception, he speaks of the perception of a round plate as being "as of something round" even when the plate is tilted (383; I've slightly altered Burge's example, but not in a way that affects the present issues). But (in a passage about the mental mechanisms that mediate the constancies) he says that "the transformational story begins with two-dimensional retinal sensory registration and ends with visual perceptions as of attributes in the physical environment" (358). This way of talking raises a crucial question that Burge doesn't answer: whether you can have a perception "as of an attribute in the physical environment" if there is, in fact, nothing in the physical environment that has that attribute; this is, in effect, the question whether perception "as of an F" can have an opaque reading. That question is crucial; we'll presently come to why it is. First, a longish digression.

8.3   A Longish, Largely Expository Digression

I think that, at several places where he shouldn't, Burge relies heavily on an unexplicated notion of "perception of an F," thus begging questions that a theory of conceptual content ought to address head on. I'll consider two examples.

First example: In the course of explaining what "anti-individualism" is, Burge opposes the thesis that *anti*-individualism "is true of how referents are established, but that some entirely different account is true of how referents are perceived or thought about" (77). (The explicit target here is the theory that, in thoughts about water, water is represented by a water stereotype.) Burge replies that "since anti-individualism concerns ways of thinking *as* … its points cannot be captured by claiming that it concerns only reference. … [Thinking of water] is a generic type of thinking that is absolutely not to be identified with thinking of water as the colorless, odorless liquid that fills lakes [etc.]" (79). Quite so. On the natural way of reading it, the thought that *water* is wet and the thought that "[insert water stereotype] is wet" both make reference to water, but they are nevertheless different thoughts; the difference between the two is thus exactly analogous to the difference between *perceives water* and *perceives as water*. But (contrary to what Burge appears to suppose) none of this even remotely suggests that the water referred to in "perceives (/*thinks about*) water" is unconceptualized. Perhaps the difference between *perceiving/thinking about water* and *perceiving/thinking about what satisfies the water stereotype* is that it is natural to read the first but not the second as transparent.[7] In any case, as far as I can tell, Burge offers no construal of perceiving/thinking about X, *conceptualist or otherwise*, except for his remark that it is "constitutively determined by patterns of interaction with the environment beyond the individual" (79), which, since it is true of *both* perceiving (/thinking about) and of perceiving (/thinking about) *as*, doesn't distinguish the two. N.b.: the complaint here isn't that Burge lacks a *reductive* theory of *perceiving (/thinking about);* it's that what he says about *them* doesn't bear on such crucial questions as, for example, whether perceiving (/thinking about) Cicero as Tully counts as perceiving (/thinking about) Cicero; or whether perceiving (/thinking about) water as H$_2$O counts as perceiving (/thinking about) water.

To put it slightly differently, Burge's way of construing anti-individualism makes it compatible with holding that the veridicality condition on *thinking about* water implicates external conditions only in the same boring way that the veridicality condition

---

7. It adds to the confusion that, like other opaque contexts, "thought about (/referred to) water" is ambiguous: roughly, it is opaque to the substitution of identicals on the reading X *thought about (/referred to) water <u>so described</u>;* but it is transparent to substitution of identicals on the reading *water is such that* X *thought about (/referred to) water.* The point, in any case, isn't really about the logical form of English "think about/refer to" sentences. Rather, it's that, on the preferred readings, water is the intensional object of thoughts about water so described but not of thoughts about water *tout court.*

on *referring* to water clearly does. It's trivially true that what a thought *refers to* when it refers to stuff in the world as water is stuff in the world (viz. water); likewise, what a thought *is about* when it's about water is also stuff in the world (viz. water). These are, if you like, both "external" constraints on the content of water-thoughts; they both constrain how the world must be in order for thoughts to represent stuff as water. But that, surely, isn't what anti-individualism is going on about when it says that content is environmentally determined. If it were, individualists and anti-individualists could very well lie down together since both agree that it's *water* that water-thoughts represent; and that is itself an "external constraint" on the content of water-thoughts. Short form: There is a robust sense in which for a thought to be about water isn't (necessarily) for it to be about water *as such*. Likewise, to perceive water isn't (necessarily) to perceive water as such. I take all that to be common ground. But it leaves wide open whether perceiving (/thinking about) requires conceptualization (which is, of course, the main issue that Burge is concerned about). The internalist/individualist says that perceiving X requires perceiving X *as* something-or-other, just as thinking about X requires thinking about X as something-or-other. So, perceiving X and thinking about X are alike in the crucial respect: both require conceptualization of X. *That's why* philosophy and psychology have traditionally embraced a conceptualist account of both perception and thinking. Pace Burge, people hold that perception implies conceptualization *not* because they overintellectualize perception; rather it's because they have recognized that perceiving (like thinking about) requires a "mode of presentation" of whatever it is that is perceived. Both require concepts under which the object perceived (/thought about) is subsumed by the perceiver (/thinker). Burge to the contrary notwithstanding, *perception really is a lot like thought.* But whereas the conceptual mediation of thought is self-evident, recognizing the conceptual mediation of perception was among the great contributions of rationalist theories of mind. It took hard work both in the library and in the laboratory to achieve. It is not to be dismissed lightly.

Second example: There is some rough going around pages 152–168 that I think traces to Burge's not having a robust notion of *seeing as*. Consider a case where a distal orange-colored orange is displayed in a green light. A subject duly reports seeing a green(ish) orange. I would think the natural way to describe this situation is that an orange orange is being seen as green, hence as a situation in which an orange orange is misperceived. This is just the sort of work that *seeing as* is good at doing. But (to repeat) Burge doesn't have a notion of *seeing as*; so what he says instead is that the representational content of the subject's perceptual state should be specified relative to the *proximal* stimulus, *not* relative to the distal stimulus. Since, as we may assume, the proximal stimulus when you see an orange orange in a green light is the same as the proximal stimulus when you see a green orange in a white light, Burge says that the content of the perceptual state that the subject is in when seeing an orange orange in green light is "as of" seeing a green orange. So, to see an orange orange in green light as green isn't, after all, to misperceive the orange. It counts as *veridical* perception according to Burge's way of counting.

But this is surely counterintuitive; and it's a strange thing for Burge, of all people, to say. Whatever else he is, Burge is a committed externalist; and an externalist should specify perceptual content relative to its *distal* cause. To see something that looks just like water *as* water is to *mis*perceive it unless the *distal* stimulus *is* water. And, anyhow, if seeing an orange orange in green light as green is veridical, what on earth is it veridical *of?* Not the distal stimulus since, by assumption, the distal stimulus is orange. Not the proximal retinal array because (unless you are very oddly wired), you can't see your retina without a mirror. Not your brain, because brains are gray (more or less). Not an intensional object that *is* green, or a green sense datum, or anything of that sort; Burge has no truck with any of those because he holds (rightly, I think) that whatever *seeing as* is, it's not a relation between a perceiver and a queer object. Indeed, it's not a relation between a perceiver and a *mental* object. So what, then, is it?

Burge says that his way of understanding this sort of case is not a matter of philosophical interpretation but "of scientific fact" (388). I suspect, however, that it's really an artifact of his failure to appreciate the extent to which psychology needs some notion of *seeing as* even to *describe* the phenomena that it is trying to explain. It's an orange (not a sense datum or a proximal array that one sees as green when one sees an orange in a green light). If that makes problems for semantics, or epistemology, or ontology (or all three at once), such problems will just have to be faced and coped with.

Summary to here: "See," "perceive," and the like are typically transparent in the sense that if you see/perceive an x, there is an x that you see. By contrast, "see as" and the like are typically opaque; you can see something as an F even though no F is in view. (Indeed, you can see something as an F if even if there isn't anything *that* you see/perceive as an F; as when, in a hallucination, you see the surround as populated by elves.) No news so far.

Suppose, then, that you can have a perception of a plate "as of something round" even though the plate is square. Then, to put it crudely, a conceptualist will want to know *where does the roundness come from?* Well, where *does* it come from? Not from the plate since, by assumption, the plate is square; but, if Burge is right, not from the plate seen (as one says) "under the concept" ROUND, because, according to Burge, *perception doesn't involve conceptualization.* This is essential to his case; indeed, Burge's argument that the philosophy of mind is hyperintellectual consists mostly of his claim that philosophers hold that perception is a species of conceptualization, which he thinks that it isn't. By contrast, the point of the conceptualist's traditional arguments from perceptual illusions, perceptual errors, and the like is that when a square plate is seen as round, the "round" has to come from somewhere; and (short of "disjunctivism," which neither Burge nor I take very seriously) the only place that it could come from is a concept that the perceiver applies to the plate.

Still, it may be that perception doesn't need *much* by way of conceptual sophistication; externalists may be *almost* right in saying that what seeing needs is mostly that the thing that's seen is causally responsible ("in the right way") for the seeing. But, that won't do except as a first approximation much in want of refinement. There is no seeing a thing without seeing it as something-or-other, and when something looks to you to be some-way-or-other, you must have some-or-other concept that it looks to you to fall under; that seems plausible, surely, whether or not your preferred ontology is committed to such things as looks. So, the chain of inference goes like this: no seeing without *seeing as*; no *seeing as* without conceptualization; no conceptualization without concepts. Thus do intentionality and conceptualization enter into the psychology of perception; *and they enter very early,* certainly not later than perceptual errors and illusions do. To that extent at least, the "argument from illusion" is vindicated, and with it the conceptualist tradition. I don't say that's all self-evident; things really are a mess in this part of the wood. But if, when you see a cat that is moving in the bushes over there, you don't see it *as* something moving in the bushes over there, why on earth do you point your head toward the bushes when you want to see it better?

"But isn't that just another instance of the very hyperintellectualization that Burge complains about? Plants don't turn towards the sun because they see it as the sun or as anything else. Plants don't have percepts; they have tropisms." Burge makes this sort of point again and again by way of deflating intellectualist accounts of perception. But it's really not relevant. Unlike plants, we *do* see things (and so surely do infants and cats), and our having seen a thing often enters into the explanation of how we behave when we see it. Our having seen a cat moving in the bushes may well be part of the story about why we turned toward the bushes; *but only if the story includes our having seen the cat as something moving in the bushes.* What enters into the explanation of our behavior isn't the *objective stimulus* (the stimulus that we actually see); it's the *effective stimulus* (the objective stimulus *as we take it to be*). When the actual and the effective stimulus diverge, the latter prevails—it controls behavior—all else equal. The constancies are there to assure that the two *don't* diverge very often in ecologically normal situations.

Take *seeing as* away and psychology loses the effective stimulus; take the effective stimulus away and psychology loses the junction between perception and action. All right so far, except that, by definition, when the effective stimulus isn't actual, *it isn't actually there*; and, it's presumably common ground that what isn't there doesn't cause things to happen. The obvious way out of this is to say that, when the two diverge, the properties of the effective stimulus are contributed not by the objective stimulus, but by the perceiver's conceptualization of the objective stimulus, that is, the objective stimulus conceptualized (as "mentally represented") by the perceiver. So, Burge to the contrary notwithstanding, perception enters into the explanation of behavior only via the assumption that percepts are conceptualized.

I don't know how Burge proposes to get around that. Gibsonians try to do so by speaking not of a creature's response to the *effective* stimulus but of its response to what the (objective) stimulus "affords." The improvement is, however, merely apparent since what a certain stimulus affords to a perceiver depends not only on how the stimulus actually is but also on what conceptual resources the creature brings to bear in the perceptual process. So we're back where we started; perception can explain behavior only on the assumption that the percept is conceptualized.

So much for a priori argument; but here empirical considerations are also germane since they strongly suggest, at the very least, that monkeys and infants do sometimes see things as *such-and-suches* even when the things they see *aren't* such-and-suches. For example, there is evidence that babies and monkeys are sensitive to the ambiguity of bi-stable figures like the Necker cube (see, e.g., von der Heydt, Qui, and Endo 2001). This is relevant not only because it involves seeing two-dimensional figures as three-dimensional, but also because there is reason to suppose that seeing a Necker cube "switch" requires seeing some of the line intersections *as* line intersections on one interpretation and seeing them *as* junctures of intersecting sides on the other. (This is, I believe, the account of such illusions that perceptual psychologists usually offer; Pylyshyn 2003.) Likewise, there is evidence that monkeys see figures in "Escher" drawings as impossible objects(!) (Shuwairi, Albert, and Johnson 2007). So it would seem, at a minimum, that Burge's anticonceptualist claims about the concepts available to the perceptual processes of baby's and infra-human creatures argue much ahead of the relevant science.[8]

Why, then, is Burge so set against conceptualist accounts of perception? There are places where he seems to argue that for a mental representation really to be a concept, it must function as a constituent of "propositional" thoughts. I suspect that Burge thinks that the constituents of one's thoughts just are one's concepts. So if (as Burge more or less takes for granted), infants/cats haven't got propositional thoughts, it then follows that they don't have concepts either.

But, as far as I can tell, Burge doesn't actually argue for any such tight connection between having concepts and having propositional thoughts of which the concepts are constituents. He therefore begs the question against a quite standard version of modularity theory, according to which the concepts available in modular systems may be encapsulated. (By definition, encapsulated concepts can't interact with thinking or any other "higher" cognitive processes). Perhaps the right thing to say is that concepts are, of necessity, the kinds of things that can be the constituents of thoughts; but

---

8. Philosophers sometimes suggest that perception is direct (that is, not conceptually mediated) *when it is veridical.* But they can get away with that only if they are prepared to assume what is patently preposterous: that the psychological mechanisms that mediate veridical perception are ipso facto different from the psychological mechanisms that mediate illusory perception. If the reply is that the philosophy of mind doesn't care about mediating psychological mechanisms, the reply is that it bloody well ought to.

whether, in a given sort of creature, they do actually perform that function depends upon the extent to which its cognitive architecture is modular (and, for all I know, on lots of other things too). In any case, Burge needs an argument why only constituents of actual propositional thoughts can be concepts; why, in particular, shouldn't mental representations that would be constituents of thoughts but for the constraints that a modular cognitive architecture imposes be good enough to qualify as concepts? And if that would be good enough, why shouldn't such concepts have a role to play in the perceptual integration of sensory registrations? This seems to be a perfect paradigm of a question that can't be settled from the armchair. To the best of my knowledge, as the empirical findings now stand, it's wide open that perceptual processes are often both encapsulated and conceptualized. If I had to make a bet, that's certainly what I'd bet on.[9]

You may think that that is the end. But it's not.

8.4 Darwin Bashing

Rather surprisingly, the question we've been discussing—how should psychology understand the distinction between *seeing* and *seeing as?*—bears interesting analogies to a problem that seems, first blush, to live in a quite different part of the woods: How should evolutionary biology understand the distinction between *selection* (as in "homo sapiens was selected, but Neanderthal became extinct") and *selection for* (as in "having an opposed thumb was selected for in monkeys because having opposed thumbs helped them to grasp things"). I want to say a bit about this, because it bears on Burge's treatment of the content of mental representations.

To begin with a couple of terminological points: Standard biological usage generally has it that the objects of *selection* are *kinds of creatures,* typically *species*. So, the monkey was selected, but the dodo was not. (Perhaps the dodo was selected *against;* or perhaps it just died out.) By contrast, the objects of *selection for* are *traits* that are innate in a species (their *phenotypic* traits). The core of the theory of natural selection (TNS)—the thesis that is common ground among Darwinists as such—is that *phenotypic traits are ones that contribute to the adaptedness/fitness of the species* that have them.[10]

So the motto is: In the paradigm cases, *the fitness of creatures' phenotypic traits explains why they have the phenotypes that they do*; which is to say that it's the fitness of their

9. Oddly enough, Burge makes a quite similar point in an argument against Spelke (cf. 439). Spelke contrasts two hypotheses about the mental representation of bodies: according to one, it is intramodal; according to the other, it is transmodal. Burge replies, "why not both?" This question is entirely pertinent; but it would seem to apply *whenever* issues about relations between perception and conceptualization arise.

10. More precisely, they're traits that contributed to the adaptedness/fitness of members of the species *in the ecology in which the species evolved.*

phenotypic traits that explains why there are the kinds of creatures that there are. This claim is, by general consensus, the heart of TNS.[11]

But here's a point of logical syntax that really does matter and that Darwinists have very largely been confused over: "select" is transparent (like "see"); but "select for" is opaque, like "see as." If an F is selected, and if being F is coextensive with being G, then the selection of an F is ipso facto the selection of a G. By contrast, even if being F and being G are coextensive, it does not follow that selection for being F is coextensive with selection for being G (unless, of course being F and being G happen to be the same traits).

So, then, suppose two phenotypic traits are so linked that a creature that has either has both. It would *not* follow that if either of these traits was selected for, so too was the other. The reason that it wouldn't follow is that the Darwinists hold it as an empirical thesis that selection is *for traits that contribute to adaptedness;* and it's easily imagined that, of a pair of linked traits, one is adaptive and the other is neutral, or even that having the other tends to *reduce* a creature's adaptedness. (By the way, it isn't *just* imaginable; it's a sort of thing that happens all the time. For examples and discussion, see Fodor and Piattelli-Palmarini 2010.) So, because "select for" is opaque to the substitution of coextensives, it's perfectly possible that a creature has some phenotypic traits that were selected for contributing to fitness *and some that were not.* But the central thesis of TNS is that selection of creatures is selection for the adaptivity of their phenotypes. So a situation of the kind just imagined would ipso facto be a counterexample to TNS. That makes TNS a shaky foundation on which to build an account of conceptual content, as we're about to see.[12]

11. It's sometimes said to be *true by definition* that the traits that are selected for are fitness producing; but that can't be right, and people really should stop saying it. For one thing, the biologists' consensus is that the measure of the fitness of a trait is *not* whether it is selected for but rather the probability of its being inherited in successor phenotypes. This would make no sense unless it is conceptually possible that some unfit traits are selected for and some fit traits are not. And, more important for present purposes, TNS is the claim that having been selected for its contribution to adaptedness *explains why* a trait belongs to a phenotype. But that couldn't be so if the connection between *being phenotypic* and *being selected for* were conceptual. John's being unmarried doesn't e*xplain* his being a bachelor; John's being unmarried *is* his being a bachelor.

12. Darwin was himself aware of the phenomenon of linkage; it shows up in breeding, where the phenotype that you breed for is often not the one that you get. But he failed to notice that "select for" like "breed for," is intensional, or that its being so undermines the general claim that phenotypes are selected for their adaptivity. For example, it might be that the posssible phenotypes are constrained "from below" (e.g., by facts of biochemistry), and, very likely, "from above" as well (e.g., by "laws of form"). See Fodor and Piattelli-Palmarini (2010) for extensive discussion of some plausible candidates for such constraints. In our view, linkage is not an odd exception to TNS but a salient example of how properties of a creature's internal structure (i.e., *non*-ecological variables) can shape the fixation of phenotypes.

That this line of thought was, and remains, widely misunderstood by the book's critics argues against the critics, not against the book.

Now back to Burge.

Burge very much needs a notion of biological function as part of his story about the content of mental states because biological function is one of the things that Burge appeals to when he wants to distinguish adventitious causes of such states from ones that are, in his term, "constitutive of" their content. It turns out, for example, that maybe you can satisfy the constitutive conditions for thinking about water at second hand (indeed at umpteenth hand) since it might be sufficient for your thoughts to be about water that *some creature you evolved from* had thoughts whose function was to represent water in thought.

So, Burge thinks that an appeal to teleology is essential to making sense of (mental) representation. But I'm not quite certain what account of teleology he endorses. Through most of the book, the view seems to be pretty straightforwardly Darwinian: to a first approximation, phenotypic traits, mental or otherwise, are selected for their contribution to the fitness of individuals (or, perhaps of species); and the function of a phenotypic trait is to do whatever it was selected for doing. Accordingly, there is, as you would expect, much talk about the "basic" biological needs of creatures, and the roles of their phenotypes in securing the satisfaction of such needs. However, there are also places where Burge suggests that traits can function to augment a creature's "flourishing," and I'm unclear how this more or less Aristotelian notion of function is supposed to fit with the Darwinian kind, where phenotypic traits are selected for their adaptivity. What does seem clear is that "flourishing" can't explain what selection for fitness purports to explain: viz. *why there are the phenotypes that there are.* Not unless flourishing somehow reliably predicts selection in the sense that TNS has in mind. For what it's worth, though it's clear enough that many creatures manage to survive, it's far from obvious that there's a lot of flourishing around. Lots of us are pretty depressed; and, for all I know, lots of dinosaurs were too. In what follows, I'll assume that Burge's notion of teleology is Darwinian, more or less.

Since their contents are constitutive of the identity of mental states, and since coextensive mental states can differ in their contents, Burge needs a story about how the process that mediates selection for fitness distinguishes among coextensive mental states that differ in content. Here's a more or less standard example of the problem: Frogs are philosophically famous for snapping at flies, which they ingest whenever they can. It's thus natural to say that flies are the "intensional objects" of fly snaps; flies are what frogs snap *at*. But what excludes the alternative thesis that it's *little ambient black dots* that frogs snap at? That is, what excludes the thesis that little ambient black dots are what frogs see the flies they snap at *as*. On this account, ambient black dots are what frogs like to eat, and catching them is what frogs have in mind when they snap at flies. In an ecology where the ambient black dots are generally flies and vice versa, a phenotypic disposition to snap at either would be equally good to satisfy the frog's appetite. So, then, which disposition do frogs have?

These kinds of puzzles about mental content are called "disjunction problems" by philosophers whom they trouble. Burge thinks that they are frivolous because they ignore the *function* of the traits that constitute a creature's phenotype. In the present case, frogs snap at flies because doing so provides them with dinner, which is among the frog's basic needs. So, a Darwinian sort of account of the evolution of fly-snapping behavior solves its disjunction problem, but only if relevant facts about the frog's ecology are borne in mind. So: the notion of *selection for* provides a notion of biological function which, in turn, fills the gap between mental states that are *merely coextensive,* on the one hand, and *identical* mental states, on the other. Putative instances of the disjunction problem are artifacts of the characteristic philosophic mistake of ignoring the empirical facts. Given TNS, there *are no* disjunction problems, so long as all of the candidates are required to meet the test of what Gibsonians call "ecological validity." So I understand Burge to claim.

But that won't do. Here as often elsewhere, Burge begs the issue by ignoring the intensionality of the key notions; in particular, the intensionality of "select for" and "needs." As previously remarked, since it's true (by assumption) that the ambient black dots generally *are* flies (and vice versa) in the frog's ecology, a snap at either will serve a frog's needs (and augment its flourishing) just as well as a snap at the other. In the ecology they inhabit, frogs can get flies to eat *by* snapping at *ambient black dots.* So the question "what does the frog see the thing it snaps at *as*" remains wide open, *even if you attend to the frog's basic needs,* as Burge suggests that you should. Likewise, of course, the question "what function was the frog's snap selected for performing?" See how high the tides of intensionality run.[13]

It is, in short, trivial to provide truth conditions for "creatures of type X need …" and for "phenotypic trait T is selected for …" when TNS is assumed and "need" and "select for" are construed *transparently*. The problem is to provide truth conditions in cases where "need" and "select for" are construed *opaquely;* it's the opaque construal of such terms that connects issues about what frogs need/want/snap at with questions about how they mentally represent what they need/want/snap at. As far as I can tell, however, the sort of account of mental content that Burge offers provides no slightest

13. I think that appealing to ecological validity is itself question begging in this context. Saying that snapping at flies is what's "ecologically valid" and snapping at ambient black dots isn't, is just a way of saying that (all else equal) the frog snap *wouldn't have evolved in nearby worlds where there aren't flies, but would have evolved in (some) nearby worlds where there aren't ambient black dots* (perhaps, in those worlds, flies are red). So the appeal to ecological validity just replaces the disjunction worry with the worry, "How could the process of selection distinguish between mental states that differ in extension only in *possible but nonactual worlds*?" After all, only *actual* causes can actually have effects. See, once again, Fodor and Piattelli-Palmarini (2010), where such matters are discussed at length. (Fat lot of good that did us.)

clue of what the difference in mental content is between frogs that want to eat some flies for dinner and frogs that want to eat some ambient black dots for dinner.[14]

Short form: It's primarily in discussing "disjunction problems" that Burge uses "perceive as" explicitly and extensively. That's not surprising since a very natural way of phrasing a disjunction problem is, "What do frogs see their prey as?" Burge likes the idea that such questions are answered (or, perhaps, dismissed) by appeals to psychological theories together with ecological facts of the sort pursued by investigations in macrobiology, physiology, zoology, and related empirical sciences. But that doesn't help; it just moves the problems about intensionality from one guy's desk to another's. "See as" is intensional; but so too are "select for," "function as," and "explain." The question "what do frogs snap at?" arises, sooner or later, in every science whose domain contains intensional systems. (Gibsonians take note: "affords" is intensional too). So, what do ambient flies "afford" to frogs? Food? Ambient flies? Dinner? Instantiated ambient-black-dotness?

8.5   Conclusion

There are lots of morals to be drawn from the discussion we've been having. One is that it's a bad idea to beg questions about intensionality; another is that it's a good idea, even for philosophers, not to ignore matters of empirical fact; another is that Darwin didn't, after all, solve the problems about the empirical underdetermination of content. I want to emphasize the first of these in rounding off the chapter.

Philosophers have, by and large, taken it for granted that intensionality is, par excellence, a topic in the theory of mind (or perhaps in modal logic, which some have hoped might solve the problem in the theory of mind). There have been various suggestions about what psychology should do about intensionality: one explicitly recommends that it should give up on the mind and make do with just the material brain. Another is that it should give up on matter and make do with just the immaterial mind. Another is that it should give up on both matter and mind since intensional explanation and neurological explanation are both just "stances" and are thus merely "optional."

14. This is, of course, not just an argument against Burge's treatment of mental content, but also against any Darwinian account of biological teleology. Biologists have told me, from time to time, that TNS must be true because biological explanation must have access to a notion of biological function, and only TNS can provide one. I don't know whether it's true that biological explanation presupposes teleology (though Burge clearly thinks that psychological explanation does); but whether it's true that biology requires an account of teleology is beside the present issues since TNS doesn't provide one. Or rather, it does so only by playing on the intensional ambiguity of "need," "snap at," "select for" (and, for that matter, "explain"), which nobody ought to be allowed to do. Not even Darwin.

And so forth. But whichever story is preferred, the view is that only psychologists and philosophers need to worry over the problems that intensional explanation would appear to raise; and, on second thought, maybe psychologists needn't bother.

In the event, however, that view has proved to be wildly optimistic. Issues about intensionality turn up all over the place, not just in psychological explanations insofar as they are teleological, but also in biological explanations insofar as they rely on such notions as *selection for*. And in historical explanations; and in explanations in economics; and in political science; and God only knows where else we would find them if we chose to look. The moral is: It's long overdue that we try to understand, in some detail, just how intensional explanation works and, in particular, when it is appropriate in science and when it isn't. My objection to Burge's book is largely that, by eliding the distinction between *see* and the like and *see as* and the like, it distracts attention from that project.

I don't know where such a serious empirical account of intensionality might lead (though I suspect that, at a minimum, major revisions are going to be required in theories about the fixation of phenotypes, TNS included). Suffice it that if, as Burge rightly urges, it would be a good idea for philosophers to pay attention to relevant findings in the sciences, it would likewise be a good idea for scientists to pay attention to relevant findings in philosophy. Just for a change.

Appendix: The Doors of Perception, the Black Swan, and the Pale Cast of Thought

If I read it right, Burge's book is committed to some or other version of this argument:

Burge's argument:
1. Concepts are constituents of thoughts.
2. Infants and animals, though they don't think (don't have "propositional thoughts"), patently do perceive.
3. Perception does not require the application (or even the possession) of concepts; in particular, it shouldn't be viewed, Kant-wise, as the integration of a sensory manifold under a concept.

By contrast, the present chapter is committed to some or other version of this argument:

4. Seeing requires *seeing as*.
5. *Seeing as* requires conceptualization.
6. There is no seeing without conceptualizing.

This does appear to be a dilemma: at least one of these arguments must be faulty. Which one?

I think it's Burge's. Because:

• 1 equivocates in a way that is important. Does it say that any concept a creature has must be a constituent of some of its thoughts? Or does it say that any concept it has *can* be a constituent of some of its thoughts (in effect, that concepts are *the kinds of things* that can be constituents of thoughts)? Notice that although the former is incompatible with the conjunction of 1 and 2, the latter is not.

I'm inclined to think that it is some sort of a priori truth that concepts are ipso facto potentially constituents of thoughts; but it's not true a priori (in fact, it's very likely just not true) that a creature's concepts are ipso facto constituents of some thoughts that it *actually has*. There are many reasons to think that it's not. For example, it seems perfectly possible that a mind should have *encapsulated* concepts, including concepts that are available for integrating sensory manifolds but not for thinking. There are, in fact, empirical reasons to suppose that sort of thing happens quite a lot.

Assume, as psychologists often do (and as practically all the linguists I know actually believe) that there is a "language module" and that the utterances a speaker/hearer understands are mentally represented within this module by parsing trees whose nodes are labeled S, NP, VP, PP, and the like. Assuming that would *not* require holding that a five-year-old who understands "that's a large cat" ever does, or even can, think the thought "large cat" is a noun phrase; it wouldn't imply that five-year-olds ever think anything at all about noun phrases. All that would follow is that children *could* think thoughts about NPs *if* they could think all the thoughts that their repertoire of concepts permits, which is exactly what modular accounts of mental processes deny. Burge, who very commendably disapproves of flying in the face of science if one can avoid so doing, would be the last philosopher to accept a concept of concept that makes generative grammar false a priori.

• The empirical status of 2 is very far from clear. Here's a finding that animal psychologists routinely demonstrate to their introductory classes: In the experiment, a rat (pigeon, whatever) is "reinforced for" pressing a bar. However, things are so arranged that a bar-press eventuates in food *only when it is made in the presence of a certain "discriminative stimulus,"* for example, only when a certain light is on. The empirical facts are not in dispute.

The following explanation is prima facie plausible: The rat learns that the reinforcement of a bar press is contingent on the presence of the discriminative stimulus. Having learned that, it reasons as follows: A bar press is reinforced if and only if the light is on; on this trial, the light is (/isn't) on; so on this trial I should (/shouldn't) press the bar. It proceeds to do so (/not do so) accordingly. Short form: the patterning of the rat's behavior is caused by its reasoning in accordance with modus ponens.

No doubt, that sort of explanation could be wrong. Perhaps the rat is a behaviorist and thus thinks that rats don't think; or perhaps it is an associationist, and thus thinks that learned behaviors are associations of stimuli with responses. But, so far at least, no remotely plausible behavioristic or associationistic explanation of the learning of discriminative responses is on offer; and the question arises why, if rats shouldn't be supposed to reason, it should be supposed that people do? But if rats can reason, surely infants can too. Consider, for example, the recent experimentations on "number constancy" in babies (reviewed in Carey 2009).

• Burge's conclusion directly contradicts the view—prominent in the psychology of visual perception—that many illusions (the Necker cube, the Müller-Lyer, the moon illusion, among lots of others) turn on what the constituents of the stimulus are seen *as;* according to one familiar account, to get the Müller-Lyer illusion, you must see the figures either as corners projecting toward you or as corners projecting away from you. It thus appears that an opaque notion of "seeing as" is sine qua non for a viable theory of perception. (Analogous examples can easily be found in the literatures on auditory perception and elsewhere.)

One might, I suppose, reply by claiming that 4 is in doubt. I don't believe that it is because I can't think of a remotely plausible counterexample. Stendhal tells us that del Dongo saw Napoleon at Waterloo, but only as a figure on a horse galloping by. He might instead have seen him only as a spot on the horizon and he would have seen Napoleon in either case; "see" is *very* transparent. But, if del Dongo did see Napoleon, he must have seen him as something-or-other. Mustn't he? If del Dongo didn't see Napoleon as something-or-other, how could he have seen Napoleon at all?

But I agree that that those are all pretty negative sorts of arguments. Here's one that's less so: Perception can affect beliefs; presumably doing so is part of its job description. Suppose you believe (wrongly) that all swans are white; and suppose you see a black swan. Then (assuming rationality) shouldn't the strength of your belief that all swans are white be shaken? Well, no; it depends on whether you see the black swan *as* a black swan. Perhaps you see it as a black channel marker (worse things happen at sea). Then, all else equal, your seeing the black swan won't (and oughtn't) affect the strength of your belief that all swans are white. "See as" is *very* much less transparent than "see." I conclude that the conceptualization of perceptual representations is prior to their effects on the fixation of beliefs; n.b.: prior, even, to their effects on the fixation of perceptual beliefs.

Versions of this line of argument have been in the philosophical literature at least since Sellars, who thought that it refutes claims for a perceptual "given" of the kind that sense-data theories endorse. But, in fact, it doesn't; Sellars apparently failed to consider the possibility that perceptual integration proceeds through several stages of mental representation, and that a sense-data analysis might be true of *some of them* even though it isn't true of *all of them.* This is essentially the view endorsed by computational theories of perception according to which the earliest mental representations of a percept are the outputs of "transducers."

Burge has, however, a reply to "black swan" arguments. "I accept Sellars's (Kant's) view that reasons that support knowledge must be propositional. ... I do not accept Sellars's assumption that reasons are the only source of epistemic warrant" (435). But that reply won't do for the present purposes. The issue isn't whether an account of perceptual information as unconceptualized would be adequate to the purposes of a normative epistemology; it's whether such an account would be adequate to the purposes of an empirical psychology. Normative issues entirely to one aside, if Burge is right and belief content is conceptualized but perceptual content is not, *how is it possible that creatures learn from their perceptual experience?* Seeing a black swan as a black swan would, really and truly, shake my belief that all swans are white. My belief that all swans are white surely counts as propositional if anything does; modulo well-known worries about generic NPs, it's logical form is (something like) *(x) x is a swan → x is white.* But then, how could I take my seeing a black swan as black to be counterinstance to my belief that all swans are white unless I mentally represent the content of my perception as (something like) *∃x (x is a swan and not white)?* How else could I learn *from my perceptual experience* that *all swans are white* isn't true?

If the mental representations that express the objects of belief have conceptual structure, then so too do the mental representations that express the objects of perception. The (dis)confirmation of beliefs by perceptions won't settle for less.

References

Burge, T. 2010. *Origins of Objectivity*. New York: Oxford University Press.

Carey, S. 2009. *The Origins of Concepts*. New York: Oxford University Press.

Fodor, J., and M. Piattelli-Palmarini. 2010. *What Darwin Got Wrong*. New York: Farrar, Straus and Giroux.

Pylyshyn, Z. 2003. *Seeing and Visualizing: It's Not What You Think*. Cambridge, MA: MIT Press.

Shuwairi, S., M. Albert, and S. Johnson. 2007. Discrimination of possible and impossible objects in infancy. *Psychological Science* 18 (4): 303–307.

von der Heydt, R., F. Qui, and K. Endo. 2001. Depth perception with ambiguous displays in humans and monkeys. *Perception* 30 (ECVP abstract supplement): 41.

9 Observational Concepts

Daniel A. Weiskopf

9.1 From Perception to Thought

How is it that we are able to think about what we perceive? More specifically, how are we able to bring the resources of conceptualized thought to bear on the objects and events that are represented to us in perception? And how much of our capacity for conceptualized thought is undergirded by, or is an extension of, our capacities for perception and action? Addressing these questions requires disentangling some of the more tightly woven strands linking perception, thought, and action.

Although one of the most distinctive features of human concepts is that they extend over indefinitely many types of things that transcend perception, we can also reflect on straightforwardly perceivable objects, and the concepts we have of these objects are often acquired by perceptually encountering and manipulating them. Additionally, how we perceive the world is infused or colored by the conceptual capacities that we possess. We don't merely see the cat, we see her *as* a cat, a visual state that depends on conceptualizing her in a certain way. And in virtue of seeing her as a cat, we may come to form perceptual beliefs concerning her presence and qualities. Thus, conceptualized perception enables conceptualized thought.

My aim here is to illuminate what happens at the interface between perception and higher cognition. On the view I develop, *observational concepts* are the pivot on which this relationship turns. Observational concepts are those that are spontaneously made available at the interface between perception-action systems and the conceptual system. They correspond to the ways we have of conceptually dividing the world based solely on the available perceptual information. We are able to treat what is perceived as evidence for what isn't directly perceived (or, indeed, perceivable at all). Observational concepts form the evidential basis for these perception-transcendent inferences. And ultimately, we acquire ways of thinking about perceived things that are not tied directly to how they are perceived; observational concepts are central to this process insofar as they provide us with an initial way of conceptually tracking categories that we will learn to represent in perception-transcendent ways.

In what follows, I situate observational concepts in the larger architecture of cognition, characterize their role and content, describe how they are learned, and show how they play a key role in learning further concepts. Along the way I distinguish them from related constructs such as recognitional concepts and show that arguments against recognitional concepts fail to work against observational concepts. I conclude by discussing what observational concepts can teach us about the extent to which perceptual systems and representations may shape higher cognition.

9.2   Interfaces

Observational concepts are distinguished by their functional role, specifically by the location they occupy in the overall architecture of cognition. Many issues about cognitive architecture remain largely unsettled, but the only architectural assumption employed here is the distinction between input-output systems and central cognitive systems. Central systems include but need not be exhausted by the conceptual system, which is not assumed to be unitary.[1]

In the simplest case, the mapping from perceptual systems to central systems is direct, so that the hierarchy of levels of sensory processing culminates in contact between sensory systems and systems of conceptual interpretation. There may, however, be complex perception-action connections that bypass higher thought, as in some forms of online sensorimotor coordination. On a more indirect arrangement, perceptual systems feed first into intermediate nonconceptual systems that preprocess sensory inputs by transforming, modifying, tagging, and re-representing them in various ways.[2] Whether the arrangement is direct or indirect, however, there must be some sort of interface between the conceptual system and these various nonconceptual processing systems. What goes on at such an interface is precisely a transition from the

1. The main views ruled out by this assumption are subsumption-style architectures and variations on them, that is, any model on which there are mainly layers of horizontal connections running directly from sensory input to motor output, with few connections between these layers (Hurley 2008). Although I will mostly speak of *the* conceptual system here, massive modularists may replace this with talk about a host of central modules.

2. This is one way of viewing the systems of core cognition discussed by Carey (2009). Core cognitive systems are domain-specific mechanisms that analyze perceptual inputs and produce conceptual outputs, including foundational concepts of objects, number, and agency. While Carey holds that these systems have "integrated conceptual content" (2009, 67), she also holds that they use iconic but nonperceptual representations. Architecturally, they are an intermediate processing stage between perception and central cognition.

way the world is represented in perception (or nonconceptually) to the way that we conceive of the world.[3]

The outputs of perception, while nonconceptual, are enormously rich, presenting us with a three-dimensional world that comes divided into distinct objects and events that are assigned locations and motion vectors in space, along with various perceivable qualities: color, shape, shading, texture, degree of solidity, and so forth (Clark 2004; Matthen 2005). These outputs constitute interface representations, inasmuch as they are accessible to both conceptual and nonconceptual systems. The job of these representations is to present a limited body of information from one system to another in a *legible* format, where a representation's format is the way in which its semantic content is encoded in the structure of the vehicle. The way a system formats information is tailored to the problem it solves or the task it carries out. Candidate formats for mental representations include icons and images, propositions, frames, maps, models, analog accumulators, and so on.

Interfaces can be classified in several ways. First, systems can make use of the same representational vehicles or different ones. Consider a parsing mechanism that contains syntactic and semantic components. The syntactic parser might construct a tree that represents constituency, dominance, and other formal relations, which is then passed to the semantic parser for interpretation. Here the same representation is transferred from one system to another. Among interfaces that use the same vehicles, some involve passing along *all* of their representational outputs across the interface, while others involve passing only *some* of them. The latter case can arise where one system interfaces with two downstream systems, each of which has access to only some of its outputs. This occurs in vision, where after the common retinocortical pathway and processing in V1, the visual output divides into the dorsal and ventral streams, which make use of different properties of the visual input (Milner and Goodale 2006). Where an interface involves passing all of one system's output to another, making use of the same vehicles, call this a *pass-through* interface; where only a subset of these representations are disseminated, call this a *filter*. Systems that compute intermediate level representations often impose filters that prevent these from being passed downstream, and some systems filter their outputs differently depending on the consumer systems they are feeding.

---

3. I have been framing things here in a way that takes sides in the debate between conceptualists and nonconceptualists about perception. While there are many ways of drawing this distinction, for present purposes we can say that nonconceptualists hold that perceptual states are not individuated by reference to the conceptual repertoire of the cognizer, while conceptualists hold that they are. I am assuming nonconceptualism in the following sense: there is at least some range of perceptual states available to cognizers that is independent of the conceptual capacities that they possess; being in these states does not involve deploying any concepts.

Finally, some interfaces occur between systems that make use of different representational vehicles. Call these *translational* interfaces: ones that transform information encoded in one format to information encoded in another. The simplest example is a digitizer, which converts a continuous analog signal into discrete bits. Cognitive systems employ many different encoding schemes for different kinds of information, so there must exist at least some translational interfaces of varying degrees of complexity. In numerical cognition, there are mappings from a display of a quantity to an analog accumulator; in visually guided reaching, a perception of an object in space is mapped to a motor representation of how it can be grasped; and in language production, a semantic representation is mapped to a phonological word form. These systems involve different codes, so their interfaces are translational.

This way of thinking about interfaces has a nice virtue: it just happens to correspond well with the major historical proposals about how concepts are acquired from perception. Empiricist theories of concepts adhere to the *shared vehicles thesis*: conceptual thought reuses the representational vehicles deployed in perception (Barsalou 1999; Prinz 2002). On classical empiricist views such as Locke's and Hume's, the relationship between percepts and concepts is described in several ways, the simplest of which involves the process of copying. In Hume's terms, ideas are less vivid copies of impressions, where copying preserves an impression's form but drains some of its "force and vivacity." Concepts are copies of percepts that play a distinctive functional role in cognition, and since copying preserves most of the properties of representational vehicles, acquiring a concept from experience involves a pass-through mechanism that causally reproduces those vehicles in a different system.

Beyond simple Humean copying, Locke sometimes describes the acquisition of complex ideas as a kind of abstraction from experience with particular category members. A Lockean abstraction mechanism selectively deletes distinctive features and retains common ones, and in this sense it is a filter for these features. The output of this process is a general concept: a stripped-down perceptual representation that captures the characteristics shared by the instances and other category members. In much this way, Locke describes the learning of a general idea like HUMAN as a process of comparing ideas of individual persons (Mama, nurse, etc.) and subtracting their distinctive qualities. As an approximation, then, we can think of Humean copying as a pass-through mechanism, and Lockean abstraction as a filter.[4]

Nonempiricist views of concepts, by contrast, see this interface as being translational, since they hold that thought employs an amodal code distinct from those used in perception. So Fodor (2008) distinguishes between perceptual and conceptual representations on the grounds that the former are *iconic* while the latter are *discursive*.

4. This is a simplification in many ways, not least of which that Locke seems to have had several theories of conceptualization running at once. See Gauker (2011, chapter 1) for an excellent discussion.

In iconic representations, every part of the representation stands for a part of what is represented, while discursive representations have a "canonical decomposition" into constituents, which are the only parts of the representation that contribute to its overall semantic interpretation. Photographs are iconic: in a photo of a koala, every part of the photo represents some part of the koala; the part containing its round, fuzzy ears represents those very ears, their shape and texture, and so forth. Sentences, on the other hand, are discursive, so that in the sentence "the koala has round and fuzzy ears," the string *the koala* represents a contextually specified bear, but the string *has round and* represents nothing, since it is not a semantically relevant part. Although every part of an icon is semantically significant, not every part of a discursive representation is. Accordingly, in moving from perceptual/iconic representations to conceptual/discursive ones, a semantically homogeneous input is discretized by a translation mechanism.[5]

The minimal conception of an interface is a device that mediates information transfer and control between two or more systems by letting the output states of the producer systems determine the input states of the consumer systems. An interface is a *normal route* for this kind of configuration. And the taxonomy of possible interfaces is one that maps onto the historically dominant accounts of conceptualization in the empiricist and rationalist traditions.

9.3 Observational Concepts Introduced

We can now reintroduce the idea of an observational concept. Where perceptual systems make contact with central cognition, there is an interface whose function is to generate a conceptual output in response to that type of perceptual input. Given the structure of the interface and the right background conditions, certain percepts will be causally sufficient to produce conceptual output states in a way that is not mediated by any other concepts.[6] Observational concepts are those concepts that are spontaneously activated or made available for use solely on the basis of a subject's being in a certain perceptual state.

Such concepts are the basic constituents of perceptual judgments, such as the belief that there is a cat on the green chair by the window, that those are sunflowers, or that there was just a loud bang to our left. These are our perceptually informed opinions

5. One needn't hold that concepts are encoded discursively to think of this interface as translational. Mental model-style views of higher cognition might employ map-like representations that nevertheless differ from the iconic representations employed in perception. See also Mandler (2004).

6. Any such mediation, should it exist, cannot go on forever—if one concept's activation is itself conceptually mediated, then that mediating concept is observational. Given the nature of interfaces, we can know that this regress must terminate, since there cannot be infinitely many representations lying along this causal pathway.

concerning the objects and events that surround us; they are the judgments that we can be in a position to make about the environment just on the basis of what perception plus our repertoire of observational concepts make available.[7]

There are two counterfactual aspects to this specification of observational concepts. First, these concepts are not *invariably* tokened when the right perceptual inputs are present. Perceiving a tree does not always lead to tokening TREE, still less to thinking THAT IS A TREE. The reference to background conditions becomes important. These conditions have to do with resources like attention and memory as well as motivational factors, goals, interests, and other ongoing thoughts one is entertaining. Perceptual inputs are sufficient for activating the appropriate observational concepts as long as the background conditions are those that dispose the creature to be conceptually responsive to its perceptual input. This is compatible with the possibility that perceptual states only ever actually lead to thoughts involving such concepts against a background of already active thoughts, plans, and broader aspects of one's mental "set." It only needs to be *possible* for these concepts to be entertained in isolation from this surrounding mental activity.

Perceptions don't dictate what perceptual judgments follow from them, nor how the perceived scene will ultimately be conceptualized. A trivial example: the visual perception of the cat dozing on the chair may give rise to the belief that the cat is on top of the chair or the (distinct) belief that the chair is under the cat. The cat itself might be represented as a cat, as an animal, or as Sophie. The same auditory perception might be equally well conceptualized as a sigh or a snort. All that is required is that some concepts are immediately made available by the occurrence of a perceptual state, though a representation's being made available, in the present sense, doesn't entail its being deployed for any particular purpose.

Second, perceptual input itself is not *necessary* for the activation of an observational concept, since being a concept requires availability for many other cognitive processes, including offline reasoning and planning, direction of other actions such as the formation of mental images, and so on. These tasks can take place under endogenous control, in the absence of any ongoing perception. So observational concepts have a distinctive set of application conditions that tie them to perception, but they also enjoy the free deployability characteristic of concepts generally.

Observational concepts are not merely *occasioned* by perceptual experience but are in a stronger sense *directed at* or *applied to* what is perceived. In a weak sense, a percept can be associatively linked with any sort of mental or behavioral state. There are direct behavioral associations such as the photic sneeze reflex, or potentially arbitrary

---

7. For an excellent discussion of the epistemology of perceptually basic beliefs in this sense, see Lyons (2008). The view being developed here does not purport to have any special epistemological status or import, although it might be developed in those directions.

psychological associations such as thoughts of springtime coming to mind whenever I see lilies. To forge a link stronger than mere association between perceiving an object and forming perceptual judgments about it, there needs to be a semantic relationship of co-application or co-indexing. A percept and concept are *co-indexed* when the concept is, or is disposed to be, applied to the very same object that the percept is tracking.[8] A function of interfaces is to provide such semantic relationships so that information about the same object can be collected across different cognitive systems and representational formats. When vision or any other object-centered sense divides the perceived environment into an array of entities, they are passed on to the conceptual system along with individuating tags that distinguish them as separate possible objects of classification and predication.

Finally, this division of representational labor gives us an account of recognitional seeing, or *seeing as*. To see a tree, and to see it *as* a tree, are two different states. The latter is more complex in that it contains the former. Seeing x involves having a representation of the perceptual qualities of x that is indexed to the object x itself; seeing x as F involves having this percept co-indexed with the concept F. States of seeing as are thus perceptual-conceptual hybrids, having one foot in each system. But notice that seeing x as F falls slightly short of seeing that x is F. Seeing as is a (partially) conceptualized state, but not a propositional state. Activating a concept, making it ready for use, is not the same as employing it in a judgment, which is the form of *seeing that*. In this sense, you can recognize x to be F without entertaining the proposition that x is F.

9.4   Against Perceptual Inflation

Observational concepts are limited by the perceptual similarities we can reliably track. In particular, it would seem we cannot have observational concepts of abstract entities (those that have no physical, perceivable manifestations at all) and categories that have overly heterogeneous perceptual presentations. Call this, following Jesse Prinz (2005), the *imperceptibility thesis*. Prinz denies the thesis and argues that we can perceive indefinitely many abstract categories; indeed, virtually anything we can form a concept of

8. Much work in midlevel vision has emphasized the need for such co-indexing representations (Pylyshyn 2001; Scholl 2001). This work is obviously relevant here, with the caveat that the instantiation tags referred to in this literature are usually opened when objects move, change, or otherwise become salient. I would expand this notion so that any object that can be distinguished from its environment can be tagged and be the subject of conceptual predication. In fact, co-indexing relationships are needed for two cognitive purposes. One is to ensure that multiple representations track the same object across processing systems and contexts. The other, emphasized by Clark (2004), is to ensure that separate representations are linked synchronically into a single representation of an object; that is, to solve the *binding problem*.

can be perceived. This includes abstract categories of things such as numbers, or properties such as *being a philosophy major* or *being an uncle*.

Prinz's argument turns on his view about recognitional perceiving. One perceives X just in case: (1) X impinges on one's sensory transducers, (2) leading to the formation of a perceptual representation, (3) which is in turn matched against stored representations of X. So to perceive something involves forming a percept of it and retrieving a representation of it, where the content of the retrieved representation determines the content of the perception one has. In addition, Prinz follows Dretske's (1986) informational semantics, on which M represents C just in case instances of C have the power to cause instances of M, and this relationship holds because M has the function of detecting C. Content is a matter of teleologically established and sustained informational connections.

Many abstract and intuitively imperceptible qualities will turn out to be perceivable on this view, since there is always some perceptual scenario that can cause us to retrieve representations of them. Consider being an uncle. Uncles have no common perceptual look, so I cannot just pick them out in a crowded room. However, if I arrange for all and only the uncles to raise their hands (assuming everyone is sincere and cooperative), they suddenly share such a look. If I arrange to get myself to think someone is an uncle just in case their hand is raised, and hand raising is a detectable look, then what I am perceiving is *unclehood*, since my UNCLE concept is activated when I see their raised hands.

Now consider number. Small numbers might be perceivable; triples of discrete objects have a distinctive look, so perhaps we can perceive *threeness* and form the corresponding observational concept. Few think that we can perceive or form such concepts of higher numbers such as fifty-seven. But we can arrange a situation in which we will activate FIFTY-SEVEN in response to a perceptual scenario: we simply count the objects, keeping track of them using number words. Our saying the numerals out loud or internally is a perceptual state, so when we run out of things to count, we have perceived the number corresponding to the last numeral that was perceptually activated. Generalizing these examples shows that we are able to perceive both abstract entities and qualities, so the imperceptibility thesis would be false.

But Prinz's account of perceptual content is implausibly permissive. Neither perception nor observational concepts themselves have contents as rich as the arbitrarily abstract categories that we can conceive of. The problem lies with the open-ended notion of recognitional perceiving. Recall that *any* sort of representation that can be retrieved as part of the comparison or retrieval process initiated by perception can contribute to what is perceived, and there are no limits on how complicated these processes may be. This lack of limits is what lets us perceive uncles by seeing raised hands—but since this connection depends on a complex cognitive arrangement that goes beyond what the perceptual system itself contributes, we should not consider it an act of perception, properly speaking. Similarly in the number case: the act of counting large numbers uses more cognitive resources (memory, language, etc.) than just what our perceptual systems provide.[9] Worries about this form of content inflation are blocked on the account of observational concepts given here by the requirement that their deployment be under the control of an interface, rather than allowing any downstream representation to count.

Susanna Siegel (2010) has also argued that the contents of perception are extremely rich, so rich that we can perceptually represent not just colors, shapes, textures, and the rest of the qualities that traditional theories of vision admit, but also so-called K-properties. These include properties covering objects (natural and artifact kinds), actions and events, mental states, and semantic facts, for example: *person, mountain, bicycle, carrying a dog, being inquisitive, being a word of Russian, being a phrase meaning "the highway exit is ahead."* According to the *rich content view*, all of these are possible contents that we can grasp in experience, and we can recognize this fact from attending to the phenomenology of the relevant experiences.

Siegel's argument runs as follows. Consider two related experiences: in E1, you are looking at a bunch of pine trees, but you do not have the ability to visually recognize pine trees; and in E2, you are looking at the same trees, but you have learned to recognize them. There is, it would seem, a phenomenological difference between these two experiences. Being able to perceptually recognize what you are looking at is different from not knowing what you are looking at, and the overall phenomenological state one occupies in each case seems different. To arrive at the rich content view, three further premises are needed: (1) if E1 and E2 differ in phenomenology, then there is a phenomenological difference between the experiences themselves; (2) if there is a phenomenological difference between them, then they differ in content; and (3) if they differ in content, it is a difference with respect to the K-properties that those experiences represent. Since we have granted that E1 and E2 differ in phenomenology, we quickly reach the conclusion that experience represents K-properties.

The account of how concepts come into play in acts of perceptual recognition gives us a response to this argument, one that focuses on the denial of premise (1). We should grant that there is a phenomenological difference for the perceiver having E1

---

9. Prinz does argue separately that our sensory systems proper can represent these abstract categories as well. Here he relies on the existence of downward projections from higher cortical centers to the sensory systems themselves. These downward projections allegedly allow conceptual information to "infuse" sensory processing. However, on Prinz's official theory of content, it is hard to see how this might work. If the dominant cause of activity in sensory systems is the perceivable object, then that is what sensory representations refer to, not abstractions. If their cause is split among external objects and higher-level systems, the theory does not assign them content, since their function and informational role is indeterminate.

versus E2, but deny that this difference is located in the visual experience proper.[10] Siegel, in sketching possible responses, considers two related objections to this premise. Both involve saying that the phenomenological difference between E1 and E2 lies not in the visual experience itself but in some associated psychological aspect, in particular in some sort of *cognitive* experience. If E1 and E2 differ only in this related respect, there is no difference in visual content, particularly not with respect to the representation of K-properties.

The candidate cognitive experiences Siegel considers, however, are all forms of propositional representation. They are either commitment-involving attitudes (e.g., beliefs or judgments) or noncommittal attitudes (e.g., hunches or merely entertained thoughts). Against the idea that the phenomenological difference comes from the presence of a commitment-involving attitude such as the belief that *that* is a pine tree, notice that I might well believe (because I am reliably informed) that the tree appearances I perceive are not real trees, but only props or holograms. Despite this belief, they might appear phenomenologically different in situations E1 and E2. So committal attitudes such as beliefs cannot make the difference between the two.

Against the idea that noncommittal attitudes might explain the difference, she presumes these attitudes to be occurrent thoughts such as *that kind of tree is familiar*. Thoughts of seeming familiarity say nothing about what the perceived objects themselves are. However, she argues, these thoughts are simply unnecessary: "There need not be, it seems, an extra episode (or occurrent state), beyond sensing, for the phenomenological change to take effect" (106). So any alleged noncommittal attitude would be redundant in explaining the E1/E2 difference. Given that (with a few caveats) these two possibilities exhaust the primary forms of nonsensory experience, we can conclude that the phenomenological differences are located in the visual experiences themselves, not in any adjoining cognitive states.

Observational concepts have a distinctive functional role that renders them well poised to thread this needle, however. First, as noted above, they are not propositional representations, and they do not *inherently* carry committal force. They may do so, if a concept becomes activated to the point where it is actually endorsed and applied to a perceived scene. The application of a concept to perception is a state that has distinctive correctness conditions, and thinkers are committed to these. But since activation is graded, these concepts may be exerting an effect even though they are not past the threshold for being applied. In the hologram case, once I am told that the trees are fake, I refrain from applying the concept, but it may retain a residual level of activation.

10. I should add that talk of experiences here is Siegel's; I am glossing *visual experiences* as being states that depend for their instantiation on activity in visual systems; similarly, *cognitive experiences* are states that depend on nonperceptual systems in some way. This gives a way of mapping experience talk onto talk of underlying cognitive systems.

What, then, of the objection that these concepts constitute merely a redundant noncommittal component? It is not clear that we have a separate occurrent state here at all. Observational concepts are distinct from their perceptual antecedents, true, but their activation levels are gradual. So the simple notion of a state's being (non)occurrent does not obviously have application here. Certainly the issue cannot be settled by intuitions about how many "episodes" are involved in an experience. Siegel suggests that if a nonsensory event is not explicit and occurrent, then "it becomes less clear that it is phenomenally conscious at all" (107). But why is this? The phenomenal properties of cognitive states, or their contribution to overall phenomenology, may in principle depend on any aspect of their functional or representational role. To take an example, tip-of-the-tongue states are cognitive, but they have a highly distinctive phenomenology that is plausibly underpinned not by explicitly entertaining any proposition, but rather by cascades of activation washing through networks of lexical and semantic memory. If these types of spreading activation can contribute to cognitive phenomenology, the same should be true of the varying levels of activation in the case of observational concepts.

What these two cases show is that attending to the role of observational concepts can help to establish boundaries on the representational power of perception. Architectural divisions determine what can be recognitionally perceived, thus blocking the sort of content inflation Prinz's account invites. Similarly, a wider range of functional interactions between perception and cognition can help us to account for the phenomenology of perceptual recognition without endorsing Siegel's rich content view.[11] The phenomenological evidence that Siegel draws our attention to needs to be explained, but only by uncovering the details of the larger architecture and how it assigns content to underlying systems and states.

9.5   Observational versus Recognitional Concepts

Observational concepts in my sense are not the same as recognitional concepts. Fodor presents a view of recognitional concepts according to which "a concept is recognitional iff: (1) it is at least partially constituted by its possession conditions, and (2) among its possession conditions is the ability to recognize at least some things that fall under the concept as things that fall under the concept" (Fodor 1998, 1). Recognitional concepts are those that are in part constituted by abilities to recognize some things in their extension. If RED and SQUARE were recognitional, then possessing them would mean

11. Although I am not necessarily endorsing the idea that all of Siegel's K-properties can be the content of observational concepts, in my sense. Addressing this issue would require more clarity both on the scope of observational concepts, and on how to fill in the list of K-properties.

necessarily being able to apply them to red things and squares, respectively, on the basis of the appropriate perceptual encounter.

Fodor argues that there cannot be any such recognitional concepts, on the grounds that recognitional abilities fail to be compositional. Since compositionality is a necessary condition on concepts, anything noncompositional cannot be part of what individuates concepts. The main premise of his argument is that the possession conditions for a complex concept must include the possession conditions for its constituents. So whatever states, capacities, dispositions, and so forth are required for having complex concepts such as RED SQUARE, FISH FOOD, or ONE-ARMED MAN necessarily include whatever is required to have the concepts that make them up. Possession conditions are inherited compositionally. But the ability to recognize instances is not inherited in this way. One can be able to separately recognize fish and food but not be able to recognize that those confetti-like flakes are fish food. Recognizing fish food depends on knowing something about what fish actually eat, not on anything one could extract from the constituent concepts themselves. Since anything that is a constitutive property of a concept must be inherited compositionally by its hosts, recognitional abilities cannot be concept constituting.

This argument doesn't work, however.[12] Suppose that some concepts have recognitional capacities c_1–c_n among their essential properties, and that these capacities must be among the possession conditions for any complex concept that hosts them. Suppose too that there is no corresponding recognitional capacity c^* for the complex concept itself—or if there is one, it is neither among c_1–c_n, nor is it derivable from them alone. This shows that not every concept composed from recognitional concepts is itself thereby recognitional. Even so, recognitional capacities are "inherited" in the relevant sense—having a complex concept entails having the capacities that are the possession conditions for its constituents, and this helps to explain why having the constituents is roughly sufficient for having the complex concept. So the fact that a wholly distinct recognitional capacity for fish food fails to be produced compositionally from the combination of FISH with FOOD doesn't argue against the existence of recognitional concepts, so long as having FISH FOOD entails having the appropriate recognitional capacities for fish and food, taken individually.[13]

12. The argument given here is similar to one advanced by Recanati (2002). For careful analysis and criticism of the notion of a recognitional concept, see Dahlgrun (2011); for a Fodorian defense of one type of recognitional concept, see Rives (2010).

13. Fodor does in fact think that "people who have the concept PET FISH do generally have a corresponding recognitional capacity" (1998, 8). It just can't be one they've derived solely from the recognitional capacities of that concept's constituents. But this is only a problem if one wants to maintain that all complex concepts formed from recognitional concepts are also recognitional, which there is no reason to do. Fodor argues that this hybrid view is arbitrary or theoretically inelegant, but the architectural considerations pointed to above show that it is, in fact, quite predictable.

The model of observational concepts gives a principled explanation for why we would not expect recognitional abilities to compose in Fodor's sense. An observational concept for FISH allows one to categorize things as fish, as long as there are good instances presented in good perceptual conditions. This ability is mediated by the structure of the interface, however, which takes a restricted set of percepts as input. Imagine the interface as consisting of a set of perceptual analyzers attuned to category appearances. These perceptual analyzers may respond to what counts as good instances of fish, and so similarly would analyzers that take appearances of food as input. But the existence of these two analyzers entails nothing about the existence of a *third* device for responding to the characteristic appearance of fish food; in fact, given that it looks rather unfoodlike, one would predict that there isn't any such device, and hence that there is no observational concept FISH FOOD.

In any event, however, observational concepts are unlike Fodorian recognitional concepts, and also unlike Peacocke's (1992, chapter. 3; 2001) perceptual concepts in that their identity *as concepts* is not constituted by their perceptual connections. Observational concepts have a certain primary perceptual affiliation, namely, a means of being directly deployed by perceptual inputs. This affiliation makes them observational, but it is not part of their possession conditions qua concepts.

Rives (2010) has defended a Fodorian notion of recognitional concepts. He argues that causal links to perception are essential to some concepts, on the basis of the general principle that scientific kinds are individuated by the laws that they participate in. For concepts, these laws include those that fix their content and causal role by connecting them with particular perceptual states. So principles of kind individuation mandate that some concepts are recognitional. Undoubtedly, the general point that kinds in the special sciences are taxonomized by their causal and functional profile is correct. But many of these causal links are *fragile*, and we should be wary of making concept identity contingent on them.

For an actual case in which observational concepts have their perceptual affiliations severed, consider associative agnosia. The core disorder involves the inability to identify visually presented objects either by naming or by nonverbal means (e.g., sorting). Patients tend to perform best with real objects or highly realistic ones such as photographs; when they hazard an identification, they often confuse visually similar objects. Associative agnosics can sometimes describe the features that objects have but seem not to know *what* the described objects are. The disorder is multifaceted, and its basis is not entirely clear (Farah 2004, chapter 5; Humphreys and Riddoch 1987, 2006), but its existence indicates that specifically visual routes to conceptual deployment can be disrupted without corresponding loss of the concepts themselves.

The patient CK, for example, was capable of providing elaborate verbal descriptions of objects that he could recognize by touch but not by sight. He could also answer specific questions about the visual properties of objects, suggesting that this fine-grained visual knowledge was usable in reasoning tasks but not in object identification (Behrmann, Moscovitch, and Winocur 1994). The patient ELM, who played in a military brass band, was able to freely describe the nonvisual properties of brass instruments in detail, and to use concepts of these instruments in an associative learning task despite his deficits in visual identification (Dixon et al. 2002). The converse pattern also appears: in some cases of category-specific semantic impairments, there is loss of almost all information that might be used in reasoning about a category, despite relatively spared ability to identify category members (De Renzi and Lucchelli 1994). So the capacity to identify category members and the capacity to reason about them are at least partially separable.

These cases suggest that agnosic patients have not *lost* the concepts of the objects that they can no longer identify, and that concepts acquired observationally can persist once these core functional links are severed. Indeed, it seems to be a general truth that concepts are *not* particularly fragile; they can survive arbitrarily many gains and losses in their representational affiliations. As a design feature, this makes sense: the more such essential links a concept has, the more difficult it is to acquire and the easier it is to lose. Concept possession should be buffered from such changes in cognitive structure, however. Given this, the notion of an observational concept seems to be a marked improvement on both the notion of a recognitional concept (as Fodor conceives it) and of a perceptual concept (as Peacocke conceives it). Both of these notions commit us to constitutive links between concepts and perception, but these, I have argued, we have ample reason to reject.

9.6   Learning Observational Concepts

Observational concepts link the conceptual system to the world in a flexible, open-ended way. Learning an observational concept involves two stages: first, the construction of a dedicated perceptual analyzer that can co-classify objects based on their appearances; second, the construction of a link between the output of that analyzer and a symbol in the conceptual system.

The main job of a perceptual analyzer is to create structure in a perceptual similarity space. There are many mechanisms for achieving this. Local, bottom-up processing has been most intensely studied in theories of object recognition, where the debate has focused on whether multiple stored views of an object or single viewpoint-independent structural descriptions are required (Feldman 2003; Riesenhuber and Poggio 2000; Pessig and Tarr 2007; Tarr 2003). These representations also need to be processed by the right sort of generalization mechanism or similarity gradient, along with a weighting matrix for assigning parts of the object greater or lesser significance. Once a set of views of an object have been stored and linked together, or once a structural description has been generated, the process of analyzing new percepts using this device depends just on the fit between the percept and the stored representations.

However, perceptual analyzers may be constructed from many different materials. How an object fits into a larger perceived scene is also relevant. Objects that appear in a familiar location, or in the context of other familiar objects, tend to be recognized faster and more accurately (Henderson and Hollingworth 1999). Analyzers take into account holistic scene-level properties in determining object categorization, not just local qualities. More interestingly, object recognition also depends on whether something is appropriately poised for action (Humphreys and Riddoch 2007). Recognition can be facilitated by the orientation of an object relative to the normal actions one performs with it, and by its orientation relative to other objects in a perceived scene, even if they are not the usual ones that it is seen to interact with.[14]

Perceptual analyzers, then, may have extremely rapid access to a large amount of information. They can integrate stored viewpoints and structural descriptions, as well as holistic scene-level properties and associations and stored or potential patterns of motor interaction and event schemas that objects can enter into. Neurally, the implementation of visual analysis seems to involve such widespread retrieval insofar as it taps massively sweeping feed-forward projections as well as recurrent projections that play a role in mediating visual awareness (Lamme 2006; Lamme and Roelfsema 2000). These analyzers may be assembled relatively quickly—seven hours of training is sufficient to induce new category-specific responses in the fusiform gyrus (Gauthier et al. 1999). None of this processing, however, needs to be conceptually mediated. Extraction of viewpoints and structural descriptions can occur prior to knowing what the object being analyzed is, as can scene analysis and co-occurrence detection. Action-based understanding may stem from keeping track of our own past actions with perceived objects as well as from on-line computation of the plausible acts and events that objects afford.

The traditional view about the scope of observational concepts is that they are situated at the "basic level" (Jacob and Jeannerod 2003, 140–141; Rosch et al. 1976). Basic categories of objects such as cats, birds, hammers, airplanes, and squares can be grouped together based on the similarities and differences detectable by the perceptual system itself, even at three to four months old (Eimas and Quinn 1994; Quinn, Eimas, and Rosenkrantz 1993). But narrower object categories also involve such similarities: ball peen hammers versus claw hammers, MD-80s versus Boeing 747s, domestic shorthairs versus Manx cats. Expert object classification treats such specific groupings

14. I should add that the view of perception I am adopting here is compatible with the existence of many tight links between perception and action systems. Indeed, there is robust evidence that the two are tightly coupled, so that sensorimotor integration rather than separation might be the norm (Prinz 1997; Schütz-Bosbach and Prinz 2007). Observational concepts, nevertheless, occur where perceptual systems interface with concepts, no matter how richly connected perception and action themselves may be.

as entry points. Most of us behave like experts when it comes to classifying well-known individuals, as shown by the fact that we can rapidly and correctly identify Bill Clinton, Golda Meir, the Mona Lisa, or the Sears Tower across different encounters (Bukach, Gauthier, and Tarr 2006; Tanaka 2001; Tanaka and Gauthier 1997. Even relatively global perceptual similarities may be detected early, such as those that unite all entities that move in the same way as animate living beings, or those that move in a way distinctive of vehicles (Behl-Chadha 1996; Mandler and McDonough 1993, 1998). Observational concepts naturally coalesce around such islands of perceptual similarity.

Having a set of perceptual analyzers causes perceived objects to cluster in similarity space, but it does not give one the ability to *think* about those objects until they are assigned to conceptual representations (Gauker 2011, chapter 3). This requires noticing the similarities that are being detected by a perceptual analyzer and coining a new mental symbol for the purpose of keeping track of *that kind of thing*, namely, the kind of thing that has the relevant appearance that the underlying analyzer tracks.

Conceptualization thus involves both a functional transformation and a shift in content. Perception knows about looks: it informs us about how things appear, and it tracks and produces detectable similarities among appearances. Concepts, in the first instance, are not for tracking appearances, but for determining what things are, and for representing them in a way that is autonomous from perception. So the content of perception informs us about the appearances of objects around us, but when we coin observational concepts they must be (as the agnosia cases show) potentially detachable from these appearances: they track categories of things that have, but are not defined by, those appearances. Perception groups things that *look F-like*, while concepts track things that *are Fs*. Part of what is involved in generating observational concepts from perceptual analyzers is shifting from content that represents only looks to content that represents categories as distinct from their looks.[15]

This point can be illustrated using Peacocke's account of perceptual content (1989, 1992). For Peacocke, the accuracy conditions for perceptual states are given in terms of abstract scenario types. A scenario is a way of filling out space in the vicinity of the perceiver; it specifies a way of locating surfaces and their properties relative to an origin point and a set of orienting axes. A perceptual scene, then, is a way that this spatial

---

15. One may object here that some perceptual representations seem to track more than mere appearances. Some models of object vision propose that there is a stage at which object-centered visual representations such as 3D models of object parts and structure are computed. These are independent of the particular viewpoint of an observer and hence may seem to be about more than looks. The difference, however, is that even these 3D models do not distinguish between being a member of one category that has a certain 3D profile and being a member of a different category that just happens to share that profile. That is, these 3D models are not yet *kind* representations and hence are still about appearances in the generalized sense meant here. Thanks to Jake Beck for raising this objection.

volume may be filled in. A filled-in scene depicts the world as containing surfaces at various distances and orientations, instantiating properties such as color, texture, shading, and solidity. This captures the look of the scene, but it does not specify what kinds of objects the world itself contains. The very same perceptual scene is compatible with many different conceptualizations. This is true not just in the sense that there may be various different entry points into scene categorization, but also in the sense that however things happen to look in a scene, they may not be what they appear on their surfaces to be. The cat may be a puppet, the tree a prop. Our recognition of this *face-value gap* is possible because the function of concepts is to provide possibilities for representation and control of thought and behavior that go beyond what perception delivers.

Conceptual content, then, reflects the appearance-transcending role of the conceptual system. This point has nothing to do with the standard way of drawing the distinction between perceptual and nonconceptual states that relies on appeals to the fine-grainedness or richness of perceptual representation (Tye 2005). There is no inherent reason that rich, fine-grained properties cannot enter into the content of some of our concepts. This is suggested by the fact that observational concepts present their content under a perceptual mode of presentation. Modes of presentation generally are ways in which categories are grasped in thought; they are *how* we are thinking about a particular category. An observational concept presents its content as being *the kind of thing that looks like THAT*, where *THAT* refers to the complex representational content that is computed by the relevant perceptual analyzer. Hence, having the concept normally involves having access to facts about looks. Given this access, we are also capable of forming the concept of *THAT* sort of look.[16] We can either think about the things that the appearance is presenting us with, or we can think about a particular kind of appearance, the difference being that in the former case, the reference of our thought "reaches through" the appearances to what possesses them, while in the latter case, we are thinking about an appearance-defined category. While observational concepts aim to track categories that have a certain appearance but also may have an appearance-transcendent nature, the interface that enables them to do this job also makes available concepts of appearances themselves.

The process of learning an observational concept bears little resemblance to traditional hypothesis-testing models of learning. For one thing, what is learned is not a hypothesis or a judgment, but rather a two-part cognitive structure composed of a perceptual similarity detector coupled to a symbol that it is capable of activating, but which is also free to function autonomously in acts of higher thought. The learning

16. This point is also made by Peacocke (2001, 258): "When some property is given to a thinker in perception in way W, then, if that thinker is sufficiently reflective, there seems to be a conceptual way C_W of thinking of that way W, where this conceptual way C_W seems to be made available to the thinker precisely by her enjoying an experience whose nonconceptual content includes that way W."

process itself may involve largely passive extraction of information from the environment, as when we store specific viewpoints on an object or when we make associations between perception and action. Sometimes it may involve task-relevant but incidental perceptual learning (Schyns 1998; Schyns, Goldstone, and Thibault 1998). Or, as in supervised learning studies, it may involve conscious, explicit learning of categorical distinctions, accompanied by environmental feedback.[17]

Nevertheless, the processes involved in building analyzers are undeniably varieties of learning—or rather, they are if we put aside our a priori prejudices about what learning must be and focus on determining what learning as an empirical phenomenon actually is (Laurence and Margolis 2011). The process of producing these new cognitive structures is environmentally sensitive in such a way that the product's detailed functioning depends on its history of interactions. The representational properties of the structures themselves reflect the kinds of inputs that shaped them. And the structures acquired tend to be both long lasting and adaptive, in the sense that they improve the organism's abilities to carry out practical and cognitive tasks. These are all stereotypical marks of learned psychological capacities (Landy and Goldstone 2005; Goldstone et al. 2008).

9.7   Observational Concepts and Conceptual Development

Once they are learned, observational concepts can resolve some longstanding puzzles in the theory of concepts.[18] One problem arises for theories that posit complex internal structure for concepts. The constituents of a concept are its *features*: they pick out the information about the concept's referent that the concept encodes. Prototypes, exemplars, causal models, and other complex types of representations are built up from such features and the relations among them. Most of the dominant models of conceptual structure depict concepts as being composed of features (Weiskopf 2009a).

As Eleanor Rosch noted some time ago, however, this view may be developmentally implausible. Describing the features elicited in some of her studies, she says: "Some attributes, such as 'seat' for the object 'chair,' appeared to have names that showed them not to be meaningful prior to knowledge of the object as chair" (Rosch 1978, 42). Moreover, "some attributes such as 'you eat on it' for the object 'table' were functional attributes that seemed to require knowledge about humans, their activities, and the real world in order to be understood" (42). The problem, in short, is that many of the features displayed by adult concepts are ones that it is not easy to think of as

---

17. For discussions of the variety of category-learning tasks and the neural bases involved in each of them, see Ashby and Maddox (2011); Segar and Miller (2010).

18. This general point is also endorsed by Roskies (2008), who argues that nonconceptual capacities are needed to explain concept acquisition. The account here aims to flesh out this picture and to show that concepts newly learned from perception can play further *bootstrapping* roles in development.

being developmentally prior to the concepts that they are part of. Call this the *feature problem*.

Conceptual atomists take the feature problem to be an objection to the view that concepts are internally complex. The fact that these features are clearly linked with concepts after they are already acquired shows that they cannot be *part* of those concepts, since coming to possess a complex concept requires first possessing its parts. Another possible interpretation, however, is that concepts are not developmentally fixed. The initial form that a concept takes is not necessarily the same as its mature form. Many concepts may start out life as simple observational concepts, later developing into complex, structured representations having many different constituents and inferential liaisons.

Suppose concepts undergo a kind of developmental cycle. They might originate as unstructured observational concepts attached to a complex perceptual analyzer. Having an observational concept allows one to attend to objects *as such*—that is, to think of them as being unified groupings that are worth keeping track of, and that may have interesting properties and behaviors to discover. Observational concepts that track especially useful categories, and that are frequently deployed in important cognitive tasks, are then vehicles for directing our attention and intentional behavior toward a category. The more we attend to a category, the more things we discover about its members, including about their perceptual properties. So we may come to analyze the appearance of a certain type of animal into its parts (legs, tail, teeth), or its observable behaviors into classes (purring, grooming). As we notice these various perceivable qualities, we can elaborate on our original observational concept and the perceptual analyzer that underlies it. Where it might have started life as an unstructured symbol, now it incorporates features corresponding to the various bits of information we have collected about the typical look of the animals it responds to. The fact that concepts undergo these types of changes in their structure and content is no surprise if we are already committed to the pluralist idea that the conceptual system makes use of various different types of representations in different domains, tasks, and contexts (Weiskopf 2009b).

One aspect of conceptual development, then, might be repeated cycles of representational redescription or reencoding such as this.[19] Concepts of types of objects might

---

19. Karmiloff-Smith (1992) also uses the term *representational redescription,* but my usage differs from hers. I mean only that the very same content can be encoded in many functionally or formally distinct representations at different stages of learning or development. Thus we might start with a purely observational concept of a certain category and then later acquire a number of exemplars from it, a prototype for it, and so on for other complex cognitive structures. These are ways of redescribing or repackaging the same conceptual content. Karmiloff-Smith, by contrast, means something slightly more specific, namely that content initially only grasped implicitly will in time pass through a number of encoding stages to become both available to explicit conscious access and linguistic formulation.

come first. An early TABLE or CAT concept might not include conceptualized information about how those entities are put together or how they function, but this information can come to be part of these concepts with time. Infant categorization, for instance, often seems to be based on perceptual sensitivity to particular parts and their structural configuration, but there is no reason to think infants conceptualize these parts until later (Rakison and Butterworth 1998a, 1998b). From object concepts emerge concepts of object parts, properties, and relations, so the fact that, for adults, TABLE has LEG as a feature says nothing about developmental priority. This kind of complex developmental pattern is consistent with the emergence of more complex concepts out of simple ones, and simple ones (ultimately) out of perception.

9.8   Conclusions

There is obviously much more to be done to flesh out the sketch of observational concepts provided here. I have spoken almost entirely about perception and said nothing about concepts that interface directly with action systems, but these are important in developing a psychologically realistic account of basic actions. I have also not worked out in detail the precise developmental trajectory of observational concepts, but doing so is needed for understanding the nature of the so-called perceptual-to-conceptual shift in infancy (Rakison 2005). Nor have I given an account of how language both adjusts the boundaries of perceptual similarity spaces and cues the creation of new concepts.

Despite these lacunae, observational concepts seem empirically well grounded, theoretically plausible, and indeed, arguably necessary in understanding the origins of thought. They also suggest a larger moral. Recent debates over empiricism, and over the extent to which thought is grounded in perception more generally, have mostly focused on sweeping claims about the nature of all our concepts. Thoroughgoing concept empiricism is unlikely to be true (Dove 2009; Machery 2007; Mahon and Caramazza 2008; Weiskopf 2007); but empiricism might be *almost* true for our observational concepts. I say *almost* here because observational concepts are not simple copies of percepts. As the feature problem indicates, not all of the structure in percepts makes it into our initial observational concepts. Although this structure may be added with time, it requires reanalysis and the construction of new representations—something that is less characteristic of a Lockean filter, and more like a translation mechanism. Observational concepts are not quite copies of percepts, but they are the concepts that are shaped most powerfully by perception, and they are where the design of our perceptual systems leaves its imprint most visibly on thought.

Claims about thought being shaped or molded by perception fall far short of committing us to strong empiricist conclusions. On the other side of the coin, amodal theorists also need to acknowledge that these shaping effects may, for all anyone knows, be profound and far reaching. If our first thoughts involve largely observational concepts, then this places us in a certain starting point in the space of possible developmental trajectories for conceptual systems to follow. Where we can go from that starting point, and what regions of conceptual space are inaccessible to us, depends on the richness of the processes available to us for amplifying and refining our conceptual repertoire. Knowing the range of observational concepts we can entertain will help to locate human thought in the space of possible conceptual schemes.

This begins to give us a sharper picture of the research directions that open up once we adopt the notion of an observational concept. There has been an enormous amount of developmental work focused on concept acquisition and the many mechanisms that are implicated in it, but little consensus on how to describe the particular functional and representational changes involved in acquiring concepts from perception. We are now in a position to start fleshing out our sketchy understanding of how the conceptual system is integrated with other faculties in our cognitive architecture. Theories of concepts have so far focused to a large extent on internal affairs: what kinds of representations concepts are, how they are processed and deployed, and so on. These accounts are important, and they tell us much about the organization of the conceptual system per se, but little about how it interfaces with the host of other cognitive systems we possess, or how concepts as a distinctive type of representation help to orchestrate cascades of cognitive processing. Describing the nature of these interfaces is an open research problem, and one worth pursuing insofar as it promises to inform us about the large-scale cognitive architecture of which our distinctively human conceptual capacities form only a part.[20]

Acknowledgments

I thank the editors for their kind invitation to participate in this volume, and for their comments on an earlier draft of this paper. Thanks to Jake Beck and Andrei Marasoiu, who also provided excellent and detailed remarks. Special thanks to Jake for inviting me to participate in a workshop on concept learning at Washington University in St. Louis in May 2010 where I presented my first attempt at organizing some of these thoughts. Finally, thanks to the organizers and participants at the workshop on Sensorimotor Representations and Concepts (Heinrich-Heine-Universität, Düsseldorf, October 2012) for a chance to discuss a more recent version. Some of the research and writing of this paper took place in Spring 2012, when a Research Initiation Grant from Georgia State University enabled me to be on leave. I gratefully acknowledge their support.

20. For some suggestions on how to distinguish higher and lower cognitive faculties, and how conceptualized thought itself might be functionally defined, see Weiskopf (2014).

References

Ashby, F. G., and W. T. Maddox. 2011. Human category learning 2.0. *Annals of the New York Academy of Sciences* 1224:147–161.

Barsalou, L. W. 1999. Perceptual symbol systems. *Behavioral and Brain Sciences* 22:577–660.

Behl-Chadha, G. 1996. Basic-level and superordinate-like categorical representations in early infancy. *Cognition* 60:105–141.

Behrmann, M., M. Moscovitch, and G. Winocur. 1994. Intact mental imagery and impaired visual perception: Dissociable processes in a patient with visual agnosia. *Journal of Experimental Psychology: Human Perception and Performance* 20:1068–1087.

Bukach, C. M., I. Gauthier, and M. J. Tarr. 2006. Beyond faces and modularity: The power of an expertise framework. *Trends in Cognitive Sciences* 10:159–166.

Carey, S. 2009. *The Origin of Concepts*. New York: Oxford University Press.

Clark, A. 2004. Feature-placing and proto-objects. *Philosophical Psychology* 17:443–469.

Dahlgrun, M. 2011. The notion of a recognitional concept and other confusions. *Philosophical Studies* 150:139–160.

De Renzi, E., and F. Lucchelli. 1994. Are semantic systems separately represented in the brain? The case of living category impairment. *Cortex* 30:3–25.

Dixon, M. J., G. Desmarais, C. Gojmerac, T. A. Schweizer, and D. Bub. 2002. The role of premorbid expertise on object identification in category-specific visual agnosia. *Cognitive Neuropsychology* 19:401–419.

Dove, G. 2009. Beyond perceptual symbols: A call for representational pluralism. *Cognition* 110:412–431.

Dretske, F. 1986. *Explaining Behavior*. Cambridge, MA: MIT Press.

Eimas, P. D., and P. C. Quinn. 1994. Studies on the formation of perceptually based basic-level categories in young infants. *Cognitive Development* 65:903–917.

Farah, M. 2004. *Visual Agnosia*. 2nd ed. Cambridge, MA: MIT Press.

Feldman, J. 2003. What is a visual object? *Trends in Cognitive Sciences* 7:252–256.

Fodor, J. 1998. There are no recognitional concepts, not even RED. *Philosophical Issues* 9:1–14.

Fodor, J. 2008. *LOT 2: The Language of Thought Revisited*. Oxford: Oxford University Press.

Gauker, C. 2011. *Words and Images*. Oxford: Oxford University Press.

Gauthier, I., M. J. Tarr, A. W. Anderson, P. Skudlarski, and J. C. Gore. 1999. Activation of the middle fusiform "face area" increases with expertise recognizing novel objects. *Nature Neuroscience* 2:568–573.

Goldstone, R. L., A. Gerganov, D. Landy, and M. E. Roberts. 2008. Learning to see and conceive. In *The New Cognitive Sciences*, ed. L. Tommasi, M. Peterson, and L. Nadel, 163–188. Cambridge, MA: MIT Press.

Henderson, J. M., and A. Hollingworth. 1999. High-level scene perception. *Annual Review of Psychology* 50:243–271.

Humphreys, G. W., and M. J. Riddoch. 1987. *To See but Not to See: A Case Study of Visual Agnosia.* Hillsdale, NJ: Erlbaum.

Humphreys, G. W., and M. J. Riddoch. 2006. Features, objects, action: The cognitive neuropsychology of visual object processing, 1984–2004. *Cognitive Neuropsychology* 23:156–183.

Humphreys, G. W., and M. J. Riddoch. 2007. How to define an object. *Mind & Language* 22:534–547.

Hurley, S. 2008. The shared circuits model (SCM): How control, mirroring, and simulation can enable imitation, deliberation, and mindreading. *Behavioral and Brain Sciences* 31:1–22.

Jacob, P., and M. Jeannerod. 2003. *Ways of Seeing: The Scope and Limits of Visual Cognition*. Oxford: Oxford University Press.

Karmiloff-Smith, A. 1992. *Beyond Modularity: A Developmental Perspective on Cognitive Science.* Cambridge, MA: MIT Press.

Lamme, V. A. F. 2006. Towards a true neural stance on consciousness. *Trends in Cognitive Sciences* 10:494–501.

Lamme, V. A. F., and P. R. Roelfsema. 2000. The distinct modes of vision offered by feedforward and recurrent processing. *Trends in Neurosciences* 23:571–579.

Landy, D., and R. L. Goldstone. 2005. How we learn about things we don't already understand. *Journal of Experimental & Theoretical Artificial Intelligence* 17:343–369.

Laurence, S., and E. Margolis. 2011. Learning matters: The role of learning in concept acquisition. *Mind & Language* 26:507–539.

Lyons, W. 2008. *Perception and Basic Beliefs*. Oxford: Oxford University Press.

Machery, E. 2007. Concept empiricism: A methodological critique. *Cognition* 104:19–46.

Mahon, B., and A. Caramazza. 2008. A critical look at the embodied cognition hypothesis and a new proposal for grounding conceptual content. *Journal of Physiology, Paris* 102:59–70.

Mandler, J. 2004. *The Foundations of Mind*. Oxford: Oxford University Press.

Mandler, J. M., and L. McDonough. 1993. Concept formation in infancy. *Cognitive Development* 8:291–318.

Mandler, J. M., and L. McDonough. 1998. On developing a knowledge base in infancy. *Developmental Psychology* 34:1274–1288.

Matthen, M. 2005. *Seeing, Doing, and Knowing*. Oxford: Oxford University Press.

Milner, A. D., and M. A. Goodale. 2006. *The Visual Brain in Action*. 2nd ed. Oxford: Oxford University Press.

Peacocke, C. 1992. *A Study of Concepts*. Cambridge, MA: MIT Press.

Peacocke, C. 2001. Does perception have a nonconceptual content? *Journal of Philosophy* 98:239–264.

Pessig, J. J., and M. J. Tarr. 2007. Visual object recognition: Do we know more now than we did 20 years ago? *Annual Review of Psychology* 58:75–96.

Prinz, J. 2002. *Furnishing the Mind*. Cambridge, MA: MIT Press.

Prinz, J. 2005. Beyond appearances: The content of sensation and perception. In *Perceptual Experience*, ed. T. Gendler and J. Hawthorne, 434–460. Oxford: Oxford University Press.

Prinz, W. 1997. Perception and action planning. *European Journal of Cognitive Psychology* 9: 129–154.

Pylyshyn, Z. W. 2001. Visual indexes, preconceptual objects, and situated vision. *Cognition* 80:127–158.

Quinn, P. C., P. D. Eimas, and S. Rosenkrantz. 1993. Evidence for representations of perceptually similar natural categories by 3-month-old and 4-month-old infants. *Perception* 22: 463–475.

Rakison, D. H. 2005. The perceptual to conceptual shift in infancy and early childhood: A surface or deep distinction? In *Building Object Categories in Developmental Time*, ed. L. Gershkoff-Stowe and D. H. Rakison, 131–158. Mahwah, NJ: Erlbaum.

Rakison, D. H., and G. E. Butterworth. 1998a. Infants' attention to object structure in early categorization. *Developmental Psychology* 34:1310–1325.

Rakison, D. H., and G. E. Butterworth. 1998b. Infants' use of object parts in early categorization. *Developmental Psychology* 34:49–62.

Recanati, F. 2002. The Fodorian fallacy. *Analysis* 62:285–289.

Riesenhuber, M., and T. Poggio. 2000. Models of object recognition. *Nature Neuroscience* 3 (supplement): 1199–1204.

Rives, B. 2010. Concepts and perceptual belief: How (not) to defend recognitional concepts. *Acta Analytica* 25:369–391.

Rosch, E. 1978. Principles of categorization. In *Cognition and Categorization*, ed. E. Rosch and B. Lloyd, 27–48. Hillsdale, NJ: Erlbaum.

Rosch, E., C. B. Mervis, W. D. Gery, D. M. Johnson, and P. Boyes-Braem. 1976. Basic objects in natural categories. *Cognitive Psychology* 8:382–439.

Roskies, A. 2008. A new argument for nonconceptual content. *Philosophy and Phenomenological Research* 76:633–659.

Scholl, B. 2001. Objects and attention: The state of the art. *Cognition* 80:1–46.

Schütz-Bosbach, S., and W. Prinz. 2007. Perceptual resonance: Action-induced modulation of perception. *Trends in Cognitive Sciences* 11:349–355.

Schyns, P. 1998. Diagnostic recognition: Task constraints, object information, and their interactions. *Cognition* 67:147–179.

Schyns, P., R. Goldstone, and J. Thibault. 1998. The development of features in object concepts. *Behavioral and Brain Sciences* 21:1–54.

Segar, C. A., and E. K. Miller. 2010. Category learning in the brain. *Annual Review of Neuroscience* 33:203–219.

Siegel, S. 2010. *The Contents of Visual Experience*. Oxford: Oxford University Press.

Tanaka, J. W. 2001. The entry point of face recognition: Evidence for face expertise. *Journal of Experimental Psychology. General* 130:534–543.

Tanaka, J. W., and I. Gauthier. 1997. Expertise in object and face recognition. *Psychology of Learning and Motivation* 36:83–125.

Tarr, M. J. 2003. Visual object recognition: Can a single mechanism suffice? In *Perception of Faces, Objects, and Scenes: Analytic and Holistic Processes*, ed. M. A. Peterson and G. Rhodes, 177–211. Oxford: Oxford University Press.

Tye, M. 2005. Nonconceptual content, richness, and fineness of grain. In *Perceptual Experience*, ed. T. Gendler and J. Hawthorne, 504–530. Oxford: Oxford University Press.

Weiskopf, D. A. 2007. Concept empiricism and the vehicles of thought. *Journal of Consciousness Studies* 14:156–183.

Weiskopf, D. A. 2009a. Atomism, pluralism, and conceptual content. *Philosophy and Phenomenological Research* 79:130–162.

Weiskopf, D. A. 2009b. The plurality of concepts. *Synthese* 169:145–173.

Weiskopf, D. A. 2014. The architecture of higher thought. In *New Waves in Philosophy of Mind*, ed. M. Sprevak and J. Kallestrup, 242–261. New York: Palgrave Macmillan.

V   Concepts and Language

10   What's in a Concept? Analog versus Parametric Concepts in LCCM Theory

Vyvyan Evans

10.1   Introduction

Any account of language and the human mind has to grapple, ultimately, with the nature of concepts. In the words of cognitive scientist Jesse Prinz, concepts are "the basic timber of our mental lives" (Prinz 2002, 1). For without concepts, there could be no thought, and language would have nothing to express. What is less clear, however, is exactly how concepts are constituted, and the relationship between language and concepts. These are the two issues I address in this chapter. I do so by posing and attempting to answer the following question: Do linguistic units (e.g., words) have semantic content independently of the human conceptual system (which, in rough terms, can be thought of as our repository of concepts)? The answer to this question is, I will argue, a clear yes.

The thrust of the argument I present in this chapter is that there is a qualitative difference between concept types. Concepts in the conceptual system, on the one hand, and in the linguistic system, on the other, are of two qualitatively different sorts, which reflect the function of the two systems. The conceptual system is, in evolutionary terms, far older than the linguistic system. And at least in outline, many other species have conceptual systems that are continuous with the human conceptual system. In contrast, language evolved, I argue, to provide an executive control function, harnessing concepts in the conceptual system for purposes of (linguistically mediated) communication. The consequence is that the concepts that inhere in each of these systems evolved to fulfill distinct, albeit complementary purposes. Moreover, the findings giving rise to a grounded (or embodied) cognition perspective has, in recent years, led to a reframing of how we should think about concepts, in both the conceptual and the linguistic systems.

Accordingly, in this chapter I present arguments for thinking that the distinction between the conceptual and linguistic systems relates to concepts that are *analog* in nature, on the one hand, and those that are *parametric* in nature, on the other. In so doing, I argue against received accounts of embodied cognition that fail to recognize such a distinction. I also argue against disembodied accounts of concepts. My overall conclusion is that parametric concepts facilitate access to analog concepts in the process of meaning construction. Although both types of concept are derived from embodied, or as I shall prefer, *grounded* experience, they are qualitatively distinct. Parametric concepts are schematic, while analog concepts are richer, more closely constituting analogs of the experience types they are grounded in. Once I have developed an account of these distinct concepts, I advance a theory of lexical representation and semantic composition, referred to as the theory of lexical concepts and cognitive models, or LCCM theory for short (Evans 2006, 2009, 2010, 2013). I use LCCM theory to show the distinct functions of parametric and analog concepts in meaning construction.

The chapter is organized as follows. In the next section, I advance a grounded cognition approach to lexical and conceptual representation. In particular, I argue that representations in the conceptual system are multimodal, being constituted of a range of information types, including sensorimotor information. I also disambiguate knowledge representation (concepts) from meaning construction (semantic composition). The two phenomena are often conflated in the cognitive science literature on concepts. But, I argue, they are, in fact, distinct. In section 10.3 I review evidence for thinking that language is subserved by analog concepts (within the conceptual system). I do so by reviewing empirical findings for what I term *grounding effects*. Section 10.4 then develops the central qualitative distinction I argue for, between nonlinguistic and linguistic concepts. I do so by first observing that extant embodied/grounded theories of concepts assume that linguistic meaning is equivalent to conceptual representation. I present arguments that lead to a distinction in terms of conceptual versus lexical representations. I then operationalize this distinction in terms of parametric concepts (linguistic system) versus analog concepts (conceptual system). Section 10.6 introduces LCCM theory, which operationalizes these distinct types of representation in terms of the theoretical constructs of *lexical concept* (linguistic system) and *cognitive model* (conceptual system). The LCCM theory framework provides a basis for understanding the respective contribution of each distinct concept type in facilitating linguistically mediated meaning construction, which is complementary, albeit orthogonal to, an account of knowledge representation (concepts).

10.2   Toward a Grounded Cognition Approach to Concepts

Broadly speaking, there are, within cognitive science, two prevalent views of concepts. The first view is, very roughly, that concepts are abstract, disembodied symbols—Barsalou (1999, 2008) describes this perspective as the amodal view of cognition—

a view that assumes that the representational format of a concept is qualitatively different from the sensory experiences concepts relate to. Although the details of specific disembodied theories vary considerably, this general perspective assumes that concepts are ultimately abstracted from the brain states that give rise to them, with information encoded in a different format. This view of concepts makes a principled distinction between conception (or cognition) and perception (and interoceptive experience more generally)—see Cisek (1999) for discussion. Representatives of this general approach include Dennett (1969), Fodor (1975, 1983, 1998, 2008), Haugeland (1985), Jackendoff (1983, 1987), Newell and Simon (1972), Pinker (1984), and Pylyshyn (1984).

More recently, a different perspective has emerged, which blurs the distinction between perception/interoception and conception/cognition. On this view, concepts are directly grounded in the perceptual and interoceptive brain states that give rise to them. Again, while details relating to specific theories differ, this *embodied, modal,* or as I prefer, *grounded* cognition perspective sees cognition as broadly continuous with perception/interoception, rather than reflecting a wholly distinct type of representation (see Barsalou 2008 and Shapiro 2010 for reviews). Notable exemplars of this view include Barsalou (e.g., 1999), Chemero (2009), Clark (e.g., 1997), Damasio (1994), Evans (2009), Gallese and Lakoff (2005); Glenberg (e.g., 1997), Lakoff and Johnson (e.g., 1999), Viglioccio et al. (2009), and Zwaan (e.g., 2004).

The grounded view assumes that concepts arise directly from representative brain states. Take the example of the experience of cats. When we perceive and interact with cats, this leads to extraction of perceptual and functional attributes of cats, which are stored in memory in analog fashion: our concept CAT, on this view, closely resembles our perception and experience of a cat. When we imagine a cat, this is made possible by reactivating, or to use the technical term, *simulating* the perceptual and interoceptive experience of interacting with a cat—these include sensorimotor experiences when we stroke and otherwise interact with a cat, as well as affective states, such as the pleasure we experience when a cat responds by purring, and so forth. But while the simulated cat closely resembles our conscious perceptual and interoceptive experience, it is attenuated.

In other words, the concept CAT is not the same as the veridical experience of perceiving a cat. When we close our eyes and imagine a cat, we are at liberty to simulate an individual cat, or a type of cat, or a cat composed of aspects of our past experiences of and with cats. But the simulation is attenuated with respect to the veridical perceptual experience of a cat. Importantly, the claim made by the embodied perspective is that the simulation is directly grounded in the same brain states—in fact, a reactivation of aspects of the brain states—that are active when we veridically perceive and interact with the cat. The simulation is then available for language and thought processes. As the reactivation of some aspects of the perceptual and interoceptive experiences of a cat is, in part, constitutive of the concept CAT, the concept is an analog of the perceptual experience.

In contrast, the disembodied view of concepts and mind assumes that perceptual experiences are redescribed into a symbol, which stands for, or *tokens,* the perceptual experience. In some disembodied theories, the symbols are represented using natural language, and the symbols are thought to comprise lists of features or attributes. In others (e.g., Fodor 1975, 2008), the concepts are represented in a format that is in some sense language-like: the idea is that the mind features its own operating system, universal to all humans—mentalese. Various approaches to mentalese have been developed in some detail (see, e.g., Fodor 2008; Jackendoff 1983).

The key difference between the two perspectives is that the disembodied view of concepts assumes that concepts are mental representations fundamentally unlike what they represent. Thus, critically, perceptual and interoceptive brain states are *not* constitutive of concepts. For embodied cognition proponents, simulations, in contrast, are analog presentations, in the sense of re-presentations of perceptual and interoceptive experiences—they are directly grounded in the body-based and subjective perceptual states that give rise to them. As such the grounded cognition view assumes that perceptual and interoceptive brain states *are* constitutive of concepts. Figures 10.1 and 10.2 capture the distinctions between the disembodied and grounded approaches to concepts.

A particular challenge that has been leveled against the disembodied view of concepts relates to what has been dubbed the "symbol grounding problem" (Harnard 1990). What is at stake is the nature of content available for semantic analysis, given that concepts presumably facilitate thought and language—about which I shall have more to say in section 10.3. In other words, if symbols are abstract, which is to say, unlike the perceptual and interoceptive mental states they represent, how do they relate to the states they are supposed to be representative of? In short, the challenge for

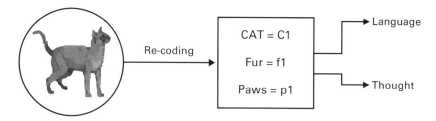

Perceptual/interoceptive experience   Feature list symbol stored in memory

Figure 10.1
Disembodied conceptual system.

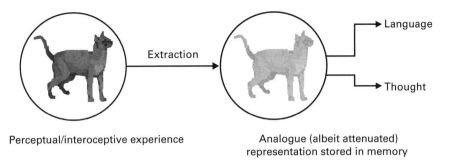

Figure 10.2
Grounded conceptual system.

the disembodied view is to show how concepts facilitate semantic analysis when they are not directly grounded in the content that they represent.

One early solution to this, in one disembodied theory of concepts, was to assume that concepts are innate. This was the proposal made by Fodor (1975), detailing mentalese (a.k.a. the language of thought). Adopting this view, Jackendoff posited a range of abstract conceptual primitives that could be combined using rules of mental syntax, facilitating a full-fledged disembodied conceptual system. In later work, Fodor (e.g., 1998) recanted, arguing that concepts were not themselves innate. Rather, concepts are grounded by virtue of a process whereby abstract symbols became *locked* to the perceptual states in the world that they represent, or *token*, in his parlance. He declined to speculate on how this locking process comes about, however, arguing that although the mechanisms that facilitate it may be innate, understanding how symbols become locked to perceptual states is not the proper concern of cognitive psychology.

The grounding problem is resolved in the grounded cognition view of concepts by positing that concepts are directly grounded in brain states: hence concepts are very much like the brain states they are representations of. Most versions of grounded cognition (e.g., Barsalou 1999; Clark 1997) assume that although brain states are constitutive of concepts, concepts are nevertheless representations, and thus distinct from brain states (e.g., sensorimotor activations). Barsalou (1999) refers to such concepts as "perceptual symbols": on this view, perceptual symbols are stored traces of prior brain states that can be reactivated, or simulated, for purposes of language and thought. Hence, the difference from the disembodied view is that perceptual symbols are directly grounded in brain states.

A more radical approach to embodied cognition removes the requirement for symbols altogether. For instance, Chemero (2009) argues that concepts are entirely constituted of brain states (rather than representations of prior brain states). Building on dynamic systems theory, and James Gibson's ecological approach to perception, Chemero thereby entirely removes the distinction between perception and conception.

Two main lines of empirical evidence support the grounded cognition view of concepts:

1. Brain-based demonstrations that the sensorimotor and other modal systems are activated during conceptual processing: a raft of studies provides clear evidence that, for instance, motor processes are automatically engaged when subjects perform perceptual and conceptual tasks. A range of different methodologies have demonstrated such automatic activation in both nonhuman primates and humans. For instance, the human motor system is automatically activated when subjects observe manipulable objects, and when they observe the actions of another individual. Methodologies deployed to demonstrate such data include studies involving functional neuroimaging, neurophysiological recordings, EEG, transcranial magnetic stimulation (TMS), and kinematic analyses. For representative reviews of the various extant findings, see Barsalou (2008), Boulenger et al. (2008), Gallese and Lakoff (2005), Pulvermüller et al. (2005), and Rizzolatti and Craighero (2004).

2. Behavioral demonstrations that activation of the sensorimotor system spread to conceptual levels of processing. Many of the relevant studies have involved sentence comprehension and lexical decision tasks. I will have more to say about the relationship between language and concepts below; however, one representative and important study is Pulvermüller et al. (2005). For instance, subjects were required to perform a lexical decision task employing action verbs relating to either arm or leg actions. A pulse of subthreshold TMS was then applied to either the *leg* or *arm* region of motor cortex immediately after exposure to the lexical cues. Pulvermüller and colleagues found that TMS exposure to the *arm* region induced a faster decision for arm action words, as opposed to leg action words. And when TMS exposure was to the *leg* region of the motor cortex, the reverse pattern in lexical decisions was found. This would appear to suggest that embodied (perceptual and interoceptive) states play a direct role in conceptual processing as it relates to language comprehension.

In the light of demonstrations such as these, the difficulty for a disembodied view of concepts—at least as classically formulated—is this: concepts are supposed to be abstract symbols, which are not constituted by sensorimotor (and interoceptive) brain states. In short, semantic analysis of concepts is independent of sensorimotor and other brain states, and hence, should not result in automatic processing of these. Although disembodied accounts would not deny that concepts for sensorimotor experience, for instance, will require activation of the relevant region of sensorimotor cortex, the point is that such activations are ancillary to the semantic analysis that the disembodied symbols furnish, for purposes of facilitating language and thought. That is, sensorimotor activation plays no role in semantic analysis during conceptual processing. Hence, this finding—that brain states such as sensorimotor activations appear to play a role in conceptual processing—would appear to falsify disembodied accounts of concepts, as classically formulated.[1]

It is also worth noting that just as the disembodied view is falsified by empirical findings briefly reviewed above, so too is the radical view of embodied cognition. The relevant finding concerns patients with apraxia—patients with impairments for using objects such as hammers are nevertheless able to name and describe in detail the nature of the same objects they cannot use (Johnson-Frey 2004; Mahon and Caramazza 2008. This illustrates that subjects appear to have some type of representation, at least for purposes of linguistic encoding, without being able to activate a supporting sensorimotor perceptual state. This finding would appear to undermine the radical claim that representations are not required for a functioning conceptual system.

The empirical findings about the role of brain states, especially sensorimotor activation in conceptual processing, appear to demonstrate that concepts, especially sensorimotor concepts, involve activation of brain states. However, this is unlikely to be the whole story: Mahon and Caramazza (2008) argue that part of the disembodied account, that concepts involve abstract (and hence non-analog) symbols, appears to be supported by findings such as patients with brain motor deficits who nevertheless retain motor concepts, as in the case of apraxia. Accordingly, they have proposed an account of concepts that can be seen as situated midway between an embodied and a disembodied account of concepts, integrating what they perceive to be the strengths of each. Mahon and Caramazza accept the empirical findings that have been used to argue for a grounded view of concepts. However, they argue that such data do not entail that a disembodied view is incorrect.

First, they argue that any embodied view is limited up front because it assumes that all concepts are constituted by sensorimotor experience. And that being so, an embodied approach inevitably cannot deal with abstract concepts such as TIME, JUSTICE, ENTROPY, or PATIENCE. For some of these concepts, they argue, there doesn't appear to be sensorimotor information that could correspond in any reliable or direct way to the abstract concept. For others, such as BEAUTIFUL, there appears not to be consistent sensorimotor experience associated with it. For instance, mountains, a lover's face, or even an idea can be beautiful: no specific type of sensorimotor information is apparently instrumental in the realization of the concept BEAUTIFUL. Second, some information is clearly abstract even for sensorimotor concepts, as evidenced in the case of apraxia, already

---

1. Some commentators have observed, however, that a suitably modified version of the disembodied account may be consistent with data that have led to the embodied/grounded cognition accounts—for discussion see Dove (2009), Mahon and Caramazza (2008), and Machery (2007). For criticism of the embodied approach on philosophical grounds, see Weiskopf (2010). I discuss proposals made by Mahon and Caramazza below.

discussed, where part of the concept is retained in the absence of the ability to simulate the motor experience associated with the concept.

In light of these observations, Mahon and Caramazza posit a "grounding by interaction" view of concepts. On this account, they retain the idea that concepts consist of abstract symbols—symbols that are non-analog in nature. Hence, they argue, concepts are not constituted by the brain's modal states, such as sensory and motor modalities. As they accept the empirical findings of the embodiment tradition, however, they assume that embodied states are not ancillary to conceptual processing. Rather, what they claim is that modality-specific activation of brain states, such as sensorimotor information, may constitute instantiations of the concept. To illustrate, reconsider the concept HAMMER. For Mahon and Caramazza, the concept consists of an abstract, disembodied symbol. And this disembodied symbol is the relevant unit for semantic analysis (upon which language and thought are contingent). That said, the referent of the concept is a concrete entity in veridical experience. And this is instantiated as sensorimotor experience. Hence, on this account, the abstract symbol HAMMER is grounded by virtue of an interaction between the abstract symbol and sensorimotor activation: they propose that the sensorimotor activation results from a cascading spreading activation from the conceptual system—where the concept is housed—to the relevant region of the motor cortex.

There are a number of problems with the grounding by interaction view. First, the assumptions it makes about the embodied cognition view are erroneous. To argue that embodied cognition researchers assume that all concepts are constituted exclusively of sensorimotor experience is patently incorrect. For instance, Barsalou's account of perceptual symbols, arguably the best-developed theoretical account of concepts from an embodied cognition perspective, explicitly includes brain states other than sensorimotor experience. Barsalou uses the term *perception* in a rather more inclusive way than is normally the case: he assumes that perceptual symbols include sensorimotor experiences as well as other sorts of more subjective modalities, such as interoceptive experience, affect, and cognitive states. In later work, Barsalou (2008) explicitly prefers the term *grounded*—rather than embodied—cognition in order to make clear that, in his view, concepts encompass all of the brain's modal systems, not just sensorimotor areas. Grounded cognition is also the nomenclature preferred in the present chapter.

Second, Mahon and Caramazza are incorrect in claiming that the embodied cognition view cannot account for abstract concepts up front. An entire research tradition associated with Lakoff and Johnson (e.g., 1980, 1999) has argued that abstract concepts are indeed largely constituted in terms of sensorimotor experience. Take for instance, the abstract concept TIME. Lakoff and Johnson argue that the domain of time is systematically structured by mappings, which inhere in long-term memory, that provide a long-term stable link from the domain of motion through space. The series of mappings that facilitate the projection of conceptual structure, asymmetrically from one domain onto another, are termed *conceptual metaphors*. These conceptual metaphors facilitate the structuring of concepts such as DURATION in terms of *physical extent* (i.e., length), as implied by linguistic examples such as (1):

(1) The relationship lasted a long time.

In (1), *long* refers to temporal rather than spatial extent (see Evans 2013 for discussion). And behavioral findings support the view that spatial extent is automatically activated by the concept of duration but not vice versa (Casasanto and Boroditsky 2008). Conceptual metaphor accounts exist for a host of abstract domains ranging from mathematics (Lakoff and Nuñez 2001) to morality (Lakoff and Johnson 1999). And behavioral studies now provide evidence that abstract concepts involve processing of sensorimotor experience—about which I shall have more to say in the next section.

That said, what has perhaps been underestimated by embodied cognition researchers, including Lakoff and Johnson, is the degree to which abstract concepts are constituted by information from modalities other than the sensory and motor modalities. With respect to time, for instance, at the neurological level, it appears that the range of phenomenologically real temporal experiences, such as duration, succession, and present/past/future, are subserved by a range of non-sensorimotor systems (for reviews, see Evans 2013; Kranjec and Chatterjee 2010). Nevertheless, representations for time also appear to be constituted, in part, in terms of sensorimotor information. Accounts differ as to the reason for this (Bonato et al. 2010 versus Bueti and Walsh 2009). But the parietal cortex appears to be implicated in linking representations for space and time.

The third problem with the grounding by interaction view is that accounting for automatic activation of sensorimotor information by allowing for interaction still doesn't provide a grounded theory of concepts. After all, the sensorimotor information still remains ancillary, as per disembodied theories: semantic analysis takes place without reference to the sensorimotor information. In essence, Mahon and Caramazza's proposal remains essentially a disembodied account, but with bells and whistles: it is arguably consistent with the empirical evidence, but the grounding problem is still not resolved because modality-specific information remains excluded from conceptual content. An alternative, which I explore below, is that concepts are of different types, some directly grounded in perceptual and interoceptive experience—what I refer to as *analog concepts*—and some that represent abstractions derived from grounded experience—*parametric concepts*. As we shall see, parametric concepts are abstract; but they are grounded in modal brain states by virtue of being schematizations, abstracted from said brain states.

The final problem is that Mahon and Caramazza conflate, and confuse, knowledge representation—the issue of *what* constitutes a concept—and meaning construction.

Their discussion of the concept BEAUTIFUL and the divergent sensorimotor properties
instantiated by this concept requires an account of meaning construction, rather than
knowledge representation. Meaning construction is, in part, a linguistically mediated
phenomenon, and it requires an appropriate account of compositional semantics. An
account of the concept BEAUTIFUL in different contexts of use turns on issues relating
to semantic composition and language use, rather than knowledge representation. It
is therefore disingenuous to criticize embodied cognition accounts of concepts when
pointing to phenomena that relate to something other than knowledge representation.
Once I have developed my account of analog versus parametric concepts, I present,
later in the chapter, an account of semantic composition within the framework of
LCCM theory, which addresses this issue.

In the final analysis, concepts appear to be constituted, in part, by multimodal brain
states, not exclusively sensorimotor experience types. A theory of conceptual representation is, in principle, distinct from that of linguistically mediated semantic composition. And as such, we must now turn to a consideration of the relationship between
concepts and language.

10.3 Grounding Effects in Language

If concepts subserve language, then it stands to reason that language relies on concepts,
at least in part, to facilitate the construction of meaning. The purpose of this section
is to review the evidence in support of such a view. Given the grounded cognition
perspective developed above, if language is subserved by concepts grounded in multimodal brain states, we should find evidence of *grounding effects* in language. A grounding effect, as I define it, constitutes an observable and intersubjectively robust intrusion
of embodied (not exclusively sensorimotor) experience in conceptual and especially
linguistic representation and processing.

Recent findings in both psychology and cognitive neuroscience now clearly reveal
a series of grounding effects when we use language (see table 10.1). First, multimodal
brain states are activated when we deploy language. Moreover, these activations are

Table 10.1
Three types of grounding effects in linguistic cognition

Automatic activation of brain regions	Brain regions that are specialized for specific types of processing are activated when the corresponding language is processed.
Immersed bodily behavior	Specialized bodily behaviors are activated by the processing of the corresponding language.
Structure and organization of language	Language appears to be structured in terms of embodied brain states, especially representations grounded in sensorimotor experience

fast—multimodal information is activated instantaneously, automatically, and cannot be avoided—and somatotopic—they relate to specific functional brain regions; for instance, action words referring to hand actions activate the *hand* area of motor cortex and not the *leg* area (Pulvermüller et al. 2005). Second, psychologists have discovered that human subjects behave as if immersed in an embodied state when using or understanding language relating to perceptual experience. Third, grounding effects show up directly in the nature and structure of language. Together, this amounts to persuasive evidence in favor of the grounded view I am advancing: the human mind is continuous with the human body and bodily experience, rather than being a separate process.

So what then are examples of grounding effects? Let's focus on the somatotopic aspect of brain activation: specific brain regions are activated when we use the corresponding words, or types of words. It is now well established that distinct parts of the cortex process and store sensory information: for instance, visual, auditory and tactile experience. Other parts of the cortex process motor information: for instance, information relating to hand or body movements. And finally, subcortical structures, such as the amygdala, process and store emotional experience. Recent findings have shown that all of these brain regions are automatically and immediately activated when corresponding body-based language is being processed.

For example, brain regions that are active during the processing of actions, such as using tools like hammers, screwdrivers, and saws, are automatically and immediately activated when we hear or read sentences relating to using tools of these kinds (Isenberg et al. 1999; Martin and Chao 2001; Pulvermüller 1999; see also Buccino et al. 2005; for a review, see Taylor and Zwaan 2009). Put another way, when you or I understand an expression such as "He hammered the nail," there is automatic and immediate activation of that part of the brain that is engaged to produce the hammering action. In addition, regions of the brain that process visual information are activated when we comprehend words and sentences relating to visual information, such as object shape and orientation (Stanfield and Zwaan 2001; Zwaan and Yaxley 2003). For instance, visual areas that process animal recognition shapes are activated when we hear or see certain animal words (Büchel, Price, and Friston 1998; Martin and Chao 2001). And finally, language involving emotional affect also results in automatic activation of the relevant brain regions. For instance, threat words such as *destroy* and *mutilate* automatically activate parts of the amygdala (Isenberg et al. 1999). This is an evolutionarily older part of the subcortical brain that neurobiologists have established as being involved in emotional processing (LeDoux 1995).

The second type of grounding effect is behavior. Human subjects, when using or understanding language, behave in myriad subtle ways, as if they are engaged in the sensorimotor activity that corresponds to the sensorimotor language; it is as if language primes language users for particular veridical actions. For instance, when

reading about throwing a dart in a game of darts, human subjects automatically activate muscle systems that ready the hand grip common to dart throwing; when we
use or hear language, our eye and hand movements are consistent with the sensorimotor activity being described (Glenberg and Kaschak 2002; Klatzky et al. 1989; Spivey
et al. 2000). It is as if language facilitates the vicarious experience of the events being
described in language.

The psycholinguist Rolf Zwaan has described this in terms of language users being
immersed experiencers. He argues that "language is a set of cues to the comprehender
to construct an experiential (perception plus action) simulation of the described situation" (Zwaan 2004, 36). And this could only be so if language provides direct access to
representations of body-based states: concepts are embodied.

Behavioral evidence for immersion in embodied states, when using language, comes
from the psychology lab. In one experiment, subjects were asked to judge whether
action sentences such as "He closed the drawer" were meaningful or not (Glenberg and
Kaschak 2002). Subjects did this by pressing one of two buttons, which were located
sequentially in front of the subject. The button signaling that a sentence was meaningful was closer to the subjects and thus involved moving their hand toward their
body, the same direction of motor control required to open a drawer. It was found that
responses to whether the sentences were correct or not were faster when the direction
of motion corresponded to that described in the sentence. This finding supports the
view that bodily motor states are automatically activated when reading a corresponding sentence. An action required by the experiment that is at odds with the motor
simulation activated by the sentence provides interference. And this, in turn, slows
down the subject's response to the semantic judgment, the ostensible purpose of the
experiment.

The third type of grounding effect derives from the structure and organization of
language: language for abstract states appears to draw on language from sensorimotor
experience in an asymmetric way. Linguistic evidence of this sort is compatible with
the grounded cognition view of concepts but not the disembodied perspective. Perhaps
the most clear evidence in language has been highlighted in the work of Lakoff and
Johnson (1980, 1999). As noted in the previous section, conceptual metaphors appear
to work by recruiting structure from sensorimotor experience in order to structure
representations relating to interoceptive experience types. For instance, various aspects
of our representations for time appear to be systematically structured in terms of
representations recruited from the domain of (motion through) space. Consider some
linguistic examples, which have been claimed to evidence this:

(2a) Christmas is fast approaching.

(2b) We are moving up on Christmas fast.

These examples suggest the following. The relative imminence of a future event, Christmas, is structured in terms of the motion of an event—an event conceptualized *as if it were* an object capable of motion—toward the ego, or the ego's motion toward Christmas, conceived as a location in space. Lakoff and Johnson posit that we structure our representations of time in terms of relative motion of objects or our relative motion with respect to stationary objects (see also Moore 2006). Moreover, the evidence for conceptual metaphors—from language, from psycholinguistic tasks (Boroditsky 2000), and from psychophysical tasks (Casasanto and Boroditsky 2008)—appears to show that the structuring is asymmetric. That is, representations for time are systematically structured in terms of representations for space and motion through space, but space appears not to be productively structured in terms of representations for time.

Interestingly, and in keeping with the proposals made by Lakoff and Johnson, a range of abstract concepts also appear to exhibit grounding effects. Lakoff and Johnson have argued that we conceptualize communication as physical transfer. Evidence for this comes from linguistic examples, as when we say things like, "I couldn't get my ideas across," "put it into words," and so on. Indeed, Glenberg and Kaschak (2002) found that the same pattern applied to abstract concepts.

Consider a sentence such as "I gave him some words of wisdom." Metaphorically, this involves transferring the "words of wisdom," some advice, from the speaker to the listener, a pattern of motion away from the body. The processing time to judge whether the sentence was semantically acceptable was quicker when the button that was required to be pressed involved an action away from rather than toward the subjects' bodies. In other words, physical action that accorded with the metaphorical action facilitated faster understanding of the linguistic expression. What this reveals is a grounding effect for abstract, as well as literal, language, a finding in keeping with the broad prediction of conceptual metaphor theory.

Further evidence for abstract concepts being structured, at least in part, by sensorimotor experience, comes from the work of Casasanto and Dijkstra (2010). In one experiment, Casasanto and Dijkstra investigated abstract concepts such as pride and shame: subjects were asked to recount experiences that had either made them proud, or ashamed. They did so while simultaneously moving marbles from a lower tray to a higher tray or vice versa. Lakoff and Johnson (1980, 1999) argue that positive experiences are metaphorically conceptualized as being up, while negative experiences are experienced as being down. Casasanto and Dijkstra found that the speed and efficiency of the autobiographical retelling was influenced by whether the direction of the marble movements was congruent with the autobiographical memory: upward for pride, downward for shame. This provides compelling evidence that even abstract language appears to involve automatic activation of sensorimotor simulations in the brain: we understand what the words *pride* and *shame* mean, in part, by virtue of the upward and downward trajectories that metaphorically structure them being activated in the brain.

More generally, an important conclusion from this discussion is the following. The traditional distinction between perception and cognition—an artifact of the earlier distinction between body and mind arising from the seventeenth-century philosophical underpinnings of psychology—may be too strong (for discussion see Barsalou 1999; Bergen 2012; Prinz 2002). Representations that arise in language use and comprehension are grounded in the same knowledge that is used in processing our experiences of the world around us. The distinction between perception and cognition, at the very least, may not be as clear-cut as some cognitive scientists have claimed. Talmy (2000), one of the pioneering linguists who first saw that language encodes embodied concepts, argued for a unified category, which he termed *ception*; Talmy sought to emphasize the continuity, rather than separation, between perception and conception (or cognition).

10.4   Conceptual Structure versus Semantic Structure

In light of the foregoing, the conclusion I draw is this: language and body-based representations would appear, together, to co-conspire in the integration process that gives rise to meaning. The question is how, a question I begin to address in this section.

From an evolutionary perspective, the perceptual and interoceptive representations in the conceptual system must have preceded language. The conceptual system allows us, and many other species, to have available for reactivation the body-based representations that arise from our interaction in our socio-physical world of experience. Humans are not alone in possessing conceptual systems and, presumably, body-based representations in those conceptual systems (Barsalou 2005; Hurford 2007, 2012). A conceptual system enables an organism to represent the world it encounters, to store experiences, and hence to respond to new experiences as a consequence. A conceptual system is what enables us and other species to be able to tell friend from foe, competitor from potential sexual mate, and to act and interact in situationally appropriate ways. Our repository of concepts facilitates thought, categorization of entities in the world, and our action and interaction with, in, and through the spatiotemporal environment we inhabit.

But complex thoughts, actions, and so on require that our concepts can be combined compositionally in order to form complex ideas. While many other species have conceptual systems, humans appear to be unique in having language. And the range and complexity of human thought appear to far exceed those of any other species. As Bertrand Russell pithily observed, "No matter how eloquently a dog can bark, it cannot tell you that its parents were poor but honest." An obvious implication, then, is that language may provide, in part at least, a means of harnessing our conceptual system, of releasing its potential—a conclusion that has been reached by a number of leading cognitive scientists (see, for example, Bergen 2012; Evans 2009; Mithen 1996,;and references therein).

Barsalou (2005; Baraslou et al. 2008; see also Evans 2009) has suggested that the function of language is to provide an executive control function, operating over grounded concepts in the conceptual system. And this view has much to commend it. The idea is that language provides the framework that facilitates the composition of concepts for purposes of communication. This is achieved by language consisting of a grammatical system, with words and constructions cuing activations of specific body-based states in the brain (see Bergen 2012, chapter 5). Their integration gives rise to complex simulations, which is the stuff of thought. On this account, language provides added value. It allows us to control and manipulate the conceptual system, which, after all, must have originally evolved for more rudimentary functions, such as object recognition and classification. Under the control of language, we can make use of body-based (not exclusively sensorimotor) concepts in order to develop abstract thought. As Barsalou et al. (2008) explain:

Adding language increased the ability of the simulation [=conceptual] system to represent non-present situations (past, future, counterfactual). Adding language increased the ability to construct simulations compositionally. Adding language increased the ability to coordinate simulations between agents, yielding more powerful forms of social organisation. (274)

However, if the function of language is to index or activate body-based concepts, we might reasonably ask what language is bringing to the table. Do words have meanings in their own right, independent of the perceptual and interoceptive representations they point to?

Some embodied mind researchers have denied that language contributes to meaning per se. Representatives of this position argue that language has no semantic properties of its own, independent of the simulations produced by grounded concepts in the conceptual system (see Glenberg and Robertson 1999; Barsalou et al. 2008).

One reason for thinking this is that decontextualized words on their own do not trigger simulations. In contrast, analog representations such as pictures and images do (Lindemann et al. 2006). For instance, being exposed to the word *cat*, unless embedded in a sentence, will not normally, on its own, give rise to a particularly rich conceptualization. In contrast, a picture of a cat, which is analog—it iconically represents our visual experience of a cat—gives rise to a simulation.

Another line of evidence relates to gist. Upon hearing a story, subjects appear to store the gist of the narrative but not the form that it was told in—subjects can recount the story, but often use quite different words to do so. This takes place after about twenty seconds, suggesting that while the language used to convey the story erodes, the story itself is represented in a nonlinguistic form, a complex representation, a simulation, in the conceptual system (Bransford and Franks 1971). This suggests that once a simulation has been achieved, language is largely irrelevant for, and hence independent of, the underlying meaning (Barsalou et al. 2008).

Barsalou and colleagues conclude from this that language processing is not very deep, in terms of the semantic representations it can evoke on its own. The role of language is to provide structure, which aids the assembly of perceptual states in the construction of meaning. In other words, simulations arise from activation of non-linguistic concepts. And it is these simulations that linguistic forms provide direct access to. According to Barsalou (e.g., Barsalou et al. 2008), language provides a level, essentially, of formal (sound or signed) representation, but no semantic content. The forms then hook up with perceptual and interoceptive states, thereby facilitating reactivations—simulations.

However, this view is likely to be too strong. First, if language has no independent semantic content, then presumably we can't use language to evoke ideas we haven't yet experienced—because the brain states don't yet exist for the experiences. Yet, we *can* use language to evoke experiences we haven't yet experienced (Taylor and Zwaan 2009; Vigliocco et al. 2009). The experiences evoked via language, in the absence of a fully "immersed" experience, such as seeing or enacting the experience, is somewhat attenuated and full of gaps. Nevertheless, language can facilitate an approximation.

By way of illustration, consider the lutz jump. Readers largely ignorant of ice-skating will also be ignorant of what this move entails. Now read the following definition of the lutz jump:

A jump in figure skating in which the skater takes off from the back outer edge of one skate and makes one full rotation before landing on the back outer edge of the other skate

Having read this, readers will have a rough idea of what the lutz jump is. They will understand it is a move in ice-skating, which involves a particular kind of footwear on a particular kind of surface. Moreover, readers will be able to close their eyes and rehearse a move in which an ice-skater takes off, performs one rotation, and lands. To be sure, many of the details will be unclear. If readers were then to look up *lutz jump* on YouTube, they would be able to watch clips of the lutz jump being performed. And this illustrates a point I will return to later: veridical experience, the experience of seeing, acting, and interacting, gives rise to body-based representations that are analog in nature. Having seen the lutz jump, readers can, thereafter, picture it in their mind's eye. Language, in contrast, doesn't work like that, I contend. The representations are more sketchy, more partial; they are not analog at all.

More troublesome for Barsalou, and for others who seek to exclude semantic content from language, is the following: although simulations arise automatically in response to language use, they are not necessary for language to be successfully used. Patients with Parkinson's disease who display difficulty in carrying out motor movements, suggesting their motor representations are damaged, are still able to use and understand, more or less, corresponding action verbs (Boulenger et al. 2008). Likewise, patients with motor neuron disease are still able to process action verbs, albeit suboptimally (Bak et al. 2001). Indeed, this was the one of the objections to an embodied approach to concepts raised by Mahon and Caramazza (2008), discussed earlier.

Taylor and Zwaan (2009) account for this by proposing what they call the *fault tolerance hypothesis*. This makes the following claim: humans construct their conceptual representations from various sources, including language. Moreover, these may be incomplete. For instance, a novice skier doesn't have the motor routines necessary for skiing; an unconventional ski instructor might ask the novice skier to imagine being a waiter, with a tray held aloft, weaving through a busy Parisian café, in order to simulate the type of body posture and motor routines required when on skis.[2] The point is that evoking such a simulation, via language, while not the same as the embodied experience of skiing, facilitates the learning of the requisite motor routines that, in time, will lead the novice to becoming an accomplished skier.

The third problem is this. The grammatical subsystem appears to encode semantic content—albeit schematic content—independently of the conceptual system (Evans 2009; Evans and Green 2006; Talmy 2000; see also Bergen 2012, chapter 5). To illustrate, if we exclude the semantic content associated with open-class elements such as nouns, verbs, adjectives, and adverbs, we are left with a type of schematic representation that is not straightforwardly imageable, or perceptual. In short, the representations associated with grammatical structure, so-called closed-class elements, appear not to relate, in a straightforward way, with perceptual representations. And yet, such representations appear to be meaningful. For instance, the distinction between the definite article *the* and the indefinite article *a* is one of specificity. But it is not clear what *the* might relate to in the conceptual system: although we can visualize open-class lexical items, such as *chair* or *tree*, and simulate the feelings and scenes associated with more abstract nouns such as *love* and *war*, we can't simulate whatever it is that *the* corresponds to, for instance.

To make this point more explicitly, consider the following:

(3) **Those** boys **are** paint**ing my** railing**s**

In this example, if we strip away the open-class elements we are left with the closed-class elements in bold—the bound morphemes (*-ing* and *-s*), and the closed-class free morphemes *those, are,* and *my.* Moreover, the state of being a noun, which is to say, the schematic category *noun*, and the schematic category *verb* (although not specific exemplars of nouns, exemplified by *boy, railing,* and *paint*) are also closed-class elements.

---

2. This example is due to Fauconnier and Turner (2002).

The composite meaning of all these closed-class elements in (3) is as follows: *Those somethings are somethinging my somethings.* This can be glossed as follows: "More than one entity close to the speaker is presently in the process of doing something to more than one entity belonging to the speaker." This actually provides quite a lot of meaning. That said, this semantic representation for the closed-class entities is schematic. We don't have the details of the scene: we don't know what the entities in question are, nor do we know what is being done by the agent to the patient.

Nevertheless, this illustration reveals the following: there appears to be a type of semantic representation that, arguably, is unique to the linguistic system. Moreover, this representation provides information relating to how a simulation should be constructed (see Bergen 2012 for a related point). After all, the grammatical organization of the sentence entails that the first entity is the agent and the second entity the patient: the first entity is performing an action that affects the second entity. This level of semantic representation derives exclusively from language, rather than from conceptual structure, providing an instruction as to the relative significance, and the relation that holds, between these two entities. In short, closed-class elements, and the grammatical configurations in which they reside—which are themselves closed-class elements—involve semantic content, albeit of a highly schematic sort (Evans 2009; Goldberg 1995, 2006; Talmy 2000).

There is one further difficulty with assuming that language has no semantic content, independent of conceptual structure. We now know that language appears to directly influence perception. In a language such as Greek, for instance, there are distinct words for light blue (*ghalazio*) and dark blue (*ble*). This contrasts with English, where there is a single word: *blue.* Neuroscientists have shown that whether one is a native speaker of Greek or of English influences how we *perceive* blueness. Using event-related potential (ERP) methodology, Thierry and colleagues (2009) found that the brain activity of Greek speakers diverged when they perceived the different shades of blue. In contrast, English speakers exhibited no divergence in brain activity across the blue shades. The conclusion that emerges from this is that there is clear relationship between a linguistic distinction in a speaker's native language—Greek divides blue color space while English doesn't—and the low-level, automatic perception of color, as measured by brain activity at the onset of preattentive awareness, before subjects become conscious of the color they are perceiving. For present purposes, the relevance of this finding is that it provides direct evidence that a parametric distinction imposed by a language—dark versus light color—modulates nonlinguistic perceptual categorization in visual experience. This could not be the case if language had no semantic content independent of the conceptual system.

Finally, language appears to induce the illusion of semantic unity. This is an effect of language rather than of the conceptual system. For instance, the word *time* in English encodes a range of different, albeit related, concepts (Evans 2004):

(4a) The time for a decision has arrived.

(4b) The relationship lasted a long time.

(4c) Time flows on forever.

(4d) The time is approaching midnight.

In these sets of examples, all involving the lexical item *time*, a different reading is obtained. In (4a), a discrete temporal point or moment is designated, without reference to its duration. The example in (4b) provides a reading relating to what might be described as "magnitude of duration." In the sentence in (4c), *time* prompts for an entity that is infinite and hence eternal. Thus, in (4c) the reading relates to an entity that is unbounded. Finally, the example in (4d) relates to a measurement system, and specifically a point that could be paraphrased as "The hour is approaching midnight."

Although English has one word for a range of (arguably) quite distinct concepts, other languages do not have a single word that covers all this semantic territory. For instance, recent research on the Amazonian language Amondawa reveals that there is no equivalent of the English word "time" in that language (Sinha et al. 2011). To give another example of typologically distinct languages, Inuit languages also don't have a single lexeme for *time* (Michael Fortescue, pers. comm.). Moreover, even genetically related languages use distinct lexical items to describe the semantic territory covered by the single lexical form *time* in English.

French is a good example of this:

(5) C'est l'heure de manger

"It's time to eat"

While the lexical form *heure* (hour) is used to describe the moment sense of time, equivalent to the English example in (4a); some of the other senses for English *time* are covered by the form *temps* (time). What this illustrates is that word forms can provide an illusion of semantic unity (Evans 2009) and give rise to the myth that time, by way of example, relates to a homogenous set of experiences. This is, I suggest, an effect of language, rather than nonlinguistic knowledge, which remains broadly similar across English and French. In short, other languages don't group the same semantic territory with a single lexeme. Still others separate out across distinct lexemes. In the final analysis, it appears that semantic unity is an illusion, an artifact of linguistic organization and use. This provides compelling evidence that language brings with it its own semantic contribution, independent of the rich and detailed knowledge representation of the nonlinguistic conceptual (or simulation) system.

In sum, it is difficult to maintain the view held by some eminent embodied/ grounded cognition researchers that semantic structure in language equals conceptual structure. There appear to be two distinct types of representations. I now turn to a consideration of what these might be.

10.5 Parametric versus Analog Concepts

In this section, I consider the distinction between representations in the linguistic system, and those that inhere in the conceptual (or simulation) system. But let's first consider what it means to say that language activates sensorimotor states. From the present perspective, the idea is that words are in fact cues that index or point to body-based states processed and stored by the brain (Evans 2009, 2013; Glenberg and Robertson 1999; Fischer and Zwaan 2009. To illustrate, consider the use of *red* in the following example sentences (adapted from Zwaan 2004):

(6a) The schoolteacher scrawled in red ink all over the pupil's homework book.

(6b) The red squirrel is in danger of extinction in the British Isles

In the first example, the use of *red* evokes a bright, vivid red. In the second, a dun or browny red is most likely evoked. This illustrates the following: The *meaning* of *red* is not, in any sense, there in the word (although I nuance this view below). Rather, words cue perceptual and interoceptive states stored in the brain. And these body-based states are reactivated during language use. Put another way, the word form *red* gives rise to distinct simulations for different hues of red. These simulations arise as a consequence of reactivating stored experience types. These reactivated experiences we might refer to as *analog concepts*—concepts that are directly grounded in the experiences that give rise to them. How then does semantic structure (in language) differ from this level of conceptual structure—which is to say, from analog concepts?

To illustrate, I consider the use of the adjective *red*, and the noun *redness*, in the following examples, adapted from a skin-care product advertisement:

(7a) Treat <u>redness</u> with Clinique urgent relief cream.

(7b) Treat <u>red</u> skin with Clinique urgent relief cream.

Both words, *red* and *redness*, relate to the same perceptual state, presumably. But the words package or serve to construe the content in a different way, giving rise to distinct simulations. In the example in (7a), *redness* gives rise to an interpretation relating to a skin condition. In the second, (7b), *red* refers more straightforwardly to an unwanted property of the skin.

The different interpretations arising from these sentences are not due to a different hue being indexed. Rather, the words (noun versus adjective) modulate the perceptual hue in a slightly different way, giving rise to slightly distinct simulations: "skin

Analogue concept:

Parametric concept:

Word forms:

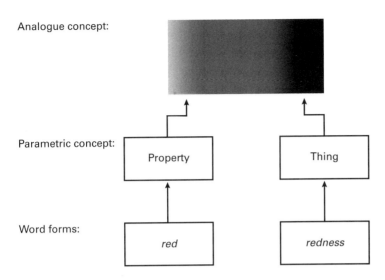

Figure 10.3 (plate 10)
Analog and parametric concepts.

condition" versus "discoloration of skin" interpretations. In other words, the grammatical distinction between the adjective (*red*) and noun (*redness*) appears to relate to a semantic distinction between the notion of property versus thing. The words *red* and *redness*, while indexing the same (or similar) perceptual state, also encode schematic concepts: PROPERTY versus THING (cf. Langacker 2008).

But unlike the body-based perceptual state—the hue of red—which is analog, PROPERTY and THING are highly schematic notions. They are what I refer to as *parametric concepts*. Unlike the perceptual experience of redness, with comes to mind when we variously imagine a fire engine, a Royal Mail post box (ubiquitous in the UK), henna, fire, the Chinese flag, or superman's cape, parametric concepts are not like veridical embodied experiences. There is nothing about the (parametric) concepts PROPERTY or THING that is akin to the perceptual experience of redness (an analog concept). Parameters are abstracted from embodied (perceptual *and* interoceptive) states, filtering out all points of difference to leave highly image-schematic content: the parameter.[3] The word form *red* encodes the parameter PROPERTY, while *redness* encodes the parameter THING. This is another way of saying that *red* is an adjective—it describes a property of a thing—while *redness* is a noun—it describes a property that is objectified in some way and established as being identifiable, in principle, in its own right, independent of other entities in world. Figure 10.3 (plate 10) captures the relationship between a word form and its parametric and analog concepts.

3. Cf. the related notion of image schema developed in the work of Johnson (1987).

My claim, then, is this. There is a distinction between analog concepts on the one hand and parametric concepts on the other. The former relate to nonlinguistic concept types that, in evolutionary terms, had to precede the existence of language. Parametric concepts constitute a species of concept that arose as a consequence of the emergence of language. They provide a level of schematic representation directly encoded by language: parametric concepts guide *how* analog concepts are activated and, consequently, *how* simulations are constructed in the service of linguistically mediated meaning construction. For instance, the forms *red* and *redness* both index the same perceptual state(s). But they parcellate the conceptual content in a different way, giving rise to distinct simulations: *redness* = condition; *red* = (unwanted) property of skin. The schematic parametric concepts, which is to say, that part of meaning that is native to language, relates to THING versus PROPERTY. Parametric concepts are language-specific affordances, rather than affordances of the simulation system.

Related proposals have been put forward by Bergen (2012) and Taylor and Zwaan (e.g., 2008, 2009). Taylor and Zwaan have captured this view in terms of what they dub the *linguistic focus hypothesis*. They argue that during language understanding, motor representations are activated that are under the governance of linguistic constructions. These serve to differentially direct focus on the referential world. Bergen's findings are consonant with this hypothesis. In one set of behavioral experiments, Bergen (2012) found that the grammatical subject, for instance, the use of *I* versus *you*, influences the perspective from which a language user perceives a scene. Bergen explains this as follows:

Grammatical person seems to modulate the perspective you adopt when performing embodied simulation. This isn't to say that every time you hear *you*, you think about yourself as a participant in simulated actions. But it does mean that the grammatical person in a sentence pushes you toward being more likely to adopt one perspective or another. What's interesting about this is that in this case, grammar appears not to be telling you what to simulate, but rather, how to simulate—what perspective to simulate the event from. Instead of acting as the script in this case, grammar is acting as the director. (114)

In the light of this discussion, what then is the function of language and, specifically, parametric concepts in embodied cognition? My answer is that parametric concepts, encoded by language, guide the formation of complex simulations for purposes of (linguistically mediated) communication. Parametric concepts guide the *parcellation* (focal adjustments, in Langacker's 2008 terms) of analog (i.e., perceptual and interoceptive) concepts, in the construction of simulations. Parametric concepts encode schematic, or *digitized,* content. Content of this sort is abstracted from analog, or perceptual (and interoceptive) representations. Hence, the parameters THING versus PROPERTY are schemas drawn from embodied experience.

Let's now examine a more complex example of a parametric concept. Consider the ditransitive construction (Goldberg 1995), as exemplified by the following:

(8) John baked Mary a cake.

Goldberg argues that this example is sanctioned by a sentence-level construction that encodes the schematic semantics in (9):

(9) X (INTENDS TO) CAUSE(S) Y TO RECEIVE Z

Goldberg's point is that the "cause to receive" meaning in (9) arises not from the semantics of *bake,* which is canonically a transitive (rather than a ditransitive) verb, but from the larger construction in which it is embedded. And there is behavioral evidence to support such a contention. Kaschak and Glenberg (2000) reported a study in which they showed sentences to participants using the novel verb *to crutch.* Some sentences employed the ditransitive construction, as in (10a), while others placed the novel verb in the transitive construction as in (10b). They then asked subjects to say which of the sentences were consistent with two inference statements, given below in (11):

(10a) Lyn crutched Tom her apple

(10b) Lyn crutched her apple

(11a) Tom got the apple

(11b) Lyn acted on her apple

The sentence in (11a) provides an inference of transfer of possession. In contrast, the inference arising from (11b) is to act on. Because the verb is novel, it has no inherent semantics associated with it. Hence, if the sentence possesses inherent semantics independently to the verb, as claimed by Goldberg, then we would expect the inference in (11a) to be judged as compatible with sentence (10a), and the inference in (11b) to be compatible with the sentence in (10b). And this is indeed what Kaschak and Glenberg found. In short, the syntactic sentence-level template appears to have a schematic representation associated with it—a complex parametric concept in present terms—which is represented in (9). Parametric concepts of this sort guide or modulate how analog concepts are parcellated, giving rise to a simulation. And a complex parametric concept such as (9) does this, in principle, in the same way as parametric concepts associated with single lexical items such as *red* and *redness.*

In essence, it turns out that working out what a concept is, is not a straightforward matter at all. Body-based representations, stored in different brain regions, form the basis of a species of concepts: analog concepts. Concepts of this kind are grounded in the veridical (perceptual) and phenomenological (interoceptive) experience types from which they arise. But a second species of concept, parametric concepts, appears

Table 10.2
Parametric versus analog concepts

Parametric concepts	Analog concepts
Specific to language	Specific to the conceptual system
Parametric (abstracted from embodied states, filtering out all points of difference to leave highly schematic properties or parameters)	Analog (albeit attenuated) representations of body-based states
	Arise directly from perceptual (conscious) experience and reside in the same neural
Underpinnings for all linguistic units (where a linguistic unit is a form or parametric content unit of any complexity)	system(s) as body-based states
	Reactivated or simulated (by language, imagination, etc.) and can be combined to form complex and novel simulations

to be directly encoded by language. Concepts of this kind are far more schematic: they encode parameters—THING versus PROPERTY, DARK COLOR versus LIGHT COLOR. They are abstracted from embodied experience but are not rich analog representations. Moreover, the parametric concepts appear to be deployed to modulate the analog concepts in giving rise to a representation known as a simulation: a complex representation that is constructed in the process of speaking and thinking. This simulation expresses an idea that language is instrumental in facilitating. Table 10.2 summarizes the distinction between parametric and analog concepts.

10.6   Access Semantics

Having distinguished between analog and parametric concepts, we now require an account of the respective contributions of parametric and analog concepts to the meaning-construction process. In other words, we need an account of how parametric concepts *access* analog concepts. To do this, in this section I develop a theory of *access semantics*. An access semantics accounts for how semantic structure (made up of parametric concepts) interfaces with, and thereby activates, the requisite aspects of nonlinguistic knowledge representation—that is, conceptual structure (made up of analog concepts)—which inheres in the conceptual system, giving rise to a simulation.

10.6.1   LCCM Theory

In Evans (2009, 2013) I have developed a theoretical account of lexical representation and semantic composition dubbed the theory of lexical concepts and cognitive models, or LCCM theory for short. LCCM theory is a theory of access semantics. The claim at its heart is enshrined in the distinction between its two foundational theoretical constructs—the *lexical concept* and the *cognitive model*: there is a qualitative distinction between these theoretical constructs, which are central to meaning construction.

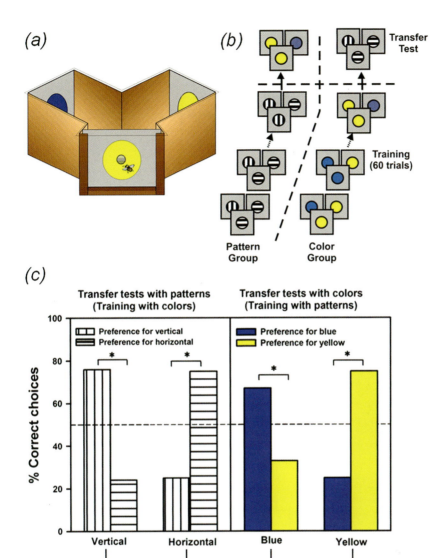

Plate 1 (Figure 1.2)

SAMENESS learning in honeybees (Giurfa et al. 2001). (a) Y-maze used to train bees in a delayed matching-to-sample task. Bees had to enter the maze to collect sugar solution on one of the back walls. A sample was shown at the maze entrance before bees accessed the arms of the maze. (b) Training protocol. A group of bees were trained during sixty trials with black-and-white vertical and horizontal gratings (pattern group); another group was trained with colors, blue and yellow (color group). After training, both groups were subjected to a transfer test with novel stimuli (patterns for bees trained with colors, colors for bees trained with patterns). (c) Performance of the pattern group and the color group in the transfer tests with novel stimuli. Both groups chose the novel stimulus corresponding to the sample although they had no experience with such test stimuli. *: $p < 0.05$.

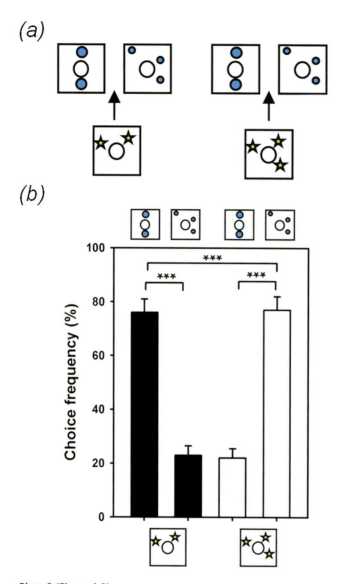

Plate 2 (Figure 1.3)
Numerosity in honeybees (Gross et al. 2009). (a) Training protocol performed in a Y-maze (see figure 1.2a). Bees were trained in a delayed matching-to-sample task to match stimuli containing two or three elements. The sample with two or three elements was shown at the maze entrance before bees accessed the arms of the maze. The bees had to choose the arm containing the stimulus composed of the same number of elements as the sample to obtain sucrose reward. The appearance of the elements and their spatial positions differed between the sample and the target (one example shown) so that bees had to focus on number and not on other perceptual cues to solve the task. (b) In transfer tests, the bees were able to match the stimuli according to the number of their composing elements, if numbers didn't exceed four. ***: $p < 0.001$.

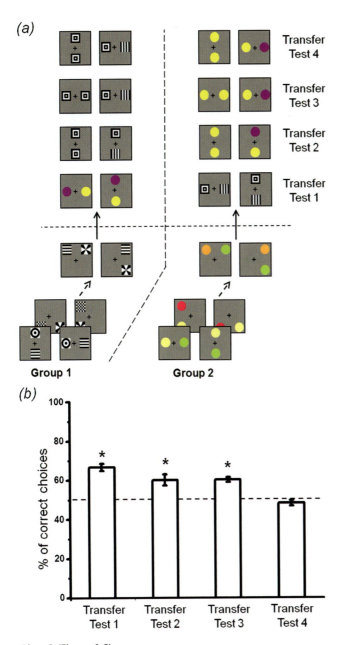

Plate 3 (Figure 1.5)

Simultaneous mastering of two concepts in honeybees (Avarguès-Weber et al. 2012). Bees learned to use two concepts simultaneously: ABOVE/BELOW (or RIGHT/LEFT) and DIFFERENCE. (a) Bees were trained with sucrose reward in a Y-maze to choose the stimulus presenting two different patterns (Group 1) or two different colored discs (Group 2) in an above/below (or right/left) relationship depending on the group of bees. Appearances and relative position of the patterns varied from trial to trial. (b) After a thirty training trials, bees succeeded in transferring the spatial relation rule to unknown stimuli presenting the appropriate spatial relationship. Bees of Group 1 trained with patterns transferred their choice to colored discs arranged in the proper spatial relationship, and bees of Group 2 trained with colored discs transferred their choice to patterns arranged in the proper spatial relationship. Additional tests (transfer tests 2 to 4) demonstrated that bees additionally learned that the patterns linked by the spatial relation had to be different. Bees used both rules simultaneously in transfer tests. *: p < 0.05.

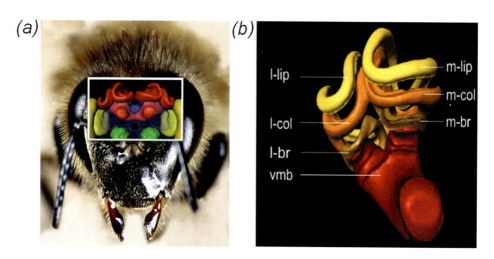

(a)

(b)

l-lip   m-lip

       m-col

l-col   m-br

l-br

vmb

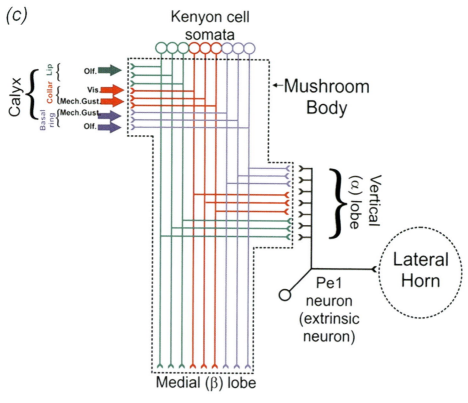

(c)

Kenyon cell
somata

Calyx

Lip — Olf.

Collar — Vis.

Mech.Gust.

Basal ring — Mech.Gust.

Olf.

← Mushroom
Body

Vertical
(α) lobe

Lateral
Horn

Pe1
neuron
(extrinsic
neuron)

Medial (β) lobe

Plate 4 (Figure 1.6)

Three-dimensional reconstruction of a honeybee brain. (a) The mushroom bodies, which are multimodal structures receiving segregated visual, olfactory, mechanosensory, and gustatory afferences, are shown in red. (b) Three-dimensional reconstruction of a mushroom body in frontal view (vmb). Two calyces, a lateral (l) and a medial one (m), fuse in a single peduncle. Each calyx is subdivided into three main regions, the lip, the collar (col) and the basal ring (br). (c) Scheme of a mushroom body (delimited by dashed straight lines), showing segregated multisensory input at the level of the calyx and integrated multimodal output at the level of the vertical (α) lobe. The somata of the Kenyon cells (KC), which integrate the mushroom body, are located in the calyx bowl. The dendrites of the KC form the calyx, which is subdivided into three main regions, the lip, receiving olfactory afferences; the collar, receiving mainly visual but also mechanosensory and gustatory afferences; and the basal ring, receiving olfactory, mechanosensory, and gustatory afferences (Mobbs 1982; Schröter and Menzel 2003; Strausfeld 2002). The axons of the KC subdivide and form the vertical (α) and the medial (β) lobe. An extrinsic, multimodal peduncle neuron, the Pe1 neuron (Mauelshagen 1993; Okada et al. 2007; Rybak and Menzel 1998), is shown, whose dendrites arborize across the vertical lobe; its axon projects to the lateral horn (delimited by a dashed circle).

◄───

A. Picture naming performance by category

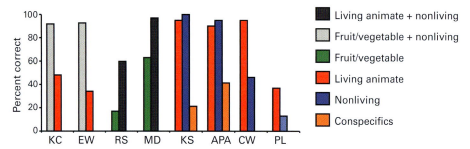

Legend:
- Living animate + nonliving (black)
- Fruit/vegetable + nonliving (light gray)
- Fruit/vegetable (green)
- Living animate (red)
- Nonliving (blue)
- Conspecifics (orange)

B. Semantic probe questions by category and modality

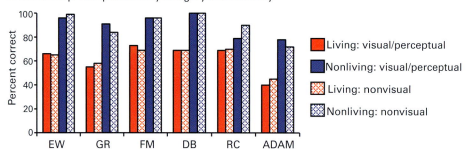

Legend:
- Living: visual/perceptual (red)
- Nonliving: visual/perceptual (blue)
- Living: nonvisual (red crosshatch)
- Nonliving: nonvisual (blue crosshatch)

Plate 5 (Figure 4.1)

Patients with category-specific semantic deficits may be differentially, or even selectively, impaired for knowledge of animals, plants, conspecifics, or artifacts. The knowledge impairment cannot be explained in terms of a differential impairment to a sensory or motor-based modality of information. While discussion and debate continues as to whether noncategorical dimensions of organization may lead to category-specific brain organization, there is consensus that the phenomenon itself is *categorical*. (A) Picture-naming performance of patients studied with materials that were carefully balanced to equate various continuous dimensions across categories (e.g., frequency, familiarity, visual complexity). The four major patterns of category-specific semantic deficits are represented. (B) Semantic attribute question performance for six representative patients with differential impairments for living animate. As shown across the patients, impairments for a category are associated with impairments for all types of knowledge about items from that category. Figure reproduced from Mahon and Caramazza (2011), with permission.

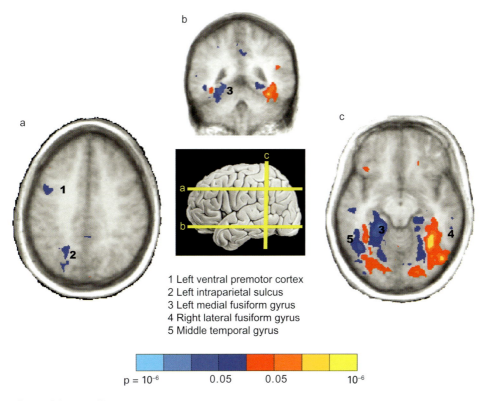

1 Left ventral premotor cortex
2 Left intraparietal sulcus
3 Left medial fusiform gyrus
4 Right lateral fusiform gyrus
5 Middle temporal gyrus

p = 10⁻⁶   0.05   0.05   10⁻⁶

Plate 6 (Figure 4.2)

Category-specific patterns of BOLD response in the healthy brain. This figure shows in red a network of regions that are differentially activated for living animate things, and in blue, a network
of regions that are differentially activated for nonliving things (Data from Chao et al 2002; figure
reproduced from Martin and Chao, 2001, with permission).

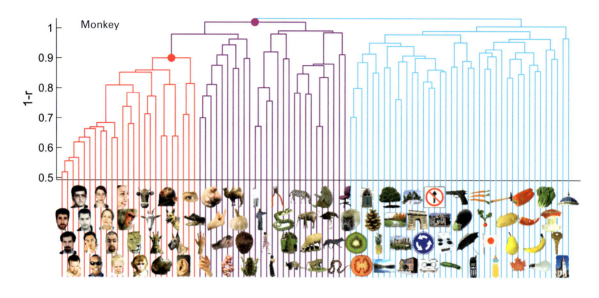

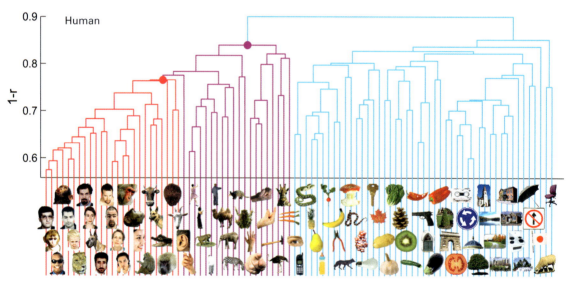

Plate 7 (Figure 4.3)

Dendrograms showing similarity of response patterns across visual stimuli in monkey inferior temporal (IT) cortex and human ventral temporal cortex. Kriegeskorte and colleagues (2008) analyzed neurophysiological data from monkey IT cortex and human fMRI data when participants (monkeys, humans) were viewing numerous stimuli from many different categories. The similarity of the neural responses across the stimuli was analyzed separately for monkeys and humans. The figures, reproduced from Kriegeskorte and colleagues (2008, figure 4.4) use hierarchical clustering to describe the similarity space of the stimuli. The fascinating aspect of these data is that they show, with entirely independent analysis pipelines, that high-level visual cortex in monkeys and humans represents largely the same similarity space for visual stimuli. Figure reproduced with permission, from Kriegeskorte and colleagues (2008).

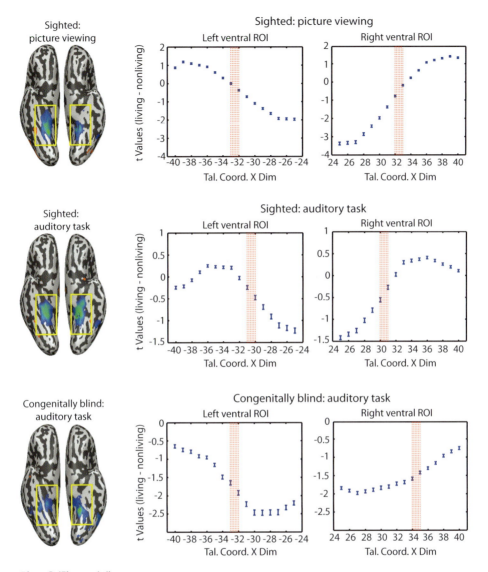

Plate 8 (Figure 4.4)

Category-specific organization does not require visual experience. Congenitally blind and sighted participants were presented with spoken words of living things (animals) and nonliving things (tools, nonmanipulable objects) and were asked to make size judgments about the referents of the words. The sighted participants were also shown pictures corresponding to the same stimuli in a separate scan. For sighted participants viewing pictures, the known finding was replicated that nonliving things such as tools and large nonmanipulable objects lead to differential neural responses in medial aspects of ventral temporo-occipital cortex. This pattern of differential BOLD responses for nonliving things in medial aspects of ventral temporo-occipital cortex was also observed in congenitally blind participants and sighted participants performing the size judgment task over auditory stimuli. These data indicate that the medial-to-lateral bias in the distribution of category-specific responses does not depend on visual experience. For details of the study, see Mahon and colleagues (2009). Figure reproduced from Mahon and colleagues (2009) with permission.

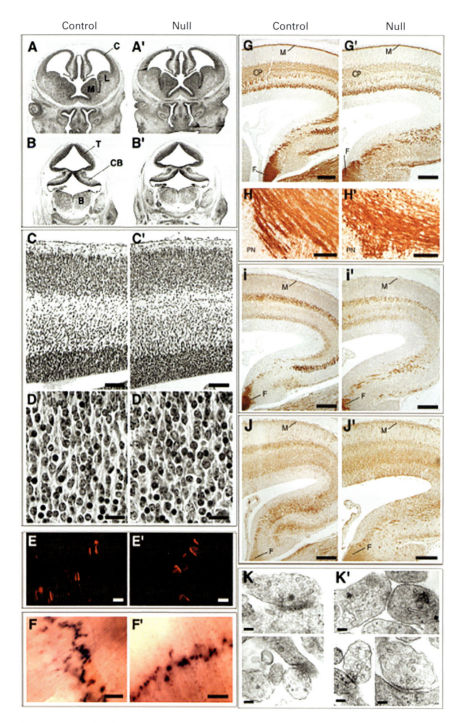

Plate 9 (Figure 5.1)
Neurological development in mutant mice that were genetically engineered to eliminate synaptic transmission (null) and in normal control mice (control). (From Verhage et al. 2000. Used with permission.)

Analogue concept:

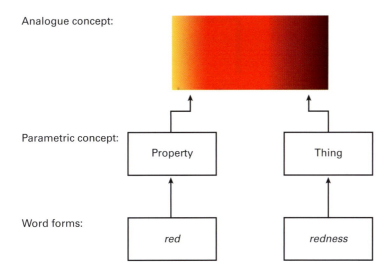

Parametric concept: | Property | | Thing |

Word forms: | *red* | | *redness* |

Plate 10 (Figure 10.3)
Analog and parametric concepts.

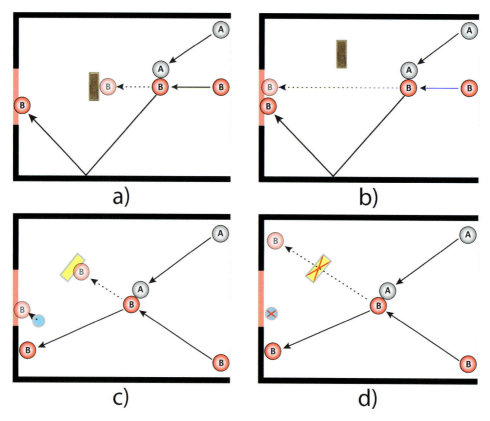

Plate 11 (Figure 22.4)

Diagrammatic illustrations of four collision events in a simple physics world. Note: Solid arrows represent the actual trajectories of ball A before the collision and of ball B before and after the collision. Dashed arrows and faded circles represent the counterfactual trajectory of ball B. The brown rectangle, yellow rectangle, and blue circle represent a brick, and the entry and exit of a teleport, respectively.

This distinction relates, ultimately, to the bifurcation between analog and parametric concepts, which respectively structure cognitive models and lexical concepts.

In keeping with the thrust of the argument developed in the foregoing, LCCM theory assumes the linguistic system emerged, in evolutionary terms, much later than the earlier conceptual system. The utility of a linguistic system, on this account, is that it provides an executive control mechanism facilitating the deployment of conceptual representations in service of linguistically mediated meaning construction. Hence, *semantic* representations in the two systems are of a qualitatively distinct kind. I model semantic structure—the primary representational substrate of the linguistic system—in terms of the theoretical construct of the lexical concept. A lexical concept is a component of linguistic knowledge—the semantic pole of a *symbolic unit* (in, e.g., Langacker's 1987 terms)—which encodes a bundle of various types of highly schematic *linguistic content* (see Evans 2006, 2009, 2013). In particular, linguistic content includes information relating to the selectional tendencies associated with a given lexical concept—the range of semantic and grammatical correlates of a given lexical concept (see Evans 2006, 2009). Hence, lexical concepts are parametric concepts.

While lexical concepts encode highly schematic linguistic content, a subset—those associated with open-class forms—are connected, and hence facilitate access, to the conceptual system. Lexical concepts of this type are termed *open-class lexical concepts*.[4] Such lexical concepts are typically associated with multiple areas in the conceptual system, referred to as *association areas*.

The range of association areas to which a given lexical concept facilitates access is termed an *access site*. LCCM theory assumes that the access site for a given *open-class lexical concept* is unique. As lexical concepts facilitate access to a potentially large number of association areas in the conceptual system, any given open-class lexical concept, in principle, facilitates access to a large *semantic potential*. However, only a small subset of this semantic potential is typically activated in *interpretation* of a given utterance.

Although the linguistic system evolved to harness the representational power of the conceptual system for purposes of communication, the human conceptual system, at least in very broad outline, is continuous with that of other primates (Barsalou 2005; Evans 2013, especially chapter 2, 2014), and shows a range of broad similarities with that of other species (Hurford 2007). In contrast to the linguistic system, the conceptual system evolved primarily to facilitate functions such as perception, categorization, inference, choice, and action, rather than communication. In LCCM theory, *conceptual structure*—the semantic representational substrate of the conceptual system—is modeled by the theoretical construct of the cognitive model. A cognitive model is a coherent body of multimodal knowledge grounded in the brain's modal systems, and derives from the full range of experience types processed by the brain, including sensorimotor

---

4. See Evans (2009) for the rationale for this position.

Lexical representation

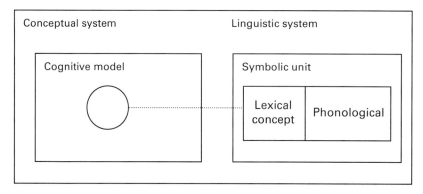

Figure 10.4
Relationship between a lexical concept and a cognitive model.

experience, proprioception, and subjective experience, including affect.[5] Hence, cognitive models are analog in nature, and as such constitute analog concepts.

The conceptual content encoded as cognitive models can become reactivated during the simulation process. Simulation is a general-purpose computation performed by the brain to implement the range of activities that subserve a fully functional conceptual system. Such activities include conceptualization, inferring, choice, categorization, and the formation of ad hoc categories.[6]

In LCCM theory, simulations are effected by a subset of lexical concepts—*open-class lexical concepts*—facilitating access to the conceptual system via a number of association areas (see figure 10.4). Each association area corresponds to a (part of a) cognitive model, as captured in figure 10.4. The range of association areas to which an open-class lexical concept corresponds makes up its access site.

10.6.2   Cognitive Model Profile
An important construct in LCCM theory, and one that is essential to providing an account of meaning construction, is that of the *cognitive model profile*. As an open-class lexical concept—a noun, verb, adjective, or adverb—facilitates access to numerous

5. The term *cognitive model* is used elsewhere in cognitive science, for instance in terms of computational modeling (e.g., in John Anderson's ACT-R theory of cognition), and is widespread in this other sense. My use of the term is not being deployed in the same way.
6. For discussion and findings relating to the multimodal nature of conceptual representations and the role of simulation in drawing on such representations in facilitating conceptual function, see, for instance, Barsalou (1999, 2008), Glenberg (1997), Gallese and Lakoff (2005), and references therein.

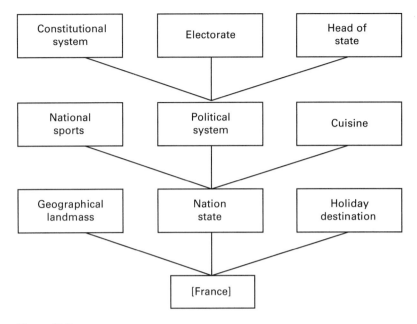

Figure 10.5
Partial cognitive model profile for the lexical concept [FRANCE].

association areas within the conceptual system, it facilitates access to numerous cognitive models. Moreover, the cognitive models to which a lexical concept facilitates access are themselves connected to other cognitive models. The range of cognitive models to which a given lexical concept facilitates direct access, and the range of additional cognitive models to which it therefore facilitates indirect access, are collectively termed its cognitive model profile.

To illustrate, consider the cognitive model profile for the lexical concept I gloss as [FRANCE], associated with the form *France*. A partial cognitive model profile for [FRANCE] is represented in figure 10.5.

Figure 10.5 is an attempt to capture the sort of knowledge that language users must presumably have access to when speaking and thinking about France. As illustrated by figure 10.5, the lexical concept [FRANCE] provides access to a potentially large number of cognitive models.[7] Because each cognitive model consists of a complex and structured body of knowledge, which, in turn, provides access to other sorts of knowledge, LCCM theory distinguishes between cognitive models that are directly accessed via the lexical concept—*primary cognitive models*—and those that form substructures of directly

7. The bracket notation used here, [FRANCE], represents the linguistic content that is encoded by the vehicle "France."

accessed models—*secondary cognitive models*. These secondary cognitive models are indirectly accessed via the lexical concept.

The lexical concept [FRANCE] affords access to a number of primary cognitive models, which make up the *primary cognitive model profile* for [FRANCE]. These are hypothesized to include GEOGRAPHICAL LANDMASS, NATION-STATE and HOLIDAY DESTINATION. And I reiterate, a cognitive model represents a coherent body of complex information, multimodal information, gleaned through sense perception, interoceptive experience, and propositional information achieved via cultural learning, language, and other channels. Each of these cognitive models provides access to further cognitive models. In figure 10.5, a flavor of this is given by virtue of the various secondary cognitive models that are accessed via the NATION-STATE cognitive model—the *secondary cognitive model profile*. These include NATIONAL SPORTS, POLITICAL SYSTEM, and CUISINE. For instance, we may know that in France, the French engage in national sports of particular types, for instance, football, rugby, and so on, rather than others: the French don't typically engage in American football, ice hockey, cricket, and so on. We may also know that as a sporting nation, they take part in international sports competitions of various kinds, including the FIFA World Cup, the Six Nations rugby competition, the Rugby World Cup, the Olympics, and so on.

That is, we may have access to a large body of knowledge concerning the sorts of sports French people engage in. We may also have some knowledge of the funding structures and social and economic conditions and constraints that apply to these sports in France as well as France's international standing with respect to these particular sports, and further knowledge about the sports themselves, including the rules that govern their practice and so forth. This knowledge is derived from a large number of sources, including direct experience and cultural transmission (including language).

With respect to the secondary cognitive model of POLITICAL SYSTEM, figure 10.5 illustrates a sample of further secondary cognitive models that are accessed via this cognitive model. In other words, each secondary cognitive model has further (secondary) cognitive models to which it provides access. For instance (FRENCH) ELECTORATE is a cognitive model accessed via the cognitive model (FRENCH) POLITICAL SYSTEM. In turn the cognitive model (FRENCH) POLITICAL SYSTEM is accessed via the cognitive model NATION-STATE. Accordingly, NATION-STATE is a primary cognitive model, while ELECTORATE and POLITICAL SYSTEM are secondary cognitive models.

Finally, it is worth highlighting a point that has been implicit in the foregoing. LCCM theory assumes that cognitive models involve content at varying degrees of abstractness, and of different types. For instance, being able to simulate the view from the top of Mont Saint-Michel on a midsummer evening, while on vacation in France, involves processing sensorimotor aspects of a scene, as well as knowledge of the affective experiences that accompany this view—pleasure, joy, awe, and so on. In addition, such information is subject to abstraction, giving rise to schematic categories, such as

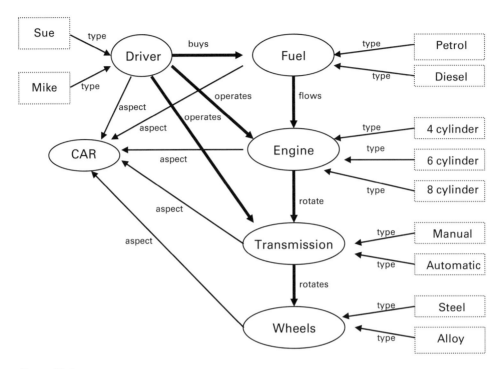

Figure 10.6
Knowledge structure for CAR concept.

"beautiful places I have seen," which may come to form part of the cognitive model profile for [FRANCE], but may also become linked to other cognitive model profiles. Moreover, cognitive models may contain information relating to entities, both individuals and types, as well as relational information. For instance, a cognitive model profile for [CAR] will include knowledge of various sorts, including, in various levels of detail contingent on the individual's knowledge base, the component parts of a car and the relations between them, as illustrated schematically in figure 10.6. Moreover, as language interfaces with the conceptual system via access sites, cultural knowledge mediated by language can come to form part of the representations associated with cognitive models. In short, LCCM theory holds that analog (body-based) content is supplemented by propositional information derived from linguistically mediated content, thus fleshing out the representations in the conceptual system.

10.6.3 Activation of Cognitive Models in Meaning Construction

The way meaning construction proceeds is by virtue of integration of parametric concepts, which give rise to a linguistic context that facilitates activation of aspects of cognitive model profiles. The outcome, then, of language understanding is activation of nonlinguistic cognitive models, guided and constrained by linguistic context. Consider the following linguistic examples:

(12a) France is a country of outstanding natural beauty.

(12b) France is one of the leading nations in the European Union.

(12c) France beat New Zealand in the 2007 Rugby World Cup.

(12d) France voted against the EU constitution in the 2005 referendum.

In each of these examples, the semantic contribution associated with the form *France* is slightly distinct. That is, the semantic contribution provided by *France* varies across these distinct utterances. The key insight of LCCM theory is that the reason for this variation is due to differential activation of nonlinguistic knowledge structures, the cognitive model profile, to which the lexical concept associated with *France* affords access.

The *informational characterization* associated with [FRANCE] in each of these examples concerns France as a geographical landmass in (12a), France as a political entity, a nation-state, in (12b), the fifteen players who make up the French rugby team in (12c), and in (12d), that proportion of the French electorate who voted "non" when presented, in a recent referendum, with the proposal to endorse a constitution for the European Union. In order to provide these distinct interpretations, this lexical concept must serve as an access site for a cognitive model profile that, at the very least, includes the sort of information indicated in figure 10.5.

The differential interpretations associated with the examples in (12) arise as follows. In (12a) the interpretation associated with the form *France*, which relates to a particular geographical region, derives from activation of the GEOGRAPHICAL LANDMASS cognitive model. That is, individual language users have knowledge relating to the physical aspects of France, including its terrain and its geographical location. In this example, the utterance context activates this part of the cognitive model profile accessed by the lexical concept [FRANCE]. In the second example, the utterance context activates a different part of the cognitive model profile to which the lexical concept [FRANCE] affords access. In this example, the informational characterization relates to the cognitive model of France as a POLITICAL ENTITY. This is due to activation of the NATION-STATE cognitive model. The use of *France* in the example in (12c) relates to the group of fifteen French individuals who play as a team and thereby represent the French nation on the rugby field. In the example in (12d), the form *France* relates not to a geographical landmass, political entity, nation-state, nor group of fifteen rugby players who happen to be representing the entire population of France. Rather, it relates to that portion of the French electorate that voted against ratification of the EU constitution in a referendum held in 2005. Accordingly, what is activated here is the ELECTORATE cognitive model.

This last example provides an elegant illustration of the way in which activation of a cognitive model provides a situated interpretation of a lexical concept by giving rise to an access route through the semantic potential. In this example, interpretation requires that an access route be established through the cognitive model profile accessed via the lexical concept [FRANCE] in a way that is consistent with the lexical concepts associated with the other linguistic forms and units in the utterance. The interpretation associated with *France* in this example has to do with the French electorate, and specifically that part of the French electorate that voted against ratification of the EU constitution. In other words, [FRANCE] in this example achieves an informational characterization that is facilitated by activating the cognitive models shown in bold in figure 10.7.

10.6.4 Matching

My final illustration speaks directly to the criticism leveled by Mahon and Caramazza (2008) against embodied/grounded approaches to concepts. They argued that an embodied account of concepts can't deal with the variable properties evoked by *beautiful* in these sorts of examples:

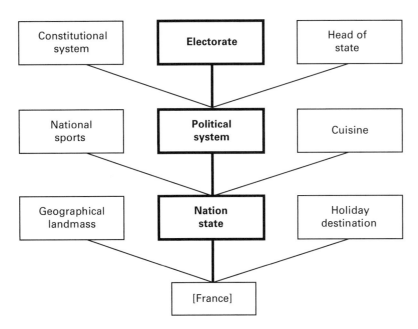

Figure 10.7
Access route established by the interpretation of [FRANCE] in the utterance "France voted against the EU constitution."

(13a) a beautiful face

(13b) a beautiful sound

(13c) a beautiful idea

On the contrary, accounting for the variable sensorimotor and affective information evoked by *beautiful* in these examples turns on the issue of meaning construction, rather than (solely) on an account of knowledge representation. As such, it is guided by the linguistic context.

The challenge, in the examples in (12), is to account for how the conceptual content for *beautiful*, and *face* are integrated. This involves, in LCCM terms, a process of *matching* across cognitive model profiles accessed by the relevant open-class lexical concepts. Moreover, this matching is based on conceptual coherence across the cognitive model profiles to ensure that the "correct" cognitive models become activated, leading to a simulation.

To begin to illustrate, consider a partial cognitive model profile for the open-class lexical concept [BEAUTIFUL]—see figure 10.8. Primary cognitive models that are accessed by [BEAUTIFUL] range from assessments relating to the receipt of or awareness of visual pleasure, particularly physical appearance, often related to perceived sexual attractiveness, to the awareness of nonvisual but physical pleasure, such as aural pleasure, as in the appreciation of music, or pleasure derived from touch, for instance. The lexical concept [BEAUTIFUL] also affords access to a cognitive model having to do with nonphysical pleasure, which I gloss as AESTHETIC PLEASURE. This relates to an appreciation for such things as art and literature from which pleasure are derived.

In the examples in (12), the linguistic context, a noun phrase (NP), gives rise to the parametric concept [A NONSPECIFIC THING WITH A PARTICULAR ATTRIBUTE]. This schematic semantic representation drives the matching process. That is, the two open-class lexical concepts, for instance [BEAUTIFUL] and [FACE], afford access to their respective cognitive model profiles. But they do so in a way that is consistent with the parcellation provided

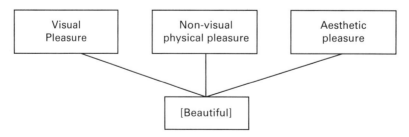

Figure 10.8
Partial cognitive model profile for the lexical concept [BEAUTIFUL].

by the parametric concept: whatever cognitive model [BEAUTIFUL] activates, this must be interpretable as an attribute associated with *face*. And vice versa, the cognitive model activated by [FACE] must be coherent with its property *beautiful*.

The process involved is thus one of matching, guided by the parametric concept. As such, because a face is a physical entity that can be seen, conceptual coherence is achieved when the VISUAL PLEASURE cognitive model is activated. In short, the language constrains the matching process involved in activation of nonlinguistic concepts, in service of linguistically mediated simulations.

10.7 Conclusion

I began this chapter by asking this question: Do linguistic units (e.g., words) have semantic content independently of the human conceptual system? Some recent theories of embodied (or grounded) cognition, for instance LASS theory, developed by Barsalou and colleagues (2008), have tended to assume that the value of language is in providing syntactic organization that facilitates the assembly of nonlinguistic concepts, and hence simulations. On this view, language has no semantic contribution independent of nonlinguistic concepts. In contrast, some psycholinguists (e.g., Taylor and Zwaan 2008, 2009) and linguists (e.g., Bergen 2012) take the view that language shapes the nature of simulations, by providing a level of focus on how the simulation should be constructed. The implication of such a view, I suggest, is that language must have a level of semantic content independent of nonlinguistic concepts. The distinction between the two, between semantic structure versus conceptual structure, I have argued, can be operationalized in terms of the distinction between what I refer to as parametric information (or concepts) and analog information (or concepts). Lexical concepts, the concepts specific to the linguistic system, are parametric, providing a level of schematic information. On this view, a lexical concept, made up of parameters, is the semantic pole of a linguistic unit, where a linguistic unit is a symbolic assembly of form and (schematic) meaning. In addition, lexical concepts facilitate access to nonlinguistic concepts, which, in LCCM theory terms, are labeled cognitive models. Cognitive models consist of analog information.

The parametric information that makes up lexical concepts can be associated with single word forms, more complex idiomatic units, and even sentence-level constructions. From this view, the parameters encoded in language actively shape, or parcellate, in my terms, the analog content to which a subset of lexical concepts (open-class lexical concepts) facilitate access. For instance, the ditransitive construction, described earlier, stipulates the relationship between the lexical concepts associated with the two NPs in the construction. One entity associated with NP1 is designated as recipient, and the other, NP2, as object of transfer. Although the open-class lexical concepts associated with these NPs access analog information, via the cognitive models that form their access sites, the simulations that are constructed arise based on the parcellation facilitated by the parametric content. In short, my argument is that there must be a distinction between parametric concepts (encoded by language) and analog concepts, associated with cognitive models, if linguistically mediated simulations are to arise in the way claimed.

The consequence of the approach to knowledge representation and meaning construction I develop is this. A grounded cognition approach to concepts has a means of addressing criticisms that an account of abstract concepts, such as BEAUTIFUL, remains intractable in this framework. On the contrary, with a descriptively adequate account of knowledge representation—recognizing the distinction between analog and parametric concepts—and an account of meaning construction—the way in which linguistic and simulation systems interface—such an account becomes conceivable, as I hope to have demonstrated.

Moving forward, I see future research on conceptual structure as having three distinct goals. First, ongoing and future research needs to develop and refine empirically verified accounts of knowledge representation. I have been assuming, based on current knowledge, that cognitive models and cognitive model profiles are based on hierarchical knowledge structures, which are relational, are dynamically updated, and feature conceptual distance between an access site—the cognitive models that interface with the linguistic system. Evidence from linguistics suggests that some types of knowledge indexed by words are more central to word meaning than others. The classic distinction between denotation and connotation is one way in which this has been operationalized (see Allan 1997). The so-called encyclopedic approach to representations underpinning words is another attempt to capture this (e.g., Langacker 1987). Moreover, experimental psychology has offered abundant evidence that knowledge is structured, ranging from classic work on typicality effects within prototype theory (e.g., Rosch 1975, 1978; Rosch and Mervis 1975) to priming studies illustrating relations between word meanings (e.g., Thompson-Schill, Kurtz, and Gabrieli 1998). Psychophysical tasks have also demonstrated that knowledge is relational (see Barsalou 1999 for a review) and is dynamically updated (Elman 2009, 2011). Further research in this view is projected under the aegis of LCCM theory, to develop an empirically robust account of knowledge representation.

A second goal for future research must be to determine the processes that facilitate access to knowledge representation. Part of this investigation must involve the compositional mechanisms that facilitate novel concept formation. For instance, what makes it possible to produce ad hoc concepts such as things to take on vacation, or things to remove from one's house in the event of fire (Barsalou 1983). Equally, how are novel blends produced, such as PET FISH—a nonprototypical fish (not gray), and a nonprototypical pet (not furry)—and mythological creatures such as UNICORNS.

Fauconnier and Turner (2002; see also Turner 2014) have argued for an integrative process termed *blending* that produces such imaginative feats. Hence, in addition to a model of conceptual structure, we also presumably require the empirical study of the conceptual integration processes that work on knowledge representation (see Coulson 2008 for a survey of preliminary work in this regard).

Third and finally, a future goal must surely be to better delineate and build on the programmatic proposals above, for understanding the way in which the linguistic system interfaces with the conceptual system in service of linguistically mediated meaning construction. One way in which this might proceed is by empirical investigation relating to the constructs of analog and parametric concepts. The claim is that parametric concepts, devoid of a linguistic context, should not result in multimodal brain activation, while analog concepts should. This prediction is something that, ultimately, should be falsifiable. Other areas of research will no doubt need to focus on the way in which linguistic constructions shape and modify simulations that arise. And behavioral and ultimately brain-imaging research will need to be brought to bear on this area.

References

Allan, K. 2007. The pragmatics of connotation. *Journal of Pragmatics* 39:1047–1057.

Bak, T. H., D. G. O'Donovan, J. H. Xuereb, S. Boniface, and J. R. Hodges. 2001. Selective impairment of verb processing associated with pathological changes in Brodmann areas 44 and 45 in the motor neuron disease-dementia-aphasia syndrome. *Brain* 124:103–120.

Barsalou, L. 1983. Ad hoc categories. *Memory & Cognition* 11 (3): 211–227.

Barsalou, L. 1999. Perceptual symbol systems. *Behavioral and Brain Sciences* 22:577–660.

Barsalou, L. 2005. Continuity of the conceptual system across species. *Trends in Cognitive Sciences* 9:309–311.

Barsalou, L. 2008. Grounded cognition. *Annual Review of Psychology* 59:617–645.

Barsalou, L. W., A. Santos, W. K. Simmons, and C. D. Wilson. 2008. Language and simulation in conceptual processing. In *Symbols, Embodiment, and Meaning*, ed. M. De Vega, A. Glenberg, and A. Graesser, 245–283. Oxford: Oxford University Press.

Bergen, B. K. 2012. *Louder than Words*. New York: Basic Books.

Bonato, M., K. Priftis, R. Marenzi, C. Umiltà, and M. Zorzi. 2010. Increased attentional demands impair contralesional space awareness following stroke. *Neuropsychologia* 48:3934–3940.

Boroditsky, L. 2000. Metaphoric structuring: Understanding time through spatial metaphors. *Cognition* 75 (1): 1–28.

Boulenger, V., L. Mechtou, S. Thobois, E. Broussolle, M. Jeannerod, and T. A. Nazir. 2008. Word processing in Parkinson's disease is impaired for action verbs but not for concrete nouns. *Neuropsychologia* 46:743–756.

Bransford, J. D., and J. J. Franks. 1971. The abstraction of linguistic ideas. *Cognitive Psychology* 2:331–350.

Buccino, G., L. Riggio, G. Melli, F. Binkofski, V. Gallese, and G. Rizzolatti. 2005. Listening to action-related sentences modulates the activity of the motor system: A combined TMS and behavioral study. *Cognitive Brain Research* 24:355–363.

Büchel, C., C. Price, and K. Friston. 1998. A multimodal language region in the ventral visual pathway. *Nature* 394:274–277.

Bueti, D., and V. Walsh. 2009. The parietal cortex and the representation of time, space, number and other magnitudes. *Philosophical Transactions of the Royal Society of London: Series B, Biological Sciences* 364:1831–1840.

Casasanto, D., and L. Boroditsky. 2008. Time in the mind: Using space to think about time. *Cognition* 106:579–593.

Casasanto, D., and K. Dijkstra. 2010. Motor action and emotional memory. *Cognition* 115 (1): 179–185.

Chemero, A. 2009. *Radical Embodied Cognitive Science.* Cambridge, MA: MIT Press.

Cisek, P. 1999. Beyond the computer metaphor: Behaviour as interaction. *Journal of Consciousness Studies* 6 (11–12): 125–142.

Clark, A. 1997. *Being There: Putting Brain, Body and World Together Again.* Cambridge, MA: MIT Press.

Coulson, S. 2008. Metaphor comprehension and the brain. In R.W. Gibbs (ed.), *Cambridge Handbook* of *Metaphor and Thought*, 177–196. Cambridge: Cambridge University Press.

Damasio, A. 1994. *Descartes' Error: Emotion, Reason and the Human Brain.* New York: Penguin.

Dennett, D. 1969. *Content and Consciousness.* London: Routledge.

Dove, G. 2009. Beyond perceptual symbols: A call for representational pluralism. *Cognition* 110:412–431.

Elman, J. L. 2009. On the meaning of words and dinosaur bones: Lexical knowledge without a lexicon. *Cognitive Science* 33:1–36.

Elman, J. L. 2011. Lexical knowledge without a mental lexicon? *Mental Lexicon* 60:1–33.

Evans, V. 2004. *The Structure of Time: Language, Meaning and Temporal Cognition.* Amsterdam: John Benjamins.

Evans, V. 2006. Lexical concepts, cognitive models and meaning-construction. *Cognitive Linguistics* 17 (4): 491–534.

Evans, V. 2009. *How Words Mean: Lexical Concepts, Cognitive Models and Meaning Construction.* Oxford: Oxford University Press.

Evans, V. 2010. Figurative language understanding in LCCM Theory. *Cognitive Linguistics* 21 (4): 601–662.

Evans, V. 2013. *Language and Time: A Cognitive Linguistics Perspective.* Cambridge: Cambridge University Press.

Evans, V. 2014. *The Language Myth: Why Language is Not an Instinct.* Cambridge: Cambridge University Press.

Evans, V., and M. Green. 2006. *Cognitive Linguistics: An Introduction.* Edinburgh: Edinburgh University Press.

Fauconnier, G., and M. Turner. 2002. *The Way We Think: Conceptual Blending and the Mind's Hidden Complexities.* New York: Basic Books.

Fischer, M. H., and R. A. Zwaan. 2009. *Grounding Cognition in Perception and Action: A Special Issue of the Quarterly Journal of Experimental Psychology.* Hove: Psychology Press.

Fodor, J. 1975. *The Language of Thought.* Cambridge, MA: Harvard University Press.

Fodor, J. 1983. *The Modularity of Mind.* Cambridge, MA: MIT Press.

Fodor, J. 1998. *Concepts: Where Cognitive Science Went Wrong.* Oxford: Oxford University Press.

Fodor, J. 2008. *LOT 2: The Language of Thought Revisited.* Oxford: Oxford University Press.

Gallese, V., and G. Lakoff. 2005. The brain's concepts: The role of the sensory-motor system in reason and language. *Cognitive Neuropsychology* 22:455–479.

Glenberg, A. M. 1997. What memory is for. *Behavioral and Brain Sciences* 20:1–55.

Glenberg, A. M., and M. Kaschak. 2002. Grounding language in action. *Psychonomic Bulletin & Review* 9 (3): 558–565.

Glenberg, A. M., and D. A. Robertson. 1999. Indexical understanding of instructions. *Discourse Processes* 28 (1): 1–26.

Goldberg, A. 1995. *Constructions: A Construction Grammar Approach to Argument Structure.* Chicago: University of Chicago Press.

Goldberg, A. 2006. *Constructions at Work: The Nature of Generalization in Language.* Oxford: Oxford University Press.

Harnad, S. 1990. The symbol grounding problem. *Physica D. Nonlinear Phenomena* 42:335–346.

Haugeland, J. 1985. *Artificial Intelligence: The Very Idea.* Cambridge, MA: MIT Press.

Hurford, J. 2007. *Origins of Meaning.* Oxford: Oxford University Press.

Hurford, J. 2012. *Origins of Grammar.* Oxford: Oxford University Press.

Isenberg, N., D. Silbersweig, A. Engelien, S. Emmerich, K. Malavade, B. Beattie, A. C. Leon, and E. Stern. 1999. Linguistic threat activates the human amygdala. *Proceedings of the National Academy of Sciences of the United States of America* 96:10456–10459.

Jackendoff, R. 1983. *Semantics and Cognition*. Cambridge, MA: MIT Press.

Jackendoff, R. 1987. *Consciousness and the Computational Mind*. Cambridge, MA: MIT Press.

Johnson, M. 1987. *The Body in the Mind*. Chicago: University of Chicago Press.

Johnson-Frey, S. H. 2004. The neural bases of complex tool use. *Trends in Cognitive Sciences* 8 (2): 71–78.

Kaschak, M., and A. Glenberg. 2000. Constructing meaning: The role of affordances and grammatical constructions in sentence comprehension. *Journal of Memory and Language* 43:508–529.

Klatzky, R. L., J. W. Pellegrino, B. P. McCloskey, and S. Doherty. 1989. Can you squeeze a tomato? The role of motor representations in semantic sensibility judgements. *Journal of Memory and Language* 28:56–77.

Kranjec, A., and A. Chatterjee. 2010. Are temporal concepts embodied? A challenge for cognitive neuroscience. *Frontiers in Psychology* 1 (240): 1–9.

Lakoff, G., and M. Johnson. 1980. *Metaphors We Live By*. Chicago: University of Chicago Press.

Lakoff, G., and M. Johnson. 1999. *Philosophy in the Flesh*. New York: Basic Books.

Lakoff, G., and R. Núñez. 2001. *Where Mathematics Comes From: How the Embodied Mind Brings Mathematics into Being*. New York: Basic Books.

Langacker, R. W. 1987. *Foundations of Cognitive Grammar*. Vol. 1. Stanford, CA: Stanford University Press.

Langacker, R. W. 2008. *Cognitive Grammar: A Basic Introduction*. Oxford: Oxford University Press.

LeDoux, J. E. 1995. Emotion: Clues from the brain. *Annual Review of Psychology* 46:209–235.

Lindemann, O., P. Stenneken, H. T. van Schie, and H. Bekkering. 2006. Semantic activation in action planning. *Journal of Experimental Psychology: Human Perception and Performance* 32:633–643.

Machery, E. 2007. Concept empiricism: A methodological critique. *Cognition* 104:19–46.

Mahon, B. Z., and A. Caramazza. 2008. A critical look at the embodied cognition hypothesis and a new proposal for grounding conceptual content. *Journal of Physiology, Paris* 102:59–70.

Martin, A., and L. L. Chao. 2001. Semantic memory and the brain: Structure and processes. *Current Opinion in Neurobiology* 11:194–201.

Mithen, S. J. 1996. *The Prehistory of the Mind: A Search for the Origins of Art, Religion, and Science*. London: Thames and Hudson.

Moore, K. E. 2006. Space-to-time mappings and temporal concepts. *Cognitive Linguistics* 17 (2): 199–244.

Newell, A., and H. A. Simon. 1972. *Human Problem Solving*. Englewood Cliffs, NJ: Prentice-Hall.

Pinker, S. 1984. *Language Learnability and Language Development*. Cambridge, MA: Harvard University Press.

Prinz, J. 2002. *Furnishing the Mind: Concepts and Their Perceptual Basis*. Cambridge, MA: MIT Press.

Pulvermüller, F. 1999. Words in the brain's language. *Behavioral and Brain Sciences* 22:253–279.

Pulvermüller, F., O. Hauk, V. V. Nikulin, and R. J. Ilmoniemi. 2005. Functional links between motor and language systems. *European Journal of Neuroscience* 21:793–797.

Pylyshyn, Z. W. 1984. *Computation and Cognition: Towards a Foundation for Cognitive Science*. Cambridge, MA: MIT Press.

Rizzolatti, G., and L. Craighero. 2004. The mirror-neuron system. *Annual Review of Neuroscience* 27:169–192.

Rosch, E. 1975. Cognitive representation of semantic categories. *Journal of Experimental Psychology* 104 (3): 192–233.

Rosch, E. 1978. Human categorization. In *Advances in Cross-Cultural Psychology*, vol. 1, ed. N. Warren, 1–72. London: Academic Press.

Rosch, E., and C. B. Mervis. 1975. Family resemblances: Studies in the internal structure of categories. *Cognitive Psychology* 7 (4): 573–605.

Shapiro, L. 2010. *Embodied Cognition*. London: Routledge.

Sinha, C., V. da Silva Sinha, J. Zinken, and W. Sampaio. 2011. When time is not space: The social and linguistic construction of time intervals in an Amazonian culture. *Language and Cognition* 3 (1): 137–169.

Spivey, M., M. Tyler, D. Richardson, and E. Young. 2000. Eye movements during comprehension of spoken scene descriptions. *Proceedings of the 22nd Annual Conference of the Cognitive Science Society*, 487–492. Mahwah, NJ: Erlbaum.

Stanfield, R. A., and R. A. Zwaan. 2001. The effect of implied orientation derived from verbal context on picture recognition. *Psychological Science* 12:153–156.

Talmy, L. 2000. *Toward a Cognitive Semantics*. 2 vols. Cambridge, MA: MIT Press.

Taylor, L. J., and R. A. Zwaan. 2008. Motor resonance and linguistic focus. *Quarterly Journal of Experimental Psychology* 61:896–904.

Taylor, L. J., and R. A. Zwaan. 2009. Action in cognition: The case of language. *Language and Cognition* 1 (1): 45–58.

Thierry, G., P. Athanasopoulos, A. Wiggett, B. Dering, and J. R. Kuipers. 2009. Unconscious effects of language-specific terminology on preattentive color perception. *Proceedings of the National Academy of Sciences of the United States of America* 106 (11): 4567–4570.

Thompson-Schill, S. L., K. J. Kurtz, and J. D. E. Gabrieli. 1998. Effects of semantic and associative relatedness on automatic priming. *Journal of Memory and Language* 38:440–458.

Turner, M. 2014. *The Origin of Ideas*. Oxford: Oxford University Press.

Vigliocco, G., L. Meteyard, M. Andrews, and S. Kousta. 2009. Toward a theory of semantic representation. *Language and Cognition* 1 (2): 219–248.

Weiskopf, D. 2010. Embodied cognition and linguistic comprehension. *Studies in History and Philosophy of Science* 41:294–304.

Zwaan, R. A. 2004. The immersed experiencer: Toward an embodied theory of language comprehension. In *The Psychology of Learning and Motivation*, ed. B. H. Ross, 35–62. New York: Academic Press.

Zwaan, R. A., and R. H. Yaxley. 2003. Hemispheric differences in semantic-relatedness judgments. *Cognition* 87:79–86.

11   Where Are the Concepts? What Words Can and Can't Reveal

Barbara C. Malt, Silvia P. Gennari, Mutsumi Imai, Eef Ameel, Noburo Saji,
and Asifa Majid

11.1   Introduction

11.1.1   Overview

To study concepts, cognitive scientists need to be able to identify them. The prevailing assumption has been that general-purpose, nonlinguistic concepts are revealed by words such as *triangle*, *table*, and *robin*. But languages vary dramatically in how they carve up the world by name.[1] Either these concepts are heavily language dependent, or the words of a language cannot be a direct route to them. In this chapter we argue that the second of these possibilities is true. We illustrate our point with a study of words for human locomotion. This study shows that shared conceptual content across four languages is distinct from the answers suggested by any single language. It supports the conclusion that words such as *triangle*, *table*, and *robin* do not individuate general-purpose concepts. However, they can identify underlying components of domain knowledge, which suggests new approaches to understanding conceptual representation.

11.1.2   The Word-Concept Problem

Smith and Medin (1981) opened *Categories and Concepts* by declaring that concepts give human experience stability and that mental life would be chaotic without concepts. Thirty years later, similar sentiments continue to be expressed. Murphy (2002) argues that concepts hold our mental world together, and Bloom (2004) suggests that a creature without concepts would be unable to learn. Concepts are considered so fundamental to human cognition that Fodor (1998) asserted, "the heart of a cognitive science is its theory of concepts" (vii). If concepts are so important for cognitive scientists to understand, then cognitive scientists need to be able to identify relevant concepts to study. In this chapter, we ask what role words can play in identifying them.

---

1. We use *names* throughout this discussion to refer to the linguistic labels given to sets of objects, actions, relations, and properties (not only to those given to individual people, places, pets, etc.—i.e., proper names).

To address this question, we need a working definition of concepts. Murphy (2002) suggests that concepts are mental representations of classes of objects in the world, and that they tell their holders what things there are and what properties they have. Carey (2009) indicates that concepts are units of thoughts that are the constituents of beliefs and theories. Bloom (2000) suggests that they are mental representations of kinds, and Solomon, Medin, and Lynch (1999) offer that concepts are building blocks of thought, and that they have, among their functions, supporting classification, inference, and conceptual combination. Taken together, such remarks suggest that concepts are stable units of knowledge in long-term memory that represent meaningful sets of entities in the world and provide the elements out of which more complex thoughts are constructed. Although many authors using the term do not provide an explicit definition, this description seems to capture the general usage (though a few propose alternatives; see Barsalou 1987; Smith and Samuelson 1997; Prinz 2002). Throughout most of this chapter, this dominant approach is what we address. In section 11.3, we revisit this use of the term and consider whether alternative ways of describing mental representations of the world may be more useful.

Among those using the general notion of concepts just described, the prevailing assumption seems to be that many important concepts can be easily identified because they are revealed by words—in fact, for many researchers, the words of English. Smith and Medin (1981) used English nouns such as *hat*, *fish*, *triangle*, *table*, and *robin* to identify concepts, as did Rosch (e.g., Rosch and Mervis 1975; Rosch et al. 1976) and Lakoff (1987). More recent investigations have continued in the same vein (e.g., Murphy 2002; Fodor 1998, who takes English nouns to reveal the stock of basic concepts that might be innate; and Carey 2009, who says that the concepts that interest her are roughly the grain of single lexical items, and that representations of word meanings are paradigm examples of concepts). Even in formal and computational models, discussions of the formalisms are illustrated with examples using English nouns (e.g., Kruschke 2005; Rogers and McClelland 2004). And this approach has not been limited to those studying "concepts" per se. Harnad (2005) declares "kinds" to be the world's potential affordances to sensorimotor systems, but he goes on to suggest finding out what those kinds are by opening a dictionary. Work on conceptual combination has taken nouns such as *chocolate* and *bee* or *zebra* and *fish* to indicate what concepts are combined (e.g., Hampton 1997, 2012; Wisniewski 1996). In work on neural representation of concepts and on deficits due to brain injury or disease, "conceptual judgment" tasks often entail responding to nouns (e.g., Kable et al. 2005; Mahon and Caramazza 2007). In cognitive development research, appeals to English nouns such as *horse*, *cow*, *boot*, and *sail* are prevalent in identifying children's concepts (e.g., Bloom 2000; Gelman 2006; Hills et al. 2009; Keil 1989; Xu 2005). Kelemen and Carey (2007) talk about the meaning of the word *accordion* and the concept of accordion interchangeably, and Gentner (2005) identifies relational concepts by reference to English nouns (*gift*, *weapon*, *predator*, etc.).

Even discussions of visual object recognition (e.g., Ullman 1998; Ullman, Vidal-Naquit, and Sali 2002) and of concept representations in nonlinguistic primates and prelinguistic infants (e.g., Phillips and Santos 2007) often identify the concepts or kinds that are to be recognized or acquired by means of English nouns.

At an intuitive level, this approach seems reasonable. After all, it makes sense to think that a person who has a grasp of the words *cat* and *chair* has concepts of cats and chairs. If entities in the world fall into natural groupings according to their shared properties—as has been argued by a number of researchers (e.g., Anderson 1991; Berlin 1992; Hunn 1977; Rosch et al. 1976; Rogers and McClelland 2004)—then it also makes sense to take English words to capture those groupings and to be associated with a coherent mental representation of those groupings. For instance, the noun *chair* will capture a set of objects sharing properties such as having a seat, a back, and legs, and supporting a human in a particular position, and people will have a concept involving knowledge about this set of things. And, if the preceding points are right, there is no need for concern about the fact that it happens to be English words that are often invoked, because other languages should have words that capture essentially the same groupings and are associated with essentially the same concepts.

But from a different perspective, this approach is startling. Word meanings are highly selective in what elements of experience they encode. Because of this selectivity, there are many possible ways to map between words and the world (Wolff and Malt 2010). Crosslinguistic research indicates that languages vary dramatically in how they carve up the world by name. Substantial crosslinguistic variation has been documented in domains including color, causality, mental states, number, body parts, containers, motion, direction, spatial relations, and terms for acts of cutting and breaking and of carrying and holding (see chapters in Malt and Wolff 2010, for detailed illustrations; also Evans and Levinson 2009; Gentner and Goldin-Meadow 2003; Gumperz and Levinson 1996; Kay et al. 1997; Majid, Boster, and Bowerman 2008; Majid, Enfield, and van Staden 2006; Majid and Levinson 2011;Malt and Majid 2013; Saji et al. 2011; Wierzbicka 2009; among others). As the list indicates, this variation occurs even in concrete domains labeled by nouns, where structure in the world might seem most likely to provide salient groupings that would be captured by the words of any language. For instance, papers in Majid, Enfield, and van Staden (2006) document diversity in how languages divide up the human body with body part terms, and Malt, Sloman, Gennari, Shi, and Wang (1999) found diversity in how languages divide up ordinary household containers (see also Malt, Sloman, and Gennari 2003). *Hand* versus *arm*, *bottle* versus *jar*, or *dish* versus *plate* may seem to English speakers to be self-evident distinctions based on obvious discontinuities in the distribution of properties in the world, but not all languages observe these same distinctions. Even when structure in the world does produce shared tendencies in meanings (e.g., the joints for body part terms; Majid 2010), it underdetermines how any given language will map words onto elements of the world. And this diversity is not only a matter of making fewer versus more distinctions. Languages often partially or substantially crosscut each other in the sets of entities they group together (e.g., Bowerman 1996a, 1996b; Malt, Sloman, and Gennari 2003). For example, whereas English speakers distinguish spatial relations of containment from support (*in* versus *on*) and ignore variations in tightness of fit or attachment to the surface, Korean speakers label relations of tight containment and attachment with one word (*kkita*), contrasting with loose containment (*nehta*), and loose support (*nohta*) (Bowerman 1996a, 1996b).

If the heart of a cognitive science is its theory of concepts, then the field risks serious, even fatal, defects by overlooking the implications of this diversity. As the just-cited work establishes, differences among languages are not merely cute examples for cocktail party conversation (cf. de Boinod 2006, on "extraordinary words from around the world"). Diversity in how languages carve up the world by name is more of a rule than an exception across many domains. In light of the documented diversity, there are three logical possibilities for the nature of the relationship between words and underlying, general-purpose concepts that serve as the elements out of which more complex thoughts are constructed. These possibilities have clear consequences for theories of mental representations, and for how researchers would need to look for concepts.

The first possibility is that the words of a language do effectively reveal much of the stock of basic concepts that a person holds. Importantly, given the pervasive crosslinguistic variability in naming patterns, this possibility implies that word learning creates much of the language user's nonlinguistic representations of the world (cf. Whorf 1956). Under this scenario, it is not possible to hold that any substantial stock of basic concepts is shared across speakers of different languages. Concepts revealed by English words will be true of English speakers, those revealed by Spanish words will be true of Spanish speakers, and so on, and these language-specific sets will be substantially different from one another. Models of semantic cognition (e.g., Rogers and McClelland 2004) would need to be taken as models of a particular language group and modified to give a larger role to names in establishing similarity among representations of entities. Under this perspective, views of conceptual development would need to grant that the end result of development is a highly language-specific set of concepts (not just word meanings), regardless of any inborn universal systems of "core cognition" (Carey 2009) or universal prelinguistic sensitivities to certain conceptual distinctions (e.g., Casasola and Cohen 2002; Gentner and Bowerman 2009; Göksun, Hirsh-Pasek, and Golinkoff 2010).

The second possibility is that the stock of basic general-purpose concepts is dissociated to some notable extent from the large differences in naming patterns, and it is therefore impossible to use words to identify these concepts. After all, much learning about the world comes from direct interaction, rather than through language. Furthermore, attention to and memory for information in the world may be shaped in part by cognitive constraints (such as limits on processing capacity) and evolutionary influences (such as special sensitivity to survival-relevant information) that are independent of the language spoken (e.g., Bock, Carreiras, and Meseguer 2012; Nairne and Pandeirada 2008; Seligman 1971; Willems et al. 2010). Although speakers of all languages do not make the same *bottle* versus *jar* naming distinction that English speakers do (Malt et al. 1999), they are likely to note the same differences among containers of different size and shape regarding their suitability for storing and extracting various types of substances. This dissociation possibility suggests that nonlinguistic representations can be substantially shared despite linguistic variability, while still allowing that language could have some influence on mental representations. Under this possibility, there may be many widely shared general-purpose representations. There may also be some nonlinguistic representations that are shaped by the language spoken, but the shaping will not necessarily fully align the conceptual content with individual words. Crucially, if linguistic and nonlinguistic representations are distinct and only loosely linked, then words are no longer direct vehicles to general-purpose concepts. The words of a language cannot routinely and straightforwardly be used to identify a person's concepts.

Empirical evidence supports a dissociation in at least some domains. Malt et al. (1999) found strong correspondence in similarity judgments for common household containers among speakers of three languages despite distinctly different naming patterns, and Ameel, Storms, Malt, and Sloman (2005) found similar results for Belgian speakers of French versus Dutch (see also Kronenfeld, Armstrong, and Wilmoth 1985). Also using artifacts, Saalbach and Imai (2007, 2012) found no influence of noun-classifier categories on Mandarin speakers' object judgments in several tasks (although they did find a small influence in two other tasks; see also Huettig et al. 2010). Similar findings also exist for other domains. Comparing seventeen languages for color naming versus color sorting, Roberson, Davies, Corbett, and Vandervyver (2005) found considerable similarity in grouping behavior despite substantial variation in naming. Munnich, Landau, and Dosher (2001) found that Korean and English speakers' memory for spatial locations varied less than their naming of the locations (see also Coventry, Valdés, and Guijarro-Fuentes 2010), and several studies have found dissociations between labeling of actions and attention to or memory for elements of the actions (e.g., Gennari et al. 2002; Papafragou, Hulbert, and Trueswell 2008; see also Sauter, LeGuen, and Haun 2011, on similar dissociations for emotional expression). If the evidence and arguments just cited are valid, this could mean that the second possibility above is right, the first is wrong, and words must be thrown out as a way of accessing concepts.

However, a third possibility, less obvious than the first two, also exists and needs to be evaluated. This third possibility is that the relation of words to the stock of general-purpose concepts is not as straightforward as current practice has taken it to be (as also suggested in the second possibility), but still, if examined in the right way, words may reveal something useful about conceptual representations shared across speakers of different languages. By looking beyond individual words from a language as if they provide a direct route to concepts, and applying more sophisticated techniques to extract structure from individual language naming or naming aggregated across languages, it may be possible to discern shared elements of meaning that indicate constraints on cross-language variability and reflect some common underlying aspects of how knowledge of the domain is represented. In this case, words may retain utility in identifying a shared understanding of a domain. What they reveal, however, may not necessarily match the traditional idea of units of knowledge representing meaningful sets of entities in the world. We consider alternative ways of thinking about conceptual representation in section 11.3.

In short, linguistic diversity in naming patterns has been well documented across many domains, but it is rarely considered in the study of concepts. It has potentially profound implications for this study, but the exact implications have not been pinned down as of yet. Next, we discuss some data that evaluate different ways of tapping into the information provided by words about conceptualization of a domain and help discriminate among the three possibilities. These data illustrate what words reveal under different approaches and what an appropriate use of words is for researchers whose interest is in underlying nonlinguistic representations rather than in knowledge about the word meanings of a particular language. In doing so, the data specify some key implications of linguistic diversity for the study of concepts.

11.1.3   Additional Considerations

Before turning to this illustration, we note two points about past treatment of the relation of words to concepts in the literature.

First, some, or perhaps many, researchers who use words of English (or another language) to point to concepts may only be using the words as convenient shorthand. They do not necessarily have an explicit commitment to a strong Whorfian position regarding the alignment of words and the stock of basic general-purpose concepts. However, being noncommittal on the issue is problematic once the pervasive crosslinguistic diversity in naming patterns is recognized. Either words must largely determine these concepts, or they cannot serve as useful shorthand for them. If the second is true, a separate account is needed of what constitutes these concepts and how they can be identified. Some researchers may also hold a somewhat more nuanced view of the word-concept relation. For instance, Murphy (2002), despite using English words to identify concepts throughout most of his book, argues in a chapter on word meaning that word meanings do not always have a simple one-to-one relation to concepts, and that meanings may be composed of a part of a concept or built out of multiple ones. If taken as his real position, this leaves Murphy the problem of how to identify what the more basic general-purpose concepts actually are—an odd dilemma in a book that is primarily about concepts. Rogers and McClelland (2004) provide their own answer to what the concepts are. Echoing Rosch and Mervis (1975) and others, they take the correlational structure of the world to provide the ultimate answer, with mental representations of objects clustering based on similarity of properties. Their inferences about what the similarity relations are, however, come only from considering English nouns. They assume that the correlational structure of the world produces concepts corresponding to *chair*, *table*, and so forth. They do not provide any independent means of verifying either structure in the world or conceptual structure—again, problematic without a commitment to the alignment of words and concepts (cf. Majid and Huettig 2008).

Second, there is one sense of the term *concept* in which it must be true that the words of a language effectively reveal the concepts held by its speakers. That is when *concept* is used to mean the knowledge associated with words. In this sense, if English *bottle* is applied to a somewhat different set of objects and carries somewhat different featural implications than Spanish *botella* (Malt et al. 1999; Malt, Sloman, and Gennari 2003), then English and Spanish speakers have acquired somewhat different concepts. To the extent that the goal of concept researchers is to study exactly those chunks of knowledge encoded by the words of a particular language (lexicalized concepts), there is nothing wrong with using words to identify the knowledge to be studied.

But there are several reasons why studying the knowledge associated with words is not sufficient for understanding conceptual representation more broadly. First, if lexicalized concepts are taken as constituting the main set of general-purpose concepts that cognitive scientists should know about, then this approach functionally makes elements of language—word meanings—the primary medium of thought, whereas cognitive scientists generally accept that there is a medium in which thought takes place that is distinct from any language used for external communication (Fodor 1975). Second, by taking word meanings to reveal the stock of basic concepts used in more complex thought, it commits cognitive science a priori to a strong version of the Whorfian hypothesis in which it is language that creates that stock of concepts. Finally, cognitive scientists who use words to identify concepts most often seem to actually have a different goal than the goal of understanding the knowledge associated with words of a specific language. Rosch (Rosch and Mervis 1975; Rosch et al. 1976) explicitly contrasts the view that segmentation of the world is arbitrary with her own hypothesis that the world contains inherent structure ready to be recognized by human perceivers. Keil (1989) appeals to "causal homeostasis," suggesting that concepts (in at least some domains) are formed in recognition of networks of properties in the world that are causally connected to one another. More recently, as just noted, Rogers and McClelland (2004) appeal to structure in the world as the determinant of conceptual content. Bloom (2004) argues at some length that language is a tool for thought but is not the mechanism that gives rise to the capacity to generate and appreciate ideas in the first place. If word meanings may be composed of a part of a concept or built out of multiple ones (Murphy 2002; see also Clark 1983), there must be some more basic stock of conceptual elements that are the building blocks of word meaning. Furthermore, any researcher interested in the possibility of innate concepts, along with those who aim to study concepts in nonlinguistic primates or in prelinguistic infants, must be seeking ones that are not created by learning of words of a language. Much of the time, then, concepts researchers seem to have a goal of studying representations that are not created by language, even while using the words of one particular language to find them.

In sum, our goal is not to argue against the idea that words may gain meaning by association with conceptual content. Nor are we arguing that the content associated with a word cannot be called a lexicalized concept. Our concern is with what role words can play in identifying concepts in the sense of general-purpose representations that are not inherently part of linguistic knowledge.

11.2   A Case Study: Words for Human Locomotion

We now turn to some data on naming patterns in English, Dutch, Spanish, and Japanese for forms of human locomotion (walking, running, skipping, hopping, and so on). Humans around the world are capable of the same forms of locomotion regardless of location or culture, suggesting that there may be substantial shared elements in their understanding of this domain. At the same time, based on previous data for a more limited sample of locomotion stimuli (produced on a treadmill that varied in speed and slope; Malt et al. 2008) we had reason to expect some diversity in naming patterns. This domain therefore provides a useful case study of the relation of naming patterns to conceptualization. The stimuli were thirty-six video clips, three to four seconds in length, depicting upright, bipedal human locomotion of as wide a variety as we could generate. All actions were demonstrated by an American college student. Figure 11.1 shows sample frames from four clips.

To determine the names each language has for the range of human locomotion depicted, we asked native speakers of the four languages, mostly undergraduates or graduate students resident in their home countries, to look at each clip and name it. Participants viewed the clips embedded in a web page, and for each one, answered the question "What is the woman doing? She is …," or its translation in the appropriate language. More details of the methods, as well as analyses not discussed here, can be found in Malt et al. (2014). Here, we consider the sets of names produced in each language, how names are distributed across actions within each language, and whether there are shared patterns in this distribution across languages. For each analysis, we consider the implications for understanding how words may relate to concepts.

Figure 11.1
Sample frames from clips used in the study, showing upright, bipedal human locomotion.

11.2.1   Name Inventories

We first determined the set of names that were used in each language for these actions. This analysis is most like the usual approach of concept researchers, except that the standard approach stops with a single language and does not compare the results with what other languages would suggest. We asked whether the different languages show consensus on what these concepts would be.

There was diversity in the surface form people used in their responses. For instance, for a given clip, in English, many participants might have said that the woman is *walking* but a few might have said *doing a walk* and some even said just *walks* or *a walk*. Some may also have said that the woman is *walking slowly*, or *walking fast with her arms swinging*. We counted as an instance of the same name all surface forms containing the same root word(s) labeling a manner of movement, and we tallied these for each clip to determine the frequency of names produced across the participants. We considered each clip's "dominant" name to be whatever word was produced most often across the participants in the language group. Clips for which fewer than 30 percent of respondents agreed on a name were considered "mixed."

Table 11.1
Inventory of locomotion names

Language			
English	Dutch	Spanish	Japanese
creep	hinkelen	caminar	aruku
gallop	huppelen	correr	hashiru
hop	joggen	marchar	**sukippu-suru**
jog	lopen	saltar	**ashibumi-suru**
jump	marcheren	trotar	**kenken-suru**
leap	rennen		**koushin-suru**
march	slenteren		**janpu-suru**
run	sluipen		
skip	springen		
stomp	stappen		
walk	wandelen		
shuffle			
tiptoe			
power walk			

Note. **Boldface** indicates terms that have more than one morpheme.

It is worth considering first what concepts would be identified by simple single-morpheme words. These words are most like the ones generally considered to pick out basic-level concepts in the psychological literature (e.g., Murphy 1988; Rosch and Mervis 1975). The monomorphemic words that emerged as dominant for at least one film clip in a language are given in table 11.1.[2] This tally makes clear that if there are universally shared concepts of this domain, these words do not directly reveal what they are. The different languages provide different answers about what that set would be.

There are also arguments for seeing if conventional names that have more than one morpheme can help reveal the most basic concepts. Brown (1958) observed that when people name at the "level of usual utility," that name is occasionally longer than a less-used name. For instance, a certain fruit is more likely to be called *strawberry* than *fruit*. A small number of Rosch and colleague's (1976) "basic level" terms were of

2. There is considerable variation between Netherlands and Belgian Dutch, and also in varieties of Spanish and English spoken around the globe. Readers may differ in their naming patterns from those reported here due to such variation. Most notably, *lopen* has a substantially different use in the Netherlands than in Belgium, being used primarily for fast locomotion in Belgium and slow locomotion in the Netherlands.

this nature (e.g., *screwdriver*, *airplane*). Furthermore, across languages, the same notion may be expressed in different forms: a male child in English is monomorphemic *boy*, but in Yucatec, it is *xi'pal*, containing morphemes for male and for child, and in Spanish, it is *muchacho* (or *niño*), a single root with a masculine suffix (Lucy 2010). Along those lines, for speakers of Japanese, limiting consideration to simple monomorphemic responses risks excluding some common action labels. Japanese speakers use a construction consisting of an action noun plus the light verb *suru* (do) to refer to some actions. Such phrases are similar to English *doing a jump* or *doing a march step*, except that some are fixed, conventional, and common labels for actions. Boldfaced names in table 11.1 are those added under this version of the tally. Under this count, the Japanese number of unique names is similar to that for Spanish, but both remain below the level of English and Dutch. The basic observations from before remain intact. The languages differ markedly in the inventory of names they display for this domain, and so names do not identify a universal set of shared concepts.

Could the speakers really vary so much in their concepts of this domain? And could they really lack concepts of some of the actions, as suggested by the clips designated *mixed*, for which there is no agreed-on name? For instance, do Japanese speakers lack a concept of running in place that the other speakers have? The remaining analyses help address this question, but for now we note that it seems unlikely that American and Belgian traditions or current lifestyles lead individuals to develop more highly differentiated locomotion concepts, overall, than Argentinean and Japanese experiences do. If there are differences in the conceptual inventory as large as is suggested by the naming differences, it seems they must be directly created by the language differences, in line with the strongest form of a Whorfian perspective.

A glance at the entire phrases participants produced, however, shows that speakers of all the languages are, in various ways, making many more distinctions among the actions than those reflected in the conventional names. For instance, Spanish speakers often used modifiers to discriminate among cases of *saltar* done on one foot versus two (*hop* versus *jump* for English speakers), and speakers of all the languages used location modifiers to point out the actions done in place. This observation suggests that people may have concepts important to the domain that are not captured in a single word. In the anthropological literature, it has been noted that many languages lack labels equivalent to English *plant* and *animal*, as well as for some groupings within these kingdoms, but the groupings still seem to be recognized as indicated by various nonverbal behaviors (e.g., Berlin 1992). If a similar situation holds here, then, again, we have to conclude that words are a poor indicator of where the concepts of interest lie (even if modest cultural differences do exist among the groups).

This first analysis points out the fundamental problem of taking individual words of any one language to directly reveal concepts: different languages will give different answers to what the concepts are, and these linguistic differences are likely to exceed the extent of any conceptual differences. We now ask whether other ways of examining the naming data do a better job at uncovering shared concepts. To the extent that they do, the results will underscore the fallacy of treating the individual words as if they directly reveal concepts. At the same time, they will suggest that naming data, examined in an appropriate way, may still provide some evidence of a shared understanding of the domain.

11.2.2   Treating Individual Languages' Naming as Similarity Data

In this analysis, we asked whether commonalities emerge from the naming data of the four languages if we make use of the full set of names produced by all participants for all stimuli. Many clips did not produce 100 percent name consensus within a language group, so even if one language has different dominant names for two clips (e.g., *walk* and *stroll*), and another gives them the same name (e.g., *caminar*), some speakers of the first language may have produced the same name for both (e.g., *walk*), pointing to a perceived similarity between them. We created name similarity matrices that reflect the extent to which each pair of objects received the same name across the speakers of a language. To do this, we assigned, for each participant, a 0 or a 1 to each possible pair of clips according to whether the person gave the two clips a different name or the same name (again, tallied according to the guidelines described above). There are 630 such pairs, given the thirty-six clips. We then constructed a similarity matrix for each language group by summing the distance values for each of the 630 pairs of clips across the participants in that language group. This use of the data is similar to using confusion matrices as similarity data (e.g., Rothkopf 1957; Shepard and Chang 1963). By taking into account the full naming array for each clip and applying scaling techniques to the similarity matrices, commonalities among languages may become more evident.

We correlated the name similarity matrices for each pair of languages to give an overall sense of the correspondence in the naming patterns, using the Mantel test for correlation of matrices (Mantel 1967). These correlations are all significant, falling between 0.65 and 0.82. The correlations indicate that the full patterns of name use, while diverse, still share substantial commonalities.

We then carried out multidimensional scaling on the matrix for each language (procedure MDS; SAS Institute 1999). To help interpret the results, additive tree clusters were drawn on the solutions (Corter 1982; Sattath and Tversky 1977). Solutions for the four languages are shown in figures 11.2–11.5, with only the top two levels of clusters for ease of viewing. Labels in the solution refer to the clip names bestowed by the experimenters (not the name given by participants) so that the solutions can be compared with regard to which clips are grouped together across the languages.

These solutions, while showing similarities, also highlight important differences. For all four languages, the horizontal dimension is interpretable in terms of the basic

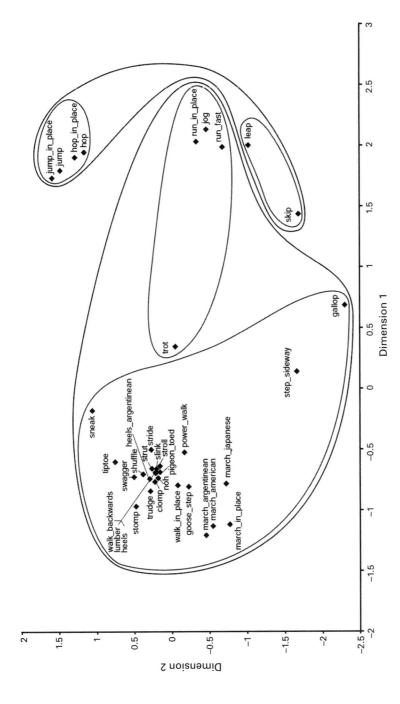

Figure 11.2

MDS solution based on American English naming data. Clip names refer to names bestowed by the experimenters, not names produced by participants.

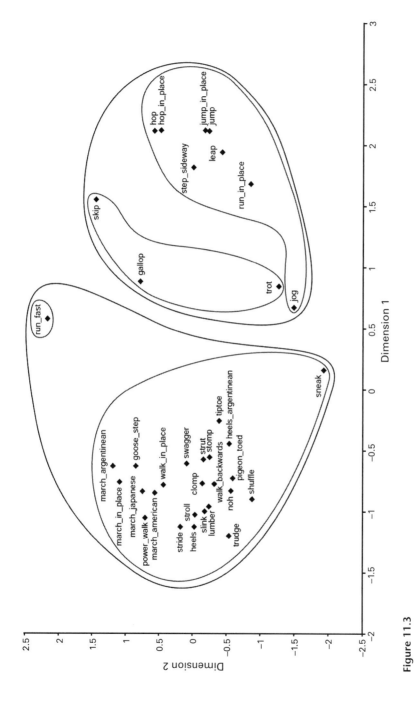

Figure 11.3

MDS solution based on Belgian Dutch naming data. Clip names refer to names bestowed by the experimenters, not names produced by participants.

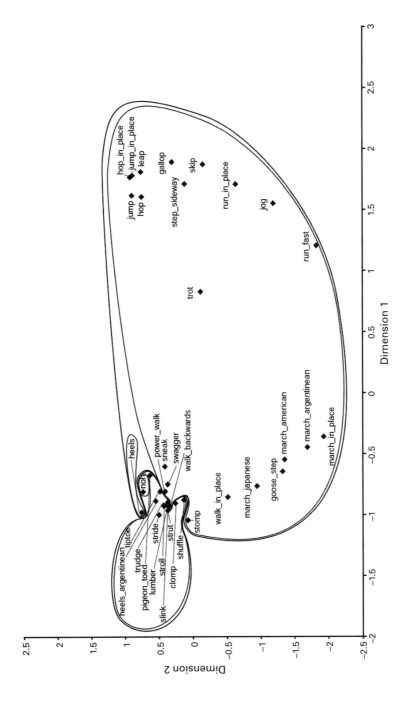

Figure 11.4

MDS solution based on Argentinean Spanish naming data. Clip names refer to names bestowed by the experimenters, not names produced by participants.

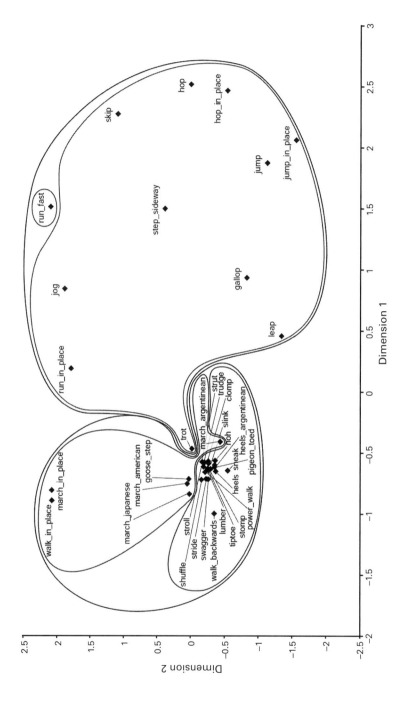

Figure 11.5
MDS solution based on Japanese naming data. Clip names refer to names bestowed by the experimenters, not names produced by participants.

biomechanical distinction between an elastic impact-and-recoil motion (characteristic of running gaits and others such as hopping and jumping) and a pendulum motion (characteristic of walking gaits), where one foot is on the ground at all times (e.g., Alexander 2002; Bennett 1992). (The pendulum-based gaits appear toward the left-hand side of each solution and the impact-and-recoil toward the right.) However, the exact spatial layout of clips varies considerably across the languages. The vertical dimension for the most part seems to reflect a dimension of speed and aggressiveness (with slower, less aggressive actions lower and faster, more aggressive ones higher for English and Spanish, and vice versa for Dutch), but the Japanese solution less clearly conforms to this possibility. The clusters resulting from the additive tree analysis reinforce the idea that the biomechanical distinction is salient for two of the languages—Dutch and Japanese—which have top-level clusters separating essentially the same sets of clips (though Dutch places the RUN_FAST clip just into the cluster of pendulum motions). English and Spanish clusters are less like the Dutch and Japanese results: for English, running actions cluster with pendulum motions at the top level, and for Spanish, walking backward and several forms of marching combine with impact-and-recoil motions, as well as walking in place. In the next level of clusters, within these top-level clusters, each language more or less separates the faster, more aggressive pendulum actions from slower, more cautious pendulum actions, but the exact composition of the clusters is variable. The Dutch solution, in particular, does not honor this separation as much as the others.

These solutions indicate that the naming patterns of the four languages reflect a shared orientation to the same dimensions of the movements. This outcome supports the idea that speakers of the four languages may have more in common in their perception of the domain than their name inventories indicate. In light of the variability of the additive tree clusters across the four solutions, though, it remains difficult to say exactly what could be identified as shared discrete concepts in the traditional sense.

11.2.3   Treating Aggregated Naming as Similarity Data

Last, we created a multidimensional scaling solution combining the naming data of participants in all four language groups. MDS by its nature looks for commonalities in the data and, to the extent that it finds them, produces a coherent solution. If a coherent solution emerges, this result would again support the idea of a shared conceptualization of the domain while underscoring the inadequacy of individual words of a single language to reveal it. Compatible with this possibility, Regier, Kay, and Khetarpal (2007) examined the highly variable color terms across 110 languages and found evidence for a general well-formedness constraint of maximizing similarity within lexical categories and minimizing it across categories. Khetarpal, Majid, and Regier (2009) obtained similar results for spatial terms of nine languages. More similar to the current analysis, Majid, Boster, and Bowerman (2008) aggregated across twenty-eight languages' verbs for cutting and breaking actions and found a shared set of dimensions underlying the different naming patterns. With only four languages to combine here, our data provide less to aggregate, but the smaller sample of languages is more like that typically available to psychologists working on concepts. From that perspective, it is particularly useful to see if a coherent conceptual space emerges from the data of only four languages.

We carried out multidimensional scaling as before. Figure 11.6 shows the two-dimensional solution, again with additive tree clusters imposed on it. This solution shows a neat horizontal separation of the impact-and-recoil motions (toward the right) from the pendulum motions (toward the left). The vertical dimension again appears to reflect something like speed and aggressiveness of the actions, with slower, less aggressive actions toward the top and faster, more aggressive ones toward the bottom.

At the top level of clustering, the impact-and-recoil motions are separated from the pendulum-based ones, with the exception of the TROT clip falling into the pendulum cluster. The placement of the TROT clip is most likely because of the qualities of the particular action implemented in the clip, which was a bouncy motion but with little or no evidence of both feet being off the ground at the same time. Within these clusters, subclusters separate the running clips from the other impact-and-recoil actions, and separate the true pendulum motion clips from the intermediate TROT clip. These clusters are thus readily interpretable, although they do not seem to map directly onto the words of any of the languages.

So, the naming data when aggregated across the four languages provide more indication of a systematic conceptual space than looking at scaling solutions of the four languages individually does. This shared space emerges out of the noisiness of the individual name inventories, which make different distinctions and numbers of distinctions. Because MDS can discover commonalities in data, but cannot invent them, the simplicity of the solution is evidence in favor of a shared underlying understanding of the domain. At the same time, though, if the identified additive tree clusters are taken to indicate discrete concepts within this space, they do not seem to be picked out by words of the languages. This outcome again suggests a shared conceptualization of the domain that is not revealed by the words of any single language.

11.2.4   Conclusions from Using Names to Reveal Conceptual Space

These analyses demonstrate that different languages would tell us different things about concepts if we were only to look at their name inventories. If there are shared general-purpose concepts, then the words of any one language do not directly reveal what they are. Moreover, different ways of counting names (monomorphemic only versus including multimorphemic ones) produce somewhat different answers. Even if we were to adopt a strong version of the Whorfian hypothesis and assume that words

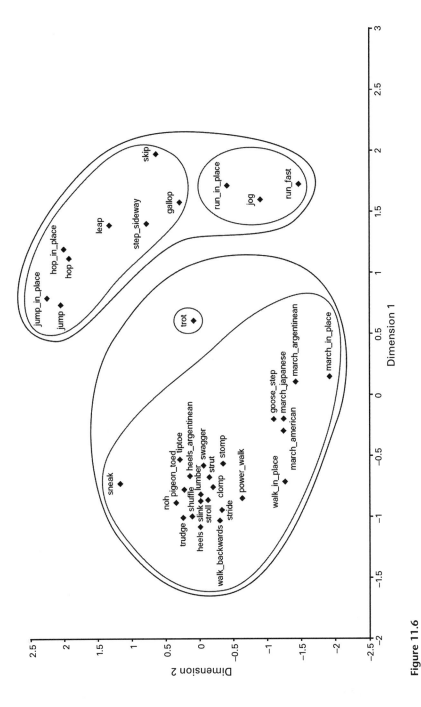

Figure 11.6

MDS solution based on the four languages' combined naming data. Clip names refer to names bestowed by the experimenters, not names produced by participants. Adapted from Malt, Ameel, Imai, Gennari, Saji, and Majid (2014).

of a language do directly reveal basic concepts for speakers of that language, it is not clear which way of counting would be the right one to use, and using names as direct pointers to concepts would remain problematic.

Despite the diversity in the name inventories, other ways of analyzing the data show commonalities underlying the naming patterns. In particular, scaling of the combined naming data of four languages produces a coherent and interpretable solution, suggesting a shared orientation to certain dimensions of the space. Still, the clusters within the scaling solution do not neatly correspond to those labeled by the names of the languages, raising questions about what, if anything, can be identified as discrete concepts in the traditional sense.

11.3   Issues and Implications

11.3.1 Implications for the Status Quo

The data make a strong case that the relation of words to concepts is not straightforward. Pervasive linguistic diversity, amply documented in other research but rarely taken into consideration within "concepts" research, is by itself cause for serious concern. It would still be possible to preserve a commitment to word-concept alignment by subscribing to a strong version of the Whorfian idea that language shapes thought. The aggregated naming data, however, suggest that any conceptual differences are less than implied by differences in word inventories. This evidence is also consistent with past findings in other domains and the observation that attention to and understanding of aspects of the world are likely shaped by multiple forces that may include but are not limited to language (see section 11.1.2). It seems unavoidable to conclude that researchers need to stop relying on the word inventories of English, or any other single language, to know what constitutes the concepts of a domain.

In light of our data and arguments, what should be made of the existing literature on concepts? We suggest that what is being studied in many cases—those where probing of knowledge comes in the form of asking for responses of various sorts to the words of English or another language—is people's knowledge associated with the words. There is nothing wrong with investigating knowledge associated with words, and making this clarification does not cast doubt on the value of the work. It does, however, suggest the need to reframe the understanding of what the work reveals, because this methodology does not directly shed light on general-purpose nonlinguistic concepts, possibly shared across speakers of different languages. The only way for researchers to argue that their work directly investigates nonlinguistic concepts is by making an explicit commitment to a strong Whorfian perspective. Whichever approach the researcher takes, it should always take into account the existing pervasive crosslinguistic diversity and the fact that word inventories can only be used as the means of tapping units of knowledge by committing to the notion that the units accessed are language specific.

It might be possible to argue for a direct alignment of words with general-purpose concepts for some domains on the grounds that in certain domains, word meanings should be broadly shared across speakers of different languages. Such word meanings could be hypothesized to exist for any innate concepts, and for concepts that are developed in a similar way across cultures due to cross-cultural recognition of structure in the world. A logistical complication still arises in that the existence of broadly shared word meanings cannot be assumed; it would have to be verified by careful crosslinguistic comparison for a domain of interest. An empirical complication also arises in that in many such domains where crosslinguistic data have been examined, word meanings have turned out to be more variable than previously imagined. Even though substantial elements of the human experience of sensory input, emotion, or space, for instance, might be universal (e.g., Clark 1973; Ekman 1992; Henning 1916), recent investigations have shown that sensory vocabularies (Majid and Levinson 2011), emotion terms (e.g., Wierzbicka 1999, 2009) and spatial term inventories and meanings (Bowerman 1996a, 1996b) are considerably variable across languages. Perception of the body or of human locomotion might be heavily constrained by structure in the stimulus domain (body joints or biomechanics of movement), but the current work and our earlier work (Majid, Enfield, and van Staden 2006; Malt et al. 2008) have shown crosslinguistic diversity in these domains, too. The body part and locomotion work does show that alongside diversity, structural constraints are reflected in shared elements of meaning. However, it seems impossible to discern from only a single language what the shared elements will be and which parts of the patterns are idiosyncratic to the language.

The domain of natural kinds is another for which it has been argued that structure in the world will give rise to shared elements of meaning (Berlin 1992; Hunn 1977)—in this case, the structure being clusters of correlated properties separating scientific genera such as bovines versus equines. Berlin (1992), Hunn (1977), and others (see Malt 1995 for review) document that nonindustrialized cultures tend to recognize by name much the same sorts of groupings that modern science and more technologically advanced cultures do. But again, the broad similarities are accompanied by differences. Primary names that label rich, important, frequently used conceptual content for members of traditional societies sometimes point to highly impoverished representations for members of urban societies (such as *elm* versus *oak* versus *chestnut*; Dougherty 1978; Wolff, Medin, and Pankratz 1999) due to attrition of knowledge bases over cultural time. Conversely, some significant groupings may lack labels in various languages, as in the case of labels for plants versus animals mentioned earlier, as well as groupings within them that are perceived but of lesser cultural utility (see Malt 1995 for review). Furthermore, although many groupings labeled with primary names may reflect structure in the world, some may depend on properties such as domesticity or use. In fact, many English names for familiar naturally occurring entities pick out groupings based on their role in human lives rather than biology, for example, *weed, tree, vegetable, dog* (see Malt 1991) and so do not reflect world structure of the sort argued to produce crosslinguistic similarities. Most likely, the degree to which words of a single language can directly reveal shared concepts for a domain for speakers of different languages will fall on a continuum from poor to better (but still imperfect). The cases just discussed indicate that it may not be possible to discern what is poor and what is better without detailed empirical study.

Despite the complex nature of the relationship between language and general-purpose concepts, our data suggest that it is still possible to use linguistic data to gain insight into something more fundamental about the nature of conceptual space. That is, combining naming information across languages does seem to provide useful information, because the aggregate allows commonalities to emerge over the "noise" of individual language idiosyncrasies. Sometimes naming data are more readily available for researchers than data such as similarity judgments. This is particularly true for those already in a position to collect data from members of different language communities through simple paper and pencil tasks, or who have access to archived data on naming for domains of interest. However, it is clear that there are also methodological challenges involved in collecting naming data across languages, in particular, gaining access to participants who speak diverse languages and having available the language expertise to administer tasks and interpret data from the various languages. For researchers whose usual methodologies entail only members of one language group, obtaining such crosslinguistic data may not be feasible. In those cases, developing other methods of avoiding the problem of faulty reliance on a word-concept equivalence will be crucial, such as finding ways to implement measures less dependent on language.

11.3.2 If There Is a Shared Conceptual Space, Why Don't Individual Naming Patterns Align Better?

The possibility of a significant dissociation of naming patterns from how people understand a domain nonlinguistically raises the question of why languages diverge in their naming patterns in the first place. If there are shared experiences across cultures in at least some domains, why wouldn't the naming patterns for those domains align more closely? The answer most likely lies in the facts that (a) words encode only a fraction of the richness of experience, and (b) the meanings encoded in any particular set are shaped in part by forces independent of the conceptual representations of current speakers. Some elements of arbitrariness in the early development of a set of meanings will exist, simply because of the limitation on how much words can encode. As the language continues to evolve, external forces such as contact with other languages, waxing or waning of the importance of a domain to the culture, the introduction of new entities within the domain that need to be named and the order in which they enter the culture, and influences from the syntax and morphology of language on how distinctions can be expressed can alter the set of words available in a domain and the meanings associated with each word (e.g., Aitchinson 2001; see Malt, Gennari, and Imai 2010 for discussion). Because each language evolves on its own path, and the current state of a language is always a function, in part, of past states (e.g., Dunn et al. 2011), languages will develop their own patterns of naming that may be only loosely related to one another, as well as only loosely related to current ways of thinking about the world by their speakers.

11.3.3 Implications for Property Projection

Promoting inferences has been taken to be a critical benefit of putting names on things (e.g., Gelman and Markman 1986; Heit 2000; Osherson et al. 1990; Quine 1970). The partially arbitrary nature of linguistic categories highlights the fact that inferences will not always be well circumscribed by named categories. For instance, consider the English names *chair, knife,* and *spoon.* A beach chair is light, but an armchair is heavy; a desk chair has a rigid seat, but a beanbag chair does not; a kitchen chair may be wood and a folding chair metal. A kitchen knife is intended for cutting but a frosting knife for spreading; a soup spoon is for scooping up liquids but a slotted spoon for draining them; a hair brush is for smoothing but a scrub brush is for scrubbing. This imperfect matching of properties to names is not limited to artifacts: although Chihuahuas and Siberian Huskies share the property of domesticity that projects across things called *dog,* other properties such as size, strength, home (small or large, indoors or out), and ability to withstand cold may be more shared with things called *cat* or *wolf.* Relying heavily on names to make inferences, then, might often produce results that would turn out to be inaccurate. To the extent that inferences about unseen properties are accurate, they may be made by projecting on the basis of observed commonalities with familiar instances more often than is generally acknowledged (see also Gelman and Davidson 1990). Despite Rogers and McClelland's (2004) problematic use of English words to identify concepts, their model provides a useful demonstration of how such inferences can be drawn without an explicit process of categorization intervening between perception of an entity and property projection.

11.3.4 Implications for the Notion of *Concepts*

The combined naming data from the four languages produces a fairly interpretable scaling solution suggesting that naming is driven by some fundamentally shared understanding of the characteristics of human locomotion. Different languages may make different numbers of distinctions and vary somewhat in what kinds of distinctions are being made, but they seem to be drawing on a shared pool of dimensions. Similar observations have been made for other domains (e.g., Jones 2010; Majid, Boster, and Bowerman 2008; see also Slobin 2010 on locomotion). Yet the scaling solutions, while suggesting some shared understanding of the domain across speakers of different languages, and some salient groupings of instances, still leave it unclear exactly what units of knowledge should count as the most fundamental, basic concepts of the domain. Different levels of the cluster analysis produce different potential answers.

The difficulty of specifying exactly what constitutes the basic concepts suggests that it may be time for psychologists to radically rethink conceptual understanding of a domain. Despite the widespread claims that cognition centrally involves concepts, it is hard to pin down a satisfying definition of what they are. The attempts that we cited at the outset of this paper by Murphy (2002), Carey (2009), and others in entire books on the topic are somewhat vague. In a review of research on concepts and categories, Medin and Rips (2005) comment, "The concept of concepts is difficult to define, but no one doubts that concepts are fundamental to mental life and human communication" (37). Smith and Medin (1981), in their seminal book that spurred much subsequent use of the term, never provided an explicit definition of what concepts are. Authors of textbooks for cognitive psychology have similar difficulties. For instance, Benjafield (2007), in a section entitled "What are concepts?" offers only that when people see something as belonging to a category, they are using a concept. Some widely used textbooks have abandoned chapters on concepts altogether in favor of discussing the contents of knowledge representations without reference to the term *concept* (e.g., Goldstein 2005; Willingham 2007). It is an unsatisfactory situation when researchers believe that something is fundamental to mental life but they cannot articulate exactly what that something is.

One alternative approach to understanding where shared elements of mental representation are to be found is represented by the search for smaller units of knowledge that are primitives, or *meaning moles,* such as EVENT, STATE, THING, PATH, PLACE, GOAL, MEANS, END, and so on (e.g., Jackendoff 1990; Landau and Jackendoff 1993; Schank and Abelson 1977; Slobin 1996b; Talmy 1985; see Pinker 2007).[3] Although psychologists interested in concepts have not looked very much in this direction in the past, more attention to this approach is emerging (e.g., Aguiar and Baillargeon 2002; Feist 2008; Göksun, Hirsh-Pasek, and Golinkoff 2010; Parish-Morris et al. 2010; Slobin 2010). For instance, researchers interested in causal verbs propose that basic notions such as CAUSE, ENABLE, and PREVENT underlie the semantics of diverse verbs in various languages (e.g.,

---

3. A related approach to the search for conceptual primitives occurs in developmental work on core cognition (e.g., Carey 2009; Csibra et al. 2003; Kinzler and Spelke 2007; Spelke 1994), in which researchers study representations (e.g., of objecthood, causality, agency, and number) that may provide the foundations of more complex conceptual understanding. This work focuses more specifically on representations hypothesized to be innate and aims to understand their nature in detail.

Also related is work in computational and human neuroscience that seeks shared features underlying semantic representations (e.g., Just et al. 2010) and argues for a continuous semantic space (Huth et al. 2012).

Wolff et al. 2005). Researchers interested in the acquisition of spatial terms have suggested notions such as CONTACT, CONTAINMENT, and SUPPORT as components of meaning (e.g., Bowerman 1996a, 1996b; Choi and Bowerman 1991). Dimensions rather than individual features (such as reversibility of an action or predictability of the outcome of an action, as suggested by Majid, Boster, and Bowerman 2008 for verbs of cutting and breaking) may also be relevant types of elements. These postulated shared elements are generally more "primitive," in the sense of isolating single properties or dimensions, than those thought of as concepts by mainstream concepts researchers and others who draw from this tradition.

Our scaling and clustering analyses suggest perceived dimensions of gait space that can contribute to this set of knowledge units. In fact, this sort of more fine-grained breakdown of knowledge is implied by the connectionist approach to modeling cognition (despite the tendency to label the inputs and outputs with words of a language). As Smolensky (1988) and others have emphasized, connectionist networks are *subsymbolic* in that the features the system uncovers, constituting its learned knowledge base, are more subtle than those labeled by many words of a human language.[4] Perhaps it is at this level of analysis that the term *concept* can be most meaningfully applied.

In this type of approach, the goal is not to identify discrete, bounded, and stable units of knowledge stored in long-term memory. As such, concerns about failure to find defining features associated with fixed categories that were raised in the early backlash against classical views of concepts and compositional approaches to word meaning (e.g., Lakoff 1987; Smith and Medin 1981) do not apply. Instead, the dimensions of experience to which people attend under various circumstances are the key point of interest. This approach is consistent with some minority views on concepts (e.g., Barsalou 1987; Imai and Saalbach 2010; Malt and Sloman 2007; Smith and Samuelson 1997; Sloman and Malt 2003) according to which the particular dimensions of focus vary depending on the context and the goals at hand. According to this perspective, what is brought to mind and experienced as a coherent grouping varies across experiences due to differing task demands. For instance, our similarity judgment task directed participants to focus attention on certain elements of the actions, but it is possible that under other circumstances, their attentional weight to various elements would have differed. When language is engaged in a task, it will require attention to the elements of a scene that are necessary for using the words of the language to be spoken, directing attention to features that may differ from when a different language is used or no language is used (e.g., Papafragou, Hulbert, and Trueswell 2008; Papafragou, Massey,

---

4. Some early precursors to modern connectionist models were more "localist" in nature, having internal nodes labeled with words of a language (e.g., McClelland, Rumelhart, and Hinton 1986), but the essential nature of current models is that knowledge is reflected in a distributed pattern of activation across nodes.

and Gleitman 2006; Slobin 1996a; see also Davidoff et al. 2012; Roberson and Davidoff 2000; and Webster and Kay 2012 in the domain of color). Thus speakers of different languages may activate similar representations under some circumstances and different ones under others. Regardless, the key point here is that the representations are flexibly used and differ from situation to situation. The variability of attention to features of a situation is supported by recent brain-imaging data showing that even in simple motion perception events, different brain regions may be activated by instructions to judge different aspects of the event (e.g., Büchel et al. 1998; Raymond 2000). It seems impossible to identify a single task that would unambiguously be the right one to decide what the discrete and stable concepts are for the domain.

   This sort of more "primitive"-oriented description of conceptual space has so far been applied mainly to actions of various sorts and spatial relations. If thought of in terms of dimensions, not just meaning moles, then it seems suitable for describing artifact conceptual representations as well, with relevant dimensions likely to include both physical attributes, such as material and shape, and affordance- or intention-related ones, such as current or potential function. In fact, given the high property diversity among objects that can share a name and the tendency for objects to be scattered with only partial clustering in similarity space (Malt et al. 1999), this sort of approach may be well suited to this object domain. Exactly how well it can work for natural kinds, and what sorts of dimensions of conceptual space would be involved for them, remains to be worked out. Given the importance of beliefs about hidden essences in conceptualization of natural kinds (e.g., Keil 1989), it will be important to consider how such beliefs can be incorporated. More abstract domains such as emotions or truth and beauty will also be a challenge for this kind of approach, but they are no less a challenge under more traditional approaches. Assuming that there are concepts called HAPPINESS or TRUTH does nothing to specify the contents of the representations.

11.3.5   Future Directions

The preceding points suggest several avenues for researchers to pursue, including extending a conceptual primitives or meaning-mole approach to additional domains and more fully understanding what elements of knowledge are activated in different task contexts. For the first of these, we have argued for the use of crosslinguistic data as one means of uncovering underlying conceptual dimensions of a domain. Development of other methodologies would also be valuable. Because paradigms for research on young infants cannot rely on linguistic stimuli or responses, work on early cognitive development that seeks conceptual primitives or studies *core cognition* (e.g., Carey 2009; Csibra et al. 2003; Kinzler and Spelke 2007; Spelke 1994) may provide some useful models for work with older children and adults (see also Kalénine et al. 2012 on the use of eye movements to evaluate activation of different types of property representations).

But acknowledging a problem is always the first necessary step to solving it, and as our opening discussion illustrated, there is currently insufficient sensitivity to the problem of assuming a close alignment of words of a given language with concepts. Much of the original problem is likely due to the predominance of monolingual English-speaking researchers in the early decades of cognitive science. Cognitive science is rapidly becoming a more international pursuit. One consequence is the participation of researchers who speak other native languages, often accompanied by proficiency in English. Along with this shift in researcher demographics has been an information technology revolution resulting in the growth of international collaborations as well as greater access to participant populations outside English-speaking parts of the world. These changes will inevitably make linguistic variation more salient in theoretical considerations, while making research across languages more feasible.

An arena where crosslinguistic variability has already come to prominence is in the study of the acquisition and use of word knowledge by bilinguals. Initial concerns for crosslinguistic variability in word meaning focused on words for abstract ideas and culture-dependent construals of aspects of the world. However, researchers have more recently begun to look at the effect of nonequivalences of concrete nouns on bilingual word knowledge (e.g., Ameel et al. 2005; Gathercole and Moawad 2010). This work highlights the issues we have raised here by proposing language-specific patterns of links from encoded features to words of each language (Ameel et al. 2005). A second arena is the renewed interest in the potential influence of language on thought. As we discussed earlier, crosslinguistic variability carries strong implications for assumptions about universality of concepts, if concepts are taken to be revealed by the words of a single language. Attention to the Whorfian hypothesis prods researchers to come to terms with the fact that if they assume word-concept equivalence, the concepts identified must be language specific. If they do not want to study language-specific concepts, they must find methodologies that do not rely on this assumption.

11.3.6   Conclusion

If the heart of a cognitive science is its theory of concepts, then cognitive scientists need to rethink how to find the concepts they want to understand. Pervasive diversity in how languages carve up the world by name is well documented but has been given little consideration in the study of concepts. Once this diversity is recognized, it creates serious challenges to business as usual. The study of locomotion presented here examines what different ways of using words to access concepts suggest about the word-concept relationship. The data show that individual words such as *walk*, *run*, and *jump*, and by implication *triangle*, *table*, and *robin*, do not directly reveal units of knowledge compatible with prevailing notions of concepts. More sophisticated techniques, however, can extract structure from language data and identify shared elements of meaning. These elements indicate constraints on cross-language variability and reflect common underlying components of domain knowledge. In doing so, they may suggest useful alternative approaches to the study of conceptual representation.

Acknowledgments

This work was supported in part by the Max Planck Gesellschaft, the Japanese Ministry of Education Grant-in-Aid for Scientific Research (#15300088), and research grants from Keio University (Keio Gijuku Academic Development Funds and Keio Gijuku Mori Memorial Research Fund). Eef Ameel was supported on a postdoctoral fellowship by the Fund for Scientific Research-Flanders (FWO-Vlaanderen). We thank Dan Slobin for helpful comments on an earlier draft and Adam Darlow, Kiri Lee, Yo Matsumoto, Kyoko Ohara, Steven Sloman, and Phillip Wolff for useful discussion. Kristine Schuster and Hiroyuki Okada developed the web experiments for data collection and Stephanie Sterrett served as walkway actor. Ludy Cilissen, Lisa Guest, Celina Hayes, and Erin Howard assisted with data collection and analysis.

An earlier analysis of some of the data discussed here was reported in Malt, Gennari, and Imai (2010). Additional analyses are reported in Malt et al. (2014).

References

Aguiar, A., and R. Baillargeon. 2002. Developments in young infants' reasoning about occluded objects. *Cognitive Psychology* 45:267–336.

Aitchinson, J. 2001. *Language Change: Decay or Progress?* 3rd ed. Cambridge: Cambridge University Press.

Alexander, R. M. 2002. *Principles of Animal Locomotion*. Princeton, NJ: Princeton University Press.

Ameel, E., G. Storms, B. C. Malt, and S. A. Sloman. 2005. How bilinguals solve the naming problem. *Journal of Memory and Language* 53:60–80.

Anderson, J. R. 1991. The adaptive nature of human categorization. *Psychological Review* 98:409–429.

Barsalou, L. W. 1987. The instability of graded structure: Implications for the nature of concepts. In *Concepts and Conceptual Development: Ecological and Intellectual Factors in Categorization*, ed. U. Neisser, 101–140. Cambridge: Cambridge University Press.

Benjafield, J. G. 2007. *Cognition*. 3rd ed. Oxford: Oxford University Press.

Bennett, M. B. 1992. Empirical studies of walking and running. In *Comparative and Environmental Physiology, vol. 11: Mechanics of Animal Locomotion*, ed. R. M. Alexander, 141–165. Berlin: Springer-Verlag.

Berlin, B. 1992. *Ethnobiological Classification: Principles of Categorization of Plants and Animals in Traditional Societies*. Princeton, NJ: Princeton University Press.

Bloom, P. 2000. *How Children Learn the Meanings of Words*. Cambridge, MA: MIT Press.

Bloom, P. 2004. *Descartes' Baby: How the Science of Child Development Explains What Makes Us Human*. New York: Basic Books.

Bock, J. K., M. Carreiras, and E. Meseguer. 2012. Number meaning and number grammar in English and Spanish. *Journal of Memory and Language* 66:17–37.

Bowerman, M. 1996a. Learning how to structure space for language: A crosslinguistic perspective. In *Language and Space*, ed. P. Bloom, M. A. Peterson, L. Nadel, and M. F. Garrett, 385–436. Cambridge, MA: MIT Press.

Bowerman, M. 1996b. The origins of children's spatial semantic categories: Cognitive versus linguistic determinants. In *Rethinking Linguistic Relativity*, ed. J. J. Gumperz and S. C. Levinson, 145–176. Cambridge: Cambridge University Press.

Brown, R. 1958. How shall a thing be called? *Psychological Review* 65:14–21.

Büchel, C., O. Josephs, G. Rees, R. Turner, C. Frith, and K. Friston. 1998. The functional anatomy of attention to visual motion: A functional MRI study. *Brain* 121:1281–1294.

Carey, S. 2009. *The Origin of Concepts*. Oxford: Oxford University Press.

Casasola, M., and L. Cohen. 2002. Infant categorization of containment, support and tight-fit spatial relationships. *Developmental Science* 5:247–264.

Choi, S., and M. Bowerman. 1991. Learning to express motion events in English and Korean: The influence of language-specific lexicalization patterns. *Cognition* 42:83–121.

Clark, E. V. 1983. Meanings and concepts. In *Handbook of Child Psychology, vol. 3: Cognitive Development,* ed. J. H. Flavell and E. M. Markman, (general editor: P. H. Mussen) 787–840. New York: John Wiley and Sons.

Clark, H. H. 1973. Space, time, semantics, and the child. In *Cognitive Development and the Acquisition of Language*, ed. T. Moore, 27–63. New York: Academic Press.

Corter, J. E. 1982. ADDTREE/P: A PASCAL program for fitting additive trees based on Sattath and Tversky's ADDTREE program. *Behavior Research Methods and Instrumentation* 14:353–354.

Coventry, K. R. Valdés, B., and P. Guijarro-Fuentes. 2010. Thinking for speaking and immediate memory for spatial relations. In *Linguistic Relativity in L2 Acquisition: Evidence for L1 Thinking for Speaking*, ed. Z.-H. Han and T. Cadierno, 84–101. Clevedon: Multilingual Matters.

Csibra, G., S. Bíró, O. Koós, and G. Gergely. 2003. One-year-old infants use teleological representations of actions productively. *Cognitive Science* 27:111–133.

Davidoff, J., J. Goldstein, I. Tharp, E. Wakui, and J. Fagot. 2012. Perceptual and categorical judgements of colour similarity. *Journal of Cognitive Psychology* 24:871–892.

de Boinod, A. J. 2006. *The Meaning of Tingo: And Other Extraordinary Words from Around the World*. London: Penguin.

Dougherty, J. W. D. 1978. Salience and relativity in classification. *American Ethnologist* 5:66–80.

Dunn, M., S. J. Greenhill, S. C. Levinson, and R. D. Gray. 2011. Evolved structure of language shows lineage-specific trends in word-order universals. *Nature* 473:79–82.

Ekman, P. 1992. An argument for basic emotions. *Cognition and Emotion* 6:169–200.

Evans, N., and S. C. Levinson. 2009. The myth of language universals: Language diversity and its importance for cognitive science. *Behavioral and Brain Sciences* 32:429–492.

Feist, M. I. 2008. Space between languages. *Cognitive Science* 32:1177–1199.

Fodor, J. A. 1975. *The Language of Thought*. Cambridge, MA: Harvard University Press.

Fodor, J. A. 1998. *Concepts: Where Cognitive Science Went Wrong*. Oxford: Oxford University Press.

Gathercole, V. C. M., and R. A. Moawad. 2010. Semantic interaction in early and late bilinguals: All words are not created equally. *Bilingualism: Language and Cognition* 13:385–408.

Gelman, S. A. 2006. Early conceptual development. In *Blackwell Handbook of Early Childhood Development*, ed. K. McCartney, and D. Phillips, 149–166. Malden, MA: Blackwell Publishing.

Gelman, S. A., and N. S. Davidson. 1990. Inductions from novel categories: The role of language and conceptual structure. *Cognitive Development* 5:151–176.

Gelman, S. A., and E. M. Markman. 1986. Categories and induction in young children. *Cognition* 23:183–209.

Gennari, S., S. A. Sloman, B. C. Malt, and W. T. Fitch. 2002. Motion events in language and cognition. *Cognition* 83:49–79.

Gentner, D. 2005. The development of relational category knowledge. In *Building Object Categories in Developmental Time. Carnegie Mellon Symposia on Cognition*, ed. L. Gershkoff-Stowe and D. H. Rakison, 245–275. Mahwah, NJ: Erlbaum.

Gentner, D., and M. Bowerman. 2009. Why some spatial semantic categories are harder to learn than others: The typological prevalence hypothesis. In *Crosslinguistic Approaches to the Psychology of Language: Research in the Tradition of Dan Isaac Slobin*, ed. J. Guo, E. Lieven, N. Budwig, S. Ervin-Tripp, K. Nakamura, and S. Özçaliskan, 465–480. New York: Psychology Press.

Gentner, D., and S. Goldin-Meadow. 2003. *Language in Mind: Advances in the Study of Language and Thought*. Cambridge, MA: MIT Press.

Göksun, T., K. Hirsh-Pasek, and R. M. Golinkoff. 2010. Trading spaces: Carving up events for learning language. *Perspectives on Psychological Science* 5:33–42.

Goldstein, E. B. 2005. *Cognitive Psychology: Connecting Mind, Research, and Everyday Experience*. Belmont, CA: Thomson Wadsworth.

Gumperz, J. J., and S. C. Levinson, eds. 1996. *Rethinking Linguistic Relativity*. Cambridge: Cambridge University Press.

Hampton, J. 1997. Conceptual combination: Conjunction and negation of natural concepts. *Memory & Cognition* 25:888–909.

Hampton, J. 2012. Thinking intuitively: The rich (and at times illogical) world of concepts. *Current Directions in Psychological Science* 21:398–402.

Harnad, S. 2005. To cognize is to categorize: Cognition is categorization. In *Handbook of Categorization in Cognitive Science*, ed. H. Cohen and C. Lefebvre, 20–45. Amsterdam: Elsevier.

Heit, E. 2000. Properties of inductive reasoning. *Psychonomic Bulletin & Review* 7:569–592.

Henning, H. 1916. Die qualitatenreihe des geschmacks (The quality series of taste). *Zeitschrift fur Psychologie mit Zeitschrift fur Angewandte Psychologie* 74:203–219.

Hills, T. T., M. Maouene, J. Maouene, A. Sheya, and L. Smith. 2009. Categorical structure among shared features in networks of early-learned nouns. *Cognition* 112:381–396.

Huettig, F., J. Chen, M. Bowerman, and A. Majid. 2010. Do language-specific categories shape conceptual processing? Mandarin classifier distinctions influence eye gaze behavior, but only during linguistic processing. *Journal of Cognition and Culture* 10:39–58.

Hunn, E. 1977. *Tzeltal Folk Zoology: The Classification of Discontinuities in Nature*. New York: Academic Press.

Huth, A. G., S. Nishimoto, A. T. Vu, and J. L. Gallant. 2012. A continuous semantic space describes the representation of thousands of object and action categories across the human brain. *Neuron* 76:1210–1224.

Imai, M., and H. Saalbach. 2010. Categories in mind and categories in language: Do classifier categories influence conceptual structures? In *Words and the Mind: How Words Capture Human Experience*, ed. B. C. Malt and P. Wolff, 138–164. New York: Oxford University Press.

Jackendoff, R. S. 1990. *Semantic Structures*. Cambridge, MA: MIT Press.

Jones, D. 2010. Human kinship, from conceptual structure to grammar. *Behavioral and Brain Sciences* 33:367–404.

Just, M. A., V. L. Cherkassky, S. Aryal, and T. M. Mitchell. 2010. A neurosemantic theory of concrete noun representation based on the underlying brain codes. *PLoS ONE* 5 (1): e8622.

Kable, J. W., I. P. Kan, A. Wilson, S. L. Thompson-Schill, and A. Chatterjee. 2005. Conceptual representations of action in lateral temporal cortex. *Journal of Cognitive Neuroscience* 17: 1855–1870.

Kalénine, S., D. Mirman, E. L. Middleton, and L. J. Buxbaum. 2012. Temporal dynamics of activation of thematic and functional knowledge during conceptual processing of manipulable artifacts. *Journal of Experimental Psychology: Learning, Memory, and Cognition* 38:1274–1295.

Kay, P., B. Berlin, L. Maffi, and W. Merrifield. 1997. Color naming across languages. In *Color Categories in Language and Thought*, ed. C. L. Hardin and L. Maffi, 21–56. Cambridge: Cambridge University Press.

Keil, F. C. 1989. *Concepts, Kinds, and Cognitive Development*. Cambridge, MA: MIT Press.

Kelemen, D., and S. Carey. 2007. The essence of artifacts: Developing the design stance. In *Creations of the Mind: Theories of Artifacts and Their Representation*, ed. E. Margolis and S. Laurence, 212–230. New York: Oxford University Press.

Khetarpal, N., A. Majid, and T. Regier. 2009. Spatial terms reflect near-optimal spatial categories. In *Proceedings of the 31st Annual Conference of the Cognitive Science Society*, ed. N. Taatgen and H. Van Rijn., 2396–2401.

Kinzler, K. D., and E. S. Spelke. 2007. Core systems in human cognition. *Progress in Brain Research* 164:257–264.

Kronenfeld, D. B., J. D. Armstrong, and S. Wilmoth. 1985. Exploring the internal structure of linguistic categories: An extensionist semantic view. In *Directions in Cognitive Anthropology*, ed. J. W. D. Dougherty, 91–113. Urbana: University of Illinois Press.

Kruschke, J. K. 2005. Category learning. In *The Handbook of Cognition*, ed. K. Lamberts and R. L. Goldstone, 183–201. London: Sage.

Lakoff, G. 1987. *Women, Fire, and Dangerous Things*. Chicago: University of Chicago Press.

Landau, B., and R. Jackendoff. 1993. "What" and "where" in spatial language and spatial cognition. *Behavioral and Brain Sciences* 6:217–238.

Lucy, J. 2010. Language structure, lexical meaning, and cognition: Whorf and Vygotsky revisited. In *Words and the Mind: How Words Capture Human Experience*, ed. B. C. Malt and P. Wolff, 266–286. New York: Oxford University Press.

Mahon, B. Z., and A. Caramazza. 2007. The organization and representation of conceptual knowledge in the brain: Living kinds and artifacts. In *Creations of the Mind: Theories of Artifacts and Their Representation*, ed. E. Margolis and S. Laurence, 157–187. New York: Oxford University Press.

Majid, A. 2010. Words for parts of the body. In *Words and the Mind: How Words Capture Human Experience*, ed. B. C. Malt and P. Wolff, 58–71. New York: Oxford University Press.

Majid, A., J. S. Boster, and M. Bowerman. 2008. The cross-linguistic categorization of everyday events: A study of cutting and breaking. *Cognition* 109:235–250.

Majid, A., N. J. Enfield, and M. van Staden. 2006. Parts of the body: Cross-linguistic categorisation. [Special issue] *Language Sciences* 28 (2–3).

Majid, A., and F. Huettig. 2008. A crosslinguistic perspective on semantic cognition. *Behavioral and Brain Sciences* 31:720–721.

Majid, A., and S. C. Levinson. 2011. The senses in language and culture. *The Senses & Society* 6:5–18.

Malt, B. C. 1991. Word meaning and word use. In *The Psychology of Word Meaning*, ed. P. Schwanenflugel, 37–70. Hillsdale, NJ: Erlbaum.

Malt, B. C. 1995. Category coherence in cross-cultural perspective. *Cognitive Psychology* 29:85–148.

Malt, B. C., S. Gennari, and M. Imai. 2010. Lexicalization patterns and the world-to-words mapping. In *Words and the Mind: How Words Capture Human Experience*, ed. B. C. Malt and P. Wolff, 29–57. New York: Oxford University Press.

Malt, B. C., S. Gennari, M. Imai, E. Ameel, N. Saji, and A. Majid. 2014. Human locomotion in languages: Constraints on moving and meaning. *Journal of Memory and Language* 74:107–123.

Malt, B. C., S. Gennari, M. Imai, E. Ameel, N. Tsuda, and A. Majid. 2008. Talking about walking: Biomechanics and the language of locomotion. *Psychological Science* 19:232–240.

Malt, B. C., and A. Majid. 2013. How thought is mapped into words. *Wiley Interdisciplinary Reviews: Cognitive Science* 4:583–597.

Malt, B. C., and S. A. Sloman. 2007. Artifact categorization: The good, the bad, and the ugly. In *Creations of the Mind: Theories of Artifacts and Their Representation*, ed. E. Margolis and S. Laurence, 85–123. New York: Oxford University Press.

Malt, B. C., S. A. Sloman, and S. Gennari. 2003. Universality and language-specificity in object naming. *Journal of Memory and Language* 49:20–42.

Malt, B. C., S. A. Sloman, S. Gennari, M. Shi, and Y. Wang. 1999. Knowing versus naming: Similarity and the linguistic categorization of artifacts. *Journal of Memory and Language* 40:230–262.

Malt, B. C., and P. Wolff, eds. 2010. *Words and the Mind: How Words Capture Human Experience*. New York: Oxford University Press.

Mantel, N. 1967. The detection of disease clustering and a generalized regression approach. *Cancer Research* 27:209–220.

McClelland, J. L., D. E. Rumelhart, and G. E. Hinton. 1986. The appeal of parallel distributed processing. In *Parallel Distributed Processing: Explorations in the Microstructure of Cognition*, vol. 1, ed. D. E. Rumelhart, J. L. McClelland, and the PDP Research Group, 3–44. Cambridge, MA: MIT Press.

Medin, D. L., and L. J. Rips. 2005. Concepts and categories: Memory, meaning, and metaphysics. In *Cambridge Handbook of Thinking and Reasoning*, ed. K. Holyoak and R. Morrison, 37–72. Cambridge: Cambridge University Press.

Munnich, E., B. Landau, and B. A. Dosher. 2001. Spatial language and spatial representation: A cross-linguistic comparison. *Cognition* 81:171–207.

Murphy, G. L. 1988. Comprehending complex concepts. *Cognitive Science* 12:529–562.

Murphy, G. L. 2002. *The Big Book of Concepts*. Cambridge, MA: MIT Press.

Nairne, J. S., and J. N. S. Pandeirada. 2008. Adaptive memory: Is survival processing special? *Journal of Memory and Language* 59:377–385.

Osherson, D. N., E. E. Smith, O. Wilkie, A. Lopez, and E. Shafir. 1990. Category-based induction. *Psychological Review* 97:185–200.

Papafragou, A., J. Hulbert, and J. Trueswell. 2008. Does language guide event perception? Evidence from eye movements. *Cognition* 108:155–184.

Papafragou, A., C. Massey, and L. Gleitman. 2006. When English proposes what Greek presupposes: The cross-linguistic encoding of motion events. *Cognition* 98:B75–B87.

Parish-Morris, J., S. Pruden, W. Ma, K. Hirsh-Pasek, and R. Golinkoff. 2010. A world of relations: Relational words. In *Words and the Mind: How Words Capture Human Experience*, ed. B. C. Malt and P. Wolff, 219–242. New York: Oxford University Press.

Phillips, W., and L. R. Santos. 2007. Evidence for kind representations in the absence of language: Experiments with rhesus monkeys (*Macaca mulatta*). *Cognition* 102:455–463.

Pinker, S. 2007. *The Stuff of Thought: Language as a Window into Human Nature*. New York: Viking.

Prinz, J. J. 2002. *Furnishing the Mind: Concepts and Their Perceptual Basis*. Cambridge, MA: MIT Press.

Quine, W. V. 1970. Natural kinds. In *Essays in Honor of Carl G. Hempel*, ed. N. Rescher, 5–23. Dordrecht: D. Reidel.

Raymond, J. 2000. Attentional modulation of visual motion perception. *Trends in Cognitive Sciences* 4:42–50.

Regier, T., P. Kay, and N. Khetarpal. 2007. Color naming reflects optimal partitions of color space. *Proceedings of the National Academy of Sciences of the United States of America* 104:1436–1441.

Roberson, D., and J. Davidoff. 2000. The categorical perception of colors and facial expressions: The effect of verbal interference. *Memory & Cognition* 28:977–986.

Roberson, D., I. R. L. Davies, G. G. Corbett, and M. Vandervyver. 2005. Free-sorting of colors across cultures: Are there universal grounds for grouping? *Journal of Cognition and Culture* 5:349–386.

Rogers, T. T., and J. L. McClelland. 2004. *Semantic Cognition: A Parallel Distributed Processing Approach*. Cambridge, MA: MIT Press.

Rosch, E., and C. B. Mervis. 1975. Family resemblances: Studies in internal structure of categories. *Cognitive Psychology* 7:573–605.

Rosch, E., C. B. Mervis, W. D. Gray, D. Johnson, and P. Boyes-Braem. 1976. Basic objects in natural categories. *Cognitive Psychology* 8:382–439.

Rothkopf, E. 1957. A measure of stimulus similarity and errors in some paired-associate learning tasks. *Journal of Experimental Psychology* 53:94–101.

Saalbach, H., and M. Imai. 2007. The scope of linguistic influence: Does a classifier system alter object concepts? *Journal of Experimental Psychology: General* 136:485–501.

Saalbach, H., and M. Imai. 2012. The relation between linguistic categories and cognition: The case of numeral classifiers. *Language and Cognitive Processes* 27:381–428.

Saji, N., M. Imai, H. Saalbach, Y. Zhang, H. Shu, and H. Okada. 2011. Word learning does not end at fast mapping: Evolution of verb meanings through reorganization of an entire semantic domain. *Cognition* 118:45–61.

SAS Institute. 1999. *SAS STAT ® User's Guide 8*. Cary, NC: SAS Institute.

Sattath, S., and A. Tversky. 1977. Additive similarity trees. *Psychometrika* 42:319–345.

Sauter, D. A., O. LeGuen, and D. B. M. Haun. 2011. Categorical perception of emotional facial expressions does not require lexical categories. *Emotion* 11:1479–1483.

Schank, R. C., and R. P. Abelson. 1977. *Scripts, Plans, Goals, and Understanding: An Inquiry into Human Knowledge Structures*. Hillsdale, NJ: Erlbaum.

Seligman, M. E. P. 1971. Phobias and preparedness. *Behavior Therapy* 2:307–320.

Shepard, R. N., and J.-J. Chang. 1963. Stimulus generalization in the learning of classifications. *Journal of Experimental Psychology* 65:94–102.

Slobin, D. 1996a. From "thought and language" to "thinking for speaking. In *Rethinking Linguistic Relativity*, ed. J. J. Gumperz and S. C. Levinson, 70–96. Cambridge: Cambridge University Press.

Slobin, D. 1996b. Two ways of travel: Verbs of motion in English and Spanish. In *Grammatical Constructions: Their Form and Meaning*, ed. M. Shibatani and S. Thompson, 195–220. Oxford: Clarendon Press.

Slobin, D. 2010. Linguistic relativity and determinism: Whence and whither? Plenary talk presented at the German Linguistics Society, Berlin, Germany, Feb. 23–27, 2010.

Sloman, S. A., and Malt, B. C. 2003. Artifacts are not ascribed essences, nor are they treated as belonging to kinds. In Conceptual representation, special issue, *Language and Cognitive Processes* 18:563–582.

Smith, E. E., and D. L. Medin. 1981. *Categories and Concepts*. Cambridge, MA: Harvard University Press.

Smith, L. B., and L. Samuelson. 1997. Perceiving and remembering: Category stability, variability, and development. In *Knowledge, Concepts, and Categories*, ed. K. Lamberts and D. Shanks, 161–196. East Sussex, UK: Psychology Press.

Smolensky, P. 1988. On the proper treatment of connectionism. *Behavioral and Brain Sciences* 11:1–74.

Solomon, K. O., D. L. Medin, and E. B. Lynch. 1999. Concepts do more than categorize. *Trends in Cognitive Sciences* 3:99–105.

Spelke, E. S. 1994. Initial knowledge: Six suggestions. *Cognition* 50:431–445.

Talmy, L. 1985. Lexicalization patterns: Semantic structure in lexical forms. In *Language Typology and Syntactic Description,* vol. 3: *Grammatical Categories and the Lexicon,* ed. T. Shopen, 56–149. Cambridge: Cambridge University Press.

Ullman, S. 1998. Three-dimensional object recognition based on the combination of views. *Cognition* 67:21–44.

Ullman, S., M. Vidal-Naquit, and E. Sali. 2002. Visual features of intermediate complexity and their use in classification. *Nature Neuroscience* 5:682–687.

Webster, M. A., and P. Kay. 2012. Color categories and color appearance. *Cognition* 122:375–392.

Whorf, B. L. 1956. *Language, Thought, and Reality: Selected Writings of Benjamin Lee Whorf.* Ed. J. B. Carroll. Cambridge, MA: MIT Press.

Wierzbicka, A. 1999. *Emotions Across Languages and Cultures*. Cambridge: Cambridge University Press.

Wierzbicka, A. 2009. Language and metalanguage: Key issues in emotion research. *Emotion Review* 1:3–14.

Willems, R. M., M. de Boer, J. P. de Ruiter, M. L. Noordzij, P. Hagoort, and I. Toni. 2010. A dissociation between linguistic and communicative abilities in the human brain. *Psychological Science* 21:8–14.

Willingham, D. T. 2007. *Cognition: The Thinking Animal*. 3rd ed. Upper Saddle River, NJ: Pearson.

Wisniewski, E. 1996. Construal and similarity in conceptual combination. *Journal of Memory and Language* 35:434–453.

Wolff, P., B. Klettke, T. Ventura, and G. Song. 2005. Expressing causation in English and other languages. In *Categorization Inside and Outside the Laboratory: Essays in Honor of Douglas L. Medin,* ed. W. Ahn, R. L. Goldstone, B. C., Love, A. B. Markman, and P. Wolff, 29–48. Washington, DC: American Psychological Association.

Wolff, P., and B. C. Malt. 2010. The language-thought interface: An introduction. In *Words and the Mind: How Words Capture Human Experience*, ed. B. C. Malt and P. Wolff, 3–15. New York: Oxford University Press.

Wolff, P., D. Medin, and C. Pankratz. 1999. Evolution and devolution of folkbiological knowledge. *Cognition* 73:177–204.

Xu, F. 2005. Categories, kinds, and object individuation in infancy. In *Building Object Categories in Developmental Time: Carnegie Mellon Symposia on Cognition*, ed. L. Gershkoff-Stowe and D. H. Rakison, 63–89. Mahwah, NJ: Erlbaum.

12   The Representation of Events in Language and Cognition

Anna Papafragou

12.1   Introduction

The world around us is full of constantly unfolding dynamic events: as I look out the window from my study, a car is honking, birds are flying, two friends are crossing the street, and the sun is moving behind the clouds. To successfully interact in the world, we must track and interpret a rich array of events to relate them to others. How do we accomplish this?

According to most theories, the way we talk about the world is limited by basic, probably universal, constraints on how we conceptualize space, objects, and events. For instance, models of language production assume that the act of speaking begins with event conceptualization (the preverbal apprehension of the broad details of an event), followed by further processes of information selection and linguistic formulation that culminate in speech execution (Levelt 1989; Bock, Irwin, and Davidson 2004; cf. also Lashley 1951; Paul 1970; Wundt 1970). Similarly, models of language acquisition generally assume that learners are equipped with a set of concepts for representing events and their components (even though the size of that set is under dispute), such that acquiring language includes mapping incoming speech stimuli onto this set of concepts (Gleitman 1990; Jackendoff 1996; Miller and Johnson-Laird 1976; Pinker 1989).

This view on how event representations make contact with language faces two challenges. First, the underlying perceptual and conceptual representations of events are elusive. Existing work on event recognition has addressed the perception of biological motion (Blake and Shiffrar 2007; Giese and Poggio 2003; Johansson 1973; Lange and Lappe 2006), the segmentation of events from dynamic displays (Newtson 1973, 1976; Zacks, Tversky, and Iyer 2001), and more recently the neural bases of human action representations (Kable and Chatterjee 2006; Tranel et al. 2003). However, little work has been done on the conceptual structure of events per se, and on the relationship between the linguistic and nonlinguistic representation of event components (see Shipley and Zacks 2008 and the infant studies reviewed in Baillargeon et al. 2011;

Göksun, Hirsh-Pasek and Golinkoff 2010; and Spelke, Phillips, and Woodward 1995 for relevant evidence). Some studies have suggested that information about individual event components (e.g., the person being affected by an action) or relationships between event components that determine whether an event is coherent can be extracted rapidly by human viewers (see, respectively, Griffin and Bock 2000; Dobel et al. 2007; cf. also Dobel et al. 2011; Webb, Knott, and MacAskill 2010). Nevertheless, these studies as a whole have focused on a limited number of events and event components and thus leave the basic building blocks and processes underlying event representation still underspecified.

Furthermore, there have been few explicit attempts to connect the process of building event representations to mechanisms of language production. In the first study of this kind, Griffin and Bock (2000) recorded speakers' direction of gaze as they visually inspected and described static line drawings of simple actions (e.g., a woman shooting a man). Analysis of the eye movements in relation to people's linguistic choices led to the conclusion that there exists an initial rapid event-apprehension stage that is temporally dissociable from any sentence-generation stage. But further eye-tracking studies using picture description tasks have shown that event apprehension and linguistic formulation overlap temporally to a greater extent than suggested by this first study (see Gleitman et al. 2007).

A second challenge for theories attempting to account for how event cognition interfaces with language is that, across natural languages, the lexical-structural representation of events varies considerably. For instance, languages have different means for encoding space, motion, number, objects, and informational access to events (see Bowerman and Levinson 2001; Gentner and Goldin-Meadow 2003; Gleitman and Papafragou, in press, for reviews, and later sections of this chapter for examples). These crosslinguistic differences raise the question whether the underlying perceptual and conceptual event representations might also vary in the minds of speakers of different languages. This possibility has been famously espoused in the past by Benjamin Lee Whorf (Whorf 1956) and has been recently revived in several neo-Whorfian theories of how perception and cognition are connected to language (e.g., Boroditsky 2001; Levinson 2003). Proponents of these theories argue that "habitual or obligatory categorical distinctions made in one's language result in language-specific categorical distortions in objective perceptual tasks," with language-specific categories being used "on-line" during perception (Winawer et al. 2007, 7783). Similarly, other researchers propose that "experience, including experience with language, can influence the perceptual system such that it is more or less attuned to particular features in the environment" (Majid et al. 2004, 113), perhaps through the selective direction of attention (Smith et al. 2002). If language can reorganize the perceptual and conceptual representation of events, then it is no longer true that (universal) event categories provide the building blocks for event encoding cross-linguistically: the causal relation can also flow in the opposite direction, with different languages having stable and permanent restructuring effects on the event concepts held by their speakers (Levinson 1996, 2003).

In this chapter, I present the results from a multipronged research collaboration between my lab and John Trueswell's lab that combines on-line, developmental, and crosslinguistic methods to address these issues. The series of studies I discuss ask two types of questions. First, how do people perceive events? Is there concrete evidence for a link between event perception and the lexical-structural representation of events in language? Second, do crosslinguistic differences in event encoding affect event apprehension? In particular, do speakers of different languages process events in distinct ways? I take up each of these types of question in turn, introduce key findings from our studies, and sketch some general implications for the interface between event representation and language.

12.2   How Are Events Perceived?

Studies of event perception need to begin with the question of what the constituents of events might be, and how these constituents contribute to event individuation and identification. Consider the simple event of a man chasing a toddler. A straightforward way of characterizing this event includes distinguishing between the role of the man, who is the causer of the action, and that of the toddler, who is the entity directly affected by that action. Inspired by linguistic analyses of events in sentences (e.g., Fillmore 1968; Chomsky 1981), one could call the first entity the *agent* of the event and the second entity the *patient*. In language, agents and patients are among several possible *thematic roles*, or relations that a sentential constituent (typically a noun phrase such as *a man* or *a toddler*) has with a main verb (Chomsky 1981; Jackendoff 1990)—see the sentence in (1a) and its representation in (1b):

(1a) A man is chasing a toddler.

(1b) [A man]$_{AGENT}$ is chasing [a toddler]$_{PATIENT}$.

It seems reasonable to assume that agents, patients, and related roles have cognitive corollaries that can be used to capture the who-did-what-to-whom structure of event representations. The idea that there is a tight relation between the cognitive and linguistic representation of events and event components is not new. Several commentators have proposed that linguistic roles such as agents and patients map relatively directly onto underlying conceptual event roles, at least in the most typical cases (see Baker 1997; Dowty 1991; Jackendoff 1990; Levin and Pinker 1991). Others have proposed that linguistic events could be individuated based on thematic roles, such that the representation of an event may have only one agent, one patient, and so forth (Carlson 1998); similar ideas can be used to characterize nonlinguistic event individuation. However, the extent to which nonlinguistic event construal is truly sensitive to components such as agents and patients as well as the processes underlying the extraction of such components remain unspecified.

In one of the first studies to investigate these issues, Hafri, Papafragou, and Trueswell (2013) asked whether the conceptual roles of agent and patient (and the events they comprise) could be rapidly extracted from visual stimuli.[1] The researchers displayed naturalistic photographs of a wide range of two-participant events (e.g., a girl punching a boy) for either 37 ms or 73 ms followed by a mask. People were then asked to identify the category of the event ("Did you see 'punching'?"), the role of agent ("Is the girl performing the action?"), the role of patient ("Is the boy being acted upon?"), or a combination of event category and roles ("The girl is punching the boy, true or false?"). It was found that people successfully recognized both event categories and event roles (and combinations of the two) even from the briefest visual displays. Further experiments revealed that the rapid recognition of event roles made use of certain physical features (e.g., outstretched extremities) that can be linked to features such as causality that typically characterize (linguistic) agenthood (e.g., Dowty 1991). Specifically, under short display durations, subjects recognized the roles of event participants less accurately when patients possessed agent-like features such as outstretched extremities (this difference disappeared with longer display durations).

These findings show that people are able to extract event role and event type information on the basis of briefly presented visual stimuli. They also show that the perceptual-conceptual representation of events is sensitive to roles such as agents and patients that are relevant for the description of events in language. Finally, the fact that event roles depend for rapid identification on certain physical features that are linked to their causal role in the event is consistent with proposals to treat linguistic thematic roles more generally as "convenient mnemonics" for prominent structural configurations of conceptual structure (Jackendoff 1990, 47).

Can these conclusions be extended to more complex events containing more participants? Consider causative events such as those in figure 12.1, in which a human agent uses an instrument to move an object toward a goal. The event in figure 12.1 would typically be described with the sentence in (2a), which has the underlying thematic-role structure in (2b):

(2a) A woman is hitting a ball into a basket with a tennis racquet.

(2b) [A woman]$_{AGENT}$ is hitting [a ball]$_{PATIENT}$ [into a basket]$_{GOAL}$ [with a tennis racquet]$_{INSTRUMENT}$.

Within linguistic theory, the thematic roles involved in (2b) would be ranked differently with respect to each other, with agents considered more prominent than patients,

---

1. All experiments in this section were conducted with English-speaking adults.

Figure 12.1
Sample stimulus from the study by Wilson et al. (2011).

and patients considered more prominent than goals; instruments would be considered least prominent. This ranking of thematic roles, otherwise known as *thematic hierarchy* (Baker 1997; Jackendoff 1990), determines the linguistic behavior of different thematic roles, affecting, for example, how each role gets mapped onto specific syntactic positions in the sentence (e.g., how agents get mapped onto sentential subjects, etc.). For present purposes, it is important to point out that the thematic hierarchy has been claimed to capture prominence relations between event roles in the nonlinguistic representation of events (see, e.g., Levin and Rappaport Hovav 2005; Baker 1997). Such claims have been difficult to evaluate, however, because of lack of evidence about how different event components are represented nonlinguistically.

In a series of experiments, we (Wilson, Papafragou, and Trueswell 2011; Wilson et al. 2011) tested how people process causative events with the goal of discovering whether there is an internal hierarchy of event components and whether that hierarchy is shared between language and perception/cognition. We used pictures of events with clearly visually defined, distinct areas corresponding to the event roles of agent, patient, goal, and instrument. (Figure 12.1 depicts an actual stimulus item.) One group of people completed a linguistic task, in which they viewed the events and were asked to describe them. A different group of people participated in a nonlinguistic task. These participants were told that they would see pictures depicting an action or event and were asked to identify certain event components by quickly looking at them and then pressing a computer key (see Griffin and Bock 2000 and especially Hafri, Papafragou, and Trueswell 2011 for similar methods). Depending on the condition they were assigned to, participants in the nonlinguistic task were told to look as quickly as possible at "the person or animal who was performing the action" (agent condition), "the object directly affected by the action" (patient condition), "the goal or destination of the action" (goal condition), or "the tool or body part used to make the action" (instrument condition). Of interest was whether the frequency with which people mentioned components of events such as agents, patients, goals, and instruments in the linguistic task would conform to the thematic hierarchy, with some components being mentioned more reliably than others. Also of interest was whether the speed of identification of individual event components in the nonlinguistic task would reveal a similar asymmetry.[2]

This dual expectation was confirmed in our data. The linguistic task revealed a difference among event components that was consistent with the thematic hierarchy: agents were mentioned most often in people's descriptions, followed by patients and goals; instruments were mentioned least often. This difference was mirrored in the eye-gaze data of the nonlinguistic task: finding an agent in a causative event (as measured by participants' eye movements to the corresponding region) occurred more quickly than finding a patient, goal, or instrument, and instruments were identified more slowly than the other event components. Further analyses ensured that this difference in speed of identification could not be due to a difference in size between the physical entities representing the different event components in our stimuli but could be confidently attributed to the role each entity played in the event.

Summarizing, the set of studies just reviewed breaks new ground by introducing a novel approach to the study of event perception and its relation to language. A major conclusion from these studies is that event perception delivers representations with internal structure (including event roles such as agents, patients, goals, and instruments). Furthermore, this structure is homologous to linguistic event structure, as evidenced by the fact that the salience of roles in complex events is similar across perception/cognition and language. Thus our results offer concrete support for the much-cited but little-tested view that the language of events builds on underlying

2. To maintain the naturalness of the events, the agents in our studies were always animate entities, and the other three components were inanimate entities. Even though we mention agents for completeness, our main focus was the asymmetry between the three components that did not differ in animacy.

nonlinguistic event concepts: as our data show, linguistic agents, patients, and so on are relational notions at the interface with conceptual structure (cf. also Jackendoff 1990; Levin and Rappaport Hovav 2005; Pinker 1989).

12.3   Do Crosslinguistic Differences in Event Encoding Affect Event Cognition?

The studies reviewed so far have dealt with event representations and the way these representations map broadly onto linguistic strings. I now turn to a separate issue: Is it possible that one's representation of events in the world depends on the language one uses to describe such events? And if so, is the representation of events different across speakers of different languages?

To address this issue, my collaborators and I focused on motion events, in which an agent moves spontaneously in a certain manner (e.g., rolling, crawling), following a specific trajectory, or path (e.g., into a cave, through a forest; Miller and Johnson-Laird 1976; Talmy 1985). Motion is an ideal domain for studying aspects of event cognition crosslinguistically. First, the representation of motion and space is a fundamental human cognitive ability (Carlson and van der Zee 2005; Hayward and Tarr 1995; Newcombe and Huttenlocher 2003; Stiles-Davis, Kritchevsky, and Bellugi 1988; and many others). Some of the spatial-mechanical conceptual machinery for representing motion is already available early in life: we know that infants in the first year of life detect changes in the path and manner of motion and find the invariant path and manner in actions (e.g., Pulverman et al. 2008; Pruden et al. 2013).

Second, and most pertinent for present purposes, despite being rooted in a shared conceptual typology, the linguistic encoding of motion and space is characterized by intense typological variability. For instance, the ways the motion primitives of manner and path are lexicalized in spatial vocabularies and the ways these primitives are conflated into sentential structure vary considerably crosslinguistically (Talmy 1975, 1985, 2000). Manner languages[3] (e.g., English, German, Russian, and Mandarin Chinese) typically encode manner in the verb (cf. English *skip, run, hop, jog*) and path in a variety of other devices such as particles (*out*), adpositions (*into the room*), or verb prefixes (e.g., German *raus-*, "out"; cf. *raus-rennen*, "run out"). Path languages (e.g., Modern Greek, Romance, Turkish, Japanese, and Hebrew) typically encode path in the verb (cf. Greek *vjeno*, "exit"; *beno*, "enter"; *diashizo*, "cross"), and manner in gerunds, adpositions, or

---

3. We adopt the distinction between path and manner languages introduced in Papafragou, Massey, and Gleitman (2002), rather than the original distinction between V-framed and S-framed languages in Talmy (1985) for ease of reference. The former distinction reflects broader lexical and morpho-syntactic asymmetries in the groups of languages involved and is therefore not specific to motion event encoding (see Beavers, Levin, and Tham 2010).

adverbials (*trehontas,* "running"; *me ta podia* "on foot"). Often, manner languages possess large and varied manner verb vocabularies, unlike path languages. The manner/path language distinction should not be taken to imply that the relevant languages lack certain kinds of verbs altogether. But the most characteristic (i.e., colloquial, frequent, and pervasive) way of describing motion in these languages involves manner and path verbs, respectively.

To illustrate these differences, the sentences in (3) and (4) describe the same event in English and in Greek. In (3), the manner of motion (*driving*) is encoded in the main verb, and the path appears as a prepositional phrase (*into the soccer net*). In (4), the same event is encoded in two different ways in Greek, none of which map directly onto their English counterpart: in (4a), the path of motion is encoded in the main verb, and the manner of motion is encoded in an optional prepositional phrase; in (4b), the event is encoded in two separate clauses, the first one containing a manner verb and the second a path verb. Of the two alternatives in (4), (4a) is more natural than (4b):

(3) A boy is driving a bike into a tent.

(4a) Ena agori beni se mia skini (me mia mihani).

lit. "A boy is-entering in a tent (with a bike)."

(4b) Ena agori odigi mia mihani ke beni se mia skini.

lit. "A boy is-driving a bike and is-entering in a tent."

The typological differences between path and manner languages are reflected in the way speakers of different languages habitually talk about motion (e.g., Özçalişkan and Slobin 1999, 2003; Papafragou, Massey, and Gleitman 2002, 2006). These differences are already in place as early as three years of age: young children quickly grasp and follow language-specific patterns for the expression of motion, such that, for instance, English learners encode path concepts in prepositions such as *in* and *out*, while Greek learners encode them in verbs with meanings such as *enter* and *exit* (Allen et al. 2007; Bunger et al. 2013; Slobin 1996, 2003; cf. Naigles et al. 1998; Papafragou, Massey, and Gleitman 2002, 2006). Furthermore, these statistical tendencies in motion descriptions affect conjectures about the meanings of novel verbs: when presented with a novel intransitive motion verb, English-speaking children and adults tend to interpret it as a manner verb, whereas Greek-speaking children and adults tend to construe it as a path verb (Papafragou and Selimis 2010b; Skordos and Papafragou 2014; cf. Maguire et al. 2010; Naigles and Terrazas 1998 for similar data from other languages).

Could such lexicalization preferences affect perceptual and conceptual motion event encoding? Some commentators have proposed that the manner of motion for speakers of manner languages is a "salient and differentiated conceptual field" compared with speakers of path languages, with potential implications for how manner of motion is perceived or attended to on-line and remembered (Slobin 2004; cf. Bowerman and Choi 2003). However, an initial series of studies with both adults and children found no evidence supporting this idea. For instance, speakers of English and Greek were equally likely to remember path and manner details of motion events, despite the differences in the way the two groups described these events (Papafragou, Massey, and Gleitman 2002). Similarly, the categorization of motion proceeded identically in speakers of the two languages (Papafragou, Massey, and Gleitman 2002; Papafragou and Selimis 2010a; see also Gennari et al. 2002).

Could linguistic encoding affect the dynamics of motion perception itself? The studies just reviewed involved slower, more complex cognitive processes, and thus leave open the possibility that on-line measures of event processing might capture early effects of language on attention. To test this possibility, we (Papafragou, Hulbert, and Trueswell 2008) conducted an eye tracking study in which adult speakers of Greek and English viewed a set of short animated motion events (e.g., a boy driving his bike into a tent). The stimuli were constructed so that linguistically relevant manner and path information could be easily defined as distinct regions spatially separated from each other: manners corresponded to the vehicle that propelled the moving agent (e.g., the bike), and paths corresponded to the object that served as the endpoint of the motion trajectory (e.g., the tent). Events unfolded for three seconds, at which point a beep was heard, and the last clip from the event remained on the screen for another two seconds. Half of the participants were asked to describe the events after hearing the beep (linguistic task). The other half were asked to watch the events carefully in preparation for a memory test (nonlinguistic task).

Of interest was to compare the way participants viewed these events. If language has deep, enduring effects on event perception, gaze patterns should differ cross-linguistically when people inspect motion events regardless of whether the task involves producing a linguistic description or not. Thus in both the linguistic and the nonlinguistic task, English speakers should look earlier and more often at manner of motion regions than Greek speakers, whereas Greek speakers should prioritize the path endpoint more.

As expected, the linguistic description data confirmed the typological difference between path and manner languages. For English speakers, 78 percent of all sentences describing an event of motion to an endpoint contained a manner verb, compared with only 32 percent for Greek speakers. Early eye movements in the linguistic task reflected this cross-linguistic difference: Greek speakers were more likely than English speakers to fixate the path endpoint first (the tent in the earlier example) rather than the manner of motion region (the bike), probably as a result of planning the informational content of the main motion verb in their sentence.

After about a second and a half, Greek speakers turned their attention to manner, while English speakers focused on the path endpoint, presumably as a result of the preparation of relevant postverbal modifiers in each language. These eye-movement patterns were repeated after the beep while people were describing aloud the events. This pattern is in accord with other eye-movement production studies, which were done within a single language, where participants' preparation to describe regions of a scene was preceded by fixations on these regions (e.g., Altmann and Kamide 2004; Griffin and Bock 2000). These results offer the first cross-linguistic evidence for the hypothesis that language production mobilizes attention: where languages differ from each other in how they encode event structure, this difference shapes how speakers visually interrogate events during speech planning (cf. also Bunger et al. 2013 for evidence that such shifts of attention during speech planning are present already in three- to four-year-old children).

Crucially, however, in the nonlinguistic task, where people were asked to simply study (but not describe) the events, attention allocation as the events unfolded was strikingly *similar* for both language groups: overall, people prioritized looks to the path endpoint and inspected the manner of motion slightly later. Thus, when inspecting the world freely, people were alike in how they perceived events, regardless of their native language. This finding argues against the hypothesis that linguistic encoding has deep and persistent effects on the way events are perceptually experienced but is entirely expected under accounts that emphasize universal aspects of event perception and cognition.

One striking finding from the nonlinguistic task introduced complexity into this picture: late in each trial, after the event had unfolded and its last frame remained on the screen, English speakers spent more time inspecting the path endpoint (e.g., the tent) rather than the manner of motion (e.g., the bike) compared with the Greek speakers, who tended toward the opposite pattern. We (Papafragou, Hulbert, and Trueswell 2008) called this a "reverse-Whorfian" finding, since each language group seemed to attend to aspects of the event that would not typically be encoded in a verb (path endpoint in English, manner in Greek).

How could this reverse-Whorfian pattern be explained? According to a first hypothesis, this effect reflects the on-line (albeit covert) use of language to help participants remember the core event and to direct attention to additional details in the scene in preparation for the memory test (see Antes 1974; Antes and Kristjanson 1993; and Loftus 1972 for evidence that participants typically begin by studying the fundamental aspects of a scene, and then increasingly fixate the "details"). Here, it appears that what was considered a detail was linguistically determined: for Greek speakers, the manner of motion was a detail of the event, because it was not preferentially encoded in the main verb of the event description, and for English speakers, the path endpoint was a detail. According to a second hypothesis, the reverse-Whorfian pattern is due to conceptual reorganization, that is, to differences in postperceptual event processing between English and Greek speakers caused by years of language use. On this hypothesis, attention was drawn late to "details" of events not because speakers used on-line (covert) verbalization as a way to remember event details but because language has created deep, stable differences in how salient manners and paths are in the minds of English versus Greek speakers.

The method and data in Papafragou, Hulbert, and Trueswell (2008) could not distinguish between the two possible explanations of the reverse-Whorfian effect, but a further study (Trueswell and Papafragou 2010) tested these alternatives directly. This study presented a new group of English and Greek speakers with motion events that were very similar to the ones in Papafragou, Hulbert, and Trueswell (2008). Participants were placed in one of three conditions. In the No Interference condition, people were asked to watch and remember the events for a later memory test, much like in the original study. In the Linguistic Interference condition, people were given the same instructions as in the No Interference condition but were additionally presented with a secondary task: they heard a series of numbers before each event (e.g., "35, 20, 76") and were asked to repeat these numbers back to the experimenter as long as the stimulus was displayed. In the Nonlinguistic Interference condition, people were given the same basic set of instructions but a different secondary task: before each event, the experimenter demonstrated a series of rhythmic taps on the table, and participants had to reproduce the taps continuously until the stimulus finished.

The logic of the experiment was as follows. If the reverse-Whorfian effect reflected the on-line use of language to recode the motion stimuli, a secondary task that blocked on-line access to the linguistic code (as in the Linguistic Interference condition) should make the effect disappear; by contrast, a secondary task that did not affect the availability of the verbal code (as in the Nonlinguistic Interference condition) should allow the effect to surface. Alternatively, if the reverse-Whorfian pattern was due to a deeper conceptual reorganization of event representations driven by language-specific forces, it should persist whether or not covert verbalization was permitted within the experimental setup (i.e., in both the Linguistic and the Nonlinguistic Interference conditions).

Results from the study supported the on-line use hypothesis over the conceptual reorganization hypothesis. Specifically, the reverse-Whorfian effect appeared strongly in the Nonlinguistic Interference condition, yielding differences in attention allocation between English and Greek speakers. However, this effect disappeared in the Linguistic Interference condition. In this condition, as in the No Interference condition, attention allocation was very similar for English and Greek speakers. These results replicate and extend the findings from the nonlinguistic task of Papafragou, Hulbert, and Trueswell

$(2008)^4$ and are consistent with prior evidence for the independence of motion cognition from linguistic-encoding patterns (Papafragou, Hulbert, and Trueswell 2008; Papafragou, Massey, and Gleitman 2002, 2006; Gennari et al. 2002; cf. also Malt et al. 2008).

The studies summarized in this section point to a few key conclusions about the relationship between crosslinguistic event encoding and event representation. First, the fact that languages differ in how they encode events has implications about the way speakers of different languages inspect events in the world before they talk about what they see. Second, such differences in attention do not percolate into situations that do not involve communication: basic patterns in event perception are independent from one's native language. Third, language can be used on-line as a tool to support memory. This implicit use of the verbal code may give rise to crosslinguistic differences in attention allocation as event details are apprehended and committed to memory (what we have called a reverse-Whorfian effect). Such on-line effects of language are distinct from effects of permanent conceptual reorganization, since they can be disrupted through processes that block access to the verbal code (e.g., Linguistic Interference). Taken together, these conclusions paint a nuanced picture of how language makes contact with event representations. In this picture, rather than permanently shaping the mechanisms supporting event perception and cognition (as proposed by recent neo-Whorfian accounts), language offers an alternative, optionally recruited system of representing, organizing, and tracking events.

4. Unlike in Papafragou, Hulbert, and Trueswell (2008), we did not observe the reverse-Whorfian effect in the No Interference condition. We suspect that the reason has to do with methodological differences between the two studies (see Trueswell and Papafragou 2010 for discussion). In our prior study, during the nonlinguistic task, participants were given examples of event changes as practice for the memory test (e.g., a woman eating an apple would turn into a woman eating a pie). Participants were also told that the memory test would involve identifying whether static images were taken from the motion events they had earlier seen. As a result, participants knew that changes relevant for the memory test would be quite subtle and that the format of the items in the memory phase would be different from the one in the presentation phase (static vs. dynamic clips). By contrast, the No Interference condition in Trueswell and Papafragou (2010) contained no practice items, and the memory items had the same format as the presentation items (dynamic events). Both of these features may have convinced participants in the earlier but not the later study that the memory task would be difficult and might have encouraged spontaneous adoption of a linguistic recoding strategy so that event details could be kept in memory. This assumption is supported by the fact that when cognitive load was increased in the Trueswell and Papafragou study (as in the Nonlinguistic Interference condition), the reverse-Whorfian effect emerged clearly and early (e.g., for English speakers, it was present after only about 800 or 900 ms from the beginning of the event).

12.4   Events and Language: Final Thoughts

The studies discussed in this chapter present a novel approach to studying the nature and building blocks of perceptual and conceptual event representations and the processes that contribute to event apprehension (especially event category and event role recognition). Additionally, these studies paint a subtle picture of how events and language interact, with language both building on event representations and also potentially affecting on-line event cognition—though not reorganizing basic perceptual-cognitive processes (for related perspectives, see Dessalegn and Landau 2008; Frank et al. 2008).

The present approach opens up several questions for further work. For instance, what is the exact nature of event representations in the first moments of observing an event? The level of specificity of these representations will presumably depend on both local features (e.g., facial expressions or eye gaze) and more global features of the scene (e.g., spatial layout of participants; Oliva 2005) in ways that remain to be specified. Relatedly, how might the recognition of an event category (e.g., punching, filming) interact with recognition of event roles? Furthermore, what are the implications of event role hierarchies for the way children learn to segment and name events? Infant work suggests that event components such as agents and patients are available to humans at a very young age (e.g., Goldin-Meadow 1985; Golinkoff 1975; Golinkoff and Kerr 1978; Gordon 2003). It remains to be seen how nonlinguistic event representations affect the acquisition of different types of event predicates (e.g., verbs or prepositions). Finally, what are the circumstances under which language is recruited in nonlinguistic event processing? Language may be particularly useful for some tasks but not others (Potter 1979), and this is bound to affect the ways in which verbal encoding is brought to bear on the representation of events.

Acknowledgments

A version of this material was presented at the Tufts Cognitive Science Conference on Language and Representation (Boston, September 2012). I thank the organizers for inviting me to speak at the conference and the audience for productive discussion. I also thank Ann Bunger, Alon Hafri, and Dimitris Skordos for their useful comments on the present manuscript. Preparation of this chapter was supported by grant 5R01HD055498–05 from the Eunice Kennedy Shriver National Institute of Child Health and Human Development.

References

Allen, S., A. Özyürek, S. Kita, A. Brown, R. Furman, T. Ishizuka, and M. Fujii. 2007. Language-specific and universal influences in children's syntactic packaging of manner and path: A comparison of English, Japanese, and Turkish. *Cognition* 102:16–48.

Altmann, G., and Y. Kamide. 2004. Now you see it, now you don't: Mediating the mapping between language and the visual world. In *The Interface between Language, Vision and Action: Eye Movements and the Visual World*, ed. J. Henderson and F. Ferreira, 347–385. New York; Hove, UK: Psychology Press.

Antes, J. R. 1974. The time course of picture viewing. *Journal of Experimental Psychology* 103 (1): 62–70.

Antes, J. R., and A. Kristjanson. 1993. Effects of capacity demands on picture viewing. *Perception & Psychophysics* 54:808–813.

Baillargeon, R., J. Li, Y. Gertner, and D. Wu. 2011. How do infants reason about physical events? In *The Wiley-Blackwell Handbook of Childhood Cognitive Development*, 2nd ed., ed. U. Goswami, 11–48. Oxford: Blackwell.

Baker, M. C. 1997. Thematic roles and syntactic structure. In *Handbook of Generative Syntax*, ed. L. Haegeman, 73–137. Dordrecht: Kluwer.

Beavers, J., B. Levin, and S. W. Tham. 2010. The typology of motion events revisited. *Journal of Linguistics* 46:331–377.

Blake, R., and M. Shiffrar. 2007. Perception of human motion. *Annual Review of Psychology* 58:47–73.

Bock, K., D. Irwin, and D. Davidson. 2004. Putting first things first. In *The Interface between Language, Vision and Action: Eye Movements and the Visual World*, ed. J. Henderson and F. Ferreira, 249–317. New York; Hove, UK: Psychology Press.

Boroditsky, L. 2001. Does language shape thought? Mandarin and English speakers' conception of time. *Cognitive Psychology* 43:1–22.

Bowerman, M., and S. Choi. 2003. Space under construction: Language-specific spatial categorization in first language acquisition. In *Language in Mind: Advances in the Study of Language and Thought*, ed. D. Gentner and S. Goldin-Meadow, 387–427. Cambridge, MA: MIT Press.

Bowerman, M., and S. Levinson, eds. 2001. *Language Acquisition and Conceptual Development*. Cambridge: Cambridge University Press.

Bunger, A., D. Skordos, J. Trueswell, and A. Papafragou. 2013. Cross-linguistic differences in event description and inspection in preschool speakers of English and Greek. Talk delivered at the 87th Annual Meeting of the Linguistic Society of America, Boston, January 3–6.

Carlson, G. 1998. Thematic roles and the individuation of events. In *Events and Grammar*, ed. S. Rothstein, 35–51. Dordrecht: Kluwer.

Carlson, L., and E. van der Zee, eds. 2005. *Functional Features in Language and Space: Insights from Perception, Categorization and Development*. Oxford: Oxford University Press.

Chomsky, N. 1981. *Lectures on Government and Binding*. Dordrecht: Foris.

Dessalegn, B., and B. Landau. 2008. More than meets the eye: The role of language in binding and maintaining feature conjunctions. *Psychological Science* 19 (2): 189–195.

Dobel, C., R. Glanemann, H. Kreysa, P. Zwitserlood, and S. Eisenbeiss. 2011. Visual encoding of coherent and non-coherent scenes. In *Event Representation in Language: Encoding Events at the Language Cognition Interface*, ed. J. Bohnemeyer and E. Pederson, 189–215. Cambridge: Cambridge University Press.

Dobel, C., H. Gumnior, J. Bölte, and P. Zwitserlood. 2007. Describing scenes hardly seen. *Acta Psychologica* 12:129–143.

Dowty, D. 1991. Thematic proto-roles and argument selection. *Language* 67:547–619.

Fillmore, C. J. 1968. The case for case. In *Universals in Linguistic Theory*, ed. E. Bach and R. T. Harms, 1–88. New York: Holt, Rinehart and Winston.

Frank, M. C., D. L. Everett, E. Fedorenko, and E. Gibson. 2008. Number as a cognitive technology: Evidence from Pirahã language and cognition. *Cognition* 108:819–824.

Gennari, S., S. Sloman, B. Malt, and T. Fitch. 2002. Motion events in language and cognition. *Cognition* 83:49–79.

Gentner, D., and S. Goldin-Meadow, eds. 2003. *Language and Mind*. Cambridge, MA: MIT Press.

Giese, M. A., and T. Poggio. 2003. Neural mechanisms for the recognition of biological movements. *Nature Reviews: Neuroscience* 4:179–192.

Gleitman, L. R. 1990. The structural sources of verb learning. *Language Acquisition* 1:1–63.

Gleitman, L., D. January, R. Nappa, and J. Trueswell. 2007. On the give and take between event apprehension and utterance formulation. *Journal of Memory and Language* 57:544–569.

Gleitman, L., and A. Papafragou. In press. New perspectives on language and thought. In *Cambridge Handbook of Thinking and Reasoning*, ed. K. Holyoak and B. Morrison. Cambridge: Cambridge University Press.

Göksun, T., K. Hirsh-Pasek, and R. M. Golinkoff. 2010. Trading spaces: Carving up events for learning language. *Perspectives on Psychological Science* 5:33–42.

Goldin-Meadow, S. 1985. Language development under atypical learning conditions: Replication and implications of a study of deaf children of hearing parents. In *Children's Language*, vol. 5, ed. K. Nelson, 197–245. Hillsdale, NJ: Erlbaum.

Golinkoff, R. M. 1975. Semantic development in infants: The concepts of agent and recipient. *Merrill-Palmer Quarterly* 21:181–193.

Golinkoff, R. M., and J. L. Kerr. 1978. Infants' perception of semantically defined action role changes in filmed events. *Merrill-Palmer Quarterly* 24:53–61.

Gordon, P. 2003. The origin of argument structure in infant event representations. In *Proceedings of the 26th Boston University Conference on Language Development*, ed. B. Skarabela, S. Fish, and A. H.-J.Do, 189–198. Somerville, MA: Cascadilla Press.

Griffin, Z., and K. Bock. 2000. What the eyes say about speaking. *Psychological Science* 11:274–279.

Hafri, A., A. Papafragou, and J. Trueswell. 2011. The gist of events: Implications for language production and scene description. Poster presented at the CUNY Conference on Human Sentence Processing, Stanford University, March 24–26.

Hafri, A., A. Papafragou, and J. C. Trueswell. 2013. Getting the gist of events: Recognition of two-participant actions from brief displays. *Journal of Experimental Psychology: General* 142: 880–905.

Hayward, W. G., and M. J. Tarr. 1995. Spatial language and spatial representation. *Cognition* 55:39–84.

Jackendoff, R. 1990. *Semantic Structures*. Cambridge, MA: MIT Press.

Jackendoff, R. 1996. The architecture of the linguistic-spatial interface. In *Language and Space*, ed. P. Bloom, M. Peterson, L. Nadel, and M. Garrett, 1–30. Cambridge, MA: MIT Press.

Johansson, G. 1973. Visual perception of biological motion and a model for its analysis. *Perception & Psychophysics* 14:201–211.

Kable, J. W., and A. Chatterjee. 2006. Specificity of action representations in the lateral occipitotemporal cortex. *Journal of Cognitive Neuroscience* 18:1498–1517.

Lange, J., and M. Lappe. 2006. A model of biological motion perception from configural form cues. *Journal of Neuroscience* 26:2894–2906.

Lashley, K. S. 1951. The problem of serial order in behavior. In *Cerebral Mechanisms in Behavior*, ed. L. A. Jeffress, 112–136. New York: Wiley.

Levelt, W. 1989. *Speaking*. Cambridge, MA: MIT Press.

Levin, B., and S. Pinker. 1991. Introduction. In Lexical and conceptual semantics, special issue, *Cognition* 41:1–7.

Levin, B., and M. Rappaport Hovav. 2005. *Argument Realization*. Cambridge: Cambridge University Press.

Levinson, S. C. 1996. Frames of reference and Molyneux's question: Crosslinguistic evidence. In *Language and Space*, ed. P. Bloom, M. Peterson, L. Nadel, and M. Garrett, 109–170. Cambridge, MA: MIT Press.

Levinson, S. C. 2003. *Space in Language and Cognition*. Cambridge: Cambridge University Press.

Loftus, G. 1972. Eye fixations and recognition memory for pictures. *Cognitive Psychology* 3:525–551.

Maguire, M., K. Hirsh-Pasek, R. M. Golinkoff, M. Imai, E. Haryu, S. Vengas, H. Okada, R. Pulverman, and B. Sanchez-Davis. 2010. A developmental shift from similar to language specific strategies in verb acquisition: A comparison of English, Spanish, and Japanese. *Cognition* 114:299–319.

Majid, A., M. Bowerman, S. Kita, D. B. Haun, and S. C. Levinson. 2004. Can language restructure cognition? The case for space. *Trends in Cognitive Sciences* 8:108–114.

Malt, B. C., S. Gennari, M. Imai, E. Ameel, N. Tsuda, and A. Majid. 2008. Talking about walking: Biomechanics and the language of locomotion. *Psychological Science* 19:232–240.

Miller, G., and P. Johnson-Laird. 1976. *Language and Perception.* Cambridge, MA: Harvard University Press.

Naigles, L., A. Eisenberg, E. Kako, M. Highter, and N. McGraw. 1998. Speaking of motion: Verb use in English and Spanish. *Language and Cognitive Processes* 13:521–549.

Naigles, L. R., and P. Terrazas. 1998. Motion-verb generalizations in English and Spanish: Influences of language and syntax. *Psychological Science* 9:363–369.

Newcombe, N., and J. Huttenlocher. 2003. *Making Space: The Development of Spatial Representation and Reasoning.* Cambridge, MA: MIT Press.

Newtson, D. 1973. Attribution and the unit of perception of ongoing behavior. *Journal of Personality and Social Psychology* 28:28–38.

Newtson, D. 1976. The perceptual organization of ongoing behavior. *Journal of Experimental Social Psychology* 12:436–450.

Oliva, A. 2005. Gist of the scene. In *Neurobiology of Attention*, ed. L. Itti, G. Rees, and J. K. Tsotsos, 251–257. San Diego: Elsevier Academic Press.

Özçalışkan, Ş., and D. I. Slobin. 1999. Learning how to search for the frog: Expression of manner of motion in English, Spanish, and Turkish. In *Proceedings of the 23rd Annual Boston University Conference on Language Development,* ed. A. Greenhill, H. Littlefield, and C. Tano, 541–552. Somerville, MA: Cascadilla Press.

Özçalışkan, Ş., and D. I. Slobin. 2003. Codability effects on the expression of manner of motion in Turkish and English. In *Studies in Turkish Linguistics*, ed. A. S. Özsoy, D. Akar, M. Nakipoğlu-Demiralp, E. Erguvanlı-Taylan, and A. Aksu-Koç, 259–270. Istanbul: Boğaziçi University Press.

Papafragou, A., J. Hulbert, and J. C. Trueswell. 2008. Does language guide event perception? Evidence from eye movements. *Cognition* 108:155–184.

Papafragou, A., C. Massey, and L. Gleitman. 2002. Shake, rattle, 'n' roll: The representation of motion in thought and language. *Cognition* 84:189–219.

Papafragou, A., C. Massey, and L. R. Gleitman. 2006. When English proposes what Greek presupposes: The linguistic encoding of motion events. *Cognition* 98:B75–B87.

Papafragou, A., and S. Selimis. 2010a. Event categorisation and language: A cross-linguistic study of motion. *Language and Cognitive Processes* 25:224–260.

Papafragou, A., and S. Selimis. 2010b. Lexical and structural biases in the acquisition of motion verbs. *Language Learning and Development* 6:87–115.

Paul, H. [1886] 1970. The sentence as the expression of the combination of several ideas. In *Language and Psychology: Historical Aspects of Psycholinguistics*, ed. A. L. Blumenthal, 34–37. New York: Wiley.

Pinker, S. 1989. *Learnability and Cognition: The Acquisition of Argument Structure*. Cambridge, MA: MIT Press.

Potter, M. C. 1979. Mundane symbolism: The relations among objects, names, and ideas. In *Symbolic Functioning in Childhood*, ed. N. R. Smith and M. B. Franklin, 41–65. Hillsdale, NJ: Erlbaum.

Pruden, S. M., T. Göksun, S. Roseberry, K. Hirsh-Pasek, and R. M. Golinkoff. 2013. Infant categorization of path relations during dynamic events. *Child Development* 84:331–345.

Pulverman, R., R. M. Golinkoff, K. Hirsh-Pasek, and J. Sootsman Buresh. 2008. Manners matter: Infants' attention to manner and path in non-linguistic dynamic events. *Cognition* 108:825–830.

Shipley, T. F., and J. M. Zacks, eds. 2008. *Understanding Events: From Perception to Action*. New York: Oxford University Press.

Skordos, D., and A. Papafragou. 2014. Lexical, syntactic, and semantic-geometric factors in the acquisition of motion predicates. *Developmental Psychology* 50:1985–1998.

Slobin, D. 1996. From "thought and language" to "thinking for speaking." In *Rethinking Linguistic Relativity*, ed. J. Gumperz and S. Levinson, 70–96. New York: Cambridge University Press.

Slobin, D. I. 2003. Language and thought online: Cognitive consequences of linguistic relativity. In *Language in Mind: Advances in the Study of Language and Thought*, ed. D. Gentner and S. Goldin-Meadow, 157–191. Cambridge, MA: MIT Press.

Slobin, D. I. 2004. The many ways to search for a frog: Linguistic typology and the expression of motion events. In *Relating Events in Narrative: Typological and Contextual Perspectives*, ed. S. Strömqvist and L. Verhoeven, 219–257. Mahwah, NJ: Erlbaum.

Smith, L., S. Jones, B. Landau, L. Gershkoff-Stowe, and L. Samuelson. 2002. Object name learning provides on-the-job training for attention. *Psychological Science* 13:13–19.

Spelke, E. S., A. T. Phillips, and A. L. Woodward. 1995. Infants' knowledge of object motion and human action. In *Causal Cognition: A Multidisciplinary Debate*, ed. D. Sperber, D. Premack, and A. Premack, 44–78. New York: Oxford University Press.

Stiles-Davis, J., M. Kritchevsky, and U. Bellugi, eds. 1988. *Spatial Cognition: Brain Bases and Development*. Hillsdale, NJ: Erlbaum.

Talmy, L. 1975. Semantics and syntax of motion. In *Syntax and Semantics*, vol. 4, ed. J. P. Kimball, 181–238. New York: Academic Press.

Talmy, L. 1985. Lexicalization patterns: Semantic structure in lexical forms. In *Grammatical Categories and the Lexicon*, vol. 3, ed. T. Shopen, 57–149. Cambridge: Cambridge University Press.

Talmy, L. 2000. *Typology and Process in Concept Structuring*. Vol. 2, Toward a Cognitive Semantics. Cambridge, MA: MIT Press.

Tranel, D., D. Kemmerer, R. Adolphs, H. Damasio, and A. R. Damasio. 2003. Neural correlates of conceptual knowledge for actions. *Cognitive Neuropsychology* 20:409–432.

Trueswell, J., and A. Papafragou. 2010. Perceiving and remembering events cross-linguistically: Evidence from dual-task paradigms. *Journal of Memory and Language* 63:64–82.

Webb, A., A. Knott, and M. R. MacAskill. 2010. Eye movements during transitive action observation have sequential structure. *Acta Psychologica* 133:51–56.

Whorf, B. L. 1956. *Language, Thought and Reality: Selected Writings of Benjamin Lee Whorf*. Ed. J. B. Carroll. Cambridge, MA: MIT Press.

Wilson, F., A. Papafragou, A. Bunger, and J. Trueswell. 2011. Rapid extraction of event participants in caused motion events. In *Proceedings from the 33rd Annual Meeting of the Cognitive Science Society*, ed. L. Carlson, C. Hoelscher, and T. F. Shipley. Hillsdale, NJ: Erlbaum.

Wilson, F., A. Papafragou, and J. Trueswell. 2011. Mapping event participants to linguistic structure. Poster presented at Structuring the Argument: A Multidisciplinary Workshop on the Mental Representation of Verbal Argument Structure, Paris, September 5–7.

Winawer, J., N. Witthoft, M. C. Frank, L. Wu, and L. Boroditsky. 2007. Russian blues reveal effects of language on color discrimination. *Proceedings of the National Academy of Sciences of the United States of America* 104:7780–7785.

Wundt, W. [1900] 1970. The psychology of the sentence. In *Language and Psychology: Historical Aspects of Psycholinguistics,* ed. A. L. Blumenthal, 20–31. New York: Wiley

Zacks, J. M., B. Tversky, and G. Iyer. 2001. Perceiving, remembering, and communicating structure in events. *Journal of Experimental Psychology: General* 130:29–58.

VI Concepts across Cultures

13   Relations: Language, Epistemologies, Categories, and Concepts

Douglas Medin, bethany ojalehto, Sandra Waxman, and Megan Bang

13.1   Introduction

For centuries, concepts have held a privileged position in inquiries about the nature of knowledge, the dawning of insight and reason, the discovery of language, and the acquisition of mind. Concepts matter, and in this chapter we argue that so does the language we use to describe them and the cultural practices in which we embed them. This position represents something of a shift from studies that have focused on properties of individual category members, such as whether they are good or poor examples of the category (e.g., Rosch and Mervis 1975), or properties of individual categories, such as whether they are subordinate, basic, or superordinate level (as in the classic studies of Rosch et al. 1976). Instead, we will take a more relational perspective, with respect to how our language and how our cultural orientations permeate conceptual behavior.[1]

Our recent work has focused on acquisition and use of concepts pertaining to the biological world and on identifying the role of language, culture, and experience in shaping them. Transparently this requires a cross-cultural and crosslinguistic developmental approach. The work we summarize here represents the efforts of longstanding collaborations with psychologists, linguists, and anthropologists from the United States and abroad. A central theme in our work, and in this chapter, is the variety of ways in which the relation between humans and the rest of the natural world can be conceptualized.

We consider this focal question from two perspectives: How are human beings conceptualized, taxonomically speaking, and how do we understand the relations between

---

1. Although we consider the interactions among concepts, cultural practices, and language, our goal in this chapter is not to resolve broad, longstanding debates about linguistic relativity. In our view, progress on this debate depends on evidence documenting *which* concepts are available in advance of (or in the absence of) language, and *how* these concepts are shaped by the availability within a language of *particular* linguistic devices. The research we present here bears on these questions, but takes no stance on whether the concepts favored by members of one language group are or are not available to members of another.

human beings and the rest of the natural world, ecologically or relationally speaking? We begin with the taxonomic question.

13.2   Biological Categories: Humans, Nonhuman Animals, Plants, and the Hierarchical Relations among Living Things

Young children acquiring biological categories (e.g., human, animal, plant, living thing) must identify not only the content or members of each category, but also the relations among categories. In this section, we focus on these relations, paying special attention to three issues in particular: (1) How do adults and children from diverse communities conceptualize the relation between human and nonhuman animals? (2) How do children come to understand the relation between the plant and animal kingdoms? (3) How are these relations shaped by cultural and linguistic forces?

13.2.1   Animals and the (Special?) Case of Humans

All animals are equal but some animals are more equal than others.

—George Orwell

What is the place of humans in the biological world? This question is intriguing because there is no one "correct" answer. As adults, we answer fluidly. In the context of Western taxonomic science, we see human beings as biological organisms (class Mammalia). In the context of Western religion, human beings typically are seen as distinct from the rest of the biological kingdom (humans alone were created in the image of God; this brings with it a notion of our dominion and the importance of stewardship over other living things). Everyday discourse is full of simile and metaphor involving comparison of humans to other animals ("I'm as hungry as a bear," "Don't eat like an animal"). How do children come to acquire and reconcile these different notions about the (biological) status of humans? As will be seen, there is an intricate interplay between linguistic and conceptual development.

Extensive evidence demonstrates that from infancy, names (and nouns in particular) are a catalyst in the formation of object categories (for evidence from infants, see Waxman and Lidz 2006; for adults, see Goss 1961; Spiker 1956). Infants' ability to form an object category (e.g., animal) when presented with a set of disparate exemplars in the absence of a name (e.g., a dog, a horse, a duck) improves dramatically when these exemplars are introduced with the same name. By fourteen months, this link between naming and object categories is specific to nouns (Echols and Marti 2004; Waxman 1999; Waxman and Booth 2001).

There is also evidence that the concept ANIMAL emerges early in development. Infants are especially interested in animate objects and are captivated by animate properties, including faces, eyes, and autonomous biological motion (Carey, Diamond, and

Woods 1980; Johnson, Slaughter, and Carey 1998; Pascalis, de Haan, and Nelson 2002; Poulin-Dubois and Shultz 1990; Scott and Monesson 2009). By three to five months, babies begin to make a principled distinction between animate and inanimate objects (Bertenthal 1993; Woodward, Sommerville, and Guajardo 2001) and between agents and nonagents (Leslie 1994; Massey and R. Gelman 1988; Newman et al. 2010; Opfer and S. Gelman 2010; see also Luo, Kaufman, and Baillargeon 2009; Pauen and Träuble 2009; Shutts, Markson, and Spelke 2009).

If names serve as invitations to form categories (Waxman and Markow 1995), then the names that children hear for biological entities should support the acquisition of biological concepts (S. Gelman 2003; S. Gelman and Markman 1986; Graham, Kilbreath, and Welder 2004; Waxman and Booth 2001; Waxman et al. 1997). A large body of ethnobiological research provides insights into how the entities in the natural world are named across diverse languages (Berlin 1992), and it shows that most languages name the concept ANIMAL. This, coupled with infants' early predisposition to link names and object concepts, likely supports the early acquisition of ANIMAL.

There is, however, one important complicating factor: the noun *animal* is polysemous. This polysemy has gripped our attention, primarily because it has consequences for children's appreciation of the relation among living things and for understanding where humans fit into the taxonomic scheme for biological kinds.

13.2.2 *Animal* Is Polysemous

For English-speaking adults, *animal* can refer either to an inclusive concept, including all animate beings (as in, "Animals have babies"), or to a more restricted concept, including nonhuman animals but excluding humans (as in, "Don't eat like an animal"). For ease of exposition, we will refer to these two nested concepts, respectively, as ANIMAL$_{inclusive}$ and ANIMAL$_{contrastive}$. Although this polysemous use of *animal* is endemic, the context in which *animal* is used commonly provides strong cues about which sense is intended.

Whatever its source, this type of polysemy could pose developmental challenges: if nouns support the formation of object categories, and if the same name *animal* points to two different but hierarchically related concepts, then it should be difficult for children to settle on its meaning.

A review of the developmental literature suggests that infants may begin to appreciate both concepts—ANIMAL$_{inclusive}$ and ANIMAL$_{contrastive}$—within the first year. Although infants and children include both humans and nonhuman animals in a concept organized around *animacy* or *agency* (Massey and R. Gelman 1988; Opfer and S. Gelman 2010; see Luo, Kaufman, and Baillargeon 2009 for discussion), they also distinguish between humans and nonhuman animals (Scott and Monesson 2009; Vouloumanos et al. 2009, 2010).

If both of these underlying concepts are represented by toddlers, which do they take to be the referent of *animal*? We have pursued this question with several different methods, from interviewing children, observing their performance in categorization tasks, and analyzing the language input they receive from their parents.

Our studies with English-speaking children suggest that they typically interpret *animal* in the contrastive sense. For example, we asked five-year-old children to name "all the animals you can think of." Children named a wide variety of animals, ranging from mammals to insects, but not a single child included humans (or "people") in their list (Winkler-Rhoades et al. 2010). We also asked three- and five-year-olds directly whether humans "are animals," and both age groups overwhelmingly denied that humans are animals. By nine years of age, roughly 40 percent of the children agreed that the name *animal* could be applied to humans (Leddon et al. 2012). In short, English-speaking children favor the contrastive sense of the term *animal*.

We also designed an experimental task to ask under what conditions young children might engage the overarching ANIMAL~inclusive~ concept (Herrmann, Medin, and Waxman 2012). We used the link between naming and object categorization as an opportunity to explore three- and five-year-old children's representations of ANIMAL. In this task, we presented children with two distinct training items, labeled them with the same novel noun, and then probed children's extensions of that noun to a range of other entities. In the first study, both training items were nonhuman animals; in the second, training items included one human and one nonhuman animal. At issue is whether they would spontaneously extend the noun to include humans along with nonhuman animals as members of the same overarching ANIMAL~inclusive~ concept.

Our materials included laminated photographs depicting humans, nonhuman animals, and inanimate objects (plants, nonliving natural kinds, artifacts). To begin, the researcher presented each card, in random order, helping the child to identify the object it depicted. Next, the experimenter introduced a hand puppet (Pinky), explaining that Pinky lived far away and used "funny words for things." The experimenter then pointed to the two training items (dog, bird) in random order, saying, "Pinky calls these both *blickets*. This one is a *blicket,* and this one is a *blicket*." The experimenter then presented each test photograph in random order, asking, "Does Pinky call this one a *blicket*?"

As expected, both three- and five-year-old children extended the novel noun to the test items that matched the training items and to the other nonhuman animals, excluding the inanimate entities. But neither the three- nor five-year-olds spontaneously extended the novel noun to include humans. In fact, they were just as unlikely to say "yes" to a human as to an inanimate object. In other words, children favored the ANIMAL~contrastive~ category. Nonetheless, this does not preclude the possibility that they also represent the more inclusive sense.

We pursued this possibility by introducing another group of children to a novel noun for a human and either a bird or a dog. Otherwise, the stimulus materials and procedure were identical to those from before. For half of the children, a human and a dog served as training items; for the others, a human and bird served as the training items. We reasoned that if three- and five-year-olds do have access to ANIMAL$_{inclusive}$, they might engage it in this naming context.

Including a human as a training item had a dramatic effect. The three-year-olds' performance fell to chance. Their unsystematic extension of the novel word signaled their difficulty accessing an overarching concept including both human and nonhuman animals. In contrast, five-year-olds extended the novel noun systematically, this time including both human and nonhuman animals. This illustrates their appreciation of ANIMAL$_{inclusive}$.

The fact that three- and five-year-olds did not spontaneously include humans in the first study suggests that humans are not prototypical animals, at least not for preschool-aged children. That three-year-olds had trouble including human and nonhuman animals in the same (newly) named category in the second study underscores the developmental challenge they face in identifying the scope of ANIMAL.

Does parents' use of language provide children with some help in identifying the relation between human and nonhuman animals? The answer seems to be no (Leddon, Waxman, and Medin, 2011). Parents of young English-speaking children offer considerable support for the concept ANIMAL$_{contrastive}$ by typically using *animal* to refer to nonhuman animals. But they offer scant support for ANIMAL$_{inclusive}$; only rarely do they invoke the term *animal* to refer to humans. This discourse practice likely highlights the uniqueness of humans and fortifies the distinction between human and nonhuman animals, but provides little support for the overarching ANIMAL$_{inclusive}$ concept spanning them.

Taking yet another tack on the conceptual polysemy, we shifted to a crosslinguistic approach, specifically focusing on the contrast between English and Indonesian. In Indonesian, *animal* is not polysemous. This has significant and sometimes counterintuitive cognitive consequences. Our work in Indonesia has been a venture with our former student Flo Anggoro (e.g., Anggoro, Waxman, and Medin 2008). Before turning to these studies, we need to broaden our conceptual focus to the concept LIVING THING.

There is strong consensus that appreciation of the concept LIVING THING (members of the plant and animal kingdoms) is a late and laborious developmental achievement. Piaget (1954) noted young children's tendency to mistakenly attribute life status to inanimate objects that appear to move on their own or to exhibit goal-directed behavior (e.g., clouds). He interpreted this "childhood animism" as a reflection of children's inchoate grasp of concepts such as ANIMAL and LIVING THING. More recent evidence indicates that even ten-year-old children have difficulty understanding the scope of LIVING THING (Hatano et al. 1993).[2]

Our studies show that how these concepts are named in a given language shapes their acquisition. The work in Indonesia provides a case in point. In Indonesian, *animal* refers to ANIMAL$_{contrastive}$; it cannot be applied to humans. The more inclusive ANIMAL$_{inclusive}$ concept remains unnamed. To examine how this crosslinguistic difference affects children's acquisition of concepts of the natural world, we recruited monolingual Indonesian-speaking children (in Jakarta) and monolingual English-speaking children (from the greater Chicago area) from urban elementary schools.

Because adult interpretations of word meanings may not mirror precisely those of children, we began by asking how Indonesian-speaking children interpret the word *animal*. The interview was identical to the one used earlier: an experimenter presented Indonesian six- and nine-year-old children with a photograph of a human and asked, "Could you call this an 'animal'?" ("Mungkinkah ini 'hewan'?"). Indonesian-speaking children uniformly endorsed the ANIMAL$_{contrastive}$ view. Recall that although English-speaking children from three to five years also favored ANIMAL$_{contrastive}$, by nine years of age, roughly 40 percent endorsed the ANIMAL$_{inclusive}$ interpretation.

To ascertain whether this difference in naming practices is reflected in children's conceptual organization, we designed two sorting tasks. In the first, we presented six- and nine-year-old children with a set of picture cards representing humans, nonhuman animals, or plants and invited them to place "the kinds of things that belong together in the same pile." If naming a concept facilitates its access, then the concept ANIMAL$_{inclusive}$ should be more accessible to English- than Indonesian-speaking children, and among the English-speaking children, it should be more accessible to older than younger children (see Anggoro, Waxman, and Medin 2008 for details).

As predicted, English-speaking children were more likely than their Indonesian-speaking counterparts to spontaneously place humans and nonhuman animals in the same category, and among the English-speaking children, nine-year-olds were more likely to do so than six-year-olds. These results suggest that children's spontaneous categorizations reflect their appreciation of the naming practices in their communities.

Next we used a more tightly structured categorization task, this time tapping into English- and Indonesian-speaking children's appreciation of the overarching concept LIVING THING. A chief goal of this study was to test Waxman's (2005) prediction about the relation between naming and the establishment of biological categories. Before presenting the prediction, a bit of background is necessary. Attributing life status to plants is a late developmental achievement. When English-speaking children are asked to sort objects on the basis of which ones are "alive," they systematically exclude plants

2. Later on, we consider the idea that natural inanimates like *rock* and *water* may be animates in other cultural schemes.

(Carey 1985; Piaget [1929] 1973; Richards and Siegler 1984; Waxman 2005). Moreover, in Japanese and Hebrew—two other languages in which the word denoting the concept ANIMAL is polysemous—children also tend to deny that plants are alive (Hatano et al. 1993; Stavy and Wax 1989). This observation, coupled with evidence that children avoid polysemy whenever possible, suggests that children should be open to aligning a word other than *animal* with the ANIMAL_inclusive concept, should a suitable candidate arise.

By Waxman's conjecture, that candidate is "alive." If English-speaking children (mis)align the word *alive* to the concept ANIMAL_inclusive, then they should have more difficulty than Indonesian-speaking children in learning the broader meaning of *alive*. By misaligning this word with ANIMAL_inclusive, they miss the insight that plants, too, are alive. Paradoxically, this difference between languages might be more pronounced in older children (nine-year-olds), for whom ANIMAL_inclusive is more firmly established.

We can now return to the structured sorting task. Children were presented with a set of cards depicting humans, nonhuman animals, plants, and artifacts, and asked to sort these cards three different times, on the basis of three different predicates—*alive, die, grow*—each of which applies to all living things. Because our primary focus was on *alive*, that predicate was always presented first, followed by the other two, in random order. If children appreciate an overarching concept LIVING THING, they should consistently distinguish the living from the nonliving entities. By comparing the sorting patterns of English- and Indonesian-speaking children, we were able to consider the consequences of polysemous and nonpolysemous *animal*.

There were two main findings. First, English- and Indonesian-speaking children's performance with the predicates *grow* and *die* showed an appreciation of the concept LIVING THING. Second, their performance with *alive* revealed special interpretive difficulties for English-speaking children, and especially at the older ages, exactly in accordance with Waxman's conjecture (English-speaking children were less likely than their Indonesian counterparts to include plants under *alive*.) Interestingly, it is not that English-speaking children were in the dark about properties of plants. In fact, they were more likely than Indonesian-speaking children to recognize that plants die and grow. Instead, it is specifically the meaning of *alive* that is harder for English-speaking children to grasp—they misalign *alive* to the node of human and nonhuman animals.

This work shows that the way in which biological concepts are named influences their acquisition. What remains unanswered is whether this difference between children acquiring Indonesian and English is attributable to the polysemy of *animal* (English) or the unnamed status of ANIMAL_inclusive (Indonesian). Answers will rest on evidence from languages that name the ANIMATE node, but in which the name is not polysemous. For example, Czech appears to be one such language: ANIMAL_inclusive is named (*živočich*), and this name is distinct from that for ANIMAL_contrastive (*zvíře*). That is a task for future work.

We have focused thus far on how children from distinct linguistic communities establish fundamental biological concepts and discover the relations among them. With this as background, we now consider how children use these biological kinds in inductive reasoning, and the role of language, culture, and expertise in reasoning.

13.3   Reasoning about Biological Kinds

We begin with a small detour. The evidence so far suggests that children have difficulty conceptualizing humans as animals, and, at best, see humans as atypical or unusual members of the animal category. This latter observation seems to imply that the category HUMAN BEING would make a poor base for generalizing (biological) properties to other biological organisms. So, for example, if I told you that humans have some property X and that dogs have some property Y and asked you whether it is more likely that squirrels also have property X or property Y, you might expect most bets to be placed on Y, because X could be some peculiarly human sort of thing. Surprisingly, however, there is a body of research and theory that comes to just the opposite conclusion: that for young children, humans are the prototype or paragon for inductive biological reasoning, and that this human-centered focus is only overturned between five and seven years of age, when children come to reason more like adults, seeing humans as an atypical instance of animal (Carey 1985).

This shift has been interpreted within a domain-specific view of human cognition. A trend in the cognitive and developmental sciences has been a shift from viewing cognition as a domain-general, general-purpose learning and thinking system to seeing cognition as a set of domain-specific mechanisms that are specialized in their processes (Cosmides, Tooby, and Barkow 1992; Medin, Lynch, and Solomon 2000). That is, learning may be guided by certain (possibly innate) skeletal principles, constraints, and assumptions about the world (e.g., R. Gelman 1990; Keil 1981; Spelke 1990). In an important book, Carey (1985) developed a theory of concept learning as built on framework theories that entail ontological commitments in the service of a causal understanding of real-world phenomena.

That's quite a mouthful; basically it means that different causal principles may operate in different domains. Consider, for example, an event in which a baseball shatters a window. The relevant features and rules underlying our appreciation of the *physical* aspect of this event (e.g., force mechanics) are quite different from the relevant features and rules that underlie our understanding of the *social* or *psychological* aspects of the same event (e.g., blame, responsibility). Developmentalists have argued that (at least) three distinct domains guide children's development of knowledge: physical processes and events (naïve or folk physics), biological processes and events (naïve or folk biology) and psychological events and processes (naïve or folk psychology).

For Carey (1985, 2009), a key childhood achievement consists of developing a (naïve) biology distinct from naïve psychology. For Western adults who tend to endorse a dualism between mind and body, psychology and biology are distinct domains with distinct causal principles. Eating a candy bar can give someone instant energy, but it will not make them a sweeter person. Carey (1985) argued that (young) children have not yet carved out a domain for biological processes. Instead, biological processes are initially interpreted within the domain of naïve psychology.

That's a strong claim, and Carey (1985) offered some striking evidence to support it. There are two steps to her argument. The first step to note is that though humans may not be prototypical within a biological domain, they are the premier psychological beings. The second step is to show that children's biological reasoning is organized around humans as the prototype. If this is the case, it would support the idea that children's biological reasoning is organized in terms of psychology.

The strongest evidence for a human-centered stance in young children's biological reasoning comes from Carey's own pioneering research (Carey 1985). In an inductive generalization task involving children (ranging from four to ten years of age) and adults from Boston, participants were introduced to a novel biological property (e.g., "has an omentum"), taught that this property is true of one biological kind (human, dog, or bee), and then a few days later asked whether other entities might have this property.

Carey reported dramatic developmental changes in inductive reasoning. If the novel property had been introduced as true of a human, four- to five-year-olds generalized, or projected, that property broadly to other biological kinds as a function of their similarity to humans. But if the identical property was introduced in conjunction with a dog or bee, four- to five-year-olds made relatively few generalizations to other animals. This produced a pattern of generalization that violates intuitive notions of similarity. For example, four- to five-year-olds generalized more from human to bug (stinkoo) than from bee to bug. Overall, Carey (1985) provided two strong indices of anthropocentric reasoning: (1) projections from humans to other animals were stronger than projections from dog or bee; and (2) there were strong asymmetries in projections to and from humans (e.g., inferences from human to dog were stronger than from dog to human).

Older children and adults gave no indications of anthropocentric reasoning. Instead they tended to generalize novel biological properties broadly from one biological kind to another, whether the property had been introduced as a property of a human or nonhuman (dog, bee) animal. Moreover, they showed no human-animal asymmetries in their reasoning. These data suggest that for older children and adults, reasoning about the biological world is organized around a concept of animal that includes both human and nonhuman animals.

Carey (1985; Carey and Spelke 1994) has argued forcefully from these data that young children hold a qualitatively different understanding of biological phenomena from that of adults. Carey (1985) entitled her book *Conceptual Change in Childhood* because her data suggested that children begin with a human-centered, psychological understanding of biology and later on must reorganize their conceptual system to reflect the understanding that, biologically speaking, humans are one kind among many.

13.3.1   A Place for Language

With these striking results as background, we are ready to turn to the role of language in children's inductive reasoning. Recall that Indonesian, unlike English, has no dedicated name for the overarching category of animate beings. Our first question (Anggoro, Medin, and Waxman 2010) was whether the ANIMAL_contrastive term in Indonesian would limit generalization of properties from humans and (other) animals and vice versa.

Following Carey, we employed a category-based induction task in which children are introduced to a novel property of an entity (the base), and then asked whether this property can be generalized to other entities (the targets). Human-nonhuman animal asymmetries should be attenuated in Indonesian-speaking children, if evident at all. Indonesian children's tendency to generalize from either a human or a nonhuman animal base should be associated with the distinctive category of the target (human or nonhuman animal).

The predictions for English-speaking children are a bit more complex. We suspected that when a nonhuman animal serves as the base, English-speaking children would favor the ANIMAL_contrastive category. Put differently, when a property is attributed to a nonhuman animal base and a human appears as the target, English-speaking children may be reluctant to generalize on grounds that "people are not animals" (this is the ANIMAL_contrastive interpretation). In contrast, when a human serves as the base, English-speaking children may access the ANIMAL_inclusive category. This category should support their generalization from a human base to nonhuman animal targets. That is, children should be less likely to make the appeal that "animals are not people." In sum, English-speaking children's access to the ANIMAL_inclusive category (a category that should be less available to Indonesian-speaking children) may account for their asymmetries favoring generalizations from humans than from nonhuman animals (see Medin and Waxman 2007 for related arguments and evidence).

Finally, because factors other than naming practices shape children's biological reasoning, we expected that the differences between English- and Indonesian-speaking children's patterns of induction would become less pronounced as children from both communities gain access to other sources of information about biological phenomena. That is, cultural practices (including naming) may have the strongest effects on the youngest children; as children get older and are exposed to a broader range of biologically relevant information, these effects may be attenuated.

Colored photographs depicting a range of living and nonliving entities served as stimuli. Four of the living things were bases; the remaining photographs were targets. We selected items that were familiar to both Chicago and Jakarta children.

Because procedural details will prove to be important, we're going to describe the task in more detail than we might otherwise. To begin, the experimenter showed the first base (e.g., a dog) and said, for example, "Dogs have some stuff inside them, and it is called *sacra*. *Sacra* is inside some kinds of things, but it is *not* inside some other kinds of things." She then presented each target picture (e.g., a bear) and asked, "Do you think bears have *sacra* inside like dogs do?" Then a different base was selected, and children were told about a different novel property (e.g., *belga*) it had and were asked what else might have it and so on for the other two bases.

We found that when a human served as the base, English-speaking children were more likely than Indonesian-speaking children to generalize to nonhuman animal target categories, but when a nonhuman animal served as the base, English- and Indonesian-speaking children performed comparably. This is exactly as predicted. These differences were much attenuated among nine-year-olds, consistent with the prediction that, with or without a dedicated name for the category that includes human and nonhuman animals, as children acquire more biological knowledge, they bring human and nonhuman animals into closer correspondence.

A closer look at children's performance as they progressed through this task revealed an intriguing finding. Thus far, we have interpreted our results as evidence that when English- and older Indonesian-speaking children are introduced to a novel property on a human base and asked to generalize to a nonhuman animal target, their access to the ANIMAL$_{inclusive}$ category results in asymmetries favoring humans. We further reasoned as follows: if this is the case, then perhaps the salience of this category will influence children's performance on subsequent trials. If on the child's first trial, a human happens to serve as the base, perhaps their use of the ANIMAL$_{inclusive}$ category would carry over to subsequent trials when a human serves as the target. But if on the child's first trial, a nonhuman animal happens to serve as the base, then their use of the ANIMAL$_{contrastive}$ category could carry over to subsequent trials.

To test this possibility, we analyzed the effect of order (human base first versus later) on children's performance. When a human was the base for the first trial, English-speaking six- and nine-year-olds and Indonesian-speaking nine-year-olds generalized strongly from a human to nonhuman animals (overall $M = 0.67$), but when the human base was introduced in subsequent trials (after human had been a target), they were much less likely to do so (overall $M = 0.37$). That is, the human-nonhuman animal asymmetries were much stronger if a human served as the initial base.

One reason order effects are important is that several claims about producing different results from Carey's (including some of our own) also have differed by, unlike Carey, using multiple bases. Consequently, it isn't clear whether the different patterns observed in other studies reflect order effects associated with multiple bases or deeper differences associated with different study populations.

In summary, young children's reasoning about this biological relation is influenced by naming practices, and this influence is attenuated over development. Clearly, then, children's biological reasoning is influenced by factors other than language alone. The developmental attenuation likely reflects the influence of learning experiences beyond naming practices. Of course, the children in Jakarta are exposed not only to a Western curriculum, but also to Western-inspired media (e.g., movies) that adopt an anthropocentric model of nonhuman animals. We'll take up this idea again shortly.

13.3.2 Responses to Carey's Arguments

Carey's provocative claims about biological reasoning stimulated a great deal of research. Some of the research showed that young children appreciate some distinctively biological mechanisms, such as growth (Hickling and S. Gelman 1995) and inheritance (e.g., Hirschfeld and S. Gelman 1994; see also S. Gelman 2003). One intriguing suggestion is that young children do begin with a distinctively biological framework theory, but it is based on the principle of "vitalistic energy" (Hatano and Inagaki 2000; Inagaki and Hatano 2002). The researchers proposed that cultural models espoused within a community shape children's biological reasoning. Their studies revealed that five- to eight-year-old Japanese children understand many bodily processes in terms of vitalism—a causal model pervasive in Japan and one that relies on the distinctly biological concept of energy. We will take up this notion of cultural models and biology again after a modest detour.

One of the most contested domain distinctions, and one that has generated a great deal of research, is that between psychology and biology.

13.3.2.1 Expertise

In the mid- to late 1990s, we teamed with cognitive anthropologist Scott Atran and a cadre of bright graduate students and postdocs to explore the role of culture and expertise in people's understanding of biology (Atran and Medin 2008). Our interest in expertise was driven by two main factors. One consisted of close parallels between Itza' Maya elders and U.S. biological experts who differed from the Maya elders in almost everything but biological expertise (Bailenson et al. 2002; Lopez et al. 1997; Medin et al. 1997; Proffitt, Coley, and Medin 2000). The other was corresponding evidence of *devolution*, or loss of biological knowledge in technologically saturated cultures such as the United States (e.g., Wolff, Medin, and Pankratz 1999).

An ingenious study by Inagaki and Hatano also pointed to the importance of experience and expertise. Inagaki and Hatano (Inagaki 1990; Inagaki and Hatano 2002) found that urban children raised in Tokyo who were closely involved with raising goldfish generalized biological facts to kinds similar to humans *and* to kinds similar to goldfish. This suggests that the relative advantage for humans over nonhuman animals as bases for induction derives from children's greater willingness to generalize from a familiar base than from an unfamiliar base. Although they did not use Carey's induction task, the anthropocentric pattern produced by urban Japanese children who did *not* raise goldfish converged well with her (1985) results. But the full pattern of results points to a different interpretation—urban children's tendency to treat humans as a privileged base may be driven by the fact that humans are the only biological kind that they know much about.

Observations like these may offer insights into children's behavior in Carey's induction task. We began to suspect that five-year-olds' human-centered reasoning patterns might reflect urban children's lack of knowledge about and intimate contact with the natural world. To pursue this idea, we employed Carey's inductive reasoning task with rural children, who presumably have "more." As we anticipated, four- to five-year-old rural children did not exhibit the asymmetries and human-centered reasoning that Carey had noted in their urban counterparts (e.g., Atran et al. 2001; Ross et al. 2003).

Medin and Waxman recall chatting with Susan Carey about these expertise effects. She offered two responses as challenges: (1) maybe all children pass through a human-centered stage but rural children do it sooner, and (2) by the way, no one had used a procedure close enough to hers to convincingly demonstrate a different pattern of results.

As we noted in reporting the Anggoro, Medin, and Waxman (2010) order effects, this second issue is not just an in principle one. Carey's procedure involved teaching a child about only one base and then bringing them back a few days later for generalization tests. In contrast, typically after using one base and one novel biological property, we went on to present another base and a new property, followed by a new set of generalization tests, and so on. Notice that these design differences (coupled with the order effects observed in Anggoro, Medin, and Waxman) raise the possibility that we might indeed have seen human-centered reasoning if we had followed Carey's procedure more closely.

We therefore adopted a closer approximation to Carey's original procedure in a series of follow-up studies with urban children, rural European American children, and rural Menominee (Native American) children. Following Carey, we taught children only about a single base and gave the generalization test a day or two later. Here's what we found (see Medin et al. 2010; Waxman and Medin 2007). First, we replicated Carey's (1985) pattern of human-centered reasoning for the urban four- to five-year-olds. These young children showed greater generalization for a human base than for a dog base, and they also showed greater generalization from human to dog than from dog to human. Second, unlike their urban counterparts, four- and five-year-old rural European American children generalized more from a dog base than from a human base. Interestingly, however, they did show greater generalization from a human base to a dog target than from a dog base to a human target. Third, and somewhat surprisingly, like their urban counterparts, four- to five-year-old Menominee children favored the human over the dog as a base when generalizing a novel property to other animals. In part, this may reflect the cultural significance of bears: generalizations from human to bear are especially strong (86%) for four- to five-year-old Menominee children, compared with the urban (67%) and rural European American (52%) children. But in contrast with urban children, young Menominee children showed no evidence of human-dog asymmetries.

In summary, we followed Carey's method with enough fidelity to replicate her finding of human-centered reasoning in four- to five-year-old urban children. With worries about procedure more or less out of the way, we found that neither rural European American children nor rural Menominee children demonstrated Carey's two markers of anthropocentrism (human-animal asymmetries and humans as a more effective base than animals).

These results have two key implications. First, human-centered reasoning in four- and five-year-old children is far from universal. Second, the two signatures of anthropocentric reasoning in Carey's account—generalization and asymmetries—do not necessarily tap into a single underlying model or construal of biological phenomena.

These results leave Carey's first point intact. Perhaps our rural children did indeed go through the stage of a human-centered biology, but passed through it earlier than urban children. The obvious way to address this question is to run younger rural children. But there's a problem—for a task like this, four years old is about as young as one can go and still get meaningful data. Three- and four-year-old children may answer the various induction questions, but may say "no" (or "yes") to everything.

To accommodate children as young as three years of age, we took our cue from developmental studies using puppets. Rather than having an experimenter provide the information, we used puppets to do so (Herrmann, Waxman, and Medin 2010). We introduced two small puppets, and in a warm-up period, showed children that each puppet was "right some of the time and wrong some of the time." In the induction task the two puppets disagreed, and the child was enlisted to cast the deciding vote. With this method (and an experimenter who has excellent rapport), three-year-olds provided systematic, meaningful data.

13.3.2.2 Cultural Models Matter We began this series of studies by focusing on three- and five-year-old urban children. We reasoned that if the human-centered reasoning pattern seen in young urban children represents the acquisition of a culturally transmitted anthropocentric model, it may be the case that urban children younger than four to five years old, who have received less exposure to the anthropocentric model, would not (yet) favor humans over nonhuman animals in their reasoning.

And that is what we found (Herrmann, Waxman, Medin 2010). Three-year-old urban children responded systematically, generalizing more from a dog base than from a human base and showing no reliable human-dog asymmetries. Moreover, with this modified puppet procedure, urban five-year-olds continue to show the now-familiar anthropocentric reasoning pattern (greater generalization from human than dog base; human-dog asymmetries). We have also used the puppet procedure with four- to five-year-old rural European American and Menominee children, just in case these design modifications change their patterns of performance. In this task, children show neither of the markers of a human-centered biology.

These results offer unambiguous evidence that the anthropocentric pattern of reasoning observed in urban five-year-old children is not an obligatory initial step in reasoning about the biological world. Instead, the results show that anthropocentrism is an acquired perspective, one that emerges between three and five years of age in American children raised in urban settings.

13.3.2.3 Summary of Induction Studies Our initial singular focus on biological expertise or lack thereof got in the way of our seeing the importance of cultural models embodying different relationships between humans and the rest of nature. Carey (1985) may have been correct in thinking that biological cognition may involve competing, incommensurable models, but we suggest that these are competing cultural models, not some acultural naïve psychology competing with an acultural naïve biology.

We now turn to the question of where humans fit with the rest of nature from an ecological and relational perspective.

13.4   Concepts of Human-Nature Relations: Ecological Reasoning

So far we have examined how the concept HUMAN is relationally positioned within broader linguistic and knowledge frameworks. We now turn to explore how what we will refer to as *epistemological orientations* affect conceptual behavior. We explore how concepts are informed by local ecological and cultural contexts, focusing on contrasts between Indigenous and majority culture communities.

Much of our thinking about human orientations to nature is grounded in a set of cultural frameworks known as *relational epistemologies*. Our notion of epistemological orientations is based on research in anthropology and in education, and this may differ somewhat from philosophical notions of epistemology. We think of relational epistemologies as sets of (often implicit) assumptions that inform skeletal principles of reasoning. Specifically, we assume, *epistemological orientations reflect the decisions, processes, and practices that determine the nature of observation, ideas about what is worthy of attention and in need of explanation (or understanding) as well as the kinds of hypotheses that are likely to be considered, and notions of what constitutes a satisfactory explanation.* On our account, epistemologies are reflected in cultural practices (in our case for engaging with nature) and these cultural practices, in turn, affect epistemological orientations.

In what follows, we describe just what aspects of Indigenous epistemologies make them *relational* epistemologies.

Note that our use of *relational epistemologies* is plural,[3] as are the Indigenous communities with whom we collaborate (e.g., Native Americans in Chicago; Indigenous Ngöbe in Panama; members of the Menominee Nation in Wisconsin). This signals our commitment to cognitive and cultural diversity within the realm of *relational frameworks*.

As a broad framework theory, relational epistemologies vary in their particulars across different geographical and cultural communities; their coherence obtains in common signatures of *relationality* structuring modes of attention to and interaction with the world. We focus on relational frameworks grounded in Indigenous Amerindian cultures, in an approach consistent with that offered by Raymond Pierotti (2011):

> The influence of local places on cultures and the corresponding diversity of peoples attached to those places guarantee the existence of variation. ... Despite this spatial variation in ecology and physical space there appears to exist a fundamental shared way of thinking and a concept of community common to Indigenous peoples of North America. (5)

We will have more to say about this in our concluding discussion, along with some observations on domain-specific causal frameworks.

Part of the power of relational epistemologies derives from their capacity to channel everyday practices and patterns of attention. Organizing knowledge along particular habitual lines of thinking changes how one attends to the environment, as patterns of expectation train our awareness, leading us to see the world in different ways. For example, if one thinks of plants as unthinking, deaf-and-dumb organisms, one will hardly be attuned to potential signs of plant communication. In contrast, attending to multiple signs of agency in plants creates the conditions for observing complex patterns of reaction, memory, anticipation, and response among the vegetal world.

The studies on relational orientations described below were conducted among Menominee, Chicago intertribal, and Ngöbe Indigenous communities.

Rural Menominee population The Menominee are the oldest continuous residents of Wisconsin. Historically, their lands covered much of Wisconsin but were reduced, treaty by treaty, until the present 95,000 hectares was reached in 1854. The present site was forested then and now—there are currently about 88,000 hectares of forest. Sustainable coexistence with nature is a strong value (Hall and Pecore 1995). Hunting and fishing are important activities, and children are familiar with both by age twelve. There are four to five thousand Menominee living on tribal lands. Over 60 percent of

3. As we will see shortly, this move is also consistent with anthropological theory on *relational epistemologies* plural (see Bird-David 1999).

Menominee adults have at least a high school education, and 15 percent have had some college.

American Indian Center of Chicago population There are approximately forty thousand Indian people in Cook County, many of whom were relocated to the area in the 1950s and 1960s, during the federal relocation era. The Chicago community is quite diverse, with individuals representing more than one hundred tribes from across the country. Native American children are scattered across a number of schools in the district and are a minority in every classroom. The AIC is the oldest urban Indian center in the country and serves as the social and cultural center of the Chicago Indian community. Menominee and other Wisconsin tribes are well represented at the AIC.

Ngöbe population The Ngöbe people of Panama are the largest Indigenous group in Central America after the Maya, with a present population of approximately 170,000 (Young unpublished ms.). We have been conducting community-based research with the Ngöbe for almost three years, and one of us has spent more than fifteen months living in the village. The Ngöbe community that collaborates with us in our research has about six hundred habitants and is located on a heavily forested island off the Caribbean coast of Panama. Community members live in family hamlets and practice agroforestry supplemented by hunting, fishing, diving, artisan crafts, or periodic wage labor (primarily in connection with the ecotourism industry and a few nearby resorts). The community hosts two Christian evangelical churches as well as the Ngöbe syncretistic Mama Tata Church. The village has a public school offering primary and partial secondary education. In most families, children are expected to achieve competence in domains beyond that of formal schooling, including farming, fishing, childcare, and other household contributions. Most families speak both Spanish and Ngöbere (the native language) in the home. Our research has been conducted in both languages.

13.4.1 Practicing Relational Epistemology: Engaging Human-Nature Relations

Different cultures have arrived at different ideas concerning the quality and extent of relations between humans and the rest of the natural world. For a child, figuring out the relation between humans and nonhuman animals depends largely on the kinds of relations their own community entertains with the nonhuman world. We have begun to explore how young children are educated into different sets of relations with the natural world through the values and activities of their communities (Bang, Medin, and Atran 2007). In a study comparing parental values, Native Americans (both Menominee and urban Natives) and rural European American parents were asked what they believed was important for their children to learn about nature and the biological world. As compared to European American parents, Native parents' values reflected more spiritual orientations (talking in terms of "Mother Earth"), holism (children should understand that they are a part of nature), and traditional values (activities that are important to pass on to future generations). While the majority of parents across communities emphasized moral values and respect for nature, European American parents tended to emphasize caregiver relations with nature (children should learn to "protect" nature), a model that reflects the stance that humans are apart from nature. In contrast, Native parents tended to focus on how people are "a part of" nature and children should learn their place and role within the world.

These self-reported values are not merely ideals but correlate with the kinds of activities children experience within their communities. Further interviews with children and parents in these same communities revealed cultural differences in practices involving nature (Bang, Medin, and Atran 2007). Native parents and children report engaging more frequently in outdoor practices that foreground nature (e.g., berry picking, forest walks) while European Americans engage relatively more in backgrounding outdoor practices (e.g., snowmobiling, playing sports). Even within the same practice type (e.g., fishing), there are significant differences in configurations of practice (e.g., fishing from a boat on a lake versus fishing on the shore of a river) that affect attentional habits and the range of content taken up in discourse and other practices (Bang 2009). These findings suggest that cultural values feed directly into the activity structures and everyday habits of children's early experiential worlds.

If cultural frameworks channel attention and observation, then they might also be reflected in the way we recall our experiences through personal narratives. The data on outdoor practices and converging measures suggest that our Native American samples are "psychologically closer" to the rest of nature. According to the Trope and Liberman (2003) construal level theory, psychological closeness is associated with greater attention to context. Building on this idea, we predicted that Native Americans and European American fishermen may tell different kinds of stories with respect to contextual information (Bang, Medin, and Atran 2007).

To test this idea, we asked rural Wisconsin adults to tell us about a recent or memorable fishing trip. Then, we measured how long it took them to "get to the point" and mention a fish (presuming that a fish was the point, of course). Greater attention to context should lead Native participants to mention the fish later in the story. This is what we found: the median number of words generated before mentioning fish was twenty-seven for European American adults and eighty-three for the Native adults, a large and reliable difference (Bang, Medin, and Atran 2007). A closer examination of these narratives found a correlation between where one fished (e.g., the shore of a river or in a boat on a lake) and the scope of ecological reasoning and biodiversity mentioned in the fishing narratives (Bang 2009).

Interestingly, the fact that different cultural groups engage with nature in different ways may be salient, even in the eyes of young children. In our work with Ngöbe children, we have found evidence that young children are attuned to distinctive cultural patterns of human-nature relations (Herrmann 2012). When Patricia Herrmann visited our Ngöbe host community in Panama in 2011, she set out to extend her previous U.S.-based research by exploring ecological reasoning among Ngöbe children. Children completed a standard triad task with three cards depicting entities from different biological categories (e.g., human, animal, plant) and asked children to choose "which two go together." The twenty triads of interest included a human (either Ngöbe [twelve sets] or non-Ngöbe Latino/Caucasian [eight sets]) and two natural entities (animals or plants). Children could choose to pair the human with one of the natural entities (a human-nature relation), or to exclude the human and pair the two natural entities together (a human exclusion).

When given a triad that included a Ngöbe person, children were more likely to pair the Ngöbe with a natural entity; but when given a triad including a non-Ngöbe person, children were more likely to exclude the human. This suggests that children saw the relations between Ngöbe people and natural entities as more pertinent and salient than for non-Ngöbe people.

In our view, these sorting patterns reveal that children see Ngöbe and non-Ngöbe relations with nature differently. Children implicitly view Ngöbe individuals as more closely related to their environments than non-Ngöbe individuals.[4] The question then arises: How do children learn to structure these human-nature correspondences? This is where cultural frameworks enter the picture and we begin to explore the cognitive consequences of different cultural orientations to the natural world.

13.4.2 Thinking Relational Epistemology: Ecological Reasoning

At this point, the reader might be wondering: If Ngöbe children recognize (implicitly or explicitly) that their own communities engage with nature in a manner distinct from non-Ngöbe communities, then what does this difference consist of? We can turn to the children themselves for an answer. When asked to explain their sorting choices, children explained the majority of Ngöbe-natural kind pairings through appeal to ecological relations. In fact, if the human included was a Ngöbe, justifications were universally ecological (e.g., "People live near cows, and they give us meat"). But if the human included was a non-Ngöbe, then justifications were more frequently taxonomic than ecological (e.g., "They are both alive"). Herrmann (2012) concluded, "When children consider the place of humans in the natural world, they take into account their knowledge about the relevant practices of particular communities. The children seemed to view the Ngöbe as more a part of nature and non-Ngöbe as more apart from nature."

---

4. In a related unpublished study we have found that Chicago area Native American children sort animals, plants, and natural inanimates differently, depending on whether we ask them to take the perspective of an elder or a science teacher.

13.4.2.1 Relational Epistemology Before describing further research findings, we first outline important dimensions of relational epistemology from the perspective of anthropology. *Relational epistemology* was a term introduced by Bird-David in an influential paper (1999) in which she critiqued previous approaches to animism as a failed epistemology or primitive religion, and argued for a new appreciation of relational ways of engaging with the nonhuman world. For our purposes, relational epistemology can be seen as closely related to relational ontologies (e.g., Ingold 2006; Santos-Granero 2009), animisms (e.g., Harvey 2006), perspectivisms (e.g., Stolze Lima 1999; Viveiros de Castro 1998), and Indigenous science and traditional ecological knowledge (e.g., Cajete 2000; Pierotti 2011).

In regard to human-nature relations, the relevant aspects of relational epistemology are (1) an appreciation of interdependencies among all components of the natural world, that is, *all things are connected* (e.g., Cajete 2000; Pierotti 2011, 62); (2) a framework for reasoning about things in terms of relationships; (3) a focus on whole organisms and systems at the macroscopic level of human perception (also a signature of complex-systems theory; Pierotti 2011, 72–73); and (4) viewing nonhumans as individual "persons" in their own right. Overall, this worldview is aptly summarized by biologist Raymond Pierotti (2011):

Indigenous understanding of the natural world emerged from conceiving of the living world as a network of relationships across communities that include humans. Because of this understanding based on relationships, Indigenous principles and insights are also superior at understanding links between systems that are often considered to be separate by the Western tradition. (76)

Building on Indigenous science and philosophy, our research has sought to explore the cognitive consequences of these cultural worldviews and practices.

13.4.2.2 Ecological Reasoning among Children One sign that ecological reasoning may play an important role in children's developing notions of human-nature relations comes from children's spontaneous discourse during the category-based induction tasks described earlier. When asked why they generalized a property attributed to bees to bears, Menominee children told us that the bee might transmit the property through the honey bears eat or by bees stinging bears (Ross et al. 2003). The standard category-based induction task was originally designed on the assumption that generalization will follow taxonomic or biological similarity, but, like biological experts and Indigenous adults in previous studies (Atran and Medin 2008), at least some Menominee children viewed ecological relations as the relevant cues for biological induction.

Do cultural orientations to nature affect cognitive development? We set out to explore this question more systematically in a comparative study among rural

European American and Menominee children in Wisconsin (Unsworth et al. 2012). Previously, we had done studies with Menominee and European American expert fishermen and found that, although the two groups had comparable knowledge bases, including ecological knowledge, there were substantial differences in how that knowledge was organized. European American experts favored a taxonomic organization, and Menominee experts an ecological organization. These differences were evident in spontaneous sorting and sorting justifications as well as in speeded probes of fish-fish interactions (Medin et al. 2006). We wondered whether there would be parallel differences in the salience of ecological relations for young Menominee and European American children.

In one study (Unsworth et al. 2012) five- to seven- year-old rural Menominee and European American children were presented with pairs of photos (including non-human animal-animal, plant-animal, and plant-plant pairs, e.g., raspberries and strawberries) and asked why the two might go together. Both groups used habitat relations equally (e.g., both are found in the forest), but Menominee children were reliably more likely to mention food-chain (e.g., the stink bug might eat the leaves of the berry bush) and biological-needs relations (e.g., both need water, sunlight, or soil).

Yet another dimension of difference that unexpectedly emerged during interviews was mimicry. Menominee children sometimes spontaneously mimicked nonhuman animal species during the interview (e.g., "bees go buzzzzz"). Strikingly, not one of the rural European American children engaged in mimicry. Unsworth and coauthors interpreted this as evidence of Menominee children's psychological closeness to nature through greater ease of perspective taking.

Given that Indigenous children and adults reason about human-nature relations in terms of ecological relations and interdependencies—both signatures of relational epistemologies—do cultural orientations have the potential to fundamentally change the way we see and think about the world around us? This brings us to the question of conceptual organization and folk theories of reality.

13.4.2.3 Conceptual Organization and Causal Reasoning

One reason that the role of Indigenous people as part of their ecological communities is so important is that they do not think of the nonhuman elements of their community as constituting "nature" or as "wilderness," but as part of their social environment.

—Raymond Pierotti (2011, 29)

Knowledge Organization: Seeing Interconnectedness How knowledge is organized— where it exists in (the ecosystem of) awareness, the roots and branches it shares with neighboring concepts—is critical to defining the *content* and *form* of that knowledge. Can a habitual focus on relational interactions train attention to reveal different aspects of the natural world? We are beginning to see evidence converging from different research sites to suggest that Indigenous communities see a wider range of cooperative and symbiotic relationships in nature when compared with their non-Indigenous local counterparts.

Engaging relational understandings of the natural world may partially determine the "nature" of the nature that you see around you. In studies in Guatemala examining the relationship between how different culture groups think about the rain forest and how they act on it, we have found striking differences between Indigenous Itza' Maya and immigrant Ladino agroforesters (e.g., Atran, Medin, and Ross 2005). In one line of studies, we directly probed for understandings of plant-animal helping and hurting relationships. We found that Maya and Ladino farmers had essentially the same understanding of how plants help animals. For Itza' Maya this was part of a rich reciprocal model where animals also help plants, but Ladino farmers overwhelmingly saw animals as having no effect on or as hurting plants. In developing our materials as part of a more open-ended interview, we asked how animals help plants. Ladino adults denied the presupposition in the question, typically saying, "Animals don't help plants; plants help animals." Other observations suggest that Ladino farmers were learning from the Itza', but this learning apparently did not include sensitivity to reciprocal relationships (Atran, Medin, and Ross 2005). It appears that a relational orientation to nature nurtures recognition of mutual dependencies and interspecies relationships in the biological world.

We have observed parallel results in a storytelling task about nonhuman animals. We used a nonfiction picture book depicting coyote and badger hunting in the American Southwest (ojalehto, Medin, Horton, Garcia, and Kays, forthcoming). When Ngöbe and U.S. undergraduates narrated the (text-free) story. Ngöbe (correctly) interpreted the hunting relationship as cooperative, while U.S. undergraduates (mis)interpreted it as competitive. (This is consistent with a broader emphasis on competitive over facilitative interactions in Western views of ecosystems; Bruno et al., 2003.) How did Ngöbe participants, who are unfamiliar with these animal species, "know" the hunt was cooperative?

Ngöbe colleagues explained that this was a case of Western versus Ngöbe sciences, which diverge on three major points: (1) an emphasis on interactions and relationships; (2) an approach to living with nature, as a system, rather than studying about nature, as isolated parts; (3) viewing nonhumans as intelligent beings worthy of respect. We do not think that Ngöbe necessarily see all relationships as cooperative, but rather that, like the Itza' Maya, they are prepared to "see" cooperation when it is present. While Indigenous sciences focus on interspecies relations and mutual dependency—supporting perceptions of cooperation and socialization among nonhuman species—Western sciences have a tradition of focusing on individual species and fitness—assuming competition among species (Pierotti 2011).

Reorganizing Domains   Earlier we suggested that a human-centered folk biology seen in young urban children may involve competing cultural models rather than some acultural naïve psychology or naïve biology. For non-Western adults who tend not to endorse a dualism between mind and body, psychology and biology may not be such distinct domains with distinct causal principles. As biologist Raymond Pierotti argues, European American folk ideas such as theory of mind have permeated academic science and invariably colored how researchers design the parameters of *relevant* inquiry:

Assuming that animals are sentient is linked to the concept referred to in Western science as a "theory of mind." Until the last few years Western science did not accept that nonhumans could have a theory of mind; however, recent discoveries have changed the way nonhuman thinking is perceived. ... These new developments reveal that Western science has had to rediscover knowledge assumed to be part of the understanding of Indigenous societies. (2011, 32)

In exploring how epistemological orientations interact with folk-biological, folk-ecological and folk-psychological knowledge, our research increasingly points to concepts that crosscut these domains, suggesting that these conceptual systems can be fruitfully studied via integrated approaches. One example of this conceptual interfacing appears in an ongoing line of research in which we are exploring how Indigenous Ngöbe adults reason about the psychological capacities of plants, animals, and other natural entities (sun, ocean) or processes (rain, clouds). The tendency to attribute mental states to nonhuman kinds is closely related to folk biology and folk ecology, with important consequences for human interactions with the natural world. Cultural framework theories organize folk-psychological knowledge around diverse concepts of MIND and INTELLIGENCE, pointing to divergent conceptual organization across cultures.

13.4.2.4 Unsettling Domains   Studying relational epistemologies with Indigenous communities has had the bottom-up effect of redirecting our conceptual boundaries of inquiry, leading us to focus on the relations *between* human, biological, and ecological worlds in a new kind of domain-like perspective. It is instructive to consider that Western psychologists proposed three *core* domains of conceptual processing based on their perceptions of the relevant metaphysics (ontological categories and correlated causal systems) and unit size (individual entities). This thinking produced folk psychology (minds), folk biology (organisms), and folk physics (things).

Domain specificity has played a key role in catalyzing understanding of conceptual development, leading to many important discoveries. Missing from this picture, however, is a framework that accommodates how people conceptualize interactions among these systems. There was no folk ecology (interactions between organisms, persons, and matter, as well as climate systems), no folk dynamics (tracking weather systems, wave systems, water-flow systems), and no folk sociology (interactions between persons, human or nonhuman). Lately, anthropologists and psychologists have been trying to make amends for this gap (see Atran, Medin, and Ross 2005; Hirschfeld 2012; White 2008).

We reckon that developing such folk theories would have required a different perception of the relevant metaphysics (process categories, or kinds of relations) and unit size (systems). In fact, it is tempting to think, based on what we have learned from our Native science colleagues, that Indigenous psychologists may have had the relevant tools and insights to develop folk ecology, folk sociology, and folk dynamics right from the start. But that's another story.

13.5   Summary and Conclusions

We continue to be immersed in these and closely related research projects and are no doubt guilty of team-centrism in focusing so much on our own research. With this apology in mind, we see these findings as carrying implications for core questions and issues in the cognitive sciences. The first question concerns the nature of concepts and categories and how we should study them. We see our research program as just one instance of groups of cognitive scientists placing the study of conceptual behaviors into broader contexts. These broader contexts include (1) analyses of information available in the environment, such as cultural artifacts (e.g., Morling and Lamoreaux 2008); (2) examining how the context of use affects conceptual representation (Markman and Ross 2003); (3) studying the interactions between language and conceptual development using crosslinguistic and developmental comparisons as a tool; and (4) assessing conceptual orientations implicit in (cultural) practices that form the background and perhaps the backbone of conceptual knowledge.

There is also a reflexive component to our research as we scramble to detect cultural or epistemological presuppositions lurking in our studies (see also Medin and Bang 2014). For example, restricting our probes of ecological relations to plants and animals may reflect our seeing natural inanimates as irrelevant, despite the fact that *niche construction* is an important construct in contemporary evolutionary theory. In our studies of folk ecology in Guatemala we also excluded natural inanimates and the "Arux" forest spirits, which is a sensible practice only if the Itza' Maya also exclude them. Even our preferred stance as "detached scientific observers" may be less about science than it is about the psychological distance that is part of a Western cultural model. We are left to wonder what the psychology of concepts would look like if it were not owned and operated by Western scientists.

References

Anggoro, F. K., D. L. Medin, and S. R. Waxman. 2010. Language and experience influence children's biological induction. *Journal of Cognition and Culture* 10:171–187.

Anggoro, F. K., S. R. Waxman, and D. L. Medin. 2008. Naming practices and the acquisition of key biological concepts: Evidence from English and Indonesian. *Psychological Science* 19 (4): 314–319.

Atran, S., and D. L. Medin. 2008. *The Native Mind and the Cultural Construction of Nature*. Cambridge, MA: MIT Press.

Atran, S., D. Medin, E. Lynch, V. Vapnarsky, E. Ucan, and P. Sousa. 2001. Folkbiology doesn't come from folkpsychology: Evidence from Yukatek Maya in cross-cultural perspective. *Journal of Cognition and Culture* 1 (1): 3–42.

Atran, S., D. L. Medin, and N. O. Ross. 2005. The cultural mind: Environmental decision making and cultural modeling within and across populations. *Psychological Review* 112 (4): 744–776.

Bailenson, J. N., M. S. Shum, S. Atran, D. L. Medin, and J. D. Coley. 2002. A bird's eye view: Biological categorization and reasoning within and across cultures. *Cognition* 84 (1): 1–53.

Bang, M. 2009. Understanding students' epistemologies: Examining practice and meaning in community contexts. PhD diss., Northwestern University.

Bang, M., D. L. Medin, and S. Atran. 2007. Cultural mosaics and mental models of nature. *Proceedings of the National Academy of Sciences of the United States of America* 104 (35): 13868–13874.

Berlin, B. 1992. *Ethnobiological Classification*. Princeton, NJ: Princeton University Press.

Bertenthal, B. I. 1993. Infants' perception of biomechanical motions: Intrinsic image and knowledge-based constraints. In *Visual Perception and Cognition in Infancy*, ed. C. Granrud, 175–214. Erlbaum.

Bird-David, N. 1999. "Animism" revisited. *Current Anthropology* 40 (S1): S67–S91.

Bruno, J. F., J. J. Stachowicz, and M. D. Bertness. 2003. Inclusion of facilitation into ecological theory. *Trends in Ecology & Evolution* 18 (3): 119–125.

Cajete, G. 2000. Indigenous knowledge: The Pueblo metaphor of Indigenous education. In *Reclaiming Indigenous Voice and Vision*, ed. M. Battiste, 181–191. Vancouver: University of British Columbia Press.

Carey, S. 1985. *Conceptual Change in Childhood*. Cambridge, MA: Bradford Books.

Carey, S. 2009. *The Origin of Concepts*. New York: Oxford University Press.

Carey, S., R. Diamond, and B. Woods. 1980. Development of face recognition: A maturational component? *Developmental Psychology* 16 (4): 257–269.

Carey, S., and E. Spelke. 1994. Domain-specific knowledge and conceptual change. In *Mapping the Mind: Domain Specificity in Cognition and Culture*, ed. L. A. Hirschfeld and S. A. Gelman, 169–200. New York: Cambridge University Press.

Cosmides, L., J. Tooby, and J. H. Barkow. 1992. *The Adapted Mind: Evolutionary Psychology and the Generation of Culture*. New York: Oxford University Press.

Echols, C. H., and C. N. Marti. 2004. The identification of words and their meaning: From perceptual biases to language-specific cues. In *Weaving a Lexicon*, ed. D. G. Hall and S. R. Waxman, 41–78. Cambridge, MA: MIT Press.

Gelman, R. 1990. First principles organize attention to and learning about relevant data: Number and the animate-inanimate distinction as examples. *Cognitive Science* 14 (1): 79–106.

Gelman, S. A. 2003. *The Essential Child: Origins of Essentialism in Everyday Thought*. New York: Oxford University Press.

Gelman, S. A., and E. M. Markman. 1986. Categories and induction in young children. *Cognition* 23 (3): 183–209.

Goss, A. E. 1961. Verbal mediating responses and concept formation. *Psychological Review* 68 (4): 248–274.

Graham, S. A., C. S. Kilbreath, and A. N. Welder. 2004. 13-month-olds rely on shared labels and shape similarity for inductive inferences. *Child Development* 75:409–427.

Hall, P., and M. Pecore. 1995. *Case Study: Menominee Tribal Enterprises*. Madison, WI: Institute for Environmental Studies and the Land Tenure Center, University of Wisconsin-Madison.

Harvey, G. 2006. *Animism: Respecting the Living World*. London: Hurst and Company.

Hatano, G., and K. Inagaki. 2000. Domain-specific constraints of conceptual development. *International Journal of Behavioral Development* 24 (3): 267–275.

Hatano, G., R. S. Siegler, D. D. Richards, K. Inagaki, R. Stavy, and N. Wax. 1993. The development of biological knowledge: A multi-national study. *Cognitive Development* 8:47–62.

Herrmann, P. 2012. Flora, fauna and familiarity: Ecological reasoning about the natural world in the Ngöbe community. SASci Symposium: Anthropological Perspectives on Space, Environment and Adaptation, Meeting of the Society for Anthropological Sciences, February 23.

Herrmann, P., S. R. Waxman, and D. L. Medin. 2010. Anthropocentrism is not the first step in children's reasoning about the natural world. *Proceedings of the National Academy of Sciences of the United States of America* 107 (22): 9979–9984.

Herrmann, P., D. L. Medin, and S. R. Waxman. 2012. When humans become animals: Development of the animal category in early childhood. *Cognition* 122 (1): 74–79.

Hickling, A. K., and S. A. Gelman. 1995. How does your garden grow? Early conceptualization of seeds and their place in the plant growth cycle. *Child Development* 66 (3): 856–876.

Hirschfeld, L. A. 2012. Seven myths of race and the young child. *Du Bois Review: Social Science Research on Race* 9 (1): 17–39.

Hirschfeld, L. A., and S. A. Gelman. 1994. *Mapping the Mind: Domain Specificity in Culture and Cognition*. Cambridge: Cambridge University Press.

Inagaki, K. 1990. The effects of raising animals on children's biological knowledge. *British Journal of Developmental Psychology* 8 (2): 119–129.

Inagaki, K., and G. Hatano. 2002. *Young Children's Naive Thinking About the Biological World*. New York: Psychology Press.

Ingold, T. 2006. Rethinking the animate, re-animating thought. *Ethnos* 71 (1): 9–20.

Johnson, S., V. Slaughter, and S. Carey. 1998. Whose gaze will infants follow? The elicitation of gaze-following in 12-month-olds. *Developmental Science* 1 (2): 233–238.

Keil, F. C. 1981. Constraints on knowledge and cognitive development. *Psychological Review* 88 (3): 197–227.

Leddon, E. M., S. R. Waxman, and D. L. Medin. 2011. What does it mean to "live" and "die"? A cross-linguistic analysis of parent-child conversations in English and Indonesian. *British Journal of Developmental Psychology* 29 (3): 375–395.

Leddon, E., S. R. Waxman, D. L. Medin, M. Bang, and K. Washinawatok. 2012. One animal among many? Children's understanding of the relation between humans and nonhuman animals. In *Psychology of Culture*, ed. G. Hayes and M. Bryant, 105–126. Hauppauge, NY: Nova Science Publishers.

Leslie, A. M. 1994. ToMM, ToBy, and agency: Core architecture and domain specificity. In *Mapping the Mind: Domain Specificity in Cognition and Culture*, ed. L. A. Hirschfeld and S. A. Gelman, 119–148. New York: Cambridge University Press.

Lopez, A., S. Atran, J. D. Coley, D. L. Medin, and E. E. Smith. 1997. The tree of life: Universal and cultural features of folkbiological taxonomies and inductions. *Cognitive Psychology* 32:251–295.

Luo, Y., L. Kaufman, and R. Baillargeon. 2009. Young infants' reasoning about physical events involving inert and self-propelled objects. *Cognitive Psychology* 58 (4): 441–486.

Markman, A. B., and B. H. Ross. 2003. Category use and category learning. *Psychological Bulletin* 129 (4): 592.

Massey, C. M., and R. Gelman. 1988. Preschooler's ability to decide whether a photographed unfamiliar object can move itself. *Developmental Psychology* 24 (3): 307–317.

Medin, D. L., and Bang, M. 2014. *Who's Asking: Native Science, Western Science, and Science Education*. Cambridge, MA: MIT Press.

Medin, D. L., E. B. Lynch, J. D. Coley, and S. Atran. 1997. Categorization and reasoning among tree experts: Do all roads lead to Rome? *Cognitive Psychology* 32:49–96.

Medin, D. L., E. B. Lynch, and K. O. Solomon. 2000. Are there kinds of concepts? *Annual Review of Psychology* 51:121–147.

Medin, D. L., N. O. Ross, S. Atran, D. Cox, J. Coley, J. B. Proffitt, and S. Blok. 2006. Folkbiology of freshwater fish. *Cognition* 99 (3): 237–273.

Medin, D. L., and S. R. Waxman. 2007. Interpreting asymmetries of projection in children's inductive reasoning. In *Inductive Reasoning: Experimental, Developmental and Computational Approaches*, ed. A. Feeney and E. Heit, 55–80. New York: Cambridge University Press.

Medin, D. L., S. R. Waxman, J. Woodring, and K. Washinawatok. 2010. Human-centeredness is not a universal feature of young children's reasoning: Culture and experience matter when reasoning about biological entities. *Cognitive Development* 25 (3): 197–207.

Morling, B., and M. Lamoreaux. 2008. Measuring culture outside the head: A meta-analysis of individualism-collectivism in cultural products. *Personality and Social Psychology Review* 12 (3): 199–221.

Newman, G. E., F. C. Keil, V. A. Kuhlmeier, and K. Wynn. 2010. Early understandings of the link between agents and order. *Proceedings of the National Academy of Sciences of the United States of America* 107 (40): 17140–17145.

ojalehto, b., Medin, D., Horton, W., Garcia, S., and Kays, E. Forthcoming. Constructing nonhuman worlds in storytelling: How folk theories diverge across cultures and converge across disciplines. Invited to appear in *Topics in Cognitive Science*. Special Issue on: *Exploring Cognitive Diversity: Anthropological Perspectives on Cognition*.

Opfer, J. E., and S. A. Gelman. 2010. Development of the animate-inanimate distinction. In *Wiley-Blackwell Handbook of Childhood Cognitive Development*, ed. U. Goswami, 213–238. Hoboken, NJ: Wiley-Blackwell.

Pascalis, O., M. de Haan, and C. A. Nelson. 2002. Is face processing species-specific during the first year of life? *Science* 296 (5571): 1321–1323.

Pauen, S., and B. Träuble. 2009. How 7-month-olds interpret ambiguous motion events: Category-based reasoning in infancy. *Cognitive Psychology* 59 (3): 275–295.

Piaget, J. 1954. *The Construction of Reality in the Child*. New York: Basic Books.

Piaget, J. [1929] 1973. *The Child's Conception of the World*. St. Albans, UK: Paladin.

Pierotti, R. 2011. *Indigenous Knowledge, Ecology, and Evolutionary Biology*. New York: Routledge.

Poulin-Dubois, D., and T. R. Shultz. 1990. Infants' concept of animacy: The distinction between social and nonsocial objects. *Journal of Genetic Psychology* 151:77–90.

Proffitt, J. B., J. D. Coley, and D. L. Medin. 2000. Expertise and category-based induction. *Journal of Experimental Psychology: Learning, Memory, and Cognition* 26 (4): 811–828.

Richards, D. D., and R. S. Siegler. 1984. The effects of task requirements on children's life judgments. *Child Development* 55:1687–1696.

Rosch, E., and C. B. Mervis. 1975. Family resemblances: Studies in the internal structure of categories. *Cognitive Psychology* 7 (4): 573–605.

Rosch, E., C. B. Mervis, W. D. Gray, D. M. Johnson, and P. Boyes-Braem. 1976. Basic objects in natural categories. *Cognitive Psychology* 8 (3): 382–439.

Ross, N., D. Medin, J. D. Coley, and S. Atran. 2003. Cultural and experimental differences in the development of folkbiological induction. *Cognitive Development* 18:25–47.

Santos-Granero, F. 2009. *The Occult Life of Things: Native Amazonian Theories of Materiality and Personhood.* Tucson: University of Arizona Press.

Scott, L. S., and A. Monesson. 2009. The origin of biases in face perception. *Psychological Science* 20 (6): 676–680.

Shutts, K., L. Markson, and E. Spelke. 2009. The developmental origins of animal and artifact concepts. In *The Origins of Object Knowledge,* ed. B. Hood and L. Santos, 189–210. New York: Oxford University Press.

Spelke, E. S. 1990. Principles of object perception. *Cognitive Science* 14 (1): 29–56.

Spiker, C. C. 1956. Experiments with children on the hypotheses of acquired distinctiveness and equivalence of cues. *Child Development* 27 (2): 253–263.

Stavy, R., and N. Wax. 1989. Children's conceptions of plants as living things. *Human Development* 32:88–94.

Stolze Lima, T. 1999. The two and its many: Reflections on perspectivism in a Tupi cosmology. *Ethnos* 64 (1): 107–131.

Trope, Y., and N. Liberman. 2003. Temporal construal. *Psychological Review* 110 (3): 403–420.

Unsworth, S. J., W. Levin, M. Bang, K. Washinawatok, S. R. Waxman, and D. L. Medin. 2012. Cultural differences in children's ecological reasoning and psychological closeness to nature: Evidence from Menominee and European-American Children. *Journal of Cognition and Culture* 12 (1–2): 17–29.

Viveiros de Castro, E. 1998. Cosmological deixis and Amerindian perspectivism. *Journal of the Royal Anthropological Institute* 4:469–488.

Vouloumanos, A., M. J. Druhen, M. D. Hauser, and A. T. Huizink. 2009. Five-month-old infants' identification of the sources of vocalizations. *Proceedings of the National Academy of Sciences of the United States of America* 106 (44): 18867–18872.

Vouloumanos, A., M. D. Hauser, J. F. Werker, and A. Martin. 2010. The tuning of human neonates' preference for speech. *Child Development* 81 (2): 517–527.

Waxman, S. R. 1999. Specifying the scope of 13-month-olds' expectations for novel words. *Cognition* 70 (3): B35–B50.

Waxman, S. R. 2005. Why is the concept "living thing" so elusive? Concepts, languages, and the development of folkbiology. In *Categorization Inside and Outside the Laboratory: Essays in Honor of Douglas L. Medin,* ed. W. Ahn, R. L. Goldstone, B. C. Love, A. B. Markman, and P. Wolff, 49–67. Washington, DC: American Psychological Association.

Waxman, S. R., and A. E. Booth. 2001. Seeing pink elephants: Fourteen-month-olds' interpretations of novel nouns and adjectives. *Cognitive Psychology* 43:217–242.

Waxman, S. R., and J. Lidz. 2006. Early word learning.In *Handbook of Child Psychology*, vol. 2, ed. D. Kuhn and R. Siegler, 299–335. Hoboken, NJ: John Wiley and Sons.

Waxman, S. R., E. B. Lynch, K. L. Casey, and L. Baer. 1997. Setters and Samoyeds: The emergence of subordinate level categories as a basis for inductive inference. *Developmental Psychology* 33 (6): 1074–1090.

Waxman, S. R., and D. B. Markow. 1995. Words as invitations to form categories: Evidence from 12-month-old infants. *Cognitive Psychology* 29:257–302.

Waxman, S. R., and D. Medin. 2007. Experience and cultural models matter: Placing firm limits on anthropocentrism. *Human Development* 50 (1): 23–30.

White, P. A. 2008. Beliefs about interactions between factors in the natural environment: A causal network study. *Applied Cognitive Psychology* 22 (4): 559–572.

Winkler-Rhoades, N., D. Medin, S. R. Waxman, J. Woodring, and N. O. Ross. 2010. Naming the animals that come to mind: Effects of culture and experience on category fluency. *Journal of Cognition and Culture* 10 (1–2): 205–220.

Wolff, P., D. L. Medin, and C. Pankratz. 1999. Evolution and devolution of folkbiological knowledge. *Cognition* 73 (2): 177–204.

Woodward, A. L., J. A. Sommerville, and J. J. Guajardo. 2001. How infants make sense of intentional action. In *Intentions and Intentionality: Foundations in Social Cognition*, ed. B. F. Malle, L. J. Moses, and D. F. Baldwin, 149–170. Cambridge, MA: MIT Press.

Young, P. Ngöbe Cultural Survival in the Twenty-first Century: Four Challenges. Unpublished manuscript, Portland, OR.

14 Innate Conceptual Primitives Manifested in the Languages of the World and in Infant Cognition

Anna Wierzbicka

14.1 The "Innate Stock of Conceptual Primitives"

In his splendid little book *Acts of Meaning*, psychologist Jerome Bruner writes:

How we "enter language" must rest upon a selective set of prelinguistic "readiness for meaning."
That is to say, there are certain classes of meaning to which human beings are innately tuned
and for which they actively search. ... Prior to language, these exist in primitive form as protolinguistic representations of the world whose full realization depends upon the cultural tool of
language. (1990, 72)

Linguist Cliff Goddard quotes Bruner's words at the outset of his own study exploring
a number of hypotheses "about the nature and identity of the innate concepts which
may underpin language acquisition" (2001a, 193). Goddard develops his hypotheses in
relation to a diary study of the semantic development of his young son, Pete (a pseud-
onym), conducted from Pete's second to fourth year.

Methodologically, Goddard's study is anchored in the NSM (natural semantic metalanguage) approach to cognitive semantics, which is also the approach underlying the
present chapter and which will be presented at some length in section 14.3. In his
study, Goddard seeks to show that "the NSM approach generates interesting research
hypotheses on language acquisition and allows for increased precision and testability
in the notoriously difficult area of child semantics." As Goddard further argues, and as
I have argued in many publications myself, the NSM approach generates interesting
research hypotheses about human cognition in general, and innate human concepts in
particular (Wierzbicka 2011).

In this chapter, I report on the latest NSM findings about the "innate stock of conceptual primitives," as they manifest themselves in the semantic systems of the languages
of the world. I also try to show that the NSM approach brings new tools to the study
of the nature, origin, and development of human concepts. In doing so, I use as my
primary reference point the developmental psychologist Susan Carey's 2009 book *The
Origin of Concepts*. In this book, Carey posits the existence of innate "core cognition,"

which is "the developmental foundation of human conceptual understanding" (11). According to Carey, "any theory of conceptual development must specify the stock of innate (unlearned) representations, as well as the mechanisms (both maturational and learning mechanisms) that underlie change" (12).

Carey sets her discussion against the background of the historical debate between rationalists (such as Descartes) and empiricists (such as Locke) and argues strongly against the empiricist thesis that the "initial state" of human cognition is restricted to sensory representations. She argues in favor of the existence of what she calls "Descartes-like innate perceptual-input analyzers" (32) —innate concepts and mechanisms present (at least latently) at birth with the help of which infants can interpret the "perceptual input" presenting itself to them. The "innate stock of primitives is not limited to sensory, perceptual, or sensori-motor primitives" (448), as the empiricists maintained. "Rather, innate primitives include the representations that articulate core cognition" (448).

Carey's exposition converges with the ideas that were put forward in my 1972 book *Semantic Primitives* and developed further in the ongoing NSM program, with benchmarks such as *Semantic and Lexical Universals* (Goddard and Wierzbicka 1994), *Meaning and Universal Grammar* (Goddard and Wierzbicka 2002), *Semantic Primes and Universal Grammar: Empirical Evidence from the Romance Languages* (Peeters 2006), *Cross-Linguistic Semantics* (Goddard 2008), and *Words and Meanings* (Goddard and Wierzbicka 2014a).

Carey is at pains to insist on the need for empirical research into innate conceptual primitives. As a developmental psychologist, she emphasizes, above all, the need for empirical research concerned with young infants, whereas for NSM semantics researchers, the focus is above all on the lexical and semantic elements apparently shared by all languages, but these two programs are clearly complementary. They both accept that there is an innate conceptual basis and a great deal of subsequent cultural shaping in human cognition. What is innate is not culturally shaped and therefore can be expected to show up in the cognition of very young infants (Carey's "core cognition") and in the shared culture-independent semantic core of all languages (NSM primes and their combinatorial properties).[1]

Framing her arguments as a debate with philosopher and logician Willard Quine, Carey writes: "I argue, contrary to Quine, that many infant representations

1. In NSM theory, *primes* are semantically basic expressions that cannot be defined any further and that appear to have lexical exponents in all languages. For example, NSM-based crosslinguistic research indicates that all languages have a word (or a morpheme, or phraseme) corresponding to the English word *say* (an English exponent of the universal prime SAY); and that all these lexical elements share certain combinatorial properties, including *valency options* such as SAY TO (an addressee option) and SAY ABOUT (a locutionary topic). For further explanations and examples, see Goddard (2011, 64–73).

are conceptual and that many of our commonsense ontological commitments are innate. However, I agree with Quine that some, indeed most, of our commonsense ontological commitments are a cultural construction" (33). NSM researchers not only accept, like Carey, that most of our "common sense ontological commitments" are culturally constructed, but point out that even concepts like *common sense* and *commitment* are cultural constructions (cf. Wierzbicka 2010a). As these two examples illustrate, the language of analysis, too, can be largely culturally constructed, and with the current dominant position of English in psychology and cognitive science, it is usually *English* vocabulary that provides most of the conceptual tools for analyzing human cognition. This impinges also on the study of the *origin of concepts* and of infant cognition.

Carey writes: "If we wish to characterize the innate representational primitives, we have no alternative but to do the hard empirical work of finding out what representations young infants have" (2009, 29). But hard empirical work always relies in some measure on a particular conceptual framework and, especially, on the conceptual vocabulary in which the experiments and other empirical studies are designed and interpreted.

Linguistic research into lexical and conceptual universals and psychological research into infant cognition must of course proceed concurrently, and independently. From a logical point of view, however, research into lexical and conceptual universals is, arguably, prior, because it is obviously desirable for the developmental psychologist to know what words can be used in analyzing infant cognition without running the risk of building an ethnocentric bias into the experimental design itself, and in particular, of falling into the trap of terminological and conceptual Anglocentrism (Wierzbicka 2014).

The main purpose of this chapter is to show how the NSM project of identifying innate conceptual primes through empirical crosslinguistic investigations fits in with the project of developmental psychologists to identify the same conceptual primitives through empirical studies of infant cognition, and how the NSM framework can provide developmental psychologists with tools allowing, as Goddard (2001a) put it, for increased precision and testability of their hypotheses.

Before engaging in direct dialogue with developmental psychologists, however, I offer a brief sketch of the historical background of the search for innate primitives: Leibniz's pursuit of the "alphabet of human thoughts" (section 14.2) and an up-to-date summary of NSM findings (section 14.3).

14.2   The Alphabet of Human Thoughts

Carey's outline of the historical background focuses on Locke and his philosophical descendants, and as a counterfigure, she mentions Descartes. One name that is conspicuously absent from this discussion is that of another key seventeenth-century thinker, Leibniz, whose theory of innate conceptual primitives was much more developed than Descartes'. As the author of the classic work *After Babel* George Steiner put it, "Leibniz was profoundly interested in the possibilities of a universal semantic system, immediately accessible to all people and based on a set of pan-human conceptual primitives" ([1975] 1998, 75). Importantly, Leibniz's lifelong search for these panhuman conceptual primitives was predicated on the assumption that once found, they can provide a basis for a reliable and insightful analysis of human thoughts—an idea with profound implications for twenty-first-century psychology, philosophy, and cognitive science.

Thus, contrasting his approach to conceptual analysis with that of inventors of artificial languages such as Wilkins, Leibniz wrote of his hypothesized innate language of the mind as promising to be at the same time an effective language for developing, storing, and comparing ideas:

For their [i.e., Wilkins and his followers'] language or script only allows a convenient form of communication to be set up between people divided by language; but the true *Characteristica Realis*, as I conceive of it, ought to be considered one of the most apt tools of the human mind, as it would have unrivaled power with respect to the development of ideas, storing those ideas, and distinguishing between them. (Gerhardt 1960–1961, 7:7 translated by A. W.)

Leibniz believed that this language—"lingua naturae"—was based on what he called the alphabet of human thoughts, *Alphabetum Cogitationum Humanarum*. The human mind, he held, is equipped with a set of simple concepts that are "letters" of an innate mental alphabet, and all human thoughts constitute combinations of those simplest concepts. To quote:

1. When thinking about these matters a long time ago, it was already clear to me that all human thoughts may be resolved into very few primitive notions. (Dascal 1987, 182).
2. Although infinitely many concepts can be understood it is possible that only few can be understood in themselves. Because an infinite number can be constructed by combining a few elements. (Couturat 1903, 430, translated by A. W.)
3. The alphabet of human thoughts is the catalogue of primitive concepts, that is those concepts which cannot be made clearer by means of any definitions. (Couturat 1903, 435, translated by A. W.)
4. The alphabet of human thoughts is the catalogue of those concepts which can be understood by themselves, and from whose combinations our other ideas arise. (Couturat 1903, 430, translated by A. W.)

Leibniz maintained that these simplest concepts are the limit of human understanding of anything: they are inherently intelligible to human beings, and everything else can be understood only through them. If no concepts were self-explanatory, we couldn't understand anything at all.

5. If nothing could be understood in itself nothing at all could ever be understood. Because what can only be understood via something else can be understood only to the extent to which that other thing can be understood, and so on; accordingly, we can say that we have understood something only when we have broken it down into parts which can be understood in themselves. (Couturat 1903, 430, translated by A. W.)

Thus, people can understand an infinite number of ideas because they possess a small number of innate simple concepts that are understandable by themselves. Different combinations of these simple concepts can generate an infinite number of complex ones.

Leibniz was convinced that the task of identifying those simplest, absolutely necessary concepts is extremely important, and he found it surprising that only very few people think about this.

6. This consideration [how some concepts arise from others] allows us to avoid vicious circles, which are constantly taken recourse to, and the mind can fasten to some firm and fixed concepts which can be decided upon. How very important this is, few people understand, because few people reflect how very important it might be to determine what the first elements in all things are. (Couturat 1903, 160, translated by A. W.)

7. The best Remedy for the Mind would be to find a small number of concepts out of which an infinite number of other concepts can be derived. In this way, from a small number of numbers [from one to ten] all other numbers can be systematically derived. (Couturat 1903, 429, translated by A. W.)

As various commentators noted, "the approach would be more convincing if one could at least gain some clue as to what the table of fundamental concepts might look like" (Martin 1964, 25). Yet Leibniz never answered "the obvious question as to the number and type of fundamental concepts" (Martin 1964, 26). From Leibniz's own perspective, two conditions for a full success of his program were lacking during his lifetime: first, the absence of collaborators, and second, lack of data from many diverse languages of the world.

Quotations that are particularly relevant to the second point include the following two—one, on languages as the best mirror of the human mind, and one on the need for extensive crosslinguistic studies:

8. Languages are the best mirror of the human mind, and ... a precise analysis of the significations of words would tell us more than anything else about the operations of the understanding. (Leibniz [1765] 1981, 330)

9. It is true that someone who wanted to write a universal grammar would be well advised to move on from the essence of languages to their existence and to compare the grammars of various languages. This would be useful not only in a practical way, but also theoretically, prompting the author himself to think of various considerations which would otherwise have escaped his notice. (Leibniz [1765] 1981, 302)

But wide-ranging typological crosslinguistic investigations were still in the distant future, and the longed-for collaborators did not materialize. In the end, Leibniz died without proposing so much as a sketch of the "alphabet of human thoughts" (and leaving most of his work in this area unpublished); and subsequently, the whole program fell into oblivion.

14.3 NSM—the Natural Semantic Metalanguage

Leibniz's search for the "alphabet of human thoughts," revived half a century ago by the Polish linguist Andrzej Bogusławski, was taken up as a research program by linguists working within the NSM paradigm, starting with my *Semantic Primitives* (1972) and developed in collaboration with Cliff Goddard and other colleagues in Australia over the last four decades (see the NSM homepage).

What was particularly distinctive about our approach was the fact that we were searching for this "alphabet of human thoughts" not only by means of experimental explications, but also by empirical investigations of many languages: we were looking, above all, for common words, that is, words with exactly the same meaning that can be found in all languages.

After decades of extensive crosslinguistic investigations by many NSM researchers (see, e.g., Goddard and Wierzbicka 1994, 2002, 2014a; Goddard 2008) this search is now regarded as very close to completion, and we can present what appears to be a full list of elementary and indispensable human concepts. An English version of this list is presented in table 14.1.[2]

Primes exist as the meanings of lexical units. Exponents of primes may be words, bound morphemes, or phrasemes. They can be formally complex. They can have combinatorial variants, or *allolexes* (indicated with ~). Each prime has well-specified syntactic (combinatorial) properties. (See note 1.)

Carey writes: "I take it that any theory of conceptual development must specify the stock of innate representations" (12). The NSM theory does just that: it specifies the stock of innate representations in the table presented above.

2. As table 14.1 illustrates, the status of an element of meaning as a universal semantic prime is indicated by means of small capitals. For example, the English words *live* and *die* are regarded as English exponents of the universal primes LIVE and DIE, and the German words *leben* and *sterben*, as German exponents of LEBEN and STERBEN. LEBEN and LIVE stand for the same prime, and so do DIE and STERBEN. The "double-barreled" items in table 14.1 indicate English allolexes. For example, *other* and *else* occur in different contexts but express the same meaning. The exponent of a prime in a particular language can be polysemous. For example, the word *live* in the sentence *I live in Cockle Street* does not stand for the universal prime LIVE, and in German it would be rendered by *wohnen*, not LEBEN. (For further explanations of NSM terminological and graphic conventions, see Goddard 2011, 64–73).

Table 14.1

Semantic primes (English exponents), grouped into related categories

I, YOU, SOMEONE, SOMETHING~THING, PEOPLE, BODY	substantives
KIND, PART	relational substantives
THIS, THE SAME, OTHER~ELSE	determiners
ONE, TWO, MUCH~MANY, LITTLE~FEW, SOME, ALL,	quantifiers
GOOD, BAD	evaluators
BIG, SMALL	descriptors
KNOW, THINK, WANT, DON'T WANT, FEEL, SEE, HEAR	mental predicates
SAY, WORDS, TRUE	speech
DO, HAPPEN, MOVE, TOUCH	actions, events, movement, contact
THERE IS, BE (SOMEWHERE), BE (SOMEONE/SOMETHING), MINE	existence, location, specification possession
LIVE, DIE	life and death
WHEN~TIME, NOW, BEFORE, AFTER, A LONG TIME, A SHORT TIME, FOR SOME TIME, MOMENT	time
WHERE~PLACE, HERE, ABOVE, BELOW, FAR, NEAR, SIDE, INSIDE	space
NOT, MAYBE, CAN, BECAUSE, IF	logical concepts
VERY, MORE	intensifier, augmente r
LIKE~AS~WAY	similarity

It goes without saying that the universal *natural language* that Leibniz envisaged, and that NSM researchers have sought to pin down, must include not only a universal mental lexicon but also a universal mental grammar, that is, some universal rules for combining mental words into sentences. Our crosslinguistic investigations have led us to believe that just as the mental lexicon of elementary concepts is equivalent to the common part of the lexicons of all natural languages, so the mental grammar is equivalent to the common part of the grammatical systems of all natural languages.

I will illustrate this with one example, directly relevant to Carey's discussion of infant cognition. Evidence suggests that all languages have a word for *something*, distinct from the word for *someone* (cf. Jackendoff 2007, 160–162), as well as words for *one*, *two*, and *many*. The word for *something* combines with the words for *one*, *two*, and *many*, creating combinations such as *one thing*, *two things*, and *many things*. These combinations constitute a conceptual foundation of numerical cognition (cf. Goddard 2009) and of the distinction between countable *things* and uncountable *stuffs*—differently elaborated in different languages.

Thus, "inside" all languages we can find a small shared lexicon and a small shared grammar. Together, this panhuman lexicon and the panhuman grammar linked with it represent a mini-language, apparently shared by the whole of humankind. On the one hand, this mini-language is an intersection of all the languages of the world. On the other hand, it is, as we see it, the innate language of human thoughts, corresponding to what Leibniz called "lingua naturae." Obviously, this language has no sound system, but it can be incarnated in the sound system of any language.

Colleagues and I have been investigating this language for many years, and we call it natural semantic metalanguage (NSM) to indicate that this language provides us with a neutral tool for describing all languages. The point is that if the meanings encoded in one language are described through the categories of another language, for example, Russian or Japanese meanings through English words, these meanings often get distorted, and an Anglo slant is imposed on them. If, on the other hand, we describe such meanings through the universal mini-language NSM, even in its English version, we can avoid such distortion.

This means that NSM is both a model of the genetic code of the human mind (cf. Wierzbicka 2011) and a practical mini-language for describing languages, and indeed, for human sciences in general (Goddard and Wierzbicka 2014a). As I illustrate in sections 14.4 and 14.5, the natural semantic metalanguage also gives us a neutral tool for exploring human cognition, including infant cognition, without relying on the historically shaped conceptual vocabulary of modern English, whether colloquial or scientific.

It is important to emphasize that the inventory of semantic primes—that is, lexico-semantic universals posited by NSM—is based on wide-ranging empirical investigations. Tables of primes comparable to table 14.1 have been drawn for over thirty languages, including languages from a wide range of language families, language types, and geographical locations. Table 14.2 gives details of a selection of languages that have been studied in depth from an NSM point of view. Languages for which a full version of the metalanguage has been documented are specially indicated. Despite some significant gaps in coverage, these studies justify a high degree of confidence that the proposed semantic primes have lexical (word-like) status in all languages of the world.

Naturally, the set of proposed universal primes emerging from this research has undergone some changes over the years. In the main, however, it has been remarkably stable for close to two decades. This can be illustrated with a version of the table included by the evolutionary psychologist and anthropologist Doug Jones in a paper published in the *Annual Review of Anthropology* in 1999 and reproduced below as table 14.3. Jones writes:

[Table 14.3] gives a provisional list of 64 panhuman conceptual primitives, divided into five domains (some of which could be merged or split). This list—but not the present division into domains—follows the cross-cultural lexical work of Wierzbicka and associates (Wierzbicka 1992, 1996, 1997). They have sought to discover a natural semantic metalanguage: a set of elementary— and presumably innate—concepts that find expression in words, inflections, or stock phrases in every language. Much of the work of this school consists of showing how secondary, culture-

Table 14.2
Selection of languages studied in the NSM framework

Language family/ type	Language(s)	Sources (not necessarily exhaustive)
Austronesian	Malay,† Mbula,† Longgu, Samoan	Goddard (2001b, 2001c, 2002), Bugenhagen (2001, 2002), Hill (1994), Mosel (1994)
Indo-European	Spanish,† Danish,† French,† Polish,† Russian†	Travis (2002, 2004, 2006), Levisen (2012), Peeters (2006, 2010), Wierzbicka (2002), Gladkova (2007, 2010)
Semitic	Amharic,† Arabic,† Hebrew†	Amberber (2008), Habib (2011a, 2011b)
Finno-Ugric	Finnish†	Vanhatalo et al. (in press)
Sinitic	Chinese (Mandarin),† Cantonese	Chappell (2002), Ye (2006, 2007, 2010), Tong et al. (1997), Tien (2009), Leung (2012), Wakefield (2011)
Algonquian	†East Cree	Junker (2003, 2007, 2008), Junker and Blacksmith (2006)
Niger-Congo	Ewe	Ameka (1994, 2006, 2009)
Japonic	Japanese†	Hasada (1998, 2001, 2008), Asano-Cavanagh (2009, 2010)
Korean	Korean†	Yoon (2006, 2008)
Tai-Kadai	Lao†	Enfield (2002)
Papuan	Koromu,† Kalam, Makasai	Priestley (2002, 2008, 2102a, 2012b), Pawley (1994), Brotherson (2008)
Pama-Nyungan (Australia)	Pitjantjatjara/ Yankunytjatjara, Arrernte	Goddard (1991, 1994), Bromhead (2011), Harkins and Wilkins (1994), Harkins (2001)
Non-Pama-Nyungan (Australia)	Bunuba	Knight (2008)
Creoles	Hawaii Creole English, Roper Kriol†	Stanwood (1997, 1999), Nicholls (2009)

†Comprehensive metalanguage studies

specific concepts can be defined by composing sentences using the conceptual primitives of a natural semantic metalanguage and a simplified version of natural language syntax. The proposal by Wierzbicka is just one regarding innate conceptual building blocks; it is included here because it is relatively accessible and because, despite differences in aims and methods, it shows a striking convergence with other work in cognitive psychology and anthropology. (1999, 560)

If we compare the NSM list of primes posited before 1999 in table 14.3 (based on Jones 1999, table 2), with the current one (table 14.1), we will see a few changes, but only a few: one element has been removed from the list, "IF … WOULD" (counterfactual); one reinterpreted, BE (SOMEONE'S) (possession); and four added, MOMENT, BE SOMEWHERE (location), BE SOMETHING/SOMEONE (specification), and DON'T WANT. The element THERE IS

Table 14.3
Conceptual domains and some (possibly) universal conceptual primitives

Things, space, and time
thing/something, have parts/part of
place/where, here, far, near, above, under, side, inside, move
time/when, now, a long time, a short time, for some time, after, before, happen
Magnitude and quantity
big, small, very
one, two, some, more, many/much
Logic and cause
this, the same, other, all, like, there is, have
not, maybe, can, if, if … would (counterfactual)
because
Natural history
body
alive/live, die, do, kind of, good, bad
Theory of mind, communication, and social life
See, hear, feel, want, know, think
Say, word, true
I, you, person/someone, mother, father (genitor), wife, husband, people

Source: Reprinted by permission from Jones (1999).

(existence), present on the current NSM list but not in Jones's version, was already on the list in my 1996 book, *Semantics: Primes and Universals*. The element DON'T WANT was on earlier NSM lists, including those in my 1972 *Semantic Primitives* and in my 1980 *Lingua Mentalis*, and has now been revived. (For the justification of these changes, see Goddard and Wierzbicka 2002, vol. 2, chap. 5; Goddard 2008, chap. 1; Goddard 2011.)

It should also be pointed out that the categories MOTHER, FATHER, WIFE, and HUSBAND in my work cited by Jones (Wierzbicka 1992, 1996, 1997) were posited as *semantic molecules* rather than *semantic atoms* (that is, primes): they are universally lexicalized, like primes, but unlike primes, they are not indefinable (Goddard 2011). The theory of semantic molecules, elaborated in recent NSM work, is beyond the scope of this chapter (Goddard 2010). In the present context, it is worth highlighting, above all, Jones's recognition of the convergence between NSM findings and the results of current work in cognitive psychology and anthropology, and of the relevance of these findings to evolutionary psychology (see also Fabrega, 2013).

What NSM researchers see as particularly important is that NSM offers a unified framework for the study of communication and cognition, of adult and child language, and of humans and nonhuman primates and early hominins (cf. Goddard et al.

2014), a framework that is independent of particular languages and cultures and free of the Anglocentrism and "scientism" that plague most contemporary debates in human sciences.

It may seem more scientific to rely in our analyses on Latinate terms such as *object, intention, agency,* and *perceive* rather than on terms like *something, want, do,* and *see.* The fact is, however, that those simpler and more naïve-sounding ones are both cross-translatable and attested in children's speech. These simpler words are *experience-near* (Geertz 1974) and therefore (in the area of human thinking) *evidence-near.* "Representational resources that get cognition off the ground" (Carey 2009, 337) cannot be dependent on "advanced" English, let alone on academic English. Thus, English exponents of universally attested concepts like DO and SEE (used in preference to AGENCY and PERCEIVE) can free our analysis from Anglocentrism and scientism at the same time.

14.4   Two Examples of Carey's "Innate Primitives": Object and Number

In this section, I seek to illustrate the danger of Anglocentrism and scientism in the study of human cognition with two examples from Carey's book (2009): *object* and *number.*

Carey distinguishes three different types of processes that "underlie the formation of human conceptual repertoire: individual learning, historical/cultural construction, and evolution." Some concepts, she writes, "such as *kayak, fraction* and *gene,* spring from human cultures," whereas others—"such as *object* and *number,* arise in some form over evolutionary time" (3).

Apart from hard-core nativists such as Jerry Fodor and Noam Chomsky (according to whom even concepts like BUREAUCRAT and CARBURETOR are innate), nobody will probably dispute the cultural origin of concepts like KAYAK, FRACTION, and GENE. But even if we fully agree with Carey's general stand on innate conceptual primitives, one must still ask: is the innateness of the concepts OBJECT and NUMBER as incontrovertible as she appears to suggest? (Admittedly, she does say "in some form," but this raises the question, In what form?)

From a linguistic point of view, the fact that the English words *object* and *number* lack counterparts in most languages of the world is a problem for these particular candidates (presented in this form) for the status of primitives. In suggesting that OBJECT is one of the innate conceptual primitives, Carey doesn't explain what exactly she means by "object," relying simply on the English word *object.* Since many languages of the world don't have such a word, to understand Carey's hypothesis from an English-independent perspective we need to ask what this English word means. We can start looking for an answer to this question by asking native speakers whether or not something is an *object.* When I did this, I found very little disagreement:

— Is the moon an *object*? — No.
— Is a car an *object*? — No.
— Is a house an *object*? — No.
— Is a nose an *object*? — No.
— Is a dog an *object*? — No.
— Is a book (ball, cup, doll) an *object*? — Yes.

These responses are remarkably consistent with the definitions of the word *object* given, for example, by the *Collins Cobuild Dictionary of English* (1991): "An object is something that has a fixed shape or form, that you can touch or see, and that is not alive"; and by the *Concise Oxford Dictionary* (1982): "object—thing placed before eyes or presented to one of the senses, material thing, thing observed with optical instrument or represented in picture."

As these dictionary definitions suggest, then, in its ordinary usage, the word *object* refers to things that can be seen or touched which have a "fixed shape" (and thus has "sides" that can be touched), and that are not living things. In fact, all this fits in with the examples of *objects* mentioned in the chapter of Carey's book titled "Core Object Cognition," which describes various experiments with "objects" and infants: "Some objects were toy models (e.g., truck, duck, elephant), whereas others were from highly familiar everyday kinds (e.g., cup, bottle, book, ball)" (79).

Accordingly, using universal human concepts, we could explicate the ordinary meaning of the English word *object* as follows:

object

one something

someone can see this something

someone can touch this something with the hands on all sides

this something is not something living

As the dictionary definitions cited earlier recognize, the concept of OBJECT is conceived in relation to a *subject,* that is, a person "before whose eyes" something is "placed"—and this is exactly what happens in the experiments with infants reported by Carey.

Are there good reasons to posit such a concept (arguably, deriving partly from a philosophical tradition opposing a *subject* and an *object*) as part of human "core cognition" and an element of a child's "initial state"? Presumably not. In fact, it appears that when Carey says "object," she doesn't necessarily mean *object* in the ordinary sense of the word. At one point, she even refers to "dog," and "table," and "man" as "kinds of objects" (249; seemingly implying that a man could also be seen as a kind of "object"), although elsewhere she refers to "representations of people and objects … in neonates"

(40), apparently excluding "people" from the broad category of "objects." This may be a standard way of using the word *object* among developmental psychologists, but it is not a use anchored in how children speak and, presumably, think.

From the perspective of cross-cultural semantics, the most likely conceptual tool that infants may have for analyzing perceptual input is not OBJECT but SOMETHING, and the neonate's responsiveness to human faces (discussed by Carey in a later chapter) suggests that, from the outset, in the infant's mind SOMETHING has its counterpart in SOMEONE, and that the two are not subsumed by the infant under one general category such as OBJECT.

The abstract words *entity* and *object* used in philosophical and semi-philosophical language have no counterparts in most natural languages. It would be hard to believe, therefore, that they could correspond neatly to one of the innate human "input analyzers." Carey insists on the "abstract" (not "spatiotemporal") character of some innate conceptual primitives, and this is quite consistent with the findings of NSM research. But the fact that the innate conceptual vocabulary needs to be stated, to some extent, in terms of "abstractions" does not mean that it is justifiable to state it in terms of *English* (and *Latinate*) abstractions, such as *object*. What all languages demonstrably share are the concepts SOMEONE and SOMETHING (*who* and *what*), not *object* and *entity*. There is no reason to assume that Latinate English words such as *object* and *agent* (to be discussed shortly) can capture innate ontological categories better than homely words such as *something, someone,* and *people,* which, evidence suggests, have exact semantic counterparts in all other natural languages.

Evidence suggests that in addition to the well-established conceptual categories of SOMEONE and SOMETHING (WHO and WHAT), most human languages have a word (or word-meaning) corresponding to the English word *thing* as used in a concrete sense (e.g., "I saw many small things lying on the ground," or "a spoon is a kind of thing that people eat with") (Wierzbicka 2015). This meaning of the word *thing* needs to be distinguished from its abstract sense, as in, for example, "A terrible thing happened to me today." The 'concrete' sense of *thing* come close to that of *object*, as defined here.[3] It is not a simple ('atomic') concept like 'something' and its acquisition requires a prior acquisition of the concept of 'hands'. Presumably, once the baby has discovered, and taken note of, its own hands and has acquired some experience in handling (exploring) toys and

3. Being conceptually somewhat simpler than *object*, *thing* can be explicated as follows:

thing

one something

someone can do something to this something with the hands

this something is not something living

other objects with the hands, the notion of a 'thing' can also emerge in its thought-world. It is, however, a conceptual 'molecule', not a conceptual primitive, and thus not an element of the "initial state" of human cognition.

The concept of NUMBER posited by Carey as one of the innate "input analyzers" is even more problematic. As discussed in detail by Goddard (2009), many languages have no word corresponding to *number,* and arguably, the concept of NUMBER is just as culturally constructed as KAYAK. What is *not* culturally constructed are the concepts ONE and TWO, which we find as words or identifiable word meanings in all languages (Wierzbicka 2012; Goddard and Wierzbicka 2012) and which arguably underlie all numerical cognition. As shown by Goddard (2009), ONE and TWO provide the foundation on which the complex and nonuniversal concept of NUMBER can be built.

Obviously, Carey does not mean that the word *number* as such is an innate conceptual primitive, but when she refers to "the concept *number*" she doesn't explain what exactly she means. As she puts it, the experiments described in chapter 2 of her book "show that infants' object representations are governed by criteria for individuation and numerical identity ... they [infants] distinguish one object seen on different occasions from two numerically distinct objects" (2009, 46). The experiments described in that chapter are impressive, but arguably, they show, above all, the presence of the concept THE SAME and the importance of the distinction between 'something' and 'one something' (ONE THING). Interpreting these findings as evidence for an innate concept of NUMBER reflects the psychologist's own perspective.

Carey might object that the NSM prime SOMETHING could not serve as a substitute for the primitive OBJECT proposed by her because "the young infant distinguishes between individuated entities such as objects and nonindividuated entities such as sand" (285). The fact that in the experiments described by Carey, babies distinguish between "things" (for example, a ball, a book, or a bottle) and "stuffs" (such as sand) needs to be accounted for, but to do so, we do not need to posit an innate concept of OBJECT. It is sufficient to posit two mutually combinable concepts SOMETHING and ONE. Sand can be thought of as *something,* but—unlike a bottle or a ball—not as *one something*: it is the concept ONE that provides the semantic core of individuation.

Carey says: "In spite of that evidence that the prelinguistic infants represent number, core cognition of number cannot have the format of a numerical list system" (391). From a linguistic point of view, given the lack of numerals in many languages of the world, one can only agree with the second clause of this sentence ("core cognition of number cannot have the form of a numerical list"). But looking at the first clause ("prelinguistic infants represent number") in the light of cross-linguistic research, some modification would seem to be indicated. This research suggests that we can expect to find evidence of ONE (THING), rather than *number* in general, in prelinguistic infants' mental world, and arguably, this is precisely what the experiments described by Carey show.

Carey properly does take an interest in linguistic data from some languages without numerals, in particular, data from the Amazonian language Pirahã, as discussed in Gordon (2004), Everett (2005), and Frank et al. (2008), and she notes the reports that the Pirahã do not have words for ONE and TWO. As argued in Wierzbicka (2012) and Goddard and Wierzbicka (2014b), however, these reports are mistaken, due to a failure to recognize the polysemy of the relevant Pirahã words (*hói*, which means "small" as well as "one," and *hoí*, which means "few" as well as "two"). Needless to say, Pirahã doesn't have a word for *number*.

Thus, linguistic evidence suggests that neither OBJECT nor NUMBER have arisen in the course of evolution (i.e., neither are innate, rather than culturally shaped). On the other hand, two pairs of simpler and somewhat less abstract concepts, SOMEONE and SOMETHING, and ONE and TWO, which we find as words or distinct word meanings in all languages, have a very good claim to having been shaped by evolution rather than culture.

Concluding her chapter on "Language and Core Cognition," Carey writes: "Natural languages most likely have the quantificational machinery they do because of the quantificational resources of prelinguistic mental representations (both ontogenetically and phylogenetically)" (2009, 283) As far as ontogenetic development goes, this is also the NSM position. Moreover, NSM formulates an explicit hypothesis as to what exactly these prelinguistic quantificational resources are—a hypothesis corroborated by empirical crosslinguistic investigations: they are the conceptual primes ONE, TWO, SOME, MANY (MUCH), FEW (LITTLE), and ALL.

In the next section, I discuss in some detail a third example of Carey's "innate primitives," that of AGENT and AGENCY. First, however, I briefly comment on the concept of PEOPLE, which is not mentioned by Carey explicitly but whose presence in "core cognition" is consistent with the spirit, if not the letter, of her discussion. To quote:

> The world of human infants is also social ... selection pressures on understanding others ... may have been a driving force in the shaping of the human brain. On this view, it would not be surprising that evolution bequeathed us humans with core cognition of agents, agents' interaction with each other, and agents' interactions with the physical world, articulated in terms of representations of goals, information, and attentional states. (157)

In a sense, this is precisely what we find in human languages: not only SOMEONE and SOMETHING, but also PEOPLE, and more specifically, PEOPLE who not only WANT, THINK, KNOW, and DO things, but also DO things WITH other people and SAY things TO other people (in the NSM model, WITH in DO WITH, and TO in DO TO, represent particular valency options of the primes DO and SAY). From a linguistic (and crosslinguistic) perspective, however, it is problematic that Carey's account of human social cognition is presented in a conceptual vocabulary derived largely from (Latinate) English, and that her key terms, such as "agent," "interaction," "information," and "attention," are complex and do not translate across languages. As a result of this terminological Anglocentrism, Carey's list of "the central concepts in the domain" is, I believe, skewed, and the account of the area of "core cognition" that involves people becomes blurred, as I illustrate in the next section.

14.5   Carey's Account of "Agency"

In this section, I try to elucidate four key statements from the section of Carey's (2009) book entitled "The Central Concepts in the Domain: Agency, Goals, Information, and Attention" (part of a chapter titled "Core Cognition: Agency").

14.5.1   Statement 1: "Inanimate Objects" versus "Agents"

Causality in the domain of inert physical objects is physical contact causality. Inanimate objects go into motion immediately upon and only upon being contacted by another moving object or by some source of physical energy. Causality in the domain of agents has a different structure. Agents are capable of self-generated motion and of resisting forces acting upon them. (158)

If we try to translate this passage into the language of simple and clear concepts that are not English bound, we can propose the following (partial) rendering:

[A] "Inanimate objects moving"
if something is not something living,
 when this something is moving, it is moving because it is like this:
  a short time before something else touched this something
  this something else was moving at that time

[B'] "Agents (e.g., animals) moving"
 if something is something living,
  when this something is moving, it can be like this:
  it is moving because it wants to be moving, not because of anything else

[B''] "Agents (e.g., people) moving"
 when someone is moving, it can be like this:
  this someone is moving because this someone wants to be moving,
  not because of anything else

Formula [A] corresponds to the first two sentences of Carey's statement quoted above, and formulas [B'] and [B''] to the second two. Despite the use of the word *agent*, on closer inspection, statement 1 appears to be concerned mainly with drawing a distinction between *living things* and *nonliving things*, in relation to what causes them to move, and not with "someone doing something," as the term *agent* might suggest. (*Animate* and *inanimate* are technical linguistic terms, whereas *living* is an ordinary word, with counterparts, evidence suggests, in all languages.)

The "translation" of Carey's statement 1 given in formulas [A], [B'] and [B''] proposed here doesn't capture the references to "some source of physical energy" in the first sentence and to "resisting forces acting upon them" in the second because their intended meaning is not quite clear to me. Perhaps the idea is that often people don't have to move (or do anything else?) if they don't want to, even if someone else wants them to do it. It is not clear, however, that the phrase "forces acting upon them" is indeed meant to refer to what other people want.

14.5.2   Statement 2: "Goals"

We explain agents' actions in terms of their goals and the state of the world that facilitates or impedes these goals. (158)

This statement refers neither to a contrast between *agents* and *inanimate objects* nor to why *inanimate objects* and *agents* move, but the word *goal* suggests that it is concerned with why *agents* do something: they do it because they want something to happen. Or at least such are the implications of the word *goal* in ordinary (non-technical) language. Unfortunately, in psychological literature one can't always take ordinary meanings for granted, and Carey, too, sometimes moves imperceptibly and without warning between ordinary and technical meanings. For example, she sometimes speaks as if she is attributing "goals" not only to children but also to plants. To quote:

We can see the difference between the richer and leaner interpretations of intentional agency by comparing how we think of light-seeking tropisms of plants and cookie-seeking actions of children. Both are goal directed, but we attribute to the child representations of their goals and beliefs about where cookies are to be found (e.g., "she wants to eat a cookie" and "she believes cookies are in the cupboard"), whereas we attribute neither to the plants. (159)

If light-seeking tropisms of plants are "goal directed," and the word *goal* is not always to be interpreted in terms of "wanting" and "doing" (as in the case of children seeking cookies), then the word *goal* is being used in two different senses. Obviously, when applied to plants it is used metaphorically. But when such metaphors are allowed into scholarly discourse without any clear distinctions being made between metaphorical and nonmetaphorical uses, then even the basic words on which the argument relies become slippery.

This is not something particularly characteristic of Carey's prose. On the contrary, I think she is generally more careful in this respect than many psychologists. So my purpose here is not to criticize Carey but rather to draw attention to some widespread conventions of psychological discourse whose legitimacy is usually taken for granted but which I believe are far less innocent than they may appear. For this reason, it is worth recalling here Locke's forceful comments on what he called the "abuse of language."

Another great abuse of words is, *inconstancy* in the use of them. It is hard to find a discourse written of any subject, especially of controversy, wherein one shall not observe, if he read with attention, the same words (and those commonly the most material in the discourse, and upon which the argument turns) used sometimes for one collection of simple *ideas*, and sometimes for another, which is a perfect abuse of language, words being intended for signs of my *ideas*, to make them known to others, not by any natural signification, but by a voluntary imposition, 'tis plain cheat and abuse, when I make them stand sometimes for one thing, and sometimes for another. ([1690] 1959, 492)

14.5.3   Statement 3: "Attention" and "Information"

We explain agents' actions in terms of their goals. ... We monitor agents' attentional focus and expect (at least in the case of people) agents to provide useful information about the world. (158)

What is meant by "attentional focus," one wonders? In ordinary English, the meaning of the word *attention* combines references to *thinking, knowing,* and *wanting.* Roughly speaking, it implies that during some time, one is thinking all the time about something (perhaps something happening "here," that is, in the place where one is) because one wants to know some things about it. Usually, some *doing* (aimed at *knowing*) also comes into play: one looks and listens because one wants to know well what is going on. It seems likely that when Carey speaks about "agents' attentional focus" she means, above all, the direction of people's gaze: when we see what someone else is looking at, we can infer from it what this other person is thinking about.

In what sense is the concept of ATTENTION part of human "core cognition"? The fact is that many (perhaps most) languages don't have such a word, so arguably, this concept, too, is culturally constructed. By contrast, the "ingredients" of this concept enumerated here, that is, the concepts THINK, KNOW, WANT, and HERE, are not culturally constructed but evidently a product of human evolution. Carey's further statement that we "monitor" other people's (*agents'*) "attentional focus" appears to refer to a situation when two people are in the same place and one of them watches the other, wanting to know what this other person intends to do. The words *want, know,* and *do* used in this formulation are simple, clear, and universally cross-translatable. The word *monitor* is not. What exactly Carey has in mind is not quite clear, but it could no doubt be clarified with the help of conceptual primitives like THINK, KNOW, WANT, and SEE.

The statement in the explanation of "agency," which says that "we ... expect (at least in the case of people) agents to provide us useful information about the world" is reminiscent of Tomasello's (2009) observations about children's desire to "inform." It is not quite clear how it is intended to fit in "core cognition."

14.5.4   Statement 4: "Intentional Agents"

The debates reviewed in the chapter do not concern whether infants are intentional agents. I have no doubt that they are, even in the strongest sense. (159)

No words used in Carey's discussion of core cognition are more difficult than *intentional* and *intentionality*—words unfortunately favored by many contemporary psychologists, and arguably a key source of obscurity in many accounts of human cognition and its evolution, functioning, and development. The main reason for this is that the ordinary language sense of *intentional* is often not distinguished from its technical philosophical use. I will illustrate this with some sentences from Carey's account of "agency" as one of the central concepts of core cognition (158–159).

First, we are told that infants are "intentional agents" ("even in the strongest sense"). If one relies on ordinary language, one could think that this phrase has something to do with *doing* (because of the word *agents*) and *wanting-cum-thinking* (because of the word *intentional*). This understanding is reinforced by statements to the effect that "their [infants'] behavior is intentional" (159). But *intentionality* is also described as "a relation between an agent and the world that is characterized by aboutness" (158). On one analysis, we are told, "having a goal is a paradigmatic intentional state: the agent desires a state of affairs ... and wanting or desiring is an intentional relation between the agent and the world" (158). However, "attending and perceiving are other paradigmatic intentional relations," and "referring is another paradigmatic intentional relation" (159).

Thus, it appears that as Carey uses it, the word *intentional* is meant to straddle, in some ways, the ordinary language word *intentional* and its technical philosophical use. *The Cambridge Dictionary of Philosophy* (Audi 1999, 441) defines *intentionality* as "aboutness" and warns: "The adjective 'intentional' in this philosophical sense is a technical term not to be confused with the more familiar sense, characterizing something done on purpose.") Given that Carey's special usage of the word *intentional,* combining some elements of philosophical and colloquial use, is never defined, the reader can't be sure what exactly is meant by it in any given context.

Moreover, Carey acknowledges that sometimes she deliberately uses the phrase *intentional agency* in different senses ("sometimes I use the term 'intentional agency' to signal that I am attributing more to the infant than representations of self-generated motion and action" [139]). Given such variable and undefined usage, the reader can't be sure what the statement "infants are intentional agents" really means. "What is at issue," we are finally told, "is whether infants *understand* intentional agency" (159). Unfortunately, as readers, we are no longer sure that we understand it ourselves.

Generally speaking, Carey's two theses—that "infants represent events in terms of agency" (172) and that "infants represent goals as goals of particular agents" (172)—are entirely persuasive. What is less than clear is what exactly she means by *agency, agents,* and *goals,* and how these terms (as used by her) are related to the simpler, intuitively more transparent and non-English-dependent terms DO, PEOPLE, WANT, KNOW, and THINK.

In some contexts, the term *agents* seems to stand for PEOPLE, as when Carey suggests that "the innate face detectors infants have may serve the purpose of identifying agents, allowing them to learn how agents typically interact" (452). Presumably, any "inner face detectors" identify *people* rather than, more specifically, *doers* (i.e., agents). In other contexts, the term *agents* appears to refer, primarily, to what people *do*. For example, "infants may initially identify agents through patterns of interaction, and they may then learn what these agents may look like" (452).

In some contexts, it sounds as if the word *agents* stood for people seen *sub specie* of what they can do. Moreover, Carey hypothesizes that there may be two distinct "input analyzers," one related to human faces (i.e., presumably, to the concept PEOPLE), and the other, to what people can DO: "A third possibility is, like mother recognition in chicks, agency detection is such an important problem for human infants that evolution built in two dedicated input analyzers to do the trick" (454).

No doubt future psychological research will bring some answers to questions such as these. Carey emphasizes that, "Characterising the conceptual repertoire of infants is a difficult work, requiring convergent evidence from many methods" (537). One could add to this that characterizing the conceptual repertoire of infants may also require convergent evidence from many disciplines, including linguistics in general and cross-linguistic semantics in particular.

14.6   Children's First Words—and Their First "Abstract" Concepts

Presumably, nobody would deny that if we want to chart "the conceptual repertoire of human infants" that underlies children's cognitive development, it makes sense to pay attention to children's first words—not only those with spatiotemporal content (i.e., the *concrete* ones) but also *abstract* ones, which intersect with the developmental psychologist's key concepts like AGENCY, GOALS, ATTENTION, INFORMATION, and INTENTIONALITY. But while the importance of listening to children's first words is generally acknowledged (cf., e.g., Bloom 1973; Bowerman 1978; Braine 1976; Clark 1993; Gopnik and Meltzoff 1997; Halliday 1975; Tomasello 1992), it is frequently assumed that to be properly understood and interpreted, these words need to be first translated into the technical language of (Anglophone) psychology. It is not widely accepted that at least some of young children's first concepts can best be understood directly through some of these children's first words—that is, not words like *object, number, agent, goal,* and *intentionality,* but words like *something, one, two, do,* and *want.*

As Carey puts it, developmental psychologists "seek to characterise the representational resources that get human cognition off the ground, in both ontogenetic and evolutionary contexts" (2009, 537). These resources include "the ontogenetic primitives from which our conceptual system is built" (537). All this is very close to the NSM research program—with one proviso: from this program's point of view, there is no need to dress the hypothesized "ontogenetic primitives" that get the human condition off the ground in the garb of the culture-specific and semi-technical vocabulary of

English, with words and phrases like *object, agency, information, intentional causality,* and so on (cf. 158–159). The "ontogenetic primitives" may well come out of the mouths of babes in the form of simple words with meanings such as SOMEONE and SOMETHING, PEOPLE, DO and SAY, WANT, KNOW and THINK, IF and BECAUSE, and a limited number of others well attested in young children's speech in many languages.

Of course, children's words are not semantically transparent and can't be taken at face value. For example, for some children the word *cat* can mean, roughly speaking, any animal with a round head. Similarly, a young child can say *I* for *you* and vice versa, or *more* for *want.* On the whole, however, evidence suggests that, more often than not, toddlers' early meanings of words like *no, more, want,* and *this* tend to match their meanings in adult speech, and that communicatively appropriate use of such words by toddlers provides reasonable evidence of the early presence of the corresponding concepts in the child's mind.

For example, Goddard (2001a) notes in his diary study of his son's semantic development that at twenty-six months, Pete, in his productive vocabulary, uses appropriately the exponents of the postulated conceptual primes GOOD, BAD, BIG, SMALL (LITTLE), WANT, MOVE, DO, NOT (NO), BEFORE (FIRST), WHERE, HERE, ABOVE, and BELOW. By the age of three and a half years, Pete has lexical exponents of nearly all proposed NSM primes in his speech. Further, Goddard argues, on the basis of his diary material, that conceptual primes appear to be present, as Bruner (1990) put it, "in protolinguistic form," some time before they emerge as spoken words: they "may be 'latent' in a child's early lexicon, in the sense of being hidden or implicit in the meanings of other, non-prime words" (Goddard 2001a, 201). Arguably, then, the best way to represent the primes in their "protolinguistic form" is to link them with words that serve as their exponents a little later, that is, in toddlers' spoken utterances.

In fact, this is in keeping with what Carey herself wrote in her earlier work (Carey 1982), when she pointed out that the majority of terms used in child language research to describe children's meanings are technical and theory laden. They represent, she argued, "a sophisticated schematization of knowledge by linguists," rather than children's "innate or at least very early-acquired concepts, out of which all other concepts are built" (351).

As noted by Goddard (2001a, 196), "this criticism cannot be levelled at the NSM system … because NSM primes are not 'abstract terms from theories which the child has not yet encountered.' On the contrary, they are plain words and expressions of ordinary language, which the child is hearing every day, and which, in many cases, exist in the child's own active vocabulary." Accordingly, the language of NSM primes offers a reliable basis for investigating children's meanings, at all levels: verbal, nonverbal, and preverbal.

I will illustrate how this could be approached by trying to clarify (in the first place, for myself) Carey's main hypotheses about *agency* (in her broad sense of the term) and its place in infant cognition. Since these hypotheses are not entirely clear to me, I regard my attempt at translating them into simple, universal, and "childish" words as a set of metahypotheses (hypotheses about hypotheses).

14.7   Interpreting Carey's Hypotheses about Infant Cognition through NSM

Human "core cognition" as conceived by Carey is not limited to a list of "ontogenetic primitives," and neither is the NSM model of the "language of the mind." Leibniz's metaphor of the "alphabet of human thoughts" is memorable, but so is his phrase "lingua naturae" ("the language of nature") and its medieval predecessor "lingua mentalis" (cf. Wierzbicka 1980, 204). Following this line of thought, one can hypothesize that there are not only innate concepts (such as, for example, *I, want, not,* and *this*) but also innate mental resources for constructing sentences, such as, for example, "I want this" and "I don't want this."

One can also hypothesize that an infant's early thoughts and messages may be holophrastic rather than configured out of conceptual primes. Thus, meanings such as "I want this" and "I don't want this" may well come before the child is able to operate with units such as *I, want,* and *this.* For the adult, however, it is natural to interpret such holophrastic messages as a (syntactically appropriate) configuration of the primes.

Such an account of children's early meanings fits in well, as far as I can see, with Carey's own view of infant cognition. For example, when she writes, "By 9 to 12 months of age, children hold up objects for others to look at, checking back and forth between the others' eyes and the object they are apparently attempting to bring to their attention" (2009, 176–177), she appears to be attributing to the child the holistic message "I-want-you-to-see-this."

But since Carey's hypotheses tend to be stated in complex and somewhat variable formulations, it is not always quite clear what exactly she has in mind. Below, I will try to clarify some of her hypotheses, as I understand them, through NSM, focusing on children's interpretation of other people as *agents.*

Carey has no doubt that children "form mental representations with symbolic content, and their behavior is intentional, goal oriented, and mediated by their representations of the world." What is at issue, in her view, "is whether infants *understand* intentional agency—whether the capacity to form representations of themselves or others as intentional agents is part of core cognition" (159). Reviewing the evidence, Carey answers the question in the affirmative: "Infants represent events in terms of agency" (172). In addition to representations of agents' goals, infants "represent agents as indicating, communicating about, and attending to objects" (173), and they "represent agents as seeking or providing information about the world" (175). Tentatively, I interpret these statements as follows:

1. An infant can think like this about someone at some time:
"this someone wants something" [cf. "attribution of wanting"]
2. An infant can think like this about someone at some time:
"this someone is doing something because this someone wants something" [cf. "attribution of a goal"]
3. An infant can think like this about someone at some time:
"this someone is thinking about this thing here" [cf. "attribution of attention"]
4. An infant can think like this about someone at some time:
"this someone wants me to see something" [cf. "indicating something"]
5. An infant can think like this about someone at some time:
"this someone wants to know something" [cf. "seeking information"]

These metahypotheses may or may not correspond exactly to Carey's conception of the relevant aspects of infants' cognition. As she notes herself, however, "building a theory of concept acquisition and a theory of concepts that fits with it is a single project" (487). A plausible theory of concepts, I believe, has to be consistent with the evidence concerning concepts that show up (as words or distinct word meanings) in all languages. It stands to reason that the "ontogenetic primitives from which our [i.e., a child's] conceptual system is built" (537) should coincide with the semantic primitives from which the conceptual systems developed in different languages are built.

The apparent existence of a common lexical (and lexico-grammatical) core in all languages of the world—independent of the cultural shaping of each language—requires an explanation, and so does the existence of "core cognition" apparently emerging from studies of infants. The simplest hypothesis consistent with the available evidence is that these "two" are in fact one, and that this one shared core of languages and cognition is innate and identifiable, in principle, through any language—through English too, of course, but only through that subset of English that coincides with similar subsets of all other languages and that can apparently be found also in child language (Goddard 2001a; Tien 2010).

If words express concepts, then children's words express children's concepts. If nothing forces us to conclude otherwise, the simplest hypothesis compatible with the available evidence is that children's earliest abstract words express their earliest abstract (nonspatiotemporal) concepts. There is simply no need to posit prelinguistic conceptual primitives such as OBJECT, NUMBER, or AGENT, which would then get transformed into linguistically embodied concepts such as *something, someone, one, two, do,* and *want.* At the same time, it is important to acknowledge that as children's vocabulary expands, their thinking becomes increasingly shaped by word meanings that are culture specific and culturally shaped themselves.

As Carey notes, "continuity theorists" such as Jerry Fodor (1975, 1998) and Steven Pinker (1984, 1994) "deny that language learning shapes our concepts in any interesting ways" (250). This reflects these scholars' limited interests and lack of attention to the literature on bilingual cognition and bilingual experience.

In mentioning the names of Fodor and Pinker as examples of "continuity theorists," Carey may seem to be lumping together two very different approaches to innate concepts: while Fodor posits "fifty thousand innate concepts" (to quote Pinker's [2007b] ironic label for Fodor's theory), Pinker himself posits only a few dozen (2007b, 81). Thus, Pinker's cast of innate concepts is in fact much closer to that posited in NSM work. When Pinker says that "word meanings can vary across languages because children assemble and fine-tune them from more elementary concepts" (150), he is saying what NSM researchers have been saying, and documenting with extensive crosslinguistic evidence, for decades.

Nonetheless, I think that Carey is right in presenting not only Fodor but also Pinker as theorists who emphasize "continuity" in children's conceptual development at the expense of discontinuities. I agree with Pinker that Fodor's claims about "fifty thousand innate concepts" (including BUREAUCRAT and CARBURETOR) are hard to take seriously; and Pinker himself does need to be taken seriously. He is an engaging and popular writer, but I believe that on these issues he, too, is wrong. Accordingly, I have sought to rebut him at some length in my book *Imprisoned in English* (Wierzbicka 2014), so here I will restate only a few key points.

As I argue in *Imprisoned,* the historically shaped vocabulary of English can be a conceptual prison for those who absolutize it and never look at it from a historical and crosslinguistic perspective, and no one stands in danger of such unwitting self-imprisonment more than theorists who see science as a foolproof guide to reality, including the reality of what goes on in human minds. This appears to apply to Pinker. To quote:

> There is no scientific evidence that languages dramatically shape their speakers' ways of thinking. The idea that language shapes thinking seemed plausible when scientists were in the dark about how thinking works or even how to study it. Now that cognitive scientists know how to think about thinking, there is less of a temptation to equate it with language just because words are more palpable than thoughts. (Pinker 1994, 58)

More than a decade later, in his book *The Stuff of Thought,* Pinker (2007b, 132) speaks in a similar tone, dismissing, for example, psycholinguist Dan Slobin's research into "thinking-for-speaking" (i.e., thinking geared toward the particular language in which one's thoughts are going to be expressed).

Pinker accepts that "every language forces speakers to pay attention to certain aspects of the world" (2007b, 131), but not that "a lifelong habit of attending to certain distinctions and ignoring others" can have an effect on how they think. In particular, he is convinced that English speakers, compared with speakers of other languages, "have no trouble grasping the distinctions that some other languages make and English doesn't" and that "clearly we command these distinctions as we negotiate the social and physical world" (2007a, 150). And so he shrugs Slobin's insight off: "It shouldn't be surprising that the effects of thinking-for-speaking on thinking itself are small at best" (2007a, 150).

The irony is that Pinker himself is an example of someone whose thinking appears to be strongly influenced by his native English—for example, when he interprets human evolution through the prism of the modern English concepts VIOLENCE and COOPERATION (Pinker 2011; cf. Wierzbicka 2014); or when he characterizes the concept of STORY—a highly culture-specific conceptual artifact of English (Wierzbicka 2010b)—as a human universal and a product of evolutionary adaptation (Pinker 2007a); or when he includes English causative verbs such as *causing, letting, enabling, preventing, impeding,* and *encouraging* (which have no counterparts in most other languages, cf. Wierzbicka 2006, chapter 6) in his list of foundational human concepts (Pinker 2007b, 81).

Speaking more generally, I would argue that if cognitive scientists are to escape Anglocentrism, they need to pay more attention to crosslinguistic evidence and to bilingual experience (e.g., Hoffman 1989; Besemeres 2002; Pavlenko 2005, 2006, 2011, 2014; Cook and Bassetti 2011). Without a perspective anchored in bilingual experience, cognitive science seems to be often unable to appreciate the reality of the effect that different languages have on the way their speakers think. To quote Eva Hoffman's bilingual memoir, *Lost in Translation: A Life in a New Language*:

"If you've never eaten a real tomato, you'll think that the plastic tomato is the real thing, and moreover, you'll be perfectly satisfied with it," I tell my friends. "It's only when you've tasted them both that you know there's a difference. ..." My friends are moved by the parable of the plastic tomato. But when I try to apply it, by analogy, to the internal realm, they balk. Surely, inside our heads and souls things are more universal, the ocean of reality one and indivisible. "No," I shout in every one of our arguments, "no!" There's a world out there; there are worlds. There are shapes of sensibility incommensurate with each other, topographies of experience one cannot guess from within one's own limited experience. (1989, 204)

I do not mean, needless to say, that one can't study human cognition if one doesn't have bilingual experience oneself. What I mean is that to appreciate the far-reaching effects of how people speak or how they think, one needs to familiarize oneself with testimonies such as Hoffman's as well as the whole broad field of bilingual and translingual experience.

14.8 Conclusion

Carey formulates the main issue that concerns her as "whether language learning (any language) leads infants to think differently about the world from how children thought about it before language learning" (2009, 248).

It seems clear that the answer to this question must be "yes and no." Acquiring the words of their native language, children also acquire a great many new concepts, but evidence suggests that the new concepts acquired through a particular language constitute culture-specific configurations of innate prelinguistic concepts. Thus, the elementary building blocks of the new thoughts are the same as those available to the child before language learning. At the same time, however, vocabulary learning leads to a radical expansion of the child's thought-world. In particular, it involves acquiring a large number of culture-specific semantic molecules, which provide prefabricated conceptual units for building new thoughts. As a result, the radically expanded thought-world is largely shaped by the culture associated with the child's first language.

Contrary to what Pinker affirms, there is massive evidence that language learning introduces the child (as well as the "language migrants," to use Mary Besemeres' [2002] term) to a wealth of new concepts, and that most of these new concepts are culturally shaped. But there is no conflict between recognizing, on the one hand, this colossal lexico-semantic diversity of languages and the concomitant diversity of concepts that children learning different languages acquire, and on the other, the existence of a shared lexico-semantic core, a part of which can be seen as matching the concepts of prelinguistic children (such as THIS, SOMETHING, ONE, SOMEONE, DO, and WANT).

Thus, NSM researchers, who posit and *specify* the stock of innate concepts, can also be called *continuity theorists,* although their position is radically different from that of scholars like either Fodor or Pinker. In the quote adduced earlier, Doug Jones justly notes that much of the work done within the NSM approach "consists of showing how secondary culture-specific concepts can be defined by comparing sentences using the conceptual primitives of natural semantic metalanguage and a simplified version of a natural language syntax" (1999, 560). But while NSM researchers do not posit radical discontinuities in children's conceptual development and show that the semantic systems of different languages are in fact commensurable, much of our work consists of demonstrating, through detailed semantic analyses, the great diversity of these systems, and by implication, the radical expansion of children's conceptual repertoire dependent on the particular language environment into which the child is born (e.g., Wierzbicka 1997; Harkins and Wierzbicka 2001; Goddard 2006).

Thus, we would like to reclaim the label of *continuity theorists* from scholars who don't recognize the radical transformation of the child's mental world that language learning (that is, learning a particular language) brings with it. Evidence suggests that continuity and transformation are both essential features of human conceptual development, just as they can both be features of an existential move from a "life in one language" to a life in another (cf. Hoffman 1989; Besemeres 2002; Slobin 1996; Pavlenko 2005, 2006; Besemeres and Wierzbicka 2007).

Carey concludes her chapter on "Language and Core Cognition" by acknowledging two areas in which language learning influences children's thought: "Language learning certainly plays a role in the construction of specific kind sortals [i.e. words for *kinds* of animals, plants, and artifacts], which are then deployed in infants' encoding of events unfolding around them. Language learning may also play a role in the availability and deployment of set-based quantification" (285).[4]

To conclude, I believe that to advance the study of concepts, we need to recognize that academic English is not an adequate metalanguage for portraying representational resources that get human cognition off the ground. To put it differently, Carey's question "What do children know innately?" cannot be answered in academic English: children may "know innately" (latently) that 'someone is not something', but not that there are *agents* and *objects*. Nor is academic English (with words like *agents, objects,* and *causation*) an adequate tool for differentiating human representational resources from those of nonhuman primates (Fabrega, 2013; Goddard et al. 2014; Wierzbicka 2004) or for comparing those resources across languages, cultures, and epochs (Goddard 2006, 2008; Wierzbicka 1999; Goddard and Wierzbicka 2014a; Bromhead 2009). I submit that the empirically established repertoire of foundational human concepts provides a more reliable toolkit for the study of concepts in a crosslinguistic, cross-temporal, evolutionary, and ontogenetic perspective.

References

Amberber, M. 2008. Semantic primes in Amharic. In *Cross-Linguistic Semantics*, ed. C. Goddard, 83–119. Amsterdam: John Benjamins.

Ameka, F. 1994. Ewe. In *Semantic and Lexical Universals: Theory and Empirical Findings*, ed. C. Goddard and A. Wierzbicka, 57–86. Amsterdam: John Benjamins.

Ameka, F. 2006. 'When I die, don't cry': The ethnopragmatics of "gratitude" in West African languages. In *Ethnopragmatics: Understanding Discourse in Cultural Context*, ed. C. Goddard, 231–266. Berlin: Mouton de Gruyter.

Ameka, F. 2009. Access rituals in West African communities: An ethnopragmatic perspective. In *Ritual Communication*, ed. G. Senft and E. B. Basso, 127–152. New York: Berg.

Asano-Cavanagh, Y. 2009. A semantic analysis of Japanese epistemic markers: chigainai and hazuda. *Language Sciences* 31 (5): 837–852.

Asano-Cavanagh, Y. 2010. Semantic analysis of evidential markers in Japanese: Rashii, yooda and sooda. *Functions of Language* 17 (2): 153–180.

4. Pinker (2007b, 137) rejects Carey's observation about the role of language in the acquisition of kind sortals by pointing out that, according to experimental work on macaque monkeys, a monkey can distinguish a carrot from a squash. He doesn't consider the possibility that in doing so, a monkey may in fact be distinguishing SOMETHING LONG from SOMETHING ROUND rather than A CARROT from A SQUASH (that is, one kind sortal from another).

Audi, R., ed. 1999. *The Cambridge Dictionary of Philosophy*. 2nd ed. Cambridge, MA: Cambridge University Press.

Besemeres, M. 2002. *Translating One's Self: Language and Selfhood in Cross-Cultural Autobiography*. Oxford: Peter Lang.

Besemeres, M., and A. Wierzbicka, eds. 2007. *Translating Lives: Living with Two Languages and Cultures*. St Lucia: University of Queensland Press.

Bloom, L. 1973. *One Word at a Time*. The Hague: Mouton.

Bowerman, Melissa. 1978. The acquisition of word meaning: An investigation into some current conflicts. In *The Development of Communication*, ed. N. Waterman and C. Snow, 263–287. New York: Wiley.

Braine, M. D. S. 1976. Children's first word combinations. *Monographs of the Society for Research in Child Development* 44 (1): 1–97.

Bromhead, H. 2009. *The Reign of Truth and Faith: Epistemic Expression in 16th and 17th Century English*. Berlin: Mouton de Gruyter.

Bromhead, H. 2011. Ethnogeographical categories in English and Pitjantjatjara/Yankunytjatjara. *Language Sciences* 33 (1): 58–75.

Brotherson, A. 2008. The ethnogeometry of Makasai (East Timor). In *Cross-Linguistic Semantics*, ed. C. Goddard, 259–276. Amsterdam: John Benjamins.

Bruner, J. 1990. *Acts of Meaning*. Cambridge, MA: Harvard University Press.

Bugenhagen, R. D. 2001. Emotions and the nature of persons in Mbula. In *Emotions in Crosslinguistic Perspective*, ed. J. Harkins and A. Wierzbicka, 69–114. Berlin: Mouton de Gruyter.

Bugenhagen, R. D. 2002. The syntax of semantic primitives in Mangaaba-Mbula. In *Meaning and Universal Grammar—Theory and Empirical Findings*. vol. II. ed. C. Goddard and A. Wierzbicka, 1–64. Amsterdam: John Benjamins.

Carey, S. 1982. Semantic development: The state of the art. In *Language Acquisition: The State of the Art*, ed. E. Wanner and L. R. Gleitman, 347–379. Cambridge: Cambridge University Press.

Carey, S. 2009. *The Origin of Concepts*. Oxford: Oxford University Press.

Chappell, H. 2002. The universal syntax of semantic primes in Mandarin Chinese. In *Meaning and Universal Grammar—Theory and Empirical Findings*. vol. I. ed. C. Goddard and A. Wierzbicka, 243–322. Amsterdam: John Benjamins.

Clark, E. V. 1993. *The Lexicon in Acquisition*. Cambridge: Cambridge University Press.

Collins Cobuild English Language Dictionary. 1991. London: Harper Collins.

Concise Oxford Dictionary of Current English. 1982. 7th ed. Oxford: Clarendon Press.

Cook, V., and B. Bassetti, eds. 2011. *Language and Bilingual Cognition*. Hove, UK: Routledge.

Couturat, L. 1903. *Opuscules et Fragments Inedits de Leibniz*. Paris: Presses Universitaires de France.

Dascal, M. 1987. *Leibniz: Language, Signs and Thought*. Amsterdam: John Benjamins.

Enfield, N. J. 2002. Combinatoric properties of Natural Semantic Metalanguge expressions in Lao. In *Meaning and Universal Grammar—Theory and Empirical Findings*. vol. II. ed. C. Goddard and A. Wierzbicka, 145–256. Amsterdam: John Benjamins.

Everett, D. L. 2005. Cultural constraints on grammar and cognition in Pirahã: Another look at the design features of human language. *Current Anthropology* 46 (4): 621–634.

Fabrega, H., Jr. 2013. *Conditions of Psychiatric Interest in Early Human History*. Lewiston, NY: Edwin Mellen Press.

Fodor, J. A. 1975. *The Language of Thought*. New York: Crowell.

Fodor, J. A. 1998. *Concepts: Where Cognitive Science Went Wrong*. New York: Clarendon Press.

Frank, M. C., D. L. Everett, E. Fedorenko, and E. Gibson. 2008. Number as a cognitive technology: Evidence from Pirahã language and cognition. *Cognition* 108 (3): 819–824.

Geertz, C. 1974. From the native's point of view: On the nature of anthropological understanding. *Bulletin - American Academy of Arts and Sciences. American Academy of Arts and Sciences*: 26–45.

Gerhardt, C. I., ed. 1960–1961. *Die Philosophischen Schriften von Gottfried Wilhelm Leibniz*. Vol. 1–7. Hildesheim: Olms.

Gladkova, A. 2007. Universal and language-specific aspects of "propositional attitudes": Russian vs. English. In *Mental States: Vol. 2: Language and Cognitive Structure*, ed. A.C. Schalley and D. Khlentzos, 61–83. Amsterdam: John Benjamins.

Gladkova, A. 2010. *Russkaja kul'turnaja semantika: èmocii, cennosti, žiznennye ustanovki* [Russian cultural semantics: Emotions, values, attitudes.] Moscow: Languages of Slavic Cultures.

Goddard, C. 1991. Testing the translatability of semantic primitives into an Australian Aboriginal Language. *Anthropological Linguistics* 33 (1): 31–56.

Goddard, C. 1994. Lexical primitives in Yankunytjatjara. In *Semantic and Lexical Universals— Theory and Empirical Findings*, ed. C. Goddard and A. Wierzbicka, 229–262. Amsterdam: John Benjamins.

Goddard, C. 2001a. Conceptual primes in early language development. In *Applied Cognitive Linguistics: Theory and Language Acquisition*, ed. M. Pütz and S. Niemeier, 93–227. Berlin: Mouton de Gruyter.

Goddard, C. 2001b. *Sabar, ikhlas, setia*—patient, sincere, loyal? A contrastive semantic study of some "virtues" in Malay and English. *Journal of Pragmatics* 33:653–681.

Goddard, C. 2001c. *Hati:* A key word in the Malay vocabulary of emotion. In *Emotions in Crosslinguistic Perspective*, ed. J. Harkins and A. Wierzbicka, 171–200. Berlin: Mouton de Gruyter.

Goddard, C. 2002. Semantic primes and universal grammar in Malay (Bahasa Melayu). In *Meaning and Universal Grammar—Theory and Empirical Findings*. vol. I. ed. C. Goddard and A. Wierzbicka, 87–172. Amsterdam: John Benjamins.

Goddard, C., ed. 2006. *Ethnopragmatics: Understanding Discourse in Cultural Context*. Berlin: Mouton de Gruyter.

Goddard, C., ed. 2008. *Cross-Linguistic Semantics*. Amsterdam: John Benjamins.

Goddard, C. 2009. The conceptual semantics of numbers and counting: An NSM analysis. *Functions of Language* 16 (2): 193–224.

Goddard, C. 2010. Semantic molecules and semantic complexity (with special reference to "environmental" molecules). *Review of Cognitive Linguistics* 8 (1): 123–155.

Goddard, C. 2011. *Semantic Analysis: A Practical Introduction*, 2nd edition. Oxford: Oxford University Press.

Goddard, C., and A. Wierzbicka, eds. 1994. *Semantic and Lexical Universals—Theory and Empirical Findings*. Amsterdam: John Benjamins.

Goddard, C., and A. Wierzbicka, eds. 2002. *Meaning and Universal Grammar: Theory and Empirical Findings*. 2 vols. Amsterdam: John Benjamins.

Goddard, C., and A. Wierzbicka. 2014a. *Words and Meanings: Lexical Semantics across Domains, Languages, and Cultures*. Oxford: Oxford University Press.

Goddard, C., and A. Wierzbicka. 2014b. Semantic fieldwork and lexical universals. *Studies in Language* 38 (1): 80–127.

Goddard, C., A. Wierzbicka, and H. Fabrega, Jr. 2014. Evolutionary semantics: using NSM to model stages in human cognitive evolution. *Language Sciences* 42:60–79.

Gopnik, A., and A. N. Meltzoff. 1997. *Words, Thoughts, and Theories*. Cambridge, MA: MIT Press.

Gordon, P. 2004. Numerical cognition without words: Evidence from Amazonia. *Science* 306 (5695): 496–499.

Habib, S. 2011a. Contrastive lexical conceptual analysis of folk religious concepts in English, Arabic and Hebrew: NSM approach. PhD thesis, University of New England.

Habib, S. 2011b. Angels can cross cultural boundaries. *RASK. International Journal of Language and Communication* 34:49–75.

Halliday, M. A. K. 1975. *Learning How to Mean—Explorations in the Development of Language*. London: Edward Arnold.

Harkins, J. 2001. Talking about anger in Central Australia. In *Emotions in Crosslinguistic Perspective*, ed. J. Harkins and A. Wierzbicka, 201–220. Berlin: Mouton de Gruyter.

Harkins, J., and A. Wierzbicka, eds. 2001. *Emotions in Crosslinguistic Perspective*. Berlin: Mouton de Gruyter.

Harkins, J., and D. P. Wilkins. 1994. Mparntwe Arrernte and the search for lexical universals. In *Semantic and Lexical Universals—Theory and Empirical Findings*, ed. C. Goddard and A. Wierzbicka, 285–310. Amsterdam: John Benjamins.

Hasada, R. 1998. Sound symbolic emotion words in Japanese. In *Speaking of Emotions: Conceptualisation and Expression*, ed. A. Athanasiadou and E. Tabakowska, 83–98. Berlin: Mouton de Gruyter.

Hasada, R. 2001. Meanings of Japanese sound-symbolic emotion words. In *Emotions in Crosslinguistic Perspective*, ed. J. Harkins and A. Wierzbicka, 221–258. Berlin: Mouton de Gruyter.

Hasada, R. 2008. Two virtuous emotions in Japanese: Nasake/joo and jihi. In *Cross-Linguistic Semantics*, ed. C. Goddard, 331–347. Amsterdam: John Benjamins.

Hill, D. 1994. Longgu. In *Semantic and Lexical Universals—Theory and Empirical Findings*, ed. C. Goddard and A. Wierzbicka, 310–330. Amsterdam: John Benjamins.

Hoffman, E. 1989. *Lost in Translation: A Life in a New Language*. New York: Dutton.

Jackendoff, R. 2007. *Language, Consciousness, Culture: Essays on Mental Structure*. Cambridge, MA: MIT Press.

Jones, D. 1999. Evolutionary Psychology. *Annual Review of Anthropology* 28:553–575.

Junker, M.-O. 2003. A Native American view of the "mind" as seen in the lexicon of cognition in East Cree. *Cognitive Linguistics* 14 (2-3): 167–194.

Junker, M.-O. 2007. The language of memory in East Cree. In *The Language of Memory in a Crosslinguistic Perspective*, ed. M. Amberber, 235–261. Amsterdam: John Benjamins.

Junker, M.-O. 2008. Semantic primes and their grammar in a polysynthetic language: East Cree. In *Cross-Linguistic Semantics*, ed. C. Goddard, 163–204. Amsterdam: John Benjamins.

Junker, M.-O., and L. Blacksmith. 2006. Are there emotional universals? Evidence from the Native American language East Cree. *Culture and Psychology* 12 (3): 275–303.

Leibniz, G. W. [1765] 1981. *New Essays on Human Understanding*. Cambridge: Cambridge University Press.

Knight, E. 2008. Hyperpolysemy in Bunuba, a polysynthetic language of the Kimberley, Western Australia. In *Cross-linguistic Semantics*, ed. C. Goddard, 205–223. Amsterdam: John Benjamins.

Leung, H. 2012. The semantics of Cantonese utterance particle laa1. Proceedings of the 2011 conference of the Australian Linguistic Society. ANU Research Collections. https://digitalcollections.anu.edu.au.

Levisen, C. 2012. *Cultural Semantics and Social Cognition: A Case Study on the Danish Universe of Meaning*. Berlin: Mouton de Gruyter.

Locke, J. [1690] 1959. *An Essay Concerning Human Understanding*. Oxford: Clarendon Press.

Martin, G. 1964. *Leibniz: Logic and Metaphysics*. Trans. K. J. Northcott and P. G. Lucas. Manchester: Manchester University Press.

Mosel, U. 1994. Samoan. In *Semantic and Lexical Universals—Theory and Empirical Findings*, ed. C. Goddard and A. Wierzbicka, 331–360. Amsterdam: John Benjamins.

Nicholls, S. 2009. Referring Expressions and Referential Practice in Roper Kriol (Northern Territory, Australia). PhD Thesis, University of New England. https://e-publications.une.edu.au/vital/access/manager/Repository/une:9244

Homepage, N. S. M. http://www.griffith.edu.au/humanities-languages/school-languages-linguistics/research/natural-semantic-metalanguage-homepage.

Pavlenko, A. 2005. *Emotions and Multilingualism*. Cambridge: Cambridge University Press.

Pavlenko, A., ed. 2006. *Bilingual Minds: Emotional Experiences, Expressions, and Representation*. Clevedon: Multilingual Matters.

Pavlenko, A., ed. 2011. *Thinking and Speaking in Two Languages*. Clevedon: Multilingual Matters.

Pavlenko, A. 2014. *The Bilingual Mind: And What It Tells Us about Language and Thought*. Cambridge: Cambridge University Press.

Pawley, A. 1994. Kalam exponents of lexical and semantic primitives. In *Semantic and Lexical Universals: Theory and Empirical Findings*, ed. C. Goddard and A. Wierzbicka, 87–422. Amsterdam: John Benjamins.

Peeters, B., ed. 2006. *Semantic Primes and Universal Grammar: Empirical Evidence from the Romance Languages*. Amsterdam: John Benjamins.

Peeters, B. 2010. La métalangue sémantique naturelle: acquis et défis. In *Grandes Voies et Chemins de Traverse de la Sémantique Cognitive*, ed. J. François, 75–101. Leuven: Peeters.

Pinker, S. 1984. *Language Learnability and Language Development*. Cambridge, MA: Harvard University Press.

Pinker, S. 1994. *The Language Instinct*. New York: Harper Perennial Modern Classics.

Pinker, S. 2007a. Critical discussion: Toward a consilient study of literature. *Philosophy and Literature* 31:161–177.

Pinker, S. 2007b. *The Stuff of Thought: Language as a Window into Human Nature*. London: Allen Lane.

Pinker, S. 2011. *The Better Angels of Our Nature: Why Violence Has Declined*. New York: Penguin.

Priestley, C. 2002. Insides and emotion in Koromu. *Pragmatics & Cognition* 10 (1/2): 243–270.

Priestley, C. 2008. The semantics of "inalienable possession" in Koromu (PNG). In *Cross-Linguistic Semantics*, ed. C. Goddard, 277–300. Amsterdam: John Benjamins.

Priestley, C. 2012a. Koromu temporal expressions: Semantic and cultural perspectives. In *Space and Time in Languages and Cultures: Language, Culture and Cognition*, ed. L. Filipović and K. Jaszczolt, 143–165. Amsterdam, Philadelphia: John Benjamins.

Priestley, C. 2012b. The expression of potential event modality in the Papuan language of Koromu. In *Proceedings of the 42nd Australian Linguistic Society Conference—2011*, M. Ponsonnet, L. Dao, and M. Bowler. ANU Research Collections. http://hdl.handle.net/1885/9422

Slobin, D. 1996. From "thought to language" to "thinking for speaking." In *Rethinking Linguistic Relativity*, ed. J. Gumperz and S. Levinson, 70–96. Cambridge: Cambridge University Press.

Stanwood, R. E. 1997. The primitive syntax of mental predicates in Hawaii Creole English: A text-based study. *Language Sciences* 19 (3): 209–217.

Stanwood, R. E. 1999. On the Adequacy of Hawai'i Creole English. PhD dissertation. University of Hawai'i.

Steiner, G. [1975] 1998. *After Babel: Aspects of Language and Translation*. Oxford: Oxford University Press.

Tien, A. 2009. Semantic prime HAPPEN in Mandarin Chinese: In search of a viable exponent. *Pragmatics & Cognition* 17 (2): 356–382.

Tien, A. 2010. *Lexical Semantics of Children's Mandarin Chinese During the First Four Years*. Munich: LINCOM.

Tomasello, M. 1992. *First Verbs: A Case Study of Early Grammatical Development*. Cambridge: Cambridge University Press.

Tomasello, M. 2009. *Why We Cooperate*. Cambridge, MA: MIT Press.

Tong, M., M. Yell, and C. Goddard. 1997. Semantic primitives of time and space in Hong Kong Cantonese. *Language Sciences* 19 (3): 245–261.

Travis, C. E. 2002. La Metalengua Semántica Natural: The natural semantic metalanguage of Spanish. In *Meaning and Universal Grammar—Theory and Empirical Findings*. vol. I. ed. C. Goddard and A. Wierzbicka, 173–242. Amsterdam: John Benjamins.

Travis, C. E. 2004. The ethnopragmatics of the diminutive in conversational Colombian Spanish. *Intercultural Pragmatics* 1 (2): 249–274.

Travis, C. E. 2006. The communicative realization of *confianza* and *calor humano* in Colombian Spanish. In *Ethnopragmatics: Understanding Discourse in Cultural Context*, ed. C. Goddard, 199–230. Berlin: Mouton de Gruyter.

Vanhatalo, U., A. Idström and H. Tissari. In press. Revisiting the universality of Natural Semantic Metalanguage: A view through Finnish. *SKY Journal of Linguistics*.

Wakefield, J. C. 2011. The English Equivalents of Cantonese Sentence-Final Particles: A Contrastive Analysis. (PhD Thesis). The Hong Kong Polytechnic University.

Wierzbicka, A. 1972. *Semantic Primitives*. Frankfurt: Athenäum.

Wierzbicka, A. 1980. *Lingua Mentalis: The Semantics of Natural Language*. Sydney: Academic.

Wierzbicka, A. 1992. *Semantics, Culture and Cognition: Universal Human Concepts in Culture-specific Configurations*. New York: Oxford University Press.

Wierzbicka, A. 1996. *Semantics: Primes and Universals*. Oxford: Oxford University Press.

Wierzbicka, A. 1997. *Understanding Cultures Through Their Key Words: English, Russian, Polish, German, Japanese*. New York: Oxford University Press.

Wierzbicka, A. 1999. *Emotions Across Languages and Cultures: Diversity and Universals.* Cambridge: Cambridge University Press.

Wierzbicka, A. 2002. Semantic primes and universal grammar in Polish. In *Meaning and Universal Grammar—Theory and Empirical Findings.* vol. II., 65–144. Amsterdam: John Benjamins.

Wierzbicka, A. 2004. Conceptual primes in human languages and their analogues in animal communication and cognition. *Language Sciences* 26 (5): 413–441.

Wierzbicka, A. 2006. *English: Meaning and Culture.* New York: Oxford University Press.

Wierzbicka, A. 2010a. *Experience, Evidence, Sense: The Hidden Cultural Legacy of English.* New York: Oxford University Press.

Wierzbicka, A. 2010b. "Story"—an English cultural keyword and a key interpretive tool of Anglo culture. *Narrative Inquiry* 20 (1): 153–181.

Wierzbicka, A. 2011. Common language of all people: The innate language of thought. *Problems of Information Transmission* 47 (4): 380–399.

Wierzbicka, A. 2012. Understanding others requires shared concepts. Special issue, *Pragmatics & Cognition* 20 (2): 356–379.

Wierzbicka, A. 2014. *Imprisoned in English: The Hazard of English as a Default Language.* Oxford: Oxford University Press.

Wierzbicka, A. 2015. The idea of a spoon: Semantics, prehistory, and cultural logic. *Language Sciences* 47 (A): 66–83.

Ye, Z. 2006. Why the 'inscrutable' Chinese face? Emotionality and facial expression in Chinese. In *Ethnopragmatics: Understanding Discourse in Cultural Context,* ed. C. Goddard, 127–169. Berlin: Mouton De Gruyter.

Ye, Z. 2007. 'Memorisation', learning and cultural cognition: The notion of bèi ('auditory memorisation') in the written Chinese tradition. In *The Language of Memory in a Crosslinguistic Perspective,* ed. M. Amberber, 127–169. Amsterdam: Benjamins.

Ye, Z. 2010. Eating and drinking in Mandarin and Shanghainese: A lexical-conceptual analysis. In *ASCS09: Proceedings of the 9th Conference of the Australasian Society for Cognitive Science,* ed. E. Christensen, E. Schier and J. Sutton, 375–383. Sydney: Macquarie Centre for Cognitive Science.

Yoon, K.-J. 2006. *Constructing a Korean Natural Semantic Metalanguage.* Seoul: Hankook.

Yoon, K.-J. 2008. The Natural Semantic Metalanguage of Korean. In *Cross-Linguistic Semantics,* ed. C. Goddard, 121–162. Amsterdam: John Benjamins.

VII Concept Acquisition and Conceptual Change

15 Why Theories of Concepts Should Not Ignore the Problem of Acquisition

Susan Carey

15.1 Introduction

The human conceptual repertoire is a unique phenomenon on earth, posing a formidable challenge to the disciplines of cognitive science. Alone among animals, humans can ponder the causes and cures of pancreatic cancer and global warming. How are we to account for the human capacity to create concepts such as CLIMATE, CANCER, ELECTRON, INFINITY, GALAXY, and WISDOM? How do such concepts arise, both over history and in ontogenesis? Rightly, most attempts to provide such an account center on what makes concept attainment possible, but the literature on concept development adds a second question. Why is concept attainment (sometimes) so easy and what (sometimes) makes concept attainment so hard? Easy: some new concepts are formed upon first encountering a novel entity or hearing a new word in context (Carey 1978). Hard: others emerge only upon years of exposure, often involving concentrated study under metaconceptual control, and are not achieved by many humans despite years of explicit tutoring in school (Carey 2009). Considering what underlies this difference illuminates both how concepts are attained and what concepts are.

A theory of conceptual development must have three components. First, it must characterize the innate conceptual repertoire—the representations that are the input into subsequent learning processes. Second, it must describe how the initial stock of representations differs from the adult conceptual system. Third, it must characterize the mechanisms that achieve the transformation of the initial into the final state.

The two projects of constructing a theory of concept acquisition and constructing a theory of concepts fit within a single intellectual enterprise. Obviously, a theory of concept acquisition must be consistent with what concepts *are*. But the relation between the two projects goes both ways, a fact that has played almost no role in the psychological literature on concepts (see, for example, the excellent reviews in Smith and Medin 1981; Murphy 2002). With the exception of developmental psychologists, cognitive scientists working on concepts have mostly abandoned the problem of characterizing

and accounting for the features that enter into their learning models, often coding them with dummy variables.

This was not always so. For example, in theorizing about concepts, the British empiricists made accounting for acquisition a central concern. They, like many modern thinkers, assumed that all concept learning begins with a primitive sensory or perceptual vocabulary. That project is doomed by the simple fact that it is impossible to express most concepts in terms of perceptual features (e.g., CAUSE, GOOD, SEVEN, GOLD, DOG, etc.). In response, some theorists posit a rich stock of innate conceptual primitives, assuming that the adult conceptual repertoire can be built from them by conceptual combination. That is, they assume that the computational primitives that structure the adult conceptual repertoire and the innate primitives over which hypothesis testing is carried out early in development are one and the same set (e.g., Levin and Pinker 1991; Miller 1977; Miller and Johnson-Laird 1976). A moment's reflection shows that this assumption is also wrong. For example, the definition of GOLD within modern chemistry might be ELEMENT WITH ATOMIC NUMBER 79. Clearly the theoretical primitives ELEMENT and ATOM are not innate conceptual features, as they arise in modern chemistry and physics only in the eighteenth and nineteenth centuries, after many episodes of conceptual change. (Of course, it is an open question whether ELEMENT and ATOM are definable in terms of developmental primitives; there are no proposals for possible definitions in terms of innately available primitives.) Or take the features that determine the prototype structure of animal concepts (e.g., BIRD: FLIES, LAYS EGGS, HAS WINGS, NESTS IN TREES, HAS A BEAK, SINGS, etc.). Participants in studies provide just these when asked to list the features of birds. Furthermore, overlap in these features with others at this grain predicts judged similarity of birds to other animals, and overlap in particular values of them (e.g., beak type), as well as other features such as color and size, predicts prototypicality within the category of birds. That is, this feature space definitely underlies adult prototypicality structure. Prototype learning models assume that learning a new concept involves constructing a summary representation of a category in terms of such features, and then using this summary representation to probabilistically determine category membership. But a moment's reflection shows that these models just help themselves to features that are not, for the most part, innate primitives—many are no less abstract nor theory laden than the concept BIRD itself.

In a recent book (Carey 2009, *The Origin of Concepts*, hereafter *TOOC*), I take on the dual projects of accounting for conceptual development and characterizing the nature of human concepts. Toward a theory of conceptual development, I defend three theses. With respect to the initial state, contrary to historically important thinkers such as the British empiricists, Quine, and Piaget, as well as many contemporary scientists, the innate stock of primitives is not limited to sensory, perceptual, or sensorimotor representations. Rather, there are also innate conceptual representations, embedded in systems of core cognition, with contents such as AGENT, OBJECT, GOAL, CAUSE, and APPROXIMATELY

TEN. With respect to developmental change, contrary to continuity theorists such as Fodor (1975), Pinker (2007), and others, there are major discontinuities over the course of conceptual development. By "discontinuity" I mean qualitative changes in representational structure, in which the later emerging system of representation cannot be expressed in terms of the conceptual resources available at the earlier time. Conceptual development consists of episodes of qualitative change, resulting in systems of representation with more expressive power than, and sometimes incommensurable with, those from which they are built. Increases in expressive power and incommensurabilities are two types of conceptual discontinuities. With respect to a learning mechanism that achieves conceptual discontinuity, I offer Quinian bootstrapping.

Toward a theory of concepts that meshes with the picture of conceptual development in *TOOC*, I support dual factor theory (e.g., Block 1986). The two factors are sometimes called "wide content" and "narrow content." The wide content of our mental representations is partly determined by causal connections between mental symbols, on the one hand, and the entities to which they refer. To the extent this is so, all current psychological theories of concepts are on the wrong track—concepts are not prototypes, exemplar representations, nor theories of the entities they represent. However, contrary to philosophical views that deny that meanings are determined in any way by what's in the head (e.g., Dretske 1981; Fodor 1998; Kripke [1972] 1980; Putnam 1975), *TOOC* argues that some aspects of inferential role are content determining (narrow content). The challenge for psychologists is saying what aspects of mental representation of entities we can think about partly determine the meaning of concepts of those entities, and which are simply what we believe about those entities (sometimes called the project of distinguishing concepts from conceptions; Rey 1983). Facts about conceptual development constrain a theory of narrow content.

While the goal of *TOOC* was to explicate and defend the above three theses about conceptual development and sketch how they mesh with a dual factor theory of concepts, I also address Fodor's (1975, 1980) two related challenges to cognitive science—first, to show how learning can possibly result in increased expressive power, and to defeat the conclusion that all concepts lexicalized as monomorphemic words are innate. The key to answering both of these challenges, as well as to understanding conceptual discontinuities in general, is to show that, and how, new conceptual *primitives* can be learned. Conceptual primitives are the building blocks of thought, the bottom level of decomposition into terms that articulate mental propositions and otherwise enter into inference. Conceived of this way, there is no logical requirement that conceptual primitives cannot be learned.

Rey (2014) denies that the project is successful in meeting Fodor's challenges, as do Fodor (2010) and Rips and colleagues (Rips, Bloomfield, and Asmuth 2008; Rips, Asmuth, and Bloomfield 2013). Although I ultimately disagree, I appreciate many of the points these critics make along the way. These debates bring into focus how the projects of understanding conceptual development and understanding the nature of concepts, learning, and the human mind are intertwined. In this chapter, I lay out these debates on the interrelated issues of conceptual discontinuity, increases in expressive power, and Quinian bootstrapping and begin to sketch how they bear on our understanding of the nature of concepts. I show how new primitives can be learned, and how this fact bears on these debates.

15.2   The Dialectic According to Fodor, Rey, Rips, Bloomfield, and Asmuth

A kind of logical constructivism is at the heart of Fodor's, Rey's, and, at least implicitly, Rips and colleagues's dialectic. These writers, like many others, take expressive power to be a function of innate primitives and of what can—in principle if not in fact—be built from them using the resources of the logic available to the learner. Expressive power is a logical and semantic notion. As long as the characterization of learning mechanisms is exhausted by specifying the set of innate primitives and the logical resources through which one builds new representations from those primitives, clearly one cannot increase expressive power by learning (Fodor 1980).

My response to this picture of learning and conceptual development is to argue that learning mechanisms can create new primitives, new primitives that cannot be constructed from antecedently existent primitives by logical combination, and thus increase the expressive power of the conceptual system. In addition, my concern is with how new primitives actually come into being; if there are processes that yield new primitives, then the question is whether such processes actually underlie the emergence of any given representation.

Fodor's (1975) second challenge to cognitive science is to defeat his argument for mad dog nativism, that is, to defeat the argument that virtually all of the over five hundred thousand concepts lexicalized by monomorphemic words in the *Oxford English Dictionary* are innate. Rey (2014) lays out Fodor's argument as follows:

Premise 1 (Hypothesis Confirmation): All learning is hypothesis confirmation.

Premise 2 (Logical Construction): One can learn new concepts only by creating and confirming hypotheses formulated in terms of logical constructions from antecedently available primitive concepts.

Premise 3 (Atomism): The concepts underlying mono-morphemic words cannot be analyzed as logical constructions of other concepts, primitive or otherwise. [Actually, Fodor says "most" monomorphemic concepts cannot be so analyzed, but for simplicity I will assume "all" rather than "most."]

Conclusion (Innateness): In order to acquire a new concept lexicalized as a mono-morphemic word, one would have to confirm hypotheses already containing the concept to be learned. Therefore, no such concept can be learned.

TOOC answers this challenge by giving reasons to deny premises 1 and 2. My basic strategy has been to provide several case studies of transitions between conceptual systems in which the later one expresses concepts that are not logical constructions from the earlier one (Carey 1985, 2009; Smith, Carey, and Wiser 1985; Wiser and Carey 1983). Sometimes this is because of local incommensurability, as in case studies of thermal concepts, biological concepts, and electromagnetic concepts in the history of science, or concepts of matter, weight, and density in intuitive physics in childhood and the concepts of life and death in childhood. Sometimes it is because of developments within mathematical representations that increase expressive power without necessarily involving local incommensurability (as in case studies of the origins of concepts of integers and rational number).[1] *TOOC* then goes on to analyze how Quinian bootstrapping plays a role in transitions of both types.

The central issue dividing my views from the critics I focus on here is discontinuity. These critics deny the very possibility of conceptual discontinuities, as well as offering a positive view of conceptual development in terms of premises 1 and 2 of Fodor's argument, which they claim shows how conceptual development is possible without discontinuity. Rips and his colleagues suggest that claims for discontinuities are incompatible with claims that concepts are learned (e.g., Rips and Hespos 2011). Again, the key is understanding that, and how, new conceptual primitives can be learned. These critics argue that my proposal for a learning mechanism that can underlie conceptual discontinuity, Quinian bootstrapping, fails, partly through failing to confront a psychologized version of Goodman's new riddle of induction (Rey 2014; Rips, Bloomfield, and Asmuth 2008).

With respect to Rips' and his colleagues' worries that concept learning and concept discontinuity are incompatible, let me clarify what the debate is *not* about. The existence of conceptual discontinuity cannot entail that it is impossible for an organism to acquire some later representations, given its initial state, except through maturation or magical processes that don't involve learning (e.g., being hit on the head). What is actual is possible. The mechanisms (there are many) that underlie the acquisition of our representational repertoire in general, and our conceptual repertoire in particular, if they are learning mechanisms, are computational processes. At stake are premises 1 and 2 of Fodor's argument, which all of these critics explicitly or implicitly endorse. I agree that most of conceptual development consists of hypothesis confirmation, where the hypotheses are articulated in terms of already available concepts. Discontinuities arise in episodes of conceptual development where this is not the right model.

1. The case study of the construction of the integers is the focus of Rey's, Rips and coauthors', and Fodor's critiques. I will discuss whether this episode of conceptual development truly involves a discontinuity, and an increase of expressive power, when I turn to it in sections 15.8 and 15.9.

With respect to the positive proposal, mad dog nativism requires that virtually all five hundred thousand concepts lexicalized in English, plus those that will come to be lexicalized in the future, are innate, existing in some way in the infant's mind. This isn't comforting as a positive proposal that obviates the need for concept learning. A priori, it is highly unlikely that QUARK and CARBURETOR and FAX are innate concepts, existing is some kind of hypothesis space available for hypothesis testing. Noting this unlikelihood, Rey (2014) distinguishes between manifest concepts (those currently available for hypothesis testing and inference) and what he calls "possessed" concepts (those that exist in the mind in some way, but are not currently available for thought, or those that can be constructed by logical combination from that initial set). Rey defines possessed concepts as those that have the *potential* to be manifest. Here I use "potential" concepts instead of "possessed" concepts to express this notion. Nobody would ever deny that an actual manifest concept had the potential to be the output of some developmental process, and in the light of characterizations of those developmental processes, we can and do explore the representational repertoire attested developmental processes can achieve. Exploring the possible outputs of the learning mechanisms we investigate is an important part of characterizing these mechanisms. Calling the potential output of concept-learning mechanisms "possessed concepts" implies something stronger, that they exist somehow in the mind prior to becoming manifest. Of course, premises 1 and 2 specify one way we can think about this stronger notion of possession: the innate primitives, along with the combinatorial apparatus of logic and language, constitute a space of alternative hypotheses about which concepts apply in particular contexts (e.g., to support the meaning of a word), and this space exhausts the potential concepts that are attainable. The writers I am criticizing here assume that potential concepts constitute a space of alternatives, lying in wait to become manifest, and that manifestation consists in *being* or *being logically constructed* from these innately possessed primitives. These assumptions follow from premises 1 and 2 of Fodor's argument, the premises I deny.

15.3   Initial Response

My project concerns manifest concepts. To reiterate, manifest concepts are those currently available for thought, inference, and guiding action. The developmental primitives I study are those we can find evidence for in the baby's or animal's behavior. They must be available to support inference and action in order to be diagnosed, that is, they must be manifest (currently available for thought). In what follows, I argue that concept manifestation is where the debates about expressive power, conceptual continuity vs. discontinuity, and induction *actually* play out.

For any representational system we posit, we are committed to there being answers to three questions. First, what is the format of the symbols in the system; second, what determines their referents; and third, what is their computational role in thought. A worked example in *TOOC* is the evolutionarily ancient system of number representations in which the mental symbols are quantities (rates of firing, or size of populations of neurons) that are linear or logarithmic functions of the cardinal values of sets, which in turn are input into numerical computations such as number comparison, addition, subtraction, multiplication, division, ratio calculations, probability calculations, and others (see Dehaene 1997 for a book-length treatment of this system of numerical representations). We can explore such systems only with psychological methods that diagnose manifest representations. The project of *TOOC* is understanding the representational resources available as the child or adult interacts with the world, how these arise and change over development. These representations are the ones available for hypothesis testing, as input into further learning, and to play a computational role in thought. And it is successive manifest conceptual systems one must analyze to establish qualitative changes (i.e., conceptual discontinuities).

In what follows I flesh out these points, explicating how *TOOC* attempts to answer Fodor's challenges to cognitive science. The issues include a characterization of the nature of learning (Fodor's first premise), the unjustified acceptance of the logical construction model as the only model of concept learning (Fodor's second premise), the misleading analogy of the totality of concepts ultimately attainable as a hypothesis space, the characterization of how primitives arise (both in cases where this is easy and in cases where this is hard), and the characterization of constraints of induction (and constraints on learning more generally, when learning does not involve induction).

Let me begin with the premises in Fodor's argument that I deny. I first comment on why these premises matter, and I then show why they are wrong.

15.4   Premise 2: Logical Construction

The premise that all concepts must be either innate or buildable by combination from innate primitives through innate logical combinatorial devices is widely adopted within cognitive science. For example, the dominant theoretical project within the field of lexical development in the 1970s was to attempt to discover the lexical primitives in terms of which lexical items are defined, and to study the intermediate hypotheses children entertain as they construct new concepts from those primitives (see Carey 1982 for a review and critique). That is, it was just assumed that definitional primitives are innate. In Carey (1982), I called this view "piece by piece construction"; Margolis and Laurence (2011) call it "the building blocks model." Here, I will call it "the logical construction model," in honor of Premise 2. In contrast, I argue (Carey 1982, *TOOC*) that computational primitives need not be innate. They can be acquired through learning processes that do not consist of logical construction from innate primitives.

One central issue is atomism. If many of the primitives in adult thought (e.g., the concepts expressed by words like "dog" or "cancer") cannot be defined in terms of innately manifest concepts, then either they must be innate primitives or it must be possible to learn computational primitives through some mechanism that does not consist of building new concepts by logical combination of antecedently available ones, and that is not exhausted by confirming a hypothesis stated in terms of the concept to be acquired. I accept Fodor's arguments that most lexical concepts are definitional primitives.

Notice that the possibility that one can learn new primitives matters to the question of expressive power of the system. The expressive power of a system of representations is a function of its atomic terms and combinatorial apparatus. The logical connectives and operators (sentential operators, modals, quantifiers) are not the only primitives that matter to expressive power. If DOG cannot be logically constructed from primitives, then acquiring the concept DOG increases expressive power of the system (see Weiskopf 2007). That is, nonlogical primitives figure into semantic-logical expressive possibilities as well as do logical ones. This is one reason that the question of whether one *learns* the concept DOG is so central to the debate between Fodor and his critics.

15.5   Premise 1: All Learning Is Hypothesis Formulation and Testing

To evaluate this proposition we must agree on what hypothesis testing is and what learning is. Bayesian models specify the essence of hypothesis-testing algorithms. Hypothesis testing requires a space of antecedently manifest concepts, each associated with prior probabilities, and each specifying likelihood functions from any possible evidence to the probability that it supports any given hypothesis. Hypothesis testing then involves choosing among the alternative hypotheses on the basis of evidence. Fodor (1975, 2008) claims that all learning mechanisms reduce to hypothesis testing, at least implicitly. I agree that any learning mechanism that revises representations as evidence accumulates (e.g., associative mechanisms that update strengths of association, supervised learning algorithms such as connectionist back propagation) do indeed do so. However, as Margolis and Laurence (2011) point out in a reply to Fodor's 2008 book (*LOT2*), a cursory examination of the variety of attested learning mechanisms in the animal kingdom shows that the generalization that *all* learning mechanisms reduce to hypothesis confirmation is wildly off the mark. Rote learning (memorizing a phone number), one-trial associational learning (e.g., the Garcia effect, the creation of a food aversion as a result of becoming nauseated some fixed time after having eaten a novel food; Garcia, Kimeldorf, and Koelling 1955), and many other types of learning do not involve choosing among multiple hypotheses, confirming one of them, in the light of accumulating evidence. And as we shall see, such mechanisms have roles to play in creating new conceptual primitives.

Of course, the claim that these are learning mechanisms depends on what one takes learning to be. Learning mechanisms share a few essential properties that allow us to recognize clear examples when we encounter them. All learning results in representational changes in response to representational inputs, where those inputs can be seen (by the scientist) to provide evidence relevant to the representational change. That is, learning is a computational process, requiring representational inputs that can be conceptualized as providing relevant *information*. Sometimes, as in the case of explicit or implicit hypothesis testing, the organism itself evaluates the information in the input with respect to its evidential status (as in all forms of Bayesian learning mechanisms). But other times, the learning mechanism is a domain-specific adaptation that responds to information by simply effecting a representational change of relevance to the organism—an example being the learning mechanism that underlies the Garcia effect mentioned above. No further evidence is evaluated, so there is no hypothesis confirmation.

15.6   The Relatively Easy Route to New Representational Primitives: Domain-Specific Learning Mechanisms

The problem of acquisition arises in the case of any representation, conceptual or otherwise, that ends up in the manifest repertoire of an animal. The literatures of psychology and ethology have described hundreds of domain-specific learning mechanisms that simply compute new representations from input, having arisen in the course of natural selection to do just that. Most of these representations are not conceptual ones, but considering how they are acquired shows that the learning mechanisms involved do not always involve hypothesis testing, thus providing counterexamples to Premise 1. They also do not implement logical construction from primitives, and thus provide counterexamples to Premise 2. Considering how they work illuminates why it's a mistake to consider potential representations as a space of existent representations, ready to be *chosen among* or *built from* in a process of manifestation.

   TOOC's example of an evolved domain-specific learning mechanism is that which underlies indigo buntings' *learning* which part of the night sky indicates north. This matters crucially to indigo buntings, for they migrate over 3,500 miles each spring (north) and fall (south), and they navigate by the stars. Because the earth tilts back and forth on its axis, what part of the night sky indicates north changes radically on a thirty-thousand-year cycle. Sometime not too far in the future, the North Star will be Vega, not Polaris. Thus, it is unlikely that an innate representation of Polaris as the North Star was created by natural selection, and indeed, Steven Emlen (1975) discovered the learning mechanism through which indigo buntings create the representation of north that will play such a crucial role in their migratory life. The learning device that achieves this analyzes the center of rotation of the night sky and stores the configuration of stars that can allow the bird to recognize the position of north from a static sighting (as it has to do every time it starts to fly during its migrations in the spring and the fall, and as it monitors its course).

This mechanism computes what it is designed to compute—nothing more nor nothing less. It creates an essential representation in the computational machinery of indigo buntings, the specification of north in the night sky. Of course, there is a prepared computational role for this representation, but the representation of north as specified by the stars must still be learned and is an essential primitive in the computational machinery underlying bunting navigation. Domain-specific learning mechanisms of this sort are often supported by dedicated neural machinery that atrophies after its work is done, leading to critical periods. This is such a case; if a bird is prevented from seeing the night sky as a nestling, no amount of exposure to the rotating night sky later in life allows the bird to identify north, and the bird perishes.

This example is worth dwelling on with respect to whether representations that can be achieved should be thought of as part of an existing space of hypotheses, and whether the acquisition mechanism involves hypothesis confirmation or logical combination. Until the learning episode is completed, there is no manifest representation that specifies north in the night sky in the bird's mind. However, this learning mechanism can learn any of a very large number of star configurations that could indicate north. Indeed, part of the evidence that this *is* the learning mechanism through which indigo buntings establish Polaris as the North Star are planetarium experiments in which the night sky is made to rotate around an arbitrarily chosen part of the night sky while the birds are nestlings. The birds then use the North Star so specified to set their course when it's time to migrate. Thus, there are a plethora of potential north pointing stars. And clearly, one can investigate limits on the system (e.g., if stars were equally distributed throughout the sky, or if they were too densely packed to be resolved, or if the patterns of stars showed large-scale repetitions, this couldn't work). It is only with an actual representational/computational characterization of this learning mechanism that the space of potential north stars the bunting could acquire representations of can be explored. Such is always the case.

What about hypothesis testing? I take the essential features of hypothesis testing to be two: (1) the learning mechanism must entertain alternatives, and (2) choice among them must be based on evidence. The space of potential representations of north that can be achieved by Buntings is in *no* way a hypothesis space. In no way does an indigo bunting's acquiring a representation of north consist of choosing among possibilities. Calling the possible specifications of north a "hypothesis space" is wildly misleading. There is no initial set of possibilities, with associated priors, with likelihood functions associated with them. The animal never considers any other than the one that is the output of the learning mechanism, and the animal has no way of testing whether the specification of north that is the output of the learning mechanism is correct. The bird simply computes it and lives or dies by it.

This case is also worth dwelling on with respect to the other issues on the table. Not only does this case not involve hypothesis formulation and testing, it also does not involve building a new representation out of primitives by logical combination. And since there is no induction involved, the issues of constraints on induction do not arise. Of course, all learning mechanisms must be highly constrained to be effective, and characterizing real learning mechanisms allows us to understand the constraints under which they operate. This is a highly constrained learning mechanism; it considers only one kind of information to create a representation that has only one computational role. It is of no use to the bird in helping it learn what to eat, who to mate with, or where its nest is in a local environment.

Navigation is not a special case. There have been hundreds of such domain-specific learning mechanisms detailed in the literatures of ethology and psychology, including the imprinting mechanisms that allow infants (animals and humans) to identify conspecifics in general and their caretakers in particular, mechanisms that allow animals to learn what food to eat (the Garcia effect just one of dozens of domain-specific learning mechanisms through which omnivores like rats and humans achieve this feat), bird song learning, and so on (see Gallistel et al. 1991 for a review of four such domain-specific information-expectant learning mechanisms, and Gallistel 1990 for a nuanced discussion of the nature of learning).

In sum, the animal literature provides many examples of learning mechanisms designed to form new computational primitives, learning mechanisms that implicate neither logical construction from existing primitives (Premise 2), nor hypothesis testing and confirmation (Premise 1). One can (and one does) explore the space of possible outputs of these mechanisms, for this is one way they can be fully characterized and their existence empirically tested, but in no way is there a space of representations lying in wait, existing ready to be manifested, existing ready to be chosen among.

15.7   The Relatively Easy Route to New Conceptual Primitives

The learning mechanism described above acquires a new primitive representation, a representation that allows the animal to identify north in the night sky, to guide navigation. One might argue it is not a new *conceptual* representation. Its format is surely iconic, and its computational role is both highly domain specific and sensorimotor. There are, however, learning mechanisms that similarly respond to inputs of certain types by simply creating new conceptual primitives, primitives that enter into representations with propositional format and participate in the full productivity of language and causal inference. These domain-specific concept-learning mechanisms need not involve hypothesis testing and do not involve constructing new concepts by logical combination. Take the Block (1986)/Macnamara (1986)/Margolis (1998) object-kind learning mechanism, for example.[2] This learning mechanism is triggered by encountering a novel object (as specified by core cognition of objects) with obviously nonarbitrary structure. As Prasada, Ferenz, and Haskell (2002) showed, there are several cues to nonarbitrary structure: the object has complex yet regular shape (e.g., symmetries, repetition), or there are multiple objects that share a complex irregular shape, or the object has functionally relevant parts, or the object recognizably falls under an already represented superordinate kind (e.g., kind of agent, kind of animal, kind of artifact). Core cognition contains perceptual input analyzers that are sensitive to cues to each of these properties of individual objects. Encountering an individual with one or more of these properties triggers establishing a new representational primitive that can be glossed SAME BASIC-LEVEL KIND AS THAT OBJECT. Reference to the kind is ensured by representation of the surface properties of the individual or individuals that occasioned the new concept (and these represented surface properties get enriched and even overturned as bases of reference and categorization as more is learned about the kind). The content of the new concept depends on the referent, the conceptual role provided by the basic-level kind schema (psychological essentialism), and the conceptual roles provided by any superordinate kind schemas that the individual is taken to fall under (e.g., AGENT, ANIMAL, ARTIFACT, these in turn being constrained by their roles in different systems of core cognition or constructed theories).

Consider encountering a kangaroo for the first time. Such an encounter might lead to the formation of a concept KANGAROO that represents animals that are the same basic-level kind as the newly encountered one. No enumerative induction is needed; the concept is what Strevens (2012) calls "introjected" into one's set of primitives. This concept, falling under psychological essentialism (as it is a kind concept), reflects the many constraints on kind concepts. That is, the conceptual role SAME KIND AS presupposes that something causes the nonrandom structure that triggered the formation of the new concept, that these underlying causes are shared by all members of the kind (now, in the past, in the future), and that the surface properties that specify the individual that occasioned the new concept may not hold for all members, possibly not even typical members. Furthermore, the current guesses about the nature of the causal mechanisms relevant to the creation of members of this kind, to determining their properties, and to tracing numerical identity though time, are taken to be open

---

2. These writers discuss this mechanism as a *natural kind* learning mechanism (e.g., kinds of animals or kinds of plants), but I believe the domain of this mechanism is object-kind representations (as opposed to object properties, individual objects, or the events in which objects participate). Roughly, kind representations are inductively deep, and kinds are construed in accordance with the constraints that constitute psychological essentialism in Strevens's (2000) sense. Artifact kinds fall under the domain of this mechanism, as do natural kinds (Kelemen and Carey 2007).

to revision. That is, there is no definition that determines membership in the kind; learners treat everything they represent about the kind up for revision (including even that there *is* a new kind—the individual we encountered might have been a mutant raccoon).

This mechanism creates new primitives, not definable in terms of other manifest concepts, and thus increases the expressive power of the conceptual system. The concept KANGAROO is not definable in terms of antecedently available primitives using the combinatorial machinery of logic. Before creating this concept, one could not think thoughts about kangaroos, just as before analyzing the center of rotation of the night sky and storing a representation of NORTH so specified, an indigo bunting could not set or guide a course of flight toward or away from north. Of course the kind-learning mechanism ensures that creating new primitives for kinds is easy; one need only encounter an individual that one takes to be an individual of a new kind and store a representation of what that individual looks like. But this process involves neither induction nor hypothesis testing among a huge space of antecedently available innate primitives. The concept KANGAROO was not lying in wait in a system of representations available for selection by a Bayesian hypothesis-testing mechanism, nor is it constructible from antecedently available primitives.

Rey (2014) discusses the Margolis kind-learning module, claiming that it falls prey to Goodman's grue problem, just as Quinian bootstrapping does (see below). There are two answers to Rey's questions regarding constraints on induction in the Margolis kind-learning module. First, as detailed above, there need be no induction. But, Rey asks, why are not kinds such as objects, animals, agents, eastern grey kangaroos, kangadiles (kangaroos until year 2040, thereafter crocodiles), undetached kangaroo parts, or an infinitude of other kinds, possible glosses of SAME KIND AS THAT OBJECT, rather than the kind kangaroo? Why does the learner not form a concept of a particular individual (Oscar) instead of a kind?

Answering this question simply *is* an important part of the project of understanding conceptual development. In the case of dedicated concept-learning devices such as the object-kind learning device, the empirical project is specifying the constraints under which the system operates. That there is a dedicated kind-concept acquisition device is an empirical discovery, and like all learning mechanisms, this one embodies strong constraints. It is a discovery that there is basic level in kind concepts, and it is a discovery that basic-level kinds are privileged in kind-concept learning (e.g., Rosch et al. 1976). It is a discovery that kind representations embody constraints derived from causal/functional analyses (see the work on psychological essentialism and the psychology of a causal-explanatory core to kind concepts in S. Gelman 2003; Keil 1989; Ahn and Kim 2000; Strevens 2000). And the existence and structure of systems of core cognition (in which the concepts AGENT and OBJECT are embedded), as well as innately supported systems of causal and functional analysis, are empirical discoveries, as is the fact that these constrain kind representations from early infancy (Carey 2009). These constraints do not rule out *ever* entertaining other concepts; after all, some of them are themselves innately manifest (e.g., AGENT) and are drawn on as important parts of the constraints on the kind module. That is, AGENT is the content of a superordinate kind that constrains a newly formed basic-level kind concept that falls under it. Others, such as subordinate and superordinate kinds, as well as stage and phase sortals like PUPPY or PASSENGER, are routinely manifested after basic-level kind representations are formed (e.g., Hall and Waxman 1993). Still others are obviously entertainable (after all, Goodman and Quine did so, and we all can join in). But these concepts simply are not the output of the dedicated basic-level kind-learning device discussed above. Furthermore, the child *can* also form a concept of a particular individual, even a newly encountered kangaroo. There is a dedicated learning mechanism for concepts of individuals, as well as for basic-level kinds (but that is another story, one that has also been told; e.g., Bélanger and Hall 2006). *Once* cognitive science has discovered the constraints under which actual learning devices operate, one can explore their possible outputs. The constraints posited are empirical proposals, falsifiable by demonstrations that they are easily violated. The empirical work strongly supports the existence of the basic-level object-kind learning module.

The basic-level kind-learning module creates new primitive concepts. Before a person has formed the concepts KANGAROO or SHOVEL, or concepts of any of infinitely many new kinds, he or she cannot think thoughts about the entities that fall under those concepts. This learning mechanism thus results in an increase in expressive power. However, like the cases of the dedicated learning mechanisms discussed in the ethology literature (those that yield representations of conspecifics, caretakers, the North Star), there is an innately specified conceptual role for kind concepts, in this case given by the abstract concept KIND OF OBJECT and by the schemas of superordinate kinds embedded in core cognition and constructed theories that the learner assigns the new concepts to. Such already existing schema and conceptual roles are always part of the relatively easy route to new primitives.

15.8 The Dual Factor Theory of Representations with Innate Conceptual Role

Dual factor theory applies straightforwardly to concepts in core cognition (AGENT, OBJECT, etc.), indeed any concept with innate conceptual role and innate perceptual input analyzers that support identification of entities that fall under it. The innate perceptual input analyzers explain how symbols are causally connected to the entities they represent, and the innate conceptual role specifies the narrow content of the concept. In core cognition, and cases like the indigo bunting representations of the azimuth, the innate conceptual role is never overturned—the narrow content of the representation of the North Star that makes it a representation of north simply *is* the suite of senso-rimotor computations supporting navigation it enters into.

The story for the Block/Macnamara/Margolis kind module is a little less straightfor-ward. In concepts created by the kind-learning device, there are innate input analyzers that trigger the establishing of a kind representation (that identify objects with nonac-cidental structure) and that support the identification of superordinate schema pro-vided by core cognition (KIND OF OBJECT, KIND OF AGENT, etc.). These innate input analyzers are part of what provides the wide content of such concepts, as they trigger forming a representation of an the entity in the world that is part of the wide content of the newly formed concept, as well as providing part of the causal connection between this wide content and the newly formed mental symbol. But there is no innate, unoverturn-able, prepared conceptual role at the level of specific kinds. Even the initial superordi-nate schema that the kind is subsumed under is revisable. However, there is an innate conceptual role for object kinds in general (i.e., given by psychological essentialism), and this specifies what sort of concept is in play and constrains its formal properties. This abstract conceptual role specifies part of the narrow content for kind concepts. As Block (1986) says, it determines the nature of the connection between symbols and the world, after a symbol is taken to be a symbol for an object kind.

15.9 The Relatively Hard Route to New Conceptual Primitives

Quinian bootstrapping also creates new primitives, thus increasing the expressive power of the conceptual system. It differs from those learning mechanisms described above in that it did not arise through natural selection to acquire representations of a particular sort. Rather, it is one of the learning mechanisms that underlie the creation of representational resources that are discontinuous (in the senses of being qualita-tively different from, or being locally incommensurable with, the representations of the same domain that were their input). It creates new conceptual roles, rather than merely creating new primitives for which there were prepared conceptual roles (as in the case in the easy route to new primitives; see above). But once created, these new conceptual roles provide constraints on the concepts that will be learned, just as in the relatively easy route to new conceptual primitives.

TOOC takes a particular episode along the way to creating a representation of inte-gers as a central worked example of conceptual discontinuity and of Quinian boot-strapping. I argue that this case involves an increase in expressive power, in that before the bootstrapping episode, the child has no manifest concepts for natural numbers, and the process of constructing the first representations of new primitive concepts, those of a subset of the natural numbers, is not exhausted by defining them in terms of primitives antecedently available. Again, let me be clear. The increase in expressive power at stake here is an increase in the expressive power of manifest concepts available to the child. Obviously, the total computational machinery available to the child has the capacity for this construction (what is actual is possible), just as the computational machinery of the child has the capacity to create representations of kangaroos in the easy route to new primitives.

Expressive power is a semantic/logical issue. Examples of questions about expressive power relative to number representations include whether arithmetic can be expressed in the machinery of sentential logic—provably no—and whether arithmetic can be expressed in the machinery of quantificational logic plus the principle that one-to-one correspondence guarantees cardinal equivalence—provably yes, if you accept Frege's proof. But the exploration of expressive power with such proofs is relevant to the question of how arithmetic arises in development *only* against empirically supported proposals for what the innate numerically relevant innate primitives are, and what form innate support for logic takes. If arithmetic can be derived from the resources of logic alone (with no numerical primitives), this is relevant to the question of the origin of arithmetic in ontogenesis *only* if the relevant logical resources are innate, and in a form that would support the relevant construction. If primitives with numerical content are needed as well (e.g., the principle that one-to-one correspondence guarantees cardinal equivalence, or the concepts ONE and SUCCESSOR), then one must account for how these arise in development. *TOOC* provides evidence that these numerical concepts are not part of the child's innate endowment, and that they arise only after the bootstrapping episode in which the numeral list representation of number is constructed.

TOOC does not consider the form innate support for logic takes or how logical resources arise in development. Indeed, I am acutely aware of this lacuna, and of its relevance to our understanding of numerical development. These questions have been the focus of research in my lab for the past several years and will be so for the next decade at least. We do not yet have answers concerning the form innate support for logic takes. My current guess is that innate logic is largely implicit, embodied in computations, and that bootstrapping is needed before children create the logical resources needed for the mathematical construction of the integers from such primitives. After all, these constructions did not arise in mathematics until after two thousand years of development of formal logic. However, as I say below, my picture of the ontogenesis of concepts of integers would be falsified by the discovery of manifest representations with numerical content in addition to the three systems for which we already have empirical support.

Thus, I acknowledge that Fodor (2010), Leslie, Gallistel, and Gelman (2007), Rey (2014), Rips, Bloomfield, and Asmuth (2008) and others *could turn out to be* right (not that they provide a shred of evidence) that a full characterization of the manifest initial state will reveal expressive power sufficient to express arithmetic. If so, I would certainly back away from my claims about this bootstrapping episode increasing expressive power, saying that my studies concern how arithmetic capacities *actually* become manifest in ontogenesis. After all, the latter is really my concern. I am quite certain that children do not construct arithmetic as Peano and Dedekind or as Frege did, and I favor my bootstrapping story about what children actually do. But, if numerical or logical primitives are needed that themselves arise as a result of bootstrapping processes, then my claims of increases in expressive power stand.

At any rate, the actual process through which representations of integers arise is an existence proof of the possibility that bootstrapping *can* yield new primitives. The case study of the ontogenetic origin of integer representations illustrates all three major theses in *TOOC*: the existence of conceptually rich innate representations, conceptual discontinuity, and Quinian bootstrapping.

15.10   Core Cognition of Number (Rich Innate Representational Resources; *TOOC*, Chapter 4)[3]

Core cognition contains two systems of representation with numerical content: parallel individuation of small sets of entities in working memory models and analog magnitude representations of number. Analog magnitude representations were briefly sketched in section 15.3 above. They are analog symbols of approximate cardinal values of sets. One signature of this system of number representation is that magnitudes are compared to one another on the basis of their ratios, and thus discriminability accords with Weber's law (discriminability is better the smaller the absolute value of the quantity) and exhibits scalar variability (the standard deviation of multiple estimates of a given quantity is a linear function of the absolute value of that quantity). Analog magnitude representations of number have been demonstrated in many animals (rats, pigeons, nonhuman primates) as well as in humans from neonates to adults.

Analog magnitude representations are the output of paradigmatic perceptual input analyzers, but the analog magnitude symbols for number that are produced are conceptual in the sense of having rich central conceptual roles, including the many different arithmetical computations they enter into, and the fact that they are bound to (quantify over) many types of individuals (objects, events, auditory individuals).

A second system of core cognition with numerical content, parallel individuation, consists of working memory representations of small sets of individuals (three or fewer). The symbols in this system represent individuals (e.g., a set of three crackers is represented CRACKER, CRACKER, CRACKER, probably with iconic symbols for each cracker). Unlike the analog magnitude number representation system, parallel individuation/

3. The evidence for central claims in *TOOC*, along with citations of relevant literature, can be found in the chapters flagged throughout the current text.

working memory is not a dedicated number representation system, nor are there any symbols that represent cardinal values (or any other quantifiers) in these models; there are only symbols for individuals. These models can then be further used to compute total volume and and total surface area of the individuals, and are input into spatial and causal representations. The numerical content in the system of parallel individuation is entirely implicit; the symbols in the models stand in one-to-one correspondence with individuals in the sets modeled. This is ensured by computations sensitive to spatiotemporal cues to numerical identity. The system must determine whether a given individual is the same one or a different one from a previously viewed individual to determine whether to add another symbol to the model. Further implicit numerical content is embodied in some of the conceptual roles these models enter into. More than one model can be entertained at any given time, and models can be compared on the basis of one-to-one correspondence to establish numerical order and equivalence. Importantly, this system of representation implicitly represents *one*. There is no explicit symbol with the content ONE, but the system updates a model of a set of one when a numerically distinct individual is added to it, yielding a model of a set of two (and ditto for sets of two and three), and the system similarly updates a model if individuals are removed from it. There is a strict upper limit to the number of individuals that can be held in working memory at any given time: three for infants. This set-size limit on performance contrasts with the ratio limit on performance that characterizes analog magnitude systems.

The parallel individuation system is perception-like in many ways, especially if the symbols for individuals are indeed iconic, as I suspect. Nonetheless, the parallel individuation models themselves are conceptual in that they are held in a working memory system that requires attention and executive function, and enter into many further computations in support of rich central inferential processes (e.g., reasoning about the actions of agents upon objects, functional analyses, causal analyses, and quantitative computations).

Systems of core cognition are not the only innate resources relevant to conceptual development. *TOOC* also assumes early linguistic resources but makes no attempt to specify their exact nature (a topic for another book). And, as commented above, the nature of logical resources available to infants and toddlers is virtually unstudied. Particularly relevant for number representations are linguistic representations that underlie the meanings of natural language quantifiers. Number marking in language (quantifiers, determiners, singular/plural morphology) requires representations of sets and individuals and provides explicit linguistic symbols (words) with numerical content: "a, all, some, most, many, few," and so on. *TOOC* reviews evidence that before age two, children have mastered some of the basic syntax and semantics of natural language quantifiers, and that these linguistic structures provide important early constraints on the meanings of verbal numerals, via syntactic bootstrapping.

15.11   Conceptual Discontinuity (*TOOC,* Chapter 8)

There are two steps to establishing discontinuities in development. The first, most important step is characterizing the nature and content of symbols in successive systems of representation: conceptual systems 1 and 2 (CS1 and CS2). These characterizations allow us to take the second step: namely, to state precisely how CS2 is qualitatively different from CS1. With respect to numerical content, there are three CS1s: analog magnitude representations, parallel individuation, and natural language quantification.

The substantive claims in *TOOC* are that these three systems of representation exist, have been characterized correctly, and are the *only* representational systems with numerical content manifest in infancy and the toddler years. *TOOC's* picture of number development would be falsified if evidence were to be forthcoming for innate numerical representations in addition to those described above, or different from them. Indeed, one aim of my current work on the logical resources of infants and toddlers is to search for such evidence.

CS2, the first explicit representational system that represents even a finite subset of the positive integers, is the verbal numeral list embedded in a count routine. Deployed in accordance with the counting principles articulated by Gelman and Gallistel (1978), the verbal numerals implicitly implement the successor function, at least with respect to the child's finite count list. For any numeral that represents cardinal value n, the next numeral in the list represents n + 1.

CS2 is qualitatively different from each of the CS1s because none of the CS1s has the capacity to represent any integers. The new primitives are the concepts of 1, 2, 3, 4, 5, 6, 7, the concepts that underlie the meanings of verbal numerals. Parallel individuation includes no summary symbols for number at all, and has an upper limit of three or four on the size of sets it represents. The set-based quantificational machinery of natural language includes summary symbols for quantity—(e.g., "some," "all") and importantly contains a symbol with content that overlaps considerably with that of "one" (namely, the singular determiner "a"), but the singular determiner is not embedded within a system of arithmetical computations. Also, natural language set-based quantification has an upper limit on the set sizes that are quantified with respect to exact cardinal values (i.e., TRIAL, along with SINGULAR and DUAL). Analog magnitude representations include summary symbols for quantity that are embedded within a system of arithmetical computations, but they represent only approximate cardinal values, and their format is analog. There is no representation of exactly 1, and therefore no representation of + 1. Analog magnitude representations cannot even resolve the distinction between 10 and 11 (or any two successive integers beyond its discrimination capacity), and so cannot express the successor function. Thus, none of the CS1s can represent 10, let alone 342,689,455.

As required by CS2's being qualitatively different from each of the CS1s that contain symbols with numerical content, it is indeed difficult to learn. American middle-class children learn to recite the count list and to carry out the count routine in response to the probe "how many" shortly after their second birthday. They do not learn how counting represents number for another one and half to two years. Young two-year-olds first assign a cardinal meaning to "one," treating other numerals as equivalent plural markers that contrast in meaning with "one." Some seven to nine months later, they assign cardinal meaning to "two" but still take all other numerals to mean essentially the same as "some," contrasting only with "one" and "two." They then work out the cardinal meaning of "three" and then of "four." This protracted period of development is called the *subset-knower* stage, for children have worked out cardinal meanings for only a subset of the verbal numerals in their count list.

Many different tasks, which make totally different information-processing demands on the child, confirm that subset-knowers differ qualitatively from children who have worked out how counting represents number. Subset-knowers cannot create sets of sizes specified by their unknown numerals, cannot estimate the cardinal values of sets outside their known numeral range, do not know what set size is reached if one individual is added to a set labeled with a numeral outside their known numeral range, and so on. Children who succeed on one of these tasks succeed on all of them. Furthermore, a child diagnosed as a "one"-knower on one task is also a "one"-knower on all the others; ditto for "two"-knowers, "three"-knowers and "four"-knowers. The patterns of judgments across all these tasks suggest that parallel individuation and the set-based quantification of natural language underlie the numerical meanings that subset-knowers construct for numeral words.

Also consistent with the claim of discontinuity, studies of nonverbal number representations in populations of humans who live in cultures with no count list (e.g., the Pirahã: Gordon 2004; Frank et al. 2008; the Munduruku: Pica, Lemer, and Izard 2004) and in populations of humans in numerate cultures with no access to a count list (e.g., homesigners; Spaepen et al. 2011) show no evidence of any number representations other than the three CS1s.

In sum, the construction of the numeral list representation is a paradigm example of developmental discontinuity. How CS2 transcends CS1 is precisely characterized, and consistent with this analysis, CS2 is difficult to learn and not universal among humans.

15.12   Greater Expressive Power?

The above analysis makes precise the senses in which the verbal numeral list (CS2) is qualitatively different from those manifest representations with numerical content that precede it: it has a totally different format (verbal numerals embedded in a count routine); none of the CS1s with numerical content can express, even implicitly, an exact cardinal value over four. But is the argument that the concepts for specific integers are new *primitives*, undefinable in terms of preexisting concepts using the combinatorial resources available to the child, actually correct? This argument, if correct, establishes the claim that acquiring the verbal count list representation of integers increases expressive power. As I comment in *TOOC*, this is on its face an odd conclusion. Integers are definable, after all, in terms of many different possible sets of primitives (e.g., *1* and the successor function, or the principle that one-to-one correspondence guarantees numerical equivalence, plus the resources of quantificational logic).

At issue is whether logical combination underlies the transition from CS1 (core cognition of number) to CS2 (representations of verbal numerals that implicitly express the successor function). This is only possible if the capacity to represent integers is innate (e.g., if there are innate concepts ONE and SUCCESSOR), or if integers are definable, by logical construction, from *manifest* innate primitives using *manifest* logical processes of conceptual combination. Whether acquiring integer representations increases expressive power simply is this question. Without a full characterization of the manifest combinatorial (logical) apparatus available to the child at the time the integers are constructed, one cannot definitively answer the question of whether the child *could in principle* construct integer representations from innate resources, quite apart from the question of whether this is how the child *does* arrive at integer representations. But one can explore how the child actually *does* do so, and in the remaining pages of this chapter, I explain why I believe the process is *not* one of logical construction.

It's true that humans must ultimately be able to formulate concepts of integers using the explicit machinery of logic, enriched by whatever numerical concepts are necessary as well (what is actual is possible). But it is only after very long historical, and ontogenetic, developmental processes that the construction of integers in terms of logic or Peano's axioms is made. We simply do not know whether part of this process involved bootstrapping new logical representations as well as new numerical primitives.

15.13   A Logical Construction of the Cardinal Principle

Piantadosi, Tenenbaum, and Goodman (2012) demonstrated that children could, in principle, construct the meanings of the words in the verbal count list representation of the integers (at least up to "ten") by conceptual combination alone, given the full general resources of logic (in the form of logical and set operations—if/ then, set difference, plus lambda calculus, including the capacity for recursion), knowledge of the structure of the count list (its order), and four numerical primitives: the concepts SINGLETON, DOUBLETON, TRIPLETON, and QUADRUPLETON (i.e., already manifest concepts of 1, 2, 3, and 4). Piantadosi and colleagues appeal to the literature on learning to count in support of the claim that these numerical concepts and a representation of the count list are manifest at the time of the induction of the counting principles, but they merely assume—without evidence—that full general resources of lambda calculus and logic are available for the generation of hypotheses about what "one," "two," "three," "four," "five," … through "ten" mean. They assume that children learn the meanings of the words "one" through "ten" from hearing words in cardinal contexts, through Bayesian enumerative induction. Thus, their model satisfies Fodor's premises 1 and 2.

The model receives input in the form of sets with one to ten items paired with the appropriate verbal numeral. It learns a function, in the language of lambda calculus, that allows it to answer the question "how many individuals?" with the correct numeral. The model's input reflects the relative frequency of verbal numerals in parental speech to children (i.e., "one" is vastly more frequent than "two," and so on.) Learning is constrained by limiting the combinatorial primitives that articulate hypotheses to be evaluated to those detailed above, by a preference for simpler hypotheses (i.e., shorter expressions in lambda calculus), and by a parameter that assigns a cost for recursion. After considering over eleven thousand (!) different hypotheses composed from these primitives, the model learns to assign the words "one" through "four" to the concepts SINGLETON, DOUBLETON, TRIPLETON, and QUADRUPLETON, and also (independently) learns a recursive cardinal-principle–knower function that assigns the numerals "one" through "ten" to sets of one through ten individuals. The recursive function tests whether the set in question (S) is a singleton, and if so, answers "one." If not, it removes an element from S and computes "next" in the count list. It then applies the same singleton probe on the resultant set. If the answer is now yes, it outputs the numeral achieved by the "next" function (i.e., "two"). If not, it recursively repeats this step, stepping up through the count list and down through the set until a singleton results from the set difference operation.

The model matches, qualitatively, several details of children's learning to count: children go through "one"-, "two"-, "three"-, and "four"-knower stages, in that order, and depending on the cost assigned to recursion, learn the CP-knower function after becoming "three"-knowers or "four"-knowers. Before the model learns the recursive CP-function, it has no way of knowing what numeral to apply to sets greater than four, and in this sense, Piantadosi and colleagues claim a discontinuity in the model's knowledge of number word meanings. Thus, they claim for this model that it puts bootstrapping on a firm computational basis, as well as focusing on the logical resources actually needed for bootstrapping to succeed.

Piantadosi and coauthors assert that combination is the source of novelty. Therefore, in the current discourse, they are denying a genuine discontinuity. There is no change in expressive power—the manifest primitives (both numerical and logical) clearly can, in combination, express the cardinal meanings of "one" through "ten." I will show why this model does not implement Quinian bootstrapping after I've discussed Quinian bootstrapping (see Rips, Bloomfield, and Asmuth 2013 for an illuminating discussion).

Here, I simply want to acknowledge that, of course, depending on the manifest concepts (both numerical and logical) actually available to the child, it certainly could be possible to learn the meanings of verbal numerals by constructing them from antecedently available concepts through logical combination.

The question that concerns me is how representations of integers *actually* arise in development. In what follows, I sketch a very different picture, one that does not rely on conceptual combination alone, and provide reasons to believe that this is the correct picture. My goal is to provide reasons to doubt that hypothesis formation by logical combination from primitives is the *only* source of new concepts.

15.14 Quinian Bootstrapping

In Quinian bootstrapping episodes, mental symbols are established that correspond to newly coined or newly learned explicit symbols. The latter are initially placeholders, getting whatever meaning they have from their interrelations with other explicit symbols. As is true of all word learning, newly learned symbols must necessarily be initially interpreted in terms of concepts already available. But at the onset of a bootstrapping episode, these interpretations are only partial—the learner does not yet have any manifest concepts in terms of which he or she can formulate the concepts the symbols will come to express.

The bootstrapping process involves aligning the placeholder structure with the structure of existent systems of concepts that are manifest in similar contexts. Both structures provide constraints, some only implicit and instantiated in the computations defined over the representations. These constraints are respected as much as possible in the course of the modeling activities, which include analogy construction. When the bootstrapping is under metaconceptual control, as is the case when it is being carried out by adult scientists, the analogical processes are explicit, and the fruitfulness of the analogies are monitored, and other modeling processes are also deployed, such as limiting case analyses and conducting thought experiments. Inductive inference is also often involved in bootstrapping, constrained by the actual conceptual structures in the process of being aligned.

In the case of the construction of the numeral list representation of the integers, the memorized count list is the placeholder structure. Its initial meaning is exhausted by the relations among the external symbols: they are stably ordered and applied to a set of individuals one at a time. "One, two, three, four, …" initially has no more meaning for the child than "a, b, c, d, …" if "a, b, c, d, …" were to be recited while attending to individuals one at a time.

The details of the subset-knower period suggest that the resources of parallel individuation, enriched by the machinery of linguistic set-based quantification, provide numerical meanings for the first few numerals, independently of their role in the memorized count routine. Le Corre and Carey (2007) proposed that the meaning of the word "one" is represented by a mental model of a set of a single individual {i}, along with a procedure that determines that the word "one" can be applied to any set that can be put in one-to-one correspondence with this model. Similarly "two" is mapped onto a long-term memory model of a set of two individuals {j k}, along with a procedure that determines that the word "two" can be applied to any set that can be put in one-to-one correspondence with this model. And so on for "three" and "four." This proposal requires no mental machinery not shown to be in the repertoire of infants—parallel individuation plus the capacity to compare models on the basis of one-to-one correspondence. Those representations available to infants are enriched with the long-term memory models that have the conceptual role of assigning "one," "two," "three," and "four" to sets during the subset-knower stage of acquiring meanings for verbal numerals. We suggested that enriched parallel individuation might also underlie the set-based quantificational machinery in early number marking, making possible the singular/plural distinction, and in languages that have them, dual and trial markers. The work of the subset-knower period of numeral learning, which extends in English learners between ages two and three and a half or so, is the creation of the long-term memory models and computations for applying them that constitute the meanings of the first numerals the child assigns numerical meaning to.

Once these meanings are in place, and the child has independently memorized the placeholder count list and the counting routine, the bootstrapping proceeds as follows: The child must register the identity between the singular, dual, trial, and quadral markers and the first four words in the count list. In the course of counting, the child notes (at least implicitly) the suspicious coincidence that the numeral reached when counting a set of three is also the word a "three"-knower takes to represent the cardinal value of that set. This triggers trying to align these two independent structures. The critical analogy is between order on the list and order in a series of sets related by additional individual. This analogy supports the induction that any two successive numerals in the child's finite count list will refer to sets such that the numeral further in the list picks out a set that is one greater than that earlier in the list.

In my earliest writings, I characterized the induction made by these young preschoolers as yielding the first representations of integers. Let me be clear, as *TOOC* is, that when the child has built the count list representation of the first ten or so verbal numerals, the child does not yet have general representation of integers. There are many further bootstrapping episodes along the way to a representation of integers, two of which are discussed in *TOOC*—about six months after becoming CP-knowers, children construct a mapping between the count list and analog magnitude representations, yielding a richer representation of the meanings of verbal numerals (chapter 9). Shortly thereafter, children abstract an explicit concept NUMBER, and explicitly induce that there is no highest number (Hartnett and Gelman 1998). And it is not until late in elementary school or even high school that children construct a mathematical understanding of division that allows them to reanalyze integers as a subset of rational numbers (chapter 9). All of these developments are along the way to richer and richer representations of integers. But without the construction of an integer list representation of a finite subset of integers, which provides children with new primitive concepts that underlie the meanings of atomic lexical items, namely verbal numerals beyond four (e.g., "seven" representing exactly seven) as well as providing new representations of "one" through "four" (in terms of their place in a count list, rather than only in terms of enriched parallel individuation), these further bootstrapping episodes never get off the ground.

This proposal illustrates all of the components of bootstrapping processes: placeholder structures whose meaning is provided by relations among external symbols, partial interpretations in terms of available conceptual structures, modeling processes (in this case, analogy), and an inductive leap.

The greater representational power of the numeral list than that of any of the systems of core cognition from which it is built derives in part from creating a new representational structure—a count list—a new conceptual role—counting, and just *using it*. Much of the developmental process involves no hypothesis testing. Just as when the child learns a new telephone number (memorizes an ordered list of digits) and learns to use it in a procedure (dial, press buttons) that results in a ring and connection to Daddy, here the child learns an ordered list and procedure for applying it to individuals as he or she touches them one at a time. This new structure comes to have numerical meaning through the alignment of aspects of its structure with aspects of the structure of manifest number representations. These, in turn, have been built from set-based quantification (which gives the child singular, dual, trial, and quadral markers, as well as other quantifiers), and the numerical content of parallel individuation (which is largely embodied in the computations carried out over sets represented in working memory models with one symbol for each individual in the set). The alignment of the count list with these manifest meanings is mediated, in part, by the common labels (the verbal numerals) in both structures. At the end of the bootstrapping episode, the child has created symbols that express information that previously existed only as constraints on computations. Numerical content does not come from nowhere, but the process does not consist of defining "seven" in terms of a logical construction from primitives available to infants. SEVEN (the meaning underlying the word "seven") is genuinely a new conceptual primitive, its content determined in part by its conceptual role in a new conceptual structure.

With this characterization in hand, one can see why the Piantadosi, Tenenbaum, and Goodman (2012) model does not implement a Quinian bootstrapping process. There are three theoretically important differences between Quinian bootstrapping and a model that formulates hypotheses at random by explicit conceptual combination from fifteen primitives, one numeral at a time, and then uses Bayesian induction to evaluate them. First, although, like Piantadosi and colleagues, I assume that children have representations with the content SINGLETON, DOUBLETON, TRIPLETON, QUADRUPLETON, before the children induces the cardinal principles, the numerical content of these representations is carried by enriched parallel individuation and is merely implicit until the child constructs the relevant structures. On this proposal there are no manifest summary discrete symbols for these concepts. The first explicit discrete symbols with these contents are "one," "two," "three," and "four," and their meanings are not already existing primitives SINGLETON, DOUBLETON, TRIPLETON, QUADRUPLETON. Similarly, the representations that underlie the meaning of "seven," after the cardinal principle induction, are largely implicit in the procedures of the count routine, not explicitly defined in a language of thought. Second, the meanings of numerals in the Piantadosi model are learned entirely independently from each other. That is, children could, in principle, compose the recursive definition of numerals first, without ever going through "one"-, "two"-, "three"-, and "four"-knower stages. In Piantadosi's model, although the primitive SINGLETON plays a role in the cardinal principle function, knowing the meaning of "one" (expressing the innate primitive SINGLETON) plays no role in learning the meanings of other numerals nor learning the cardinal principle underlying how counting expresses number. In Quinian bootstrapping, the structure created by interrelations of the newly learned words, plus their partial meanings from initial mappings to prelinguistic thought, play an essential, constitutive role in the learning process. Third, and relatedly, the Quinian bootstrapping story takes seriously the question on the source of constraints on the learning process. It empirically motivates its claims of the exhaustive set of primitives with numerical content (the three CS1s) and provides evidence for syntactic bootstrapping as an account for how the child breaks into the meanings of the first numerals. As Rips, Asmuth, and Bloomfield (2013) point out in their illuminating discussion of the Piantadosi model, this model does not provide an account for how the hypothesis space is conveniently limited to just the fifteen numerically relevant primitives it randomly generates hypotheses from. The child has much other numerically relevant knowledge at the time of the CP induction. If that knowledge were included in the set of primitives, the hypothesis space created by random combination from the primitives would explode beyond the already entirely unrealistic eleven thousand hypotheses considered and rejected by the model. If numerically irrelevant primitives are included (how does the child decide which primitives are relevant?), the problem would quickly become entirely intractable.

In sum, Quinian bootstrapping is very different from the Piantadosi logical combination model, but which model provides better insight into how children actually learn how counting represents number? Two recent animal studies clarify the nature of bootstrapping, allowing us to see that it does not involve hypothesis testing over a huge space of existing concepts, nor does it involve logical combination of primitives.

These studies also increase the plausibility that young children have the computational resources to engage in Quinian bootstrapping.

15.15   Animal Models

In *TOOC* I speculated that Quinian bootstrapping might well be uniquely human (depending on external explicit symbols as it does), and thus might provide part of the explanation for the uniquely human conceptual repertoire. Since then, two studies have convinced me that other animals have the capacity for Quinian bootstrapping.

15.15.1   Alex

The first study (Pepperberg and Carey 2012) drew on explicit numerical representations created by Alex, an African gray parrot, who had been trained by Irene Pepperberg for over thirty years. He had a vocabulary of over two hundred words, including object labels, color words, relational terms such as "same," and several other types of labels. Alex had been taught to produce the words "three" and "four" in response to "how many *x*'s" for sets of three and four respectively. During this initial training, Alex was also shown mixed sets of objects (e.g., four blue balls, five red balls, and three yellow balls) and asked, for example, "what color three," responding "yellow." In other words, he was first taught to produce and comprehend "three" and "four" as symbols for cardinal values three and four. After this training was in place, he was similarly taught to produce and comprehend "two" and "five" as symbols for cardinal values two and five. And then "one" and "six"were added to his repertoire.

We do not know what nonlinguistic numerical representations underlie these explicit numeral representations, because we do not know the sensitivity of Alex's analog magnitude representations or the set-size limit of his parallel individual system. Analog magnitude representations themselves could have done so, or both parallel individuation and analog magnitudes could have been drawn on. As he is a nonlinguistic creature, he doesn't have the resources of set-based quantification that is part of the language acquisition device to draw on. What the quantificational resources of nonlinguistic thought are has not been studied, but Alex clearly had the capacity to selectively attend to small sets and evaluate whether any given set had a cardinal value of one through six.

After he had a firm understanding of the cardinal meanings of "one" through "six," Pepperberg taught him to label plastic tokens of Arabic numerals "1," "2," "3," "4," "5," and "6," with the words "one" through "six." Arabic numerals were never paired with sets of individuals. The only connection between Arabic numerals and set sizes was through the common verbal numeral (e.g., "two" for "2" and "two" for a set of two individuals.) He quickly learned to produce and comprehend the verbal numeral labels for the Arabic numerals. Then with no further training, Pepperberg posed him the following question for each pair of Arabic numerals between "1" and "6": "Which color bigger?" He was to choose, for example, between a blue "3" and a red "5," the plastic Arabic numeral tokens being the same size, and the correct answer being "red." He succeeded at this task when first presented it; it required no further training. Not only had he not been given any positive evidence that "2" refers to a cardinal value, the only context in which he had answered questions about "bigger" and "smaller" previously was in regard to physical size (i.e., "which color bigger" of two objects that differed in size).

Please dwell on this finding. It must be that the common labels (e.g., "two") had allowed him to connect a representation of the Arabic digits (e.g., "2") with the cardinal values (e.g., two), and it must be that the intrinsic order in his nonverbal representations of cardinal values allowed him to say which Arabic numeral was bigger or smaller than which others. Although Alex had never been taught a count list (and had been taught the cardinal meanings of numerals in the order "three"/"four," "two"/"five," and finally "one"/"six"), by the time we began our study, Alex could produce and comprehend the words "one" through "six" as labeling both cardinal values of sets and Arabic digits, and could use the intrinsic order among set sizes to order his verbal numerals.

We were thus in a position to teach Alex to label Arabic numerals "7" and "8," "seven" (pronounced by him "sih-none") and "eight." This training took about a year, and during it he had no evidence that "7" or "8" were numerals. He was then taught that "6" is a smaller number than "7," which in turn is a smaller number than "8," by posing the "which color number bigger/smaller" task, giving him feedback if he guessed wrong. This was the first evidence he had that "7" and "8" are numerals, as are "1" through "6." It took only a few hours to train him to answer which color number bigger or which color number smaller for each of the pairs: "6"/"7," "6"/"8," and "7"/"8." After he had reached criterion on this task, he was probed which color number bigger and smaller for each pair of numerals "1," "2," "3," "4," "5," "6" with respect to "7" and "8," and succeeded at this task with no further training. Thus, at this point he knew that "7" and "8" are verbal numerals, labeled "sih-none" and "eight," and he knew that "8" is a bigger number than "1" through "7," and "7" is a bigger number than "1" through "6." Importantly, he had never been given any information about which cardinal values "sih-none/7" and "eight/8" referred to.

The question of this study was whether he would make the (wildly unwarranted) induction that "sih-none/7" expresses cardinal value seven and "eight/8" expresses cardinal value eight. He did. The very first time he was asked to label a set of seven objects "how many treats?" he answered "sih-none," and the first time he was asked to label a set of eight objects "how many treats?" he said "sih-none" and immediately self-corrected to "eight." Over a two-week period he was asked to label sets of different sizes (these questions were probed by many different experimenters, only a few questions a day, intermixed with many other questions currently under study, concerning visual illusions and many other things). He performed better than chance producing both "sih-none" and "eight" (p < 0.01 in each case). He was also given comprehension trials (e.g., "what color seven" and "what color eight," probed with three sets of either six, seven, eight, nine, or ten colored blocks), and got eleven of twelve correct (p < 0.01). Thus, Alex had inferred the cardinal meanings of "eight" and "seven/sih-none" from knowledge of the cardinal meanings of "one" through "six" and from the fact that six is a smaller number than seven and seven is a smaller number than eight.

The Piantadosi model could not possibly apply here. This learning episode did not involve hypothesis confirmation. Alex never got any feedback as to whether his answers were correct. Nor was he ever given the pairings between "seven" ("sih-none") and sets of seven and "eight" and sets of eight that constitute the data for the Piantadosi model. Alex *must* have made an inductive inference based on the meanings of numerals he had already constructed. Given that his knowledge of the use of numerals was exhausted by just a few procedures they entered into (answering questions about set size and numerical order, labeling cardinal values of sets, and labeling Arabic numerals), and by the mappings he had already made between representations of sets, verbal and Arabic numerals, his induction was subject to strong constraints. He clearly had not searched through a vast unconstrained hypothesis space specified by logical combination of all 250 or so concepts he had that were lexicalized (or even a larger set of conceptual primitives he may manifest). As mentioned, this induction was wildly unwarranted; what he had been taught was consistent with "7" referring to any set size greater than "6," and with "8" referring to any set size greater than whatever "7" refers to. But in his thirty years of working with numerals, they had been introduced as related by +1 ("three" vs. "four," then "two" and "five," and then "one" and "six" added to his repertoire in turn). His induction was not mathematically or logically warranted, but it was sensible, given his actual experience with numerals. So too is the child's.

Piantadosi, Tenenbaum, and Goodman might reply that Alex may have made the leap to CP-knower, having engaged in the same conceptual combination process as hypothesized by their model that children do, during the period of learning when he was taught "one" through "six." In that case, the induction he made here was that "seven" and "eight" were the next two numerals, in that order, in the relevant list after "six." This is also not possible, because Alex lacked an essential set of primitive functions for the Piantadosi model during this earlier period: namely, he did not have a count list. He was never taught a list, per se, nor ever taught to count. Thus he could not form any generalizations carried by the function "next" applied to a count list. He wasn't even taught the numerals in numerical order (remember he learned first "three" and "four," then "two" and "five," and finally "one" and "six"). It's true that he explicitly knew his numerals were ordered, but that order had to be derived from the intrinsic order of cardinal values that were expressed by numerals and could not have been part of the source of the mapping between numerals and cardinal values. That order was not carried by a count routine and a memorized ordered list. Further insight into the process of learning that Alex was more likely engaged in is provided by a recent study of rhesus macaques.

15.15.2   Rhesus Macaques

Livingstone, Srihasam, and Morocz (2009) taught four juvenile male rhesus macaques (one year old at beginning of training), to choose the larger of two dot arrays, or to choose a symbol that came later in an arbitrary list. The dot arrays varied between one and twenty-one dots, and the arbitrary list of symbols was "1, 2, 3, 4, 5, 6, 7, 8, 9, X, Y, W, C, H, U, T, F, K, L, N, R." The monkeys were trained on the dot arrays and on the symbol list on alternate days. Training in both cases involved giving the monkey a choice between two stimuli (e.g., two dots and seven dots, or "2" and "7") on a touch screen. When the monkey touched one of the arrays, it was rewarded with the number of pulses of juice or water that corresponded to its choice. Thus it was always rewarded but got bigger rewards for picking the larger dot array or the symbol later in the list. The monkeys learned to pick the stimulus that led to the larger reward with both stimuli sets and were extremely accurate with both types of stimuli, making errors only for closely adjacent values.

Two extremely interesting results emerged from this study. First, with no training, the first time monkeys were given a choice between dot arrays and symbols (e.g., four dots and "7"), they chose the stimulus that would lead to the larger reward. That is, they had automatically integrated the two predictors of quantity of liquid—dot arrays and discrete symbols ordered in a list. Clearly this integration had to be mediated by the fact that the dot array and discrete list tasks established a common context (same testing chamber, same dependent measure of touching one of two stimuli on a screen), and the outcomes predicted were from the same scale of quantities of liquid. Still, they had integrated them. This is the structural alignment process drawn on in bootstrapping.

Second, when making a choice between dot arrays, the noise in choices among large sets (e.g., 19 vs. 21) was greater than that between smaller sets (e.g., 9 vs. 11 or 3 vs. 5). In fact, the choices showed scalar variability, the marker of analog magnitude values (see above). But errors when choosing values on the ordered list of discrete symbols did not increase as the list got longer. Livingstone and colleagues interpreted this difference as showing that the mapping from dot arrays to liquid quantity showed scalar variability, whereas the mapping from the list to hedonic value was linear. A more likely interpretation is that the mapping, during learning, reflected recognizing the relevance of each type of order (order among set sizes in analog magnitude representations of number of dots, and linear order in an arbitrary list) and inducing a rule that one should pick the stimulus later in each ordering. Analog magnitude representations of dots showed scalar variability, and representations of the linear order in the list did not. It's true that some mapping between each ordering and quantity of liquid was constructed in the process, because the two orderings were integrated. But if choosing between predicted quantities of liquid underlay each choice, both tasks should have shown scalar variability, since quantity of liquid is represented with an analog magnitude value. I suggest that the structure of an ordered list of symbols is a linear order, supported by the discriminability of each symbol from each other, and this order directly determined choice once the task was learned. This structure, after being constructed, was alignable with the intrinsic order of representations of quantity of liquid, and then with the other predictor of quantity of liquid (dot arrays). This is structurally the same as the alignment between an ordered list and analog magnitude representations of number achieved some six months after children have become cardinal-principle-knowers.

Livingstone's rhesus macaques did not induce the cardinal meaning of a new symbol from its place in a count list, but nonetheless they exhibited several components of the extended bootstrapping process that supports children's (and Alex's) doing so. They did build a representation of an ordered list (twenty-one elements long!) and align it with a representation that was itself intrinsically ordered. Also, they automatically aligned two different ordered representations (the list, the dot arrays), which were separately aligned to quantity of liquid. Clearly, finding the structural correspondence between an ordered list and increasing magnitude (whether that magnitude is number or a continuous variable like quantity of liquid) is a natural computation, at least for primates.

15.15.3 Conclusions Concerning the Nature of Bootstrapping

As the historical examples discussed in *TOOC* make clear, bootstrapping episodes are often under metaconceptual control; the scientist is consciously engaged in exploring mappings between mathematical structures and physical, biological, and psychological phenomena. But as the above examples show, metaconceptually explicit hypothesis-testing and modeling procedures are not necessary.

I now turn to the questions of whether the representations achievable by bootstrapping should be thought of as part of a preexisting hypothesis space, or otherwise as a process of formulating and confirming hypotheses in terms of concepts that are logical constructions from primitives in a preexisting hypothesis space.

Prior to the bootstrapping processes, neither children, nor Alex, nor rhesus macaques have any representations for exact cardinal values outside the range of parallel individuation. A representation of 341,468, or of 7, does not exist in some preexisting hypothesis space ready to become manifest. Nor is representation of 7 constructed by conceptual combination of innate primitives. Of course, children, Alex, and the rhesus macaques must have the capacity to represent linear order and to construct an explicit mapping between different ordered representations, but this process does not involve constructing definitions. Some of the learning processes involved in the extended episode of bootstrapping are certainly not hypothesis testing (e.g., memorizing the ordered list of numerals), and some are subpersonal (as Shea [2011] put it, "not explainable by content"; see also Strevens' [2012] proposal that introjection involves subpersonal processes). That is, the connection of the "three" in a count list with the THREE of enriched parallel individuation is most probably mediated simply by the shared label and associative machinery, just as Alex's aligning of his representations of verbal numerals, set sizes, and Arabic numerals is based first on common labels, which then supports ordering them according to the intrinsic order among cardinal values within analog magnitude and parallel individuation systems of representations. Similarly, the rhesus's aligning of an ordered list of twenty-one discrete symbols with set sizes from one to twenty-one depends on shared associations with quantities of liquid. Such alignment processes are not processes of logical combination (although logical combination is involved in building the placeholder structures). Also, Alex never got any feedback regarding the pairing of "seven" and "eight" with cardinal values, so no hypothesis confirmation or Bayesian enumerative induction was involved. I conclude that Quinian bootstrapping yields new primitives in this case, representations of integers embedded in a count list, and is a learning mechanism that does not conform to premises 1 and 2 of Fodor's argument.

15.16   Critiques of Quinian Bootstrapping

Rey (2014), Fodor (2010), and Rips, Asmuth, and Bloomfield (2013) deny Quinian bootstrapping is a learning mechanism that can increase expressive power by creating new primitives not lying in wait. They deny that Quinian bootstrapping actually creates new primitives. It may create new concepts, but they are not primitives; they must be constructible by logical combination from others. Specific versions of the challenges include (1) analogy cannot create new representational resources, because analogies require alignable structures antecedently; (2) the induction the child makes requires an antecedent appreciation of the successor function; and (3) the bootstrapping proposal fails to confront Goodman's grue problem, the problem of constraints on induction. As I hope is already clear, I believe all of these challenges to be off the mark.

With respect to the challenge that analogy requires already available representations to be aligned, I agree. The bootstrapping process is an extended one. The new representational resource is not created at the moment of the analogy and the induction alone. By the time of the induction of the counting principles, the child has indeed created the alignable structures needed for the limited induction he or she makes, just as Alex had. In the case of the child, these structures are, by hypothesis, the count list and representations of the cardinal values of the numerals "one" through "four" supported by enriched parallel individuation. The whole process begins with the innate numerical resources (the CS1s described above), the enrichment of parallel individuation during the subset-knower stage, and the creation of the meaningless placeholder structure. Of course, one needs both structures to align them. My account of the bootstrapping process specifies the origin of each structure and shows what new arises from their alignment.

I also don't agree with the second critique, that to notice sets of two differ from sets of three by a single individual, one must already represent the successor function. All one must be able to do is subtract two individuals from three individuals, and one individual from two individuals, computations that both parallel individuation and analog magnitude representations support. The successor function, in contrast, generates an infinite series of cardinal values, whereas the knowledge the child has is initially restricted to the relations among sets of one, two, three, and four (because of the set-size limit on parallel individuation and the sensitivity of analog magnitude representations being limited to 3:4 or 4:5 among young preschoolers). But of course, without the capacity to subtract two individuals from a set of three individuals, and one individual from a set of two individuals, yielding a single individual in each case, the child could not make the induction concerning how his or her short count list works. I do not deny that this knowledge must be in place for the induction; rather I present *evidence* that it is, including *how* it is (within the system of enriched parallel individuation in the case of children's learning to count), and *evidence* that precisely that induction separates subset-knowers from cardinal-principle-knowers. Again, one must consider the format and computational roles of the actual representations involved. The induction the child most probably makes is that when you add an individual to a set for which you would reach numeral "N" when applying the count routine, if you count the resulting set, you will reach the next word on the count list. This is not yet the successor function and certainly doesn't presuppose the successor function.

The heart of Rey's and Rips and colleagues' criticism is that I failed to take on Goodman's new riddle of induction. Rips, Asmuth, and Bloomfield's extended example of a possible induction consistent with the data children have available at the time of inducing the counting principles is modular arithmetic. They ask, why do children not hypothesize that the counting sequence begins at "1" again after reaching some value (e.g., "10" in a mod-10 system)? That is, why do they not consider the hypothesis that the list cycles, just as "Monday, Tuesday, Wednesday, … Sunday, Monday" does. Rey asks why children do not take "two" to be a proper name for a set, or any myriad other hypotheses. There are, of course, an infinite number of hypotheses consistent with any finite set of data. Human inductive inference is profligate; so too, apparently, is parrot inductive inference. Accounting for the constraints on induction is everybody's problem.

This chapter has been an extended response to Rey's, and to Rips' and colleagues' critique that Quinian bootstrapping fails by failing to address Goodman's new riddle of induction. One place where both writers go wrong is closely related to the view of possessed concepts as a vast hypothesis space, lying in wait to become manifest. If this were right (think Piantadosi, Tenenbaum, and Goodman), the issue of constraints on induction would indeed be trenchant. As I have repeatedly said, any actual learning mechanism imposes constraints on what can be learned. Thus, part of the project of exploring an actual learning mechanism is studying what constraints are imposed by it, including constraints on induction. Of course children *could* learn a modular arithmetic (as adults can), but once integrated with analog magnitude representations, their actual hypotheses about meanings of numerals are constrained by the structure of the analog magnitude system (which extends open-endedly toward higher values) and constraints that the same words do not apply to discontinuous regions of it. Induction, in this case, is constrained by the only three systems of representation with numerical content (parallel individuation, analog magnitude representations, and natural language quantification) that are manifest at the time of learning.

One understands the constraints on the inductions made by three-year-olds and by Alex by attending to the extremely limited contexts in which these inductions (and most inductions) are actually drawn (think Alex and the rhesus macaques, as opposed to the model of Piantadosi, Tenenbaum, and Goodman, selecting among over eleven thousand hypotheses consistent with the data it has received, where that large hypothesis space has been artificially constrained). The induction made during the hypothesized bootstrapping episode is constrained by the structures being aligned, and by their very local conceptual roles. The scientific work involved in understanding episodes of Quinian bootstrapping is characterizing those structures, showing how they arise, and showing what new is achieved by aligning them.

15.17   A Dual Factor Theory of Bootstrapped Concepts

In section 15.8, I argued that dual factor theory straightforwardly applies to concepts that are easily acquired, for they are supported by innate conceptual roles that are never overturned (partially determining narrow content) and by innate perceptual input analyzers that guarantee a causal connection between entities in the world and the symbols that refer to them (partially determining wide content).

In chapter 13 of *TOOC,* I argue that dual factor theory is also needed to understand the nature of concepts that are the output of bootstrapping episodes that underlie the origin of hard-to-attain concepts. Space does not permit a full discussion of this issue here. Briefly, newly coined concepts are ultimately mapped to antecedent ones that were supported by innate conceptual roles and innate input analyzers, and they inherit their wide content from that of those antecedent concepts. The placeholder structures in terms of which new concepts are introduced consist of interrelations among new concepts directly represented in an external language, not yet mapped to any already existing concepts that play any role in thought or refer to anything in the world. That is, they have *only* conceptual roles to provide their content. Bootstrapping proceeds by mapping these newly coined symbols to related symbols that are already interpreted. This process is often mediated by shared labels but requires changes within the antecedently represented concepts, changes effected by aligning the two structures though modeling processes such as analogical mapping.

In *TOOC* (chapter 13), I consider whether any of the conceptual roles that play such an important role in this process determine the content of the final representations, given that they are all up for revision (and indeed, are revised in every episode of bootstrapping). The issue is that conceptual role has many roles to play in a full theory of concepts that do *not* specify narrow content, such as underlying inferences and being part of the sustaining mechanisms that connect concepts to their referents. The challenge to a dual factor theory is specifying which aspects of conceptual role, if any, actually determine content.

The proposal I make in *TOOC* is that the conceptual role that exhausts the meaning of the terms introduced in newly coined placeholder structures, and that constrains the structural alignment process through which these terms come to have wide content, is part of narrow content. But how can this be so, given that the relations expressed in placeholder structures are not analytic, but rather fall under the assumptions of psychological essentialism, and thus are assumed to be (and are) up for revision? The solution, I suggest, is to take seriously the relation between ancestor and descendant concepts in cases of true conceptual change (as opposed to cases of belief revision). Narrow content is that part of conceptual role that was part of the initial placeholder structure, or the aspects of conceptual role that led to changes at the level of individual concepts (differentiations, coalescences, changes in conceptual core) in the descendants of that initial placeholder structure.

15.18   Conclusions

As has long been recognized, a theory of concepts must include an account, at least in principle, of how it is possible that they are acquired, both over historical time and in ontogenesis. This problem has largely been ignored in the psychological literature on concepts within cognitive psychology. I have argued here that taking this problem seriously constrains our understanding of what concepts are. There are two broad routes to concept acquisition: the easy route that underlies episodes of fast mapping and the hard route that underlies conceptual discontinuities and requires bootstrapping. The lesson that emerges from considering the two cases side by side is the crucial contribution of conceptual role in determining content. In the easy cases, there are innate conceptual roles for the new concepts to play (e.g., north in the night sky has an innate role to play in bunting navigation; kind concepts are supported by an innate schema within the constraints of psychological essentialism). The hard cases differ from these in that there is no innate conceptual role for the new primitives; the new inferential role and the primitives that fill those roles must be co-constructed. The bootstrapping process includes constructing new placeholder structures whose symbols get meanings entirely in terms of their interrelations with each other, and this conceptual role then comes to have wide content through modeling processes that connect it to antecedently available representations. It is not a hard sell for psychologists to consider that inferential role must have a role to play in individuating concepts and specifying their content. Considerations of acquisition show how deeply this is so and provide suggestive evidence concerning the questions of which aspects of conceptual role might be content determining.

15.19   New Directions

There is much work do be done, both on what I am calling the easy cases of concept acquisition and on what I am calling the hard cases. But here I want to draw attention to an urgent problem in this discourse that is virtually unstudied—specifying what form innate support for logic takes. We cannot evaluate Premise 2 of Fodor's argument without knowing this; we cannot know whether later developing concepts can be built from earlier available primitives by straightforward conceptual combination without this. One of the deepest issues in cognitive science is at stake. Many hold (e.g., Bermúdez 2007; Penn, Holyoak, and Povinelli 2008) that nonhuman animals do not have a logic-like language of thought formulated over language-like representations of propositions, and many have suggested that these arise in development only upon learning natural language. Others (e.g., Braine and O'Brien 1998; Crain and Khlentzos 2010; Fodor 1975) hold that it is obvious that nonhuman animals have such representational capacities, and that babies could not learn language without it. Actually, it is not obvious one way or the other. It is possible that the capacity for logic-like conceptual combination may be part of the evolved capacity for human language, and that it emerges in ontogenesis only in the course of language acquisition. More radically, it is possible that logical content is initially embodied only in computations defined on explicit representations, like the numerical content of parallel individuation, and that bootstrapping is needed to yield meanings of language-like symbols for logical connectives.

In *TOOC*, I speculate that the format of representation of all core cognition systems is iconic and provide evidence for this in the case of core cognition of number (both analog magnitude and parallel individuation representations). But systems of core cognition do not exhaust the innate representational repertoire. At the very least there are perceptual representations as well, and *perhaps* abstract central representations of relations such as *cause* or *same*. It is less plausible that the format of these latter types of representations is iconic. Furthermore, it is completely unstudied whether infants have mental representations in their language of thought with the content of the logical connectives in language and logic, such as "and," "or," or "not," but if there are, their format of representation is certainly not iconic. There is simply no research on logical symbols and reasoning schema in infancy using the productive methods of modern studies of infant cognition. There should be.

Acknowledgments

Parts of this chapter are based on Carey (2014).

References

Ahn, W., and N. S. Kim. 2000. The role of causal features in categorization: An overview. In *Psychology of Learning and Motivation*, vol. 40, ed. D. L. Medin, 23–65. New York: Academic Press.

Bélanger, J., and D. G. Hall. 2006. Learning proper names and count nouns: Evidence from 16- and 20-month-olds. *Journal of Cognition and Development* 7:45–72.

Bermúdez, J. L. 2007. Thinking without words: An overview for animal ethics. *Journal of Ethics* 11 (3): 319–335.

Block, N. J. 1986. Advertisement for a semantics for psychology. In *Midwest Studies in Philosophy*, ed. P. A. French, 615–678. Minneapolis: University of Minnesota Press.

Braine, M. D. S., and D. P. O'Brien, eds. 1998. *Mental Logic*. Mahwah, NJ: Erlbaum.

Carey, S. 1978. The child as word learner. In *Linguistic Theory and Psychological Reality*, ed. J. Bresnan, G. Miller, and M. Halle, 264–293. Cambridge, MA: MIT Press.

Carey, S. 1982. Semantic development, state of the art. In *Language Acquisition, State of the Art*, ed. L. Gleitman and E. Wanner, 347–389. Cambridge: Cambridge University Press.

Carey, S. 1985. *Conceptual Change in Childhood*. Cambridge, MA: Bradford Books, MIT Press.

Carey, S. 2009. *The Origin of Concepts*. New York: Oxford University Press.

Carey, S. 2014. On learning new primitives in the language of thought: Reply to Rey. *Mind & Language* 29:133–166.

Crain, S., and D. Khlentzos. 2010. The logic instinct. *Mind & Language* 25 (1): 30–65.

Dehaene, S. 1997. *The Number Sense*. New York: Oxford University Press.

Dretske, F. 1981. *Knowledge and the Flow of Information*. Cambridge, MA: MIT Press.

Emlen, S. T. 1975. The stellar-orientation system of a migratory bird. *Scientific American* 233:102–111.

Fodor, J. A. 1975. *The Language of Thought*. Cambridge, MA: Harvard University Press.

Fodor, J. A. 1980. On the impossibility of acquiring "more powerful" structures: Fixation of belief and concept acquisition. In *Language and Learning*, ed. M. Piatelli-Palmerini, 142–162. Cambridge, MA: Harvard University Press.

Fodor, J. A. 1998. *Concepts: Where Cognitive Science Went Wrong*. New York: Oxford University Press.

Fodor, J. A. 2008. *LOT 2: The Language of Thought Revisited*. Oxford: Oxford University Press.

Fodor, J. A. 2010. Woof, woof. Review of *The Origin of Concepts*, by S. Carey. *Times Literary Supplement*, October 8, 7–8.

Frank, M. C., D. L. Everett, E. Fedorenko, and E. Gibson. 2008. Number as a cognitive technology: Evidence from Pirahã language and cognition. *Cognition* 108:819–824.

Gallistel, C. R. 1990. *The Organization of Learning*. Cambridge, MA: MIT Press.

Gallistel, C. R., A. Brown, S. Carey, R. Gelman, and F. Keil. 1991. Lessons from animal learning for the study of cognitive development. In *The Epigenesis of Mind: Essays in Biology and Cognition*, ed. S. Carey and R. Gelman, 3–36. Hillsdale, NJ: Erlbaum.

Garcia, J., D. J. Kimeldorf, and R. A. Koelling. 1955. Conditioned aversion to saccharin resulting from exposure to gamma radiation. *Science* 122 (3160): 157–158.

Gelman, R., and C. R. Gallistel. 1978. *The Child's Understanding of Number*. Cambridge, MA: Harvard University Press.

Gelman, S. A. 2003. *The Essential Child: Origins of Essentialism in Everyday Thought*. New York: Oxford University Press.

Gordon, P. 2004. Numerical cognition without words: Evidence from Amazonia. *Science* 306 (5695): 496–499.

Hall, D. G., and S. R. Waxman. 1993. Assumptions about word meaning: Individuation and basic-level kinds. *Child Development* 64:1550–1570.

Hartnett, P., and R. Gelman. 1998. Early understandings of numbers: Paths or barriers to the construction of new understandings? *Learning and Instruction* 8 (4): 341–374.

Keil, F. C. 1989. *Concepts, Kinds, and Cognitive Development*. Cambridge, MA: MIT Press.

Kelemen, D., and S. Carey. 2007. The essence of artifacts: Developing the design stance. In *Creations of the Mind: Theories of Artifacts and Their Representation*, ed. E. Margolis and S. Lawrence, 212–230. New York: Oxford University Press.

Kripke, S. [1972] 1980. *Naming and Necessity*. Cambridge, MA: Harvard University Press.

Le Corre, M., and S. Carey. 2007. One, two, three, four, nothing more: An investigation of the conceptual sources of the verbal counting principles. *Cognition* 105:395–438.

Leslie, A. M., C. R. Gallistel, and R. Gelman. 2007. Where integers come from. In *The Innate Mind: Foundations and Future*, ed. P. Carruthers, S. Laurence, and S. Stich, 109–138. Oxford: Oxford University Press.

Levin, B., and S. Pinker. 1991. *Lexical and Conceptual Semantics*. Cambridge, MA: Blackwell.

Livingstone, M. S., K. Srihasam, and I. A. Morocz. 2009. The benefit of symbols: Monkeys show linear, human-like accuracy when using symbols to represent scalar value. *Animal Cognition* 13:711–719.

Macnamara, J. 1986. *Border Dispute: The Place of Logic in Psychology*. Cambridge, MA: MIT Press.

Margolis, E. 1998. How to acquire a concept. *Mind & Language* 13:347–369.

Margolis, E., and S. Laurence. 2011. Learning matters: The role of learning in concept acquisition. *Mind & Language* 26:507–539.

Miller, G. A. 1977. *Spontaneous Apprentices: Children and Language*. Seabury Press.

Miller, G. A., and P. N. Johnson-Laird. 1976. *Language and Perception*. Cambridge: Cambridge University Press.

Murphy, G. 2002. *The Big Book of Concepts*. Cambridge, MA: MIT Press.

Penn, D. C., K. J. Holyoak, and D. J. Povinelli. 2008. Darwin's mistake: Explaining the discontinuity between human and nonhuman minds. *Behavioral and Brain Sciences* 31 (2): 109–129.

Pepperberg, I., and S. Carey. 2012. Grey parrot number acquisition: The inference of cardinal value from ordinal position on the numeral list. *Cognition* 125:219–232.

Piantadosi, S. T., J. B. Tenenbaum, and N. D. Goodman. 2012. Bootstrapping in a language of thought: A formal model of numerical concept learning. *Cognition* 123:199–217.

Pica, P., C. Lemer, and V. Izard. 2004. Exact and approximate arithmetic in an Amazonian indigene group. *Science* 306 (5695): 499–503.

Pinker, S. 2007. *The Stuff of Thought: Language as a Window into Human Nature*. New York: Viking.

Prasada, S., K. Ferenz, and T. Haskell. 2002. Conceiving of entities as objects and stuff. *Cognition* 83:141–165.

Putnam, H. 1975. The meaning of meaning. In *Language, Mind, and Knowledge*, ed. K. Gunderson, 131–193. Minneapolis: University of Minnesota Press.

Rey, G. 1983. Concepts and stereotypes. *Cognition* 15:237–262.

Rey, G. 2014. Innate and learned: Carey, mad dog nativism, and the poverty of stimuli and analogies (yet again). *Mind & Language* 29:109–132.

Rips, L. J., J. Asmuth, and A. Bloomfield. 2013. Can statistical learning bootstrap the integers? *Cognition* 128:320–330.

Rips, L. J., A. Bloomfield, and J. Asmuth. 2008. From numerical concepts to concepts of number. *Behavioral and Brain Sciences* 31:623–642.

Rips, L. J., and S. J. Hespos. 2011. Rebooting the bootstrap argument: Two puzzles for bootstrap theories of concept development. *Behavioral and Brain Sciences* 34:145–146.

Rosch, E., C. B. Mervis, W. Gray, D. Johnson, and P. Boyes-Braem. 1976. Basic objects in natural categories. *Cognitive Psychology* 8:382–439.

Shea, N. 2011. Acquiring a new concept is not explicable-by-content. *Behavioral and Brain Sciences* 34:148–150.

Smith, C., S. Carey, and M. Wiser. 1985. On differentiation: A case study of the development of size, weight, and density. *Cognition* 21 (3): 177–237.

Smith, E., and D. Medin. 1981. *Categories and Concepts*. Cambridge, MA: MIT Press.

Spaepen, E., M. Coppola, E. Spelke, S. Carey, and S. Goldin-Meadow. 2011. Number without a language model. *Proceedings of the National Academy of Sciences* 108 (8): 3163–3168.

Strevens, M. 2000. The essentialist aspect of naïve theories. *Cognition* 74:149–175.

Strevens, M. 2012. Theoretical terms without analytic truths. *Philosophical Studies* 160:167–190.

Weiskopf, D. 2007. The origins of concepts. *Philosophical Studies* 140:359–384.

Wiser, M., and S. Carey. 1983. When heat and temperature were one. In *Mental Models*, ed. D. Gentner and A. Stevens, 267–297. Hillsdale, NJ: Erlbaum.

16 Conceptual Innovation on the Frontiers of Science

Nancy J. Nersessian

16.1 Introduction

Conceptual innovation is a hallmark of scientific change. It is implicated in numerous scientific and technological breakthroughs. *Conceptual innovation* can mean both the creation of historically novel concepts and the modification of existing ones, though the former have attracted more attention from historians, philosophers, and psychologists of science. The creation of historically novel concepts through which to understand and explain phenomena has marked all major changes in scientific theory (*scientific revolutions*). Indeed, examining conceptual innovation shows that understanding, explanation, and representation are deeply entwined in science practice. Conceptual innovation is, thus, central to the much discussed problem of conceptual change. Despite its importance, scant research has been conducted into the processes of conceptual innovation. In *Creating Scientific Concepts* (Nersessian 2008; hereafter referred to as *CSC*), I advanced this argument: (1) conceptual innovation occurs in problem-solving contexts that are extended in time, dynamic in nature, and embedded in social, cultural, and material contexts, and (2) features of a particular kind of reasoning that makes use of analogies, visual representations, and thought experiments (and other forms of mental simulation)—*model-based reasoning*—make it especially productive of novel scientific concepts.

The primary task of *CSC* was to determine the nature of model-based reasoning and how it can be productive of conceptual innovation. The argument of that book was made on the basis of a cognitive-historical analysis that examined historical records to determine how scientists create new concepts through constructing and reasoning by means of conceptual models and analyzed these practices with respect to the broader framework of research on human cognitive capacities. Since that work, my research group has been conducting cognitive ethnographies of cutting-edge research in the bioengineering sciences to further articulate the notion of model-based reasoning by extending models to include physical and computational models. My claim is not that model-based reasoning is always productive of, nor the only means of, conceptual innovation in science. However, there are features of this form of creative reasoning that promote innovative representational change. In this chapter, I briefly reprise my earlier argument and augment and extend it to include the range of model-based reasoning practices. In historical cases, with the benefit of hindsight, it is possible to select productive cases of conceptual innovation, which is not possible in ethnographic research of ongoing science. In both kinds of investigation, however, cognitive historical and cognitive ethnographic, I follow the strategy of studying modeling practices in frontier areas of science, where novel problem solutions often require conceptual innovation. My research group was fortunate to capture interesting and perhaps what will be historically significant instances of it in our ethnographic studies.

16.2   What Is Model-Based Reasoning?

Model-based reasoning is a form of reasoning in which inferences are made by means of constructing, manipulating, evaluating, and adapting models. A model can be characterized broadly as a representation of a system with interactive parts and with representations of those interactions. Model-based reasoning can be performed through the use of conceptual, physical, mathematical, and computational models, or combinations of these. Models are designed to be structural, functional, or behavioral analogs of target phenomena that capture relevant features of phenomena of interest and, themselves, serve as the objects of investigation. Analogical, visual, and simulative processes are means of manipulating and transforming models. For instance, future states of a model can be determined through simulating the model. Although it is possible that a problem can be solved with only one version, model-based reasoning often involves bootstrapping, which consists of cycles of construction, simulation, evaluation, and adaptation of models that serve as interim interpretations of the target problem. Target problems in frontier science are ill-formed and become further specified through interaction with models in these processes.

Model-based reasoning is widely used in problem solving, ranging from mundane to highly creative usage. On a cognitive-historical account, these uses are not different in kind but lie on a continuum. Studying one end of the spectrum will illuminate the other, but a deep understanding requires examining the range. In creative scientific usage, we see, for instance, that different representational modalities are often exploited in a single problem-solving episode. The historical exemplar in *CSC* details how Maxwell, in creating the concept of electromagnetic field, used visual representations of analogical models (see section 16.3). The models were conceived as dynamic—to be thought of as animated in time—and the visual representations of these are accompanied by text instructing the reader how to animate them mentally. Reasoning by means of model construction and manipulation, he derived mathematical equations, theoretical hypotheses, and experimental predictions. Scientific uses, such as Maxwell's, are likely to be more explicit and reflective than ordinary uses because the problem situation comprises deep knowledge of a repertoire of methods, domain-specific knowledge, and significant problem-solving experience. The second exemplar in *CSC*, however, is a protocol study of a person solving a much simpler problem (to determine what makes a spring stretch evenly) that exhibits much the same kind of model-based reasoning as in the Maxwell case. In coming to understand how model-based reasoning can lead to conceptual innovation in science, we understand something about the intellectual work that is accomplished through model-based reasoning across the spectrum.

16.3 What Cognitive Processes Underlie Model-Based Reasoning?

To understand how model-based reasoning leads to conceptual innovation requires detailed investigations both of its use in scientific practice and of its basis in human cognition. These requirements are consistent with a *naturalist* perspective, which holds that the problem-solving practices of scientists arise out of and are constrained by basic cognitive capacities exhibited also in mundane problem solving, though of course not from these alone. For instance, the normally functioning human cognitive apparatus is capable of mental modeling, analogy making, abstraction, visualization, and simulative imagining. Humans also have the capacity for metacognitive reflection and reasoning. The *continuum hypothesis* proposes that the sciences, through individual and collective efforts, have over centuries extended and refined these basic capabilities by means of consciously reflective development of methods of investigation aimed at gaining specific kinds of understanding and insight into nature, such as quantitative understanding, and methods aimed at eliminating error and individual bias in data analysis. Of course, the development of these methods has been and continues to be a complex interaction among scientists and their creation of rich material and sociocultural environments of practice (Nersessian 2012). Nevertheless, examining these practices in relation to the mundane cognitive capabilities out of which they arise is an important part of explaining how the investigative strategies of scientists are quite successful in fulfilling their objectives. Creative scientific practices are of far greater complexity and sophistication than any of those studied in current cognitive investigations and cannot be explained by reducing them to psychological theories or computational implementations based on the experimental studies. Further, cognitive processes underlying these practices are usually studied separately in cognitive science, but integration is required for explaining the data on science. Nevertheless, the cognitive science literature does provide important insights for my account, and in *CSC* I provided an extended analysis of relevant literature in the context of how it relates to scientific model-based reasoning practices to which I refer the reader. In this section I summarize the main conclusions I draw from that analysis.

The primary cognitive process underlying model-based reasoning is the capacity for mental modeling, and simulative, analogical, imagistic, and various abstractive processes all contribute to mental modeling. Although the mental models framework is still under development in cognitive science, we can make progress toward understanding conceptual innovation and model-based reasoning, more generally, by advancing what I have called a Craikian view of mental modeling. In his 1943 book (which was reissued in 1967 and spurred the research into mental models in cognitive science), Craik proposed that in many situations, people reason by carrying out thought experiments on internal models, where a mental model is a structural, functional, or behavioral analog representation of a real-world or imaginary situation, event, or process (Craik 1943). It is analog in that it preserves constraints inherent in what is represented. On Craik's conception, *simulation* is a fundamental aspect of mental modeling and is likely to have evolved as an efficient, though fallible, means of navigating the environment, anticipating situations, and projecting solutions to problems of significance to daily existence (see also Shepard 1988). Humans have extended its use to more esoteric situations, such as science. In reasoning processes, simulation can be understood as an epistemic endeavor, the purpose of which is to foster insight and inference through predicting future states of models and examining the consequences of these. A simple and familiar example is mentally simulating how to orient a large sofa so as to move it though a doorway. In creating new states, simulative model-based reasoning takes advantage of the tacit information embedded in the constraints of a representation. To be effective in mundane cases, at least tacit knowledge of real-world constraints is needed, such as that the sofa cannot simply pass through the wood of the door frame or that the frame of the sofa will not bend or be capable of squishing as does a cushion. In the case of science, implicit and explicit knowledge of constraints relating to general principles of the domain and of mathematical equations plays a role. This knowledge, such as of causal coherence and mathematical consistency, is likely to be represented in different informational formats. Inferences stemming from mental modeling can, of course, be erroneous, but scientists go to great lengths to reflect critically on the information used in constructing and manipulating models, and in their evaluation of the outcomes.

A mental model, then, is a conceptual system representing the physical situation, event, or process that is being reasoned about. It is an abstraction—idealized and schematic in nature—that represents a physical system by having surrogate objects or entities and properties, relations, behaviors, or functions of these that are in correspondence with it. In mundane reasoning situations, mental models are likely homomorphic (many-one), but in scientific reasoning, the intended relation is isomorphic (one-to-one with respect to dimensions salient to the problem-solving goals). Mental models embody and comply with the constraints of the phenomena being reasoned about, and enable inferences about these through simulation processes. Inferences made in simulation processes create new data that play a role in evaluating and adapting models. In reasoning processes, mental models interact with other representations—external diagrams, written equations, verbal representations such as written or oral descriptions or instructions, and gestural representations. I have called the notion of interaction among internal and external resources during reasoning *representational coupling*—a process that *interlocks* mental and real-world models such that inferences derive from the coupled system; that is, manipulations of the external model lead to corresponding transformations of the mental model (Nersessian 2008, 2009).

One kind of coupling is with external diagrammatic representations. In *CSC*, I argued that many of the diagrammatic representations found in the notebooks, diaries, and papers of historical scientists are like snapshots—or what David Gooding (2004) called momentary arrested processes"—that in reasoning are coupled with dynamical mental model simulations. Modern science extends this coupling beyond pen and paper resources to physical and computational simulations. One bioengineering researcher in our ethnographic studies aptly characterized what they do in experimenting by means of simulation models as "putting a thought into the bench top and seeing whether it works or not." As an instantiated thought, the real-world model maintains correspondences with the researcher's mental model. It is a tangible artifact with an interpretation that evolves along with the researcher's understanding. Construed in this way, the physical or computational model is a site of simulation not just of some biological or mechanical process, but also of the researcher's knowledge. Similar to the ways in which microscopes and telescopes have extended scientists' capacity to see, external simulation models have extended their cognitive capacity to reason through simulating (Chandrasekharan, Nersessian, and Subramaninan 2012; Nersessian 2002, 2008). The simulation model is an extension of the scientific thought experiment—more complete and complex, with more possibilities for manipulation, and less subject to individual bias and error.

More prosaically, another researcher explained: "We typically use models to predict what is going to happen in a system [in vivo]. So like people use mathematical models to predict … what's going to happen in a mechanical system? Well, this is an experimental model that predicts what would happen—or you hope that it would predict—what would happen in real life." On the representational coupling account, the "experimental model that predicts" is a coupled model system that requires co-processing information in human memory and in the environment (see also Greeno 1989). This processing can comprise concurrent mental and external simulations, or an external simulation might possibly "off-load" the simulation part of the process, with results from it leading to changes in mental representations. This *distributed* notion of simulative model-based reasoning casts inference as processes of co-constructing and manipulating the researcher's mental models of the phenomena and of the external model along with the external model itself—each incomplete.

How mental models are created, what neurological mechanisms underlie simulation, how coupling with the external world takes places are all open questions for cognitive science research. Craik rooted his proposal about mental modeling in research in neurophysiology that indicated that the ability to "parallel or model external events" (Craik 1943, 51) is fundamental to the brain. He further proposed that mental simulation occurs by means of the "excitation and volley of impulses which parallel the stimuli which occasioned them" (60) and leads to inferences that "might have been reached by causing the actual physical processes to occur" (51). Increasingly, contemporary cognitive research is demonstrating that simulation is constitutive of human cognition, where the human conceptual system is predicated on forms of reenactment (see, e.g., Barsalou 1999; Prinz 2002). Recent research in the theoretical perspective called *ideomotor theory* and the common coding hypothesis (see, e.g., Brass and Heyes 2005; Chandrasekharan 2009; Prinz 2005) points to a way to investigate the idea that simulation involves representational coupling. These perspectives interpret experimental data that show automatic activation of motor processes by perception as demonstrating that brain states automatically mimic movements in the world. Neuroimaging experiments show that the same brain areas are activated during action and motor imagery of the same action. For instance, Gallese and colleagues (2002) report that when study participants observe goal-related behaviors executed by others (with effectors as different as the mouth, the hand, or the foot), the same cortical sectors are activated as when they perform these actions. Such studies lead to the conclusion that whenever people look at someone performing an action, in addition to the activation of various visual areas, there is a concurrent activation of the motor circuits that are recruited when they perform that action themselves. Although this line of research has not yet been extended to mental modeling, it does suggest the possibility that perceptual and motor processes can be recruited in model simulation and representational coupling.

Simulation provides a means of creating and manipulating models, which then can be evaluated and adapted in further constructive processes. Additionally, analogy and imagistic representation and reasoning are significant cognitive processes that contribute to mental modeling, and they are widely implicated in data on conceptual innovation. One possible reason they are used so frequently is that they (as with simulation) are means of transforming representations. Making an analogy, for instance, involves understanding target phenomena or a system in terms of a representation common to it and a different system, about which more is known. An analogy between the atom and the solar system, for instance, requires each system to be re-represented more abstractly as a centrally located entity around which other entities orbit (what I call a *generic* model). Once this is done, one can then examine to what extent problem solutions in the solar system domain, such as the inverse square law for forces between the entities, transfer to the atom. Imagistic representation can involve many different kinds of transformations. Some kinds of imagistic representation involve change in format, such as changing a propositional or a mathematical representation into a visual one. The claim that "a face is like a car," for instance, might only be intelligible through a sketch representing a car schematically with prominent headlights (eyes), grill (nose), and bumper (mouth) as in cartoons. Another type of change through imagistic representation is creating an external visualization of an internal imagining, which can fix an image and add detail, such as the stripes of a zebra. Both kinds of transformations can make evident salient features not recognized before and can enable new ways of manipulating representations.

Although productive analogy in model-based reasoning has many of the features attributed to analogy by current cognitive theories, there is a significant way in which analogy as often used in problem solving in science differs from the studies that have gone into those theories. What is called *retrieval* is customarily considered a process of finding an analogical source in memory, whereas in frontier science, solving an ill-structured problem can require building a model to serve as an analogical source. There are, of course, numerous instances of conceptual innovation that use ready-to-hand analogical sources, such as Galileo's analogy between the moon and a wall made of stone through which he cast doubt on the "perfect" nature of the heavenly bodies. But there are also numerous significant instances in which there is no problem solution to retrieve that can serve as a ready-made analogical source, and a model needs to be built explicitly to serve this purpose, as in the Maxwell case examined at length in *CSC*. In the practices of physical and computational modeling we have studied in the bioengineering sciences, a major goal of the problem-solving process is to design and build a model from which insight can be transferred by analogy to the target problem. This kind of *building to discover* practice provides insight into why model-based reasoning is productive of conceptual innovation.

16.4   What Features of Model-Based Reasoning Make It a Particularly Effective Means of Conceptual Innovation?

Model-based reasoning is a widespread and significant means of problem solving across the sciences. It is ampliative and can be creative. Through it, understanding is enlarged or deepened, often in ways that lead to novel insights and even conceptual innovation. Not all problem solutions require conceptual innovation, but it occurs frequently in research on the frontiers of science, where representational problems abound. Conceptual innovation is found more readily in ethnographic research than in historical records, since innovations that are not adopted by the scientific community often do not make it into those records. Two interrelated features of model-based reasoning make it productive of conceptual innovation: analogical source building and abstraction; that is, (1) models are built explicitly to serve as analogical sources, and (2) model building requires abstraction and integration of multiple constraints from different origins. The interaction of these constraints can give rise to heretofore unrepresented structures or behaviors in the built models.

16.4.1 Analogical Source Building

In tackling complex, ill-defined problems, a common practice across the sciences is to create models through which to reason about the target phenomena. These kinds of models are constructed in accord with the epistemic goals of the scientist to serve as analogical sources for the target domain. That is, the constructed model is built explicitly to provide a comparison to the target phenomena based on analogy, with potential target solutions obtained first in the model and then transferred to and evaluated for the target. Further, although a constructed model might be a specific instance, in reasoning it is understood as a generic model, that is, as applying to the class of phenomena under investigation, not a specific instance. The way in which the model is constructed determines the nature of the analogical comparison between target and model objects, entities, or processes.

Although it is not possible to go into detail here, some exemplars of how models are built to serve as analogical sources will help clarify this notion. The main exemplar of the *CSC* book was that of James Clerk Maxwell's construction of the concept of electromagnetic field by means of building a series of conceptual models through which he derived its mathematical representation. Figure 16.1 is a schematic representation of Maxwell's modeling processes.

The objective of formulating a continuous action representation of electric and magnetic forces led to Maxwell's using continuum mechanics as a general analogical source domain. He was able to narrow the source further to that of an elastic fluid by guiding the selection with constraints from the electromagnetic target domain, specifically the experimental constraints that a model would need to be capable of rotational motion (plane of polarized light is rotated by a magnetic force) and result in certain kinds of geometric configurations so as to give rise to observed lines of force (such as iron filings forming around a magnet). Thus the resulting model was a hybrid of constraints from both domains. The hybrid models possessed their own, emergent constraints that figure into the analytical mix. Maxwell's initial hybrid model, for instance, led to the constraint of friction between vortices when in motion. It is likely that he recognized the friction constraint though attempting to simulate the model imaginatively. In such a simulation, one could notice the vortices touching and infer friction between them. Following out the problem of accommodating the model constraint of friction led him to another source domain, machine mechanics, and a new representational resource, the *idle wheel,* from which he constructed a more complex hybrid model (see figure 16.2). This model proved capable of representing additional electromagnetic constraints as well as possessing emergent constraints. The emergent constraints between the idle wheels and vortices enabled his derivation of a novel behavior: propagation of

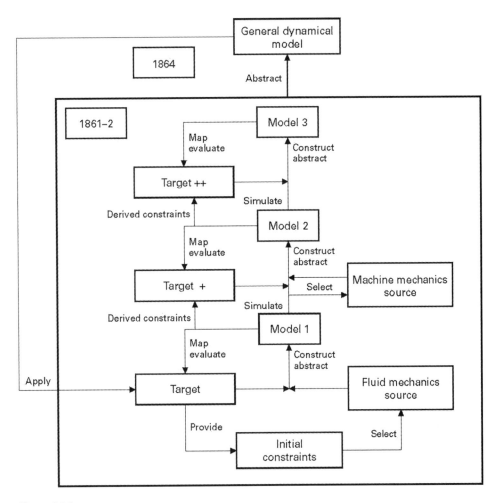

Figure 16.1

Maxwell's modeling process.

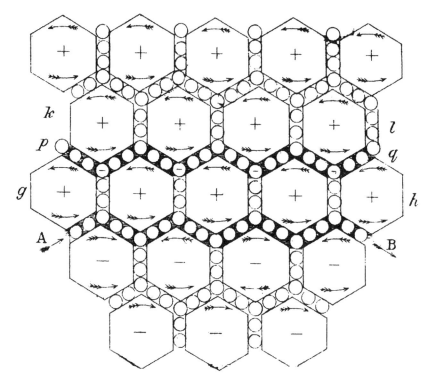

Figure 16.2
Maxwell's drawing of the idle-wheel vortex model (Maxwell 1890, 1:463).

a *wave* of electromagnetic action through the model medium. Determining the propagation speed of the wave provided the insight that light might also be an electromagnetic field phenomenon, and with further analysis, Maxwell proposed this hypothesis, which Hertz established experimentally several years later.

Another exemplar comes from the neural engineering lab (Lab D) my research group studied over the course of four years. The major problem-solving episode we captured and analyzed involved the interaction of a physical model and a computational model. Because of ethics and control issues, it is often not possible to experiment on in vivo phenomena of interest in research in the bioengineering sciences, and so this research relies almost exclusively on modeling. Researchers design, build, and experiment with physical (in vitro) and computational (in silico) model systems that serve as analogical sources from which to form hypotheses about the in vivo phenomena. The goal of the research of Lab D is to investigate learning and memory in the brain through studying living networks of neurons. For this purpose, the lab director designed, built, and optimized over many years a bioengineered model system—a *dish* of living cortical neurons plated on a multielectrode array (MEA) for stimulating and recording. The dish is designed to be a generic model of cortical processing behavior and function. It is a hybrid model that integrates constraints from neuroscience, biology, chemistry, and electrical engineering. Model constraints have contributed to its design; for instance, technological hurdles with keeping the neurons alive limit the model to a monolayer of neurons. To "embody" the dish, the researchers develop computational worlds with simulated creatures (*animats*) and real-world robotic devices (*hybrots*) to provide feedback systems controlled by the dish (*brain*). These embodied model systems, in turn, satisfy and produce new constraints.

When we entered the lab, the researchers were trying to induce learning in the dish, which they understood would require developing a control structure for supervised learning that would enable the dish to direct specific movements of the various embodiments. Our analysis of their major conceptual innovation, *center of activity trajectory* (CAT), and a related cluster of novel concepts is too complex to even summarize here. I will instead point out features pertinent to this section of the chapter. The group was having a problem controlling the dish because of repeated dish-wide spontaneous *bursts* of electrical activity. Their software tool provided a visual representation of burst output as electrical spikes per electrode (channels) of the MEA dish (64 in all); figure 16.3A shows a sample visualization. They conceptualized *bursts* in terms of the engineering concept of *noise*—interference that needs to be eliminated. One researcher focused her energies on "quieting" the dish by providing it electrical *sensory* stimulation (thinking sensory stimulation might be what prevents bursting in the brain). For months she made no progress in quieting the dish, and during that period, one of the other researchers decided to branch off and construct a computational dish model that might, if the project worked out, serve as an analogical source for developing insight about the living dish and how to control it.

As with Maxwell's conceptual model, the in silico dish was built incrementally toward becoming an analogical source for the in vitro dish (a process of nearly a year), as represented by my figure 16.4. The construction of the in silico dish model incorporated constraints from the modeling platform (CSIM); experimental findings in neuroscience literature on brain slice studies, single neuron studies, and other in vitro dish studies; and structural constraints only from their own in vitro dish (8 x 8 electrode grid; random location of the neurons). Only after the computational model replicated the experimental results in the literature were data from their own in vitro dish used to optimize it. Building the computational model created a dynamic simulation that integrated a range of experimental data—a synthesis of the literature that exists nowhere else and can yield novel behaviors. These behaviors are understood not as pertaining to a specific system (e.g., their in vitro dish), but to the class of systems of that kind.

As the researcher was developing a "feel for the model," he wanted to be able "to see" what was going on in the model, so he decided to create a dynamic visualization

A

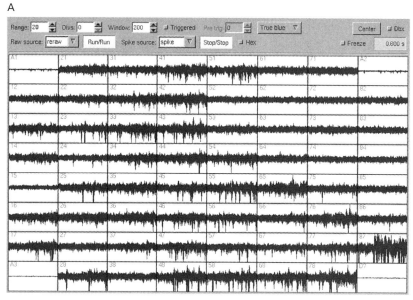

B

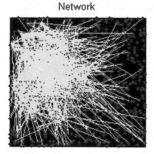

Figure 16.3
Computer screen shots of (A) per-channel visualization of in vitro dish-bursting activity; (B) network visualization of in silico dish-bursting activity.

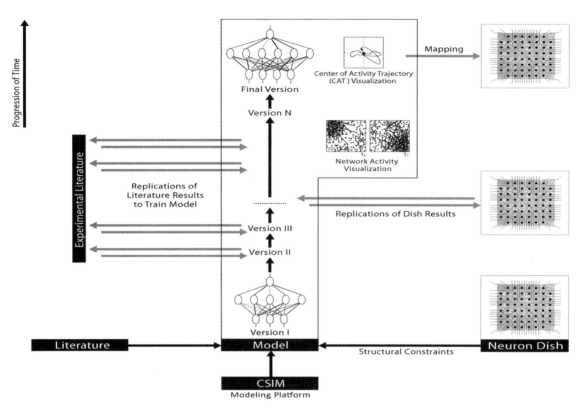

Figure 16.4
Lab D researcher's in silico modeling process.

of the simulation. The choice of how to visualize a computational model is largely arbitrary, and he could have visualized it using their earlier per-channel representation. However, since the network properties of the dish were most salient in the way he imagined what he would see if he were able to see into the dish, he visualized it as a network (figure 16.3B). The network visualization showed the in silico dish to have novel behaviors with respect to what they understood about the in vitro dish; specifically, it enabled him and the other researchers literally to see that what they had thought were *random* bursts appeared to have a limited number of *patterns*. Patterns might be exploited as signals (rather than noise), so they developed a mathematical analysis to track the burst patterns across the dish (CAT), first for the computational dish and then modifying it as needed in the process of mapping to the in vitro dish (e.g., replacing individual neurons in the computational model with individual electrodes in the in vitro model). With further work, the new concept of bursts as signals led to their solving the problem of controlling supervised learning in the in vitro dish model system (with embodiments) for the first time in the field. The analysis of the in vitro dish in turn led them to hypothesize that epilepsy might be a form of bursting in the brain and could possibly also be controlled in a manner paralleling the control structure of the dish, which other researchers started to examine experimentally.

The information one could bring to bear on a complex problem is considerable; thus the selectivity in representation afforded by focusing on specific constraints makes reasoning cognitively tractable. In *CSC*, using the Maxwell exemplar, I developed the argument that model building is a constraint satisfaction process. The second exemplar illustrates that the argument extends to physical and computational simulation models as well. For instance, any type of model would need to satisfy as constraints the known experimental results of the target domain. Constraints of the target determine a likely source domain and which constraints of the source domain are potentially relevant, and which can be ignored as potentially not germane. These are incorporated into a *hybrid* model—related to both domains. Hybrid models embody novel combinations of constraints, which lead to emergent constraints specific to the model and others previously not recognized as specific to the target phenomena that contribute to further model-building cycles. The kind of iterative model building fits the metaphor of a *bootstrapping* process. Each constructed model is built on the previous model, based on the evaluation of how well that model fits the target constraints and enhanced understanding of the target that the evaluation provides. The evaluation can yield new constraints that the next model in the process needs to satisfy. Changing representational format can facilitate bypassing constraints of existing representations that might be impeding the problem-solving process and can make evident novel constraints. Fitting the constraints stemming from different sources together requires various abstractive processes, which leads to a consideration of the role of these in conceptual innovation.

16.4.2   Abstraction

Model-based reasoning involves iterative processes of constructing, evaluating, and revising models that correspond to features considered relevant to the phenomena under investigation. Selective abstraction is needed for this kind of representation building. Many abstractive processes enable model construction, including idealization, limiting case, simplification, approximation, and generic abstraction. Although different kinds of abstraction often occur in tandem, differentiating them calls attention to a kind of abstraction that is especially productive in merging constraints from multiple sources, and thus is highly significant for the problem of conceptual innovation. I have called this *abstraction via generic modeling,* or, simply, *generic abstraction.* For instance, in considering the behavior of a physical system, such as a spring, scientists often draw a specific instance but then reason with it as without specificity as to the number and width of coils. To reason about it as a generic simple harmonic oscillator requires further suppressing features of its spring-like structure and behaviors. As Berkeley noted, one cannot imagine a triangle in general but only some specific instance. However, in considering what it has in common with all triangles, we are able to reason with the specific triangle but without specifying the lengths of the sides and degrees of the angles.

In model-based reasoning, constraints drawn from different sources need to be understood at a level of generality sufficient for retrieval, integration, and transfer. Furthermore, inferences made from the specific models need to be grasped as pertaining to the generic case. The relation between the specific instance of a model and a generic model is akin to the distinction between an instance and a type. Generality in representation is achieved by interpreting the components of the representation as standing for object, property, relation, or behavior types rather than instances of these.

The Maxwell exemplar shows this mode of abstractive reasoning in action. Maxwell started from thinking about specific connecting mechanisms, such as idle wheels, and abstracted from the specific model to what the dynamical relations between idle wheels and vortices have in common with the category of "general dynamical relational structures that capture the motion of a connected system in which one part imparts motion to another in a continuous fashion." Through reasoning about this generic abstraction, he arrived at a mathematical formulation of continuous-action transmission of electromagnetic forces, that is, a concept of field—a heretofore unrepresented structure in physics. Generic abstraction is central also to Lab D's physical and computational modeling in that the specific built models were understood not as representing any specific instance of the system under investigation, but as pertaining to the class of such systems.

Model-based reasoning involves selectively bracketing (potentially) irrelevant features and focusing attention on those features relevant to the problem-solving context. Abstractive and evaluative processes enable the reasoner to disregard irrelevant factors. Features not relevant to the problem solving can be instantiated in a model and can serve as scaffolding for the germane features. But to reason correctly by means of models requires recognizing which features are germane and which are cognitively inert within that problem-solving context. In the next section, I introduce the notion that the cognitively germane features are those that are *exemplified* in the model.

16.4.3   Exemplification

To understand how model-based reasoning is an effective means of conceptual innovation, we need, finally, to address the question of what enables the scientist to have some assurance that he or she is on a productive path with a built model. Models—whether conceptual, physical, or computational—are all abstractions, constructed to selectively instantiate features thought relevant to the phenomena of interest. Inferences made from a model can, of course, be formulated as propositions that are true or false of the phenomena. But the most that reasoning from the model can do is provide inferences about targets that are warranted to pursue by other means. From what does the warrant derive? For a model to be productive of warranted inferences, it needs to capture the relevant features of the target problem with respect to the scientist's epistemic goals. The problem, then, is how does the scientist determine whether the features germane to the target have been represented in the model? Here we can gain some insight from recent work in epistemology.

The model-building processes often require many iterations, because salient features of ill-defined problems only become evident through evaluating the fit of a proposed model to the target phenomena. The central criterion of evaluation is that the model satisfy the requirement to capture features that are of the "same kind as"—or belong to the same class as—the target phenomena along the relevant dimensions. I have argued in earlier work that the *same kind as* criterion indicates that *isomorphism,* rather than just similarity, is the basis of productive model-based reasoning in science. However, although isomorphism narrows the notion of degrees, isomorphic matching structures can be accidental as well (Suarez 2003), and so there needs to be a means to determine which structures are relevant. This requires further explicating of the *same kind as* criterion. The notion of *exemplification* is useful for this purpose.

What Nelson Goodman (1968) broadly calls a *symbol* exemplifies certain features or properties if it "both is and refers to" something that has those feature or properties; that is "exemplification is possession plus reference" (53). One of his examples is that of a tailor's fabric swatch, which "is a sample of color weave, texture, and pattern; but not of size, shape, or absolute weight or value" (53). I concur with Catherine Elgin (1996, 2004, 2009) that the notion of exemplification can productively be extended to certain practices of scientists in which representations are constructed to stand for selected features of phenomena. She argues that practices such as limiting case demonstrations, idealizations, curve smoothing, and computational modeling lead clearly to falsehoods if we insist on equating truth and epistemic acceptability. Yet science accepts the outcomes of such practices as advancing scientific goals. We can conclude from this either that science is cognitively defective or allow that scientific understanding "is often couched in and conveyed by symbols that are not and do not purport to be true" (Elgin 2004, 116). She advocates that the epistemic value of these strategies and symbols used by science lies in their ability to exemplify, that is, to "at once refer to and instantiate a feature" (1996, 171).

The notion is easy to grasp for physical exemplifications, such as those routinely created for experimental purposes, as when a lump of ore is refined to consist only of iron. The physical object, then, affords epistemic access to the properties of iron in the context of real-world experimentation. The notion of exemplification readily applies to physical models such as the dish of neurons or living tissue models of vascular processes that biomedical engineers use in performing simulations (Nersessian and Patton 2009), since these both refer to and physically instantiate the features. But how it would apply to conceptual and computational models can be more difficult to see. Elgin's discussion of fictional narratives points the way toward understanding how abstractions can also function as exemplifications. She argues, for instance, that some stories are crafted to exemplify (and thus provide insight into) aspects of human relations, such as *Middlemarch* exemplifying the dynamics of family life within the claustrophobic atmosphere of a nineteenth-century English village (2009). Likewise, I have argued that thought-experimental narratives are crafted to aid in constructing mental models with entities, events, situations, or processes corresponding to those of the intended real-world correlate. A productive thought-experimental model is the mental equivalent of the purified iron in that it, too, makes clear which features instantiated in the model are germane and which can be discounted.

Applied to models, generally, the notion of exemplification captures both requirements of models whose inferences are warranted: that they be selective representations that focus attention on features relevant to epistemic goals and that the representations fit the *same kind as* criterion. For example, the vortex idle-wheel model refers to and has the causal relational structure of the electromagnetic phenomena Maxwell was investigating. The fact that the idle wheels were introduced to solve a model constraint—that if the vortices were touching, this would produce friction and jamming of the mechanism of the imaginary model—is not germane to electromagnetic phenomena. What is germane is that the model captures the causal structure between electricity and magnetism. As Maxwell noted in later work, any mechanism that would capture this relational structure could serve as a model. In the Lab D case, the computational model exemplifies (refers to and exhibits) the bursting behavior of the in vitro dish and dynamic network visualization (figure 16.3B) exemplifies the network structure of the dish. However, the per-channel representation (figure 16.3A) does not capture that structure, and relying on it initially was not productive. This case demonstrates that *how* the information is represented in the model is cognitively significant for the inferences that can be made from it. That the researchers were able to map and transfer the novel CAT concept appropriately from the computational model to the in vitro model indicates, as one researcher explained, that they "had the information; the information was always there" in the living dish. However, it was represented in a way that did not exemplify the major network behavior constraint of the model and thus did not afford their noticing that there were patterns of burst propagations across the network.

In sum, exemplification is a goal of the iterative modeling process, and satisfying this goal provides a means of determining that the relevant constraints have been met. As the Maxwell example illustrates, the modeler often has latitude in how the correspondences are built and the constraints are met. Selectively constructing the models to satisfy constraints deemed germane enables the reasoner to bracket irrelevant (or potentially irrelevant) features and fixes attention on those features relevant to the problem-solving context. The modeling cycles aid in determining what those cognitively germane factors are and whether they have in fact been exemplified in the model. Further model building is required when they have not. Once a model is judged to exemplify target features relevant to the epistemic goals of the modeler, he or she is warranted in pursuing where the inferential outcomes deriving from the model might lead with regard to the target phenomena.

16.5 Conclusion

Conceptual innovation in science is tightly bound with model-based reasoning. By examining the nature of the model-based reasoning, we gain insight into a central problem of conceptual innovation and change: Given that conceptual innovation starts from existing representations, how is it possible for a genuinely novel representation to be created? Analogical, imagistic, and mental modeling processes are especially effective means of abstracting and integrating constraints from existing representations to allow for novel combinations to occur. These combinations can produce heretofore unrepresented structures and behaviors that can be formulated as novel scientific concepts.

Conceptual innovation, that is, how novel concepts are formed, is a relatively recent topic for the philosophy of science. The proposal that model-based reasoning is generative of scientific concepts, although it appears to transfer to innovation across the sciences, is based largely on cases from physics and the bioengineering sciences, so research in other domains is needed to see how broadly it transfers. In addition, as indicated in the Lab D case especially, model-based reasoning is situated in problem-solving environments with material and sociocultural affordances and limitations that contribute to the iterative modeling processes, and more detailed analyses of their contribution are needed. Further, there are undoubtedly other reasoning processes implicated in conceptual innovation that need to be ascertained. Finally, the account of model-based reasoning presented here provides novel insight into analogical reasoning, specifically that in creative reasoning, there is often no ready-to-hand analogical source, thus building the analogical source is central to the creative process. This insight warrants further investigation in the analogy research of both philosophy and psychology.

Acknowledgments

I appreciate the support of the National Science Foundation grant DRL097394084 and the comments of Lisa Osbeck and Miles MacLeod on drafts of this chapter.

References

Barsalou, L. W. 1999. Perceptual symbol systems. *Behavioral and Brain Sciences* 22:577–609.

Brass, M., and C. Heyes. 2005. Imitation: Is cognitive neuroscience solving the correspondence problem? *Trends in Cognitive Sciences* 9:489–495.

Chandrasekharan, S. 2009. Building to discover: A common coding approach. *Cognitive Science* 33 (6): 1059–1086.

Chandrasekharan, S., N. J. Nersessian, and V. Subramaninan. 2012. Computational modeling: Is this the end of thought experiments in science? In *Thought Experiments in Philosophy, Science and the Arts*, ed. J. Brown, M. Frappier, and L. Meynell, 239–260. London: Routledge.

Craik, K. 1943. *The Nature of Explanation*. Cambridge: Cambridge University Press.

Elgin, C. Z. 1996. *Considered Judgment*. Princeton, NJ: Princeton University Press.

Elgin, C. Z. 2004. True enough. *Philosophical Issues* 14:113–131.

Elgin, C. Z. 2009. Exemplification, idealization, and understanding. In *Fictions in Science: Essays on Idealization and Modeling*, ed. M. Suárez, 77–90. London: Routledge.

Gallese, V., P. F. Ferrari, E. Kohler, and L. Fogassi. 2002. The eyes, the hand, and the mind: Behavioral and neurophysiological aspects of social cognition. In *The Cognitive Animal*, ed. M. Bekoff, C. Allen, and M. Burghardt, 451–462. Cambridge, MA: MIT Press.

Gooding, D. C. 2004. Cognition, construction, and culture: Visual theories in the sciences. *Journal of Cognition and Culture* 4 (3–4): 551–593.

Goodman, N. 1968. *Languages of Art*. Indianapolis: Hackett.

Greeno, J. G. 1989. Situations, mental models, and generative knowledge. In *Complex Information Processing*, ed. D. Klahr and K. Kotovsky, 285–318. Hillsdale, NJ: Erlbaum.

Maxwell, J. C. 1890. *The Scientific Papers of James Clerk Maxwell*. Ed. W. D. Niven. 2 vols. Cambridge: Cambridge University Press.

Nersessian, N. J. 2002. The cognitive basis of model-based reasoning in science. In *The Cognitive Basis of Science*, ed. P. Carruthers, S. Stich, and M. Siegal, 133–153. Cambridge: Cambridge University Press.

Nersessian, N. J. 2008. *Creating Scientific Concepts*. Cambridge, MA: MIT Press.

Nersessian, N. J. 2009. How do engineering scientists think? Model-based simulation in biomedical engineering research laboratories. *Topics in Cognitive Science* 1:730–757.

Nersessian, N. J. 2012. Engineering concepts: The interplay between concept formation and modeling practices in bioengineering sciences. *Mind, Culture, and Activity* 19:222–239.

Nersessian, N. J., and C. Patton. 2009. Model-based reasoning in interdisciplinary engineering: Two case studies from biomedical engineering research laboratories. In *Philosophy of Technology and Engineering Sciences*, ed. A. Meijers, 678–718. Amsterdam: Elsevier Science.

Prinz, J. J. 2002. *Furnishing the Mind: Concepts and Their Perceptual Basis*. Cambridge, MA: MIT Press.

Prinz, W. 2005. An ideomotor approach to imitation. In *Perspectives on Imitation: From Neuroscience to Social Science*, ed. S. Hurley and N. Chater, 141–156. Cambridge, MA: MIT Press.

Shepard, R. N. 1988. Imagination of the scientist. In *Imagination and the Scientist*, ed. K. Egan and D. Nadaner, 153–185. New York: Teachers College Press.

Suarez, M. 2003. Scientific representation: Against similarity and isomorphism. *International Studies in the Philosophy of Science* 17 (3): 225–244.

VIII Concepts and Normativity

17 Does the Infant Possess a Moral Concept?

J. Kiley Hamlin

17.1 Introduction: The Origins of Moral Concepts

As soon as ancient philosophers began contemplating the origins of concepts in general, they contemplated the origins of moral concepts in particular. For instance, in Plato's *Meno*, Meno asks Socrates: "Can you tell me, Socrates, is virtue something that can be taught? Or does it come by practice? Or is it neither teaching or practice but natural aptitude or instinct?" Although Meno questioned Socrates in the year 380 BCE, his inquiry into the origins of virtue illustrates what continues to be one of the most critical theoretical divides in contemporary cognitive science, one that has been applied to many human traits. By questioning the role of teaching and practice versus instinct in human virtue,[1] Meno asks whether it is more appropriate to describe the origins of moral concepts from an "empiricist" or a "nativist" perspective.

In this chapter I argue for a nativist account of the acquisition of moral concepts. To support this argument, I present evidence that, from early in the first year of postnatal life, human infants evaluate others for their prosocial and antisocial actions, including some that fall squarely within the moral realm. Crucially, infants' evaluations appear to rely specifically on the moral characteristics of others' actions, rather than on their physical or even their social ones. From this evidence I will argue that infants' evaluations emerge too early and are too sophisticated to be solely the result of experience, whether it be low-level perceptual processing, observations of or interactions with social others, or implicit or explicit internalization of cultural norms. Instead, there appears to be one or more extremely early developing—but nonetheless complex—*intuitions* about which actions and individuals are better than others. These intuitions presumably constrain each child's earliest experiences with the social and moral world, thereby influencing the nature and process of acquiring mature moral concepts.

1. "Virtue" has both general and specific referents; for the purposes of this chapter, we will assume that Meno was using it generally, as one might use "morality" today.

17.2   The Nativist-Empiricist Debate

Before launching into a nativist account of morality, some discussion of the nativist-empiricist debate is in order. Historical philosophers (Aristotle, Descartes, Hume, Kant, Leibniz, Locke, and many others) vigorously debated the interplay between experience and innate cognitive architecture in the acquisition of psychological traits such as concepts, behaviors, abilities, and personality. The debate rages on today in cognitive science (for in-depth reviews from various perspectives see Carruthers, Laurence, and Stich 2005–2007; Johnson 2010; Margolis and Laurence 1999; Oakes et al. 2010; Xu 2012). The nativist-empiricist divide is sufficiently wide that it has been given descriptions laypeople recognize; for instance, "Nature versus nurture," "Innate versus learned," or the dreaded "'Natural state' versus 'blank slate.'" Although the colloquial use of such phrases suggests that the general public is aware of the nativist-empiricist distinction, it is not necessarily the case that individuals—even those within the cognitive sciences—agree even on what makes a particular argument nativist versus empiricist: defining the debate's boundary conditions sometimes seems as controversial as the debate itself. As a result, it seems possible that some of the most heated disagreements between self-described nativists and empiricists are exacerbated to the extent that each side believes the other is committed to some extreme form of their preferred "ism," even if very few individuals actually ascribe to such extreme positions. Therefore, before addressing the origins of moral concepts specifically, I will outline what I do (and do not) believe is entailed by adopting "empiricist" versus "nativist" perspectives on the origins of psychological traits[2]—in the hopes of alleviating concerns that my particular nativist claims are more radical than they are.

17.2.1   Empiricism

For the purposes of this chapter, I take empiricist developmental accounts to be those that claim psychological traits are the product of environmental inputs interacting with general-purpose learning systems. Commonly cited learning systems include conditioning, associative learning, selective attention, memory, statistical learning, explicit instruction, complex conscious reasoning, and others; such systems are considered sufficient to drive learning across a wide variety of domains. Distinct psychological traits, then, result from distinct environmental inputs acting upon general-purpose systems during development. For example, the acquisition of distinct moral and numerical concepts results from different experiences with the moral and numerical world (for instance, being taught about right and wrong versus being taught about mathematics).

2. For careful discussion, definitions, and additional references, see Carruthers, Laurence, and Stich (2005–2007); Griffiths, Machery, and Linquist (2009); Mameli and Bateson (2006); Marcus (2004); Margolis and Laurence (2012).

Empiricists do not consider the *timing* of developmental emergence to be critical. Some domain-general systems are clearly functional at or before birth (several or all of our senses; the ability to form associations), whereas others become increasingly functional as the brain matures (conscious reasoning abilities). Empiricists even allow that specialized systems could emerge quite early (for instance, systems tuned for perceiving faces might result from only a few hours of facial experience); they simply claim that whenever a specialized system does emerge, its emergence is the result of varied inputs to general-purpose learning systems. In other words, domain-specific systems can be built by domain-general ones, but they cannot emerge on their own.

17.2.2   Nativism

Nativist developmental accounts posit that psychological traits are based in some part on systems that evolved to perform domain-specific functions. Though nativists vary in how specific they posit these systems to be, some of the most commonly cited are those designed to process basic aspects of everyday life, such as objects, people, and language. Some nativists assert that domain-specific systems include actual conceptual *content* (for example, the belief that objects persist when out of sight), while others posit *constraints* on how experience influences development (for example, a bias to pay close attention to physical continuities during object perception, but not during agent perception). These viewpoints are not mutually exclusive: nativist domain-specific systems might consist of both conceptual content and learning constraints, or they might have one and not the other. Unlike empiricists, then, nativists claim that the acquisition of distinct psychological traits is at least partially the result of differences that are within domain-specific acquisition systems themselves; distinct traits are not solely the result of differences in input. Thus, humans acquire distinct moral and numerical concepts *both* because of different experiences with the moral and numerical world *and* because the human mind evolved to treat those experiences differently.

Although nativist claims are often seen as equivalent to claims about presence or absence at birth, nativists, like empiricists, make no demands on the timing of developmental emergence. Though domain-specific systems could operate from birth, they need not do so. First, some systems might emerge at some point during development due to biological maturation rather than experience (for instance, systems for assessing potential sexual partners). Alternatively, domain-specific systems might be present from birth but be essentially nonfunctional due to domain-general immaturities (such as a poorly calibrated visual system or underdeveloped long-term memory). Finally, domain-specific systems may be in place and functional, even from birth, and yet contemporary experimental methodologies may not be sufficiently sensitive to detect them. Overall, a lack of evidence for domain-specific systems at particular developmental stages does not in itself necessitate that domain-general systems are responsible for building them.

17.2.3 Arguments against Nativism

As my endeavor is a nativist one, I will quickly note some of the arguments commonly raised against nativism and why I consider them misplaced. One common argument is that to claim something is innate[3] is equal to saying that it does not develop (see Prinz 2012). This cannot be true: everything about humans develops. Every person begins life as a single cell, but not since the time of Aristotelian homunculi has anyone believed that single cells have legs or eyelashes, much less high-level social or cognitive capacities. Rather, nativists attempt to use the timing of developmental emergence to constrain the hypothesis space of experiential causes of a particular capacity. For example, because the womb is dark but the newborn sees, it is unlikely that the light sensitivity of the human eye is primarily the result of experiencing light. Yet eyes develop their sensitivity to light during ontogeny: single cells are not light sensitive. In sum, the fact that something comes into existence when it did not previously exist is unrelated to whether it is innate: everything develops. The nativist-empiricist question, then, is to elucidate the role of the environment in driving that development.

Malleability, or the tendency to be influenced by the environment during development, is a related argument commonly brought against nativism: the assumption is that if a trait changes over the course of development such that outcomes differ based on varied inputs, then that trait must not be innate. But surely all kinds of innate processes are influenced by experience. Humans' gustatory system "prefers" sweet to bitter tastes, and presumably this preference is not learned via experience. And yet, giving infants experience with bitter liquids over their first year can influence this preference, making bitterness less aversive than it once was (e.g., Mennella and Beauchamp 1996). Similarly, the tendency to find painful stimuli aversive is surely innate, but atypical early experiences with pain (for instance, in a neonatal intensive care unit) have been demonstrated to lead to hyper- or hypo-pain sensitivity later in life (e.g., Johnson and Stevens 1996). The possibility that taste and pain can change based on varied experience does not make the notion that they are organized in advance of such experience any less accurate.

To return to the purpose of this chapter, by arguing for a nativist account of moral concepts, I do not claim (nor do I believe) that moral development does not exist, is not critically important, or that both typical and atypical moral-developmental outcomes are not largely the result of experience and other domain-general processes. I do claim that, in principle, issues of development and plasticity are orthogonal to those of innate foundations: experience and psychological processes might operate on a moral "blank slate," or they might operate on a rudimentary system that has some content and/or is prepared to process experience in particular ways. Clearly, documenting moral

---

3. I use "innate" herein as synonymous with being to any extent "organized in advance of experience" (Marcus 2004, 40), or as generally "describable via nativist accounts of development."

developmental change across the lifespan and discovering how this change occurs is fantastically important. Decades of careful developmental work have been devoted to this question (see Killen and Smetana 2006, 2013, for extensive review); this work has lead to critical discoveries regarding the component processes involved in the development of mature moral judgment and action, as well as how best to foster moral development. That said, nativist accounts are focused not on whether moral *maturity* is innate, but on whether humans' basic cognitive building blocks contain *anything more than nothing* of morally specific content or biases, which should be considered some part of subsequent moral development. Put another way, I aim to determine whether, on a "moral development scale" from 0 to 100 (in which 0 = completely amoral and 100 = ideal moral maturity), the postnatal developmental process begins at 0, or 5, or 20, and to characterize the nature of this postnatal starting point as accurately as possible. Indeed, surely whatever the outcome of such a pursuit, knowledge of where moral development begins can only increase the accuracy of our understanding of its progress, facilitate the detection of cases in which that progress is delayed, and boost the effectiveness of our attempts to improve developmental outcomes.

17.2.4   Examining Nativist Claims: The Study of Preverbal Infants

Although neither nativists nor empiricists make specific claims about the timing of developmental emergence, the study of preverbal infants is often at the forefront of the nativist-empiricist debate.[4] Critically, the applicability of infant data to the debate relies heavily on the claim that very young infants simply *could not have acquired* some concept or another so early in development via domain-general learning alone. This is often referred to as the "argument from the poverty of the stimulus," and suggests that young infants lack sufficient inputs—be they sensory, linguistic, pedagogical, or other—to have acquired a particular psychological trait without necessitating support from innate conceptual structures or domain-specific learning systems. That is, if developmental psychologists were to provide evidence that a particular competence exists in infants too young to have gained such competence via domain-general learning, then the nativist hypothesis is supported. In particularly telling cases, nativists argue that experience is not only *insufficient* to explain a particular pattern of infant behavior, but also that the nature of infants' performance is actually *opposed* to what one might expect if domain-general learning systems were responsible for it. In these ways, the study of preverbal infants can be used to constrain the hypothesis space for accurately describing the acquisition of psychological traits.

4. For examples of the application of infant cognition research to nativist arguments, see Gelman and Baillargeon (1983); Baillargeon, Scott, and He (2010); Carey (2009); Gergely and Csibra (2003); Leslie and Keeble (1987); Kovács, Téglás, and Endress (2010); Spelke (1990, 1994); Wynn (1992); Xu and Spelke (2000).

17.3   How to Define Morality

Although nativist claims are always controversial, nativist claims regarding human morality are particularly so. This is hardly surprising. In order to examine the origins of any concept, one must first define it, identifying what counts as a member of a category and a reliable way to distinguish category members from nonmembers. Though this is not trivial for any concept (see Margolis and Laurence 1999), there are several ways in which moral concepts are *particularly* difficult to define. At a semantic level, "moral" refers both to the general state of possessing any morally relevant content (the opposite of "amoral"), as well as to the more specific state of being morally good (the opposite of "immoral"). On the former distinction, hitting persons is moral but hitting buttons is not; on the latter, hugging persons is moral but hitting persons is not. In addition, "moral" can refer to actions, to outcomes, or to individuals: the judgment "X is morally wrong" could refer to an act of hitting (wrong in itself), to the pain of an individual who was hit (a regrettable outcome), or to the individual who performed the hitting (who was wrong for doing so).

Scholars also disagree, often vehemently, on whether normative considerations should be included in the definition of moral. They disagree in particular on whether there exist universal moral laws that everyone's moral concept should include. Those who include normative considerations in their definitions have tended to study the process by which humans come to deem some specific things universally right and other specific things universally wrong (and what drives the process of reaching these conclusions); these scholars see the ultimate goal of moral development as reaching some normatively correct end state (e.g., Kohlberg 1969, 1981; Piaget 1932; Piaget and Inhelder 1956; Rest et al. 1999). In contrast, others exclude normative considerations from their definition of morality, claiming that while moral judgments and actions are universal—in that all cultures have notions that some things are right and others are wrong—opinions of moral value differ too widely between individuals, groups, and societies to allow for normative definitions.[5] Instead, these individuals focus on the processes by which any individual comes to *any* morally relevant behavior or judgment: as long as the (or some) individual conceives of a particular issue as within the moral domain, it is treated as though it is within the moral domain (e.g., Brown 1991; Haidt and Graham 2007; Kelly et al. 2007; Shweder, Mahapatra, and Miller 1987).

Another common definitional disagreement rests on the relative roles of reason and emotion in morality. Some believe that morality consists first and foremost of the capacity to reason through abstract moral dilemmas, perhaps discounting how one personally feels about a situation in order to reach an objective judgment or planned course of action. The most famous supporter of reason-focused morality was Immanuel

---

5. That is, these individuals reject normativity in the psychological study of morality; this does not necessarily mean that they personally ascribe to moral relativism.

Kant ([1781] 1998), who claimed that "thoughts without contents are empty; intuitions without concepts are blind" (A 51, B 75) (see also Kant [1785] 2012; Kohlberg 1969; 1981; Piaget 1932; Piaget and Inhelder 1956; Rawls 1971). Kant believed that not only were emotions not enough to support morality, they would often lead individuals astray, as they are likely to hinder rational decision making. In contrast, others assert that morality is fundamentally emotional and intuitive, and that, to the extent that reason plays a role in moral judgment and action, it is small and often post hoc. The most famous supporter of emotion-focused morality was David Hume, who stated ([1739] 1978) "reason is, and ought only to be a slave to the passions" (217) (see also Aquinas 2006; Blair 1995; Damasio 1994; de Waal and de Waal 1996; Eisenberg and Hussen 1989; Greene et al. 2001; Haidt 2001; Hoffman 2001; Macnamara 1991; Pizarro, Inbar, and Helion 2011; Smith 1759).

Despite—or perhaps as a result of—these definitional debates, scholarly interest in humans' moral origins has grown rapidly in recent years, in particular in social, developmental, and comparative psychology (e.g., Anderson et al. 2013; Bloom 2013; Cushman, Young and Hauser 2006; Gray, Young, and Waytz 2012; Greene 2007; Haidt and Joseph 2007; Hamlin 2013a; Hauser 2006; Joyce 2006; Katz 2000; Killen and Smetana 2006; Macnamara 1991; Mikhail 2011; Premack and Premack 1994; Wynn 2008). A particular interest in nativist accounts of humans' moral origins has been spurred by the hypothesis that human morality is an evolved propensity for sustaining collective action and cooperation among large groups of unrelated individuals (see Alexander 1987; Cosmides and Tooby 1992; de Waal 2008; Henrich and Henrich 2007; Joyce 2006; Katz 2000; Price, Cosmides, and Tooby 2002; cf. DeScioli and Kurzban, 2013). That is, large-scale cooperation and prosociality are highly beneficial at an individual and a societal level, but they can endure only to the extent that there are mechanisms for discouraging behaviors that threaten such systems, such as cheating and other forms of antisociality. These mechanisms may consist of cognitive and motivational capacities to detect, to avoid or exclude, and to punish antisocial individuals: these are basic components of morality.

17.4 A Working Definition of Morality

For the purposes of this research, the term "moral" refers to the state of *possessing any morally relevant content*—that is our everyday, commonsense notion of the term. Under this definition, killing, helping, stealing, and sharing are all moral actions, whereas baking, skiing, doing math problems, and hearing are not. Of course, I could bake a poisoned cake to kill my friend, or you could do math problems in the process of building a bomb. Acts like stealing and helping, however, are clearly more prototypical instances of moral actions than are baking and math, and it is practical to start with the obvious cases before moving on to the subtleties. Under this definition of moral, "moral judgment" refers to an evaluation of something or someone that is *based on* its morally relevant content: the general tendency to evaluate some actions and individuals as right, good, and deserving of reward, and others as wrong, bad, and deserving of punishment. While there is considerable cross-cultural variation in exactly which things are considered morally good and bad, across cultures everyone finds some things morally relevant and good, some things morally relevant and bad, and some not morally relevant at all, and everyone feels some urge to punish others' immoral acts (e.g., Brown 1991; Herrmann, Thöni, and Gächter 2008). This research concerns itself with the origins of these universal tendencies.

This is a rather liberal definition, but it is not so liberal to allow the word "moral" to apply to anything people happen to like or dislike. First and foremost, moral judgments are social: they do not apply to inanimate objects. For instance, though anyone would be upset to discover his or her windshield broken, it would make a big moral difference to the owner whether it was a tree limb or an ex-lover that caused the damage. Second, moral judgments apply to social agents who are capable of directing their own behavior: coma patients, newborns, and the coerced tend to be exempt from blame and praise, even if they cause harmful outcomes (e.g., Fincham and Roberts 1985; Gray, Gray, and Wegner 2007; Newman and Weitzer 1956). Third, the target of a social agent's (potentially) morally relevant action matters: kicking rocks is morally different from kicking people.[6] Fourth, moral evaluations should be able to be made by individuals who are not themselves personally involved in a situation, in which "interest or revenge or envy perverts not our disposition" (Hume [1751] 2008, 96). Finally, the moral status of actions varies tremendously based on *why* a particular person performed a particular action: What was the goal? What was the motivation? For example, some abstract notion of helping others pursue their goals is not always morally good: to assist a baby in its quest to touch a hot stove would certainly not be praiseworthy. In addition, moral actions do not always result in someone being helped or harmed: plenty of morally relevant actions involve an individual who attempts to help or harm someone else but fails to do so. Relatedly, sometimes an individual is helped or harmed but the helper or harmer's moral responsibility is attenuated, as in the case of accidents.

These examples illustrate just how much identifying an action as morally relevant, and engaging in moral evaluation, rely on basic social-cognitive capacities. Our commonsense notions of moral responsibility are filled with notions of agency, patiency, relationship, goal directedness, intention, and motivation (e.g., Baird and Moses 2001; Cushman 2008; Gray, Young, and Waytz 2012; Killen and Smetana 2008; Malle 1999; Rai and Fiske 2011; Robinson and Darley 1995; Young et al. 2007); it is nearly impossible to imagine a moral concept that does not include these component social-cognitive

---

6. Moral actions typically involve an agentic or experiencing recipient (a moral "patient" who is helped or harmed by the moral "agent"), but technically they need not: moral actions can involve a physical patient (for instance, harm of the environment), or they can be directed at the self (for example, purity violations or self-harm).

concepts. Thus, before beginning a discussion of whether preverbal infants possess any moral concepts, it seems necessary to demonstrate that they possess the underlying social-cognitive abilities that moral concepts require.

17.5 Social Cognition in Preverbal Infants

Decades of research into infant social cognition suggests that within the first year of life, infants have a remarkable understanding of social agents and their actions. During the first year, infants distinguish agents (things with minds) from nonagents (things without minds) on several dimensions, including how they move (e.g., Bertenthal 1993; Leslie 1994; Mandler 1992; Premack 1990; Simion, Regolin, and Bulf 2008) and how they act on the world (e.g., Carlson 1980; Leslie 1982; Watson 1979). In addition, infants analyze others' actions in terms of their goal-relevant properties: they expect that an agent will pursue a goal he or she has pursued before, as efficiently as possible, even if this pursuit requires a change in behavior (e.g., Gergely et al. 1995; Csibra et al. 1999; Woodward 1998). Although this interpretation is controversial (e.g., Gergely and Csibra 2003; Ruffman, Taumoepeau, and Perkins 2012), a growing body of evidence suggests that infants' analysis of agentive action is specifically mentalistic: infants recognize that the mental states driving goal-directed actions are (1) unique to individuals, (2) separable from physical aspects of behavior (outcomes may be accidental or intentions may go unfulfilled), and (3) the product of what an agent perceives, knows, and believes (see Baillargeon et al. 2014 for extensive review of the literature on infant mentalizing).

An overwhelming majority of infant social-cognition work to date has examined infants' understanding of agents' *object-directed* behaviors. As a social species, however, humans are typically far more concerned with the mental states underlying agents' *agent-directed* behaviors—with social interactions—than those underlying actions in the physical world. Indeed, agent-directed behaviors are considerably more likely than object-directed ones to have moral relevance: prototypical moral acts like hitting, helping, sharing, stealing, and so forth all involve behaviors that one individual does directly to another individual or that have consequences for another individual.

Although the data are more limited, there is evidence that infants have some grasp of *their own* social interactions by early in the first year of life. For example, three-month-olds become agitated by "still face" interactions, in which an interaction partner ceases to respond to their communication attempts, suggesting that they find the interruption to be unexpected or otherwise distressing (e.g., Tronick et al. 1978). Intriguingly, just how upset infants become during an interaction pause depends on cues that signal *why* the partner stopped responding: three-month-olds are less distressed if the partner turns away after being distracted by an outside event than if he or she turns away for no apparent reason (e.g., Legerstee and Markova 2007). In a similar set of studies, infants from five months of age become more agitated when interacting

with someone who intentionally withholds a toy (that is, has a fulfilled negative intention) than when interacting with someone who tries but fails to give them a toy (that
is, has an unfulfilled positive intention; e.g., Behne et al. 2005; Marsh et al. 2010; see
also Dunfield and Kuhlmeier 2010). Together, these "unwilling/unable" results suggest
that infants actively analyze the mental states of their own interaction partners in the
first year of life.

Infants also have some understanding of social interactions that occur between
unknown third parties, in which they are not personally involved. For instance, ten-
month-olds expect communicative partners to look at one another (Beier and Spelke
2012) and expect larger social agents to dominate smaller ones (Thomsen et al. 2011;
see also Mascaro and Csibra 2012). Securely attached twelve-month-olds expect caregivers to respond to their dependents' distress calls, but insecurely attached infants do not
(Johnson, Dweck, and Chen 2007). Finally, ten- to twelve-month-olds expect an agent
who is helped by one individual and hindered by another to subsequently approach
one and avoid the other (e.g., Kuhlmeier, Wynn, and Bloom 2003; Fawcett and Lisz-
kowski 2012; see also Hamlin, Wynn, and Bloom 2007), and twelve-month-olds associate different social interactions by their valence rather than their physical similarities
(e.g., helping with caressing, and hindering with hitting; Premack and Premack 1997).

In sum, studies with preverbal infants suggest that infants interpret social goals, even
those involving morally relevant acts such as helping, harming, giving, and failing to
give. Moral concepts, however, involve more than identifying underlying intentions
and predicting future behaviors. In particular, the human moral sense also involves
evaluation, by which certain kinds of social goals are seen as good and others as bad,
and (critically) the individuals who possess and act on such goals are themselves evaluated as good and bad. Although these kinds of evaluations can certainly be applied to
valenced first-party interactions, to have relevance for a *moral* concept, they must also
be applicable to situations in which one has no immediate personal interest; that is, to
valenced interactions among unknown third parties.

17.6   Do Preverbal Infants Evaluate Third Parties for Their Prosocial and Antisocial Goals?

The first test of whether infants evaluate others based on their prosocial and antisocial
actions toward unknown third parties adapted animated stimuli from Kuhlmeier and
colleagues' "helper/hinderer" paradigm (2003), involving a character being helped and
hindered in its goal to reach the top of a hill. Ten- and six-month-old infants watched
live puppet shows starring three individuals: a "Protagonist" (P) with an unfulfilled
goal to reach the top of a hill, a "Helper" who facilitated P's goal (pushed P up), and
a "Hinderer" who blocked P's goal (pushed P down). Each puppet was made of wood,
was distinguishable by both color and shape, and had two large googly eyes for a face
(see figure 17.1). During each act, P repeatedly moved up and then back down the hill's

A. Helper - pushes P up hill

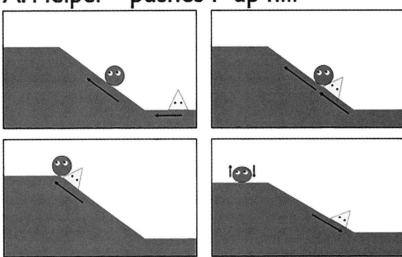

B. Hinderer - pushes P down hill

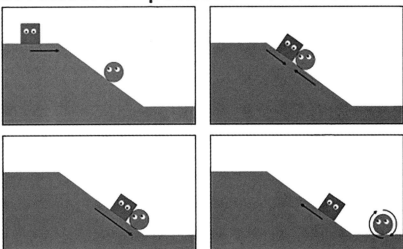

Figure 17.1
(A) Hill Helper event. Protagonist (P) tries but fails to climb steep section of hill twice; on third attempt Helper enters and pushes P up the hill twice, allowing P to reach the top. P bounces up and down upon reaching the top while Helper goes back down hill and offstage. (B) Hill Hinderer event. P tries but fails to climb hill twice; on third attempt Hinderer enters and pushes P down the hill twice, forcing him to the bottom. P rolls end-over-end to very bottom of hill; Hinderer goes back up hill and offstage.

steepest slope, decelerating on the way up—suggesting an increasingly effortful strug-
gle—and accelerating on the way down—suggesting an unintentional fall. Because gaze
direction is an important cue to others' goals (e.g., Hood, Willen, and Driver 1998), P's
eyes were fixed pointing up the hill throughout, such that all of P's upward movements
were consistent with his gaze—implying upward movement was intentional—whereas
all of P's downward movements were inconsistent with his gaze—suggesting downward movement was unintentional.[7] Both "Helping" and "Hindering" events began in
this same way.

During Helping events, on P's third attempt, the Helper puppet entered from below
and pushed P up twice, to the top of the hill (figure 17.1A). During Hindering events,
on P's third attempt, the Hinderer puppet entered from above and pushed P down
twice, to the bottom of the hill (figure 17.1B). To further demonstrate P's successes and
failures, P bounced up and down several times at the top of the hill at the end of Helping events, and rolled end over end to the very bottom of the hill at the end of Hinderer
events. Infants viewed Helping and Hindering events repeatedly until a preset looking
criterion was reached, indicating that they had sufficiently processed the events (minimum six, maximum fourteen events).

Following habituation, infants were turned away from the stage and presented with a
choice between the Helper and the Hinderer puppets. "Choice" was determined online
as the first intentional touch of a puppet (looking must precede touching; see figure
17.2).[8] Ten- and six-month-olds both tended to choose the Helper over the Hinderer:
88 percent of ten-month-olds and 100 percent of six-month-olds did so. In additional
conditions, equally high rates of infants at each age preferred (1) a Helper to a Neutral
character, suggesting they positively evaluate Helpers; and (2) a Neutral character to
a Hinderer, suggesting they negatively evaluate Hinderers. Together, these results are

---

7. We piloted this project with stimuli in which P's eyes remained "googly," but infants did not
show the effects outlined below, leading us to adjust our methodology. Although in a previous
study (Kuhlmeier, Wynn, and Bloom 2003), infants seemed to infer P's goal solely via P's body
movements, in this case, P had no eyes at all; it seems that if an agent *has* eyes, then its eyes
should point toward its goal. This is relevant to a recent study in Scarf et al. (2012), which
offered an alternative explanation for the Hamlin, Wynn, and Bloom (2007) findings. Importantly, Scarf and colleagues' Protagonist's eyes were unfixed, making it difficult to compare their
results to our own (see comment to Scarf et al. by Hamlin, Wynn, and Bloom [both 2012]). We
have replicated infants' failure in an unfixed eye condition in the laboratory (Hamlin, unpublished ms.).

8. The experimenter who presented the choice was unaware of which puppet was which for
each infant. In addition, in several conditions of this original study (and in all subsequent studies), parents closed their eyes during choice and therefore were unable to influence infants'
responses.

Choice: Shape puppets

Choice: Hand puppets

Preferential Looking

Figure 17.2
(Top) Choice: Shape puppets. Parents close eyes. Shapes placed on white board facing infant, board brought within reach. Choice recorded as first shape touched via a visually guided reach. (Middle) Choice: Hand puppets. Parents close eyes. Experimenter kneels in front of infant with puppets behind back; gets infant's attention by saying "hi" and making eye contact. Experimenter holds up puppets in view but out of reach; ensures infant looks at each one briefly before saying hi and making eye contact again. Experimenter moves puppets within reach; choice recorded as first puppet touched via a visually guided reach. (Bottom) Preferential looking. Parents close eyes. Experimenter kneels in front of infant with puppets behind back; gets infant's attention by saying "hi" and making eye contact. Experimenter holds up puppets in view but out of reach, looks down at infant's chest and counts to 30. Attention to each puppet subsequently coded from video.

consistent with the conclusion that both positive and negative social evaluations are operative by six months of age: infants appear not only to *understand* prosocial and antisocial actions, but also to *evaluate* prosocial and antisocial others.

17.7   But Is This Really Social Evaluation?

There are, of course, several alternative explanations for infants' choices; a "rich" interpretation of these data—that infants make third-party social evaluations—requires ruling out lower-level alternatives. For instance, rather than *socially evaluating* the actions of the Helper and Hinderer, infants' may have *physically evaluated* them: perhaps infants simply like upward pushing and dislike downward pushing, or perhaps they find entities associated with bouncing to be positive or those associated with rolling to be negative (see Scarf et al. 2012). To examine the first of these possibilities, new groups of six- and ten-month-olds viewed physical control events involving "Pusher Uppers" and "Pusher Downers"; these puppets pushed an inanimate object up and down a hill but did not engage in any socially relevant actions. Infants at both ages chose Pusher Uppers and Pusher Downers equally, suggesting that choices in the social conditions were not due to preferring agents who push up versus down (e.g., Hamlin, Wynn, and Bloom 2007). To examine whether infants' choices resulted from liking bouncing or disliking rolling, a new group of six- to ten-month-olds viewed an animate, upward-gazing Protagonist try but fail to get up the hill and be Helped and Hindered by other animate characters who pushed him up from below or down from above, as in Hamlin, Wynn, and Bloom (2007). In contrast to previous research, however, P neither bounced at the top of the hill during Helper events nor rolled end over end to the bottom of the hill during Hinderer events. Despite the absence of bouncing and rolling, a significant majority of infants chose the Helper over the Hinderer (Hamlin, unpublished ms.). This result is consistent with the hypothesis that infants engage in social, rather than physical, evaluation.

To further support the claim that evaluations of pro- and antisociality, rather than physical cues, drove infants' choices, we conceptually replicated the basic preference for prosocial over antisocial individuals in several other goal scenarios (Hamlin and Wynn 2011). The "Ball" scenario (figure 17.3) represented the simple goal to retrieve a dropped ball. To start both Helper and Hinderer events, a Protagonist (an animal hand puppet) played with a ball and accidentally dropped it toward another puppet. P then "asked" for the ball back by opening its arms repeatedly. When the Helper was asked for the ball, he returned it to P (figure 17.3A); when the Hinderer was asked for the ball, he ran offstage with it (figure 17.3B). The "Box" scenario (figure 17.4) represented an action or means-ends goal: opening a transparent box containing a toy. An animal Protagonist repeatedly struggled to open the box's lid; during Helper events, the Helper opened the box with P (figure 17.4A), who grasped the toy inside; during Hinderer

A. Helper - Gives ball

B. Hinderer - Takes ball

Figure 17.3

(A) Helper. Cat Protagonist (P) enters stage, runs forward and grabs ball, jumping and bouncing the ball up and down three times. On the fourth jump-bounce, P drops the ball to one side; the ball is retrieved by the Helper. P turns toward the Helper and opens its arms as though asking for the ball twice; on P's third turn the Helper turns, rolls the ball back to P, and runs offstage. (B) Hinderer. P enters stage, runs forward and grabs ball, jumping and bouncing the ball up and down three times. On the fourth jump-bounce, P drops the ball to one side; the ball is retrieved by the Hinderer. P turns toward the Hinderer and opens its arms as though asking for the ball twice; on P's third turn the Hinderer runs offstage with the ball.

A. Helper - Opens box

B. Hinderer - Closes box

Figure 17.4

(A) Helper. Cow Protagonist (P) enters stage, runs to side of box, and looks inside twice. P grasps front corner of box lid and tries but fails to open it four times. On fifth attempt, Helper on opposite side of box runs forward, grasps corner of box lid and opens lid together with P. P lays down on top of toy in open box; Helper runs offstage. (B) Hinderer. P enters stage, runs to side of box, and looks inside twice. P grasps front corner of box lid and tries but fails to open it four times. On fifth attempt, Hinderer on opposite side of box runs forward and jumps sideways onto box lid, slamming it shut. P lays down next to closed box; Hinderer runs offstage.

events, the Hinderer slammed the box lid shut, and P could not access the toy (figure 17.4B). Of note is that these studies minimized potential physical confounds. Unlike in the Hill scenario, P's behaviors were physically identical in the Ball and Box scenarios: P jumped up and down at the end of every Ball event and lay down at the end of every Box event.[9] In addition, during the physical control conditions, characters performed *physically identical* giving/taking and opening/closing actions as in the social conditions, which lead to exactly the same physical outcomes (ball on-/offstage; box open/closed). However, the actions were directed toward a mechanical claw: an inanimate object that possesses no volitional mental states and is therefore unworthy of being helped and hindered (claws are common in studies of infant social cognition; e.g., Meltzoff 1995; Woodward 1998). Despite physical similarities within and across conditions, infants chose "Givers" over "Takers" and "Openers" over "Closers" *only* when these characters' actions were directed toward an animate Protagonist.

These initial studies suggest that in the first half year of life, preverbal infants actively evaluate individuals based on their third-party social behaviors, positively evaluating prosocial individuals and negatively evaluating antisocial ones. Both the variety of goal scenarios and the physical control conditions suggest that infants evaluate others based on their tendency to *be helpful* or to *be unhelpful*, rather than on a tendency to perform a particular physical act or to cause a particular physical outcome. These results are noteworthy for at least two reasons. First, infants evaluated characters despite the infants' status as passive observers: infants had no prior knowledge of any of the individuals involved, nor did they stand to personally gain or lose from any of the actions they saw.[10] Second, infants' preferences are extremely robust: the majority of infants in *every single social condition* preferred the more helpful character. These results have since been replicated many times, across two laboratories, using videos rather than live stimuli, and even when infants view each puppet's action only once—more closely resembling how social evaluations must work in the real world (both published and unpublished data).

17.8   How Does Social Evaluation Get off the Ground?

17.8.1   Active Personal Experience?

We found no differences in infants' tendency to prefer more-helpful characters between five and ten months. In an attempt to further illuminate the foundations of these

9. This was true specifically for five-month-olds; nine-month-olds were shown Box puppet shows in which P raised the toy out of the box at the end of Helper events.
10. This is not to say that no personal-interest processes are involved in these judgments, either consciously or unconsciously. Yet, there was no obvious or direct way in which infants were personally involved in the interactions they evaluated.

abilities, we examined even younger, three-month-old infants (e.g., Hamlin and Wynn 2011; Hamlin, Wynn, and Bloom 2010). Although examining younger and younger infants can certainly bolster innateness claims, simply moving down the postnatal age ladder was not the principal motivation for testing three-month-olds. Rather, the motivation was to examine social evaluation in a population who (1) may or may not be able to reason about others' goals at all (see mixed evidence from Luo 2011; Sommerville, Woodward, and Needham 2005), and (2) itself can perform an extremely limited repertoire of goal-directed actions. That is, although three-month-olds are clearly *social beings* (they have begun to smile socially [Wolff 1963], recognize certain individuals [e.g., Barrera and Maurer 1981; Bartrip, Morton, and de Schonen 2001], hold eye contact well [e.g., Haith, Bergman, and Moore 1977], and show distress during the "still face" paradigm [e.g., Tronick et al. 1978]), behaviorally they are not particularly proficient with goal-directed action: they have not even begun reaching (McDonnell 1975). As it has been claimed that infants' emerging ability to interpret others' actions as goal directed is based on their own ability to *produce* goal-directed actions (i.e., that mentalizing occurs via a "like me" simulation process; for reviews, see Gerson and Woodward 2010; Meltzoff 2007; Woodward 2009), it is possible that infants' tendency to evaluate helpers and hinderers of others' goals reflects their own experiences being helped and being hindered in such goals. That is, perhaps infants process our events (implicitly or explicitly) in something like the following: *"I can tell that the Protagonist has X unfulfilled goal because I perform those same actions when I have X goal. I know that the Hinderer is responsible for preventing the Protagonist from reaching X goal, because my caretakers perform those actions when they block me from reaching X goal. I don't like it when my goals are blocked. Therefore, I don't like the Hinderer."* A similar process could lead infants to positively evaluate helpers. But does this kind of experiential account explain social evaluation in prereaching, prelocomoting three-month-olds?

I think not, and I think it could not happen by a more general process of *"I don't like it when my goals are blocked, regardless of what or how that happens,"* either. Of course, three-month-olds are being "helped" and "hindered" all the time (fed/not fed, held/not held, changed/not changed). Yet, within these experiences there is no clear *coupling* of any actions that infants themselves perform to signal their goals with any specific actions that caregivers perform that facilitate or block those goals; there is no sense that *"when I move like this and my caretaker moves like that, I get/do not get what I want."* Instead, young infants cry to communicate all their unfulfilled goals, and caregivers (who at first can only guess what infants want) respond with several possible "helpful" acts, perhaps repeatedly, until they find one that works. In most situations with very young infants, it is presumably the *failure* to fulfill a goal that is unhelpful. Thus, it follows that if three-month-olds form social evaluations of those whose *overt behaviors* influence others' *goal-directed behaviors*, it seems impossible that this evaluation could stem solely from personal experience: they just do not have these experiences.

Therefore, examining whether three-month-olds evaluate helpers and hinderers proves to be theoretically meaningful indeed.

Studying three-month-olds requires adjusting one's choice methodology: as mentioned above, three-month-olds do not reliably reach for objects (McDonnell 1975) and cannot participate in a reaching task. Instead, we measured three-month-olds' evaluations via a "preferential looking" procedure, in which relative attention to one stimulus versus another (when the two stimuli are presented side by side) is considered a measure of discrimination and preference (e.g., Fantz 1958).[11] After three-month-olds were habituated to helping and hindering events, the Helper and the Hinderer were held in front of their face for thirty seconds (see figure 17.2), and attention to each puppet was later coded from video. Using both parametric and nonparametric analyses, we discovered that like older infants, three-month-olds significantly preferred (looked longer toward) Helpers versus Hinderers in the social conditions of both the Hill and the Ball scenarios. Also like older infants, they did not distinguish puppets in physical control conditions. Interestingly, although three-month-olds preferred Helpers to Hinderers, and Neutral characters to Hinderers, at the same rate as older infants did (over 80 percent per group), we observed one age difference: three-month-olds did *not* discriminate Helpers from Neutral characters in the Hill scenario (Hamlin, Wynn, and Bloom 2010). These results suggest that negatively evaluating Hinderers may emerge prior to positively evaluating Helpers in development. Although this difference was not observed with older infants, it is both functional (all else equal, avoiding harm is presumably more important than pursuing help) and consistent with extensive documentation of a general "negativity bias" in social, cognitive, and emotional processes throughout the lifespan (e.g., Abelson and Kanouse 1966; Aloise 1993; Ito et al. 1998; Kanouse and Hanson 1972; Knobe 2003; Leslie, Knobe, and Cohen 2006; Rozin and Royzman 2001; Skowronski and Carlston 1989; Vaish, Grossmann, and Woodward 2008; but see Farroni, Menon, et al. 2007; LaBarbera et al. 1976).

17.8.2   Observational Experience?

If infants' evaluation of helpers and hinderers does not result from personal experience being helped and hindered in specific goal-directed acts, perhaps it stems from observational experience. For instance, perhaps infants see *others* with unfulfilled goals, and these others appear happier after being helped and less happy after being hindered. Over time, infants might develop an association between positivity, goal completion, and helpful actions, and between negativity, goal failure, and unhelpful actions. If so,

---

11. The validity of this methodology was first explored via measuring older infants' relative attention to Helpers versus Hinderers *prior to* their reaches; infants looked longer at the puppet they eventually chose (e.g., Hamlin, Wynn, and Bloom 2010).

infants could apply these associations to the helping and hindering scenarios they see in the laboratory.

While possible, such a process seems unlikely to account for social evaluation in three-month-olds. First, although very young infants can sometimes *distinguish* different emotional expressions, they do not seem to recognize what those expressions mean until well into the first year (e.g., Caron, Caron, and Myers 1985; Farroni, Massaccesi et al. 2007; Walker-Andrews 1997). In addition, throughout this research we have observed no differences in the preferences of infants who presumably have less, versus more, experience with observing antisocial actions in their environment: those with older siblings and those without. Although it is unlikely that firstborn infants under three months of age see much, if any, hindering occurring between their *caregivers* (surely parents of young infants have conflict, but most conflict presumably manifests itself vocally rather than behaviorally), a young infant who is the second- or third-born might see hindering behaviors fairly regularly (in interactions between two older siblings, or between one older sibling and a parent). One could imagine this experiential difference going both ways: firstborns might do worse because they have less experience with different sorts of actions and others' emotional reactions to helping and hindering; later-borns might do worse because they have been sensitized to hindering actions because they see them all the time. Yet, currently across studies and laboratories, we have observed no differences between first- and later-born infants' evaluations (typically a little over 50 percent are singleton children at the time of testing).

Individual variation in experience aside, most infants see a lot more helpful actions than unhelpful ones in their daily lives and are probably helped more than they are hindered.[12] Perhaps infants prefer helpers to hinderers in the laboratory because they see helping as familiar and pursue familiarity; indeed, "familiarity preferences" are fairly common in infancy research (Burnham and Dodd 1998; Houston-Price and Nakai 2004; Rose et al. 1982). However, detailed analyses from infants' habituation data render a familiarity explanation of infants' choices unlikely: across studies, infants *look equally* to helpful and unhelpful events during habituation trials, suggesting they do not find helpful or unhelpful actions more or less familiar. Thus it is unclear why they would come to prefer helpers via a familiarity account, as they have no differential experience with these particular characters before the study, and gain no differential experience with them during the study itself. Finally, infants show an aversion to hinderers versus neutral before they show a preference for helpers versus neutral (Hamlin, Wynn, and Bloom 2010), which only makes a "helping is familiar and familiar is good" account less likely: if helping is most familiar, infants should be best at distinguishing helpers from other individuals.

---

12. Precrawling infants, that is; this might shift as infants become increasingly mobile.

17.9   So *What* Are Infants Evaluating? Elucidating Early "Evaluation Rules"

Across several social scenarios and age groups, preverbal infants prefer prosocial to antisocial individuals. I have argued that this preference emerges *too soon* to be the result of
experience alone, either from interactive experience being helped and hindered themselves, or from observational experience seeing others be helped and hindered. In addition, infants' social preferences do not differ based on what surely amounts in varied
input (birth order), nor from a tendency to attend more to one kind of action versus
another during habituation. Furthermore, physical control conditions rule out the possibility that infants' evaluations are simply *physical*: exactly the same individuals can
perform exactly the same actions toward inanimate objects (Hamlin and Wynn 2011)
or toward a Protagonist without a clear goal (Hamlin, unpublished ms.) and infants do
not distinguish them, even if P acts in exactly the same manner after being helped and
hindered. Overall, then, whatever it is that leads infants to distinguish the prosocial
from the antisocial characters in these studies, there does not seem to be some "evaluation rule" in the infant mind that takes the form PERFORMING X BEHAVIOR = GOOD/BAD, or
CAUSING (OR BEING ASSOCIATED WITH) SOCIAL AGENT P'S PERFORMANCE OF X ACTION = GOOD/BAD.

But then what evaluation rules *are* infants using? Understanding the specific mechanisms by which infants (consciously or unconsciously) arrive at their social evaluations has two main benefits. First, it allows one to rigorously approach the question of
whether infants' evaluations seem moral or not, by comparing infants' evaluation rules
with whatever moral evaluation rules one chooses as the gold standard (mine were
listed in the introduction). In particular, one can define what does *not* count as moral:
if infants' rules fall squarely into one's "not moral" category, then one would be forced
to conclude that infants' evaluations are (merely) social. In this way, my approach is
actually rather *like* classic developmental studies of moral cognition: the goal is to elucidate the specific cognitive processes that underlie analyses of morally relevant actions
(e.g., Nucci and Turiel 1978; Piaget 1932; Piaget and Inhelder 1956; Kohlberg 1969;
Smetana 1981; Turiel 1983). I simply think these analyses begin during infancy, and
that they need not be verbally reportable. The second benefit to expounding infants'
evaluation rules is that, similarly to specifying the chronological age at which evaluations first occur, understanding how infants interpret helpful and unhelpful actions
necessarily constrains accounts of how these preferences emerge. In this section, I will
summarize several pieces of evidence from my laboratory demonstrating that there
are some critical ways in which infants' evaluation rules resemble those of a morally
mature adult.

17.9.1   Mental States versus Outcomes

The social scenarios presented thus far have represented unambiguously good and bad
acts: helpers have intended to help third parties and successfully done so; hinderers

have intended to hinder third parties and successfully done so. The question remains, however, whether the tendency to prefer helpers to hinderers is based on an analysis of the actor's intentions or motives (e.g., helpers are good because they intend to help), or rather on the outcomes they cause (e.g., helpers are good because they bring about positive effects in the world). The relationship between mental states and outcomes is critical to the assignment of moral and criminal responsibility in adults (e.g., Baird and Moses 2001; Cushman 2008; Hart 1968; Killen and Smetana 2008; Malle 1999; Mikhail 2007; Robinson and Darley 1995; Young et al. 2007), and young children's failure to consider mental states in their explicit moral judgments is often considered the defining feature of their moral immaturity (e.g., Piaget 1932; Piaget and Inhelder 1956).[13] Thus, determining whether and when infants' social evaluations incorporate mental state analyses would help shed light on the relationship between infants' social evaluations and actual moral ones.

17.9.1.1 Failed Attempts to Help and Harm   One common scenario in which mental states and outcomes diverge is in situations of "failed attempts": an individual might intend to help but fail to do so, or intend to harm but fail to do so, leading to outcomes that are opposed or unrelated to the individual's initial desires. Although several studies have demonstrated that infants correctly infer third parties' object-directed goals during failed attempts by seven to ten months (e.g., Brandone and Wellman 2009; Hamlin, Newman, and Wynn 2009; Hamlin, Hallinan, and Woodward 2008), and become less frustrated by situations that involve unsuccessful attempts to help *them* (e.g., Behne et al. 2005; Marsh et al. 2010), it is unclear whether they can identify others' failed attempts to help and hinder others, in particular whether failed attempts to help or harm inform infants' social evaluations.

To examine this question, I showed infants a modified version of the Box scenario described above (from Hamlin and Wynn 2011; see figure 17.5). Some individuals were *successful* in their prosocial or antisocial goals, while others *failed* to complete their prosocial or antisocial goals. When Successful puppets tried to help P open the box, P did so; when they tried to prevent P from opening the box, he did not. When Failed puppets tried to help P open the box, they failed to help, and P did not open the box (figure 17.5A); when they tried to prevent P from opening the box, they failed to hinder, and P did open the box (figure 17.5B). Essentially, during Successful events, the valence of the Helper or Hinderer's intention matched that of the outcome for P; during Failed events the valence of the Helper or Hinderer's intention was opposed to that of the outcome for P. Eight-month-olds were shown various pairs of Successful and Failed Helpers and Hinderers: for some infants, characters had the same intentions, but P's outcomes differed; for other infants, characters had different intentions, but P's outcome was the

13. But perhaps not their implicit judgments; see Piaget (1932); Piaget and Inhelder (1956).

A. Failed Helper - Tries to open box with P; fails; P does not get toy

B. Failed Hinderer - Slams box closed; P opens box alone; P gets toy

Figure 17.5

(A) Failed Helper. Cow Protagonist (P) enters stage, runs to side of box, and looks inside twice. P grasps front corner of box lid and tries but fails to open it four times. On fifth attempt, Failed Helper on opposite side of box runs forward, grasps corner of box lid and unsuccessfully attempts to open it three more times. On third failed attempt, lid slams shut, P lays down next to box and Failed Helper runs offstage. (B) Failed Hinderer. P enters stage, runs to side of box, and looks inside twice. P grasps front corner of box lid and tries but fails to open it four times. On fifth attempt, Failed Hinderer runs forward, slams the box closed, jumps off the box and pauses. P successfully opens box lid, and lays down on toy inside box. Failed Hinderer runs offstage.

same; and for still other infants, characters' intentions always opposed P's outcomes. A very clear pattern of results emerged. Eight-month-olds *always* preferred characters with prosocial intentions over those with antisocial intentions, regardless of outcomes: they preferred a Successful Helper to a Failed Hinderer, a Failed Helper to a Successful Hinderer, and a Failed Helper to a Failed Hinderer (Hamlin 2013b). Notably, they did so at the same rate that infants preferred Successful Helpers to Successful Hinderers in previous studies—over 80 percent per condition. Consistent with previous results suggesting that infants at this age understand the role of mental states in failed attempts (e.g., Brandone and Wellman 2009; Hamlin, Newman, and Wynn 2009; Hamlin, Hallinan, and Woodward 2008), intention/outcome conflict did not influence eight-month-olds' evaluations at all.

Intriguingly, eight-month-olds did *not* distinguish characters whose intentions matched but who differed on outcome: they chose equally between a Successful Helper and a Failed Helper and between a Failed Hinderer and a Successful Hinderer. That is, their evaluations seem to be *solely* based on intention. These results are consistent with previous work with toddlers, who do not preferentially help an individual who gave them a toy over one who tried but failed to do so (Dunfield and Kuhlmeier 2010); but the results raise the possibility that infants' responses in the other conditions were about distinctive physical characteristics of prosocially versus antisocially motivated actions, rather than to the distinct motivations that drove them. For example: positively intended individuals (whether successful or not) engaged in coordinated action with the Protagonist, moving upward and downward in sync; whereas negatively intended individuals (whether successful or not) loudly slammed the box lid closed. To examine this possibility, a new group of eight-month-olds chose between a puppet who engaged in coordinated action with the Protagonist, moving upward and downward in sync, and a puppet who slammed the box lid closed. Crucially, in this condition, neither puppet's actions implied a prosocial or an antisocial motivation. Eight-month-olds chose randomly in this condition, supporting the conclusion that infants' preferences in previous conditions were not driven by these physical cues.

Unlike eight-month-olds, five-month-olds did not distinguish puppets in any condition involving failed attempts. There are many possibilities for these null results: five-month-olds may not privilege the intentions behind social acts, they might be confused by failed attempts of any kind, or they might be confused by actions that contain conflicting information of any sort. Distinguishing these possibilities is essential to accurately portraying the development of social evaluations in the first year; we are currently attempting to distinguish these possibilities in the laboratory.

17.9.1.2 The Role of Knowledge in Helping and Hindering   In all the cases presented above, what makes an action prosocial versus antisocial is how it *looks*: regardless of whether they are successful or not, attempts to help look very different from attempts to hinder. Yet, there are lots of cases in which exactly the same intentional action could be prosocial, antisocial, or neither, depending specifically on the mental states of everyone involved. To borrow an example from Liane Young and her colleagues (e.g., Young et al. 2007), consider a girl who intentionally puts white powder into a cup of coffee, with the intention to give that coffee to another person (making the action socially relevant). If the powder is sugar, and the girl knows the coffee recipient likes sweet coffee, then this powder-placing action is prosocial. If the powder is sugar, and the girl knows the coffee recipient hates sweet coffee, then the powder placing is antisocial. If the powder is sugar and the girl does not know what the coffee recipient's preference is, then the action is neither particularly prosocial nor particularly antisocial (though perhaps it leans slightly prosocial, depending on exactly what the girl believes to be the base rate of sugar liking in the population of coffee drinkers). Yet if the powder is actually *poison* and the girl knows it, everything flips: what was prosocial becomes antisocial. This rather confusing example illustrates that many actions have no particular valence; adults distribute praise and blame via a complex understanding of knowledge, preference, and other circumstantial information.

Hamlin, Ullman, Tenenbaum, Goodman, and Baker (2013) explored whether infants' evaluations incorporate such subtleties by showing ten-month-old infants a

Protagonist demonstrating a clear preference for a duck over a flower,[14] by selectively grasping the duck four times (see figure 17.6, and see Luo and Baillargeon 2007 for evidence that infants attribute a preference to P from this behavior). Two additional puppets sat onstage during P's actions, to imply that they "knew" P's preference. Subsequently, P lost access to both toys and jumped up and down indicating an unfulfilled goal. In this "Preference-Knowledge" condition, one of the observing puppets lifted a door that allowed P to reach the toy he preferred, and the other observer lifted a door that allowed P to reach the toy he had avoided. In this condition, despite the fact that the Lifters' behaviors were essentially identical (both lifted a door), adults would consider one Lifter to be better than the other. Infants' choices suggest that they thought so too: they preferred the Lifter who facilitated P's goal. Two control conditions suggest that infants' evaluations were not based simply on one Lifter having *happened to* facilitate P's goal without knowing it, nor that one Lifter knowingly led P to act as he had before. In the "Preference-Ignorance" control condition, the Lifters were offstage during P's grasps of the duck and not the flower and were therefore unaware of P's preference (infants themselves watched the whole thing and knew which toy P preferred). In the "No Preference-Knowledge" condition, the Lifters were onstage during P's grasps, but the duck was the only object available at the time (the flower came out later), and so no preference was attributable to him by either the Lifters or the infants. Infants chose Lifters equally in both the Preference-Ignorance and the No Preference-Knowledge conditions, suggesting that their evaluations depended specifically on the mental states of both the Lifters and the Protagonist: helpers were those who knowingly facilitated P's goal and hinderers were those who knowingly prevented it.

17.9.2   Intentional Antisocial Behaviors

Evaluation rules like INTENDING TO FACILITATE OTHERS' GOALS = GOOD and INTENDING TO BLOCK OTHERS' GOALS = BAD seem fairly sophisticated, especially if those rules incorporate things like KNOWLEDGE and PREFERENCE. Yet, these rules are insufficient to encompass a large portion of adults' moral evaluations, even within the domain of helpful and unhelpful acts. Specifically, these rules apply only to those cases in which the recipients of helpful and unhelpful acts are unknown third parties, ones who are seen as both *capable* of making their own decisions and *deserving* of help. For instance, young children seem to consistently desire things they should not: to stick their fingers in light sockets, stay up all night, eat candy for every meal, and so on. It is a virtuous caregiver who intentionally blocks all their children's inadvisable goals, and a negligent caregiver who facilitates them; there is no shortage of moral condemnation directed toward permissive parenting styles.

---

14. Or a flower over a duck; this was counterbalanced across infants in each condition.

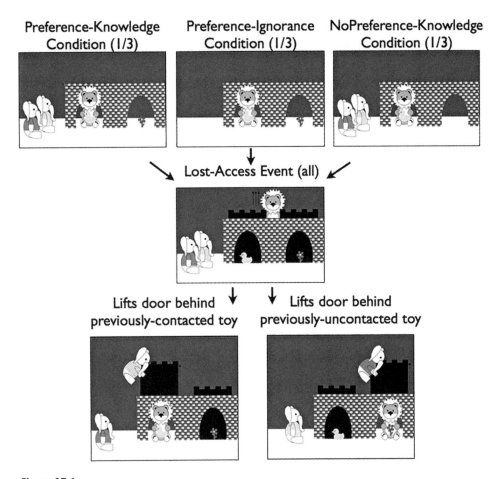

Figure 17.6
Preference-Knowledge Condition. Top row: Elephant puppets rest next to colored wall; flower and duck objects rest in front of wall openings. Lion puppet peeks through one opening, then the other, then grasps toy in front of first opening. Toys switch places; Lion peeks and chooses the same toy (four total grasping events). Middle row: Elephant puppets rest next to colored wall; flower and duck objects rest in front of wall openings; white doors now block openings. Lion puppet jumps up and down three times behind wall, as though cannot get through (one event). Bottom row: One elephant lifts door blocking previously contacted toy; Lion grasps contacted toy. Other elephant lifts door blocking previously uncontacted toy; Lion grasps uncontacted toy (six alternating events). Preference-Ignorance Condition. Identical to Preference-Knowledge condition except that elephants not onstage during initial toy grasps (top row). NoPreference-Knowledge Condition. Identical to Preference-Knowledge condition except that only one toy is available during initial toy grasps (top row).

Another case in which intentional goal blocking is positively evaluated is when it is directed toward those who have themselves been antisocial before, whom adults see as deserving of punishment. Although punishment is a "locally" antisocial act (Heider 1958), adults are personally motivated to punish those who have harmed third parties (e.g., Boyd and Richerson 1992; de Quervain et al. 2004; Fehr and Gächter 2002; Henrich et al. 2006; Wiessner 2005) and positively evaluate individuals and institutions that punish appropriately (Barclay 2006; Kurzban and DeScioli 2008; Gürerk, Irlenbusch, and Rockenbach 2006; Maurer 1999; Price, Cosmides, and Tooby 2002; Robinson, Kurzban, and Jones 2007). These tendencies suggest that adults' evaluation rules are not restricted to notions of local value in which facilitating is always good, but instead encompass some notion of an action's global or "total" value (Heider 1958), in which those who intentionally hinder others can be viewed positively in some circumstances.

17.9.2.1 Infants' Evaluations of Reward and Punishment

To examine whether preverbal infants can evaluate individuals for the "total" value of their acts, Hamlin, Wynn, Bloom, and Mahajan (2011) showed infants a two-phase puppet show involving both the Box and the Ball scenarios from Hamlin and Wynn (2011). Instead of habituating infants to puppet events, infants saw each event only once, more closely resembling how evaluation occurs in the real world. In phase 1, infants viewed an unknown Protagonist try to open a box; P was helped once by the Prosocial puppet and hindered once by the Antisocial puppet. In phase 2, subjects in the Prosocial Target condition saw two events in which the Prosocial puppet from phase 1 was playing with a ball: his ball was returned by a Giver and stolen offstage by a Taker. In the Antisocial Target condition, Giving and Taking events were directed toward the Antisocial puppet from phase 1. After viewing the Giving and Taking events, infants in each condition chose between the Giver and the Taker. Eight-month-olds showed a pattern of response suggesting that they appreciated the total value of the Giving and Taking acts: they chose the character who gave to (versus took from) the Prosocial Target and the character who took from (versus gave to) the Antisocial Target. To ensure that infants were not simply matching the valence of events throughout the study phases, we ran an additional control condition in which a victim, rather than a perpetrator, of antisocial box hindering was the target of Giving and Taking. This control appealed to the notion that to adults, only *agents* of antisocial acts deserve punishment; *patients* do not. Eight-month-olds chose the puppet who gave to the Victim Target, suggesting that preferences in the Antisocial Target condition cannot be accounted for by valence matching. These results demonstrate that by eight months, infants engage in nuanced evaluations: they like those who treat prosocial others well and antisocial others poorly.

In the same study, we found that five-month-olds showed no evidence of nuanced evaluation: they always preferred Givers to Takers regardless of whether the target of the action was prosocial or antisocial. Although this result suggests that the ability to evaluate total value emerges between five and eight months, it is also possible that five-month-olds failed due to some domain-general limitation (e.g., poor memory) rather than to a domain-specific limitation (e.g., inability to make nuanced evaluations). Indeed, the memory demands for this study were extremely high: infants saw five different characters across the two study phases, and each prosocial/antisocial action occurred only once (four total events). Thus, it was possible that five-month-olds chose the Giver over the Taker after phase 2 of the Antisocial Target condition because they simply *forgot* what the Antisocial Target had done during phase 1. To examine this possibility, I have since replicated the original methodology with one change: 4.5-month-olds were habituated to the original box helping and hindering events in phase 1, in order to boost their likelihood of remembering who had done what when they moved on to phase 2. This was the only methodological change from Hamlin et al. (2011): infants saw one Giving and one Taking action in phase 2, and subsequently chose between the Giver and the Taker. Confirming the hypothesis that it was memory limitations and not an inability to engage in nuanced evaluations that underlay five-month-olds' previous failure, 4.5-month-olds chose the character who *took from* the Antisocial Target (but more chose the character who *gave to* the Victim Target; Hamlin 2014).

17.9.2.2 Liking Punishers: What's the Mechanism? By four and a half months of age, infants evaluate others based not only on who *intended* to do what, but also on who did what *to whom*. Although I introduced these studies as related to notions of reward and punishment, there are at least two reasons why adults like those who punish wrongdoers, and it is unclear whether one, the other, or some combination of both drove infants' choices. The first possibility is that infants grasp some notion of deservingness, in which those who harm others should themselves be harmed. If so, infants would positively evaluate punishers because they positively evaluate the punishing action itself; those who punish are *doing the right thing*. Alternatively, infants might be attending to social alliances, in which those who punish individuals who infants dislike are seen to share the infants' opinion about the value of the Antisocial Target. That is, infants may not like the punishing *action*, but rather they may like what the action says about the opinions of the punishing *individual*. This notion is captured in the common phrase "the enemy of my enemy is my friend" and its iterations, and is reflected in the social preferences and cognitive processing of both children and adults (e.g., Aronson and Cope 1968; Cvencek, Greenwald, and Meltzoff 2012; Gawronski, Walther, and Blank 2005; Heider 1958; Pietraszewski and German 2013). These two possibilities for infants' preference for punishers are not mutually exclusive: both operate in adults.

In a study of similar design to Hamlin et al. (2011), we explored the "enemy of my enemy" account of infants' antisocial preferences (Hamlin, Mahajan, et al. 2013). In previous work (Mahajan and Wynn 2012), infants were shown to prefer a puppet who shared their food preference (either for graham crackers or green beans) over a puppet who held the opposite food preference. These results suggest that like adults and children, infants like similar others and/or dislike dissimilar others (e.g., Byrne 1971; Fawcett and Markson 2010). In Hamlin, Mahajan, et al. (2013), we capitalized on infants' distaste for dissimilar others and habituated nine- and fourteen-month-olds to Ball scenario puppet shows in which the Target of Giving and Taking actions was either a puppet who shared their preference or one who held an opposite preference. At both age groups, infants strongly preferred the character who gave to (versus took from) the Same-Preference Target, and preferred the character who took from (versus gave to) the Opposite-Preference Target. These results mirror those of Hamlin et al. (2011) above, and suggest that simply disliking the Target of an antisocial behavior is enough to lead infants to prefer antisocial others, even when the Target does not actually (by adult standards) deserve punishment. It is certainly possible that in fact infants believe that those who do not share their preference *do* deserve punishment; food preferences in particular are good cues to distinguish individuals from different cultures and groups (for discussion, see Shutts, Kinzler, and DeJesus 2013). In any case, these results suggest that the mechanism underlying infants' nuanced evaluations can take the form "the enemy of my enemy is my friend."

Results suggesting that infants sometimes positively evaluate antisocial individuals, though not particularly heartening, are significant for discussions regarding the role of input in the development of social evaluation. In particular, *these judgments are not being socialized*. One does not need to spend much time with the parent of a young infant to get the sense that "niceness" in any form is encouraged—parents praise their infants for gently touching animals, "giving" disgusting spit-ridden toys and soggy food to others, and so on. Simply put, parents readily communicate the value of prosocial acts to their infants (although this is not solely what motivates prosociality; e.g., Hoffman 2001; Warneken and Tomasello 2008). On the other hand, the idea that parents socialize the value of punishment, or the value of harming those one dislikes, seems so unlikely it approaches the realm of ludicrous. Even if a five-month-old sometimes *sees* punishment (probably *only* if they have older siblings, and—in our subjects—*only* in the form of "time outs"), it is unclear how a five-month-old would learn from this input that such acts are better than helping all the time. Rather, it appears that infants' judgments stem from cognitive mechanisms for nuanced social evaluation, ones that are themselves unlearned.

17.9.3 And the Evaluation Rules Are …? Summary and Future Directions
To quickly summarize the findings presented herein:

1. Basic social evaluations by three months of age: Helpers better than Hinderers; Neutral better than Hinderers.

2. Nuanced social evaluations by four and a half months of age: Appropriately Antisocial better than Inappropriately Prosocial.

3. Mental states (intention) privileged over outcome by eight months: Failed Helpers better than Failed Hinderers.

4. Mental states (knowledge) privileged by ten months: Knowledgeable Helpers better than Knowledgeable Hinderers; Ignorant Helpers not better than Ignorant Hinderers.

As perhaps is clear from this list, from the current state of the data on infants' social evaluations, it is not particularly easy to determine a single evaluation rule that covers all of infants' social preferences. The "highest-level" rule we can currently attribute to three-month-olds is BLOCKING OTHERS' GOALS = BAD; but by one and a half months later, BLOCKING OTHERS' GOALS = GOOD GIVEN THE OTHER IS ANTISOCIAL seems to apply too. By eight months of age, infants demonstrate a clear role for intention in their judgments—inasmuch as INTENDING TO FACILITATE OTHERS' GOALS = GOOD while INTENDING TO BLOCK OTHERS' GOALS = BAD—but given that 4.5-month-olds show nuanced evaluations, presumably this would not apply if the targeted others were themselves antisocial. By ten months, infants demonstrate rules that include analyses of both agents' and patients' unique mental states (KNOWLEDGE and PREFERENCE, respectively); this includes considerations of whether patients' preferences are shared by the infants themselves.

I list this mishmash of evaluation rules for two reasons. The first is to be up front about the fact that the developmental story of social evaluation in infancy, even within the domain of helping and hindering, is not well fleshed out by the current results. In many cases, younger age groups simply have not yet been tested on relevant tasks, and in others, null results may reflect domain-general limitations rather than changes in evaluation rules (e.g., Hamlin et al. 2011; Hamlin, 2014). There is still much, much more work to be done to be able to confidently describe which capacities are and are not present at different points in infancy, and I believe that we must do so before accurately accounting for processes of change. Thus, I will be the first to admit that I did not present an adequate developmental story of social evaluation in the first year, regardless of the mechanism by which evaluative processes emerge.

Beyond the need for additional data in the domain of helping and harming, there are great opportunities for future research into the roots of socio-moral cognition and evaluation more broadly. Entire domains of the "moral" world have not been addressed in infancy to date, including but not limited to domains of generosity, duty, and purity. Infants' understanding of *fair* versus *unfair* object distributions (and their evaluations of fair versus unfair object distributors) has recently been documented in the second year (e.g., Geraci and Surian 2011; Schmidt and Sommerville 2011; Sloane, Baillargeon, and Premack 2012); much more remains to be discovered. Perhaps most interesting will be to elucidate whether and how abilities across distinct domains fit together into an overarching system: Are certain domains more influential than others? What domain-general cognitive skills are required to incorporate information across versus within domains? Thankfully, work with children in other morally relevant domains has set the stage for their exploration in infancy (see, e.g., McCrink, Bloom, and Santos 2010; Olson and Spelke 2008; Stevenson et al. 2010; Warneken et al. 2011).

The need for further exploration aside, the research described herein suggests that infants' evaluation rules are to some essential extent *moral*. To return to the definition put forth in section 17.4, infants' judgments (1) are specifically *social*, (2) apply to social *agents* (not victims), (3) apply to *unknown third parties*, (4) privilege *intention*, (5) incorporate *agent knowledge*, (6) incorporate *patient desires*, and (7) support intuitions about *punishment*. Some of infants' judgments seem markedly less moral than others, even *immoral*, such as liking those who harm individuals who do not share one's food preferences (Hamlin, Mahajan, et al. 2013). And yet, it is not so difficult to think of scenarios in which adults show similar antisocial preferences (for instance, regarding sports rivals); there are even cases in which acting on one's antisocial preferences is considered morally good (for instance, religious warfare). Overall, the similarities in infants' and adults' evaluation rules are striking, in some ways more striking than their differences.

17.10   Final Thought

I return to Meno's question from the introduction, whether "virtue" is the result of teaching, of practice, or of instinct. If one were to interpret Meno's use of the word "virtue" to refer not to the desire to engage in virtuous actions oneself, but as the tendency to judge others for their virtuous or wicked acts, then this chapter suggests an answer: "all three." Specifically, this work adds to what is already known about the important role of socialization and practice in moral development, and suggests that part of human moral judgment is the instinctual tendency to evaluate others for their helpful and harmful acts.

References

Abelson, R. P., and D. E. Kanouse. 1966. Subjective acceptance of verbal generalizations. In *Cognitive Consistency: Motivational Antecedents and Behavioral Consequents*, ed. S. Feldman, 171–197. New York: Academic Press.

Alexander, R. D. 1987. *The Biology of Moral Systems*. New York: De Gruyter.

Aloise, P. A. 1993. Trait confirmation and disconfirmation: The development of attribution biases. *Journal of Experimental Child Psychology* 55 (2): 177–193.

Anderson, J. R., H. Kuroshima, A. Takimoto, and K. Fujita. 2013. Third-party social evaluation of humans by monkeys. *Nature Communications* 4:1561.

Aquinas, T. 2006. *Summa Theologiae, Questions on God*. Ed. B. Davies and B. Leftow. New York: Cambridge University Press.

Aronson, E., and V. Cope. 1968. My enemy's enemy is my friend. *Journal of Personality and Social Psychology* 8 (1): 8–12.

Baillargeon, R., R. M. Scott, and Z. He. 2010. False-belief understanding in infants. *Trends in Cognitive Sciences* 14 (3): 110.

Baillargeon, R., R. M. Scott, Z. He, S. Sloane, P. Setoh, K. Jin, D. Wu, and L. Bian. 2014. Psychological and sociomoral reasoning in infancy. In *APA Handbook of Personality and Social Psychology*, vol. 1: *Attitudes and Social Cognition*, ed. E. Borgida and J. Bargh (P. Shaver and M. Mikulincer eds.-in-chief). Washington, DC: APA.

Baird, J. A., and L. J. Moses. 2001. Do preschoolers appreciate that identical actions may be motivated by different intentions? *Journal of Cognition and Development* 2 (4): 413–448.

Barclay, P. 2006. Reputational benefits for altruistic punishment. *Evolution and Human Behavior* 27 (5): 325–344.

Barrera, M. E., and D. Maurer. 1981. Recognition of mother's photographed face by the three-month-old infant. *Child Development* 52:714–716.

Bartrip, J., J. Morton, and S. de Schonen. 2001. Responses to mother's face in 3-week to 5-month-old infants. *British Journal of Developmental Psychology* 19 (2): 219–232.

Behne, T., M. Carpenter, J. Call, and M. Tomasello. 2005. Unwilling versus unable: Infants' understanding of intentional action. *Developmental Psychology* 41:328–337.

Beier, J., and E. Spelke. 2012. Infants' developing understanding of social gaze. *Child Development* 83 (2): 486–496.

Bertenthal, B. I. 1993. Infants' perception of biomechanical motions: Intrinsic image and knowledge-based constraints. In *Visual Perception and Cognition in Infancy*, ed. C. Granrud, 175–214. Hillsdale, NJ: Erlbaum.

Blair, R. J. R. 1995. A cognitive developmental approach to morality: Investigating the psychopath. *Cognition* 57 (1): 1–29.

Bloom, P. 2013. *Just Babies: The Origins of Good and Evil*. New York: Crown Publishing.

Boyd, R., and P. J. Richerson. 1992. Punishment allows the evolution of cooperation (or anything else) in sizable groups. *Ethology and Sociobiology* 13 (3): 171–195.

Brandone, A. C., and H. M. Wellman. 2009. You can't always get what you want: Infants understand failed goal-directed actions. *Psychological Science* 20 (1): 85–91.

Brown, R. E. 1991. *Human Universals*. New York: McGraw-Hill.

Burnham, D., and B. Dodd. 1998. Familiarity and novelty preferences in infants' auditory-visual speech perception: Problems, factors and a solution. In *Advances in Infancy Research*, vol. 12, ed. C. K. Rovee-Collier, L. P. Lipsitt, and H. Hayne, 170–184. Stamford, CT: Alex Publishing.

Byrne, D. E. 1971. *The Attraction Paradigm.* Vol. 11. New York: Academic Press.

Carey, S. 2009. *The Origin of Concepts.* New York: Oxford University Press.

Carlson, V. 1980. *Differences between social and mechanical causality in infancy.* Paper presented at the International conference on Infant Studies, New Haven, CT.

Caron, R. F., A. J. Caron, and R. S. Myers. 1985. Do infants see emotional expressions in static faces? *Child Development* 56 (6): 1552–1560.

Carruthers, P., S. Laurence, and S. Stich. 2005–2007. *The Innate Mind,* vols. 1–3. New York: Oxford University Press.

Cosmides, L., and J. Tooby. 1992. Cognitive adaptations for social exchange. In *The Adaptive Mind: Evolutionary Psychology and the Generation of Culture,* ed. J. Barkow, L. Cosmides, and J. Tooby, 163–228. New York: Oxford University Press.

Csibra, G., G. Gergely, S. Bíró, O. Koos, and M. Brockbank. 1999. Goal attribution without agency cues: The perception of "pure reason" in infancy. *Cognition* 72 (3): 237–267.

Cushman, F. 2008. Crime and punishment: Distinguishing the roles of causal and intentional analyses in moral judgment. *Cognition* 108 (2): 353–380.

Cushman, F., L. Young, and M. Hauser. 2006. The role of reasoning and intuition in moral judgments: Testing three principles of harm. *Psychological Science* 17 (12): 1082–1089.

Cvencek, D., A. G. Greenwald, and A. N. Meltzoff. 2012. Balance identity theory: Evidence for implicit consistency in social cognition. In *Cognitive Consistency: A Unifying Concept in Social Psychology,* ed. B. Gawronski and F. Strack, 157–177. New York: Guilford Press.

Damasio, A. 1994. *Descartes' Error: Emotion, Reason, and the Human Brain.* New York: Putnam.

DeScioli, P., and R. Kurzban. 2013. A solution to the mysteries of morality. *Psychological Bulletin* 139:477–496.

De Quervain, D. J.-F., U. Fischbacher, V. Treyer, M. Schellhammer, U. Schnyder, A. Buck, and E. Fehr. 2004. The neural basis of altruistic punishment. *Science* 305 (5688): 1254–1258.

De Waal, F. B. 2008. Putting the altruism back into altruism: The evolution of empathy. *Annual Review of Psychology* 59:279–300.

De Waal, F. B., and F. B. M. De Waal. 1996. *Good Natured: The Origins of Right and Wrong in Humans and Other Animals.* Cambridge, MA: Harvard University Press.

Dunfield, K. A., and V. A. Kuhlmeier. 2010. Intention-mediated selective helping in infancy. *Psychological Science* 21 (4): 523–527.

Eisenberg, N., and P. H. Hussen. 1989. *The Roots of Prosocial Behavior in Children.* Cambridge: Cambridge University Press.

Fantz, R. L. 1958. Pattern vision in young infants. *The Psychological Record.* Retrieved from http://psycnet.apa.org/?fa=main.doiLandinganduid=1959-07498-001.

Farroni, T., S. Massaccesi, E. Menon, and M. H. Johnson. 2007. Direct gaze modulates face recognition in young infants. *Cognition* 102 (3): 396–404.

Farroni, T., E. Menon, S. Rigato, and M. H. Johnson. 2007. The perception of facial expressions in newborns. *European Journal of Developmental Psychology* 4 (1): 2–13.

Fawcett, C., and U. Liskowski. 2012. Infants anticipate others' social preferences. *Infant and Child Development* 21 (3): 239–249.

Fawcett, C. A., and L. Markson. 2010. Similarity predicts liking in 3-year-old children. *Journal of Experimental Child Psychology* 105 (4): 345–358.

Fehr, E., and S. Gächter. 2002. Altruistic punishment in humans. *Nature* 415 (6868): 137–140.

Fincham, F. D., and C. Roberts. 1985. Intervening causation and the mitigation of responsibility for harm doing: II. The role of limited mental capacities. *Journal of Experimental Social Psychology* 21 (2): 178–194.

Gawronski, B., E. Walther, and H. Blank. 2005. Cognitive consistency and the formation of interpersonal attitudes: Cognitive balance affects the encoding of social information. *Journal of Experimental Social Psychology* 41 (6): 618–626.

Gelman, R., and R. Baillargeon. 1983. A review of some Piagetian concepts. In *Handbook of Child Psychology*, vol. 3, ed. P. H. Musssen, 167–230. New York: Wiley.

Geraci, A., and L. Surian. 2011. The developmental roots of fairness: Infants' reactions to equal and unequal distributions of resources. *Developmental Science* 14 (5): 1012–1020.

Gergely, G., and G. Csibra. 2003. Teleological reasoning in infancy: The naïve theory of rational action. *Trends in Cognitive Sciences* 7 (7): 287–292.

Gergely, G., Z. Nádasdy, G. Csibra, and S. Bíró. 1995. Taking the intentional stance at 12 months of age. *Cognition* 56 (2): 165–193.

Gerson, S., and A. L. Woodward. 2010. Building intentional action knowledge with one's hands. In *Neo-constructivism*, ed. S. P. Johnson, 295–313. New York: Oxford University Press.

Gray, H. M., K. Gray, and D. M. Wegner. 2007. Dimensions of mind perception. *Science* 315 (5812): 619.

Gray, K., L. Young, and A. Waytz. 2012. Mind perception is the essence of morality. *Psychological Inquiry* 23 (2): 101–124.

Greene, J. D. 2007. The secret joke of Kant's soul. In *Moral Psychology*, vol. 3: *The Neuroscience of Morality: Emotion, Disease, and Development*, ed. W. Sinnott-Armstrong, 59–66. Cambridge, MA: MIT Press.

Greene, J. D., R. B. Sommerville, L. E. Nystrom, J. M. Darley, and J. D. Cohen. 2001. An fMRI investigation of emotional engagement in moral judgment. *Science* 293 (5537): 2105–2108.

Griffiths, P., E. Machery, and S. Linquist. 2009. The vernacular concept of innateness. *Mind & Language* 24 (5): 605–630.

Gürerk, Ö., B. Irlenbusch, and B. Rockenbach. 2006. The competitive advantage of sanctioning institutions. *Science* 312 (5770): 108–111.

Haidt, J. 2001. The emotional dog and its rational tail: A social intuitionist approach to moral judgment. *Psychological Review* 108 (4): 814–834.

Haidt, J., and J. Graham. 2007. When morality opposes justice: Conservatives have moral intuitions that liberals may not recognize. *Social Justice Research* 20 (1): 98–116.

Haidt, J., and C. Joseph. 2007. The moral mind: How five sets of innate intuitions guide the development of many culture-specific virtues, and perhaps even modules. In *The Innate Mind,* vol. 3: *Foundations and the Future,* ed. P. Carruthers, S. Laurence, and S. Stich, 367–392. Oxford: Oxford University Press.

Haith, M. M., T. Bergman, and M. J. Moore. 1977. Eye contact and face scanning in early infancy. *Science* 198 (4319): 853–855.

Hamlin, J. K. 2013a. Moral judgment and action in preverbal infants and toddlers: Evidence for an innate moral core. *Current Directions in Psychological Science* 22 (3): 186–193.

Hamlin, J. K. 2013b. Failed attempts to help and harm: Intention versus outcome in preverbal infants' social evaluations. *Cognition* 128 (3): 451–474.

Hamlin, J. K. 2014. Context-dependent social evaluation in 4.5-month-old human infants: the role of domain-general versus domain-specific processes in the development of social evaluation. *Frontiers in Psychology* 5: 614.

Hamlin, J. K. Unpublished ms. The eyes have it: The role of cues to agency and goal-directedness in infants' social evaluations.

Hamlin, J. K., E. V. Hallinan, and A. L. Woodward. 2008. Do as I do: 7-month-old infants selectively reproduce others' goals. *Developmental Science* 11 (4): 487–494.

Hamlin, J. K., N. Mahajan, Z. Liberman, and K. Wynn. 2013. Not like me: Bad infants prefer those who harm dissimilar others. *Psychological Science* 24 (4): 589–594.

Hamlin, J. K., G. E. Newman, and K. Wynn. 2009. Eight-month-old infants infer unfulfilled goals despite ambiguous physical evidence. *Infancy* 14 (5): 579–590.

Hamlin, J. K., T. Ullman, J. Tenenbaum, N. Goodman, and C. Baker. 2013. The mentalistic basis of core social cognition: Experiments in preverbal infants and a computational model. *Developmental Science* 16 (2): 209–226.

Hamlin, J. K., and K. Wynn. 2011. Young infants prefer prosocial to antisocial others. *Cognitive Development* 26 (1): 30–39.

Hamlin, J. K., K. Wynn, and P. Bloom. 2007. Social evaluation by preverbal infants. *Nature* 450 (7169): 557–559.

Hamlin, J. K., K. Wynn, and P. Bloom. 2010. Three-month-olds show a negativity bias in their social evaluations. *Developmental Science* 13 (6): 923–929.

Hamlin, J. K., K. Wynn, and P. Bloom. 2012. Reply to Scarf et al.: Nuanced social evaluation: Association doesn't compute. *Proceedings of the National Academy of Sciences of the United States of America* 109 (22): E1427.

Hamlin, J. K., K. Wynn, P. Bloom, and N. Mahajan. 2011. How infants and toddlers react to antisocial others. *Proceedings of the National Academy of Sciences of the United States of America* 108 (50): 19931–19936.

Hart, L. A. 1968. *Punishment and Responsibility*. Oxford: Oxford University Press.

Hauser, M. D. 2006. *Moral Minds: How Nature Designed Our Universal Sense of Right and Wrong*. New York: Ecco.

Heider, F. 1958. *The Psychology of Interpersonal Relations*. Hillsdale, NJ: Psychology Press.

Henrich, J., and N. Henrich 2007. *Why Humans Cooperate: A Cultural and Evolutionary Explanation*. New York: Oxford University Press. Henrich, J., R. McElreath, A. Barr, J. Ensminger, C. Barrett, A. Bolyanatz, J. C. Cardenas, M. Gurven, E. Gwako, N. Henrich, E. Lesorogol, F. Marlowe, D. Tracer, and J. Ziker. 2006. Costly punishment across human societies. *Science* 312:1767–1770.

Herrmann, B., C. Thöni, and S. Gächter. 2008. Antisocial punishment across societies. *Science* 319 (5868): 1362–1367.

Hoffman, M. L. 2001. *Empathy and Moral Development: Implications for Caring and Justice*. Cambridge: Cambridge University Press.

Hood, B. M., J. D. Willen, and J. Driver. 1998. Adult's eyes trigger shifts of visual attention in human infants. *Psychological Science* 9 (2): 131–134.

Houston-Price, C., and S. Nakai. 2004. Distinguishing novelty and familiarity effects in infant preference procedures. *Infant and Child Development* 13 (4): 341–348.

Hume, D. [1739] 1978. *A Treatise of Human Nature*. London: John Noon.

Hume, D. [1751] 2008. *An Enquiry Concerning the Princples of Morals*. Oxford: A. Miller.

Ito, T. A., J. T. Larsen, N. K. Smith, and J. T. Cacioppo. 1998. Negative information weighs more heavily on the brain: The negativity bias in evaluative categorizations. *Journal of Personality and Social Psychology* 75:887–900.

Johnson, C. C., and B. J. Stevens. 1996. Experience in a neonatal intensive care unit affects pain response. *Pediatrics* 98:925–930.

Johnson, S. C., C. S. Dweck, and F. S. Chen. 2007. Evidence for infants' internal working models of attachment. *Psychological Science* 18 (6): 501–502.

Johnson, S. P. 2010. *Neoconstructivism: The New Science of Cognitive Development*. New York: Oxford University Press.

Joyce, R. 2006. *The Evolution of Morality*. Cambridge, MA: MIT Press.

Kanouse, D. E., and L. R. Hanson. 1972. Negativity in evaluations. In *Attribution: Perceiving the Causes of Behavior*, ed. E. E. Jones, D. E. Kanouse, H. H. Kelley, R. E. Nisbett, S. Valins, and B. Weiner, 47–62. Morristown, NJ: General Learning Press.

Kant, I. [1781] 1998. *The Critique of Pure Reason*. Trans. P. Guyer and A. W. Wood. Cambridge: Cambridge University Press.

Kant, I. [1785] 2012. *Groundwork of the Metaphysic of Morals*. Ed. M. Gregor and J. Timmermann. New York: Cambridge University Press.

Katz, L. D. 2000. *Evolutionary Origins of Morality: Cross-Disciplinary Perspectives*. Bowling Green, OH: Imprint Academic.

Kelly, D., S. Stich, K. J. Haley, S. J. Eng, and D. M. Fessler. 2007. Harm, affect, and the moral/conventional distinction. *Mind & Language* 22 (2): 117–131.

Killen, M., and J. G. Smetana. 2006. *Handbook of Moral Development, Vol 1*. Mahwah, NJ: Erlbaum.

Killen, M., and J. G. Smetana. 2013. *Handbook of Moral Development*. vol. 2. New York: Psychology Press.

Killen, M., and J. G. Smetana. 2008. Moral judgment and moral neuroscience: Intersections, definitions, and issues. *Child Development Perspectives* 2 (1): 1–6.

Knobe, J. 2003. Intentional action and side effects in ordinary language. *Analysis* 63 (279): 190–194.

Kohlberg, L. 1969. *Stage and Sequence: The Cognitive-Developmental Approach to Socialization*. New York: Rand McNally.

Kohlberg, L. 1981. *The Philosophy of Moral Development: Moral Stages and the Idea of Justice*. Vol. 1 of *Essays on Moral Development*. San Francisco: Harper and Row.

Kovács, Á. M., E. Téglás, and A. D. Endress. 2010. The social sense: Susceptibility to others' beliefs in human infants and adults. *Science* 330 (6012): 1830–1834.

Kuhlmeier, V., K. Wynn, and P. Bloom. 2003. Attribution of dispositional states by 12-month-olds. *Psychological Science* 14 (5): 402–408.

Kurzban, R., and P. DeScioli. 2008. Reciprocity in groups: Information-seeking in a public goods game. *European Journal of Social Psychology* 38 (1): 139–158.

LaBarbera, J. D., C. E. Izard, P. Vietze, and S. A. Parisi. 1976. Four- and six-month-old infants' visual responses to joy, anger, and neutral expressions. *Child Development* 47:535–538.

Legerstee, M., and G. Markova. 2007. Intentions make a difference: Infants' responses to still-face and modified still-face interactions. *Infant Behavior and Development* 30:232–250.

Leslie, A. M. 1982. The perception of causality in infants. *Perception* 11:173–186.

Leslie, A. M. 1994. ToMM, ToBy, and agency: Core architecture and domain specificity. In *Mapping the Mind: Domain Specificity in Cognition and Culture*, ed. L. Hirschfeld and S. Gelman, 119–148. New York: Cambridge University Press.

Leslie, A. M., and S. Keeble. 1987. Do six-month-old infants perceive causality? *Cognition* 25 (3): 265–288.

Leslie, A. M., J. Knobe, and A. Cohen. 2006. Acting intentionally and the side-effect effect: Theory of mind and moral judgment. *Psychological Science* 17 (5): 421–427.

Luo, Y. 2011. Three-month-old infants attribute goals to a non-human agent. *Developmental Science* 14:453–460.

Luo, Y., and R. Baillargeon. 2007. Do 12.5-month-old infants consider what objects others can see when interpreting their actions? *Cognition* 105 (3): 489–512.

Macnamara, J. 1991. The development of moral reasoning and the foundations of geometry. *Journal for the Theory of Social Behaviour* 21 (2): 125–150.

Mahajan, N., and K. Wynn. 2012. Origins of "us" versus "them": Prelinguistic infants prefer similar others. *Cognition* 124 (2): 227–233.

Malle, B. F. 1999. How people explain behavior: A new theoretical framework. *Personality and Social Psychology Review* 3 (1): 23–48.

Mameli, M., and P. Bateson. 2006. Innateness and the sciences. *Biology and Philosophy* 21 (2): 155–188.

Mandler, J. M. 1992. The foundations of conceptual thought in infancy. *Cognitive Development* 7 (3): 273–285.

Marcus, G. F. 2004. *The Birth of yhe Mind: How a Tiny Number of Genes Creates the Complexities of Human Thought*. New York: Basic Books.

Margolis, E., and S. Laurence. 1999. *Concepts: Core Readings*. Cambridge, MA: MIT Press.

Margolis, E., and S. Laurence. 2012. In defense of nativism. *Philosophical Studies* 165:693–718.

Marsh, H. L., J. Stavropoulos, T. Nienhuis, and M. Legerstee. 2010. Six-and 9-month-old infants discriminate between goals despite similar action patterns. *Infancy* 15 (1): 94–106.

Mascaro, O., and G. Csibra. 2012. Representation of stable dominance relations by human infants. *Proceedings of the National Academy of Sciences of the United States of America* 109 (18): 6862–6867.

Maurer, M. 1999. Why are tough on crime policies so popular? *Stanford Law & Policy Review* 11:9–22.

McCrink, K., P. Bloom, and L. Santos. 2010. Children's and adults' judgments of equitable resource distributions. *Developmental Science* 13 (1): 37–45.

McDonnell, P. M. 1975. The development of visually guided reaching. *Perception & Psychophysics* 18 (3): 181–185.

Meltzoff, A. N. 1995. What infant memory tells us about infantile amnesia: Long-term recall and deferred imitation. *Journal of Experimental Child Psychology* 59 (3): 497–515.

Meltzoff, A. N. 2007. "Like me": A foundation for social cognition. *Developmental Science* 10 (1): 126–134.

Mennella, J. A., and G. K. Beauchamp. 1996. Developmental changes in the acceptance of protein hydrolysate formula. *Journal of Developmental and Behavioral Pediatrics* 17:386–391.

Mikhail, J. 2007. Universal moral grammar: Theory, evidence and the future. *Trends in Cognitive Sciences* 11 (4): 143–152.

Mikhail, J. 2011. *Elements of Moral Cognition: Rawls' Linguistic Analogy and the Cognitive Science of Moral and Legal Judgment.* New York: Cambridge University Press.

Newman, L., and L. Weitzer. 1956. Duress, free will and the criminal law. *Southern California Law Review* 30:313.

Nucci, L. P., and E. Turiel. 1978. Social interactions and the development of social concepts in preschool children. *Child Development* 49 (2):400–407.

Oakes, L. M., C. H. Cashon, M. Casasola, and D. H. Rakison. 2010. *Infant Perception and Cognition: Recent Advances, Emerging Theories, and Future Directions.* New York: Oxford University Press.

Olson, K. R., and E. S. Spelke. 2008. Foundations of cooperation in young children. *Cognition* 108:222–231.

Piaget, J. 1932. *The Moral Judgment of the Child.* London: Kegan Paul, Trench, Trubner.

Piaget, J., and B. Inhelder. 1956. *The Child's Concept of Space.* New York: Humanities Press.

Pietraszewski, D., and T. C. German. 2013. Coalitional psychology on the playground: Reasoning about indirect social consequences in preschoolers and adults. *Cognition* 126 (3): 352–363.

Pizarro, D., Y. Inbar, and C. Helion. 2011. On disgust and moral judgment. *Emotion Review* 3 (3): 267–268.

Premack, D. 1990. The infant's theory of self-propelled objects. *Cognition* 36 (1): 1–16.

Premack, D., and A. J. Premack. 1994. Levels of causal understanding in chimpanzees and children. *Cognition* 50 (1): 347–362.

Premack, D., and A. J. Premack. 1997. Infants attribute value to the goal-directed actions of self-propelled objects. *Journal of Cognitive Neuroscience* 9 (6): 848–856.

Price, M. E., L. Cosmides, and J. Tooby. 2002. Punitive sentiment as an anti-free rider psychological device. *Evolution and Human Behavior* 23 (3): 203–231.

Prinz, J. P. 2012. *Beyond Human Nature: How Culture and Experience Shape the Human Mind*. London: Allen Lane.

Rai, T. S., and A. P. Fiske. 2011. Moral psychology is relationship regulation: Moral motives for unity, hierarchy, equality, and proportionality. *Psychological Review* 118 (1): 57–75.

Rawls, J. 1971. *A Theory of Justice*. Cambridge, MA: Harvard University Press.

Rest, J. R., D. Narvaez, S. J. Thoma, and M. J. Bebeau. 1999. DIT2: Devising and testing a revised instrument of moral judgment. *Journal of Educational Psychology* 91 (4): 644–659.

Robinson, P. H., and J. M. Darley. 1995. *Justice, Liability, and Blame: Community Views and the Criminal Law*. San Francisco: Westview Press.

Robinson, P. H., R. Kurzban, and O. D. Jones. 2007. Origins of shared intuitions of justice. *Vanderbilt Law Review* 60:1633.

Rose, S. A., A. W. Gottfried, P. Melloy-Carminar, and W. H. Bridger. 1982. Familiarity and novelty preferences in infant recognition memory: Implications for information processing. *Developmental Psychology* 18 (5): 704.

Rozin, P., and E. B. Royzman. 2001. Negativity bias, negativity dominance, and contagion. *Personality and Social Psychology Review* 5 (4): 296–320.

Ruffman, T., M. Taumoepeau, and C. Perkins. 2012. Statistical learning as a basis for social understanding in children. *British Journal of Developmental Psychology* 30:87–104.

Scarf, D., K. Imuta, M. Colombo, and H. Hayne. 2012. Social evaluation or simple association? Simple associations may explain moral reasoning in infants. *PLoS ONE* 7 (8): e42698.

Schmidt, M. F. H., and J. A. Sommerville. 2011. Fairness expectations and altruistic sharing in 15-month-old human infants. *PLoS ONE* 6 (10): e23223.

Shutts, K., K. D. Kinzler, and J. M. DeJesus. 2013. Understanding infants' and childrens' social learning about foods: Previous research and new prospects. *Developmental Psychology* 3:470–479.

Shweder, R. A., M. Mahapatra, and J. G. Miller. 1987. Culture and moral development. In *The Emergence of Morality in Young Children*, ed. J. Kagan and S. Lamb, 1–82. Chicago, IL: University of Chicago Press.

Simion, F., L. Regolin, and H. Bulf. 2008. A predisposition for biological motion in the newborn baby. *Proceedings of the National Academy of Sciences of the United States of America* 105 (2): 809–813.

Skowronski, J. J., and D. E. Carlston. 1989. Negativity and extremity biases in impression formation: A review of explanations. *Psychological Bulletin* 105 (1): 131.

Sloane, S., R. Baillargeon, and D. Premack. 2012. Do infants have a sense of fairness? *Psychological Science* 23 (2): 196–204.

Smetana, J. G. 1981. Preschool children's conceptions of moral and social rules. *Child Development* 52 (4):1333–1336.

Smith, A. 1759. *The Theory of Moral Sentiments*. London: A. Millar.

Sommerville, J. A., A. L. Woodward, and A. Needham. 2005. Action experience alters 3-month-old infants' perception of others' actions. *Cognition* 96 (1): B1–B11.

Spelke, E. S. 1990. Principles of object perception. *Cognitive Science* 14 (1): 29–56.

Spelke, E. S. 1994. Initial knowledge: Six suggestions. *Cognition* 50 (1): 431–445.

Stevenson, R. J., M. J. Oaten, T. I. Case, B. M. Repacholi, and P. Wagland. 2010. Children's response to adult disgust elicitors: Development and acquisition. *Developmental Psychology* 46 (1): 165–177.

Thomsen, L., W. E. Frankenhuis, M. Ingold-Smith, and S. Carey. 2011. Big and mighty: Preverbal infants mentally represent social dominance. *Science* 331:477–480.

Tronick, E. Z., H. Als, L. Adamson, S. Wise, and T. B. Brazelton. 1978. The infants' response to entrapment between contradictory messages in face-to-face interaction. *Journal of the American Academy of Child Psychiatry* 17:1–13.

Turiel, E. 1983. *The Development of Social Knowledge: Morality and Convention*. Cambridge: Cambridge University Press.

Vaish, A., T. Grossmann, and A. Woodward. 2008. Not all emotions are created equal: The negativity bias in social-emotional development. *Psychological Bulletin* 134 (3): 383.

Walker-Andrews, A. S. 1997. Infants' perception of expressive behaviors: Differentiation of multimodal information. *Psychological Bulletin* 121 (3): 437.

Warneken, F., K. Lohse, A. P. Melis, and M. Tomasello. 2011. Young children share the spoils after collaboration. *Psychological Science* 22 (2): 267–273.

Warneken, F., and M. Tomasello. 2008. Extrinsic rewards undermine altruistic tendencies in 20-month-olds. *Developmental Psychology* 44 (6): 1785–1788.

Watson, J. S. 1979. Perceptions of contingency as a determinant of social responsiveness. In *The Origins of the Infant's Social Responsiveness*, ed. E. B. Thoman, 33–64. Hillsdale, NJ: Erlbaum.

Wiessner, P. 2005. Norm enforcement among the Ju/'hoansi bushmen: A case of strong reciprocity? *Human Nature* 16 (2): 115–145.

Wolff, P. H. 1963. Observations on early development of smiling. In *Determinants of Infant Behavior*, vol. 2, ed. B. M. Foss, 113–138. New York: Wiley.

Woodward, A. L. 1998. Infants selectively encode the goal object of an actor's reach. *Cognition* 69 (1): 1–34.

Woodward, A. L. 2009. Infants' grasp of others' intentions. *Current Directions in Psychological Science* 18 (1): 53–57.

Wynn, K. 1992. Addition and subtraction by human infants. *Nature* 358 (6389): 749–750.

Wynn, K. 2008. Some innate foundations of social and moral cognition. In *The Innate Mind*, vol. 3: *Foundations and the Future,* ed. P. Carruthers, S. Laurence, and S. Stich, 330–347. Oxford: Oxford University Press.

Xu, F. (Ed.) 2012. *Advances in Child Development and Behavior,* vol. 43: *Rational Constructivism in Cognitive Development.* New York: Academic Press.

Xu, F., and E. S. Spelke. 2000. Large number discrimination in 6-month-old infants. *Cognition* 74 (1): B1–B11.

Young, L., F. Cushman, M. Hauser, and R. Saxe. 2007. The neural basis of the interaction between theory of mind and moral judgment. *Proceedings of the National Academy of Sciences of the United States of America* 104 (20): 8235–8240.

18 Normative Concepts

Charles W. Kalish

18.1 Introduction

A central debate in the psychology of concepts is whether mental representations are just records of frequency distributions, or whether there is something more to them. The concept DOG may be characterized as a memory trace or record of the features that have tended to be associated with the term. Barking is part of the concept because the label "dog" and barking tend to co-occur. In contrast, other accounts hold that concepts involve some modal content in addition to frequencies. That modal content can be semantic: barking is a feature of the abstract kind or concept DOG, not (or not just) a feature of individuals (Khemlani, Leslie, and Glucksberg 2012; Prasada and Dillingham 2009). The modal content can also be causal: something about being a dog causes barking (Gelman 2003; Keil 1989). The purpose of this chapter is to consider another sort of modal content: normativity. There is some obligatory or normative constraint on what goes into a concept: concepts are not just records of what happens to be experienced.

The issue of the normativity of meaning is well recognized (and debated) in philosophy (Boghossian 1989; Davidson 1984; Kripke 1982). However, norms have not been a central focus of psychological research on concepts. This chapter will introduce two senses in which normativity may play an important role in the psychology of concepts. First, concepts are subject to normative evaluation. This is the sense in which one's concept DOG ought to include barking and ought not to include meowing. Second, NORM is itself an important concept, especially developmentally. How do concepts acquire a normative structure, and how do children acquire the concept NORM? Humans clearly have capacities to make judgments of obligations, permissions, and prohibitions. Such capacities would seem to depend on possessing certain kinds of concepts. Theories of concepts must explain and accommodate normative content. Moreover, studying norms may also shed new light on the nature and acquisition of concepts.

Although the concept NORM is addressed later in the chapter, it is useful to provide a bit of description to start. In the broad sense, norms involve evaluative standards: they concern how things ought to be rather than how they are. Normative evaluations contrast with descriptions. There can be many types of evaluation. For example, a simple judgment of liking or pleasurableness is normative in the broad sense. "I like that" is a standard against which experiences can be measured. More narrow senses of NORM involve specific types of evaluation. In particular, many hold that there is a special standard of moral norm distinct from likes and preferences. To judge that killing is wrong is different than judging that anyone dislikes killing. Exactly how this might be different is the subject of the second part of the chapter: Roughly, how do children acquire norms that go beyond likes and dislikes? At that point it will be important to distinguish broad evaluations from more narrow norms. To begin, though, it will suffice to consider norms without specifying the kind of evaluation involved.

18.2   Empirical and Descriptive Concepts

Most psychological theories identify concepts with representations of feature co-occurrences (see Murphy 2002 for review). A concept can be a parametric description of associations that is stored and recalled across situations (e.g., a prototype). A concept can be a set of stored exemplars, or a distributed pattern of activation in a network, dynamically changing with context. This large family of theories may be characterized as descriptivist (Millikan 1998). Although descriptivist concepts could be innately specified, they are usually understood to be records or memory traces of experience. After a number of experiences with objects in the environment, the learner might notice that animals called "whale" live in water and have fins. The representation of these (and other) associations is the WHALE concept. The concept is a kind of description, a record, of those associations.

Concepts give rise to expectations and perceptions of relatedness. Upon hearing an animal labeled as a *whale*, people expect the animal to have fins. The concepts of WHALE and FISH encode many of the same associations, so people perceive the two to be similar. The similarities and expectations generated by concepts are kinds of experiences; they are features of the conceptualizer's mind. They are not, in and of themselves, expectations or beliefs about objects in the world. As such, the similarities are neither right nor wrong. People perceive many associations. For example, Paul Rozin and colleagues (Rozin, Millman, and Nemeroff 1986) have noted that people prefer not to eat fudge shaped in the form of feces. People would also rather wear a well-laundered sweater that once belonged to a loved one, instead of one that once belonged to Hitler. Such reactions reflect mental associations. Although the actions taken based on the mental associations are subject to evaluation as rational or mistaken, the associations are not. One cannot object, "It is a mistake to associate that fudge with filth." The perceived similarities are not defeasible because they are not claims or inferences about anything.

In the same way, the similarity between whales and fish is a kind of mental experience. The human conceptual system delivers such experiences.

Of course, the reason that perceptions of association and similarity are of such interest is that they are used to guide behavior and inference. From the perception that whales are similar to fish, people tend to expect that they eat the same foods, reproduce in the same manner, and so on. As in the case with disgust, associations might lead to maladaptive actions or mistaken predictions. There is a temptation to say that the concepts are mistaken, especially as concepts are often modified in response to failures of prediction (as in error-driven learning). However, such modifications are best understood as updating: a new association is incorporated into the concept. The concept, as a record of past associations, cannot be wrong. In the same sense, a weather forecaster's data cannot be wrong. When the forecaster states, "There is an 80 percent chance of rain today," he is reporting that rain has occurred on 80 percent of the past days like this one. The inference based on that record might be wrong (it may not rain), but the record is not.

Of course, there is a sense in which weather forecasters may be wrong. Their data may be understood not as records of historical events, but as models of reality. A model is correct or incorrect (or correct to some degree). As models, concepts have an empirical character (Millikan 1998) as well as a descriptive character. Concepts are representations, not simply records.

The empirical sense of concepts implies a connection to an external reality. The concept WHALE is not (just) a memory trace of experiences; it is somehow connected to a real kind in the world. The concept WHALE is a representation of whales. As a representation, a concept may be correct or incorrect. If the concept misrepresents the kind or property it is connected to, then it should be changed. People whose concept WHALE contains the feature "is a fish" do not just have a particular association (that may be more or less useful or consistent with future experience), they have a mistaken representation. Given that these people understand their concepts to be representations, they have an interest in keeping them accurate. Here is the normative aspect of concepts: the world provides a standard against which the content of concepts may be evaluated.

The empirical sense of concepts is most evident with respect to natural kinds. To understand some kind or property as natural is to believe it is real and objective. The function of a concept is to link the conceiver to that property (Margolis 1998). The empirical quality of concepts, however, extends beyond natural kinds. Concepts may be linked to descriptions (Burge 1979). For example, a child's concept UNCLE will be evaluated against the community's definition. If the child believes that all uncles are adults, and thus his or her father's two-year-old brother is not the child's uncle, the child's concept is wrong (Keil and Batterman 1984). Children and adults believe that some concepts are representations of real kinds in the world, while others are representations of more or less arbitrary conventions (e.g., what counts as a *touchdown*? Kalish

1995, 1998a; Rhodes and Gelman 2009). The key feature of an empirical concept is not what it represents (natural kind, artifact), but that it is understood as a representation.

18.2.1 Psychological Differences between Empirical and Descriptive Concepts

The difference between an empirical and descriptive concept is one of attitude: What does the possessor think about the concept? Having empirical concepts requires treating or taking concepts as representations. That is, it is not sufficient to have representational mental states; some understanding of representational relations is required as well. The idea of understanding concepts as empirical raises a number of psychological questions. For example, are there distinct systems of empirical and descriptive concepts in the mind (Smith and Grossman 2008)? Which tasks involve which kind (or sense) of concept? It seems plausible that descriptive concepts are more basic: Do children and nonhumans have empirical concepts? At least part of the difference in attitude is whether concepts are evaluated against a normative standard. Thus, one avenue for research on the psychology of concepts is exploring when people treat concepts as matters of right and wrong.

One difference between empirical and descriptive attitudes is the disposition to defer to experts regarding the content of one's concepts. If a concept is an empirical representation of reality, then possessors have an interest in keeping their concepts accurate. As any individual's experience with the world will be limited and potentially misleading, it makes sense to rely on expert judgments about the concepts. Experts know what is true. This empirical attitude underlies ideas about division of cognitive labor and external determinants of reference (Kripke 1980; Putnam 1982). In contrast, experts have no special claim or power to determine descriptive concepts. Of course, an expert's usage may be part of the associations encoded in a concept, perhaps a very salient or significant part.

Consider a child who believes that whales are fish who now hears a teacher say that whales are mammals. If the child has an empirical concept WHALE, he has reason to change his concept, at least to the extent that the teacher is believed to have more accurate beliefs. What about a descriptive concept WHALE? The teacher has provided a new association with the concept: whale and mammal become connected. The strength of that connection depends on the child's past history of associations. If fish was only weakly associated, mammal may come to dominate. If teachers have been very influential sources in the past, mammal may become a dominant association (see Rogers and McClelland 2004 on context effects). When someone asks, "What is a whale?" the child hears the teacher's voice and replies "a mammal." To be an expert just is to be influential. While empirical concepts imply deference to experts, descriptive concepts imply responsiveness to experts. In practice it may be difficult to distinguish these two types of effect. In principle, though, what makes a source an expert is very different for descriptive than for empirical concepts.

Both descriptive and empirical concepts are subject to revision based on experience. How that revision is understood or motivated represents an important difference between the two kinds of concepts. For empirical concepts, experience is evidence. A concept is a kind of hypothesis about a population or generative process. Experience provides evidence about the nature of that population or process. The individual whales one has encountered, or the statements about whales one has heard, constitute the evidence one has available to form a hypothesis, concept, about whales. This idea that concepts are hypotheses and responsive to evidence is central to theory-based (Murphy and Medin 1985) and Bayesian (Xu and Tenenbaum 2007) accounts of concepts and concept acquisition. Experts, or any other experiences, are influential to the degree they are understood to provide good evidence. Conceptual change is an inferential process (Kalish, Kim, and Young 2012). One of the most active areas of research and debate in the psychology of concepts is whether people are sensitive to evidential properties of experience (e.g., relations between samples and populations; see debate in Chater, Tenenbaum, and Yuille 2010; McClelland et al. 2010; also Kalish and Thevenow-Harrison, 2014).

Descriptive concepts change in response to experience just because they are descriptions of that experience. The change in description associated with a particular experience need not be simple or additive. In some models, concepts are represented as distributed patterns of activation within a network (see Rogers and McClelland 2004). The network is set up to maintain some sort of consistency or constraint satisfaction among descriptions. If the world is saying "mammal," but one's conceptual system is delivering "fish," then there is a conflict. One way to respond to the inconsistency is to modify the conceptual system so that it becomes more likely to deliver "mammal." Such modifications can have unexpected and nonlinear consequences throughout the network. Although it is tempting to view the system as developing a more accurate representation, and becoming better at prediction, representation and prediction really play no role in the process. We can suppose that evolution selected for this particular way of recording descriptions of experience because it tends to produce more accurate predictions than does some other way of forming descriptions. Accuracy and representation are the designer's goals, not the network's.

18.2.2 Development of Descriptive and Empirical Concepts

Adult humans seem to have goals not just to describe their experience but also to form accurate representations. Proponents of descriptivist models of concepts hold that the concern with accurate representations is a rarified metacognitive attitude: that is what scientists worry about. However, even regular folk seem to worry about the accuracy of their beliefs and representations of the world, at least at times. Among cognitive developmentalists, many feel that young children are adopting empirical attitudes and actively testing and evaluating their concepts against reality. It is unclear how deeply or generally this empirical attitude is to be ascribed. Do infants have empirical concepts? Nonhumans? We can characterize this as the developmental question. It seems plausible that descriptive concepts are more basic; simple cognitive systems have descriptive concepts. What does it take to have empirical concepts?

One hypothesis is that empirical concepts are products of language. On this view, empirical concepts are more properly characterized as word meanings. Concepts are descriptive records of associations; word meanings are conventionalized sets of such associations. For example, the concept BOTTLE involves a large and unstable system of associations, related to, and overlapping with, JAR, CAN, and GLASS (Sloman and Malt 2003). Conceptualizers are not attempting to represent some kind in the world. When using the word *bottle,* however, people are required to bring some order to their associations and conform to a conventional set of meanings. It is as the meaning of the word *bottle* that a network of associations becomes a representation: a representation of the meaning of the word. There does seem to be a close connection between language and empirical attitude. Anyone who could not adopt an empirical attitude could acquire descriptive concepts, but not word meanings (see Clark 1992). Whether language provides the ability to adopt empirical attitudes, or vice versa, is unclear. However, it seems acquisition and use of language is one important indicator of empirical concepts.

Some evidence bearing on the developmental question is that young children seem to distinguish descriptive and empirical applications of concepts and words. For example, preschool-aged children accept that people may differ in their judgments about which objects are most similar (is a novel animal more like a dog or a cat?). However, these children reject diversity in judgments of identity. If one person asserts that an unfamiliar animal "is the same kind of thing" as a dog, while the other asserts it is the same kind as a cat, children believe that one of the people must be wrong (Kalish 2007). Judgments of labeling (which two should have the same name?) are intermediate. The hypothesis is that the identity judgment is understood as a claim about reality, and such a claim is either correct or incorrect. In contrast, a judgment of similarity is taken as a subjective report. Presumably these children would see an obligation for one party to change their beliefs in the identity condition, but not in the similarity condition. Just when and how children hold people responsible for their thoughts and judgments, however, is something of an open question (Chandler and Lalonde 1996; Koenig 2002; Pritchard and Kalish 2001). For example, young children may not recognize that people have control over their beliefs. If having empirical concepts requires engaging in normative evaluations, then only beings able to understand and reason about norms will have such concepts.

18.3   Concept(s) of Norms and Evaluations

The cognitive requirements for descriptive concepts seem fairly minimal; most creatures have such concepts. Many philosophers have argued that true concepts must be something more than collections of associations. Moreover, the conditions for possessing such concepts are quite stringent. Having a concept involves being able to give and appreciate reasons for belief, to have some notions of justification and warrant. For an individual to have mental states to which it is possible to ascribe meaning, such as the concept X, the individual must understand the conditions under which the state is an accurate representation of *x* (Boghossian 1989; Kripke 1982). The individual must appreciate the normative constraint to have adequate reasons for his or her beliefs and representations (e.g., why believe that whales are mammals rather than fish?) (Brandom 1998; McDowell 1994). On this account, concepts require acting (or believing) according to epistemic norms. Empirical concepts as described above seem to fit with this epistemic norms account of concepts. The concept holder takes the world as the standard against which concepts are evaluated. That one's concepts match the world is a reason for believing one thing rather than another. This suggests that the ability to give and understand reasons is necessary for empirical concepts. When do children acquire this understanding: When do they acquire normative concepts?

18.3.1 Norms and Other Evaluations

Even young infants can make instrumental evaluations: they prefer some states to others. We often think that the concepts involved in instrumental evaluation, LIKE and DISLIKE, are foundational. Such evaluations are normative in a very broad sense. Liking and disliking, however, are not sufficient to provide a foundation for empirical concepts. That one likes or dislikes the associations produced in the mind, or the consequences of those associations, does not make them empirical. For example, a child's concept WHALE might lead to the expectation that whales breathe water (like fish). When she later learns that whales breathe air, there is some conflict or disequilibrium. Most theories of concepts ascribe motivational significance to such conflict. The cognitive system works to maintain equilibrium and reduce conflict. This is not the same, however, as seeking to maintain accurate concepts. That is, a child with an empirical concept WHALE would revise her concept because it is inaccurate. This account differs in two ways from a dispreference for conflict: it involves a concept of accuracy and the idea of acting *because* of accuracy. Both these components involve more complex normative concepts.

18.3.2 Accuracy and Inaccuracy

Understanding a concept as empirical seems to require the ability to distinguish between accurate and inaccurate: that is, the concept can match or mismatch the world. Recognizing truth or accuracy as an evaluative standard provides a kind of norm. Infants seem sensitive to such norms. For example, they react to mismatches between labels and referents (Koenig and Echols 2003). Toddlers will correct speakers who make mistakes (Pea 1982). These children also prefer to learn new words from speakers who have previously been accurate rather than inaccurate (Harris 2007; Koenig and Woodward 2010). Preschool-aged children can identify failures of communication but have difficulty identifying the form of an utterance as the source (Robinson and Robinson 1976). For example, an ambiguous message that leads to successful performance is not seen as problematic (Robinson and Whittaker 1986). Although young children seem to make evaluations of accuracy, it is not clear exactly what is involved in such evaluations. In particular, an ability to identify matches between words and referents as well as a preference for matches over mismatches seem sufficient to account for the data.

The concept ACCURACY involves or depends on some additional concepts, notably the concept REPRESENTATION. It is only as a representation that an utterance can be accurate or not. The concept REPRESENTATION, that one thing can stand for or symbolize another, emerges over the first few years of life. Preissler and Carey (2004) found that eighteen-month-old infants who learned a novel word by seeing pictures of the referent identified the actual object (e.g., a real whisk) rather than the picture as the referent (also Ganea et al. 2009). Children understand the word (and picture) to represent the real thing. Young children, however, often have difficulty focusing on the representational content of symbols, especially when the symbols are complex concrete objects (DeLoache 2004). For example, a scale model of a room is not seen as representing the real room, because the scale model is interesting and significant in its own right.

With age, children get better at identifying when and how one thing represents another. In particular, they come to understand referential claims. For example, preschool-aged children often conflate pretending and lying (Taylor, Lussier, and Maring 2003). Three-year-olds (but perhaps not two-year-olds) distinguish the *direction of fit* of descriptions and commands (Rakoczy and Tomasello 2009): they recognize that only the former are to be evaluated by their match to the current state of the world. Some of the most difficult representational relations are those involving belief: not until age four years or so do children appreciate that beliefs may misrepresent (Wellman, Cross, and Watson 2001; though see Onishi and Baillargeon 2005). One influential account of the *false-belief error* holds that the empirical possibility of misrepresentation poses the problem (Wellman 1992). Children recognize that people think *about* objects in the world, but their understanding is that the causal process producing such thoughts cannot result in errors. Clearly, there is a protracted process of learning about representations, but the basic concept seems present quite early. Thus, young children seem to have the conceptual capacities to make judgments of accuracy and inaccuracy, even if they may not be expert in knowing when and how to deploy such evaluations.

Part of having empirical concepts is understanding them as representations that can be evaluated as more or less accurate. A second part of an empirical attitude is seeing accuracy/inaccuracy as a motive, a reason for changing one's beliefs. When a symbol is seen to be inaccurate, it is often also understood to be wrong. Indeed, much of the evidence that children make evaluations of accuracy depends on their recognition and response to error. For example, part of recognizing an inaccurate statement is the sense that it ought to be changed to be accurate. However, judgments of correctness and error, of right and wrong, are a distinct kind of evaluation. A representation can be inaccurate without being an error. An old photograph might be an inaccurate representation of the current state of the world without being an error or mistake. A Picasso portrait may not look much like its subject. It seems possible to evaluate accuracy and inaccuracy without understanding the result of the evaluation as a reason for action (e.g., changing beliefs).

18.3.3   Reasons

One of the central prerequisites for fully normative concepts is the concept REASON. Explaining or evaluating behavior using normative concepts involves treating the behavior as part of a particular kind of causal process. Only individuals who understand themselves (and/or others) as having or being subject to reasons may understand themselves (and/or others) in normative terms. A natural disaster may be terrible, but it cannot be wrong: natural disasters are not caused by or subject to reasons. Similarly, conceiving of whales as fish may lead to disastrous (or at least dispreferred) outcomes. Those outcomes provide a reason to change the concept, but only for certain kinds of agents. Having normative concepts requires having concepts of those special kinds of agents.

Research on developing theories of mind provides some insight into how and when children come to understand people as acting for reasons. Interestingly though, most work has focused on concepts of representational mental states with little discussion of the related concept REASON. Gergely and Csibra (2003) have argued that quite young infants understand rational action, which would seem to involve understanding of reasons (see also Perner 1991). For example, infants view certain kinds of agents as goal directed (Woodward, Sommerville, and Guajardo 2001). If an agent has a goal, say, to reach a piece of food, then the agent would seem to have reasons to do some things rather than others: approach (rather than avoid) the food, alter its path to avoid obstacles, and so forth. A theory of rational action is understood to be distinct from a theory of mind. There are no mental state ascriptions, just a kind of logic of goal-directed action. This logic provides a basis for evaluation. Numerous studies show that infants are surprised when agents behave "unreasonably" (Gergely and Csibra 2003). It is irrational for an agent to alter its path in the absence of a barrier to a goal, for example. Such evaluations are part of the concept GOAL (or goal-directed behavior).

Evaluations of goal-directed behavior may not be sufficient to demonstrate the concept REASON. The reasons involved in rational action seem importantly limited. A full concept involves understanding how reasons relate to action. In particular, reasons can only affect behavior via mental states: the effects of reasons are mind dependent. This is not to say that reasons are mental states. People may have reasons they are unaware of. Sally has a reason not to touch the hot stove, whether or not she is aware of the danger. However, reasons themselves are causally inert; they need to get into people's heads to do anything. For people to act on reasons, they must have the kind of heads reasons can get into. Sally may not be aware of any particular reason (that the stove is hot), but her behavior is guided by some reasons, and potentially affected by others. The theory of rational action is a model that can be applied irrespective of underlying causal structure, akin to using a mathematical model for physical phenomena. There does seem to be an important distinction, however, between actually having reasons, acting on reasons, and just being interpreted as such. That distinction turns on an understanding of mental causation.

The false-belief task (Wimmer and Perner 1983) was designed as test of children's understanding of the representational nature of mental states. The task also provides information about children's understanding of mental causation, of the mind-dependent nature of acting for a reason. One interpretation of behavior on false-belief tasks is that preschool-aged children do not appreciate that reasons must be represented (believed) in order to affect behavior. When Maxi's chocolate is moved from the cupboard to the basket without his seeing, he has a reason to search in the basket (that's where the chocolate is), but he is unaware of this reason. Nonetheless, young children predict Maxi will look in the basket. It is as if the state of the world is directly influencing his behavior, without having to go through his mental states. If that is how a preschooler understands causes of behavior, then the preschooler lacks a concept REASON. The presence of chocolate in the basket exerts some influence on Maxi's behavior, but it is not a reason.

However, there is an alternative interpretation of failures on false-belief tasks. Perhaps young children just misunderstand the conditions under which people are aware of their reasons: if Maxi has a reason to look in the basket, then he probably represents that reason and can act on it. Some evidence for this interpretation is that children do understand ignorance (Wellman 1992).[1] If Maxi walks into a room where chocolate is hidden, without ever being *cognitively connected* (Flavell 1988) to the treat, children do not expect him to find it. In this condition, Maxi's reason for looking in the basket is not expected to drive his behavior. Reluctance to ascribe false beliefs could reflect a kind of *cognitive charity*: generally, it is good practice to ascribe true rather than false beliefs. Young children may take this charity to a greater extreme. For example, when confronted by a mistake, such as an actor pouring the contents of an orange juice box on cereal, children tend to invent good reasons: the person probably likes orange juice on cereal (Schult and Wellman 1997). Young children may have different ideas than

---

1. Further support for this interpretation comes from evidence that even infants may recognize false belief (Onishi and Baillargeon 2005). Perhaps the developmental story is not one of coming to understand representation, but one of developing more-sophisticated and flexible abilities to reason about how represented and nonrepresented (but nonetheless true) information actually affects people's behavior (see Perner and Roessler 2010).

adults about which reasons people recognize, but the basic concept of a reason, as only causing behavior via representation, may be shared.

The same sort of ambiguous evidence of understanding the mind dependence of reasons occurs in the context of normative evaluations. It often seems that children think that norms have direct causal influences on behavior. Piaget (1965) described the classic error of *immanent justice*. For example, a thief who steals food will become sick (Jose 1990). The natural operation of the world tends to reward good behavior and punish bad. Rules inform predictions of behavior independent of ascriptions of belief (Clement, Bernard, and Kaufmann 2011). For example, preschool-aged children believe that actors will follow rules the actors are unaware of (Kalish 1998b; Kalish and Cornelius 2007). Similarly, young children often deny that people can avoid following rules, even if they intend not to (Kalish 1998b; Kushnir, Wellman, and Chernyak 2009). However, such findings may reflect further operations of charity. The expectations that people know the rules and want to follow them may override the explicit instructions in an experiment.

As in other contexts, children may show more appreciation of reasons in their explanations or responses to violations (Wellman 2011). They recognize that a violator may be called on to give an account of his or her actions, and can evaluate the quality of the reasons provided (though younger children seem to find apologies more important than excuses; Banerjee, Bennett, and Luke 2010). Young children will often inform violators of correct rules with the goal of changing their behavior (Rakoczy, Warneken, and Tomasello 2008). These behaviors suggest a recognition of the role that mental states play in reason-guided behavior. Of course, the same responses could reflect learned scripts or patterns of discourse. Perhaps children just know that when someone violates the rule, the thing to do is teach or tattle. One direction for future research is to more carefully assess children's responses to norm violations (see below). For example, do they teach only ignorant violators, but tattle on knowing?

Understanding behavior as governed by reasons involves a complex set of concepts and causal beliefs. A full account of the development of concepts of reasons will go beyond conceptions of representational mental states. The general question is how children come to understand mental causation, which involves conceptions of mind dependence and perhaps even ideas about free will (Kalish 1998b; Kushnir, Wellman, and Chernyak 2009). If the possession of empirical concepts requires understanding reasons, then there is a fairly high bar for such concepts. However, it is possible that the bar for empirical concepts is even higher. Empirical concepts were characterized as motivated by a particular kind of reason: a criterion of accuracy or truth. There is a reason to believe that whales are mammals, and that reason is that whales really are mammals. There may be many other reasons to hold the belief; for example, it may be more functional (leads to useful predictions about whales) or more socially acceptable. However, those reasons do not seem empirical. To believe something because it is true is to adhere to a particular kind of norm, an epistemic norm. Thus, a further constraint or requirement for empirical concepts is having concepts of norms distinct from other reasons. Only individuals who can understand themselves (and others) not just as having reasons, but as having normative reasons, will have empirical concepts.

18.3.4 Normative Concepts

The acquisition of normative concepts has been the focus of considerable research in the area of moral development. Kohlberg's classic theory (1981) described a series of stages in which children's concepts moved from utilitarian (will I/others benefit?) to conventional (is this legal?), to principled (is this just?). More recent theories hold that quite young children distinguish different domains of normative evaluation: they recognize that stealing is wrong because it violates a moral principle, and that eating spaghetti with one's fingers is wrong because it violates a conventional practice (Turiel 1998). There has been considerable debate concerning just how to distinguish different types of normative evaluations (Sripada and Stich 2006). However, there has been little discussion about just what makes any of these evaluations truly normative. For example, why is the judgment that stealing is wrong (because it is unfair) indicative of a normative evaluation? Couldn't the child be making a more basic evaluation of disliking? To judge stealing as wrong is to report disliking stealing. Note that this is not to suggest that stealing is wrong *because* people dislike it (a utilitarian norm). The question is whether evaluations of wrong (and right) involve distinctly normative concepts rather than some other kind.

The challenge is to identify some behavior or judgment that is evidence of normative evaluation that cannot be accounted for by ascribing the agent more basic evaluative concepts (such as liking or accuracy). There is some reason to believe that there will be no definitive evidence forthcoming. Normative evaluations may just be types of preferences (as in the stealing example above). For example, perhaps people's sense that they ought to have accurate concepts stems from a preference for accuracy (including both expected outcomes as well as a possible preference for rule following in its own right). In this case the person recognizes accuracy as a reason for holding certain beliefs, however that reason is not a norm.

In his analysis of social facts, Searle (1995) develops an account of what is distinctive about normative evaluations. He argues that normative evaluations cannot be identified with subjective states such as likings or preferences. Similarly, Sripada and Stich (2006) identify norms as ultimate ends: people are motivated to comply with norms because they are norms, not because doing so will achieve some other goal (such as satisfying a desire). Searle imagines a case in which one enters into an obligation with no desire to fulfill it, for example ordering a beer at a bar but not wanting to pay.

Having the obligation is different from any preferences about its fulfillment. It seems possible to have absolutely no desire to fulfill one's obligations. That (alone) does not dissolve the commitments; the drinker still has a reason to pay the tab. An epistemic norm involves a commitment to believe something because it is true, not because the belief will lead to other outcomes (e.g., conformity, utility; Kornblith 1993; Stich 1990). For Searle, the distinctive feature of normative evaluations is that they involve *desire-independent reasons*: people recognize reasons that are not grounded in preferences. The challenges are to identify such reasons, and to explain what they may be based on if not preferences. This characterization provides a basis for exploring the development of normative concepts: Does the child have a concept of desire-independent reason?

18.3.5   Desires and Norms

Having to do things you do not want to is more or less what childhood is all about. Children are frequently constrained by reasons that seem not their own. They readily recognize the force of norms, even norms governing behavior that has no obvious significance. For example, young children who see a person demonstrate a particular way to play a game will object when a different person uses a different strategy (Rakoczy, Warneken, and Tomasello 2008). The exact conditions that lead a child to object, to believe the actor has a reason to conform, are unclear, but they do not seem to require any expectation of benefit either to the child or to the actor (Kenward 2012; Schmidt, Rakoczy, and Tomasello 2011).

Importantly, children will not always object to nonstandard behaviors. For example, if a group has established a joint pretense, members of the group are expected to adhere to the pretense stipulations, but nongroup members are not (Kalish, Weissman, and Bernstein 2000; Schmidt, Rakoczy, and Tomasello 2012). These results suggest that children do not have a simple preference for conformity. Similarly, norms cannot be identified with pleasing others. Kalish and Cornelius (2007) asked children about changed desire scenarios. During school a teacher requests one behavior (do your homework in pen). After school, the teacher changes her mind and comes to prefer another behavior (homework in pencil). Does this change in preference change her students' obligation? Young school-aged children (seven-year-olds) recognized that the students have a reason to perform the old behavior (pen) even though the teacher would be happier with the alternative. Preschool-aged children thought the students were supposed to do what the teacher wants. In these stories, the students have reasons for both pen and pencil. Younger children may have been less sensitive to the particular evaluation requested: the language of evaluations is complex and generally ambiguous.

Empirical work suggests that young children do recognize desire-independent reasons. However, such results are not definitive. It is always possible to impute a desire that could be motivating children's evaluations (e.g., preferring conformity by game players but not nonplayers). But note that this ambiguity cuts both ways. Is it clear that young children recognize desire-based reasons? Perhaps all their reasons are desire independent. The key feature of a desire-based reason is subjectivity. Norms are objective, or at least intersubjective (Searle 1995). Young children tend to objectify the sources of mental states (another interpretation of the false-belief task). Perhaps it is the idea of a subjective reason that requires development. Although desire is often thought to be a more basic concept than norm, this may not be the case in terms of reasons.

Young children do appreciate something of the subjectivity of desires. They know that people may have different, even conflicting, motives (Rakoczy, Warneken, and Tomasello 2007; Repacholi and Gopnik 1997). Such motives are usually glossed as desires or preferences but could just as likely reflect conflicting obligations.[2] Kalish and Shiverick (2004) found that preschool-aged children often conflated preferences and obligations: they expected that a person would to want to follow a rule rather than want to do what he or she liked. There is some suggestion that young children look to norms and expectations in the environment to identify their desires. For example, they state they do not like forbidden toys (Costanzo, Grumet, and Brehm 1974). Desirability is often seen as an objective feature of the environment, rather than a subjective response (Yuill et al. 1996). Things are desired because they are good, not good because they are desired. The hypothesis is that the sources of motivation are not reliably distinguished as either subjective or objective. That something is good or right is not distinct from whether it is liked or desired.

18.4   Summary: Norms and Other Evaluations

This review of the developmental literature has not provided any definitive answers about the course of acquisition of normative and evaluative concepts. There is, however, a consistent theme: it is very difficult to sort out just how children appreciate the mind-dependent nature of reasons and motives. Quite young children have concepts that are at least important precursors of norms. Infants understand goal-directed actions (Gergely and Csibra 2003) and can evaluate behaviors as effective or efficient means to achieve goals. Toddlers have some conception of representation and seem able to evaluate accuracy (e.g., correct speakers' mistakes). And, of course, infants make positive and negative evaluations, likes and dislikes. Such evaluative abilities do not add up to a concept NORM, however. Norms are reasons, and understanding reasons requires understanding mental causation. In particular, reasons are not themselves mental states, but only influence behavior via mental states. A similar issue of mind dependence arises

2. For example, the language used in Rakoczy, Werneken, and Tomasello (2007) was suggestively normative (at least in English translation). Characters expressed opinions about what should be done.

when distinguishing different types of reasons. Norms are special types of reasons: reasons that do not depend on subjective evaluations of liking (desires). In neither case is it completely clear just when young children come to understand the relation between mind-dependent and mind-independent aspects of rational action.

Two points follow from this argument. First, more work needs to be done to understand young children's concepts of mental causation. The false-belief task has become caricatured as just a litmus test for "having" a theory of mind. In reality, this task, and others like it, are parts of a complex account of a wide range of conceptual abilities. Indeed, children's abilities to serve as moral agents, to make and be subject to normative evaluations, depends critically on their conceptions of mental causation. The second implication is that characterizing early conceptions of reasons as a "belief-desire" psychology is potentially misleading. Work on belief has pointed out that children's concept may be quite different from adults'. Young children emphasize objective determinants and have a narrower view of the conditions of misrepresentation. The same seems true of the concept DESIRE. Young children may have a more general concept PRO-ATTITUDE that does not distinguish (clearly) between objective and subjective determinants. If this is the case, then young children would seem to appreciate *desire-independent* reasons, in virtue of lacking the concept DESIRE. It may be that the concept NORM requires contrast with DESIRE: one can only appreciate a normative *should* by comparing with an instrumental *should*. In any case, it may be incorrect to think of young children as understanding themselves and others as motivated by intrinsic, personal, desires. Young children may begin their thinking about reasons with a much more objective focus (Kalish 2013; Perner and Roessler 2010).

18.5   Back to Concepts

Normative concepts are among the most important and distinctive components of the human cognitive repertoire. Arguably, what distinguishes human cognition from that of other animals is our ability to engage in cooperative interactions with normative structure (Tomasello and Rakoczy 2003). Some philosophers have taken the centrality of norms even further, arguing that the very possession of any concepts at all requires norms (Davidson 1984).

This chapter began by distinguishing two different senses of concepts and concept possession. Descriptive concepts as traces of past experiences seem very basic: almost any organism with memory would qualify as having concepts. In contrast, the conditions for empirical concepts ultimately involve rich understandings of norms and reasons. Indeed, empirical concepts involve so many components, or prerequisite concepts, it may be useful to think of a continuum of concepts. Each sense of concept involves increasingly complex understanding of norms and evaluation. The first step along the continuum is treating concepts as representations, or at least as systems of belief that may match or mismatch an external standard. The concept WHALE is not simply a record of associations, but is taken to be a more or less accurate record. A second step is appreciating that accuracy provides a reason for belief or conceptual change. Someone who learns that his or her concept WHALE is inaccurate has a reason to change that belief. Finally, the reasons motivating beliefs and concepts can be understood to be normative (epistemic norms) rather than prudential.

It is not clear exactly what level of empirical conception is required for various psychological functions of concepts. For example, when do concepts serve as or support word meanings? What level of concept underlies deference to experts? The more complex functions seem to depend on increasingly complex understanding of norms and reasons. Similarly, it seems plausible that conceptual development involves increasing appreciation of the empirical nature of concepts. Young children clearly have some evaluative concepts. They recognize inaccuracies and correct their own (and others') behavior. Certainly young children are active and responsive learners and give evidence of trying to adapt their beliefs to standards provided. Whether they are fully "reasonable" creatures, understanding rational action and normative evaluations is less clear.

It may be that a strict divide between descriptive and empirical concepts is too simple. There may be many ways to possess concepts, many different types of concepts. Understanding concepts as representations may not always involve understanding reasons for belief. Understanding reasons for belief may not always entail understanding normative commitment (versus instrumental goals). At least part of what distinguishes different types of concepts are the normative commitments and evaluations they entail. It is in this sense that norms are not just important examples of concepts; norms are central to the study of concepts at all.

References

Banerjee, R., M. Bennett, and N. Luke. 2010. Children's reasoning about the self-presentational consequences of apologies and excuses following rule violations. *British Journal of Developmental Psychology* 28:799–815.

Boghossian, P. 1989. Rule-following considerations. *Mind* 98:507–549.

Brandom, R. 1998. *Making It Explicit*. Cambridge, MA: Harvard University Press.

Burge, T. 1979. Individualism and the mental. *Midwest Studies in Philosophy* 4:73–121.

Chandler, M., and C. Lalonde. 1996. Shifting to an interpretive theory of mind: 5- to 7-year-olds' changing conceptions of mental life. In *The Five to Seven Year Shift: The Age of Reason and Responsibility*, ed. A. J. Sameroff and M. M. Haith, 111–139. Chicago: The University of Chicago Press.

Chater, N., J. B. Tenenbaum, and A. Yuille. 2010. Probabilistic models of cognition: Exploring the laws of thought. *Trends in Cognitive Sciences* 14:357–364.

Clark, E. V. 1992. Conventionality and contrast: Pragmatic principles with lexical consequences. In *Frames, Fields, and Contrasts: New Essays in Semantic and Lexical Organization*, ed. A. Lehrer and E. F. Kittay, 171–188. Hillsdale, NJ: Erlbaum.

Clement, F., S. Bernard, and L. Kaufmann. 2011. Social cognition is not reducible to theory of mind: When children use deontic rules to predict the behaviour of others. *British Journal of Developmental Psychology* 29:910–928.

Costanzo, P. R., J. F. Grumet, and S. S. Brehm. 1974. The effects of choice and source of constraint on children's attributions of preference. *Journal of Experimental Social Psychology* 10:352.

Davidson, D. 1984. *Inquiries into Truth and Interpretation*. Oxford: Clarendon Press.

DeLoache, J. S. 2004. Becoming symbol-minded. *Trends in Cognitive Sciences* 8:66–70.

Flavell, J. H. 1988. The development of children's knowledge about the mind: From cognitive connections to mental representations. In *Developing Theories of Mind*, ed. J. W. Astington and P. L. Harris, 244–267. Cambridge: Cambridge University Press.

Ganea, P. A., M. A. Allen, L. Butler, S. Carey, and J. S. DeLoache. 2009. Toddlers' referential understanding of pictures. *Journal of Experimental Child Psychology* 104:283–295.

Gelman, S. A. 2003. *The Essential Child: Origins of Essentialism in Everyday Thought*. New York: Oxford University Press.

Gergely, G., and G. Csibra. 2003. Teleological reasoning in infancy: the naive theory of rational action. *Trends in Cognitive Sciences* 7:287–292.

Harris, P. L. 2007. Trust. *Developmental Science* 10:135–138.

Jose, P. E. 1990. Just-world reasoning in children's immanent justice judgments. *Child Development* 61:1024–1033.

Kalish, C. W. 1995. Essentialism and graded membership in animal and artifact categories. *Memory & Cognition* 23:335–353.

Kalish, C. W. 1998a. Natural and artifactual kinds: Are children realists or relativists about categories? *Developmental Psychology* 34:376–391.

Kalish, C. W. 1998b. Reasons and causes: Children's understanding of conformity to social rules and physical laws. *Child Development* 69:706–720.

Kalish, C. W. 2007. Pragmatic and prescriptive aspects of children's categorization. In Conventionality in cognitive development: How children acquire shared representations in language, thought, and action, ed. C. Kalish and M. Sabbagh, special issue, *New Directions in Child and Adolescent Development* 115: 39–52.

Kalish, C. W. 2013. Status seeking: The importance of roles in early social cognition. In *The Development of Social Cognition*, ed. M. Banaji and S. A. Gelman, 216–210. New York: Oxford University Press.

Kalish, C. W., and R. Cornelius. 2007. What is to be done? Children's ascriptions of conventional obligations. *Child Development* 78:859–878.

Kalish, C. W., S. Kim, and A. G. Young. 2012. How young children learn from examples: Descriptive and inferential problems. *Cognitive Science* 36:1427–1448.

Kalish, C. W., and S. M. Shiverick. 2004. Children's reasoning about norms and traits as motives for behavior. *Cognitive Development* 19:401–416.

Kalish, C. W., and J. Thevenow-Harrison. 2014. Descriptive and inferential problems of induction: Toward a common framework. In B. Ross (Ed.) *Psychology of Learning and Motivation*, vol. 61, 1–39. San Diego: Academic Press.

Kalish, C. W., M. Weissman, and D. Bernstein. 2000. Taking decisions seriously: Young children's understanding of conventional truth. *Child Development* 71:1289–1308.

Keil, F. C. 1989. *Concepts, Kinds, and Cognitive Development*. Cambridge, MA: MIT Press.

Keil, F. C., and N. Batterman. 1984. A characteristic-to-defining shift in the development of word meaning. *Journal of Verbal Learning and Verbal Behavior* 23:221–236.

Kenward, B. 2012. Over-imitating preschoolers believe unnecessary actions are normative and enforce their performance by a third party. *Journal of Experimental Child Psychology* 112:195–207.

Khemlani, S., S. J. Leslie, and S. Glucksberg. 2012. Inferences about members of kinds: The generics hypothesis. *Language and Cognitive Processes* 27:887–900.

Koenig, M. A. 2002. Children's understanding of belief as a normative concept. *New Ideas in Psychology* 20:107–130.

Koenig, M. A., and C. H. Echols. 2003. Infants' understanding of false labeling events: The referential roles of words and the speakers who use them. *Cognition* 87:179–208.

Koenig, M. A., and A. L. Woodward. 2010. Sensitivity of 24-month-olds to the prior inaccuracy of the source: Possible mechanisms. *Developmental Psychology* 46:815–826.

Kohlberg, L. 1981. *The Philosophy of Moral Development: Moral Stages and the Idea of Justice*. vol. 1 of *Essays on Moral Development*. New York: HarperCollins.

Kornblith, H. 1993. Epistemic Normativity. *Synthese* 94:357–376.

Kripke, S. 1980. *Naming and Necessity*. Oxford: Basil Blackwell.

Kripke, S. 1982. *Wittgenstein on Rules and Private Language*. Cambridge, MA: Harvard University Press.

Kushnir, T., H. M. Wellman, and N. Chernyak. 2009. Preschoolers' understanding of freedom of choice. Paper presented at the 31st annual meeting of the Cognitive Science Society, July 29 to August 1, Amsterdam.

Margolis, E. 1998. How to acquire a concept. *Mind & Language* 13:347–369.

McClelland, J. L., M. M. Botvinick, D. C. Noelle, D. C. Plaut, T. T. Rogers, M. S. Seidenberg, and L. B. Smith. 2010. Letting structure emerge: Connectionist and dynamical systems approaches to cognition. *Trends in Cognitive Sciences* 14:348–356.

McDowell, J. 1994. *Mind and World*. Cambridge, MA: Harvard University Press.

Millikan, R. G. 1998. A common structure for concepts of individuals, stuffs, and real kinds: More Mama, more milk, and more mouse. *Behavioral and Brain Sciences* 21:55–65.

Murphy, G. L. 2002. *The Big Book of Concepts*. Cambridge, MA: MIT Press.

Murphy, G. L., and D. L. Medin. 1985. The role of theories in conceptual coherence. *Psychological Review* 92:289–316.

Onishi, K. H., and R. Baillargeon. 2005. Do 15-month-old infants understand false beliefs? *Science* 308:255–258.

Pea, R. D. 1982. Origins of verbal logic: Spontaneous denials by two- and three-year olds. *Journal of Child Language* 9:597–626.

Perner, J. 1991. *Understanding the Representational Mind*. Cambridge, MA: MIT Press.

Perner, J., and J. Roessler. 2010. Teleology and causal reasoning in children's theory of mind. In *Causing Human Action: New Perspectives on the Causal Theory of Action*, ed. J. Aguilar and A. A. Buckareff, 199–228. Cambridge, MA: MIT Press.

Piaget, J. 1965. *The Moral Judgment of the Child*. New York: Free Press.

Prasada, S. S., and E. M. Dillingham. 2009. Representation of principled connections: A window onto the formal aspect of common sense conception. *Cognitive Science* 33:401–448.

Preissler, M. A., and S. Carey. 2004. Do both pictures and words function as symbols for 18- and 24-month-old children? *Journal of Cognition and Development* 5:185–212.

Pritchard, C., and C. W. Kalish. 2001. Working at thought: Children's understanding of epistemic states and scientific reasoning. Paper presented at the meetings of the Cognitive Development Society, October 26–27, Virginia Beach, VA.

Putnam, H. 1982. *Reason, Truth, and History*. New York: Cambridge University Press.

Rakoczy, H., and M. Tomasello. 2009. Done wrong or said wrong? Young children understand the normative directions of fit of different speech acts. *Cognition* 113:205–212.

Rakoczy, H., F. Warneken, and M. Tomasello. 2007. This way! No! That way! 3-year-olds know that two people can have mutually incompatible desires. *Cognitive Development* 22:47–68.

Rakoczy, H., F. Warneken, and M. Tomasello. 2008. The sources of normativity: Young children's awareness of the normative structure of games. *Developmental Psychology* 44:875–881.

Repacholi, B. M., and A. Gopnik. 1997. Early reasoning about desires: Evidence from 14- and 18-month-olds. *Developmental Psychology* 33:12–21.

Rhodes, M., and S. A. Gelman. 2009. A developmental examination of the conceptual structure of animal, artifact, and human social categories across two cultural contexts. *Cognitive Psychology* 59:244–274.

Robinson, E. J., and W. P. Robinson. 1976. The young child's understanding of communication. *Developmental Psychology* 12:328–333.

Robinson, E. J., and S. J. Whittaker. 1986. Children's conceptions of meaning: Message relationships. *Cognition* 22:41–60.

Rogers, T. T., and J. L. McClelland. 2004. *Semantic Cognition: A Parallel Distributed Processing Approach*. Cambridge, MA: MIT Press.

Rozin, P., L. Millman, and C. Nemeroff. 1986. Operation of the laws of sympathetic magic in disgust and other domains. *Journal of Personality and Social Psychology* 50:703–712.

Schmidt, M. F. H., H. Rakoczy, and M. Tomasello. 2011. Young children attribute normativity to novel actions without pedagogy or normative language. *Developmental Science* 14:530–539.

Schmidt, M. F. H., H. Rakoczy, and M. Tomasello. 2012. Young children enforce social norms selectively depending on the violator's group affiliation. *Cognition* 124:325–333.

Schult, C. A., and H. M. Wellman. 1997. Explaining human movements and actions: Children's understanding of the limits of psychological explanation. *Cognition* 62:291.

Searle, J. R. 1995. *The Construction of Social Reality*. New York: Free Press.

Sloman, S. A., and B. C. Malt. 2003. Artifacts are not ascribed essences, nor are they treated as belonging to kinds. *Language and Cognitive Processes* 18:563–582.

Smith, E. E., and M. Grossman. 2008. Multiple systems for category learning. *Neuroscience and Biobehavioral Reviews* 32:249–264.

Sripada, C., and S. Stich. 2006. A framework for the psychology of norms. In *The Innate Mind, Volume 2: Culture and Cognition,* ed. P. Carruthers, S. Laurence, and S. Stich, 280–301. New York: Oxford University Press.

Stich, S. 1990. *The Fragmentation of Reason*. Cambridge, MA: MIT Press.

Taylor, M., G. L. Lussier, and B. L. Maring. 2003. The distinction between lying and pretending. *Journal of Cognition and Development* 4:299–323.

Tomasello, M., and H. Rakoczy. 2003. What makes human cognition unique? From individual to shared to collective intentionality. *Mind & Language* 18:121–147.

Turiel, E. 1998. The development of morality. In *Social, Emotional, and Personality Development*, 5th ed., vol. 3 of *Handbook of Child Psychology,* ed. W. Damon and N. Eisenberg, 863–932. New York: Wiley.

Wellman, H. M. 1992. *The Child's Theory of Mind*. Cambridge, MA: MIT Press.

Wellman, H. M. 2011. Reinvigorating explanations for the study of early cognitive development. *Child Development Perspectives* 5:33–38.

Wellman, H. M., D. Cross, and J. Watson. 2001. Meta-analysis of theory-of-mind development: The truth about false belief. *Child Development* 72:655–684.

Wimmer, H., and J. Perner. 1983. Beliefs about beliefs: Representation and constraining function of wrong beliefs in young children's understanding of deception. *Cognition* 13:103–128.

Woodward, A. L., J. A. Sommerville, and J. J. Guajardo. 2001. How infants make sense of intentional action. In *Intentions and Intentionality: Foundations of Social Cognition*, ed. B. F. Malle, L. J. Moses, and D. A. Baldwin, 149–170. Cambridge, MA: MIT Press.

Xu, F., and J. B. Tenenbaum. 2007. Word learning as Bayesian inference. *Psychological Review* 114:245–272.

Yuill, N., J. Perner, A. Pearson, and D. Peerbhoy. 1996. Children's changing understanding of wicked desires: From objective to subjective and moral. *British Journal of Developmental Psychology* 14:457–475.

IX Concepts in Context

19 All Concepts Are Ad Hoc Concepts

Daniel Casasanto and Gary Lupyan

19.1 Overview

To explain how people think and communicate, cognitive scientists posit a repository of concepts, categories, and word meanings that are stable across time and shared across individuals. But if concepts are stable, how can people use them so flexibly? Here we explore a possible answer: maybe this stability is an illusion. Perhaps all concepts, categories, and word meanings (CC&Ms) are constructed ad hoc, each time we use them. On this proposal, which we call the *ad hoc cognition* (AHC) framework, all words are infinitely polysemous, all communication is "good enough," and no idea is ever the same twice. The details of people's ad hoc CC&Ms are determined by the way retrieval cues (such as words) interact with the physical, social, and linguistic context. Commonalities across instantiations of CC&Ms yield some emergent stability and create the illusion of context-independent core properties. Here we argue that even the most stable-seeming CC&Ms are instantiated via the same processes as those that are more obviously ad hoc, and they vary (a) from one microsecond to the next within a given instantiation, (b) from one instantiation to the next within an individual, and (c) from person to person and group to group as a function of people's experiential history. If this is true, then a central goal of research on language and cognition should be to elucidate the fleeting, idiosyncratic neurocognitive representations that people actually use for thinking and communicating, rather than to discern the nature and origin of context-independent CC&Ms, which, we argue, only exist as theoretical abstractions. Thinking depends on brains, and brains are always changing; therefore thoughts are always changing. Rather than trying to explain concepts, categories, and word meanings as things that we *have in* our minds, like entries in a mental dictionary or mental encyclopedia, it may be more fruitful to build theories of conceptualizing, categorizing, and constructing word meanings: things that we *do with* our minds.

19.2   Concepts, Categories, and Word Meanings as Scientific Constructs

What's in our minds? How is our knowledge organized, stored, and used? Two millennia ago, these questions could only be addressed through allegory. For example, Plato considered whether the mind might be like an aviary, and each bird in it a piece of knowledge (*Theaetetus*, ca. 360 BCE). When the birds are not in use, they are free to flap about the cage of our memories. To use a piece of knowledge, we just need to catch (i.e., retrieve) the right bird.

It was clear then, as it is now, that there are not actually birds in our heads. But today, many people believe that the mind is populated by much more elusive creatures: concepts, categories, and word meanings. Aspects of the bird-catching model of the mind remain strongly entrenched insomuch as CC&Ms are often characterized as discrete entities that exist fully formed, even when we are not using them, to be summoned as needed.

According to the AHC framework we sketch here, concepts, categories, and word meanings only exist as "analytic fictions created by those who study them" (Barsalou 1987, 119), rooted in folk-psychological notions (e.g., concepts are entries in a mental encyclopedia, word meanings in a mental dictionary). As scientific constructs, these fictions can be useful for describing the neurocognitive states and processes that cognitive scientists seek to characterize, as long as one's "concept of X" or "the meaning of word Y" are not mistaken for natural kinds whose true essence can be discovered. Barrett, Mesquita, and Smith (2010) observe:

Scientific disciplines categorize. They divide their universe of interests into groupings of "kinds," name them, and then set about the business of understanding those kinds. … This categorization process functions like a sculptor's chisel, dividing up the world into figure and ground, leading scientists to attend to certain features and to ignore others. One consequence of scientific categorization is that we sometimes *essentialize* our subject matter, then search for evidence of those essences, without considering how context might influence or contribute to its very nature. (1; italics added)

Many researchers in the physical and biological sciences have shed the illusion that there exist observer-independent natural kinds. This belief is untenable in light of their fields' emerging understanding of ways in which the act of observing the world changes it, and in light of repeated illustrations that today's scientific constructs may become tomorrow's quaint footnotes in history. "Natural kinds" like phlogiston (the fire-like element chemists once believed to cause combustion reactions), the élan vital (the animating force believed, as recently as the twentieth century, to separate the living from the nonliving), and the brontosaurus (a chimera accidentally created out of two other species' bones) were once the subjects of serious scientific inquiry and popular belief. For many researchers, the scientist's job is now to construct useful models of the natural world, rather than to discern some latent "true" structure in it (see Chomsky 2002; Dunham and Banaji 2010).

We suggest that progress toward a scientific understanding of thinking and language use would be accelerated if researchers were to consider that (a) CC&Ms are human creations rather than natural kinds, and (b) the patterns of neurocognitive activity that CC&Ms are meant to provide a model of are constructed ad hoc and shaped by the physical and social contexts in which they are instantiated, on various time scales. Aspects of this proposal overlap with other proposals that emphasize the importance of context and the dynamism of language and thought (e.g., Barsalou 1987; Churchland 1986; Clark 1996, 1997; Elman 2004, 2009; Evans 2009; Hampton 2012; Machery 2009; Prinz 2002; Rogers and McClelland 2004; Smith and Samuelson 1997; Spivey 2007; Taylor and Zwaan 2009; Weiskopf 2009; Wittgenstein 1953).

We argue that it is necessary not only to acknowledge that thinking happens on the fly, but also to abandon the idea that CC&Ms have stable *cores* or *defaults* that people simply access whenever they instantiate CC&Ms (cf. Armstrong, Gleitman, and Gleitman 1983; Osherson and Smith 1981). Instead, each instantiation of CC&Ms is constructed on the basis of retrieval cues (internal and external) embedded in an ever-changing physical, social, and internal biological context.

Proposals in various literatures have argued that some circumstances can lead to the creation of ad hoc concepts (e.g., Allott and Textor 2012) or categories (e.g., Barsalou 1983). According to these proposals, however, ad hoc concepts and categories are created only when "common" concepts and categories—from which the ad hoc versions are qualitatively different—are unsuitable. We will argue here that common CC&Ms *are* ad hoc CC&Ms.

Across the cognitive sciences, concepts, categories, and word meanings are treated as distinct constructs for some purposes but as interdependent constructs for others: typically, *concepts* are what allow us to categorize, *categories* are the extensions of concepts, and *words have meanings* by virtue of activating (lexical) concepts. Accordingly, we will treat CC&Ms as indistinguishable throughout much of the chapter (thus their amalgamation in the term "CC&M"), but we will also treat them separately in order to engage with the distinct literatures about concepts, categories, and word meanings.[1]

In what follows, we first sketch an account of CC&Ms according to the ad hoc cognition framework, and then review evidence of the pervasive instability of mental representations that motivates this view. We illustrate this instability on three overlapping

---

1. We recognize that notions like concepts and categories, and the desiderata for what work they should do, may differ between psychologists and philosophers (Hampton 2012; Margolis and Laurence 2008; Machery 2009). In general, we will be writing from the perspective of researchers primarily interested in advancing theories in psychology and cognitive neuroscience.

time scales: *activation dynamics*, *local context effects*, and *experiential relativity*. We then offer some explanations of why, in spite of this demonstrable variability, people find it hard to escape the intuition that invariant CC&Ms exist, and briefly suggest ways in which the focus of research in the cognitive sciences should change in light of the ad hoc nature of cognition.

19.2.1   From *Concepts* to *Conceptualizing*

We will use the term *concept* to mean a dynamic pattern of information that is made active in memory transiently, as needed, in response to internally generated or external cues. Activating a "concept of X" is thinking about X; this should be uncontroversial. More controversially perhaps, we suggest that concepts exist only when they are being used. Concepts are not something we *have in* the mind, they are something we *do with* the mind. The word *concept* is, itself, problematic (though hard to avoid) insomuch as naming something with a noun seems to imply it is an object, but *conceptualizing* is a process (see Barsalou, Wilson, and Hasenkamp 2010; Spivey 2007).

Rather than a process of accessing a preformed package of knowledge, instantiating a concept is always a process of activating an ad hoc network of stored information in response to cues in context. These cues may be verbal (e.g., the word *dog*) or nonverbal (e.g., a barking sound), exogenous (coming from the outside world) or endogenous (internally generated). Cues may be processed consciously or unconsciously. Even if the exact same cue could be experienced repeatedly, the context in which it is experienced can never be re-created exactly, since one's internal neurocognitive state is part of the context. At minimum, the contexts at time 1 and time 2 differ because, at time 2, one's neurocognitive state has been altered by the processes that occurred at time 1.

As such, no two instantiations of "the same" concept are ever identical. In William James's words, "a permanently existing 'idea' ... which makes its appearance before the footlights of consciousness at periodic intervals is as mythological an entity as the Jack of Spades" (1890, 230). Different responses to the same cue (or similar cues) may be very similar, and this similarity may contribute to the illusion that concepts are stable over time, but as we argue in section 19.5.3, the unity of concepts has been greatly overestimated.

19.2.2   From *Categories* to *Categorizing*

In his landmark paper introducing the term *ad hoc categories* to psychology, Barsalou (1983) showed that goal-derived, for-the-nonce categories like *things to sell at a garage sale* are structured similarly to "common" categories like *vehicles*. According to Barsalou, the main distinction between ad hoc and common categories is that only common categories are well entrenched in memory. As evidence for this distinction, he reported single dissociations between behavioral responses to stimuli designed to activate ad hoc versus common categories. Arguably, however, the apparently categorical differences these studies showed could be artifacts of using categorical experimental designs, which artificially dichotomize a continuum of entrenchment in memory. Consistent with this assertion, Barsalou wrote that raising the frequency with which an ad hoc category is activated can turn it into a common category (at least for the individual who's doing the categorizing), and lowering the frequency of use can turn a common category into an ad hoc category.

Since there appears to be no categorical difference between these supposedly different types, we suggest that the terminological distinction between common (i.e., stable) and ad hoc categories has outlived its usefulness. In later writing, Barsalou (1987) appears amenable to the proposal that all categorizing is ad hoc:

Knowledge in long-term memory ... is relatively undifferentiated and continuous. ... It may be extremely difficult, if not impossible, to identify where the knowledge for a particular category in long-term memory begins and ends. To the extent that this is true, it is hard to imagine how there could be invariant representations for categories stored in long-term memory. (121)

On our view, *categorizing* (i.e., forming equivalence classes that support generalization and inference) is surely among the most important functions of the brain and mind, but *categories* as static structures in long-term memory—or as observer-independent collections of entities in the world—are a theoretical dead end.

19.2.3   From Accessing Word Meanings to Constructing Them

On standard views of language understanding, words have a finite variety of meanings and senses, and the context determines which of these gets "accessed." Accessing a word's meaning (or sense) means retrieving the appropriate concept (e.g., Jackendoff 2002; but see Elman 2004; Evans 2009). From the concept, activation often spreads to other information in long-term memory, which on many theories, is held to be *associated* with the concept or word meaning but is not *part of* it (e.g., Mahon and Caramazza 2008).

By contrast, within the AHC framework, word forms are cues to activate stored information, as needed and as determined by the specifics of the internal neurocognitive and external physical and social contexts. There is no principled distinction between information cued by a word-in-context that is *constitutive* of the meaning versus merely *associated* with it. The pattern of activity that constitutes a word's ad hoc meaning can be called the ad hoc concept that it activates in a given instance, but there is no memorized mapping between word forms and concepts. AHC, therefore, rejects an assumption that cuts across many otherwise divergent theories of language: that word meanings consist of memorized, conventionalized form-meaning pairings (e.g., Evans 2009; Jackendoff 2002; Langacker 2008; Snedeker and Gleitman 2004).

In short, according to AHC, words do not *have* meanings; rather, a word-in-context is a cue to construct what can be called its meaning for a given instantiation (see also Elman 2004). The meaning that gets activated in response to a word depends on the individual's history of processing this cue, as well as its current context. Meanings may be similar across instances, but they are always constructed in response to words-in-context functioning as complex retrieval cues. Since a given internal and external context can never be duplicated, no word ever has exactly the same meaning twice.

There is no principled distinction between the role that a word plays in cuing a neurocognitive representation and the role that its context plays. The impossibility of such a distinction becomes clear as soon as language use is considered in more ecologically valid settings than laboratory experiments involving exposure to single words. People don't activate meanings in response to words: they activate meanings in response to words-in-context. (This is true even when words appear in isolation, in the lab, as we will argue in the "local context" section, 19.5.2.)

Because words are not normally isolated but occur in the context of other linguistic, physical, and social (e.g., pragmatic) cues, people do not need to wait to hear a word in order to start understanding it: language users *predict* meaning. In a seminal study, participants who were presented with an array of objects (e.g., pictures of a ball, a train, a truck, and a cake) were likely to start looking at the cake upon hearing "*the boy will eat …,*" apparently finishing the sentence in their minds before hearing "*the cake*" (Altmann and Kamide 1999). The proportion of looks to the cake increased smoothly over the time that participants heard *eat … the … cake,* indicating that their representations of cake were constructed incrementally (see also DeLong, Urbach, and Kutas 2005; Dikker et al. 2010). Although the context rarely fully constrains what will follow, ordinary language understanding relies on the same predictive processes shown in this study: people begin to partially construct the meanings of words before they hear (or read) them, tuning the network of activated information gradually as the context constrains their predictions.

19.3   There Are No Context-Independent CC&Ms

Is a word's meaning *always* co-determined by its context, or are some words' meanings (or some aspects of word meaning) invariant across all contexts? Barsalou (1982) proposed that some features of concepts and word meanings are *context independent* (CI) and are activated maximally and obligatorily whenever a word is perceived, irrespective of its context. Other features are *context dependent* (CD): activated by the context, and *not* by the word that names the concept. The notion of CI features follows from the standard assumption that words activate fixed concepts, or conceptual cores, and the notion of CD features follows from the assumption that words are separable from their contexts; neither assumption is compatible with AHC. Even while arguing for the flexibility of concepts, Barsalou (1987) maintained the distinction between CD and CI properties, which still figures prominently in theories of concepts decades later (e.g., Machery 2009).

The experimental results supporting the CD-CI distinction (Barsalou 1982), however, like the results supporting the distinction between ad hoc and common categories, may primarily reflect the categorical distinctions imposed on the stimulus materials by the experimenters: if you ask a dichotomous question, often you get a dichotomous answer.

The properties that Barsalou identified as CD and CI appear to lie along a continuum of automaticity and context dependence—but it seems unlikely that any are context invariant. Barsalou suggested, for example, that the property "has a smell" is a context-invariant property of skunks, which is always maximally activated in response to this word. Is this true? In Barsalou's (1982) experiments, the target word (e.g., skunk) was always presented *before* the contextual information that determined whether the putatively invariant property was relevant. What if the contextual information had come first? If the prior context had made it clear that the skunk was a toy skunk, or a taxidermied skunk, or a lithograph of a skunk, wouldn't smell-related information have been activated less strongly than in other contexts involving, say, lifted tails? Crucially, Barsalou (1982) compared the activation of putatively context-invariant properties in contexts that supported the property versus neutral contexts: there were no tests of whether the supposedly CI properties were equally activated in contexts that were clearly *unsupportive* of the property, which would provide a stronger test of the property's context independence.

We suggest that there is no principled way to distinguish between context-dependent and context-independent information cued by words because there is no such thing as context-independent information. A given word may tend to activate some information more frequently and more automatically than other information, but all information is context dependent. Consistent with this assertion, Barsalou (1982, 1987) suggested that, over the course of experience, properties that start out as *context independent* in an individual's mind can become context dependent, and vice versa, belying any categorical distinction.[2]

---

2. In personal communication with D. C. (October 20, 2012), L. Barsalou agreed that the CI-CD distinction has outlived its usefulness. We consider Barsalou's studies establishing the constructs of ad hoc categories (1983) and context-dependent features of concepts (1982) to be of great theoretical importance, even though we disagree with their conclusions. These forward-thinking studies arguing that *some* CC&Ms are ad hoc paved the way for the proposal that *all* CC&Ms are ad hoc. Barsalou's contemporary writings on the dynamism of concepts (e.g., Barsalou, Wilson, and Hasenkamp 2010) are compatible with what we propose here and provide inspiration to further develop the AHC framework.

Demonstrations of context dependence are abundant (see section 19.5); here we focus on Barsalou's (1982) study because it represents a considered attempt to demonstrate that some properties of concepts are truly context independent, as posited by some influential theories of word meaning (e.g., Katz and Postal 1964), forming a fixed core of a word's meaning that is activated "on all occasions" and is "unaffected by contextual relevance" (Barsalou 1982, 82). In light of subsequent research, however, it seems unlikely that any aspects of concepts or word meanings fulfill these criteria.

The Stroop effect (Stroop 1935), which has been replicated in more than five hundred experiments (Besner, Stolz, and Boutilier 1997), is often interpreted as evidence that concepts are activated automatically in response to words. In a classic Stroop task, participants see the names of colors printed in ink that is either congruent in color (e.g., *blue* printed in blue ink) or incongruent (e.g., *blue* printed in red ink). Participants are instructed to ignore the words' meanings and simply to name the color of ink in which each word appears. Across many studies, reaction times (RTs) suggest it is impossible to comply with the instruction to ignore the words' meanings: naming the color of the ink is faster when it is congruent with a word's meaning than when it is incongruent. When we see the word *blue,* we can't help reading it; when we read it, we can't help activating its core meaning, the concept BLUE. Such data seem to support the claim that concepts—or at least their cores—are activated reflexively (i.e., automatically and maximally; Barsalou 1982), whenever we perceive the words that name them, independent of their processing context (which, in the case of the Stroop task, includes instructions *not* to activate words' meanings).

Yet, a small twist on the classic Stroop task shows this conclusion to be a fallacy. Besner and colleagues (1997) posited that the presence of congruent Stroop trials (which typically compose up to 50 percent of the trials in an experiment) were largely responsible for what appeared to be an irrepressible color-meaning interference effect. According to Besner and colleagues, seeing that the ink color matches the meaning of the word on many of the trials reinforces participants' expectation that these elements of the stimulus should match, creating or enhancing the RT disadvantage found for the trials on which they mismatch. If so, then the Stroop effect is, itself, a context effect: congruent trials establish a processing context that makes the incongruent trials especially difficult. To test this account of Stroop interference, rather than comparing RTs for incongruent trials to congruent trials, Besner and colleagues (1997) compared incongruent trials to neutral trials. In one condition, participants named the ink colors for color words printed in the wrong color (e.g., *blue* printed in red ink), and in the other (color-neutral) condition they named the ink colors for meaningless nonwords (e.g., *blat* printed in red ink). Besner and colleagues found the usual large RT disadvantage when responses to incongruent color words were compared to congruent color words (103 millisecond difference), but this effect was reduced to one-third of its size when incongruent color words were compared to color-neutral nonwords (34 millisecond difference). In another condition, Besner and colleagues found the Stroop effect was eliminated completely when only one of the letters in each word or nonword was colored, rather than all the letters.

In principle, it might be possible to explain away any results showing a failure to activate putatively "core" aspects of a word's meaning by positing that those aspects must not be part of the true core. But this strategy is fraught: How can we ever know what information is in a putative "core" (see section 19.4)? Furthermore, it is hard to imagine any theory of conceptual cores that does not hold "blueness" to be at the core of the concept BLUE. As such, it seems hard to imagine any theory of conceptual cores or default word meanings that can accommodate evidence that blueness is not reflexively activated when people read the word *blue*. Meaning is not a reflex.

19.4   Dissolving the Distinction between *Core* and *Periphery*

We argue that there are no cores to CC&Ms (cf. Margolis and Laurence 2008). The more frequently a piece of information is activated in response to a cue, and the more narrow the range of likely contexts, the more core-like that information may appear. Setting aside experimental results like those of Besner and colleagues (1997) reviewed above, a priori there is no principled way to distinguish an ad hoc concept's *core* from its *periphery*.

As Wittgenstein (1953) illustrated, if we really look for cores, we realize there is nothing to find. It is impossible to identify necessary or sufficient features that could serve as the invariant core of a common artifact concept like GAME, or even of a more constrained-seeming concept like NUMBER (Wittgenstein 1953, sections 66–100). Given a moment's reflection, it becomes clear that even those properties that seem the most likely candidates for core-hood are context dependent. What are the core features, for example, of TIGER? Surely *living* (but what if it's dead?); OK, *animate* (but what if it's a toy tiger?); *striped* (but what if it's bleached, or painted, or selectively bred?); *fierce* (but what if it's tame or lame?); *large* (but what if it's a baby, a dwarf, or a scale model?) If we cannot locate the invariant core of simple concrete ideas like TIGER, how can we hope to find the core of more abstract ideas like LOVE and JUSTICE that are notoriously vague and context dependent? To paraphrase Wittgenstein, there is no way to draw a boundary around a region of property space that includes all and only "core" properties and is valid for all instantiations of a concept or word meaning.

Some concepts like TRIANGLE, ODD NUMBER, and GRANDMOTHER may appear to be definable in terms of certain core, necessary, and sufficient conditions (Armstrong, Gleitman, and Gleitman 1983). Yet, even when people know the conditions and can articulate them, their classification behavior is not predicted by these conditions. For example, although people can articulate the definitions of odd and even numbers, their categorization behavior—both timed and untimed—shows that a number like 798 is *more odd* than a number like 400. Participants reliably miscategorize nonprototypical even numbers like 798 as odd numbers, misclassify scalene triangles as nontriangles, and believe that grandmothers with fewer grandchildren have a lower chance of winning a contest whose only criterion is being a grandmother (Lupyan 2013). Thus, even though people's explicit definitions of notions like *even number* may be core-like and invariant (e.g., an even number is one that yields an integer when divided by two), their actual categorization behavior cannot be explained by concepts with a fixed core. The apparently crisp definitions available to people metacognitively are not reflected in their cognition.[3]

Arguably, if one averages all the various instantiations of TIGER or GRANDMOTHER over time, people, and contexts, a conceptual core could be said to emerge at their intersection. But this intersection (which could be thought of as a point or as a probability density function in some state space) is a figment of the cognitive scientist's imagination. There is an old joke about three statisticians who go duck hunting. When a duck flies across the horizon, the first statistician shoots one meter above the duck, and the second shoots one meter below the duck. The third statistician calls out, "We got him!" Universal, invariant, conceptual cores can be said to "exist," created by averaging over everyone's idiosyncratic neurocognitive representations, in the same sense that those statisticians can be said to have bagged that duck.

In contrast with theorists who posit that conceptual cores are always activated (e.g., Barsalou 1982; Machery 2009), some theorists posit a kind of core that serves as a default representation that gets activated "most of the time" (Prinz 2002, 157), "when no context is specified" (Prinz 2002, 154). We argue below that a context is *always* specified (though not always explicitly), that the specifics of the context are always in flux (especially when the internal neurocognitive context is taken into account), and that myriad aspects of the internal and external context shape the representations that people form, on multiple time scales.

19.5   Variability of CC&Ms on Three Time Scales

The proposal that all CC&Ms are constructed ad hoc is motivated by the observation that CC&Ms are inherently variable: much more variable than they appear on most characterizations in cognitive science—a field where "representations" were once implemented in punch cards. Unlike the invariant representations in a punch card

---

3. Explaining these effects as being products of a peripheral "identification procedure" (Armstrong, Gleitman, and Gleitman 1983) hits a dead end when all aspects of categorization of formal concepts are shown to be subject to graded typicality effects (Lupyan 2013). As articulated by Greg Murphy, "At the end of the day, the core serves only as a security blanket to make linguists and philosophers feel better about their concepts, but the behavior all seems to be controlled by the identification procedure. So, if you got rid of the core, your theory's explanatory power would be equal to that of one with a core" (personal communication with G. L., August 13, 2013).

stack, representations in the human mind vary on at least three partly overlapping time scales: (a) from one microsecond to the next within a given instantiation (what we will call *activation dynamics*), (b) from one instantiation to the next within an individual as a function of the *local context*, and (c) from person to person and group to group as a function of people's experiential history (*experiential relativity*; Casasanto and Henetz 2012).

19.5.1   Activation Dynamics

Thinking happens in brains, and brains are always changing. As a consequence, thoughts are always changing. When someone reads the word *dog*, sees a picture of a dog, or sees a dog, what happens after the eyes send the retinal image to V1? When can it be said that they have *seen* the dog or activated the concept DOG, and where in the brain do these acts of perception and conception occur? As information flows from V1, it disperses: some follows the dorsal *where* pathway into the parietal cortex, carried primarily by fast magnocellular connections. Other information follows the ventral *what* pathway carried by the relatively slow parvocellular system.

Even though the new visual information has passed through nearly all the responsive areas within the first 150 milliseconds of this initial "forward sweep" through the brain, visual cortex neurons keep firing at increased rates for hundreds of milliseconds more. During this continued firing, lower-level neurons are responding to feedback from higher brain areas, presumably coordinating the activity in visual areas with distinct receptive fields, composing a coherent percept through dynamic feed-forward, feedback, and lateral connections. The visual brain reconfigures itself continuously throughout the act of seeing (e.g., Lamme and Roelfsema 2000). In parallel, the evolving activity in the visual system engages frontally mediated retrieval processes that incrementally activate relevant information in posterior areas involved in episodic and semantic memory processes.

Where and when, then, is a dog percept or a dog concept activated? The act of perceiving and conceptualizing a dog is not circumscribed, spatially or temporally. The distribution of neurocognitive representations over both time and space makes it impossible to delineate either a moment or an anatomical location in which CC&Ms reside. The perceiver's neurocognitive response to the *dog* stimulus is continuous with their prior neurocognitive activity and with their responses to the context in which the stimulus occurred; it fades gradually into their response to subsequent endogenous and exogenous cues (Spivey 2007).

19.5.2   Local Context

In cognitive psychology, researchers generally try to eliminate effects of context as much as possible, in order to isolate their processes of interest. It is easy to imagine, for example, that by presenting participants with single words or sentences, in randomized order, it should be possible to observe the concepts they "correspond to" in their pure, default form. But there are at least two major problems with this assumption.

The first problem is that, outside the lab, people don't just rely on the cues they're receiving in the experiments to construct an understanding of them; they rely on these cues-in-context. Clark (1997) illustrates how the representations people construct in response to linguistic cues depend critically on their physical and social environments. Even a simple utterance like "I'm hot" may be impossible to interpret in any way approximating its intended meaning unless the listener knows who is saying it and where, when, why, and to whom it is being said. Depending on these factors, this utterance could mean, for example, that the speaker is (1) physically warm, (2) sexually aroused, (3) stolen, (4) radioactive, or (5) on a lucky streak. It is likely that, in the lab, participants might reliably converge on the literal "physical warmth" interpretation of this utterance—but this could be a response to the pragmatics of the experimental context, and could mask other ordinary processes of meaning construction.

There is a second problem with the assumption that we can study CC&Ms in a "neutral context": Even in the most sterile of experimental settings, participants are immersed in a physical context (that of the university psych lab), a social context (interacting with the experimenter, playing the role of the subject, etc.), and their internal biological and neurocognitive context, all of which have consequences for the representations they form. These implicit aspects of the context mold people's minds, in real time, all the time.

A growing catalog of studies at the intersection of metaphor research, emotion, and judgment and decision making illustrates how the incidental physical context affects thinking and language understanding. For example, the spatial metaphor "to move *forward* in time" is ambiguous: it can mean to move earlier or later, depending on the comprehender's spatial perspective. In one study, people's understanding of *forward* was found to vary as a function of their spatial location in a cafeteria line: participants near the end of the line interpreted *forward* to mean earlier in time, whereas those at the front of the line (who had just moved forward through space) thought the same word meant later (Boroditsky and Ramscar 2002). In other studies, the physical context affects memory retrieval. Participants retrieve positive memories more efficiently when they are sitting up tall, and negative memories more efficiently when they are slumping down (Riskind 1983). Likewise, given the same set of memory prompts like "tell me about something that happened last summer," people are more likely to retrieve happy memories when they are assigned to move objects upward during retrieval, and more likely to retrieve sad memories when assigned to move objects downward (Casasanto and Dijkstra 2010). Our actions form one dynamic aspect of the context that shapes our thoughts.

Quirks of the physical context affect aspects of the self that people normally think of as stable, such as their morality or their political orientation. In one study, participants in a room with slightly dim lighting were more likely to cheat than those in a room with brighter lighting (Zhong, Bohns, and Gino 2010). This was true even though their cheating was not actually less detectable. In another study, participants were seated in an office chair with one wheel removed, forcing them to lean to the left or the right, while completing a political attitudes questionnaire. Participants who leaned to the left (literally) were more sympathetic to liberal views than those who were induced to lean to the right (Oppenheimer and Trail 2010).

Context is ubiquitous and varied, and so are its effects on the neurocognitive representations people form. Most of the time, the effects of local context on our mental functions are, paradoxically, both dramatic and nearly invisible to us—like the effect of the air around us on bodily functions.

19.5.3 Experiential Relativity

Some aspects of context are more enduring than those reviewed above, such as the language spoken in people's community, their cultural conventions, and the peculiarities of their bodies. Patterns of linguistic, cultural, and bodily experience influence people's minds; people with different patterns of experience tend to think differently, in predictable ways. Together, the influences of these separable streams of experience can be called *experiential relativity* effects (Casasanto and Henetz 2012).

19.5.3.1 Linguistic Relativity *Linguistic relativity*, the idea that people who speak different languages think differently as a consequence, was once rejected for lack of empirical support. But accumulating evidence suggests that lexical and grammatical differences across languages cause their speakers to form systematically different representations, in fundamental cognitive domains such as *time* (e.g., Boroditsky et al. 2001), *space* (Majid et al. 2004), *motion* (Papafragou, Hulbert, and Trueswell 2008), and *color* (Regier and Kay 2009). Beyond influencing high-level language-mediated thinking, experience using language can also influence low-level perceptual and motor representations, as evidenced by nonlinguistic psychophysical experiments (Casasanto 2008; Dolscheid et al. 2013; see also Lupyan and Spivey 2010a, 2010b; Lupyan and Ward 2013; Thierry et al. 2009). Once we give up the idea of fixed concepts that languages map onto, language can be more productively viewed as a system for activating and manipulating CC&Ms (see Lupyan 2012; Willems and Casasanto 2011; Zwaan 2004).

19.5.3.2 Cultural Relativity Experiential relativity extends beyond language: Patterns of cultural experience and bodily experience also shape the brain and mind, via some of the same mechanisms by which language does. In one example of *cultural relativity*, across cultures people implicitly conceptualize time as flowing either from left to right or from right to left. This difference cannot be attributed to patterns in language (i.e., no language uses "earlier is *left*" metaphors), or physical experience (i.e., it is not the case that earlier events happen on our left and later events on our right in the natural world). Rather, this habit of thinking appears to be established as people use the particular reading and writing system in their culture (Casasanto and Bottini 2014) and interact with culture-specific artifacts like calendars and graphs (Tversky, Kugelmass, and Winter 1991).

Much broader forms of cultural relativity have also been documented. According to Nisbett and colleagues (2001), members of East Asian and Western cultures have predictably different cognitive styles: whereas Westerners (Europeans and Americans) tend to think individualistically, Easterners (Chinese, Japanese, and Koreans) think more collectivistically, in terms of relationships among members of a society and between people and their environment. Early tests of this proposal seemed too poetic to convince some scientists. For instance, when asked to describe an underwater scene, American participants were likely to start off by mentioning the most prominent individual fish ("there's a big fish …"). By contrast, Japanese participants began by describing the surroundings ("there's a pond …"). Yet, on a skeptical interpretation, such results could merely show that Americans and Japanese people describe things differently, not that they perceive or conceptualize them differently.

Further studies challenged this skeptical position. In one study, Japanese and Americans were shown a box with a vertical line inside of it. They were then shown a second box of a different size and asked to draw a vertical line inside it that matched the one in the first box. Half of the time, participants were told to make the line "the same" as the original, meaning the same absolute length (absolute condition). The other half of the time, they were told to draw a line that was the "same" length as the first in proportion to the surrounding box (relative condition). Results showed that Americans were more accurate in the absolute task, which required focusing on an individual object and ignoring its surroundings, but Japanese participants performed better on the relative task, which required perceiving and remembering an object in its context (Kitayama et al. 2003).

The conclusions about the extent of cross-cultural differences in thinking that are supported by these laboratory tests, for which researchers prioritized experimental control and sought to test cognitive mechanisms, appear dwarfed by field anthropologists' reports of differences in culture-specific practices and attitudes. For example, Henrich and colleagues (2010) report the following difference between cultures:

In the tropical forests of New Guinea, the Etoro believe that for a boy to achieve manhood he must ingest the semen of his elders. This is accomplished through ritualized rites of passage that require young male initiates to fellate a senior member. ... In contrast, the nearby Kaluli maintain that male initiation is only properly done by ritually delivering the semen through the initiate's anus, not his mouth. The Etoro revile these Kaluli practices, finding them disgusting. (61)

To many readers, these rituals may seem immoral; to the Etoro and the Kaluli, apparently they do not, suggesting that concepts like morality and manhood are not universal; they are shaped by specifics of our cultures.

19.5.3.3 Bodily Relativity Beyond linguistic and cultural relativity, different bodily experiences produce *bodily relativity* effects (Casasanto 2011, 2014). For example, right- and left-handers, who typically perform actions like throwing and writing with different hands, also use premotor regions in opposite hemispheres to represent the meanings of the verbs that name these actions (Willems, Hagoort, and Casasanto 2010). Contra all previous models of language in the brain (including those that posit a role for the motor system in constructing verb meanings; e.g., Pulvermüller 2005), right-hemisphere motor areas are activated by action verbs in people who use these areas to perform common manual actions, demonstrating how small differences in habitual motor actions can induce gross changes in cortical representations of language.

Bodily differences can also affect people's conceptualizations of things they can never see or touch, including their notions of good and bad. Implicitly, right-handers associate positive qualities like honesty, kindness, and intelligence with the right side of space, but left-handers associate positive things with the left, in spite of patterns in language and culture that link *good* with *right*. When asked to decide which of two products to buy, which of two job applicants to hire, or which of two alien creatures looks more trustworthy, right- and left-handers tend to respond differently: right-handers tend to prefer the product, person, or creature presented on their right side, but left-handers prefer the one on their left (Casasanto 2009). This pattern persists even when people make judgments orally, without using their hands to respond. Children as young as five years old already make evaluations according to handedness and spatial location, judging animals shown on their dominant side to be nicer and smarter than animals on their nondominant side (Casasanto and Henetz 2012).

Beyond the laboratory, the association of *good* with the dominant side can be seen in left- and right-handers' spontaneous speech and gestures. In the final debates of the 2004 and 2008 U.S. presidential elections, positive speech was more strongly associated with right-hand gestures and negative speech with left-hand gestures in the two right-handed candidates (Bush, Kerry), but the opposite association was found in the two left-handed candidates (McCain, Obama; Casasanto and Jasmin 2010). In a simulated election, left-handers were more likely than right-handers to vote for a candidate listed on their "good side" of a ballot, suggesting these body-based implicit associations could have significant influences on real-world decisions (Kim, Krosnick, and Casasanto 2014).

19.5.3.4 Flexibility of Experiential Relativity Effects

Importantly, the effects of experiential relativity are enduring but also flexible. Habits of mental representation can be changed rapidly when people are exposed to new patterns of linguistic, cultural, or bodily experience. For example, English speakers, who normally conceptualize time as a horizontal line, can be induced to think about time vertically after about twenty minutes of exposure to Mandarin-like up-down metaphors (Boroditsky 2001), or to think about time in terms of three-dimensional space after exposure to Greek-like metaphors that express duration in terms of volume rather than length (Casasanto 2008). Exposing members of a left-to-right-reading culture to a few minutes of mirror-reversed writing can *reverse* the flow of time in their minds, as indicated by RT tests of implicit space-time associations (Casasanto and Bottini 2014). Handedness-based judgments about the abstract ideas of goodness and badness can also be completely reversed, after long-term changes in functional handedness due to unilateral stroke, and even after short-term motor training in the laboratory (Casasanto and Chrysikou 2011).

Are these demonstrations of rapid retraining a problem for interpreting longer-term experiential relativity effects? Only if one adheres to a traditional view of concepts and assumes that "true" relativity effects should result in alterations to concepts' stable cores. If all concepts are constructed ad hoc, in response to cues in context, both long-term and transient relativity effects are demystified. Language, culture, and the body are ubiquitous parts of the context in which people use their minds. To the extent that these aspects of context are constant over time, the mental representations people form will tend to appear constant, exhibiting commonalities across instantiations. To the extent that these aspects of the context vary, the representations people form may vary accordingly (Casasanto 2011, 2014).

19.6   The Illusion of Invariant CC&Ms

The patterns of neurocognitive activity that cognitive scientists characterize as concepts, categories, and word meanings vary according to the contexts in which people instantiate them: from millisecond to millisecond, instantiation to instantiation, individual to individual, and group to group. Why, then, in the face of this pervasive and demonstrable variability, do people have the illusion that CC&Ms are generally stable, across time and across people? We briefly sketch three sources of this illusion.

19.6.1 Conceptual Change Blindness

Observers are often unaware of changes in the visible world around them from one moment to the next, giving rise to phenomena like change blindness. For example, when a participant's face-to-face conversation with an experimenter is briefly interrupted, they often fail to notice changes that occur—even enormous changes—like having their interlocutor vanish and be replaced by a different person (Simons and Levin 1998).

The illusion of stable CC&Ms may arise, in part, from what we will call *conceptual change blindness*. Most of the time, people probably do not introspect on the contents of their ordinary mental representations. But even if they tried, they might be unable to notice, for example, the many ways in which representations cued by a given word differ from one instantiation to the next.

This suggestion is consistent with evidence that, although people generally think they understand how common devices work (e.g., a lock, a zipper), their actual understanding is surprisingly shallow (Keil 2003). As Keil argues, our skeletal knowledge appears more fleshed out than it is, in part because people enrich their theories of how things work on the fly, incorporating information that the current context makes available, ad hoc.

The notorious fallibility of eyewitness memory, in particular people's willingness to substitute incorrect details of a witnessed event for correct ones (e.g., Loftus 1979), provides another line of support for the existence of conceptual change blindness. If conceptual change blindness is anything like visual change blindness, people may intuit invariance even when they are faced with enormous variability in their own mental representations and others'.

19.6.2 The Power of Words

One factor that may contribute to conceptual change blindness, and more broadly to the illusion of invariant CC&Ms, is the use of words to label our ideas—particularly the use of nouns (Barsalou, Wilson, and Hasenkamp 2010). As William James (1890) observed:

Whenever we have a word … to denote a certain group of phenomena we are prone to suppose a substantive entity existing beyond the phenomena, of which the word shall be the name (Barrett, Mesquita, and Smith 2010, 195).

Words encourage psychological essentialism: If we have a word, it is tempting to assume that there must be some observer-independent category of entities that the word names (Barrett, Mesquita, and Smith 2010; Waxman 2004). Verbal labels may help speakers construct representations that are, indeed, more stable across time and across individuals than representations constructed without labels (Lupyan, Rakison, and McClelland 2007; Lupyan and Thompson-Schill 2012), but verbal labeling also contributes to the *illusion* that different representations activated by the same label are identical to one another.

19.6.3   The Fallacy of Shared Concepts and Mutual Understanding

If CC&Ms are not stable across instances and individuals, how do people ever understand each other? The short answer is: they don't—at least not as well as they might think they do.

On traditional theories of language processing, the result of the comprehension process is a detailed, accurate representation of the input. In reality, however, the representations people form appear to be shadowy reflections of the input, merely "good enough" to achieve communicative goals, at least partially, at least much of the time (Ferreira et al. 2002). Comprehenders typically overlook semantic anomalies in sentences like "the authorities had to decide where to bury the *survivors*." Likewise, they often miss syntactic complexities of sentences like "the dog was bitten by the man," interpreting this unlikely scenario as sensible.

Comprehension failures in these carefully constructed cases may reveal the kind of good-enough processing that people engage in routinely. Rather than a precise, complete, and fully combinatorial process, language use is a process of constructing ad hoc representations cued by words and constructions in context, which may often be shallower, more error prone, and more context dependent than language researchers have suspected (Clark 1996, 1997).

Moreover, successful communication should not be interpreted as evidence that interlocutors shared matching CC&Ms. Suppose, for example, that a speaker says "I saw Julio yesterday." The speaker's memory of "seeing Julio" may involve seeing him in the morning, whereas the listener activated a representation of seeing Julio in the afternoon. This discrepancy may be inconsequential and go unnoticed: we suspect this is the case for innumerable discrepancies between what speakers say and what listeners understand. Understanding is always incremental, is partial, is usually full of errors that go unnoticed, and never represents an exact match between speaker and listener.

In some cases, a match between the speaker's and listener's neurocognitive representations would be undesirable; communicative success often depends on *complementarity* between interlocutors' mental representations. For example, if a speaker says, "I'm freezing!" this speech act would be unsuccessful if what the listener represents is also "I am freezing," or even "He is freezing." It would be a success if this utterance results in the listener representing the intention, "I think I'll close the window" (Grice, Cole, and Morgan 1975; Van Ackeren et al. 2013). Communication is successful to the extent that communicative goals are achieved despite the inevitable mismatches between interlocutors' neurocognitive representations.

19.7   Conclusions

In the effort to explain how people think and communicate, cognitive science has created some of its own hardest problems: mistaking human inventions for natural kinds, and then struggling to explain their "true" nature. Common assumptions about CC&Ms made by cognitive scientists and laypeople are at odds with what is known about the brain and behavior. By rethinking these constructs, it is possible to dissolve some of the classic quandaries at the heart of cognitive science, and to frame a new set of challenges for research on language and mind.

According to the AHC framework, all concepts, categories, and word meanings are constructed ad hoc and differ from one instantiation to the next, within and between individuals and groups. CC&Ms are inseparable from their contexts, and are shaped by the contexts in which they are instantiated on every time scale, from the millisecond to the lifetime. Even in "fictive preparations" of CC&Ms in the psychology lab, they are not context independent; experiments occur in specific physical and social contexts. More generally, people's memories, languages, cultures, and bodies are ubiquitous parts of the context in which they use their minds.

If future research can demonstrate the kind of invariance in CC&Ms that is commonly assumed, AHC will have to be revised or abandoned. We have argued, however, that past research that has been interpreted as evidence of invariance in CC&Ms is not convincing; despite people's intuitions, invariance is an illusion. If this is true, then a central goal of research on language and cognition should be to elucidate the fleeting, idiosyncratic neurocognitive representations that people *actually use* for thinking and communicating—and to explain how apparent stability emerges from pervasive variability.

References

Allott, N., and M. Textor. 2012. Lexical pragmatic adjustment and the nature of ad hoc concepts. *International Review of Pragmatics* 4 (2): 185–208.

Altmann, G., and Y. Kamide. 1999. Incremental interpretation at verbs: Restricting the domain of subsequent reference. *Cognition* 73 (3): 247–264.

Armstrong, S. L., L. R. Gleitman, and H. Gleitman. 1983. What some concepts might not be. *Cognition* 13 (3): 263–308.

Barrett, L. F., B. Mesquita, and E. R. Smith. 2010. The context principle. In *The Mind in Context*, ed. B. Mesquita, L. F. Barrett, and E. R. Smith, 1–21. New York: Guilford Press.

Barsalou, L. W. 1982. Context-independent and context-dependent information in concepts. *Memory & Cognition* 10:82–93.

Barsalou, L. W. 1983. Ad hoc categories. *Memory & Cognition* 11:211–227.

Barsalou, L. W. 1987. The instability of graded structure: Implications for the nature of concepts. In *Concepts and Conceptual Development*, ed. U. Neisser, 101–140. Cambridge: Cambridge University Press.

Barsalou, L. W., C. D. Wilson, and W. Hasenkamp. 2010. On the vices of nominalization and the virtues of contextualizing. In *The Mind in Context*, ed. B. Mesquita, L. Feldman-Barrett, and E. Smith, 334–360. New York: Guilford Press.

Besner, D., J. A. Stolz, and C. Boutilier. 1997. The Stroop effect and the myth of automaticity. *Psychonomic Bulletin & Review* 4 (2): 221–225.

Boroditsky, L. 2001. Does language shape thought? English and Mandarin speakers' conceptions of time. *Cognitive Psychology* 43 (1): 1–22.

Boroditsky, L., and M. Ramscar. 2002. The roles of body and mind in abstract thought. *Psychological Science* 13 (2): 185–188.

Casasanto, D. 2008. Who's afraid of the Big Bad Whorf? Cross-linguistic differences in temporal language and thought. *Language Learning* 58 (1): 63–79.

Casasanto, D. 2009. Embodiment of abstract concepts: Good and bad in right- and left-handers. *Journal of Experimental Psychology: General* 138 (3): 351–367.

Casasanto, D. 2011. Different bodies, different minds: The body specificity of language and thought. *Current Directions in Psychological Science* 20 (6): 378–383.

Casasanto, D. 2014. Bodily relativity. In *Routledge Handbook of Embodied Cognition*, ed. L. Shapiro, 108–117. New York: Routledge.

Casasanto, D., and R. Bottini. 2014. Mirror reading can reverse the flow of time. *Journal of Experimental Psychology: General* 143(2): 473–479.

Casasanto, D., and E. G. Chrysikou. 2011. When left is "right": Motor fluency shapes abstract concepts. *Psychological Science* 22 (4): 419–422.

Casasanto, D., and K. Dijkstra. 2010. Motor action and emotional memory. *Cognition* 115 (1): 179–185.

Casasanto, D., and T. Henetz. 2012. Handedness shapes children's abstract concepts. *Cognitive Science* 36:359–372.

Casasanto, D., and K. Jasmin. 2010. Good and bad in the hands of politicians. *PLoS ONE* 5 (7): e11805.

Chomsky, N. 2002. *On Nature and Language*. Cambridge: Cambridge University Press.

Churchland, P. S. 1986. *Neurophilosophy: Toward a Unified Science of the Mind/Brain*. Cambridge, MA: MIT Press.

Clark, H. H. 1996. *Using Language*. Cambridge: Cambridge University Press.

Clark, H. H. 1997. Dogmas of understanding. *Discourse Processes* 23 (3): 567–598.

DeLong, K. A., T. P. Urbach, and M. Kutas. 2005. Probabilistic word pre-activation during language comprehension inferred from electrical brain activity. *Nature Neuroscience* 8 (8): 1117–1121.

Dikker, S., H. Rabagliati, T. A. Farmer, and L. Pylkkänen. 2010. Early occipital sensitivity to syntactic category is based on form typicality. *Psychological Science* 21 (5): 629–634.

Dolscheid, S., S. Shayan, A. Majid, and D. Casasanto. 2013. The thickness of musical pitch: Psychophysical evidence for linguistic relativity. *Psychological Science* 24 (5): 613–621.

Dunham, Y., and M. R. Banaji. 2010. Platonic blindness and the challenge of understanding context. In *The Mind in Context*, ed. L. Feldman-Barrett, B. Mesquita, and E. Smith, 201–213. New York: Guilford.

Elman, J. L. 2004. An alternative view of the mental lexicon. *Trends in Cognitive Sciences* 8 (7): 301–306.

Elman, J. L. 2009. On the meaning of words and dinosaur bones: Lexical knowledge without a lexicon. *Cognitive Science* 33 (4): 547–582.

Evans, V. 2009. *How Words Mean*. Oxford: Oxford University Press.

Ferreira, F., V. Ferraro, and K. Bailey. 2002. Good-enough representations in language comprehension. *Current Directions in Psychological Science* 11:11–15.

Grice, H. P., P. Cole, and J. Morgan. 1975. Logic and conversation. In *Syntax and Semantics,* vol. 3: *Speech Acts,* ed. P. Cole and Jerry L. Morgen, 45–47. New York: Academic Press.

Hampton, J. A. 2012. Thinking intuitively: The rich (and at times illogical) world of concepts. *Current Directions in Psychological Science* 21 (6): 398–402.

Henrich, J., S. J. Heine, and A. Norenzayan. 2010. The weirdest people in the world? *Behavioral and Brain Sciences* 33 (2–3): 61–83, discussion 83–135.

Jackendoff, R. S. 2002. *Foundations of Language: Brain, Meaning, Grammar, and Evolution*. Oxford: Oxford University Press.

James, W. 1890. *Principles of Psychology*. Vol. 1. New York: Holt.

Katz, J., and P. Postal. 1964. *An Integrated Theory of Linguistic Descriptions*. Cambridge, MA: MIT Press.

Keil, F. 2003. Folkscience: Coarse interpretations of a complex reality. *Trends in Cognitive Sciences* 7 (8): 368–373.

Kim, N., J. Krosnick, and D. Casasanto. 2014. Moderators of candidate name order effects in elections: An experiment. *Political Psychology* doi: 10.1111/pops.12178.

Kitayama, S., S. Duffy, T. Kawamura, and J. T. Larsen. 2003. Perceiving an object and its context in different cultures: A cultural look at new look. *Psychological Science* 14:201–206.

Lamme, V., and P. Roelfsema. 2000. The distinct modes of vision offered by feedforward and recurrent processing. *Trends in Neurosciences* 23 (11): 571–579.

Langacker, R. 2008. *Cognitive Grammar: A Basic Introduction*. New York: Oxford University Press.

Loftus, E. F. 1979. *Eyewitness Testimony*. Cambridge, MA: Harvard University Press.

Lupyan, G. 2012. What do words do? Towards a theory of language-augmented thought. In *The Psychology of Learning and Motivation*, vol. 57, ed. B. H. Ross, 255–297. London: Academic Press.

Lupyan, G. 2013. The difficulties of executing simple algorithms: Why brains make mistakes computers don't. *Cognition* 129 (3): 615–636.

Lupyan, G., D. H. Rakison, and J. L. McClelland. 2007. Language is not just for talking: Labels facilitate learning of novel categories. *Psychological Science* 18 (12): 1077–1082.

Lupyan, G., and M. Spivey. 2010a. Making the invisible visible: Auditory cues facilitate visual object detection. *PLoS ONE* 5 (7): e11452.

Lupyan, G., and M. Spivey. 2010b. Redundant spoken labels facilitate perception of multiple items. *Attention, Perception & Psychophysics* 72 (8): 2236–2253.

Lupyan, G., and S. L. Thompson-Schill. 2012. The evocative power of words: Activation of concepts by verbal and nonverbal means. *Journal of Experimental Psychology: General* 141 (1): 170–186.

Lupyan, G., and E. J. Ward. 2013. Language can boost otherwise unseen objects into visual awareness. *Proceedings of the National Academy of Sciences* 110(35): 14196–14201.

Machery, E. 2009. *Doing Without Concepts*. New York: Oxford Univ. Press.

Mahon, B. Z., and A. Caramazza. 2008. A critical look at the embodied cognition hypothesis and a new proposal for grounding conceptual content. *Journal of Physiology, Paris* 102 (1): 59–70.

Majid, A., M. Bowerman, S. Kita, D. B. M. Haun, and S. C. Levinson. 2004. Can language restructure cognition? The case for space. *Trends in Cognitive Sciences* 8 (3): 108–114.

Margolis, E., and S. Laurence. 2008. Concepts. In *The Blackwell Guide to Philosophy of Mind*, vol. 10, ed. S. Stich and T. Warfield, 190–213. Oxford: Wiley-Blackwell.

Nisbett, R. E., K. Peng, I. Choi, and A. Norenzayan. 2001. Culture and systems of thought. *Psychological Review* 108:291–310.

Oppenheimer, D. M., and T. E. Trail. 2010. Why leaning to the left makes you lean to the left: Effect of spatial orientation on political attitudes. *Social Cognition* 28 (5): 651–661.

Osherson, D., and E. Smith. 1981. On the adequacy of prototype theory as a theory of concepts. *Cognition* 9:35–58.

Papafragou, A., J. Hulbert, and J. Trueswell. 2008. Does language guide event perception? *Cognition* 108 (1): 155–184.

Prinz, J. 2002. *Furnishing the Mind*. Cambridge, MA: MIT Press.

Pulvermüller, F. 2005. Brain mechanisms linking language and action. *Nature Reviews. Neuroscience* 6 (7): 576–582.

Regier, T., and P. Kay. 2009. Language, thought, and color: Whorf was half right. *Trends in Cognitive Sciences* 13:439–446.

Riskind, J. H. 1983. Nonverbal expressions and the accessibility of life experience memories: A congruence hypothesis. *Social Cognition* 2:62–86.

Rogers, T. T., and J. L. McClelland. 2004. *Semantic Cognition: A Parallel Distributed Processing Approach*. Cambridge, MA: MIT Press.

Simons, D. J., and D. T. Levin. 1998. Failure to detect changes to people during a real-world interaction. *Psychonomic Bulletin & Review* 5:644–649.

Smith, L. B., and L. K. Samuelson. 1997. Perceiving and remembering: Category stability, variability and development. In *Knowledge, Concepts, and Categories*, ed. K. Lamberts and D. Shanks, 161–196. Cambridge, MA: MIT Press.

Snedeker, J., and L. Gleitman. 2004. Why is it hard to label our concepts? In *Weaving a Lexicon*, ed. D. G. Hall and S. R. Waxman, 257–294. Cambridge, MA: MIT Press.

Spivey, M. 2007. *The Continuity of Mind*. New York: Oxford University Press.

Stroop, J. R. 1935. Studies of interference in serial verbal reactions. *Journal of Experimental Psychology* 18 (6): 643–662.

Taylor, L. J., and R. A. Zwaan. 2009. Action in cognition: The case of language. *Language and Cognition* 1:45–58.

Thierry, G., P. Athanasopoulos, A. Wiggett, B. Dering, and J.-R. Kuipers. 2009. Unconscious effects of language-specific terminology on preattentive color perception. *Proceedings of the National Academy of Sciences of the United States of America* 106 (11): 4567–4570.

Tversky, B., S. Kugelmass, and A. Winter. 1991. Cross-cultural and developmental trends in graphic productions. *Cognitive Psychology* 23:515–557.

Van Ackeren, M., D. Casasanto, H. Bekkering, P. Hagoort, and S. A. Rueschemeyer. 2012. Pragmatics in action: Indirect requests engage theory of mind areas and the cortical motor network. *Journal of Cognitive Neuroscience* 11 (4): 2237–2247.

Waxman, S. R. 2004. Everything had a name, and each name gave birth to a new thought: Links between early word-learning and conceptual organization. In *Weaving a Lexicon*, ed. D. G. Hall and S. R. Waxman, 295–335. Cambridge, MA: MIT Press.

Weiskopf, D. 2009. The plurality of concepts. *Synthese* 169:145–173.

Willems, R. M., and D. Casasanto. 2011. Flexibility in embodied language understanding. *Frontiers in Psychology* 2 (116): 1–11.

Willems, R. M., P. Hagoort, and D. Casasanto. 2010. Body-specific representations of action verbs: Neural evidence from right- and left-handers. *Psychological Science* 21 (1): 67–74.

Wittgenstein, L. 1953. *Philosophical Investigations*. Ed. G. E. M. Anscombe and R. Rhees. Trans. G. E. M. Anscombe. Oxford: Blackwell.

Zhong, C., V. K. Bohns, and F. Gino. 2010. Good lamps are the best police: Darkness increases dishonesty and self-interested behavior. *Psychological Science* 21:311–314.

Zwaan, R. A. 2004. The immersed experiencer: Toward an embodied theory of language comprehension. In *The Psychology of Learning and Motivation*, vol. 44, ed. B. H. Ross, 35–62. New York: Academic Press.

20 By Default: Concepts Are Accessed in a Context-Independent Manner

Edouard Machery

20.1 Introduction

In previous work (Machery 2005, 2009, 2010a), I have argued that the notion of concept should be eliminated from the theoretical vocabulary of psychology on the grounds, first, that what psychologists call *concepts* do not form a natural kind, and second, that keeping this notion would have several drawbacks. A key step of this argument is the characterization of a concept about x as "a body of knowledge about x that is stored in long-term memory and that is used by default in the processes underlying most, if not all, higher cognitive competences when these processes result in judgments about x" (2009, 12).[1] This characterization has been criticized, particularly on the grounds that the notion of default was either unclear or empirically invalid. The goal of this chapter is to clarify and defend the role played by the notion of default in the characterization of concepts (see also Mazzone and Lalumera 2010).

In section 20.2, I briefly summarize the argument for the elimination of the notion of concept from the theoretical vocabulary of psychology, so as to bring to the fore the role played by the characterization of the notion of concept I offer. In section 20.3, I clarify the notion of default, and I will contrast two conceptions of knowledge retrieval from long-term memory, *invariantism* and *contextualism*. In section 20.4, I briefly discuss some behavioral evidence that seems to cast doubt on the idea that some bodies of knowledge are retrieved by default from long-term memory, but I argue that my picture of retrieval from long-term memory can in fact account for this body of evidence. In sections 20.5 and 20.6, I present some behavioral and cognitive-neuroscientific evidence that strongly supports the claim that some bodies of knowledge are retrieved by default from long-term memory.

1. Following psychologists' use of this word, *knowledge* will be used here as a rough synonym of *information*.

20.2   The Eliminativist Argument and the Notion of Default

20.2.1   The Eliminativist Argument against the Notion of Concept

It is common among philosophers of science (and occasionally among scientists themselves) to conclude that some theoretical notion should be eliminated from the theoretical vocabulary of some science. Thus, Paul Griffiths has extensively argued that the notion of innateness should be eliminated from developmental psychology (Griffiths 2002; Griffiths, Machery, and Linquist 2009), and, particularly relevant for our concerns in this chapter, psychologist Linda Smith has argued that the notion of concept should be eliminated from psychology (Smith and Samuelson 1997). Although this kind of inference can be justified on various grounds, in *Doing without Concepts,* I compare two forms of eliminativism, semantic eliminativism and scientific eliminativism, arguing that semantic eliminativism is a deficient form of argument, and that scientific eliminativism should be preferred. The former, illustrated by Stich's (1983) eliminativist argument about propositional attitudes, argues that there are no *x's* on the grounds that nothing satisfies the functional definition of the concept of *x*: for instance, there are no beliefs because nothing satisfies the functional definition of the concept of belief (for discussion of this kind of argument, see Mallon et al. 2009). The latter argues that the notion of *x* should be eliminated from the theoretical vocabulary of a science if this notion does not help fulfill the goals of this science and, a fortiori, if it prevents or delays the fulfillment of these goals. The goals of many sciences include classificatory goals: scientists intend to develop notions that identify natural kinds (roughly, kinds about which numerous causally grounded generalizations can be made) in their domains of investigation. Thus, the notion of *x* should be eliminated if the following two conditions are met. First, the notion of *x* should not pick out a natural kind—that is, the *x's* should not form a natural kind. This condition, however, is not sufficient for the elimination of the notion of *x* since this notion could play other useful roles in a given science. Whence the second condition: keeping the notion of *x* does not contribute to the progress of the relevant science. Together these two conditions are sufficient for the elimination of the notion of concept.

The argument for the elimination of the notion of concept applies the scientific-eliminativist strategy to the notion of concept:

1. *Concept* refers to the class of bodies of knowledge that are used by default in the cognitive processes underlying most higher cognitive competences.
2. The best available evidence suggests that for each category (each substance such as water, or each event such as going to the dentist, etc.), an individual typically has several concepts (at least, a prototype, an exemplar, and a theory).
3. Co-referential concepts have very few properties in common. Thus, co-referential concepts belong to very heterogeneous kinds of concepts.

4. Thus, concepts do not form a natural kind, and *concept* does not refer to a natural kind.
5. Keeping *concept* would impede progress in psychology.
6. *Concept* should be eliminated from the theoretical vocabulary of psychology.

Much has to be said to defend the premises of this eliminativist argument, and I have done it at length elsewhere (Machery 2009, 2010a, 2010b, 2010c, 2011). For the purposes of this chapter, I merely want to highlight the fact that this eliminativist argument depends on the validity of the characterization of concept offered in premise 1.

20.2.2 Criticisms

The characterization of concepts I have offered has been criticized on several grounds. In *Doing without Concepts*, I argue that *concept* is ambiguous between philosophy and psychology, a claim that has been criticized (Margolis and Laurence 2010; Gauker 2011; for a response, see Machery 2010a). Others have argued that my characterization of the notion of concept has problematic consequences for the individuation of concepts (Hill 2010; for a response, see Machery 2010b). Yet others have insisted on alternative characterizations of the notion of concept (e.g., Gauker 2011). Since I have already answered these concerns at length elsewhere, I will overlook them in what follows.

Instead, I will focus on the concerns elicited by the use of the notion of default to characterize the notion of concept. In particular, Hill (2010, 417) has written that "a theoretician who wishes to base an account of concepts on the notion of default knowledge has a rather large burden of proof," while Malt (2010, 626) has asserted that "it may be impossible in principle to segregate default knowledge in some domain from associated general background knowledge, and thus impossible to define concepts as Machery has done with reference to what is retrieved by default" (see also Rice, forthcoming).

Hill's, Malt's, and others' concerns are in fact twofold (for a response to the specifics of Hill's criticism, see Machery 2010b; for a response to the specifics of Malt's criticisms, see Machery 2010c). First, the notion of being used by default has been insufficiently clarified in my previous work. Second, it is unclear whether any knowledge is retrieved by default from long-term memory to be used in cognitive processes. I will address these two concerns in the remainder of this chapter.

20.3 The Notion of Default

20.3.1 What Is Default Knowledge?

In previous work (see the quotation from *Doing without Concepts* in the introduction of this chapter), I applied the notion of default to the use of knowledge in cognitive processes. However, it is better to apply it to the retrieval of knowledge from long-term memory in order to distinguish two types of knowledge: the knowledge that is retrieved by default from long-term memory (or, as I will occasionally say, *default knowledge*), and the knowledge that isn't (which I will call *background knowledge*). Naturally, retrieval from memory and use of knowledge aren't entirely disconnected since knowledge is typically retrieved from memory to be used in cognitive processing. Still, the two notions are not equivalent because the knowledge that is retrieved by default need not be automatically used in cognitive processing. So, for instance, it could be that during speech perception, we access by default the body of knowledge associated with each open-class word in a sentence, but that the information that is not relevant in the linguistic context is discarded or inhibited and does not contribute to the construction of the meaning of the sentence (see Greenspan 1986 for discussion).

So, what does it mean to say that knowledge is retrieved by default from long-term memory? In previous work (2009, 12–13), I used some synonyms ("default knowledge" is "preferentially available") and some metaphors to clarify this notion, proposing in particular that default knowledge "spontaneously comes to mind." Although this approach may help the reader identify the phenomenon I am interested in, it casts insufficient light on what default knowledge is.

Knowledge is retrieved by default if and only if retrieval possesses the three following properties:

- *Speed* Default knowledge is *quickly* retrieved from long-term memory.
- *Automaticity* Default knowledge is *automatically* retrieved from long-term memory.
- *Context independence* Default knowledge is retrieved from long-term memory *in every context*.

The first characteristic that distinguishes default from background knowledge is how long it takes to retrieve it from memory. The second characteristic is the nature of control: roughly, the retrieval of a particular body of knowledge is under intentional control when retrieval requires the intention and the use of some attentional resources to access it. Although the literature on automaticity (e.g., Bargh 1994) often treats this dimension as categorical (a process is either controlled or automatic), control may well be a continuum. If that is the case, default bodies of knowledge are those that are on its automatic end. The third characteristic is context dependence: some bodies of knowledge are retrieved only in a particular context that primes their retrieval, while other bodies of knowledge are retrieved in all contexts. It is not entirely clear whether context dependence is a categorical or a continuous property. If it is a continuum, default bodies of knowledge are on its context-independent end.

The three properties of default knowledge are logically distinct and could be combined in various ways: that is, retrieval from long-term memory could have one of them without the other. For example, context-dependent retrieval could be quick and automatic, although it could also be slow and under intentional control. On the other hand, being fast, automatic, and context independent plausibly form a homeostatic cluster: if some body of knowledge is retrieved in all contexts, then its retrieval can be automatic since no attentional resources are required to decide whether to retrieve it, and its retrieval is probably fast since the retrieval process can be simple. In fact, on my view, context independence is the most important of the three properties that are independently necessary and jointly sufficient for a body of knowledge to be retrieved by default, and the two other properties are consequences of context independence. Finally, background knowledge retrieval does not need to be uniformly slow or under intentional control. What really characterizes this type of retrieval is its context dependence. So, retrieval of background knowledge is always context dependent, and it could occasionally be automatic or fast.

20.3.2 Invariantism and Contextualism

Now that the notion of default has been clarified, we can contrast two distinct conceptions of knowledge retrieval from long-term memory: the invariantist conception (or *invariantism*) and the contextualist conception (or *contextualism*). Invariantism holds that knowledge in long-term memory is of two kinds: some of it is retrieved in a context-independent manner, and as a result, quickly and automatically; some of it is not retrieved in a context-independent manner. The knowledge about *x* that constitutes the concept of *x* is retrieved by default. Keil captures the gist of invariantism as follows:

Shared mental structures are assumed to be constant across repeated categorizations of the same set of instances and different from other categorizations. When I think about the category of dogs, a specific mental representation is assumed to be responsible for that category. (1994, 169)

To illustrate, consider our knowledge about dogs. Invariantism holds that in all contexts, automatically, and quickly, we retrieve a specific body of knowledge—say, the knowledge that dogs are four-legged furry animals that bark, are good companions for people, and have a specific shape—and this body of knowledge constitutes the concept of dogs. Everything else we know about dogs (e.g., that dogs are mammals and vertebrates, that dogs and wolves are related, that I have a dog called *Fido*, that Labradors are dogs, etc.) is part of the background knowledge about dogs: this knowledge is retrieved in a context-dependent manner.

By contrast, contextualism holds that knowledge retrieval is always context dependent. Furthermore, contextualism is noncommittal about automaticity and speed. Thus, in the case of our knowledge about dogs, contextualism holds that *all* our knowledge about dogs is retrieved in a contextual manner. In some contexts, we retrieve the knowledge that dogs are furry, in other contexts, that they are mammals, in yet other contexts, that they herd, and so on. No body of knowledge is privileged and retrieved in a context-independent manner.

Contextualism has been defended by influential psycholinguists (e.g., Tabossi), psychologists (e.g., Barsalou, L. Smith, and Malt), cognitive neuroscientists (e.g., Kiefer), and philosophers of psychology (e.g., Prinz and Carston).[2] For instance, Barclay, Bransford, Franks, McCarrell, and Nitsch (1974) have argued that access to lexical meaning was characterized by "a semantic flexibility": as Greenspan put the idea, they proposed "that the comprehension of a noun in a sentence involves the selective activation (or instantiation) of only those semantic features or meaning postulates that are relevant to the specific linguistic context" (1986, 539–40). Similarly, Barsalou writes:

A loose collection of property and relation simulators is available for interpreting the instances of a category. On a given occasion, a temporary online abstraction is constructed dynamically to interpret the current instance. (2005, 417)

Hoenig, Sim, Bochev, Herrnberger, and Kiefer describe their views about concepts as follows:

Concepts are situational-dependent mental entities. They are composed of semantic features which are flexibly recruited from distributed, yet localized, semantic maps in modality-specific brain regions depending on contextual constraints.[3] (2008, 1799)

It is clear that, if contextualism is correct, it would be a mistake to appeal to the notion of default to spell out the notion of concept.

20.4   Evidence for Contextualism?

20.4.1   The Argument for Contextualism

Barsalou, Malt, Smith, and others allude to a particular kind of empirical result in support of contextualism (Barsalou 1987, 1999, 2003; Smith and Samuelson 1997; Malt 2010). Performance in a range of tasks meant to elicit retrieval from knowledge in long-term memory (e.g., from people's knowledge of dogs) varies from context to context and even from occasion to occasion. In particular, in a property-listing task, participants are asked to list the properties that are true of, or typical of, the members of various categories, for example, bachelors, birds, chairs, and so forth. Completing this task requires accessing one's knowledge about these categories in long-term memory.

2. See, for example, Barclay et al. (1974); Tabossi and Johnson-Laird (1980); Barsalou (1987, 1999, 2003, 2005); Smith and Samuelson (1997); Carston (2002); Prinz (2002); Kiefer (2005); Yeh and Barsalou (2006); Rice (forthcoming).
3. Although Kiefer aligns his views about concepts with contextualism, it is not entirely clear that he is correct. On his view, the properties that a concept of x represents x as having are more or less "dominant," and, together with "conceptual constraints," dominance influences knowledge retrieval (e.g., Hoenig et al. 2008, 1780). This hypothesis is very similar to my interpretation of invariantism and to the conception of knowledge retrieval proposed in *Doing without Concepts*.

Barsalou (1989) reports that participants tend to list different properties on different occasions. Overlap in the properties mentioned by different subjects on a given occasion and by the same subject across the two occasions was calculated, and it was found that only 44 percent of the properties mentioned by a given subject were mentioned by another subject, and that only 66 percent of the properties mentioned by a subject on a given occasion were mentioned by this very subject on the other occasion. Barsalou concludes that there was "substantial flexibility in how an individual conceptualized the same category on different occasions" (1993, 32). Proponents of contextualism then hold that contextualism provides a better explanation of this finding and related results than invariantism since the former clearly predicts variation across instances of memory retrieval. They conclude that memory retrieval is thoroughly context dependent, and that there is no body of knowledge that is retrieved in a context-independent manner—thus no body of knowledge that is retrieved by default (see also Machery 2009, 21–24).

In the remainder of this section, I briefly assess the second premise in this inference-to-the-best-explanation argument—that is, the claim that contextualism provides a better explanation of the empirical findings about the variation in participants' performance in tasks tapping into knowledge in long-term memory.

20.4.2 Comparing the Explanatory Power of Contextualism and Invariantism

To assess which of contextualism and invariantism best explains the alleged evidence for contextualism, it is important to clarify what each conception exactly entails. Contextualism entails that, when people think about x (e.g., dogs) in different contexts, they retrieve different bodies of knowledge about x, and that the knowledge retrieved will somehow be relevant to the context of retrieval.[4] Of course, contextualism does not entail that when people think about x (e.g., dogs) in different contexts, they retrieve bodies of knowledge about x that are entirely different, since the bodies of knowledge about x that are relevant in these contexts may overlap. While these consequences are clear, there is some vagueness in the consequences of contextualism since the notion of context is left unexplained. No individuation conditions for contexts have been provided, and we are not told how to assess the similarity and difference between two contexts. It is also not obvious how these two shortcomings could be remedied.

Invariantism does not deny that the knowledge retrieved from long-term memory varies to some extent across contexts (Machery 2009; Mazzone and Lalumera 2010). Quite the contrary in fact: it predicts that when people think about x (e.g., dogs) in different contexts, they retrieve different relevant elements of knowledge from their

---

4. How we retrieve the knowledge that is relevant remains a mystery, but this is a problem for both views about knowledge retrieval since invariantism also assumes that relevant information is retrieved from our background knowledge in a context-dependent manner.

background knowledge about x. So, variation across contexts of retrieval is consistent with, indeed predicted by, invariantism. Where invariantism and contextualism disagree is about whether the bodies of knowledge retrieved in different contexts always overlap: Invariantism entails that claim (since the default body of knowledge is always retrieved); contextualism denies it.

It is clearly not obvious to determine which of contextualism and invariantism best explains the alleged evidence for contextualism. The consequences of contextualism are not very precise because the notion of context is left vague. Finding that the bodies of knowledge retrieved differ when one is thinking about x in some different contexts does not favor contextualism over invariantism since, as we have just seen, the latter predicts that retrieval from background knowledge about x varies with context. Because both predict that in numerous contexts where one is thinking about x, the knowledge about x that is retrieved will overlap, finding some overlap across contexts does not support one conception over the other.

That said, three points challenge the second step in the argument for contextualism presented above. First, without any additional auxiliary assumptions, contextualism does not predict some of the findings put forward by contextualists such as Barsalou and Smith. In particular, although contextualism does predict that when one is thinking about x in distinct contexts, one will retrieve different (albeit possibly overlapping) bodies of knowledge, it does not predict that, in the same context, one will retrieve different bodies of knowledge. But some of the findings alleged to support contextualism actually amount precisely to this. So, for instance, the low test-retest reliability of the feature-listing task does not show that people retrieve different bodies of knowledge in different contexts because the context of the task is the same the first and the second time it is completed: in both cases, the task is completed in a lab, under the guidance of a psychologist, and so on. Of course, contextualists could respond that the context is in fact different: participants may come to the second experiment with different thoughts and concerns, for instance. But, first, even if that is right, contextualists need this auxiliary assumption to explain a kind of finding that is prominent in their criticism of invariantism. Second, unfortunately, because the individuation conditions for the notion of context are unclear, it is difficult to decide whether the auxiliary assumption needed by contextualists is in fact correct. At the very least, I conclude, some of the findings put forward by contextualists do not clearly support their view.

Second, both contextualists and invariantists predict that knowledge retrieval will often in part, and only in part, vary across contexts. As a result, it is dubious that contextualism provides a better explanation of many of the findings alleged to support it. Rather, contextualism and invariantism seem both able to explain these findings, which as a consequence cannot be appealed to in an inference-to-the-best-explanation argument. Instead of a clear victory of contextualism, what we really have is a draw between these two theories about knowledge retrieval from long-term memory.

Third, the more different the knowledge retrieved from long-term memory across contexts, the stronger the evidence for contextualism over invariantism because, according to the latter, when people think about x, there is a core of knowledge that is automatically retrieved in all contexts—namely the concept of x. But the findings put forward by contextualists show a large amount of overlap across the knowledge retrieved on different occasions, exactly as invariantists would have predicted (more on this in Machery 2009, 23).

20.4.3   Upshot

The argument for contextualism over invariantism takes the form of an inference to the best explanation. Contextualism is said to provide a better explanation of a range of findings about memory retrieval. However, we have briefly seen that the second step of this argument is dubious, and I thus conclude that the findings presented by contextualists do not support contextualism over invariantism.

20.5   Behavioral Evidence for Invariantism

In the remainder of this chapter, I consider a range of findings that support invariantism over contextualism, starting with behavioral evidence in this section.[5]

20.5.1   Evidence for Automatic, Context-Independent Memory Retrieval

Whitney, McKay, Kellas, and Emerson (1985) used a version of the Stroop task to examine how context influences access to lexical meaning. Target words were printed in a colored ink, and participants had to name the color. The target word could either denote a *high-dominant* property (e.g., "has fur") of the objects denoted by a noun (e.g., "rabbit")—where a property is dominant if it is semantically strongly associated with the relevant noun[6]—or a *low-dominant* property ("hop"). Before seeing the word, participants heard a sentence. In one condition, this sentence ended with the noun the target word was semantically related to, and it emphasized the high-dominant property ("The child touched the rabbit"). In a second condition, the sentence also ended with the noun the target word was semantically related to, but it emphasized the low-dominant property ("The child chased the rabbit"). Finally, in the third condition, participants heard a control, irrelevant sentence. Finally, the target word could be

5. For further behavioral evidence, see the literature review in Mazzone and Lalumera (2010, 63–65).
6. High dominance is operationalized as a high-occurrence frequency in property-listing tasks (Ashcraft 1976).

Table 20.1
Reaction times (ms) in Stroop task

	Delay					
	0 ms		300 ms		600 ms	
Prime	High	Low	High	Low	High	Low
Appropriate	914	930	980	968	984	975
Inappropriate	908	926	984	894	977	926
Control	876	880	815	907	919	927

presented after a 0, 300, or 600 ms delay. Response times were measured. The longer the response time, the stronger the interference between the meaning of the target word (e.g., "has fur" or "hop") and the name of the color, and thus, the stronger the target word's meaning has been primed by the noun.

Whitney and colleagues found that in the 0 ms delay condition, for both the high-dominant and the low-dominant properties, response times were identical when the sentence primed the predicate denoting the property (*appropriate context*) and when it did not (*inappropriate context*), and these response times differed from the response times in the control condition (establishing that semantic priming had occurred). Thus, context did not influence access to information about either kind of property. By contrast, in the 300 and 600 ms delay conditions, for the high-dominant properties, but not for the low-dominant ones, response times were identical in the appropriate and inappropriate contexts, and they differed from the response times in the control condition. For the low-dominant properties, response times were longer in the appropriate context than in the inappropriate one (table 20.1, based on table 1 of Whitney et al. 1985), and the response times in the latter condition did not significantly differ from the response times in the control condition (suggesting that no semantic priming had occurred). Thus, in these two conditions, context did matter for the low-dominant properties, but not for the high-dominant properties: the former remain accessible independently of the context, while access to the latter is dependent on the right context.

These results undermine contextualism since they speak against the proposal that retrieval from long-term memory is always context dependent. Context made no difference in access to long-term memory in the 0 ms delay condition, and it made no difference for the continuing access to a subset of the properties—the high-dominant properties—in the 300 ms and 600 ms conditions.[7]

7. It is puzzling that context did not matter in the 0 ms condition.

20.5.2   Evidence for the Distinction between Context-Insensitive and Context-Sensitive Knowledge

In a remarkable article, Barsalou (1982) provided some further evidence for the claim that access to some information in long-term memory is context independent. In Experiment 1, participants were asked to complete a property-verification task: they had to decide whether the objects denoted by a noun (e.g., "skunk") possess a particular property. The study compared two types of properties, those that are assumed to be *context independent,* and those are assumed to be *context dependent.* That skunks smell was taken to be a context-independent component of our knowledge of skunks: it was hypothesized that knowledge of this fact is retrieved whenever one thinks about skunks. By contrast, that roofs can be walked on was taken to be a context-dependent component of our knowledge of roofs: it was hypothesized that knowledge of this fact is retrieved only in appropriate contexts. The study also compared two types of priming situations: before having to make their property-verification judgment about a target predicate (e.g., "can be walked on" or "smells"), participants were presented with three possible kinds of prime: *unrelated context, related context,* and *control.* In the unrelated context condition, they were presented with a priming sentence that did not highlight the connection between the property denoted by the target predicate and the objects denoted by the relevant noun (e.g., "roof" or "skunk"). For example, for a context-independent property, they could be told, "The skunk was under a large willow," and for a context-dependent property, they could be told, "The roof had been renovated prior to the rainy season." By contrast, in a related context condition, participants were presented with a priming sentence that highlighted the connection between the property denoted by the target predicate and the objects denoted by the relevant noun. For example, for the context-independent property *smells*, they could be told, "The skunk stunk up the whole neighborhood," and for the context-dependent property *can be walked on*, they could be told, "The roof creaked under the weight of the repairman." When participants were in the control condition, the priming sentences had nothing to do with the objects denoted by the relevant noun. For instance, for a context-independent property about skunks, participants could be told, "The fire was easily visible through the trees." Latencies and percentage of mistakes were measured as dependent variables.

What does the hypothesis that some bodies of information are retrieved by default from long-term memory predict in Barsalou's (1982) Experiment 1? Assuming that Barsalou's distinction between context-dependent and context-independent properties taps into the knowledge that is constitutive of, respectively, concepts and background knowledge, this hypothesis makes the following two predictions:

1. Context (unrelated vs. related context) should make no difference in how quickly knowledge about context-independent properties is retrieved, while knowledge about

Table 20.2
Reaction times (ms) in property-verification task

Condition	Control	Unrelated	Related
Context independent	1,335	1,113	1,145
Context dependent	1,098	1,404	1,259

the context-dependent properties should be retrieved more quickly in related contexts than in unrelated contexts: that is, an interaction between context and type of property is predicted.
2. Information about context-independent properties should be retrieved faster than information about context-dependent properties: that is, a main effect of type of property on time latency is predicted.

By contrast, the hypothesis that all knowledge is retrieved in a context-dependent manner makes the following predictions:

3. Knowledge about all (i.e., context-dependent and context-independent) properties, should be more quickly retrieved when the context is related than when it is not related: that is, no interaction between context and type of property is predicted.
4. No main effect of type of property is predicted.

As can be seen in table 20.2 (based on table 3 of Barsalou 1982), the two predictions derived from invariantism turned out to be correct. For the context-independent properties, no statistical difference was found between the latencies in the unrelated (1,113 ms) and related (1,145 ms) context, while the context-dependent properties were retrieved significantly more quickly in the related (1,259 ms) than in the unrelated (1,404 ms) context. Additionally, information about the context-independent properties was retrieved faster than information about the context-dependent properties. These results clearly support the notion that some information is retrieved by default, that is, automatically, quickly, and in a context-independent manner.

20.5.3 Further Evidence for the Distinction between Context-Dependent and Context-Independent Memory Retrieval

One may suspect that Barsalou's findings are due to the strategies of knowledge retrieval elicited by the task he used, and one may wonder whether findings similar to Barsalou's (1982) would be found in other behavioral tasks tapping into conceptual knowledge. Greenspan's (1986) studies show that the answer is affirmative: he used three distinct experimental tasks to provide further evidence for the distinction between context-dependent and context-independent memory retrieval.

In Experiment 1, participants had to complete a cued-recall task. They were presented with sentences. After a delay, they were presented with cues, and they were asked to write which sentence each cue reminded them of. Half of the sentences indirectly highlighted a property semantically strongly associated with the noun ending the sentence ("While she drank the coffee, Mary looked through the newspaper"); the other half a property semantically weakly associated with it ("On the bottom of the birdcage, John placed some newspaper"). Half of the cues denoted the strongly associated properties (e.g., "print"), the other half the weakly associated properties ("lining"). The relevance of the sentence barely made a difference for the frequency of recall for the strongly associated properties (65 percent vs. 52.5 percent), while it mattered a lot for the weakly associated properties (62.5 percent vs. 12.5 percent). Experiment 1 suggests that, even in irrelevant contexts, some, but not all, knowledge is accessed, providing support for the distinction between context-dependent and context-independent knowledge.

In Experiment 2, participants had to complete a semantic-relatedness task: they were asked to judge the association between sentences and target words. The sentences indirectly emphasized a property strongly semantically associated with the word ending them, or they indirectly emphasized a property weakly semantically associated with the word ending them, or they were control sentences. The target words denoted either the strongly associated or the weakly associated properties. Again, context mattered for the latter kind of property, but not for the former (table 20.3, based on table 2 of Greenspan 1986): when the context was not appropriate, information about the weakly associated properties that are possessed by the objects denoted by a noun was not retrieved from memory, and people did not see any semantic relation between a noun and a predicate denoting the relevant property.

In Experiment 3, participants completed a cross-modal semantic priming task: they heard a sentence before being visually presented with a series of letters (1s delay), and they had to decide whether these letters formed a word or not. Compared to a baseline, reaction times indicated whether the sentence had primed access to the representation of the property denoted by the target word. As in Experiments 1 and 2, two types of target words were used: those that denoted a

Table 20.3

Mean association on a 7-point scale

Condition	Central property	Peripheral property
Emphasized	5.5	5.4
Non-emphasized	4.2	2.5
Control	1.6	1.9

Table 20.4
Reaction times (ms) in cross-modal semantic priming task

Condition	Central property	Peripheral property
Emphasized	558	579
Non-emphasized	583	611
Control	617	621

property strongly semantically associated with the last word of the priming sentence and those that denoted a property weakly semantically associated with it. Three kinds of sentences were associated: some indirectly highlighted the first kind of property, some indirectly highlighted the second kind of property, and some were control sentences. The pattern of results is similar to the results found in Experiments 1 and 2 (table 20.4, based on table 3 of Greenspan 1986): for the strongly associated properties, facilitation is context independent, while it is context dependent for the weakly associated properties.

Greenspan's studies provide strong evidence that the distinction between the knowledge that is accessed in a context-dependent manner and the knowledge that is accessed in a context-independent manner is an important feature of knowledge retrieval. This conclusion is in line with Greenspan's interpretation of his findings:

Results from a cued-recall task, a semantic judgment task, and a semantic priming (lexical decision) task suggested that properties which are central to the typical use of an object tend to be instantiated in the representation of sentence that mentions the object, independent of sentence emphasis. However, properties that are peripheral to the object's typical use tend to be instantiated only when emphasized by the sentence. (1986, 539)

20.5.4 Upshot

The behavioral results discussed in this section strongly suggest that knowledge in memory is not a seamless, undifferentiated whole; rather, knowledge is clumped. Some of it is accessed automatically, quickly, and in all contexts; some of it is accessed in a context-dependent manner.

20.6 Cognitive-Neuroscientific Evidence for Invariantism

In this final section, I describe some cognitive-neuroscientific evidence about knowledge retrieval: it too supports the proposal that some information is retrieved from long-term memory by default.

20.6.1   Automatic Access to Irrelevant Perceptual Knowledge Elicited by Visual Stimuli

James and Gauthier (2003) were interested in providing evidence for the neo-empiricist view of concepts, according to which, roughly, to entertain a concept consists of entertaining some perceptual representations (Barsalou 1999; Prinz 2002; for discussion, see Machery 2007). They trained participants to associate different kinds of properties with unfamiliar objects, that is, with objects that participants were not previously acquainted with (*greebles*), which were divided into four different sets (James and Gauthier 2003, figure 1). Three kinds of properties were of interest: sounds made by objects, motions, and character properties (e.g., intelligence). These properties were presented orally (i.e., they were named), while the greebles were presented visually: for instance, participants may be told that a visually presented greeble roars, that it crawls, or that it is gentle. Participants were then presented with a visual-matching task: they were shown two pictures of greebles, and they had to decide whether they were the same greeble or not. Importantly, completing this task does not require accessing any knowledge about the stimuli; it merely requires using the visual shapes of objects. Participants were scanned by fMRI while completing the visual-matching task in order to determine whether the brain areas associated with sound perception or biological motion (identified for each subject by a region-of-analysis methodology) were incidentally activated during the visual presentation of the stimuli.

As they had predicted, James and Gauthier found that the right superior temporal gyrus, which is involved in auditory perception, was more activated by objects that had been associated with sounds during training than by objects associated with actions.[8] By contrast, the right posterior superior temporal sulcus, which is involved in the perception of motion, was more activated by objects that had been associated with motions during training than by objects associated with sounds (James and Gauthier 2003, figures 2 and 3).

For the purpose of this chapter, what matters is that this knowledge was retrieved despite its utter irrelevance for completing the task. Thus, people retrieved some knowledge about the stimuli in a context-independent manner and, plausibly, in an automatic manner too.[9] This finding is predicted by the hypothesis that some informa-

---

8. A caveat is that objects associated with sounds did not activate the superior temporal gyrus more than objects associated with character traits. It may thus be that the difference between objects associated with sounds and objects associated with motions is that the latter deactivated the superior temporal gyrus. A second caveat is that, unexpectedly, no effect was found for the left hemisphere.

9. It is dubious that participants intentionally retrieved this irrelevant knowledge.

tion represented in long-term memory is accessed by default, and it is surprising if all knowledge is retrieved in a context-dependent manner.

20.6.2   Automatic Access to Irrelevant Functional Knowledge Elicited by Visual Stimuli

One may wonder whether James and Gauthier's (2003) findings would generalize to other kinds of knowledge, in addition to the perceptual information (auditory and visual knowledge about biological motion) participants had to learn. What about, for example, functional information—information about how to use objects? Weisberg, van Turennout, and Martin's (2007) study suggests that the answer is affirmative.

Weisberg and colleagues (2007) trained participants to use unfamiliar objects to solve particular tasks (Weisberg, van Turennout, and Martin 2007, figure 1). Presumably, while doing so, participants acquired some knowledge about the uses these objects can be put to. Participants were then presented with a visual-matching task (determining whether two pictures were of the same object viewed from two distinct perspectives) while their brain was scanned by fMRI. Importantly, completing this task did not require accessing the acquired knowledge about the tools' uses. Still, Weisberg and colleagues found enhanced activity in the left middle temporal gyrus, left intraparietal sulcus, and left premotor cortex, areas that have been involved in numerous tasks tapping into people's conceptual knowledge about object use (e.g., recognition tasks, property verification tasks, etc.; for discussion and references, see Weisberg, van Turennout, and Martin 2007).

Just like James and Gauthier's (2003) study, the Weisberg, van Turennout, and Martin (2007) study suggests that information that is not relevant for solving a task—in this case, functional information—is accessed during task completion. This information is plausibly accessed automatically since it is unclear why participants would have the intention to retrieve this useless information.

20.6.3   Automatic Access to Irrelevant Semantic Information Elicited by Visual Stimuli

Both James and Gauthier (2003) and Weisberg and colleagues (2007) examined the incidental retrieval of information that is, in some ways, connected to our peripheral faculties—vision, audition, or action. Would their findings generalize to other forms of knowledge? James and Gauthier's (2004) study suggests that they would.

James and Gauthier (2004) examined whether the inferior frontal cortex, which research has associated with semantic processing, would be automatically activated in a task that did not require any semantic knowledge. Their method was similar to the one used in James and Gauthier (2003): participants were either trained to associate semantic information or proper names with greebles. Then they were given a visual-matching task, while their brain was scanned by fMRI. As James and Gauthier had predicted, greater activation was found in the inferior frontal cortex for the visual stimuli associated with semantic information than for those merely associated with a proper name, even though, again, retrieving this information was not useful for completing the task. In line with the idea that some knowledge is retrieved by default from long-term memory, James and Gauthier summarize their study as follows:

Because the task required no semantic retrieval, access to semantics appears to be involuntary. The brain regions involved have been implicated in semantic processing, thus recently acquired semantics activate a similar network to semantics learned over a lifetime. (2004, 249)

20.6.4   Automatic Access to Context-Independent Knowledge Elicited by Verbal Stimuli

The three studies I have discussed so far in this section used visual stimuli, and they provided evidence for an automatic retrieval of irrelevant information, undermining the hypothesis that all information is retrieved in a context-dependent manner. But they do not provide direct evidence for the distinction between context-dependent and context-independent knowledge retrieval. Hoenig and colleagues' (2008) study provides the missing evidence.

Embracing a neo-empiricist view of concepts, Hoenig and colleagues intended to provide evidence against the view that "concepts are situational invariant mental knowledge entities (conceptual stability)" (2008, 1799), and they interpret their results as supporting a contextualist conception of knowledge retrieval from long-term memory (see their quotation earlier in this chapter). However, a closer look at their findings supports the opposite conclusion: pace Hoenig and colleagues (2008), their results provide evidence for invariantism.

Participants were asked to complete a semantic-congruence task with verbal stimuli (deciding whether a predicate, e.g., "elongated" or "cut" is semantically related to a noun, e.g., "knife" or "ball"), while their brain was scanned by fMRI. The stimuli used in this semantic-congruence task were of two kinds: nouns of artifacts and nouns of natural objects (fruits, vegetables, and animals). "Knife" illustrates the first kind of stimuli, and "banana" the second kind. Two types of predicates were used: visual property predicates and action predicates (what the stimulus does or what can be done with it). For the artifact noun "knife," "elongated" illustrates the first kind of predicate, "cut" the second kind; and for the natural object noun "banana," "yellow" illustrates the first kind of predicate, and "peel" the second.

When participants were asked to decide whether a visual property predicate was semantically related to an artifact noun, activation was found, unsurprisingly, in the middle temporal and inferior temporal gyri: this is consistent with evidence suggesting that, to determine whether an object has a visual property, we imagine seeing this object. More interesting for the purpose of this chapter is an incidental finding of Hoenig and colleagues' study, which is well illustrated by figure 4 of Hoenig et al. (2008): activation was also found in the inferior frontal gyrus (i.e., the premotor cortex), which is activated when people imagine using an object. Even though information about artifact use was of no relevance to complete the task, it seems to have been accessed. The reverse was not true. When participants were asked to assess the semantic affinity between an artifact noun and a particular action predicate, no activation was found in the middle temporal and inferior temporal gyri (in fact, a significant deactivation seems to have been found). A similar but inverted phenomenon was found for natural objects. When participants were asked to determine the semantic affinity between a natural object and an action predicate, activation was unsurprisingly found in the inferior frontal gyrus: this is consistent with evidence showing that to determine whether an object can do something or whether it can be used in a particular manner, we imagine using this object. What is more surprising, however, is the fact that in this condition, activation was also found in the middle temporal and inferior temporal gyri. Even though information about the visual appearances of natural objects was of no relevance to completing the task, it seems to have been accessed. The reverse was not true. When participants were asked to assess the semantic affinity between a natural object noun and a particular visual predicate, no activation was found in the middle temporal and inferior temporal gyri (in fact, a significant deactivation seems to have been found).

It is unfortunate that Hoenig and colleagues misinterpret their own findings and conclude, "Together, these findings support the proposed perspective change toward conceptual flexibility and seriously question the traditional notion of conceptual stability" (2008, 1808). This misinterpretation occurs in part because they take invariantism to entail a complete lack of flexibility: any evidence of flexible context retrieval is then interpreted as providing evidence for contextualism. However, as we have seen in section 20.3, invariantism allows for a fair amount of flexibility in knowledge retrieval.

A more accurate interpretation of their results goes as follows. Different kinds of concepts, specifically concepts of artifacts and of natural objects, store different kinds of knowledge: the former are more likely to store knowledge about use, the latter about visual properties. Consistent with the idea that concepts are constituted by knowledge retrieved by default, knowledge about visual properties, but not about use, is retrieved in a context-independent manner (i.e., whether or not this retrieval is relevant) when one is thinking about natural objects, while knowledge about use, but not about visual properties, is retrieved in a context-independent manner when one is thinking about artifacts. Brain activation in the middle temporal and inferior temporal gyri and in the inferior frontal gyrus in the different conditions of Hoenig and colleagues' experiment reflects this difference.

This interpretation is consistent with a large body of evidence in experimental psychology and in neuropsychology, suggesting, first, that concepts of natural objects (animals, plants, fruits, etc.) store more information about visual properties than about how they are used, and second, that concepts of artifacts store more information about use than about visual properties (see, e.g., McRae and Cree 2002 for an analysis of a property-listing task).

To conclude, Hoenig and colleagues' findings provide some further evidence for the claim that some task-irrelevant information about categories is retrieved automatically, which provides support for invariantism over contextualism. More important, they also provide support for the distinction between knowledge that is retrieved in a context-dependent manner and knowledge that is retrieved in a context-independent manner, which the three other studies reviewed in this section did not do.

20.6.5 Upshot

The cognitive-neuroscientific evidence reviewed in this section provides strong support for the validity of the distinction between bodies of knowledge retrieved by default and bodies of knowledge retrieved in a context-dependent manner. A diverse range of information (perceptual, functional, etc.) that is not relevant for a task is retrieved automatically, whether the stimuli are visual or verbal. Furthermore, among the knowledge that is retrieved from long-term memory, some, but not all of it, seems to be retrieved in a context-independent manner, very much in line with Barsalou's (1982) behavioral results.

20.7 Conclusion

In this chapter, I have addressed two worries about the use of the notion of default to characterize concepts. First, I have clarified this notion. I now conceive of this notion as qualifying access to memory (or memory retrieval) instead of concept use. In addition, a body of knowledge is accessed by default if it possesses three homeostatic properties: context independence, automaticity, and speed. Second, I have argued that understood in this way, the notion of default is empirically valid. Behavioral findings and more recent brain imagery results suggest that some knowledge in long-term memory, but not all, is retrieved by default. Thus, contextualism, one of the most influential approaches to concepts in contemporary psychology (Barsalou, Malt, Smith), neuroscience (Hoenig), and philosophy (Prinz), seems to mischaracterize the nature of knowledge retrieval from long-term memory. Of course, this chapter is not the final word on the debate between contextualism and invariantism. More research may undermine the latter and provide some support for the former. In particular, the behavioral evidence presented here (but not the neuroscientific evidence) involved linguistic tasks, and there may be more context dependency to be found in nonlinguistic tasks.

Furthermore, invariantism calls for further empirical and theoretical research since it is so far unclear what determines whether a piece of information belongs to a concept of a category, an event, or a substance, or to background knowledge.

References

Ashcraft, M. H. 1976. Priming and property dominance effects in semantic memory. *Memory & Cognition* 4:490–500.

Barclay, J. R., J. P. Bransford, J. J. Franks, N. S. McCarrell, and K. Nitsch. 1974. Comprehension and semantic flexibility. *Journal of Verbal Learning and Verbal Behavior* 13:471–481.

Bargh, J. A. 1994. The Four Horsemen of automaticity: Awareness, efficiency, intention, and control in social cognition. In *Handbook of Social Cognition*, 2nd ed., ed. R. S. Wyer, Jr., and T. K. Srull, 1–40. Hillsdale, NJ: Erlbaum.

Barsalou, L. W. 1982. Context-independent and context-dependent information in concepts. *Memory & Cognition* 10:82–93.

Barsalou, L. W. 1987. The instability of graded structure: Implications for the nature of concepts. In *Concepts and Conceptual Development: Ecological and Intellectual Factors in Categorization*, ed. U. Neisser, 101–140. Cambridge: Cambridge University Press.

Barsalou, L. W. 1989. Intraconcept similarity and its implications for interconcept similarity. In *Similarity and Analogical Reasoning*, ed. S. Vosniadou and A. Ortony, 76–121. Cambridge: Cambridge University Press.

Barsalou, L. W. 1993. Flexibility, structure, and linguistic vagary in concepts: Manifestations of a compositional system of perceptual symbols. In *Theories of Memory*, ed. A. C. Collins, S. E. Gathercole, and M. A. Conway, 29–101. Erlbaum.

Barsalou, L. W. 1999. Perceptual symbol systems. *Behavioral and Brain Sciences* 22:577–609.

Barsalou, L. 2003. Abstraction in perceptual symbol systems. *Philosophical Transactions of the Royal Society of London* 358:1177–1187.

Barsalou, L. 2005. Abstraction as dynamic interpretation in perceptual symbol systems. In *Building Object Categories*, ed. L. Gershkoff-Stowe and D. Rakison, 389–431. Mahwah, NJ: Erlbaum.

Carston, R. 2002. *Thoughts and Utterances*. Malden, MA: Blackwell.

Gauker, C. 2011. *Words and Images: An Essay on the Origin of Ideas*. New York: Oxford University Press.

Greenspan, S. L. 1986. Semantic flexibility and referential specificity of concrete nouns. *Journal of Memory and Language* 25:539–557.

Griffiths, P. E. 2002. What is innateness? *Monist* 85:70–85.

Griffiths, P. E., E. Machery, and S. Linquist. 2009. The vernacular concept of innateness. *Mind & Language* 24:605–630.

Hill, C. 2010. I love Machery's book, but love concepts more. *Philosophical Studies* 149:411–421.

Hoenig, K., E.-J. Sim, V. Bochev, B. Herrnberger, and M. Kiefer. 2008. Conceptual flexibility in the human brain: Dynamic recruitment of semantic maps from visual, motor, and motion-related areas. *Journal of Cognitive Neuroscience* 20:1799–1814.

James, T. W., and I. Gauthier. 2003. Auditory and action semantic features activate sensory-specific perceptual brain regions. *Current Biology* 13:1792–1796.

James, T. W., and I. Gauthier. 2004. Brain areas engaged during visual judgments by involuntary access to novel semantic information. *Vision Research* 44:429–439.

Keil, F. C. 1994. Explanation based constraints on the acquisition of word meaning. *Lingua* 92:169–196.

Kiefer, M. 2005. Repetition priming modulates category-related effects on event-related potentials: Further evidence for multiple cortical semantic systems. *Journal of Cognitive Neuroscience* 17:199–211.

Machery, E. 2005. Concepts are not a natural kind. *Philosophy of Science* 72:444–467.

Machery, E. 2007. Concept empiricism: A methodological critique. *Cognition* 104:19–46.

Machery, E. 2009. *Doing without Concepts*. New York: Oxford University Press.

Machery, E. 2010a. Précis of *Doing without Concepts*. *Behavioral and Brain Sciences* 33:195–244.

Machery, E. 2010b. Replies to my critics. *Philosophical Studies* 149:429–436.

Machery, E. 2010c. Reply to Barbara Malt and Jesse Prinz. *Mind & Language* 25:634–646.

Machery, E. 2011. Replies to Lombrozo, Piccinini, and Poirier and Beaulac. *Dialogue* 50:195–212.

Mallon, R., E. Machery, S. Nichols, and S. P. Stich. 2009. Against arguments from reference. *Philosophy and Phenomenological Research* 79:332–356.

Malt, B. 2010. Why we should do without concepts. *Mind & Language* 25:622–633.

Margolis, E., and S. Laurence. 2010. Concepts and theoretical unification. *Behavioral and Brain Sciences* 33:219–220.

Mazzone, M., and E. Lalumera. 2010. Concepts: Stored or created? *Minds and Machines* 20:47–68.

McRae, K., and G. S. Cree. 2002. Factors underlying category-specific semantic deficits. In *Category-Specificity in Mind and Brain*, ed. E. M. E. Forde and G. W. Humphreys, 211–249. New York: Psychology Press.

Prinz, J. J. 2002. *Furnishing the Mind: Concepts and Their Perceptual Basis*. Cambridge, MA: MIT Press.

Rice, C. Forthcoming. Concepts as pluralistic hybrids. *Philosophy and Phenomenological Research*.

Smith, L., and L. K. Samuelson. 1997. Perceiving and remembering: Category stability, variability, and development. In *Perceiving and Remembering: Learning, Memory and Cognition*, ed. K. Lamberts and D. Shanks, 161–196. Cambridge, MA: MIT Press.

Stich, S. P. 1983. *From Folk Psychology to Cognitive Science: The Case Against Belief*. Cambridge, MA: MIT Press.

Tabossi, P., and P. N. Johnson-Laird. 1980. Linguistic context and the priming of semantic information. *Quarterly Journal of Experimental Psychology* 32:595–603.

Weisberg, J., M. van Turennout, and A. Martin. 2007. A neural system for learning about object function. *Cerebral Cortex* 17:513–521.

Whitney, P., T. McKay, G. Kellas, and W. A. J. Emerson. 1985. Semantic activation of noun concepts in context. *Journal of Experimental Psychology: Learning, Memory, and Cognition* 11:126–135.

Yeh, W., and L. W. Barsalou. 2006. The situated nature of concepts. *American Journal of Psychology* 119:349–384.

X Concepts and Conceptual Individuation

21 Logical Concepts and Associative Characterizations

Elisabeth Camp

21.1 Introduction

Recent theorizing about concepts has been dominated by two broad models: crudely speaking, a philosophical one on which concepts are rule-governed atoms, and a psychological one on which they are associative networks.[1] The debate between these two models has often been framed in terms of competing answers to the question of "cognitive architecture" or "the nature of thought." I argue that this is a false dichotomy, because thought operates in both these ways. Human thought utilizes word-like representational structures that function as stable, arbitrary, recombinable bits. This supports a version of the language of thought hypothesis—though a significantly more modest one than its advocates typically assume. But human thought also employs representational structures that are contextually malleable, intuitive, and holistic, which I call *characterizations*. *Dual systems* models of cognition (e.g., Sloman 1996; Evans 2008; Evans and Frankish 2009) recognize this multiplicity of mental processes but posit largely separate structures, and emphasize conflicts between them. By contrast, I argue that the two forms of representation are more closely integrated, and more symbiotic, than talk of duality suggests.

21.2 Logic and Systematicity: Concepts as Words

The starting point for much philosophical theorizing about concepts is that conceptual thought is *systematic*. That is, either as an a priori or an empirical matter, the ability to think one thought, *a is F*, is intertwined with the ability to think a host of other, related thoughts, *b is F, c is F, d is F ...; a is G, a is H, a is I. ...* Systematicity is generally

1. This description is crude both because it neglects important variations among views within each model, and because it ignores psychologists who adopt the word-like model (e.g., Bloom 2002; Carey 2011; Pinker 1994) as well as philosophers who adopt a more associationist or at least holistic one (e.g., Prinz 2004; Davidson 1973, 1975).

taken to be fundamental for several reasons. Most importantly, it produces cognitive *flexibility*: the ability to track objects and properties across a wide range of situations. It also underwrites *productivity*: acquiring one new concept brings with it the capacity to think a wide range of other thoughts. Finally, the structural similarities and differences among these various thoughts also entail certain inferential relations among them: for instance, because the thoughts that *a is F* and *b is F* share a common concept, *F*, when combined with the thought that *a is not b*,[2] they entail the thought that *at least two things are F*. Thus, systematicity supports the ability to *reason*.

Many philosophers believe that if conceptual thought is systematic in these ways, it must also be fundamentally linguistic. Systematic representational abilities, the argument goes, must be implemented by a systematic mechanism, which in turn requires a vehicle with a compositional format. And this, it is claimed, is tantamount to accepting a language of thought. Jerry Fodor is most closely associated with this view (e.g. Fodor 1987; Fodor and Pylyshyn 1988); but Georges Rey (1995), Martin Davies (1991), José Bermudez (2003), and Michael Devitt (2005) are among the many others who have endorsed and developed arguments along these lines.[3]

I agree that conceptual thought does—indeed must—involve a significant degree of systematicity; but I reject the inference that it must therefore be linguistic in any interesting sense. One major weakness of the language of thought hypothesis has been lack of specificity about exactly what systematicity is, and why it is so important for conceptual thought. A second weakness has been lack of specificity about exactly what language is, and so about what it means to claim that thought is language-*like*. In this section, I address both shortcomings by unpacking three major features that are closely tied to systematicity: semantic arbitrariness, combinatorial neutrality, and digitality. In each case, I argue that language (either natural or formal) constitutes a paradigmatic instance of the relevant feature, but also that the feature comes in degrees and is manifested in formats that are clearly nonlinguistic. Thus, to insist that conceptual thought must be language-like either begs the question under discussion or trivializes the notion of language. The upshot is that there are indeed good reasons to hold that a significant portion of human thought is importantly language-like, because it deploys arbitrary

---

2. Or at least with a de jure non-co-indexing of *a* and *b*.

3. A second philosophical tradition is more skeptical about the idea that thought requires a stable representational vehicle, but still ties thought tightly to language. Here the claim is that genuine thought, as opposed to mere stimulus response, requires the capacity for higher-order reflection, especially on one's epistemic credentials; and it is further assumed that only language enables such reflection. This position is most strongly associated with Davidson (1982), but versions of it have been articulated by Peacocke (1992), McDowell (1994), Dummett (1994), and Bermudez (2003). I have argued (2009b) against this that the crucial differentiation from stimulus response can be satisfied in a more minimal manner, as long as the thinker's representational capacities are capable of being exercised in a wide variety of circumstances.

recombinable representational bits. But this conclusion follows not from inherent features of thought or concepts per se, but rather from the fact that some human thought happens to exhibit these three features to an exceptionally high degree.

If we step back to consider what concepts are for—their most fundamental job—perhaps the most basic thing we can say is that concepts bring together multiple instances as belonging to the same kind, either by ascribing a common property to multiple objects or by re-identifying a single object as it gains and loses properties. This already constitutes a weak species of systematicity, insofar as a concept treats all of its instances as the same. It also means that concepts are inherently *abstract*, in at least three respects. First, they are not essentially tied to any one instance: they apply in the same way and with the same results to multiple instances. Second, concepts are not essentially tied to any particular attitude: conceptual thought enables thinkers to enter into multiple mental states—say, to wonder whether a is F, to fear or desire that a be F, and eventually to believe that a is, or is not, F—with the represented content remaining constant across those attitudinal changes. Finally, concepts are arguably abstract, not just in terms of what they represent and what attitude the thinker takes, but of when the thinker deploys them. That is, conceptual thought goes beyond mere differential response in that a concept can be exercised in a variety of cognitive contexts, independent of any particular triggering stimulus. In this sense conceptual thought is importantly *active* or under the thinker's control (Camp 2009b).

So far, I have merely argued that an extremely minimal interpretation of systematicity, which follows from concepts' most basic function, entails that concepts are abstract in being essentially independent of both represented and representing contexts. But for concepts to be context-independent in this sense, they must also be cross-contextually stable: the same concept must be able to be *redeployed* on different occasions and in different applications with a common representational import. Cross-contextual stability is an important feature of systematicity in its own right, and one might simply want to stop there. However, it has seemed to many philosophers and psychologists that a capacity for stable cross-contextual redeployment in turn requires that concepts be construed, not merely as representational abilities, but as items in a representational vehicle: as entities with ultimately physical (e.g., neural) properties, albeit individuated in functional terms. This inference from abilities to vehicles is controversial; Gareth Evans (1982, 100), for one, resisted it, and as an abductive ("how else?") argument, it is vulnerable to alternative explanations and accusations of imaginative failure. I take such worries seriously. But supposing one does accept a need for representational vehicles, then the above criteria of abstractness and redeployability together imply that the relation in virtue of which instances of a particular vehicular type, C, represent a particular object or property type, F, must be at least somewhat *arbitrary*. That is, the various instances of C must have some stable formal property in virtue of which they count as tokens of C; but this property cannot simply be that of replicating the appearance of *F*, because there is in general no constant appearance for the content of *being F* to have across all the contexts in which it can occur and be represented.

The paradigmatic case of an arbitrary principle mapping representational vehicle to content is the conventional linguistic connection between word and object. However, semantic arbitrariness is a matter of degree, and can be achieved in a variety of ways. In particular, a range of nonpictorial systems, like maps and diagrams, employ semantic principles which are partially resemblance-based but also significantly formalized: thus, city maps often employ iconic elements, such as a cross for a church or a picnic table for a park. (And indeed, there are pictographic written languages.) These icons are partially perceptual, insofar as *C*s represent *F*s because they look (sound, etc.) like them in important respects. But they are also formalized or stylized first because only some of *C*'s physical properties are semantically significant, and second because those properties of *C* that are significant do not reflect the full determinacy of the corresponding properties as instantiated by particular *F*s.

To the extent that a representational system does employ an arbitrary semantic principle, it can achieve at least two key representational advantages. First, arbitrary semantic principles permit flexible implementation: any type of token can be deployed as a symbol, subject only to constraints like ease of production and discrimination. Second, they permit *topic neutrality*: any sort of content can be the value of a symbol. By contrast, the more heavily a system relies on resemblance to underwrite semantic significance, the more constrained its representational range is. At the limit, pictorial systems can only represent objects and properties with distinctive visual appearances——a quality that many properties it is quite useful to represent, such as tastiness, obviously lack. Conversely, though, greater semantic arbitrariness also compromises certain representational advantages that are possessed by resemblance-based systems; in particular, such systems require less translation from perceptual inputs, which can facilitate both acquisition and integration between perception and cognition.

By themselves, these three key features abstractness, redeployability and arbitrariness can all be implemented with unstructured representational abilities: thus, a simple thinker might represent a single situation-type across multiple occasions by using an atomic representation *P* (simply deleting *P* should contravening evidence arise). But in that case there would be no point in ascribing concepts to the thinker, as opposed to whole undifferentiated thoughts; and his or her thoughts would be systematic only in the comparatively minimal sense of treating a variety of situations the same way across various representing contexts and attitudes. The core of the intuition that conceptual thought is systematic is the assumption that concepts are *compositional*: that they form a base of recurrent elements, which combine in different ways to produce wholes whose representational significance is a rule-governed function of the significances of those constituents and their mode of combination. Here again, the driving idea is that concepts remain stable across redeployment in various contexts; what we now add is the idea that those contexts include other concepts, in addition to represented contents and representing attitudes.

Above, I described the principle that maps vehicles to contents as semantic, and argued that redeployability and abstractness together entail semantic arbitrariness. With the shift to compositionality, we turn to questions of syntax; and here too, redeployability and abstraction are closely connected, with important consequences for how and what a system can represent. In order for one and the same concept to be retokened across multiple combinations, the result of combining that concept with some other(s) must not depend on specific interactions between those concepts; otherwise we couldn't ascribe a stable representational contribution to each of them individually. But this in turn means that the principle or operation that combines those concepts must itself apply generally, depending only on the type of concept in question (e.g., predicative or singular), and abstracting away from the particular contents represented.

We can say that a combinatorial principle is abstract in this sense insofar as it makes only a minimal contribution to the representational significance of the resulting whole, and so is relatively *neutral* about which types of concepts it can combine. Natural languages and formal logics are, of course, highly abstract in this sense. For instance, predication can combine any predicate phrase (e.g., "is an F" or "Fs") with any noun phrase (e.g., "a G" or "the G"), regardless of what objects and properties those phrases denote; and the representational significance of that combination is just that the object denoted by the noun phrase *possesses* the property denoted by the predicate.[4] By contrast, many nonlinguistic systems employ combinatorial principles that make a much more robust representational contribution to the whole. For instance, maps employ a spatial combinatorial principle such that the spatial arrangement of vehicular items represents an isomorphic spatial structure among the corresponding represented entities (up to a distance metric). The fact that these systems employ such representationally robust combinatorial principles significantly limits their expressive flexibility (Camp 2007). For instance, because placing items on a map necessarily represents their referents as arranged in an isomorphic spatial structure, maps are only capable of representing objects and properties as *having* spatial structures and locations. (Similarly, because phylogenetic trees employ a spatial structure of branching lines representing differentiation with common descent, they can only represent objects as having ancestors and descendants (Camp 2009).)

In principle, the more neutral a representational system's combinatorial principle is, the wider a range of concepts it can combine: the relative abstractness of its syntactic operation(s) permits correlatively greater compositional systematicity. As with semantic arbitrariness, it is natural to think of formal and natural languages as paradigms of abstractness. And indeed, the relative neutrality of predication as a combinatorial

4. For simplicity, I focus on predication; the point holds a fortiori for other combinatorial principles, such as functional application and Merge.

principle, added to a high degree of semantic arbitrariness, does make language distinctively topic neutral. This is obviously an advantageous feature for a conceptual system to possess. Moreover, to the extent that a thinker's conceptual abilities display a high degree of topic neutrality, this suggests that it is employing something like a linguistic format (Camp 2007; Carruthers 2006).

I believe that an argument from topic neutrality along these lines—along with the more quotidian fact that we talk so much—does support an inference to the conclusion that much of human thought is language-like in a fairly strong sense. More precisely, the fact that humans can think about such a wide range of things suggests that our thinking takes place in a highly abstract, semantically arbitrary, and combinatorially neutral medium. However, we need to lodge two crucial caveats about the combinatorial properties of language, and in turn about just how language-like human concepts must be.

First, combinatorial neutrality, like semantic arbitrariness, is not distinctive to language, because some diagrammatic systems also employ combinatorial principles whose representational contribution is similarly minimal. For instance, Venn diagrams work by combining circles (along with some other symbols, like shading and dots) such that the spatial relations among those circles represent isomorphic logical relations among the denoted sets; but set union and intersection are just as if not more abstract than the possession relation denoted by predication. Their comparatively neutral combinatorial principles and relatively arbitrary semantic principles gives such diagrammatic systems significant expressive power; indeed, Shin (1994) demonstrates that a sophisticated version of Venn diagrams is expressively equivalent to first-order predicate calculus. Thus, the first caveat is that by itself, evidence from topic neutrality only supports the claim that the conceptual system's underlying format is either linguistic *or* diagrammatic. Moreover, it may also be possible to achieve topic neutrality by employing multiple distinct formats in combination.[5]

5. Diagrammatic systems like Venn diagrams do still exhibit significant expressive limitations relative to language because their combinatorial principles are less abstract than language's in a second sense: with respect to the way they relate to their representational vehicle. Diagrammatic systems deploy physical, specifically spatial, relations among vehicular constituents to represent logical or other relations among represented constituents; by contrast, linguistic syntactic principles are defined entirely in terms of *operations* on the semantic *values* of the system's basic constituents (Rey 1995). As a result, the linguistic vehicle (the sentence) only needs to signal the appropriate order of operations on constituents, which can be done by any implementationally convenient means. By contrast, Venn diagrams can only represent logical relations that are isomorphic to intersecting figures drawn in a single plane (Lemon and Pratt 1998). Discussion about vehicular format is complicated here by the fact that the vehicle is to be understood at a functional, rather than physically implementing, level (e.g., Fodor and Pylyshyn 1988). I believe it does make sense to talk about differences in format at the functional level (Camp 2007), but such talk must be interpreted carefully.

The second caveat is that natural languages fall far short of full systematicity. Semantically, the intuitive meaning of whole phrases and sentences often appears to depend on interactions among their constituent words, as well as their contexts of utterance and interpretation. Thus, "cut" intuitively seems to make substantially different contributions to "Jane cut the grass," "Jane cut the cake," and "Jane cut her finger" (Searle 1978; Travis 1994); similarly for the contribution of "soccer" to "soccer shirt," "soccer fan," and "soccer mom." More importantly, preserving the assumption that language employs one or a few generally applicable combinatorial principles has forced linguists to posit massive hidden complexity in logical form, by means of covert movement, deletion, and type-shifting (Szabo 2012).

Worse, many syntactically and semantically similar expressions, such as "put" and "stow" in "John put/stowed his gear down," cannot be freely intersubstituted. As a result, the claim that language permits general recombinability of items within a given syntactic type is either false or relies on a typology that is so fine grained as to trivialize the claim to systematicity (Johnson 2004). One might dismiss these restrictions as the result of contingent limitations arising from the interface between syntax and lexical or phonological systems, rather than from the fundamental nature of language per se (Hauser, Chomsky and Fitch 2002). But many philosophers and linguists have also wanted to restrict the systematicity of language and thought at a more fundamental, purely semantic level. Thus, Strawson (1970, 95), Evans (1982, 101), and Peacocke (1992, 42) all follow Ryle (1953, 76) in assuming that category mistakes like "Julius Caesar is a prime number" are nonsense, because their correlative concepts cannot be meaningfully combined. I have argued (2004) that such cross-categorial strings do have comprehensible inferential roles, and that there is no compelling reason to deny them truth conditions; indeed, I'll suggest in section 21.5 that such apparently absurd combinations are an important source of human cognition's imaginative power. A well-formed sentence is a powerful communicative and cognitive tool; however, it cannot be constructed simply by repeatedly subsuming pairs of words under universal concatenation rules, as a simple view of compositionality would allow. By contrast, diagrams and many maps are significantly more compositionally straightforward in this respect.[6]

With these two caveats noted, we can reiterate the main point thus far: compared with other representational systems, language is extremely abstract, both in employing a highly arbitrary semantic principle mapping vehicular items to contents, and in employing a highly neutral syntactic principle combining vehicular items into representational wholes. Languages combine these two forms of abstractness to produce

6. The corollary is that such non-linguistic systems only need so few syntactic types because their more robust combinatorial principles restrict what sorts of things their basic constituents can represent; hence, they achieve maximal systematicity within a more restricted domain.

a high degree of topic neutrality, and hence of expressive power. To the extent that human conceptual thought displays a similar degree of systematicity and topic neutrality, this provisionally suggests that it may employ similarly abstract semantic and combinatorial principles as well. In this sense, human conceptual thought is like language and concepts are like words.

The third major feature I want to draw out of systematicity also follows from the requirement of recombinability and also supports the analogy between concepts and words. We can only identify concepts as forming a stable, systematic structure if it is possible to segment representational wholes into parts that can be retokened in different combinations on different occasions. And this in turn appears to entail that a systematically recombinable representational system must be *digital*. Here again, language provides a paradigm of digitality. Words are (assumed to be) stable atoms of meaning; and predication or functional application are highly discrete functions that takes two such atoms to produce a determinate result. By contrast, pictures approach continuity (or, in Nelson Goodman's [1968] terms, *density*), both in terms of which syntactic features of the vehicle make a representational difference and of which semantic values they denote. (For instance, in a color photograph any difference in the picture's color represents a correlative difference in the color of the represented scene.) More importantly, it is not clear that elements in a picture can even be isolated *as* syntactic units independently of assigning them a semantic interpretation; and to the extent this is possible, the semantic significance of such elements—say, of three lines coming to a point—often depends heavily on their role within the larger representing context.

One might think that all that matters for systematicity is *that* a representational system be digital, so that it has recombinable parts with stable semantic significance. And one might think further that any digital representational system is *de facto* linguistic, because a language just is a representational system with semantically stable, recombinable atoms.[7] However, digitality too is a matter of degree, with a system's degree of digitality again making a substantive difference for what and how it represents. For instance, some map systems, like city maps and seating charts, employ a finite base of recurrent elements (e.g., crosses for churches, green squares for parks, circles for sites of historical interest), but permit those icons to be placed in very many—perhaps indefinitely many—locations, with the representational significance of the whole being a rule-governed function of the representational significance of those icons and their

7. Thus, Eliot Sober (1976, 141) claims that "where [picture-like representational systems] are digital, they simply *are* linguistic systems of a certain kind." This also seems to be what Fodor (2007, 107–108) is thinking when he argues that "'iconic' and 'discursive' are mutually exclusive modes of representation," where the distinction between the two modes is defined in terms of whether the representational whole has "a canonical decomposition."

spatial arrangement. The system is still technically digital or discrete as long as there is some lower bound on the fineness of grain of the semantically significant locations at which icons can be placed; but its relative density stands in clear contrast to the relative sparseness of language.

The fact that linguistic systems are highly digital renders them robust against certain kinds of error in production and interpretation, by making many small differences in the vehicle's physical properties representationally inert. Thus, distinct utterances of a word can differ significantly in their pronunciation or inscription without producing correlative representational differences, where analogous differences in a map or diagram would be significant. Conversely, though, when a word is misinterpreted—say, when we hear *set* instead of *let* or *can* instead of *can't*—the resulting representational error is also one of kind rather than degree, with correlatively radical representational results.

In addition to being more dense, many representational systems are also more highly *relational* than language. Thus, maps, phylogenetic trees, and Venn diagrams all work by placing many elements in relation, with no upper limit on the number of items, and with every represented object or property thereby automatically placed in a substantive semantic relation to all the others. By contrast, language has as its fundamental unit a propositional or sentential phrase. Below that level, additional information can be included as qualifications of verb and noun phrases, while above it sentential connectives can link propositions together, in both cases indefinitely. But the basic unit of linguistic significance contains less information than in other representational systems, and stores that information as a discrete unit. Again, relationality brings both advantages and disadvantages. On the one hand, compiling and manipulating information that would require active, unwieldy inference in language comes along as a "free ride" in a map or diagram, because adding or altering one symbol automatically updates the represented relations to all the other symbols' referents (Shimojima 1996). On the other hand, those systems' high degree of relationality can also make it difficult or impossible to extract isolated bits of information, and especially to represent general states of affairs without representing specific instances (Camp 2007). Thus, insofar as humans are adept at manipulating isolated units of abstract quantificational information, this again suggests that their underlying conceptual format is strongly language-like.

In this section, I have offered a tempered justification of the analogy between concepts and words by motivating the intuition that conceptual thought is systematic. The basic job of concepts is to classify multiple distinct instances as belonging to the same kind. This means they must *abstract* away from many features of those instances and remain stable while being *redeployed* across a variety of contexts. If we assume that thought requires a vehicle at all, then these intertwined features of abstractness and redeployability entail that the relation which assigns contents to vehicles must be at least somewhat *arbitrary*. The heart of systematicity is the requirement that conceptual thought be compositional. But if concepts are to retain stable significance across combinations and enter into a wide range of combinations, then their operative syntactic principle must be *combinatorially neutral*, making only a minimal contribution to the representational import of the whole. Finally, a system with recombinable elements must be *digital*, so that representational wholes can be segmented into parts with independent representational import.

Putting these features together makes the conclusion that conceptual thought is fundamentally linguistic seem very natural: if concepts must be arbitrary recombinable bits, they must also be a lot like words. Further, our initial considerations in support of systematicity were highly plausible. Thinking of the same thing as a single thing on multiple occasions and subsuming multiple instances under the same kind; using inference to produce belief in new thoughts; changing one's attitude about the same thought—these are fundamental tasks for a conceptual system to perform. Moreover, it is highly plausible that humans do actually perform these tasks on a regular basis. We also excel at thinking about an enormous range of topics, without obvious limitation; and we are capable of, and sometimes quite good at, manipulating abstract, especially quantificational information. These abilities require a high degree of semantic and syntactic abstractness, of the sort paradigmatically encountered in language.

However, we've also seen that the usual argument from systematicity to a language of thought is too quick, in at least three respects. First, semantic arbitrariness, syntactic neutrality, and digitality can all be satisfied by nonlinguistic representational systems, and all are a matter of degree. Thus, instead of a sharp dichotomy between imagistic and discursive systems, we have a variety of systems that are more or less arbitrary, combinatorially flexible, and digital. Language lies at or near the top of the continuum along each of these dimensions, while other formats display each feature to different degrees and in different ways. The differences among these formats are not merely notational: they produce substantive differences in ease of use, expressive power, and types of error and breakdown, delivering distinctive profiles of representational advantage and weakness.

Second, the connection between conceptual thought and language cannot therefore be justified by a general inference about thought per se, but must rely on the contingent fact that human conceptual thought manifests a distinctive pattern of abilities (and limitations) that mirrors the distinctive features of language. Other creatures display different profiles of ability and limitation, suggesting that their thought may employ a different format(s) (Camp 2007, 2009a). So long as their cognition is significantly systematic and stimulus-independent, it should be treated as conceptual in a substantive sense of that term (Camp 2009b).

Third, the conclusion that human conceptual thought is language-like must be tempered by the realization that natural languages do not fit the paradigm suggested by the language of thought hypothesis. In particular, natural languages exhibit significant limitations on recombinability; and the intuitive meaning of whole sentences often appears to depend on their internal and external context in ways that cannot be traced back to obvious semantically legislated context sensitivity plus general compositional rules. Thus, it is controversial whether words themselves are systematically recombinable representational atoms. The assumption that they are should instead be seen as a methodological commitment, borne out of the desire to explain how speakers and hearers converge on common communicative contents (Szabo 2012). The model of "language" assumed by the language of hought hypothesis is an idealization, much closer to that of artificial formal logics like the predicate calculus.

21.3   The Malleability of Association: Characterizations as Contextual Gestalts

Faced with the above considerations about the systematicity of conceptual thought, many psychologists are likely to diagnose a typical case of philosophical imperialism: of stipulating features that thought must exemplify if it is to fulfill a philosopher's fantasy of rationality. I noted at the end of section 21.2 that human thought does at least sometimes fit this model. But it is also undeniable, and important, that much of our thought is not systematic or logical, but *associative*: intuitive, holistic, and context sensitive. Much of the research on associative thinking has focused on how it interferes with logical thought, causing us to respond in ways that are absurd by our own reflective lights. Perhaps the most famous example of this is the *conjunction fallacy* (Tversky and Kahneman 1982): the tendency to rank a conjunction of two conditions as more probable than one subcondition when the entire conjunction better fits a stereotype. Here is the classic example:

Linda is 31 years old, single, outspoken, and very bright. She majored in philosophy. As a student, she was deeply concerned with issues of discrimination and social justice, and also participated in antinuclear demonstrations.
   Which is more probable?

1. Linda is a bank teller.
2. Linda is a bank teller and is active in the feminist movement.

When posed this question, 85 percent of subjects opted for the second response, even though logically (and as subjects themselves willingly concede), no conjunction can be more probable than either of its conjuncts.
   More generally, it is increasingly well established that intuitive, stereotypical thinking drives a wide range of our everyday engagement with the world, by disposing us to *frame* or *gestalt* subjects in certain ways. These effects are especially palpable and influential, and have been especially well studied, in the context of judgments of probability and actuality, and in the domains of emotional and moral response. In

particular, a wide range of studies has demonstrated that presenting the same set of facts against the background of different interpretive perspectives, or through descriptions that emphasize different features, can produce dramatically different emotional and moral responses, as well as different estimates of probability and assignments of causal responsibility.[8] More generally, stereotypes, perspectives, and "framing" play a pervasive role in our thinking even when we aren't explicitly focused on emotion, moral evaluation, probability, or causality.

The considerations about systematicity from section 21.2 show that if human concepts are indeed arbitrary, recombinable representational bits, then they are ill-equipped to support associative thinking. For instance, concrete images play an important role in associative thought, especially in facilitating rapid recognition and motivating emotion and action. But insofar as concepts employ an arbitrary semantic principle, they can only access such images indirectly. Similarly, associative thought is highly context sensitive: the same feature can be framed in dramatically different terms, and produce dramatically different responses, when embedded in different situations. But the most fundamental feature of concepts is their cross-contextual stability. Finally, associative thought is highly synthetic, bundling lots of information into intuitive clusters; but the digitality of linguistic systems leads them to store much information as discrete bits, with many connections retrievable only through active inference.

It should not be controversial that associative thought employs intuitive, context-driven, synthetic classifications that rely on images and emotions and depart from the deliverances of logic. However, many philosophers appear to assume, at least implicitly, that there is nothing of theoretical substance to say about how associative thought works. The extreme version of this view is that outside the domain of rational concepts, there are only idiosyncratic "trains of images suggested one by another," as William James ([1890] 1950, 325) says, where these trains are purely causal processes, grounded in the spatial and temporal contiguity of their sources. Thus, Proust's bite into a madeleine reminds him of his Aunt Leonie not for any logical reason but only because

8. On the effects of framing on evaluative response, see Tversky (1981), Kahneman and Tversky (1982), Bartels (2008), and Bartels and Medin (2007). See Levin, Schneider, and Gaeth (1998) and Iliev et al. (2009) for overviews of framing effects, especially in moral contexts. See Wallbott and Scherer (1986), Ortony, Clore, and Collins (1988), Smith (1989), and Mauro, Sato, and Tucker (1992) for discussions of connections between cognitive appraisal and emotional response. See Judd and Park (1993), Ryan, Judd, and Park (1996), and Nelson, Acker, and Manis (1996) for discussion of the effect of stereotypes on judgments of probability. Conversely, priming for different emotions also affects how subjects frame the presented situation, which in turn alters which features they notice, what causal explanations they assign, and the valence and intensity of their moral judgments; see Forgas (1990), Keltner, Ellsworth, and Edwards (1993), Lerner et al. (2003), Small, Lerner, and Fischhoff (2006), and Dasgupta et al. (2009); see Musch and Klauer (2003) for an overview of affective priming.

she used to give him a bite of the cookie on Sunday mornings. If this is all association amounts to, we shouldn't expect much in the way of interesting generalizations.

Against such pessimism, I think we can identify a more substantive, nuanced cognitive structure in play—one that merits theoretical investigation in its own right and that interacts in interesting ways with the sort of conceptual thought discussed in section 21.2. We do sometimes engage in purely Proustian association, but associative thought comprises a variety of distinct, partially overlapping capacities and dispositions (Evans 2008), at least some which manifests a sufficiently high degree of functional integration and interpersonal similarity to warrant independent classification. I call these patterns of thought *characterizations*; they are close to what many psychologists have thought of as concepts, and especially to stereotypes and prototypes (Rosch 1978).[9] However, as we will see, they depart markedly from concepts as philosophers conceive of them. I am not interested in legislating the use of terminology; but because most advocates of prototype and "theory" theories of concepts have taken prototypes and theories to perform the basic cognitive tasks identified in section 21.2—specifically, the classification of instances under kinds in a way that permits redeployment, thereby underwriting inference and attitude revision—when I speak of *concepts,* I will mean concepts as described there. By limning the distinct functional roles played by concepts and characterizations, I will argue, we achieve a clearer overall picture of the overall cognitive terrain; perhaps more importantly, we free ourselves to appreciate characterizations for the tasks that they perform well, rather than simply treating them as concepts manqué.

As I think of them, characterizations are constituted by three main features: their *content*, the sort of *endorsement* they involve, and their *structure*. First, characterizations apply collections of properties, often quite rich, to their subjects. For instance, my characterization of quarterbacks includes their being natural leaders, affable, and a bit shallow. In addition to such general traits, characterizations also often include more specific, experientially represented properties: thus, I think of quarterbacks as having a certain sort of square, clean-shaven jaw, gleaming teeth, and a ready smile. Some such properties, like certain ways of walking or talking, are so specific and experientially dependent that we lack established expressions for them and can only refer to them demonstratively.[10] Importantly, these include affectively laden properties concerning

9. Recently, Tamar Szabo Gendler has drawn philosophers' attention to a related range of phenomena, which she collects under the term "alief" (Gendler 2008). Like characterizations, aliefs are intuitive and associative, but they include much more basic reflexes and "action potentials," and hence are typically less cognitively sophisticated and contextually malleable than characterizations. I believe that aliefs and characterizations are both theoretically rewarding constructs, with overlapping but distinct extensions. A more systematic comparison remains a topic for further work.

10. Or metaphorically; see Camp (2006).

how the subject in question tends to or should make one feel: for instance, the terror one feels upon encountering a stern professor in the hallway, or the awe one feels upon entering a sunlit cathedral.

I take the characterization of quarterbacks alluded to above to be in line with an entrenched (and very American) cultural stereotype. And stereotypes are the most obvious class of characterizations. But where stereotypes are ways of thinking about *types*, characterizations can also represent individual persons, objects, and events, such as Barack Obama, the Notre Dame Cathedral, or the March on Washington.[11] Further, where stereotypes are communally shared ways of thinking, characterizations can be quite idiosyncratic: my characterization of a romantic afternoon excursion may not match yours (or sadly, anyone else's), and I may have a characterization of something the rest of the community simply doesn't notice, such as my route to work. Thus, stereotypes are a special case of the broader category of characterizations.

The second major feature of characterizations is that they don't require commitment to their subjects actually possessing the properties ascribed to them. Thus, I'm under no illusion that quarterbacks are especially likely, in fact, to have gleaming teeth or square jaws. Still, there is a species of commitment involved in my characterizing quarterbacks this way: I take those features to be *fitting* for them. If I were casting a quarterback in a movie, for instance, I would look for an actor with those features. Similarly, some features in my characterization of an individual might be "just-so" or apocryphal facts that I take to be fitting albeit false: thus, John might be the kind of guy who *should* have locked the principal out of his office in high school, even if he never actually did any such thing. Conversely, I might also marginalize some features that I acknowledge a subject does in fact possess because they don't fit the rest of my characterization: thus, I might tend to ignore or forget that John once attended seminary, because I take it not to fit with his sporty, carefree manner.

When assessments of fittingness do come apart from how we take a subject to actually be, it's often because we believe that an individual is exceptional or aberrant for its type. (In particular, the generic force of stereotypes allows us to maintain them in the face of exceptions.) Although it might be nice if fittingness could be straightforwardly reduced to statistical norms, intuitions of fittingness often appear to have a more squarely aesthetic basis, which Arthur Danto (1981) nicely articulates in connection with style:

The structure of a style is like the structure of a personality. ... This concept of consistency has little to do with formal consistency. It is the consistency rather of the sort we invoke when we say

---

11. Where it obviously makes an enormous difference whether a concept represents a type or an individual, or an object or a property, the sort and specificity of what a characterization represents makes no inherent difference to its basic structure; in particular, characterizations of types can include equally precise, vivid properties as those of individuals.

that a rug does not fit with the other furnishings of the room, or a dish does not fit with the structure of a meal, or a man does not fit with his own crowd. It is the fit of taste which is involved, and this cannot be reduced to formula. It is an activity governed by reasons, no doubt, but reasons that will be persuasive only to someone who has judgment or taste already. (207)

If we were more fully rational, we would sharply distinguish what we take to be fitting from we believe to be actual or even probable. But in fact, we often allow intuitions about fit, especially in the form of stereotypes, to drive our beliefs about probability and actuality, with highly problematic, sometimes repugnant, results.[12]

The third major feature of characterizations is that they don't merely consist of collections of attributed properties, but *structure* those properties in a complex pattern with powerful cognitive effects. Characterizations' structures involve at least two distinct dimensions of psychological importance. Along the first dimension, some features are more *prominent* than others. Prominence is roughly equivalent to what Amos Tversky (1977) calls "salience," which he in turn defines in terms of intensity and diagnosticity. A feature is *intense* to the extent that it has a high signal-to-noise ratio: it sticks out relative to the background, like a bright light or a hugely bulbous nose. A feature is *diagnostic* to the extent that it is useful for classifying objects as belonging to a certain category, like the number of stripes on a soldier's uniform. Both intensity and diagnosticity are highly context sensitive: in a room full of bulbous noses, or on a heavily scarred face, an ordinary bulbous nose will not stand out; and in such a room, knowing that the man I'm looking for has a bulbous nose won't help me to identify him.[13]

Along the second dimension, some features are more *central* than others, insofar as the thinker treats them as causing, motivating, or otherwise explaining many of the subject's other features (Thagard 1989; Sloman, Love, and Ahn 1998; Murphy and Medin 1985). For instance, I take a quarterback's being a natural leader to explain more of his other features—why he's popular and confident, why he smiles so readily, indeed why he's a quarterback at all—than his having a square jaw does. A good measure of centrality is how much else about the subject one thinks would change if that feature were removed.[14]

Structures of prominence and centrality are highly intuitive and holistic, in a way that the oft-cited analogy with seeing-as and perceptual gestalts makes vivid. Contrast

12. I discuss the role of perspectives and fittingness (and stereotypes) in connection with slurs in Camp (2013).

13. I take it that prominence is the most influential determinant of a feature's prototypicality relative to some class of objects—although this is a matter for empirical investigation.

14. The "theory theory" of concepts (e.g., Murphy and Medin 1985) is often presented as antidote to prototype theory, replacing the purportedly vacuous notion of similarity with more substantive attributions of causal relations. Centrality is a broader genus of which attributions of causation are the most important species.

Figure 21.1
The Old Woman/Young Lady.

the two ways of seeing figure 21.1. On either way of seeing the figure, the structural role of each constituent element depends on the roles of many other elements. When I switch from seeing the figure one way to the other, the relative prominence and centrality of those various elements shift dramatically. Further, this can cause those basic elements themselves to represent different things: the same set of pixels comes to be seen as a nose, say, or as a wart.

Much the same effect applies with characterizations: the same property may be assigned different structural roles within the same overall set of elements, which in turn can imbue that property with different emotive, evaluative, and even conceptual significance. Thus, if I take Bill's jovial sociability to be central to his personality, then his teasing remarks might seem like harmless attempts at bonding; while if I emphasize his desire to be in control, those same remarks will appear malicious and manipulative.[15] In each case, I acknowledge both that he is sociable and that he values control; the difference lies in how I weigh those features and connect them to others, and these differences may in turn underwrite different judgments about Bill's future actions and about what evaluations of and responses to him are warranted. Such holistic, structural context-dependence is especially obvious and forceful in the case of emotional significance, which "colors" a wide range of features and can engender markedly distinct evaluations and responses without necessarily changing our outright beliefs about which lower-level features are actually possessed. Many philosophers have argued that emotions impose an intuitive gestalt on a field of constituent features;[16] and as noted above, there is ample psychological evidence that different characterizations of the same set of facts both produce and are produced by different emotions.

21.4   Concepts and Characterizations: Differences

Given this sketch, it is obvious that characterizations cannot be straightforwardly identified with concepts as discussed in section 21.2. Among other things, many concepts, such as 1/4 INCH HEX NUT or SQUARE ROOTS OF 4, lack corresponding characterizations with any intuitive substance for most people. More fundamentally, the role of fittingness in characterizations precludes them from fixing the references of what they represent, since thinkers don't typically take either the presence or absence of fitting features to determine category membership, but readily classify counter-stereotypical birds or quarterbacks *as* birds or quarterbacks.[17] It also means that characterizations cannot be equated with what are sometimes called *conceptions* (e.g., Woodfield 1991): that is, a richer and potentially more idiosyncratic "theory" (Murphy and Medin 1985) associated with a conceptual core, which can shift while the core remains constant. Beyond these relatively obvious differences, the discussion in section 21.2 allows us to identify

---

15. Such interpretive effects have been especially well documented in the case of stereotypes. Devine (1989) found that nonconscious priming with stereotypically associated traits for blacks led white subjects to interpret ambiguous actions by racially unspecified actors as more hostile, even though no traits directly related to hostility were primed. Likewise, Duncan (1976) found that whites interpreted the same ambiguous move as a hostile, violent shove when the actor was black, and as just playing around when the actor was white. Sager and Schofield (1980) replicated these findings in children.

16. For instance, Noël Carroll says, "The emotions focus our attention. They make certain features of situations salient, and they cast those features in a special phenomenological light. The emotions' 'gestalt', we might say, situations" (2001, 224). See also Rorty (1980), de Sousa (1987), Calhoun (1984), Robinson (2005), and Currie (2010, 98).

17. This is a familiar philosophers' complaint against prototype theories of concepts: see for example, Rey (1983), Fodor and Lepore (1996), and Laurence and Margolis (1999).

three more basic differences between concepts and characterizations, grounded in the fundamental functions we identified concepts as performing.

The first fundamental job of concepts is to be capable of stable redeployment across cognitive and environmental contexts, so that the thinker can subsume different instances under the same concept, track the same object as it gains and loses properties, and take different attitudes toward the same content. By contrast, characterizations' basic job is to enable thinkers to engage intuitively with their current cognitive and environmental context. As the special case of stereotypes brings out, thinkers do have some default, cross-contextual dispositions to characterize certain subjects in certain ways. But as work on stereotypes, specifically on combating stereotype threat, also shows, priming for different concepts, even briefly, can alter thinkers' cognitive contexts significantly, with dramatic consequences for how they intuitively construe and act toward the focal subject.[18] More generally, much of the cognitive work—and cognitive and imaginative interest—of personal conversations and of reading historical and fictional narratives consists in temporarily aligning one's own intuitive characterizations and overall perspective with someone else's.[19]

Context plays a direct role in structuring characterizations through prominence, both in determining the background "noise" against which a particular feature's intensity is defined, and in fixing the cognitive interests and needs that determine a feature's degree of diagnosticity. It also plays a role in determining centrality, by affecting which sorts of properties, and which connections among properties, are explanatorily relevant. Finally, a thinker's emotional state or mood can dramatically affect a characterization's overall structure, and in turn the significance of particular constituent features.

If we think of characterizations as implementing the functional role of concepts, then their contextual malleability seems like a drawback or a bug: a failure of full rationality. But if we instead think of them as functional structures in their own right, and in particular as patterns of thought whose primary task is to enable thinkers to engage with their environments in an intuitive, nuanced way, then context sensitivity becomes an important desideratum. Different features really do matter more or less in different contexts and for different purposes, and thinkers need to be immediately and intuitively sensitive to these variations. This is not to deny that there are real conflicts between the deliverances of the two functional roles, but only to emphasize that they may occur for good reason.

Characterizations' pervasive contextual malleability also means that questions of individuation are much harder to settle, but also considerably less important, than they are in the case of concepts. Although individuation is obviously a contentious

18. See, for example, Steele and Aronson (1995), Steele, Spencer, and Aronson (2002), Marx and Roman (2002), McIntyre, Paulson, and Lord (2003), and Martens et al. (2006).
19. See Camp (unpublished ms.).

topic, concepts are often individuated by some appeal to reference plus inferential role (e.g. Block 1987). Intrapersonally, concepts differ just in case a thinker could rationally believe a thought containing one while disbelieving an otherwise identical thought containing the other (Frege 1892; Peacocke 1992); interpersonally, two thinkers possess the same concept if they endorse many of the same inferences and would apply their concept to many of the same instances. Because redeployability is such an important feature of concepts, most theorists reject strong holism, restricting a concept's individuating inferential role to a small subset of its inferential connections (weighted by degree of importance if not identified as absolutely analytic). By contrast, characterizations need to be informationally rich, relating as many properties, images, and responses as possible into intuitive wholes. Further, because not just which features but also how those features are structured is crucial for characterizations, and because this structure is itself strongly responsive to context-specific factors like intensity, diagnosticity, and centrality, characterizations of the same subject will usually differ in at least some functionally important ways both interpersonally and intrapersonally across time. We can say that two people, or the same person on different occasions, are employing the same characterization just in case there is a sufficiently large overlap in their characterizations' constituents and structure for our current cognitive or communicative purposes—but we shouldn't expect there to be any robust standard of identity that applies across the various occasions on which we classify characterizations as same or different.

The second fundamental job of concepts is to combine with a wide range of other concepts to produce whole thoughts. This compositional structure accounts for concepts' productivity and underwrites inferential relations among thoughts. By contrast, characterizations lack such general recombinability: just because I have characterizations of two types, or of an individual and a property, it does not follow that I also have a characterization of their combination. For instance, I have a characterization (or stereotype) of bank tellers, and another of feminists, but none of feminist bank tellers. Similarly, I have a rich characterization of Anna Karenina, and another of what's involved in being president of the United States, but no characterization of Anna Karenina as president. More importantly, when characterizations do combine, the resulting combination may include features not contained in either individual characterization, which *emerge* from their combination. Thus, I have a characterization of Napoleon, and another of mistresses, and I can form a characterization of Napoleon's mistress, but it contains many features (hairstyle, dress, personality) that are not part of my characterization of mistresses per se (nor of Napoleon). Again, when we think of characterizations as performing the tasks of concepts, failures of combination and emergent features look like serious problems.[20] But if we acknowledge characterizations as having

20. Again, these are familiar objections to prototypes as candidates for concepts; see for example, Margolis (1994) and Fodor and Lepore (1996).

their own representational function, these results make sense. Characterizations cannot retain the richness, specificity, and relational structure that makes them so intuitively powerful and cognitively useful while also being sufficiently abstract to combine in stable ways with a wide range of other characterizations. Further, when characterizations do combine, it is our knowledge of the referent(s) of the combined concepts—of NAPOLEON'S MISTRESS, say—that determines which features go into the resulting characterization, and how those features are structured.

The third fundamental difference between concepts and characterizations has to do with characterizations' intuitive gestalt structure. Because a fundamental function of concepts is to be redeployable across various combinations and attitudes, merely entertaining or endorsing a propositional thought containing a concept is both necessary and sufficient for exercising the corresponding conceptual ability. By contrast, characterizing a subject requires structuring one's thinking about the subject in such a way that the relevant lower-order features really do play appropriately prominent and central roles in one's overall intuitive thinking about that subject. As a result, it is neither necessary nor sufficient for having a characterization that one explicitly entertain or endorse any particular propositional thought; in particular, it is neither necessary nor sufficient for characterizing something in a certain way that one entertain thoughts about the prominence, centrality, or fittingness of the characterization's constituent features. Rather, what matters is just that one actually structure one's thoughts in the relevant intuitive way.

The analogy with perception is helpful here. There is a phenomenologically striking and practically efficacious difference between "seeing-as" and "looking plus thinking" (Wittgenstein 1953 197); for instance, I might know that *this* feature in figure 21.1 represents the old woman's nose, and *that* one a wart, without successfully seeing the figure *as* (a picture of) an old woman. So too with characterizing in thought. Suppose John tells me, in detail, about his characterization of Bill: which features he takes to be especially important and why, the explanatory relations among them, and so on. I might endorse all of these propositions, because I trust John's judgment, without ever managing to "get" the relevant characterization, because the operative features don't intuitively leap out as prominent or central for me. Further, just as with literal seeing-as, getting the relevant propositions to play the relevant organizational role is partly, but not entirely, under one's willful control: directing one's attention toward some particular features may help induce a certain characterization, but ultimately the "click" of holistic understanding is something that just happens—or doesn't.

Despite this importantly nonpropositional dimension of characterizations, we can still endorse, reject, and argue about them. Even though they are complex, nuanced, context sensitive, and intuitive, and even though they can be highly idiosyncratic, they are not just Jamesian causal associations. Endorsing a characterization amounts to accepting that its assignments of fittingness, prominence, and centrality are consistent with the objective distribution of properties in the world (modulo discrepancies introduced by fittingness) and conducive to achieving one's current cognitive goals. And although I cannot compel you by propositional means to even entertain my characterization, let alone endorse it, I can help you to "get it" by directing your attention toward the features that are most prominent and central for me, and explaining why I take them to be highly intense, diagnostic, central, and fitting.

21.5   Concepts and Characterizations: Connections

The details of my presentations of concepts and especially characterizations may be novel. But talk of two representational dimensions, one systematic and logical and the other associative and holistic, is familiar. In particular, advocates of a *dual systems* approach to cognition argue that humans employ two distinct modes of cognition: an evolutionarily more basic system that is fast, heuristic, and imagistically and affectively laden; and another, more recent and distinctively human system that is effortful, abstract, and logical.[21] The standard picture is that the associative system shoulders the bulk of unreflective, relatively automatic interaction with a messy, rapidly changing environment, with the logical system serving as a kind of overseer, stepping in when the stakes are high or the associative system delivers an especially implausible verdict. A raft of psychological evidence supports the claim that the logical system plays such a checking role; and as Sloman (1996) notes, it is methodologically easiest to discern both systems in operation in cases where they conflict. Although a full exploration of the interaction between concepts and characterizations is beyond the scope of this article, I want in this section to suggest, first, that talk of two distinct "systems" is overblown; and second, that the relationship between the two types of cognitive structure is often more symbiotic than antagonistic.

There is a fairly clear sense in which characterizations are more basic than concepts. They are less abstract and more closely tied to perceptual inputs and immediate action. Further, the tasks that concepts need to perform, for which systematic redeployability is so crucial, result from a demand for cross-contextual stability that, while clearly advantageous, is not essential to cognition as such. Cognitive agents could, after all, represent and respond to multiple instances in similar, but only roughly similar, ways—in which case they couldn't really entertain the same thought twice, adopting different attitudes toward it on different occasions. These are the sorts of considerations that have led to classifying System 1, associative thinking as basic and System 2, logical thought as a secondary overseer. At the same time, within the context of adult human

21. See, for example, Sloman (1996), Stanovich and West (2000), Kahneman (2003), Carruthers (2006), and Evans (2008); for recent discussion, see the essays in Evans and Frankish (2009). As noted above, Gendler's (2008) distinction between alief and belief is also relevant here.

cognition, there is an important sense in which concepts are more basic. Concepts are recombinable representational bits with stable referential and inferential significance. Given this, the conditions on possessing a concept (as opposed to full mastery) are comparatively minimal: one only needs to be able to think *about* the relevant object or property and draw a few core inferences; in many cases, not much more than hearing a word in the public lexicon is required. As noted in section 21.4, however, we lack substantive characterizations for many of our concepts.

Further, concepts provide the stable anchors that preserve characterizations' referential import through changes in their contents and structure. Because characterizations have their referents determined by way of concepts (as well as having the contents of their constituent features determined via concepts), it appears not to be possible for "Frege cases" to arise between characterizations and concepts.[22] That is, if a thinker has a concept and a characterization for the same individual or kind but fails to recognize that they are co-referential, this will only be because he or she possesses two distinct concepts for that thing, with the failure to recognize co-referentiality between the concept and the characterization holding in virtue of a failure to recognize co-referentiality between those two concepts.[23] In this sense at least, the two "systems" cannot be entirely distinct.

A better metaphor for the relationship between concepts and characterizations than laborer and overseer, then, might be of characterizations as roiling electron clouds orbiting concepts' more stable nuclear structures. Although characterizations do filter and color, and sometimes distort, our intuitive access to the "bare" truth-conditional facts, they do not operate on their own, in isolation from concepts; they piggyback off of them.

In this respect, my view can be seen as a species of the "pluralism" advocated by Laurence and Margolis (1999, 2003), according to which concepts function as representational atoms around which a variety of further informational structures, like prototypes and theories, are organized without actually contributing to the core concept's individuating referential and inferential content. In section 21.4, I resisted full-blown pluralism, by emphasizing the fundamental differences between concepts' and characterizations' functional roles. I think that much philosophical and psychological

---

22. As noted above, Frege (1892) individuated concepts in terms of the criterion of cognitive significance: the possibility that a thinker might rationally believe a thought containing concept *A* while not believing the same thought differing only in the substitution of *B* for *A*. A "Frege case" is one in which a thinker takes different attitudes toward the same state of affairs because he or she fails to realize that two concepts are in fact coextensional.

23. One can also associate multiple characterizations with a single concept, perhaps in virtue of having access to sociologically distinct sets of assumptions about the kind in question. Again, though, distinctness of characterizations cannot produce Frege cases except through distinctness of concepts.

confusion has been sown by thinking of characterizations *as* concepts, and that we gain a clearer understanding of each by separating them—and by collecting some but not all of the psychological phenomena that have been subsumed under prototypes, theories, and conceptions under the distinct category of characterizations. My current point, though, is that acknowledging the distinction between concepts and characterizations should not blind us to their deeply intimate relationship; and for this purpose, the pluralist model is helpful.

More specifically, I want to suggest that the minimal, abstract, systematic structure of concepts serves as a scaffold undergirding characterizations' contextually malleable complexity, and that the combination of both structures is key to the fertile imagination distinctive of human creativity.[24] As we saw in section 21.2, multiple representational formats can produce thought that is conceptual in the sense of being systematic, abstract, and flexible. But linguistic systems achieve these qualities to an exceptionally high degree. In particular, because language employs highly digital, semantically arbitrary representational atoms, and combines them using just one or a few combinatorially neutral syntactic operations, it is distinctively topic neutral. Moreover, semantic arbitrariness makes language especially well equipped for achieving a high degree of stimulus independence: the capacity to represent a wide range of contents in the absence of a directly triggering stimulus. Stimulus independence is an important condition on conceptual thought in its own right; but even more clearly, it is an essential condition for imagination (Camp 2009b; Carruthers 2006).

By itself, however, merely possessing a representational system with the capacity to represent a wide range of nonactual states of affairs doesn't give a thinker any motivation to exploit this capacity, or even to realize that he or she has it (Camp 2009b). Here again, linguistic systems are distinctively well equipped for exploring the space of unrealized possibilities, not just because languages are potentially topic neutral and stimulus independent, but because they permit hierarchically recursive representations, of a sort that can underwrite the ability to represent one's thoughts explicitly to oneself (McGeer and Pettit 2002).[25] Explicitly representing the compositional structure of one's own representations may also help to draw one's attention to new potential combinations of concepts, including those one lacks any direct, practical reason to entertain (Camp 2004).

The representational structures constructed by the conceptual system are, however, fairly thin, encompassing only a limited set of formal and material implications. For absurdly impractical combinations of concepts, like "Julius Caesar is a prime number,"

24. I think an analogous interplay is displayed even more clearly in the context of linguistic communication, but that lies even further outside the scope of the current discussion.
25. Although some other representational systems, such as phylogenetic trees, permit hierarchical recursion, their operative syntactic principles lack the semantic neutrality required to underwrite a general metacognitive ability.

this might seem like such a minimal variety of comprehension that it doesn't amount to genuine understanding. I've argued (2004) that such inferential roles do matter, not least because they allow us to make arguments. My current suggestion is that these minimal conceptual structures often serve as seeds for associative thought, including not just Jamesian or Proustian streams, but also for the construction of more substantive, structured, norm-governed characterizations. Sometimes, the result is a novelistic or poetic flight of fancy: thus, although I have no ready-made characterization for Anna Karenina as president of the United States, or for death as an overworked Joe, a writer might take these bare propositions as invitations to traverse new imaginative terrain (Camp 2009c). At other times, the result is a scientific revolution, as occurred when physicists took seriously the possibility that time is a fourth dimension, or that light is both particle and wave, or that the mind is the software of the brain. The insights that followed from exploring these possibilities did not follow as a matter of conceptual necessity from the (then) apparently absurd propositions expressed by those sentences; rather, they required ingenuity and a series of reconstruals of the characterizations associated with the operative terms.

21.6   New Directions for Investigation

Human thought is—or at least has the capacity to be—systematic. Among other things, this means that it is abstract, flexible, and productive. This in turn requires that concepts function as arbitrary recombinable representational bits. The specific contours of human thought, in particular its high degree of topic neutrality, adeptness at manipulating quantificational information, and capacity for truth-preserving inference, suggest that at least some human cognition is in language—or perhaps, in a logical format like a predicate calculus.

At the same time, human thought also is—or at least has the capacity to be—associative. Among other things, this means that it is experientially grounded, holistic, and intuitive. This in turn requires some representational structures—call them characterizations—that are rich, contextually malleable, and imagistically and affectively laden. For better and for worse, characterizations operate throughout our everyday engagement with the world. But in doing so, they build on the more minimal and general structure of concepts, which also permits them to play an essential role in metaphor, fiction, and scientific and philosophical exploration. Instead of arguing for a single answer to "how the mind works," then, we should probe, and appreciate, the multiplicity of functions that cognition performs, and the interactions between the structures underwriting them.

Given these conclusions, I see three main areas for future research. First, more attention needs to be paid to representational formats that fall between the extremes of pictures and language. There has recently been a renewed interest in the semantics and even syntax of pictures (e.g., Kulvicki 2006; Greenberg 2011). This is a vitally important project in its own right. But too often philosophers assume a sharp dichotomy between pictorial and sentential modes of representation. As we glimpsed in section 21.2, various other formats mix different degrees of semantic arbitrariness, combinatorial neutrality, and relationality, producing significant differences in what sorts of information they are capable of representing and how they manipulate it. A close examination of the resulting patterns of representational strength and vulnerability may in turn provide clues to what representational formats are employed by different thinkers, of various species, at different times.

Second, we need to further investigate forms of associative thought that are not merely idiosyncratic chains of association, but display significant structure. This involves, at a minimum, getting clearer on the causal mechanisms that underlie characterizations, on their connections to emotion and other aspects of our cognitive lives, and on what (if any) representational format they might have. In particular, in what ways are characterizations subject to voluntary control, both at a given moment or in the longer term, through cultivating habits of attention and response? (In this context, a sustained comparison with *aliefs* (Gendler 2008) would be especially useful.) It also involves getting clearer on the distinctive norms governing characterizations. Assignments of fittingness involve a crucial aesthetic dimension; but prominence and centrality are both functionally responsive to cognitive interests and explanatory purposes in ways that go beyond the straightforward tracking of objective statistical profiles. More generally, how are individual characterizations linked together into coherent overall perspectives, both for particular domains and about the world at large? How do we pick up and modulate these overall perspectives, through conversation and sustained imaginative exercises like fiction? (Camp 2009c, ms.)

Third, we need to attend to ways in which concepts and characterizations interact, both antagonistically and symbiotically. I have argued that distinguishing their functional roles enables us to acknowledge each representational structure as appropriately accomplishing a distinct cognitive task. Where "dual systems" approaches emphasize the ways associative thought fails to meet logical norms, I have suggested that the two structures often support and enrich one other. This includes not just standard tasks probed by psychologists, like object classification and judgments of probability, but also more idiosyncratic, contextually sensitive, and imaginatively demanding tasks like reading fiction and poetry. Finally, philosophers (and psychologists) generally assume that the job of language is to express thought, and that words have concepts as their lexical values. But many words and ways of using language have the function of expressing and manipulating characterizations and perspectives; among these are metaphor (Camp 2006, 2008), slurs (Camp 2013), and generics (Leslie 2007). This again suggests that characterizations and related associative structures are not merely concepts manqué, but representational structures in their own right, which find systematic expression in and through language.

References

Bartels, D. 2008. Principled moral sentiment and the flexibility of moral judgment and decision making. *Cognition* 108 (2): 381–417.

Bartels, D., and D. Medin. 2007. Are morally-motivated decision makers insensitive to the consequences of their choices? *Psychological Science* 18 (1): 24–28.

Bermudez, J. L. 2003. *Thinking without Words*. Oxford: Oxford University Press.

Block, N. 1987. Functional role and truth conditions. *Proceedings of the Aristotelian Society* 61:157–181.

Bloom, P. 2002. *How Children Learn the Meanings of Words: Learning, Development, and Conceptual Change*. New York: Bradford Books.

Calhoun, C. 1984. Cognitive emotions? In *What Is an Emotion?* ed. C. Calhoun and R. Solomon, 327–342. Oxford: Oxford University Press.

Camp, E. 2004. The generality constraint and categorial restrictions. *Philosophical Quarterly* 54 (215): 209–231.

Camp, E. 2006. Metaphor and that certain "Je ne sais quoi." *Philosophical Studies* 129 (1): 1–25.

Camp, E. 2007. Thinking with maps. In *Philosophical Perspectives,* vol. 21, *Philosophy of Mind,* ed. J. Hawthorne, 145–182. Oxford: Blackwell.

Camp, E. 2008. Showing, telling, and seeing: Metaphor and "poetic" language. In *The Baltic International Yearbook of Cognition, Logic and Communication,* vol. 3, *A Figure of Speech,* ed. E. Camp, 1–24. Manhattan, KS: New Prairie Press.

Camp, E. 2009a. A language of baboon thought? In *Philosophy of Animal Minds*, ed. R. Lurz, 108–127. Cambridge: Cambridge University Press.

Camp, E. 2009b. Putting thoughts to work: Concepts, systematicity, and stimulus-independence. *Philosophy and Phenomenological Research* 78 (2): 275–311.

Camp, E. 2009c. Two varieties of literary imagination: Metaphor, fiction, and thought experiments. *Midwest Studies in Philosophy: Poetry and Philosophy* 33:107–130.

Camp, E. 2013. Slurring perspectives. *Analytic Philosophy* 54(3): 330–349.

Camp, E. Unpublished ms. Perspective in imaginative engagement with metaphor.

Carey, S. 2011. *The Origin of Concepts*. New York: Oxford University Press.

Carroll, N. 2001. Simulation, emotion, and morality. In *Beyond Aesthetics: Philosophical Essays*, 306–316. Cambridge: Cambridge University Press.

Carruthers, P. 2006. *The Architecture of the Mind: Massive Modularity and the Flexibility of Thought*. Oxford: Oxford University Press.

Currie, G. 2010. *Narratives and Narrators*. Oxford: Oxford University Press.

Danto, A. 1981. *The Transfiguration of the Commonplace: A Philosophy of Art*. Cambridge, MA: Harvard University Press.

Dasgupta, N., D. DeSteno, L. Williams, and M. Hunsinger. 2009. Fanning the flames of prejudice: The influence of specific incidental emotions on implicit prejudice. *Emotion (Washington, DC)* 9 (4): 585–591.

Davidson, D. 1973. Radical interpretation. *Dialectica* 27:314–328.

Davidson, D. 1975. Thought and talk. In *Mind and Language*, ed. S. Guttenplan, 7–23. Oxford: Oxford University Press.

Davidson, D. 1982. Rational animals. *Dialectica* 36:317–328.

Davies, M. 1991. Concepts, connectionism, and the language of thought. In *Philosophy and Connectionist Theory*, ed. W. Ramsey, S. Stich, and D. Rumelhart, 229–257. Hillsdale, NJ: Erlbaum.

de Sousa, R. 1987. *The Rationality of Emotion*. Cambridge, MA: MIT Press.

Devine, P. 1989. Stereotypes and prejudice: Their automatic and controlled components. *Journal of Personality and Social Psychology* 56 (1): 5–18.

Devitt, M. 2005. *Ignorance of Language*. Oxford: Oxford University Press.

Dummett, M. 1994. *The Origins of Analytic Philosophy*. Cambridge, MA: Harvard University Press.

Duncan, B. L. 1976. Differential social perception and attribution of intergroup violence: Testing the lower limits of stereotyping of blacks. *Journal of Personality and Social Psychology* 34:590–598.

Evans, G. 1982. *The Varieties of Reference*. Oxford: Oxford University Press.

Evans, J., and K. Frankish. 2009. *In Two Minds: Dual Processes and Beyond*. Oxford University Press.

Evans, J. S. B. T. 2008. Dual-processing accounts of reasoning, judgment, and social cognition. *Annual Review of Psychology* 59:255–278.

Fodor, J. 1987. *Psychosemantics*. Cambridge, MA: MIT Press.

Fodor, J. 2007. The revenge of the given. In *Contemporary Debates in Philosophy of Mind*, ed. B. McLaughlin and J. Cohen, 105–116. Oxford: Blackwell.

Fodor, J., and E. Lepore. 1996. The red herring and the pet fish: Why concepts still can't be prototypes. *Cognition* 58:253–270.

Fodor, J., and Z. Pylyshyn. 1988. Connectionism and cognitive architecture: A critical analysis. *Cognition* 28:3–71.

Forgas, J. 1990. Affective influences on individual and group judgments. *European Journal of Social Psychology* 20:441–455.

Frege, G. 1892. Über sinn und bedeutung. *Zeitschrift für Philosophie und Philosophische Kritik, NF* 100:25–50.

Gendler, T. S. 2008. Alief and belief. *Journal of Philosophy* 105 (10): 634–663.

Goodman, N. 1968. *Languages of Art: An Approach to a Theory of Symbols*. Indianapolis: Bobbs-Merrill.

Greenberg, G. 2011. The semiotic spectrum. PhD diss., Rutgers University, New Brunswick.

Hauser, M, N. Chomsky, and T. Fitch. 2002. The Language Faculty: What is it, who has it, and how did it evolve? *Science* 298: 1569–1579.

Iliev, R., S. Sachdeva, D. Bartels, C. Joseph, S. Suzuki, and D. Medin. 2009. Attending to moral values. In *Moral Judgment and Decision Making: The Psychology of Learning and Motivation*, vol. 50, ed. D. Bartels, C. Bauman, L. Skitka, and D. Medin, 169–190. San Diego: Elsevier.

James, W. [1890] 1950. *The Principles of Psychology*. New York: Dover.

Johnson, K. 2004. On the systematicity of language and thought. *Journal of Philosophy* 101 (3): 111–139.

Judd, C., and B. Park. 1993. Definition and assessment of accuracy in social stereotypes. *Psychological Review* 100 (1): 109–128.

Kahneman, D. 2003. A perspective on judgement and choice. *American Psychologist* 58:697–720.

Kahneman, D. and A. Tversky, 1981. The framing of decisions and the psychology of choice. *Science* 211 (4481): 453–458.

Keltner, D., P. Ellsworth, and K. Edwards. 1993. Beyond simple pessimism: Effects of sadness and anger on social perception. *Journal of Personality and Social Psychology* 64:740–752.

Kulvicki, J. 2006. *On Images: Their Structure and Content*. Oxford: Oxford University Press.

Laurence, S., and E. Margolis. 1999. Concepts and cognitive science. In *Concepts: Core Readings*, ed. E. Margolis and S. Laurence, 3–81. Cambridge, MA: MIT Press.

Laurence, S., and E. Margolis. 2003. Concepts. In *The Blackwell Guide to Philosophy of Mind*, ed. S. Stich and T. Warfield, 190–213. Oxford: Wiley-Blackwell.

Lemon, O., and I. Pratt. 1998. On the insufficiency of linear diagrams for syllogisms. *Notre Dame Journal of Formal Logic* 39 (4): 573–580.

Lerner, J., R. Gonzalez, D. Small, and B. Fischhoff. 2003. Emotion and perceived risks of terrorism: A national field experiment. *Psychological Science* 14 (2): 144–150.

Leslie, S. J. 2007. Generics and the structure of the mind. *Philosophical Perspectives* 21 (1): 375–403.

Levin, I., S. Schneider, and G. Gaeth. 1998. All frames are not created equal: A typology and critical analysis of framing effects. *Organizational Behavior and Human Decision Processes* 76 (2): 149–188.

Margolis, E. 1994. A reassessment of the shift from the classical theory of concepts to prototype theory. *Cognition* 51:73–89.

Martens, A., M. Johns, J. Greenberg, and J. Schimel. 2006. Combating stereotype threat: The effect of self-affirmation on women's intellectual performance. *Journal of Experimental Social Psychology* 42:236–243.

Marx, D. M., and J. S. Roman. 2002. Female role models: Protecting women's math performance. *Personality and Social Psychology Bulletin* 28:1183–1193.

Mauro, R., K. Sato, and J. Tucker. 1992. The role of appraisal in human emotions: A cross-cultural study. *Journal of Personality and Social Psychology* 62:301–317.

McDowell, J. 1994. *Mind and World*. Cambridge, MA: Harvard University Press.

McGeer, V., and P. Pettit. 2002. The self-regulating mind. *Language & Communication* 22 (3): 281–299.

McIntyre, R. B., R. M. Paulson, and C. G. Lord. 2003. Alleviating women's mathematics stereotype threat through salience of group achievements. *Journal of Experimental Social Psychology* 39:83–90.

Murphy, G., and D. Medin. 1985. The role of theories in conceptual coherence. *Psychological Review* 92:289–316.

Musch, J., and K. C. Klauer, eds. 2003. *The Psychology of Evaluation: Affective Processes in Cognition and Emotion*. Hillsdale, NJ: Erlbaum.

Nelson, T., M. Acker, and M. Manis. 1996. Irrepressible stereotypes. *Journal of Experimental Social Psychology* 32 (1): 13–38.

Ortony, A., G. Clore, and A. Collins. 1988. *The Cognitive Structure of Emotions*. Cambridge: Cambridge University Press.

Peacocke, C. 1992. *A Study of Concepts*. Cambridge, MA: MIT Press.

Pinker, S. 1994. *The Language Instinct: How the Mind Creates Language*. New York: Harper Collins.

Prinz, J. 2004. *Furnishing the Mind: Concepts and Their Perceptual Basis*. New York: Bradford Books.

Rey, G. 1983. Concepts and stereotypes. *Cognition* 15:237–262.

Rey, G. 1995. A "not merely" empirical argument for the language of thought. In *Philosophical Perspectives*, vol. 9, *AI, Connectionism and Philosophical Psychology*, ed. J. Tomberlin, 201–222. Atascadero, CA: Ridgeview Publishing.

Robinson, J. 2005. *Deeper than Reason: Emotion and Its Role in Literature, Music, and Art*. Oxford: Oxford University Press.

Rorty, A. 1980. Explaining emotions. In *Explaining Emotions*, ed. A. Rorty, 103–126. Berkeley: University of California Press.

Rosch, E. 1978. Principles of categorization. In *Cognition and Categorization*, ed. E. Rosch and B. B. Lloyd, 27–48. Hillsdale, NJ: Erlbaum.

Ryan, C., C. Judd, and B. Park. 1996. Effects of racial stereotypes on judgments of individuals: The moderating role of perceived group variability. *Journal of Experimental Social Psychology* 32 (1): 91–103.

Ryle, G. 1953. Categories. In *Logic and Language*, 2nd series, ed. A. Flew, 65–81. Oxford: Blackwell.

Sager, H. A., and J. W. Schofield. 1980. Racial and behavioral cues in black and white children's perceptions of ambiguously aggressive acts. *Journal of Personality and Social Psychology* 39:590–598.

Searle, J. 1978. Literal meaning. *Erkenntnis* 13 (1): 207–224.

Shimojima, A. 1996. Operational constraints in diagrammatic reasoning. In *Logical Reasoning with Diagrams*, ed. J. Barwise and G. Allwein, 27–48. Oxford: Oxford University Press.

Shin, S. J. 1994. *The Logical Status of Diagrams*. Cambridge: Cambridge University Press.

Sloman, S. 1996. The empirical case for two systems of reasoning. *Psychological Bulletin* 119:3–22.

Sloman, S., B. Love, and W. K. Ahn. 1998. Feature centrality and conceptual coherence. *Cognitive Science* 22 (2): 189–228.

Small, D. A., J. S. Lerner, and B. Fischhoff. 2006. Emotion priming and attributions for terrorism: Americans' reactions in a national field experiment. *Political Psychology* 27 (2): 289–298.

Smith, C. 1989. Dimensions of appraisal and physiological response in emotion. *Journal of Personality and Social Psychology* 56:339–353.

Sober, E. 1976. Mental representations. *Synthese* 33:101–148.

Stanovich, K., and R. West. 2000. Advancing the rationality debate. *Behavioral and Brain Sciences* 23:701–726.

Steele, C. M., and J. Aronson. 1995. Stereotype threat and the intellectual test performance of African Americans. *Journal of Personality and Social Psychology* 69:797–811.

Steele, C. M., S. J. Spencer, and J. Aronson. 2002. Contending with group image: The psychology of stereotype and social identity threat. In *Advances in Experimental Social Psychology*, vol. 34, ed. M. Zanna, 379–440. New York: Academic Press.

Strawson, P. F. 1970. Categories. In *Ryle: A Collection of Critical Essays*, ed. O. Wood and G. Pitcher, 181–211. Garden City, NY: Doubleday Anchor Books.

Szabo, Z. 2012. The Case for Compositionality. In, *The Oxford Handbook of Compositionality*, ed. M. Werning, W. Hinzen and E. Machery, 64–80. New York, NY: Oxford University Press.

Thagard, P. 1989. Explanatory coherence. *Behavioral and Brain Sciences* 12:435–502.

Travis, C. 1994. On constraints of generality. *Proceedings of the Aristotelian Society* 94:165–188.

Tversky, A. 1977. Features of similarity. *Psychological Review* 84:327–352.

Tversky, A. 1981. The framing of decisions and the psychology of choice. *Science* 211 (4481): 453–458.

Tversky, A., and D. Kahneman. 1982. Judgments of and by representativeness. In *Judgment Under Uncertainty: Heuristics and Biases*, ed. D. Kahneman, P. Slovic, and A. Tversky, 3–22. Cambridge: Cambridge University Press.

Wallbott, H., and K. Scherer. 1986. The antecedents of emotional experience. In *Experiencing Emotion: A Cross-Cultural Study*, ed. K. R. Scherer, H. G. Wallbott, and A. B. Summerfield, 69–83. Cambridge: Cambridge University Press.

Wittgenstein, L. 1953. *Philosophical Investigations*. Trans. G. E. M. Anscombe. Oxford: Basil Blackwell.

Woodfield, A. 1991. Conceptions. *Mind* C (400): 547–572.

22 Concepts in a Probabilistic Language of Thought

Noah D. Goodman, Joshua B. Tenenbaum, and Tobias Gerstenberg

22.1 Introduction

Knowledge organizes our understanding of the world, determining what we expect given what we have already seen. Our predictive representations have two key properties: they are productive, and they are graded. Productive generalization is possible because our knowledge decomposes into *concepts*—elements of knowledge that are combined and recombined to describe particular situations. Gradedness is the observable effect of accounting for uncertainty—our knowledge encodes degrees of belief that lead to graded probabilistic predictions. To put this a different way, concepts form a combinatorial system that enables description of many different situations; each such situation specifies a distribution over what we expect to see in the world, given what we have seen. We may think of this system as a *probabilistic language of thought* (PLoT), in which representations are built from language-like composition of concepts, and the content of those representations is a probability distribution on world states. The purpose of this chapter is to formalize these ideas in computational terms, to illustrate key properties of the PLoT approach with a concrete example, and to draw connections with other views of conceptual structure.

People are remarkably flexible at understanding new situations, guessing at unobserved properties or events, and making predictions on the basis of sparse evidence combined with general background knowledge. Consider the game of tug-of-war: two teams matching their strength by pulling on either side of a rope. If a team containing the first author (NG) loses to a team containing the third author (TG), that might provide weak evidence that TG is the stronger of the two. If these teams contain only two members each, we might believe more in TG's greater strength than if the teams contain eight members each. If TG beats NG in a one-on-one tug-of-war, and NG goes on to beat three other individuals in similar one-on-one contests, we might believe that TG is not only stronger than NG but strong in an absolute sense, relative to the general population, even though we have only directly observed TG participating in a single match. However, if we later found out that NG did not try very hard in his match against TG, but did try hard in his later matches, our convictions about TG's strength might subside.

This reasoning is clearly statistical. We may make good guesses about these propositions, but we will be far from certain; we will be more certain of TG's strength after seeing him play many games. But our reasoning is also highly abstract. It is not limited to a particular set of tug-of-war contestants. We can reason in analogous ways about matches between teams of arbitrary sizes and composition, and are unperturbed if a new player is introduced. We can also reason about the teams as collections: if team Alpha wins its first four matches but then loses to team Bravo, whom it has not faced before, we judge team Bravo very likely to be stronger than average. The smaller team Bravo is, the more likely we are to judge a particular member of team Bravo to be stronger than the average individual. And similar patterns of reasoning apply to inferences about skill and success in other kinds of team contests: We could be talking about math teams, or teams for doubles Ping-Pong, and make analogous inferences for all the situations above.

Our reasoning also supports inferences from complex combinations of evidence to complex conclusions. For example, suppose that participants have been paired up into teams of two. If we learn that NG was lazy (not trying hard) whenever his team contested a match against TG's team, but NG's team nonetheless won each of these matches, it suggests both that NG is stronger than TG and that NG is often lazy. If we then learned that NG's teammate is stronger than any other individual in the population, we would probably revise the former belief (about NG's strength) but not the latter (about his laziness). If we learned that NG's team had won all of its two-on-two matches, but we were told nothing about NG's teammate, it is a good bet that the teammate—whoever he is—is stronger than average; all the more so if we also learned that NG had lost several one-on-one matches while trying hard.

Finally, our reasoning in this one domain can be modularly combined with knowledge of other domains, or manipulated based on subtle details of domain knowledge. If we observed TG lifting a number of very heavy boxes with apparent ease, we might reasonably expect his tug-of-war team to beat most others. But this would probably not raise our confidence that TG's math team (or even his Ping-Pong team) are likely to be unusually successful. If we know that NG is trying to ingratiate himself to TG, perhaps to receive a favor, then we might not weight his loss very heavily in estimating strength. Likewise if we knew that NG had received a distracting text message during the match.

We will return to this extended example in more detail in section 22.3, but for now we take it merely as an illustration, in one simple domain, of the key features of human cognition that we seek to capture in a general computational architecture. How can we account for the wide range of flexible inferences people draw from diverse patterns of evidence such as these? What assumptions about the cognitive system are needed to explain the productivity and gradedness of these inferences? What kind of representations are abstract enough to extend flexibly to novel situations and questions, yet concrete enough to support detailed quantitative predictions about the world? There are two traditional, and traditionally opposed, ways of modeling reasoning in higher-level cognition, each with its well-known strengths and limitations. Symbolic approaches (e.g., Newell, Shaw, and Simon 1958) can naturally formulate a wide array of inferences but are traditionally confined to the realm of certainty. They would be challenged to capture all the gradations of reasoning people find so intuitive and valuable in an uncertain world. Probabilistic network approaches—whether based on neural networks (Rumelhart and McClelland 1988) or Bayesian networks (Pearl 1988, 2000)—support graded inferences based on sparse or noisy evidence, but only over a fixed finite set of random variables. They lack the representational power and productivity of more structured symbolic approaches and would be hard pressed to formulate in a coherent fashion all the inferences described above—let alone the infinite number of similar inferences we could have listed but did not.

More recently, researchers have begun to move beyond the dichotomy between statistical and symbolic models (Anderson 1996) and have argued that much of cognition can be understood as probabilistic inference over richly structured representations (Tenenbaum et al. 2011). This has led to a proliferation of structured statistical models, which have given real insight into many cognitive domains: inductive reasoning (Kemp and Tenenbaum 2009), causal learning (Griffiths and Tenenbaum 2009; Goodman, Ullman, and Tenenbaum 2011), word learning (Frank, Goodman, and Tenenbaum 2009; Piantadosi, Tenenbaum, and Goodman 2012), and mental state inference (Baker, Saxe, and Tenenbaum 2009), to name a few. But the computational tools used for these different models do not yet amount to a truly general-purpose or integrated approach. They are both insufficiently flexible—requiring new models to be described for each different situation—and idiosyncratic—requiring different representational tools across different specific domains.

We require a new computational architecture for cognition, grounded in a new theory of concepts—a theory that does justice to two distinct but equally important roles that concepts play in mental life. On the one hand, concepts enable predictive generalization: they summarize stable regularities, such as typical distributions of objects, properties, and events. This is the role primarily addressed by prototype (Rosch 1999), exemplar (Nosofsky 1986) and other *statistical* accounts of concepts. On the other hand, concepts provide the basic building blocks of compositional thought: they can be flexibly combined with other concepts to form an infinite array of thoughts in order to reason productively about an infinity of situations. They can be composed to make new concepts, which are building blocks of yet more complex thoughts. Indeed, concepts get much of their meaning and their function from the role they play in these larger-scale systems of thought. These are the roles primarily addressed (albeit it in different ways) by classical (rule-based) theories of concepts (Bruner, Goodnow, and Austin 1967), and by the *theory theory* (Gopnik 2003) and other accounts based on inferential or conceptual roles (Block 1997). While these theories differ in crucial ways, we group them under the heading of *symbolic* approaches, because they highlight the compositional aspects of concepts that require a powerful symbol-processing architecture.

Our goal in this chapter is to sketch a new account of concepts that combines these two aspects, their statistical and symbolic functions, and to show how this account can explain more of the richness of human reasoning than has been previously captured using traditional approaches. We can phrase our hypothesis, somewhat informally, as follows:

Probabilistic language of thought hypothesis (informal version): Concepts have a language-like compositionality and encode probabilistic knowledge. These features allow them to be extended productively to new situations and support flexible reasoning and learning by probabilistic inference.

This view of the nature of concepts provides a deeper marriage of statistical inference and symbolic composition. Because they are probabilistic, concepts support graded reasoning under uncertainty. Because they are language-like, they may be flexibly recombined to productively describe new situations. For instance, we have a set of concepts, such as STRENGTH and GAME, for the tug-of-war reasoning domain described above that we may compose with each other and with symbols referring to entities (individuals and teams) in the domain. These combinations then describe distributions on possible world states, which we may reason about via the rules of probability. Our proposal for the PLoT can be seen as making the statistical view of concepts more flexible and systematic by enriching it with a fine-grained notion of composition coming from symbolic approaches. It can also be seen as making symbolic approaches to concepts more useful for reasoning in an uncertain world, by embedding them in a probabilistic framework for inference and decision.

The level of description intended in the PLoT hypothesis is neither the highest level, of input-output relations, nor the lower level of psychological processing. Instead, we aim to use the PLoT to describe conceptual representations and the inferences that they license across situations and domains. The process by which these inferences are implemented is not directly part of the hypothesis, though it can be very useful to consider the possible implementations when evaluating connections between the PLoT and other views of concepts.

22.2 Formalizing the PLoT

The PLoT hypothesis as stated above is an evocative set of desiderata for a theory of concepts, more than a concrete theory itself. Indeed, it is not a priori obvious that it is possible to satisfy all these desiderata at once in a concrete computational system. We are in need of a compositional formal system—a language—for expressing probability distributions over complex world states. Our first clue comes from the idea of representing distributions as *generative processes*: a series of random steps by which the world comes to be as it is. But while generative processes are a useful way to represent probabilistic knowledge, adopting such a representation only transforms our problem into one of finding a compositional language for generative processes. The solution to this problem comes from a simple idea: if you have described a deterministic process compositionally in terms of the computation steps taken from start to end, but then inject noise at some point along the way, you get a stochastic process; this stochastic process unfolds in the original steps, except where a random choice is made. In this way a distribution over outputs is determined, not a single deterministic output, and this distribution inherits all the compositionality of the original deterministic process. The stochastic λ-calculus realizes this idea formally, by extending a universal computational system (λ-calculus) with points of primitive randomness. The *probabilistic programming language* Church (Goodman, Mansinghka, et al. 2008) extends the sparse mathematical system of stochastic λ-calculus into a more usable system for describing statistical processes.

We now give a brief introduction to the syntax and ideas of probabilistic modeling using Church, sufficient to motivate a more formal version of the PLoT; further details and many examples can be found at http://probmods.org. Church uses a syntax inherited from the LISP family of languages (McCarthy 1960). Thus, operators precede their arguments and are written inside grouping parentheses: for example, (+ 1 2) encodes the operation "add 1 and 2." We use define to assign values to symbols in our program and lambda for creating functions. We could, for example, create a function double that takes one number as an input and returns its double. The code would look like this: (define double (lambda (x) (+ x x))). Applying this function to 2 would look like (double 2) and result in the value 4.

What differentiates Church from an ordinary programming language is the inclusion of random primitives. For example, the function (flip 0.5) can be interpreted as a simple coin flip with a weight (i.e., a Bernoulli random draw) outputting either true or false. Every time the function is called, a new random value is generated—the coin is flipped. These random primitives can be combined just as ordinary functions are—for instance (and (flip 0.5) (flip 0.5)) is the more complex process of taking the conjunction of two random Booleans. A Church program specifies not a single computation but a distribution over computations. This *sampling semantics* (see Goodman, Mansinghka, et al. 2008 for more details) means that composition of probabilities is achieved by ordinary composition of functions, and it means that we may specify probabilistic models using all the tools of representational abstraction in a modern programming language. We will not provide a primer on the power of function abstraction and other such tools here, but we will use them in what we hope are intuitive and illustrative ways in the examples below.

A number of language features in Church parallel core aspects of conceptual representation. Perhaps the most familiar (and most controversial) for cognitive modeling is the use of arbitrary *symbols*. In Church (as in LISP) a symbol is a basic value that has only the property that it is equal to itself and not to any other symbol: (equal? 'bob 'bob) is true, while (equal? 'bob 'jim) is false. (The single quote syntax simply indicates that what follows is a symbol). Critically, symbols can be used as unique identifiers on which to hang some aspect of conceptual knowledge. For instance, they can be used to refer to functions, as when we used define to create the double function above and then reused this doubling function by name. Symbols can also be used together with functions to represent knowledge about (an unbounded set of) objects. For instance, the function

```
(define eyecolor (lambda (x) (if (flip) 'blue 'brown)))
```

takes a person x and randomly returns an eye color (e.g., (eyecolor 'bob) might return 'blue). That is, it wraps up the knowledge about how eye color is generated *independently* of which person is asked about—a person is simply a symbol ('bob) that is associated with another symbol ('blue) by the eyecolor function.[1]

Of course, the above representation of an object's property has a flaw: if we ask about the eye color of Bob twice, we may get different answers! Church includes an operator mem that takes a function and returns a *memoized* version: one that makes its random choices only once for each distinct value of the function's arguments, and thereafter, when called, returns the answer stored from that first evaluation. For instance, a memoized version of the eye color function,

```
(define eyecolor (mem (lambda (x) (if (flip) 'blue 'brown))))
```

could output either 'blue or 'brown for Bob's eye color, but only one of these possibilities, to be determined the first time the function is called. This ensures that (equal? (eyecolor 'bob) (eyecolor 'bob)) is always true.

Thus symbols can be used as *indices* to recover random properties or as labels that allow us to recover stored information. These uses are conceptually very similar, though they have different syntax, and they can be combined. For instance, we can access one function in another by its name, passing along the current objects of interest:

```
(define eyecolor
    (mem (lambda (x)
        (if (flip 0.1)
            (if (flip) 'blue 'brown)
            (if (flip) (eyecolor (father x))
                       (eyecolor (mother x)))))))
```

1. In Church the conditional has a traditional but cryptic syntax: (if a b c) returns b if a is true, and c otherwise. Thus (if (flip) b c) randomly returns b or c.

This (false, but perhaps intuitive) model of eye color asserts that the color is sometimes simply random but most of the time depends on the eye color of one of a person's parents—which is accessed by calling the `father` or `mother` function from inside the `eyecolor` function, and so on. Symbols and symbolic reference are thus key language constructs for forming complex concepts and situations from simple ones.

How does reasoning enter into this system? The fundamental operation of belief updating in probabilistic modeling is *conditioning*. We can define conditioning within Church via the notion of rejection sampling: if we have a distribution represented by `dist` (a stochastic function with no input arguments) and a predicate `condition` (that takes a value and returns `true` or `false`), then we can define the distribution conditioned on the predicate being true via the process:

```
(define conditional
    (lambda ()
        (define sample (dist))
        (if (condition sample) sample (conditional))))
```

That is, we keep sampling from `dist` until we get a sample that satisfies `condition`, then we return this sample.[2] It can be cumbersome to split our knowledge and assumption in this way, so Church introduces a syntax for conditionals in the form of the `query` function:

```
(query
    ...definitions...
    query-expression
    condition-expression)
```

Our initial distribution is the `query-expression` evaluated in the context of the `...definitions...`, and our predicate is the `condition-expression` evaluated in the same context.

For instance, referring again to the eye color example, we could ask about Bob's mother's likely eye color, given that Bob has blue eyes:

```
(query
    (define eyecolor ...as above...)
    (eyecolor (mother 'bob))
    (equal?    'blue (eyecolor 'bob)))
```

Notice that there is a distinction between the definitions, which represent probabilistic knowledge reusable across many queries, and the query and condition expressions, which represent the particular question of interest at the moment. In this example, the

---

2. For readers familiar with Bayesian belief updating in probabilistic models, this process can be seen as taking a prior model specified by `dist` and generating a sample from the posterior corresponding to `dist` conditioned on the evidence that `condition` is `true`.

particular people need to be introduced only in the question of interest because the conceptual knowledge is defined over arbitrary symbols.

Equipped now with a compositional formal language for representing distributions and performing conditional inference, we can revisit the probabilistic language of thought hypothesis. Within a probabilistic language like Church, knowledge is encoded in stochastic function definitions. These functions describe elements of stochastic processes that can be composed together to describe various situations, to pose various questions and to answer those questions with reasonable probabilistic guesses. Indeed, just as concepts are the stable and reusable components of human thinking, stochastic functions are the units of knowledge encoded in a Church program. Motivated from this observation, we can formulate a stronger PLoT hypothesis:

Probabilistic language of thought hypothesis (formal version): Concepts are stochastic functions. Hence they represent uncertainty, compose naturally, and support probabilistic inference.

Notice that this formal version realizes the informal PLoT in a precise way, showing that the hypothesis is coherent and allowing us to ask more detailed questions about plausibility. For instance we can begin to ask the usual philosophical questions about concepts of this system: What constitutes meaning? How are concepts related? How are they acquired and used? The answers to these questions can be subtle, but they are determined in principle from the basic claim that concepts are stochastic functions. For instance, on the face of it, the meaning of a stochastic function is simply its definition, and the relation between concepts is determined by constituency—in the example above, the meaning of eyecolor is its definition, and it is related to other concepts only by its use of mother and father functions. However, when we consider the inferential relationships between concepts that come from conditional inference—query—we see additional aspects of meaning and conceptual relation. Conditioning on parentage can influence eye color, but also vice versa; conditioning on hair color could influence judgments about eye color indirectly, and so on. In the next section we give an extended example in the domain of simple team games, illustrating these foundational issues as well as exploring the empirical adequacy of the PLoT hypothesis.

22.3   Example: Ping-Pong in Church

Consider the information shown in figure 22.1. Most people conclude that TG is relatively strong, while BL is average to weak. Below we describe various patterns of evidence that we displayed to people in the guise of a Ping-Pong tournament. How can we account for people's sensitivity to the uncertain nature of the evidence in such situations? While capturing the abstract structure that remains invariant between this

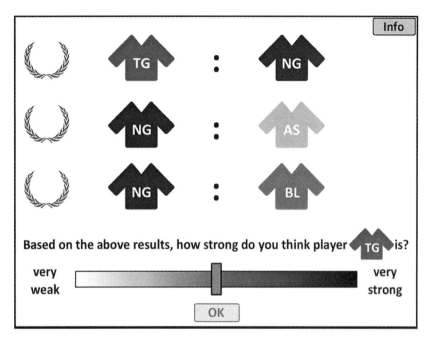

Figure 22.1
Screenshot of a single-player tournament. The winner of each match is indicated by a laurel wreath.

particular situation and other similar situations involving different players, teams, and outcomes?

This simple sports domain is built around people, teams, and games. In Church, we can use symbols as placeholders for unspecified individuals of these types. This means that we do not need to define in advance how many people participate, what the size of the teams will be, or how many games a tournament will have. Instead, we begin by describing a lexicon of abstract concept definitions useful for reasoning about these games. We define an individual player's strength (i.e., skill at Ping-Pong), `personstrength`, via a function that draws from a Gaussian distribution (with arbitrary $M = 10$ and $SD = 3$):

```
(define personstrength (mem (lambda (person) (gaussian 10 3))))
```

Memoization ensures that the strength value assigned to a person is persistent and does not change between games. However, we assume that players are sometimes lazy in a given match. The chance of a person being lazy in a particular game is 10 percent:

```
(define lazy (mem (lambda (person game) (flip 0.1))))
```

The overall strength of a team, in a given game, is the sum of the strength of each person on the team. If a person on the team is lazy, however, he plays with only half of his actual strength.

```
(define teamstrength
    (mem (lambda (team game)
        (sum (map (lambda(person)
                        (if (lazy person game)
                            (/ (personstrength person) 2)
                            (personstrength person)))
                team)))))
```

Finally, we specify how the winner of a game is determined. We simply say that the team wins who has the greater overall strength:

```
(define winner
    (mem (lambda (team1 team2 game)
        (if (> (teamstrength team1 game) (teamstrength team2 game))
            'team1 'team2))))
```

This set of function definitions specifies a simple lexicon of concepts for reasoning about the Ping-Pong domain.

The way in which we can define new concepts (e.g., teamstrength) based on previously defined concepts (personstrength and lazy) illustrates one form of compositionality in Church. The set of concept definitions refers to people (teams, etc.) without having to declare a set of possible people in advance: instead we apply generic functions to placeholder symbols that will stand for these people. That is, the concepts may be further composed with symbols and each other to describe specific situations. For instance, the inference in figure 22.1 can be described by:

```
(query
      ...CONCEPTS...
      ;The query:
      (personstrength 'TG)
      ;The evidence:
      (and
            (equal? 'team1 (winner '(TG) '(NG) 1))
            (equal? 'team1 (winner '(NG) '(AS) 2))
            (equal? 'team1 (winner '(NG) '(BL) 3))))
```

Here ...CONCEPTS... is shorthand for the definitions introduced above—a lexicon of concepts that we may use to model people's inferences about a player's strength not only in the situation depicted in figure 22.1, but in a multitude of possible situations with varying teams composed of several people, playing against each other with all

Table 22.1
Patterns of observation for the single-player tournaments

Confounded evidence (1,2)	Strong indirect evidence (3,4)	Weak indirect evidence (5,6)	Diverse evidence (7,8)
A > B[*]	A > B	A > B	A > B
A > B	B > C	B < C	A > C
A > B	B > D	B < D	A > D
lazy,game: B,2	B,1	B,1	C,2

Note: An additional set of four patterns was included for which the outcomes of the games were reversed. The bottom row shows the omniscient commentator's information in experiment 2. For example, in the confounded case, player B was lazy in the second game.
[*]A > B means that A won against B

thinkable combinations of game results in different tournament formats. This productive extension over different possible situations including different persons, different teams, and different winners of each game renders the Church implementation a powerful model for human reasoning.

Gerstenberg and Goodman (2012) wanted to explore how well our simple Church model predicts the inferences people make, based on complex patterns of evidence in different situations. In Experiment 1, participants' task was to estimate an individual player's strength based on the outcomes of different games in a Ping-Pong tournament. Participants were told that they would make judgments after having seen single-player and two-player tournaments. The different players in a tournament could be identified by the color of their jersey as well as their initials. In each tournament, there was a new set of players. Participants were given some basic information about the strength of the players, which described some of the modeling assumptions we made. That is, participants were told that individual players have a fixed strength that does not vary between games, and that all the players have a 10 percent chance of not playing as strongly as they can in each game. This means that even if a player is strong, he can sometimes lose against a weaker player.[3]

Table 22.1 shows the patterns of evidence that were used for the single-player tournaments. Table 22.2 shows the patterns for the two-player tournaments. In all tournaments, participants were asked to judge the strength of player A. For the single-player tournaments, we used four different patterns of evidence: *confounded evidence*,

3. Demos of the experiments can be accessed here: http://web.mit.edu/tger/www/demos/BPP _demos.html.

Table 22.2

Patterns of observation for the two-player tournaments

Confounded with partner (9,10)			Confounded with opponent (11,12)			Strong indirect evidence (13,14)		
AB	>	CD	AB	>	EF	AB	>	EF
AB	>	EF	AC	>	EG	BC	<	EF
AB	>	GH	AD	>	EH	BD	<	EF

Weak indirect evidence (15,16)			Diverse evidence (17,18)			Round robin (19,20)		
AB	>	EF	AB	>	EF	AB	>	CD
BC	>	EF	AC	>	GH	AC	>	BD
BD	>	EF	AD	>	IJ	AD	>	BC

Note: An additional set of six patterns was included in which the outcomes of the games were reversed.

in which A wins repeatedly against B; *strong* and *weak indirect evidence*, where A wins only one match herself, but B either continues to win or lose two games against other players; and *diverse evidence*, in which A wins against three different players. For each of those patterns, we also included a pattern in which the outcomes of the games were exactly reversed. For the two-player tournaments, we used six different patterns of evidence: in some situations, A was always on the same team as B (*confounded with partner*), and in other situations, A repeatedly played against the same player E (*confounded with opponent*). As in the single-player tournaments, we also had patterns with mostly indirect evidence about the strength of A by having her partner in the first game, B, either win or lose against the same opponents with different teammates (*weak/strong indirect evidence*). Finally, we had one pattern of *diverse evidence*, in which A wins with different teammates against a new set of opponents in each game, and one *round robin* tournament, in which A wins all her games in all possible combinations of a four-player tournament. Further experimental details can be found in appendix A.

In order to directly compare the model predictions with participants' judgments, we z-scored the model predictions and each individual participant's judgments. Furthermore, we reverse coded participants' judgments and the model predictions for the situations in which the outcomes of the games were reversed so that both strength and "weakness" judgments go in the same direction.

Figure 22.2 shows the mean strength estimates (gray bars) together with the model predictions (black bars) for the single- and two-player tournaments. The top

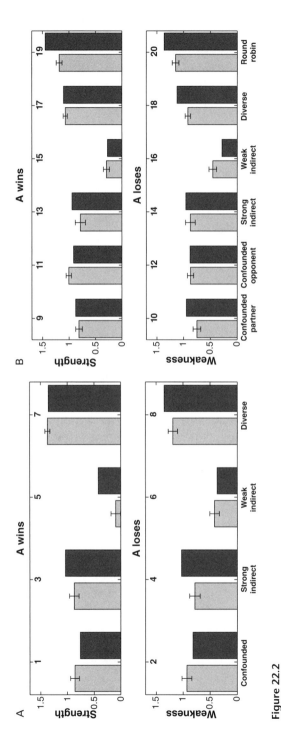

Figure 22.2

Mean strength estimates (gray bars) and model predictions (black bars) for the single-player (left) and two-player tournaments (right). The top row shows strength judgments for cases in which player A won her game(s). The bottom row shows weakness judgments for cases in which player A lost. Numbers above the bars correspond to the patterns described in tables 22.1 and 22.2. Error bars indicate ±1 standard error of the mean.

panels display the situations in which A won her game(s). The bottom panels show the situations in which A lost. Our model predicts participants' judgments in the single- and two-player tournaments very well with $r = 0.98$ and $RMSE = 0.19$. A very high median correlation with individual participants' judgments of $r = 0.92$ shows that the close fit is not merely due to an aggregation effect. These results show that our model predicts participants' inferences very accurately—a single, concise representation of the task is sufficient to predict people's inferences for a great diversity of patterns of evidence.

A still greater variety of evidence is available by composing the basic concepts together in different ways: there is no reason for evidence not to directly refer to a player's strength, laziness, and so on. For instance:

```
(query
    ...CONCEPTS...
    ;The query:
    (personstrength 'TG)
    ;The evidence:
    (and
        (equal? 'team1 (winner '(TG) '(NG) 1))
        (equal? 'team1 (winner '(NG) '(AS) 2))
        (equal? 'team1 (winner '(NG) '(BL) 3))
        (lazy 'NG 1)))  ;additional kinds of evidence (Expt. 2)
```

While in Experiment 1, the match results were the only source of information participants could use as a basis for their strength judgments, Experiment 2 introduced an omniscient commentator who gave direct information about specific players. After participants saw a tournament's match results, an omniscient commentator, who always told the truth, revealed that one player was lazy in a particular game. We were interested in how participants updated their beliefs about the strength of player A given this additional piece of evidence. Importantly, we do not need to change anything in the concept definitions to derive predictions for these situations, since only the way they are composed into evidence changes.

Figure 22.3 shows the mean strength judgments (gray bars) together with the model predictions (black bars; see table 22.1 for the different patterns of evidence). The dark gray bars indicate participants' first judgments based on the tournament information only. The light gray bars indicate participants' second judgments after they received the commentator's information. The model predicts participants' ratings very accurately again with $r = 0.97$ and $RMSE = 0.29$. The model's median correlation with individual participants' judgments is $r = 0.86$. These results show that participants, as well as our model, have no difficulty in integrating different sources of evidence to form an overall judgment of a player's likely underlying strength. The model predicts participants' judgments very accurately by being sensitive to the

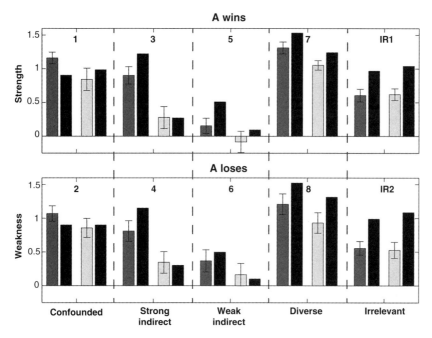

Figure 22.3

Mean strength estimates and model predictions. Dark gray bars = estimates after tournament information only, light gray bars = estimates after omniscient commentator info, black bars = model predictions. Error bars indicate ±1 standard error of the mean. Note: Situations IR1 and IR2 were cases in which the information given by the commentator was irrelevant; see appendix B for details.

degree to which the initial strength estimate should be updated in light of new evidence provided by the commentator.

22.4 Intuitive Theories

The examples above provide concrete illustrations of how to represent concepts as functions in a probabilistic language of thought, how a system of such concepts supports inferences that are both productive and probabilistic, and how these inferences can capture the outputs of human reasoning at a high level of quantitative accuracy. But while reasoning about team games like Ping-Pong is very illustrative, it is of relatively limited scope compared with many of the concepts involved in everyday human reasoning. In this section, we discuss how the same machinery can describe abstract concepts that are the backbone of thinking about everyday life, and that have often not fit easily into more traditional formal frameworks.

Intuitive theories (Gopnik and Wellman 2012; Wellman and Gelman 1992; Carey 2009), like their more familiar scientific counterparts, comprise a system of interrelated and interdefined concepts articulating a basic ontology of entities, the properties of and relations between those entities, and the causal laws that govern how these entities evolve over time and interact with each other. For instance, intuitive physics is a system for reasoning about physical objects, and intuitive psychology for reasoning about intentional agents. These are called *theories* because, like in scientific theories, the essential constructs of intuitive theories are typically not directly observable. Yet intuitive theories also specify how unobservable states, properties, and processes affect observable experience—and thus how they support competencies such as prediction, explanation, learning, and reasoning.

Intuitive theories can be found in some form in young infants, and are also to some extent shared with many other species; they are arguably the earliest and oldest abstract concepts we have (Carey 2009). They provide the scaffolding for many of children's conceptual achievements over the first few years of life. They also provide core building blocks for meaning in natural language, at the same time as they are enriched and transformed fundamentally as children develop their natural language abilities. Through adulthood, they continue to serve as the basis for our common-sense understanding of the world. Yet while these intuitive theories have long been a prime target for exploration by developmental and cognitive psychologists, linguists, and philosophers, they have not received much treatment in the literature on formal models of concepts. This may be because they do not fit well into the general-purpose mathematical and computational modeling frameworks that have been available and useful for more mundane category concepts—prototypes, exemplars, and logical accounts. Starting around ten years ago, several authors began to consider Bayesian networks as formal models for intuitive theories (Tenenbaum and Griffiths 2003; Gopnik et al. 2004; Rehder 2003; Goodman et al. 2006), focusing on their causal aspects. These efforts were ultimately limited by the fact that Bayesian networks, like neural networks before them, fail to capture genuine productivity in thought. An intuitive theory of physics or psychology must be able to handle an infinite range of novel situations, differing in their specifics but not their abstract character, just as we illustrated above on a much smaller scale for an intuitive theory of tug-of-war or Ping-Pong. Hierarchical Bayesian models have been proposed as one way to increase the representational power of Bayesian networks, and they have given reasonable accounts of some aspects of abstract causal theories (e.g., Tenenbaum et al. 2011). But hierarchical Bayesian models on their own still lack sufficient representational power to address the fine-grained compositionality inherent in our intuitive theories. The PLoT allows us to take a major step forward in this regard. Both Bayesian networks and hierarchical Bayesian models of intuitive theories can be naturally written as Church programs, preserving their insights into causal reasoning and learning, but

Church programs go much further in letting us capture the essential representations of common-sense physics and psychology that have defied previous attempts at formalization within the probabilistic modeling tradition.

To illustrate, consider how we might capture the core concepts of an intuitive psychology—a probabilistic model of how agents act rationally in response to their mental states, aiming to satisfy their desires as efficiently as possible given their beliefs. As an initial step, imagine extending the game model above to take into account the fact that laziness for a particular player in a given game may be not simply a random event, but an intentional choice on the part of a player—he may estimate that the other team is so weak that it is not worth his effort to try hard. We pose this as a Church model by imagining that a player asks himself, "How should I act such that my team will win?":

```
(define lazy (mem (lambda (person game)
     (query
          (define action (flip L))
          action
          (equal? (teamof person)
                   (winner (team1of game) (team2of game) imagined-game))))))
```

where we have helped ourselves to some helper functions to look up the team of a player and so on (and notionally extended the game into an imagined-game index). The parameter L controls the a priori tendency to be lazy; this gives a simple way of including a principle of efficiency: a tendency to avoid undue effort. The condition statement of the query specifies the player's goal—for his team to win the game— hypothetically assuming that this goal will be achieved. The output of the query is an action (trying hard, or not) that is a reasonable guess on the player's part for how that goal may be achieved. An inference about which team will win a match now leads to a subinference, modeling each player's choice of whether to exert his or her full effort, given the players on each team. We could further extend this model to take into account private evidence that each player might have about the strengths of the other players, expressing his or her process of belief formation about the total strengths of the two teams as an additional set of nested subinferences.

The pattern of using an embedded query to capture the choices of another agent is a very general pattern for modeling intuitive psychology (Stuhlmüller and Goodman 2013). We could write down the abstract structure schematically as:

```
(define choice (lambda (belief state goal?)
     (query
          (define action (action-prior))
          action
          (goal? (belief state action)))))
```

where `belief` is taken to be the agent's summary of the world dynamics (transitions from states and actions to resulting states), and `goal?` is a goal predicate on states, picking out those that the agent desires. Of course, many additional refinements and additions may be needed to build an adequate model of human intuitive psychology—agents form beliefs, experience emotions, and so on. Yet we hope that the ease of writing down even a simple version of a theory of mind that captures both the theory's abstractness and its potential for productive probabilistic inferences illustrates the power of the PLoT view.

22.5   Mental Simulation and Sampling

There is a central link between the sampling semantics of Church programs, mental simulation, and the causality central to many intuitive theories. A Church program naturally expresses the causal, generative aspect of people's knowledge through the function dependencies in the program. The function dependencies dictate the causal flow of the sampling process: functions whose outputs serve as an input to another function must be evaluated first. Each run of a Church program can be interpreted as the dynamic generation of a possible world that is consistent with the causal laws as specified in the program (Chater and Oaksford 2013). Because the sampling process is stochastic, a Church program specifies a probability distribution over possible worlds, and different modes of reasoning can be seen as different forms of mental simulation on top of this basic sampling process. Although the notion of mental representation and simulation of possible worlds has had many advocates (Craik 1967; Hegarty 2004; Johnson-Laird 1983, 2006), the PLoT view integrates this idea naturally into a view of mental models that is also probabilistic, causal, and sufficiently expressive to capture core intuitive theories.

We will illustrate the implications of this view via a concrete example from the domain of intuitive physics: people's judgments about the causal relations among the trajectories of physical objects in motion. We are concerned with judgments of *actual causation*: whether one specific event caused another specific event to happen. Consider a relatively simple scenario that consists of two billiard balls *A* and *B*, some solid walls with an opening gate, a brick, and a teleport gate that can be either active or inactive. Figure 22.4 (plate 11) shows diagrammatic illustrations of causal interactions between *A* and *B* in this world, assuming simple Newtonian elastic collisions between moving bodies. The question of interest is whether ball *A*'s collision with ball *B* caused ball *B* to go through the red gate on the left of the screen, prevented it from going through, or did neither. The tools of probabilistic programs and sampling-based inference allow us to give a precise formal account of these causal judgments, which also accords well with intuitions of mental simulation and gives strong quantitative fits to behavioral experiments.

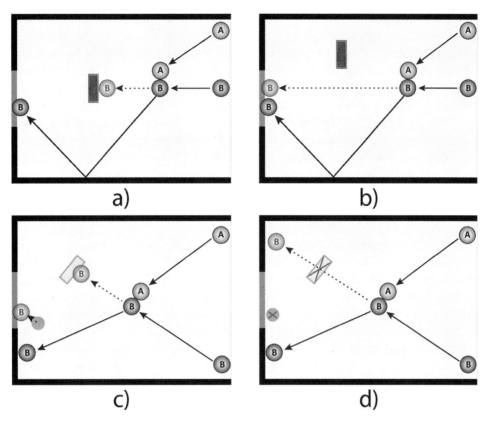

Figure 22.4 (plate 11)

Diagrammatic illustrations of four collision events in a simple physics world. Note: Solid arrows represent the actual trajectories of ball A before the collision and of ball B before and after the collision. Dashed arrows and faded circles represent the counterfactual trajectory of ball B. The brown rectangle, yellow rectangle, and blue circle represent a brick, and the entry and exit of a teleport, respectively.

To explain these judgments, we first need to be able to represent the relevant physical knowledge at the right level of abstraction. Despite its simplicity, our domain already affords an infinite number of interactions between *A* and *B,* and we want a model that yields a causal judgment for each possible situation. Rather than having to specify a new model for each causal interaction of interest (as we would have to do if we adopted a Bayesian network formulation; Pearl 2000), we want to represent the general laws that govern the interactions between the objects in our world. One way of representing people's knowledge of physical object motion in Church is by writing down a probabilistic and approximate version of some aspects of Newtonian mechanics. Functions in the Church program compute the inertial time evolution and the outcome of collisions by taking as input the mass and velocity of objects as well as more general aspects of the world such as friction and gravity. So far these are standard, deterministic simulation routines (so we leave out details). Critically, we also assume that some noise in each object's momentum is inserted just after each collision, and perhaps at other times as well, resulting in trajectories that are noisy versions of their Newtonian counterparts. Recent research has shown that people's intuitive physical judgments in several domains are well described by such noisy Newtonian simulations (Sanborn, Mansinghka, and Griffiths 2013; Battaglia, Hamrick, and Tenenbaum 2013; Smith et al. 2013; Smith and Vul 2012). Once we have a Church program that captures people's intuitive physics, we can model predictions about the future (e.g., will ball *B* go through the gate?) as simple forward simulations, and inferences about the past (e.g., where did ball *B* likely come from?) by a query of the past given the present—simulating possible histories that could have led up to the current state.

More subtly, a Church program can also be used to evaluate counterfactuals (e.g., would ball *B* have gone through the gate if the collision with *A* hadn't happened?). In line with Pearl (2000), the evaluation of counterfactuals in a Church program involves three steps: First, we condition all the random choices in the program based on what actually happened to estimate the unobserved values of the actual world. Second, we realize the truth of the counterfactual antecedent (e.g., that the collision did *not* happen) by intervening in the program execution that generated the actual world. This intervention breaks the normal flow of the program by setting some function inputs to desired values. For example, to model what would have happened if there had been no collision between *A* and *B*, we could set ball *A*'s velocity to zero or move ball *A* outside of the scene shortly before the time of collision. Finally, to evaluate the truth of the counterfactual, we reevaluate all the functions downstream from the point at which we intervened in the program. This process generates a sample over counterfactual world states, and repeatedly running this process allowing for different stochastic function evaluations can be used to express people's uncertainty over what would have happened in the relevant counterfactual world. Notice that the key feature of Church that allows this process to work is that it specifies a process for sampling particular situations and makes explicit the steps of the causal history that led up to a situation (in the form of a program execution trace). Counterfactuals are then evaluated by a series of *simulation* steps that result in imagined counterfactual worlds.

In a series of empirical studies, we have shown that people's quantitative judgments of actual causation are closely linked to such a probabilistic counterfactual analysis (Gerstenberg et al. 2012). When judging whether one event caused another event to happen, people compare what actually happened with what they think would have happened in the counterfactual world in which the candidate causal event had been absent. They appear to estimate something like the probability that the candidate cause was *necessary* to produce the outcome event: the probability that the outcome, which did in fact occur, would not have occurred in a counterfactual world where the candidate cause was absent. Consider the top pair of diagrams shown in figure 22.4 (plate 11). In both clips, what actually happened is identical. However, the outcome in the relevant counterfactual worlds would have been different. In figure 22.4a, ball *B* would have bounced off the brick if it hadn't collided with ball *A*. In contrast, in figure 22.4b, ball *B* would have gone through the gate even without the collision with ball *A*. As predicted by our account, people's judgments about whether *A* caused *B* to go through the gate are significantly higher for figure 22.4a than for figure 22.4b (Gerstenberg et al., 2014). In the bottom pair of cases, the contrast in the relevant counterfactual worlds was realized by comparing situations in which a teleport was either on (figure 22.4c) or off (figure 22.4d). Although people judged that *A* prevented *B* from going through the gate in figure 22.4c, they didn't think that *A* prevented *B* in figure 22.4d. In figure 22.4c, ball *B* would have gone through the gate via the teleport if it hadn't collided with *A*. In figure 22.4d, in contrast, the teleport was off, and *B* would not have gone through the gate even if there had been no collision with *A*. The fact that people's judgments differ dramatically between situations in which what actually happened was held constant supports the idea that causal and counterfactual judgments are inextricably linked. It also shows that it is not possible to give an account of people's causal judgments just in terms of what actually happened (e.g., Wolff 2007). Finally, it demonstrates the flexibility of people's intuitive theories and the critical way in which this flexibility supports mental simulation, counterfactual, and causal reasoning. Once people have learned how the teleport works, they have no trouble imagining its effects and incorporating these into their counterfactual simulations, whose outcome in turn influences their causal judgments.

Although we have focused here on the example of how we can explain people's causal judgments in the domain of intuitive physics, the general framework applies equally well to any domain for which we are able to represent our knowledge in terms of a Church program. For example, we could model people's judgments about whether agent *A*'s argument convinced agent *B* to try harder as a function of what actually happened and people's subjective degree of belief that *B* would still have tried harder had *A* not said anything. A Church program that captures people's intuitive understanding of psychology looks different from a Church program that captures people's intuitive understanding of physics, but we can understand people's causal judgments in terms of the same process that compares the actual outcome with the outcomes of mental simulations (sampling) of the relevant counterfactual worlds.

22.6 Concepts and Natural Language

Thus far we have sketched a notion of concepts as stochastic functions in Church, and intuitive theories as systems of interrelated concepts. We have also described how such intuitive theories can be used to describe the complex causal knowledge that people use to reason about the world. We would additionally like a theory of concepts to help us formulate the meanings of words, and more generally the ways in which natural language can be used to convey thought. In Goodman and Lassiter (forthcoming), we use Church to formulate an architecture for language understanding in which word meanings are grounded into intuitive theories, and utterance interpretation is a rich inferential process starting with these meanings. We summarize here the parts of this architecture that illuminate the role of concepts in thought.

As described above, we view intuitive theories as collections of function definitions; together they form a distribution over all the expressions that can be composed from these functions—this constitutes prior knowledge of the domain. We posit that the foundational operation of natural language interpretation is to update this prior belief distribution into a posterior distribution. Because belief update in a probabilistic system happens by conditioning, we need utterances to lead to conditions that can be used in a query. That is, there must be a meaning function that maps from strings of words to Boolean-valued expressions in the PLoT (i.e., expressions that can be the condition of a query). This meaning function is essentially the *narrow* language facility (Hauser, Chomsky, and Fitch 2002), mapping from sound strings to the PLoT. In Goodman and Lassiter (forthcoming), we describe the meaning function in two (fairly standard) steps: first we look up the PLoT expression for each word in a linguistic lexicon (an association between words and PLoT expressions), then we compose these expressions recursively until we have built a meaning for the whole sentence. These steps may be nondeterministic, but additional uncertainty causes no difficulties since we are already within a probabilistic framework. Thus, the meaning function lets us construct from a natural language expression a condition expression that can be used in query to update beliefs about some question—the query expression. But notice that although they are constructed in the same PLoT, these two expressions play very different cognitive roles: the query expression is a question about the world; the condition expression is a constraint on the causal process that generates the answer to this question.

The architecture is reminiscent of Jackendoff's "languages of thought" (Jackendoff 1995), in which there are several modules (for example, natural language and cognition), each with their own representation language and interfaces for translating from one module to another. In our approach the representation languages are mathematically similar for natural language and cognition (based in the stochastic lambda calculus) and their "interface" is defined by their roles in the inference (query) of language interpretation. Despite their mathematical similarities, the different cognitive roles of these different kinds of expressions imply two different, but interlocking, principles of compositionality in the cognitive architecture. One instance of compositionality allows us to build rich (distributions on) generative histories, while the other allows us to build up complex conditioning statements to constrain these histories. A naïve approach would try to make these two kinds of composition directly compatible, by requiring that each natural language constituent describe a probability distribution and relying on linguistic composition to combine these distributions. Our approach allows these distinct modes of composition to apply separately in natural language and thought, resulting in complex interactions that can look noncompositional when only one type of representation is considered.

Meaning conveyed by natural language is further enriched by pragmatic inference. As described elsewhere (Stuhlmüller and Goodman 2013; Goodman and Stuhlmüller 2013; Frank and Goodman 2012; Goodman and Lassiter, forthcoming) a broad range of pragmatic inferences can be understood as the output of conditioning in an intuitive theory of communication and can also be formalized using the PLoT tools described above. Adding this layer of inference results in further complexities and context sensitivities to the effective relationship between words and concepts, but is essential for understanding how we talk about our thoughts and understand what other people mean to say.

22.7   Concept Acquisition

If concepts are definitions in a library of useful (stochastic) functions, what is concept learning? Forming new concepts from examples is fundamentally a problem of induction—in our case, the problem of program induction. This can be formulated as Bayesian inference of a set of concepts that best explain the experience we have in the world: Conditioned on generating the examples we have seen, what is the likely new concept? Hypothesized concepts are formed in an effective language of thought based on the concepts learned so far—all the expressions that can be formed by composing the underlying PLoT and the already-defined function symbols. We can view these hypotheses as being generated by a higher-order *program-generating program,* a stochastic function that generates candidate stochastic functions that might explain a given set of observed examples. Concept learning as probabilistic program induction is philosophically and mathematically well posed, but a great deal of research is needed both to reduce it to useful engineering practice and to validate it as a model of human concept learning. Induction over such an infinite combinatorial space is simply stated as probabilistic conditioning, but such inferences are extremely challenging to implement in general. Yet recent progress has shown that this approach can be successful in certain cases: grammar-based program induction has been used to describe category learning (Goodman, Tenenbaum, et al. 2008), learning relational concepts (Kemp, Goodman, and Tenenbaum 2008), learning simple visual concepts (Lake, Salakhutdinov, and Tenenbaum 2013), and learning number concepts (Piantadosi, Tenenbaum, and Goodman 2012).

Notice that in this notion of inductive program elaboration, each concept begins life as simply a new symbol to which a function will come to be attached. The impetus to add such a placeholder symbol may come from natural language (upon hearing a new word), from the interaction of knowledge about natural kinds and specific examples (as suggested by Margolis 1998 and Carey, chapter 15, this volume), or from other explanatory pressures. Richer content and relationships to other concepts would be incorporated into the web of function definitions inductively, as the learner encounters additional examples and gains experience in the new domain.

Language, social context, and other factors may play a critical role in positing both the existence and the content of new concepts. For instance, Shafto, Goodman, and Frank (2012) argue that the social context of examples (for instance, that they are generated communicatively by a helpful person) can strongly affect the inferences made. Similarly, language can provide a strongly constraining form of evidence for concept formation—for instance, Piantadosi, Tenenbaum, and Goodman (2012) use a linguistic count list as a key input in learning numerical concepts. The PLoT offers a powerful way to think about these and other bootstrapping phenomena at the interface of social interaction, language acquisition, and concept acquisition, such as the contributions of syntactic and semantic bootstrapping in learning verbs, or the contributions of pragmatic inference in learning quantifiers. Again, further research is needed to understand how these factors integrate with inductive learning from examples in a full theory of concept acquisition; what is important for us here is that the PLoT provides us with a theory of concepts, and an approach to concept learning as probabilistic inference, that is able to explore these interactions in a productive way.

One important implication of the inductive view just indicated is that concept learning changes the effective language of thought. While this effective language has the same mathematical expressivity as the underlying PLoT, particular thoughts may be vastly simpler (and thus more cognitively tractable) in the effective language. Changing the effective language, by adding a new concept, then affects a number of cognitive functions. For instance, future concept induction will take place in the new effective language, which provides a different inductive bias than the original. In this way, concepts that are complex and unlikely to be constructed by a learner initially may become simpler and more plausible later on in the process of elaborating the learner's conceptual library. This process may be a critical driver of children's long-term cognitive development.

22.8   Summary and Next Steps

We have argued that concepts should be viewed as the stable representations of a *probabilistic language of thought*—more formally, as functions in an enriched stochastic lambda calculus. This view allows fine-grained compositionality while supporting reasoning by probabilistic inference. Compositionality is key to explaining the productivity of thought, while probabilistic inference explains graded and successful reasoning in an uncertain world. The PLoT hypothesis seeks to explain complex human cognition in a way that previous formal theories of concepts have not, and helps us to understand many topics in everyday cognition with both new qualitative insights and quantitative accuracy.

Importantly, the PLoT hypothesis builds on and unifies many attractive aspects of previous views on concepts. Like classical and symbolic theories, the PLoT puts compositionality and symbolic scaffolding at center stage. Unlike these theories however, but very much in the spirit of prototype, exemplar, and connectionist approaches, the PLoT explains why human reasoning is graded and why this is useful. It does so by borrowing from probability theory, and from modern Bayesian modeling approaches, the basic mechanics of reasoning under uncertainty. This reliance on probabilistic inference makes a natural connection to inferential role notions of concept meaning: it is not merely the proximal definitions, but the complex ways that information flows under inference that matter in practice. Rather than working at the level of monolithic probability distributions, the stochastic lambda calculus and Church allow us to work from the point of view of generative, sampling systems. This in turn makes a key connection to mental simulation and—poetically, but perhaps also literally—the importance of *imagination* in thinking.

For work on Bayesian models of cognition, the PLoT view holds particular importance. Recent advances in building probabilistic models of higher-level cognition share the basic mechanics of probabilities and many aspects of their philosophy, but they bring a bewildering and heterogenous array of additional representational tools and claims. The view presented here serves as a key unification by showing that all of these Bayesian models can be represented in, and hence reduced to, a simple system built from little more than function abstraction and random choice. It gives hope that advances in probabilistic models of targeted domains are compatible with each other and can ultimately be combined into a broader architecture for modeling human knowledge, reasoning, and learning.

Church models, and the PLoT more generally, are intended to capture the representations of knowledge people use to reason about the world, and the inferences that are supported by this knowledge. They are not intended to convey the algorithmic *process* of this inference, much less the neural instantiation. Indeed, establishing connections to these other levels of psychological analysis is one of the key future challenges for the PLoT hypothesis; others being further broadening of scope and demonstration of empirical adequacy within higher-level cognition. The implementations of Church, at the engineering level, suggest one set of ideas to motivate psychological process models. Indeed, implementations of Church query work through various combinations of caching and Monte Carlo simulation, which provide a very different view of computation than one might expect from a course on probability: not so much arithmetic tabulation as noisy dynamical systems tuned to result in samples from the desired distributions. Long engineering practice shows that these algorithms can give efficient solutions to tough statistical inference problems; recent work on probabilistic programming languages (e.g., Wingate, Stuhlmüller, and Goodman 2011) shows that they can be realized in general-purpose ways suitable to a PLoT. Furthermore, initial connections between such inference algorithms and human cognitive processes have been made (e.g., Griffiths, Vul, and Sanborn 2012). Yet classic and ongoing work on cognitive architecture, concepts, and neural dynamics all have additional insights that must also be understood in moving the PLoT toward the process and neural levels.

Acknowledgments

This work was supported by NSF STC award CCF-1231216, ONR awards N00014-09-1-0124 and N00014-13-1-0788, and a John S. McDonnell Foundation Scholar Award.

References

Anderson, J. R. 1996. Act: A simple theory of complex cognition. *American Psychologist* 51 (4): 355–365.

Baker, C. L., R. Saxe, and J. B. Tenenbaum. 2009. Action understanding as inverse planning. *Cognition* 113:329–349.

Battaglia, P. W., J. B. Hamrick, and J. B. Tenenbaum. 2013. Simulation as an engine of physical scene understanding. *Proceedings of the National Academy of Sciences of the United States of America* 110 (45): 18327–18332.

Block, N. 1997. Semantics, conceptual role. In *The Routledge Encyclopedia of Philosophy, vol. 8,* ed., E. Craig, 652–657. London: Routledge.

Bruner, J., J. Goodnow, and G. Austin. 1967. *A Study of Thinking.* New York: Science Editions.

Carey, S. 2009. *The Origin of Concepts.* New York: Oxford University Press.

Chater, N., and M. Oaksford. 2013. Programs as causal models: Speculations on mental programs and mental representation. *Cognitive Science* 37(6): 1171–1191.

Craik, K. J. W. 1967. *The Nature of Explanation.* Cambridge: Cambridge University Press Archive.

Frank, M., and N. Goodman. 2012. Predicting pragmatic reasoning in language games. *Science* 336 (6084): 998.

Frank, M. C., N. D. Goodman, and J. B. Tenenbaum. 2009. Using speakers' referential intentions to model early cross-situational word learning. *Psychological Science* 20:578–585.

Gerstenberg, T., and N. D. Goodman. 2012. Ping Pong in Church: Productive use of concepts in human probabilistic inference. In *Proceedings of the 34th Annual Conference of the Cognitive Science Society*, ed. N. Miyake, D. Peebles and R. P. Cooper, 1590–1595. Austin, TX: Cognitive Science Society.

Gerstenberg, T., N. D. Goodman, D. A. Lagnado, and J. B. Tenenbaum. 2012. Noisy Newtons: Unifying process and dependency accounts of causal attribution. In *Proceedings of the 34th Annual Conference of the Cognitive Science Society*, ed. N. Miyake, D. Peebles and R. P. Cooper, 378–383. Austin, TX: Cognitive Science Society.

Gerstenberg, T., N. D. Goodman, D. A. Lagnado, and J. B. Tenenbaum. 2014. From counterfactual simulation to causal judgment. In *Proceedings of the 36th Annual Conference of the Cognitive Science Society*, ed. P. Bello, M. Guarini, M. McShane, & B. Scassellati, 523–528. Austin, TX: Cognitive Science Society.

Goodman, N. D., C. L. Baker, E. B. Bonawitz, V. K. Mansinghka, A. Gopnik, H. Wellman, L. Schulz, and J. B. Tenenbaum. 2006. Intuitive theories of mind: A rational approach to false belief. In *Proceedings of the 28th Annual Conference of the Cognitive Science Society*, ed. R. Sun & N. Miyake, 1382–1387. Mahwah, NJ: Erlbaum.

Goodman, N. D., and D. Lassiter. Forthcoming. Probabilistic semantics and pragmatics: Uncertainty in language and thought. In *Handbook of Contemporary Semantics,* ed. S. Lappin and C. Fox. Oxford: Wiley-Blackwell.

Goodman, N. D., V. K. Mansinghka, D. Roy, K. Bonawitz, and J. B. Tenenbaum. 2008. Church: A language for generative models. In *Uncertainty in Artificial Intelligence,* ed. D. McAllester and P. Myllymaki, 220–229. Corvallis, OR: AUAI Press.

Goodman, N. D., and A. Stuhlmüller. 2013. Knowledge and implicature: Modeling language understanding as social cognition. *Topics in Cognitive Science* 5 (1): 173–184.

Goodman, N. D., J. B. Tenenbaum, J. Feldman, and T. L. Griffiths. 2008. A rational analysis of rule-based concept learning. *Cognitive Science* 32 (1): 108–154.

Goodman, N. D., T. D. Ullman, and J. B. Tenenbaum. 2011. Learning a theory of causality. *Psychological Review* 118 (1): 110–119.

Gopnik, A. 2003. The theory theory as an alternative to the innateness hypothesis. In *Chomsky and His Critics*, ed. L. M. Antony and N. Hornstein, 238–254. Oxford: Blackwell.

Gopnik, A., C. Glymour, D. M. Sobel, L. E. Schulz, T. Kushnir, and D. Danks. 2004. A theory of causal learning in children: causal maps and Bayes nets. *Psychological Review* 111 (1): 3–32.

Gopnik, A., and H. Wellman. 2012. Reconstructing constructivism: Causal models, Bayesian learning mechanisms, and the theory theory. *Psychological Bulletin* 138 (6): 1085–1108.

Griffiths, T. L., and J. B. Tenenbaum. 2009. Theory based causal induction. *Psychological Review* 116 (4): 661–716.

Griffiths, T. L., E. Vul, and A. N. Sanborn. 2012. Bridging levels of analysis for probabilistic models of cognition. *Current Directions in Psychological Science* 21 (4): 263–268.

Hauser, M. D., N. Chomsky, and W. T. Fitch. 2002. The faculty of language: What is it, who has it, and how did it evolve? *Science* 298 (5598): 1569–1579.

Hegarty, M. 2004. Mechanical reasoning by mental simulation. *Trends in Cognitive Sciences* 8 (6): 280–285.

Jackendoff, R. 1995. *Languages of the Mind: Essays on Mental Representation*. Cambridge, MA: MIT Press.

Johnson-Laird, P. N. 1983. *Mental Models: Towards a Cognitive Science of Language, Inference, and Consciousness*. Cambridge, MA: Harvard University Press.

Johnson-Laird, P. N. 2006. *How We Reason*. New York: Oxford University Press.

Kemp, C., N. D. Goodman, and J. B. Tenenbaum. 2008. Learning and using relational theories. *Advances in Neural Information Processing Systems* 20:753–760.

Kemp, C., and J. B. Tenenbaum. 2009. Structured statistical models of inductive reasoning. *Psychological Review* 116 (1): 20.

Lake, B. M., R. Salakhutdinov, and J. Tenenbaum. 2013. One-shot learning by inverting a compositional causal process. In Advances in Neural Information Processing Systems 26, ed. C. J. C. Burges, L. Bottou, M. Welling, Z. Ghahramani, and K. Q. Weinberger, 2526–2534. Cambridge, MA: MIT Press.

Margolis, E. 1998. How to acquire a concept. *Mind & Language* 13 (3): 347–369.

McCarthy, J. 1960. Recursive functions of symbolic expressions and their computation by machine, part i. *Communications of the ACM* 3 (4): 184–195.

Newell, A., J. C. Shaw, and H. A. Simon. 1958. Elements of a theory of human problem solving. *Psychological Review* 65 (3): 151–166.

Nosofsky, R. M. 1986. Attention, similarity, and the identification-categorization relationship. *Journal of Experimental Psychology: General* 115 (1): 39–57.

Pearl, J. 1988. *Probabilistic Reasoning in Intelligent Systems: Networks of Plausible Inference*. San Francisco: Morgan Kaufmann.

Pearl, J. 2000. *Causality: Models, Reasoning and Inference*. Cambridge: Cambridge University Press.

Piantadosi, S. T., J. B. Tenenbaum, and N. D. Goodman. 2012. Bootstrapping in a language of thought: A formal model of numerical concept learning. *Cognition* 123 (2): 199–217.

Rehder, B. 2003. A causal-model theory of conceptual representation and categorization. *Journal of Experimental Psychology: Learning, Memory, and Cognition* 29 (6): 1141–1159.

Rosch, E. 1999. Principles of categorization. In *Concepts: Core Readings*, ed. E. Margolis and S. Laurence, 189–206. Cambridge, MA: MIT Press.

Rumelhart, D. E., and J. L. McClelland. 1988. *Parallel Distributed Processing*. Cambridge, MA: MIT Press.

Sanborn, A. N., V. K. Mansinghka, and T. L. Griffiths. 2013. Reconciling intuitive physics and Newtonian mechanics for colliding objects. *Psychological Review* 120 (2): 411–437.

Shafto, P., N. D. Goodman, and M. C. Frank. 2012. Learning from others: The consequences of psychological reasoning for human learning. *Perspectives on Psychological Science* 7 (4): 341–351.

Smith, K., E. Dechter, J. Tenenbaum, and E. Vul. 2013. Physical predictions over time. In *Proceedings of the 35th Annual Meeting of the Cognitive Science Society*, ed. M. Knauff, M. Pauen, N. Sebanz, and I. Wachsmuth, 1342–1347. Austin, TX: Cognitive Science Society.

Smith, K. A., and E. Vul. 2012. Sources of uncertainty in intuitive physics. In *Proceedings of the 34th Annual Conference of the Cognitive Science Society*, ed. N. Miyake, D. Peebles, and R. P. Cooper, 995–1000. Austin, TX. Cognitive Science Society.

Stuhlmüller, A., and N. D. Goodman. 2013. Reasoning about reasoning by nested conditioning: Modeling theory of mind with probabilistic programs. *Cognitive Systems Research* 28:80–99.

Tenenbaum, J. B., and T. L. Griffiths. 2003. Theory-based causal inference. *Advances in Neural Information Processing Systems 15*, ed. S. Becker, S. Thrun, and K. Obermayer, 43–50. Cambridge, MA: MIT Press.

Tenenbaum, J. B., C. Kemp, T. L. Griffiths, and N. D. Goodman. 2011. How to grow a mind: Statistics, structure, and abstraction. *Science* 331 (6022): 1279–1285.

Wellman, H. M., and S. A. Gelman. 1992. Cognitive development: Foundational theories of core domains. *Annual Review of Psychology* 43 (1): 337–375.

Wingate, D., A. Stuhlmüller, and N. Goodman. 2011. Lightweight implementations of probabilistic programming languages via transformational compilation. In *Proceedings of the 14th International Conference on Artificial Intelligence and Statistics*, 131.

Wolff, P. 2007. Representing causation. *Journal of Experimental Psychology: General* 136 (1): 82–111.

Appendix A. Experiment 1

A.1 Participants

Thirty participants (twenty-two female) recruited through Amazon Mechanical Turk participated in the experiment. The mean age was 31.3 ($SD = 10.8$).

A.2 Materials and Procedure

The experiment was programmed in Adobe Flash CS5. Participants viewed twenty tournaments in total: first, one block of eight single-player tournaments, and then another block of twelve two-player tournaments. The order of the tournaments within each block was randomized. Participants could remind themselves about the most important aspects of the experiment by moving the mouse over the Info field on the top right of the screen (see figure 22.1). Based on the results of the three matches in the tournament, participants estimated the strength of the indicated player on a slider that ranged from -50 to 50. The endpoints were labeled "very weak" and "very strong." It took participants 7.4 ($SD = 3.3$) minutes to complete the experiment.

A.3 Design

Table 22.1 shows the patterns of evidence that were used for the single-player tournaments. Table 22.2 shows the patterns for the two-player tournaments. In all tournaments, participants were asked to judge the strength of player A. For the single-player tournaments, we used four different patterns of evidence: *confounded evidence,* in which A wins repeatedly against B; *strong* and *weak indirect evidence,* where A wins only one match herself but B either continues to win or lose two games against other players; and *diverse evidence,* in which A wins against three different players. For each of those patterns, we also included a pattern in which the outcomes of the games were exactly reversed.

Appendix B. Experiment 2

B.1 Participants

Twenty (eleven female) recruited through Amazon Mechanical Turk participated in the experiment. The mean age was 34 ($SD = 9.8$).

B.2 Materials, Procedure, and Design

Participants viewed ten single-player tournaments, which comprised the eight situations used in Experiment 1 plus two additional patterns (IR 1, 2). Participants first judged player A's strength based merely on the match results in the tournament. Afterwards, participants received information from the omniscient commentator about one player who was lazy in a particular match. Participants then rated A's strength for a second time, whereby the slider was initialized at the first judgment's position. It took participants 9.4 ($SD = 4$) minutes to complete the experiment.

The bottom row of table 22.1 shows what information the omniscient commentator revealed in each situation. For example, in situation 3 in which participants first saw strong indirect evidence, the commentator then said: "In game 1, Player B was lazy." In the additional pattern (IR 2), A wins against B, B wins against C, and D wins against E. The commentator then reveals that E was lazy in game 3. For the patterns in which A lost her game, the results of each match as shown in table 22.1 were reversed, and the corresponding losing player was indicated as having been lazy. For example, in situation 2, A lost all three games against B, and the commentator revealed that A was lazy in game 2.

23   Concepts in the Semantic Triangle

James A. Hampton

23.1   Introduction

Looking at the range and variety of contributions to this volume, it is evident that *concept* is a term that means many things to many people, a fact that has been widely acknowledged (Dove 2009; Machery 2009; Weiskopf 2009). Probably the most central issue of all, the one over which there is least agreement, is how to explain or describe the meaning or content of concepts. What information do they carry, and how do they do so?

The aim of this chapter is to describe three different ways in which it has proved useful to talk about the meaning or content of concepts. The first comes primarily from philosophy and uses the notion of *reference*. When we think a thought, or utter a statement, the words that we use refer to particular things in the world. Each concept term has its *denotation*, the class of things to which it refers. A second way to think about conceptual meaning is by looking at *language use*. When we use a word, we can do so either appropriately in a way that others will readily understand, or inappropriately in a way that others will object to. For this approach, meaning is a matter of social convention or practice. The third way to look at meaning is to ask what information is represented in a person's mind at the time that they have a thought or express an idea. As well as asking what a concept refers to, and what the appropriate use of the term in language might be, we can also ask *how* an individual mind achieves this result. What must we assume about the representation of information in the mind that enables a possessor of a concept to use it in these ways?

These three approaches to concepts and meaning lead to very different accounts of what a concept is. While not promising to unravel the tangled knot of how the accounts relate to each other, I hope at least to lay out some of the issues involved.

23.2   The Semantic Triangle

An early view of the relation between different forms of meaning was the classic *Meaning of Meaning* by Ogden and Richards (1923). Figure 23.1 uses their famous semantic triangle to illustrate the complex relations that we are considering here.

Ogden and Richards were more interested in illustrating the ways in which misunderstanding can occur as people communicate their thoughts through the use of words. For the present purpose, I have relabeled the links to make a rather different point. The three corners of the triangle turn out to represent the three accounts of concept identity that I will be discussing. Taking the accounts in reverse order, at the top of the triangle is the psychology of the individual. In psychology, researchers investigate concepts by interrogating individuals about their conceptual knowledge and intuitions. Psychologists aim to uncover the *meaning* of a concept by direct and indirect measurement of how individuals represent the concept and what function it plays in directing their behavior. This behavior will include (among other things) memory, judgments of similarity, inductive reasoning, categorization, naming, and language comprehension. For the psychologist, then, a concept is a postulated entity whose character can be inferred from its effects on behavior. Like many other theoretical terms in psychology since the behaviorist revolution (intelligence, personality, and motivation would be cases in point), the theoretical notion of concept is defined operationally in terms of its observed effects on measured behaviors.

The approach that focuses on words on the left of the triangle is to be found in linguistics, as represented, for example, by lexical semantics. The study of lexical semantics takes a language such as English as its basic object of study. Pinning down the meaning of a concept, and differentiating it from others, is a matter for cultural study— in effect developing a natural history of the concepts deployed in a given linguistic-cultural group. For example, one might try to understand how conceptual terms (the

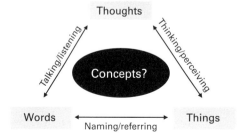

Figure 23.1
The Semantic Triangle redrawn to illustrate the three different notions of concept and their interrelations.

substantive words in a language) can be differentiated into classes such as verbs of motion, animate nouns, adjectives of degree, and so forth, in a way that explains their behavior in different linguistic contexts. The "English language" is of course an abstraction or idealization based on empirical observation of texts and the intuitions of speakers averaged across a given language group. So whereas the psychology of concepts is primarily about individuals trying to understand and negotiate their way through the world, the linguistic approach is primarily about the net effect that social communities speaking a common dialect or language and achieving shared meaning have on the standard use and meaning of linguistic terms.

Finally, the bottom right corner of the triangle emphasizes the crucial role that concepts play in our interaction as a sociocultural species with the real world. Thoughts and utterances can have a semantic value, in the sense that they can be *true* or *false*. Broadly speaking, being true means corresponding to the way things actually are. So an equally important part of the triangle is to provide a "reality check" or constraint on thoughts and words, keeping them in touch with the way the world actually is. The development of science, in the broadest sense, is not just the accumulation of facts. Equally important is the evolution across the centuries of the appropriate concepts with which to articulate hypotheses and theories (Kuhn 1962). In parallel with this positive evolution of "correct" concepts, there will be the gradual extinction of concepts that don't do the job of providing us with terms for understanding the world.

Writing in 1851, Herman Melville (1951) has his narrator Ishmael define the whale thus:

How shall we define the whale, by his obvious externals, so as conspicuously to label him for all time to come? To be short, then, a whale is A SPOUTING FISH WITH A HORIZONTAL TAIL. There you have him. However contracted, that definition is the result of expanded meditation. (*Moby-Dick*, chapter 32)

Classification of animal and plant species into the now widely accepted scientific taxonomy taught in schools is a relatively recent achievement of biology. Classifying a whale as a mammal and not as a fish provides a classification that makes sense of a range of data—facts about the anatomy and physiology of the whale, such as that it breathes air and suckles its young, but also about the evolutionary history of species and how and where they branched off from other life forms in the past. Humans are free to create whatever concepts or classifications they choose. In the nineteenth century, the fact that whales and cod were in a similar category for the purposes of commercial fishing meant that it was intuitively evident that they should both be classed as fish (at least to those who had direct experience of them). Subsequently, increasing education and biological understanding in the population has led to a shift in classification (but see Dupré 1999 for an alternative view).

The third approach to considering the real world of things serves to tie together the other two corners of the triangle. If we first of all assume that there is a real class of things—for example, whales—in the world out there, then we can use that to say both what someone is thinking about (their idea or conception of whale as it plays a role in whale thoughts), and what someone is talking about (the meaning of the word *whale* in the language). It has therefore proved tempting to rely heavily on this third corner of the triangle as the cornerstone for fixing the meaning of concepts. Note, however, that having first to assume the real existence of the class may raise problems for this approach (Wikforss 2005).

23.2.1 Psychology and Concepts

My own interest in concepts has followed the path taken by psychology. As readers may be aware, interest in how people categorize and conceptualize the world took a great leap forward with the work of Rosch and Mervis in the 1970s (Rosch 1975; Rosch and Mervis 1975). Previous work on concepts in psychology had followed two main paths. The Piagetian tradition concentrated on conceptual development and saw concepts as logically structured schemas that organized the perceptions and actions of an individual (Piaget 1953). Although consistent with modern approaches to understanding concepts as complex representations, Piaget's theory of adult cognition was effectively an idealization. In Chomskyan terms, it was an account of adult competence, in that it sought to explain and elaborate the developmental processes that lead to the full power of hypothetico-deductive thought in the adult. The overly strong focus on logic and the overelaborated descriptive aspect of the theory meant that with the advent of cognitive experimental psychology in the 1960s, developmental and reasoning psychologists tended to see Piagetian theory as a target for criticism. New methodological developments revealed more about the conceptual abilities of infants and young children, while the reasoning of adults was discovered to be at odds with the Piagetian account (Wason 1960). The continuation of this tradition has seen children portrayed as ever more intelligent at ever younger ages (see, for example, Gelman 2003), and adults as ever more likely to fall into logical fallacy and error (e.g., Kahneman, Slovic, and Tversky 1982).

The other way in which concepts were traditionally considered in psychology was as an offshoot of learning theory in the behaviorist tradition, with concepts treated as classification rules that were learned through a process of hypothesis formation and testing (e.g., Bourne and Restle 1959). Another classic set of studies from this era was by Bruner, Goodnow, and Austin (1956), who explored how people set about discovering categorization rules of a given logical form through entertaining hypotheses and sampling exemplars in order to test them.

Whereas psychologists had previously been mainly content to define concepts in terms of simple conjunctive rules, Rosch and Mervis set out to discover how actual concepts were represented within individuals. The most direct way to do this is to ask them, and Rosch and Mervis did just this. Their participants described their understanding of terms like *lemon, trout, chair,* or *hammer* by listing descriptive properties. From the results of this listing exercise came the idea of prototype concepts. As I have argued in Hampton (2006), the key insight here is that people represent the central tendency of a class rather than its boundaries. It is as if when defining London, you specified the center of the city (Trafalgar Square, say), and gave an indication of its approximate size. The rest is left vague. What you don't do is trace on the map the actual boundary of the city. Indeed people's understanding of geographical features such as mountains often works in much this way (Fisher et al. 2004). In a similar way, people's concept of a HAMMER is represented by an idealized notion of what most typical hammers are like, without a clear rule for deciding when something is or is not a hammer.

The initial idea of a prototype as just a list of features or properties clearly lacked sufficient representational power. There was also considerable confusion about whether prototypes were intended to be primarily *visual* (e.g., Osherson and Smith 1981; Rips 1989). Some theorists assumed that the notion of *similarity* appealed to by prototype theory was akin to *surface similarity* or *similarity in appearance.* They therefore argued that prototype theory could not account for categorization on the basis of deeper or more abstract properties such as function or historical origin. It can be argued, for example, that the (presumably sincere) intention of a designer to create a particular kind of artifact is the single necessary defining property of artifact kinds. Their appearance and their actual ability to perform the intended function are irrelevant (see Bloom 1998). In Hampton et al. (2009), we provided evidence that while originally intended function does influence categorization, it is treated along with current function and appearance as one feature among many affecting the likelihood of being included in the concept class. Similarly, Malt and Johnson (1992) showed that the function of an artifact is neither necessary nor sufficient for determining its kind. Prototype concepts should therefore be considered as integrating multiple sources of information, including perceptual, functional, and historical features as required.

Another source of confusion comes from the claim that prototype concepts lack necessary and sufficient conditions for membership. On the one hand, such conditions can easily be formulated using similarity—to be a category member, it is both necessary and sufficient to be more similar to the prototype than some threshold level (Hampton 1995). On the other hand, concepts that do have necessary and sufficient defining features may still be represented as prototypes. When two or three features are individually given maximal weight such that each on its own outweighs the sum of all other features, then a threshold can be set that renders the features singly necessary, and jointly sufficient, for category membership.

In any case, the notion of prototypes was largely supplanted in psychology in the mid-1980s with the notion of causal schemas (Murphy and Medin 1985). When more is known about a domain, then knowing about the relations among the features becomes increasingly important. Perceptual similarity is only a starting point for forming conceptual categories. A child just observing how a word is used may form a simple prototype on the basis of associating the word with the appearance of a set of objects. Most creatures appear to have the ability to learn on the basis of similarity of appearance. Conditioned responses generalize to novel situations to the extent that the new situations are similar to those in which the responses were learned. Initial prototype formation on the basis of sensory features is therefore a fundamental process. Even young children quickly learn, however, that appearances may be misleading (Gelman et al. 1994), and adults understand that a range of different features and the right kind of relations among them are important for determining kinds (Rehder 2003).

Current psychological accounts of concepts and categorization are consequently keen to emphasize the role of concepts in understanding and causal explanation. Even so, the key insight described above remains critical. Our causal schemas still provide a descriptive account of the central or typical cases of a conceptual category. Only rarely will they provide a clear rule for deciding category membership at the boundary. In this sense, the causal schemas are still prototypes.

23.2.2 Possible Problems with the Psychological Approach

As an account of concepts in general, there are several well-known problems with the path that psychology has followed. These problems relate to the difficulty of using the contents of an individual's mental representation as a means of pinning down a concept's meaning.

The first difficulty is the problem of error. People's concepts may in fact contain incorrect information about the world. For example, many people think that snakes are slimy to the touch. Never having felt one, and seeing the shininess of their skins, it is a reasonable inference to draw but happens to be false. The problem is that if we take the concept SNAKE to be whatever people understand by that term, then we would have to agree that snakes are slimy. The proposition "snakes are slimy" would be evaluated as true or false, not by looking at actual snakes, but by looking at people's beliefs about snakes. This problem led Rey (1983) to propose, along with other philosophers, that the psychological notion needs a different name—say, *conception*—to differentiate it from the correct concept, which allows truth to be determined in relation to the actual world. Otherwise, if it were the case that everyone in a given community believed that snakes were slimy, then their concept SNAKE would in fact refer to nothing in the actual world, thus remaining in the realm of fantasy. It is more plausible to suppose that their concept SNAKE still refers to the actual set of snakes, but that what the concept actually denotes is not just determined by the contents of their beliefs about snakes.

A second difficulty arises from the impossibility of having a debate about a topic that doesn't just descend into a question of terminology. Suppose that Joanna is a zookeeper and believes that snakes are dry to the touch. Then along comes Katy, who thinks that they are slimy. When they find that they disagree, all that we should be able to say using the psychological sense of concept is that they have different concepts of snake. They don't disagree about the facts, because the way Joanna uses the word *snake* is different from the way Katy does. Their different beliefs lead to different concepts, so all factual disagreement turns into terminological disagreement.

The third difficulty is closely related to this one. To be useful, the meaning of a concept needs to have some means of differentiating the information that constitutes its meaning from information that is otherwise true of it (Miller and Johnson-Laird 1976). Compare the information that you would find about snakes in a dictionary as opposed to an encyclopedia. The average person may be able to tell you all kinds of things about snakes, but most of it may be incidental to the question of what type of thing a snake actually is—its conceptual definition. Being cold blooded and reptilian and lacking limbs seem to be core parts of the meaning of the concept, whereas being used for making handbags or being a Christian symbol of the temptation of Eve do not. In spite of models that try to make the distinction between defining and characteristic features of concepts (e.g., Smith et al. 1974), no good way of differentiating the two psychologically has been found. For example, all species of birds have two legs, but only some species fly, yet when describing birds, these two features are equally likely to be produced and are rated equally important to the concept.

23.3   External Definitions—A Solution to the Problem

To resolve the problem of error and of disagreement, a good solution is to fix a concept meaning in relation to reference. If the meaning of a concept is tied to the class of things to which it refers, then these difficulties do not arise. Conceptual classes according to this proposal are the real classes of things that actually exist in the world. Deciding whether snakes are slimy is not a psychological question but one about biology. People's mental representations of the world in their conceptual store are not concepts themselves, but are representations *of* concepts —what Rey called conceptions. (For Fodor [1998], they are atomic unanalyzed symbols in an internal language of thought.) Thus we can say that Joanna and Katy disagree about a fact, rather than just having different concepts, since the question of sliminess versus dryness is to be resolved by examining the class of things being talked about (which for both of them is just the actual class of snakes).

To handle the problem of the dictionary versus the encyclopedia, and assuming that the differentiation cannot be achieved by psychological methods (i.e., through behavioral measures), then there are two possible solutions. One possibility is to follow Melville's Ishmael and attempt a definition. A definition is an explicit verbal formula that will correctly classify cases that fall under the concept and discriminate them from those that do not. For example:

Snakes are elongated, legless, carnivorous reptiles of the suborder Serpentes that can be distinguished from legless lizards by their lack of eyelids and external ears. ("Snake," *Wikipedia*)

This is a concept definition in a form of which Aristotle (and indeed Linnaeus) would have approved. A set of properties are described that are all true of all snakes, and all true only of snakes. Any beliefs not included in the definition (e.g., relating to the texture of the skin) would be part of the encyclopedia and not the dictionary. As we saw with Ishmael's definition of a whale, however, definitions can change over time. The evolution of science and culture frequently require a change in concept definitions, and in this case, the question arises of when they should be treated as the same concept—with an evolving definition—rather than as two different concepts.

The other way to resolve the dictionary/encyclopedia problem is to follow Fodor's (1998) informational atomism. For Fodor there are no definitions, so that concepts are simply abstract unitary symbols that stand for the appropriate classes or properties in the world. Thoughts, then, are "just" structured sets of symbols, much as this text is represented on the computer's hard disk just as a series of 1s and 0s on a magnetic medium. They derive their meaning through their relation to the external world. For Fodor, all the properties of snakes are encyclopedic, with the exception of "is a snake." Effectively, the problem of discovering the meaning of a concept is passed over to other disciplines—in particular to the sciences—while the problem of how humans come to possess concepts is a part of evolutionary psychology.

23.4   Meaning as Use

23.4.1   The Meaning as Use Proposal

Let us turn next to the "words" corner of the triangle. Wittgenstein famously wrote: "For a large class of cases—though not for all—in which we employ the word 'meaning,' it can be defined thus: the meaning of a word is its use in the language game" (1953, section 43). Perhaps then, language behavior, or how people use words when talking to each other, might provide a way around the problem of deciding the content of a concept.

Consider the case of adjectives describing simple properties. What is the meaning of a color term like *beige* or of a height term like *tallish*? It is not obvious how we can use the external route here (but see Williamson 1994). We believe that whales and snakes have a real existence as kinds, because of our scientific and cultural knowledge of what it is to be a natural kind, what determines species boundaries, and so forth (I leave aside the interesting question of the difficulty of defining the concept of species in biological theory; Mayr 1982). But we cannot turn to any equivalent set of validated knowledge to tell us that beige or tallish things constitute a class independent of our own understanding of them. There is no theory of beigeness or tallness.

How do we fix the content of these concepts? We could take a psychological view, and say that each person has their own concept of beige and their own concept of tallish. But that will again raise the problem of error. If Jed likes to call anything that is deep purple (to us) *beige,* we will be justified in calling him to account—he is just wrong about that word and its meaning. On the other hand a difference of opinion about just where on the spectrum beige turns into a light tan or a pink would not be grounds for denying that someone possesses the concept.

In cases like these, the most sensible course is to define concepts by the consensus that exists among a group of speakers. To have the "correct" concept of beige cannot be a matter of being in possession of a symbol or definition that correctly picks out the real class of beige things in the world, since there is no independent way of saying whether that class really exists. To have the correct concept is rather to use the word in a way that would be considered acceptable or normal by most other speakers of one's dialect. Partly these "others" will be one's peers with whom one interacts, but they will also include the full range of social and cultural influences to which one is exposed.

This proposal makes good sense for a whole range of concepts. For example, it provides a reasonable account of how children learn the meaning of many words. They hear and observe how words are used in different contexts and then gradually learn to use them in the same way. Keil and Batterman (1984) showed how young children first attach the meaning of words to the most obvious characteristic features of the named class. A bowl of cornflakes is breakfast regardless of the time of day at which it is eaten. A robber is a man with a gun who takes your TV away, even if he has your permission to do so. Similarly Satlow and Newcombe (1998) found that children's classification of geometric shapes as triangles or circles were based on broad similarity rather than defining rules. If children form hypotheses of word meaning on the basis of what they find interesting to attend to in the context in which they hear the word used, and a general notion of similarity, then one would expect just this kind of result. Interestingly, Lupyan (2013) has evidence that adults also may categorize triangles by similarity rather than by their strict definition. Triangles that were judged as atypical were also more likely to be rejected as being triangles.

The proposal also provides a way of rescuing the validity of psychological research tools for uncovering people's prototypes and conceptual schemas. In an unpublished study I ran with Danièle Dubois in 1995, we explored whether people would see any distinction between how words are used and conceptual classification. We selected eight common categories like tools, sciences, and fruits, and created a list of twenty-four items for each category. The list included a full range of degrees of membership in the category. For sciences, for example, it included typical sciences (chemistry), atypical sciences (dentistry), and a range of less and less scientific disciplines down to a clear

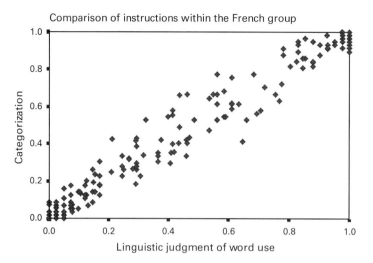

Figure 23.2

Comparing group decision probabilities for judgments of category membership (a walnut is a fruit) and for judgments of language use (I would spontaneously use the word "fruit" to refer to walnuts).

nonmember (literature). Two groups of participants then made yes or no decisions about each category list. The first group was asked to decide for each item whether it belonged in the category. Is chemistry a science? Is literature a science? The second group was asked to make a judgment about word use. Participants were asked, "As a speaker of your language, do you think that you would spontaneously use the word *science* to refer to each of these items?" The study was conducted on two groups of students in France, in the French language.

The results were very clear, as can be seen in figure 23.2, which plots the probability of people saying yes to each item, either in the categorization task (the vertical axis) or the linguistic judgment task (the horizontal axis).

The correlation between the two groups was near perfect, with no systematic variation beyond that expected by the error of measurement of the probabilities. In addition, these probabilities of categorization or agreement with word use were closely correlated with the data from a third group, that was asked to judge how typical each item was of the category. In sum, there is just one underlying representation of the concept here. The closer an item comes to matching the expected prototype of the category, the more typical it is judged to be, the more likely people are to endorse it as a category member, and the more likely they are to imagine themselves using the category label to refer to the item. According to the *meaning as use* account, this prototype is the result of generalizing across many contexts of use in which the word has been heard or successfully used in communication. The mental lexicon evolves through coordination with other speakers.

The evidence then suggests that asking people about the extensions of concepts (as in whether bananas are in the extension of fruits) is equivalent to asking them about the use of words (as in whether they would refer to a banana using the word fruit). Traditional psychological tasks such as typicality ratings, attribute listing, and category membership judgments are therefore reasonably valid ways of getting at the social consensus about concepts.

23.4.2   Problems with the Meaning as Use Proposal

Recent work by Barbara Malt and colleagues has thrown some doubt on the utility of the *meaning as use* proposal for fixing conceptual content. The difficulty arises from data that she has been collecting on the use of different terms in a language to refer to subclasses of artifacts or functional objects around the home. Malt and colleagues (1999) took photographs of a large number of simple containers such as cartons, boxes, bottles, and jars, then showed the photographs to different groups of speakers of English, Chinese, and Spanish. Some groups judged similarity of the objects, while others had to name them in their own language. Remarkably, although there was a good correlation ($r > 0.9$) in overall similarity across the different language groups, the naming data showed only weak correlations ($0.35 < r < 0.55$). There was clearly a disjunction between how the different cultures saw the similarity between the objects, in much the same way, and how they named the objects, using very different name categories. Note that the disparity was not just because different languages divided up the similarity space in different ways (as, for example, when Russian divides the English color range for BLUE into a dark and a light category). The conceptual categories derived from similarity were just a poor foundation on which to base the classes with a common name. Objects that were similar could have different names, and objects that were dissimilar could have the same name, and different languages mapped onto the space in very different ways.

This result and subsequent research by Malt and colleagues throws some doubt on treating language use as a basis for exploring underlying concepts—especially for artifacts. The traditional "survey" method of asking people whether some object is (for example) an instance of BOTTLE may not provide a clear picture of how objects are classed into conceptual types in people's minds. The difficulty, as identified by Malt and colleagues, is that naming is affected by the pragmatics of communication and also reflects historical change. A pair of similar artifacts may start out with the same name, but over time they may evolve in different ways so that while they still keep the same name, their similarity can be lost.

So although the usage of the language community certainly provides a way of coordinating one's own concepts with those of others, the relation between knowing how to use words and possessing particular concepts is not as direct or straightforward as one might hope. In fact, how things are named may not provide a reliable or valid basis for describing the underlying conceptual structure in people's minds.

Malt and Sloman (2003) go so far as to argue that many artifact concepts are not treated as kinds. They argue that classifying something as a weapon, or furniture, or a hammer is highly context dependent. These concepts have strong functional properties. A weapon is something used to harm another. But there is no stable category of weapons, since not only objects created with this intention, but almost any other object becomes a weapon in the context of a person intending to use it to harm another. Thus the police may bring a charge against someone for being in possession of a baseball bat if they have reason to believe it is intended for use as a weapon.

23.5 How to Ensure that We Are Talking about the Same Thing

When we communicate with others, the very definition of successful communication is clearly going to depend crucially on our ability to know when we are talking about the same thing. Otherwise we might not be speaking the same language, and disagreement and agreement would be meaningless. If by *fish* I mean what biologists mean by fish, while Ishmael means something like "fish-shaped creatures of the deep," unless we are aware that we have these different concepts, we will be open to all kinds of misunderstanding.

From the discussion so far, I have outlined two ways in which we might achieve this coordination of meanings. One is to pin meaning to external classes that exist in reality. This approach works well for concepts that contribute to scientific understanding. Snakes and whales exist independently of humans (so we have reason to believe), and so the most natural way to fix the meaning of concepts such as these will be in terms of the actual class. The second way is to pin meaning to implicit social conventions about word use. Just as it is appropriate to say "thank you" when receiving something positive from another, so it is appropriate to say "red" when asked the color of a particular shade. Both ways of coordinating meaning, either by the external world or by language convention, imply that it is possible for a person to represent a concept either correctly or incorrectly. As a consequence, concepts and meanings are not "in the head" to use Putnam's phrase (Putnam 1975). An individual who wishes both to understand the world and to be understood by others has a responsibility to represent the correct concepts.

Interestingly, the problem of error works differently for things and for words. It is quite conceivable (indeed it has happened) that everyone in a cultural group has the wrong concept of (say) disease. They can all identify cases of individuals who are sick, but they believe that disease is caused by witchcraft and the malign attentions of invisible spirit forces, and that treatment involves invocation of spells and sacrifices. But it would be very odd to say that they all have the wrong *meaning* for the word *disease* in their language. When concepts are tied to language use, then either a majority of speakers or a powerful minority (for example the priesthood or an educational elite) must be the "keepers" of the correct use. Although everyone's concepts can be incorrectly attached to the world, meanings cannot all be incorrectly attached to the language group.

There will be situations where the two principles may come into conflict. Obviously the question of what real classes actually exist is not always easy to answer. Most people take it as a given that the natural world exists and that modern science provides the best account of the kinds of things that are out there. But the scope of science is very narrow in relation to the full repertoire of concepts a person will have. Consider the realm of psychological disorders. To advance their science, psychiatrists and clinical psychologists need to determine what categories of psychological disorder are to be found in the population. (Their decisions are crucial, since deciding on the existence of these categories of disorder is also of vital importance for putative sufferers if they are to gain access to medical care funded by the state or other agencies.)

Early theorists distinguished those conditions that were considered disorders of the nervous system (neuroses) from those that were disorders of thought (psychoses), but this distinction is far from easy to draw, and the term neurosis was dropped from the classification scheme currently in use by the American Psychological Association. The DSM IV-TR, a text revision of the fourth version of the *Diagnostic and Statistical Manual of Mental Disorders* (American Psychiatric Association, 1994) was created by explicitly using prototypical descriptions of the behavioral symptoms associated with each condition. Classification based on theory (largely psychodynamic theory) had been earlier rejected in favor of categorization based on observable indicators (Robins and Guze 1970). Thus, for example, the diagnosis of schizophrenia in DSM-IV includes a set of five characteristic symptoms any two of which need to be present over a period of a month for diagnosis to be triggered (unless one symptom is very severe). It is therefore possible for two people in the same category to share no symptoms in common. The question of whether there is a single "real" condition or many different conditions with similar symptoms is left unanswered by the DSM. Only with a better theory of the underlying causes of the problem would such an account be possible.

Within the semantic triangle, we find that in the absence of an understanding of the real nature of the condition (the "things" corner), we fall back on the common usage among experts—the "words" corner of the triangle. The DSM attempts to codify this common usage but acknowledges that the definitions may need to be revised as knowledge advances. In 2013, the fifth edition of DSM appeared, with the declared aim of using neuroscience and genetics to provide a classification that should take more account of causal etiology and depend less on clusters of symptoms (Kupfer and Regier 2011). Many patients were consequently concerned to discover whether their former condition still existed in the new classification scheme.

In medicine, because a cure is best achieved by identifying the cause of an illness (for example, a virus or other infection), "real" conditions are often understood as those with a single cause, in keeping with psychological evidence that people in categorization experiments in the laboratory will place greater weight on causal properties than on effects (Ahn et al. 2000). Thus malaria is an infection by the *Plasmodium* parasite. Having the symptoms without this infection is not a case of malaria. There is a single necessary and sufficient criterion.

However, a medical category can also be defined by properties that are further along the causal chain. Primary hypertension is the condition of raised blood pressure and is attributable to a combination of different causal factors that converge on the same effect. Given a diagnosis of hypertension, further effects and symptoms can be predicted, so the conceptual category still provides predictive value. Hypertension is not itself diagnosed on the basis of a single cause, but as a category, it exists at an intermediate level, providing an explanation of further medical problems.

On the other hand, a diagnosis of arthritis refers to a condition of inflammation in the joints and can have over one hundred different causes and related treatments. Diagnosis of arthritis therefore carries almost no information beyond its presenting symptom of persisting joint pain. It is at the end of the causal chain.

What can be learned about how concepts are defined from these examples? Medics have found a need for conceptual categories at all levels of causal depth. While real-world categories with common primary causes provide the most useful source of concepts, there are also categories that are defined at intermediate levels in the causal path, or even just in terms of their effects. Although it is possible to be wrong about a diagnosis of malaria, it seems highly implausible that a doctor could be wrong about a diagnosis of arthritis. Having the concept of arthritis is just a matter of knowing how to apply the word.

In sum, the concepts that evolve within fields such as psychiatry and medical sciences generally have to serve many purposes. They can be pinned to the cause or etiology of a condition, they can be pinned to intermediate changes in physiology that have negative consequences, or they can refer to those consequences themselves. The selective pressures that lead to particular concepts becoming established must be a complex interaction of their real-world status as providing explanatory and predictive potential and their communicative value in describing cases to expert and nonexpert audiences. For concepts fixed to deep causal principles in the real world, we could all be wrong—for example, schizophrenia may turn out to have no single cause or theory to explain it. But for concepts fixed by language use, we cannot all be wrong. It could not turn out that no doctors had really been using the word *arthritis* correctly.

23.6   Fixing Conceptual Contents by Explicit Definition

In what other ways are individual concept users constrained in the way they represent concepts? A third way of fixing meaning is by explicit definition. Concepts of this kind conform to what Smith and Medin (1981) called the classical model of concepts. For example, a bank note is a piece of paper that has a particular origin in a particular place of manufacture (e.g., a central bank or mint). One can specify the precise conditions of whether something belongs to this class. Indeed it is vitally important economically to be able to do so. The distinction between valid and invalid currency absolutely requires an explicit definition if people are to have faith in it. The construction of categorization schemes such as the DSM described above seeks to provide explicit operational definitions for psychiatric conditions.

To take another practical application, when lawmakers create a new law, they have to provide definitions of concepts in a way that can be applied by the courts. When jurors in the UK have to judge the evidence concerning a charge of receiving stolen goods, the judge instructs them that the offense requires three things to be established beyond reasonable doubt. The accused must have received the goods, those same goods must have been previously stolen, and the accused must have had knowledge at the time they were received that the goods were stolen.

This is not to say that courts do not have to make difficult decisions about the meaning of concepts enshrined in the law. In fact, Endicott (2000) argues that vagueness is a necessary feature of the law, given the need to allow judges discretion to take into account all the possible circumstances in any given case. Explicit definitions do not preclude difficult decisions, and lawyers spend many happy and lucrative hours trying to persuade the courts of the interpretation that best suits their clients. But one function of civil society has been to provide explicit definitions for concepts that were originally based on social consensus about typical exemplars. Once these definitions are in place, then we have a third means of ensuring that people are talking about the same thing. The individual who accepts the rule of law thereby accepts the way in which the law defines particular concepts.

As a final example, stipulation of definitions can also be found in the physical sciences. In 2006, following a period of consultation, the International Astronomical Union created by a vote of its general assembly a new classification of large objects orbiting the sun, by which Pluto was "demoted" to the status of a dwarf planet. The types of argument and debate around this controversial move make for fascinating reading for those interested in concepts, and how the choice of particular definitions affects the practice of science (Messeri 2010).

23.7   Fixing Concepts by Their Mental Representation

The discussion so far has focused on two sources of conceptual content. There is the real nature of the world and the kinds that are found there, and there is the existence of socially coordinated terms in language that require individuals to adapt their concepts according to word use, including socially stipulated definitions of concepts provided by those in a position of authority to centralize and regulate this process of coordination.

What, then, of the last corner of the triangle—the idea of concepts as mental representations of kinds? We have seen how the problems of error and disagreement make it difficult to fix meaning in terms of thoughts. One can also see, however, that only through concepts' appearance in thoughts themselves do we know anything at all about concepts. So one notion of *concept* that can be defended is that one cannot have concepts without people to conceive of them.

The right way to understand this corner is as the place where the other two sources of constraint come together. I doubt that there are concepts that exist in our minds that are tied neither to real classes in the world nor to the classes resulting from learning how others use words to label things. But the last corner of "thoughts" is in a way the most interesting, both psychologically and philosophically. It is in how our minds come to represent concepts that we must look to explain how people think, communicate, and understand the world.

As I discuss in Hampton (2012), we have learned a great deal about concepts from looking at how individuals think and reason. In everyday cognition, people categorize the world according to prototype similarity, and this leads to errors in reasoning. In that paper, I review a range of examples to illustrate this point. One example is the well-known conjunction fallacy reported by Tversky and Kahneman (1983). They showed that when judging the probability that some individual is in a given class, people do not use the logic of sets and class inclusion, but instead turn to judgments based on similarity and representativeness. Tversky and Kahneman called this type of reasoning "intuitive." Here I will briefly discuss an example of this intuitive mode of thought, based on recent research I have conducted with Martin Jönsson and Alessia Passanisi (Jönsson and Hampton 2006, 2012; Hampton, Passanisi. and Jönsson 2011).

Our research was triggered by an effect discovered by Connolly and colleagues (2007). They asked people to judge how likely it was that certain sentences were true. Among their sentences were some simple generic statements such as "ravens are black," and others in which the same statements had modified subject nouns, as in "feathered ravens are black" or "jungle ravens are black." They observed that when the subject noun was modified, ratings of likelihood decreased relative to the unmodified forms. Moreover, the effect was larger if the modifier was atypical (as in jungle ravens) than typical (as in feathered ravens). Connolly and colleagues used this effect to argue that the view of concepts as prototypes is incorrect. We were naturally concerned, therefore, to explore the underlying basis of the phenomenon.

In Jönsson and Hampton (2012), we replicated the effect and explored people's explanations for choosing the unmodified sentence as more likely. Primary reasons were based on pragmatic considerations of trying to be maximally informative and knowledge-based reasons of imagining a scenario in which the modifier would affect the property (for example, that jungle ravens might be camouflaged for jungle living). We concluded that, contrary to the argument advance in Connolly et al., most of the time people do in fact assume that a modified concept will inherit the properties of its unmodified parent concept.

Following from this study, we ran a study considering what would happen to the likelihood of modified and unmodified statements when they were expressed as universally quantified—"all ravens are black" versus "all jungle ravens are black" (Jönsson and Hampton 2006, which actually appeared before the Connolly et al. paper because of publication lag). In this situation, a rational answer should not allow that it is possible for a property to be true of a whole class if it is not also true of a subclass. If jungle ravens are not all black, then clearly it cannot be true that all ravens are black. However, our participants continued to rate the unmodified version of the statement as more likely to be true—just as if the universal quantifier had not been present. Similar results showing that people ignore the logical implications of universal quantification have been reported by Leslie, Khemlani, and Glucksberg (2011) in what they term the generic overgeneralization effect. In their studies, participants judged sentences like "All ducks lay eggs" to be true despite the experimenters' best efforts to remind them that male ducks do not lay eggs.

From these two examples, we can see that mental logic works in a different fashion from the logic that one would use when defining actual classes in the world. If conceptual contents are fixed by reference to real-world classes, then the logic of real-world classes should equally apply to conceptual contents as we represent them. Logics (including fuzzy logics—see Hampton 2011) provide a poor model of how people reason conceptually. For a psychological theory of concepts and conceptual thinking, we must be able to explain people's behavior as well as people's idealized competence. The parallel with other forms of reasoning is a good one. While the "words" and "things" corners of the triangle are concerned with ensuring correct or accurate conceptual frameworks, the "thoughts" corner provides us with insight into the messy heuristics that underlie actual behavior.

23.8   Conclusion

In this chapter, I have considered three approaches to fixing conceptual meaning, and it should be clear that there is no one right approach. The example of snakes and people's mistaken beliefs about them shows how people's mental representation of concepts can be in error. To explain how we can have incorrect conceptions, we have to be willing to let the real world be the arbiter of the meaning of our concepts. On the other hand, there are equally clear cases where it is not the physical world but rather the social world that fixes concepts—either through informal coordination among speakers of a language, or through the social power structures that permit particular bodies to stipulate how words and concepts should be defined. It is hard to escape the view that the fixation of conceptual meaning has more than one source. Rather than seeing this as an indication of heterogeneity or plurality of concepts, I would argue that the different sources actually come together and are integrated in our mental representation of the concepts. Possessing a concept, in the "thoughts" corner of the triangle, is a matter of building a schematic or prototypic representation of a concept that will be tied to the real world, to the use of language, and to the social constructions of one's society. Many of the most important social and moral issues of the day, be it abortion, drugs legislation, same-sex marriage, mental disorders, or human rights, are debates about concepts. Is an embryo a human being? Can one define a category of dangerous substances that includes cannabis but excludes alcohol? Is it a defining feature of the concept of marriage that it should be between a man and a woman? Is sexual fetishism a mental disorder? The list of such debates is extensive, and an understanding of both the social influences on how concepts are negotiated and the psychological barriers to conceptual change are central to understanding the debates as they evolve.

23.9   Future Directions

Concepts provide an exciting area in which all the cognitive sciences—particularly philosophy, psychology, social anthropology, and linguistics—can develop useful and mutually enlightening collaborations. It is important for researchers to recognize that there is no single answer to the question of what concepts are, or where their meanings reside. There are a variety of concepts, some clearly grounded in physical reality, while others are grounded in culture and language. The mind itself has been shown to have different systems for categorization, involving both rules and similarity and associations (Ashby et al. 1998). All interested parties need to expand the range and variety of the concepts that they use in their thought experiments, their linguistic analyses, and their behavioral experiments. Often the literatures have failed to engage with each other because of an insufficiently broad view of the range of different concepts that humans possess. For this reason, the development of experimental philosophy as a discipline is to be welcomed. Not only is it valuable to test and explore the intuitions underlying different philosophical positions, but the very act of conducting empirical tests leads to interesting reflection and debate on the value of the evidence. A philosophical argument that is based on the philosopher's clear intuition that in circumstances Y, people would think X, is clearly open to empirical test by placing people in circumstances Y and measuring what they think. This suggestion can be countered, however, with the argument that we should not be doing philosophy by conducting opinion surveys. The correct answer is not necessarily the one that attracts the largest endorsement. So some important work needs to be done to develop better guidelines on just which questions can be settled by behavioral experiment, and which should be answered by rational argument.

Acknowledgments

This chapter benefited greatly from discussion at an ESF-funded Eurounderstanding Symposium held at the London meeting of the European Society for Philosophy and Psychology, August 2012. I have also to acknowledge my great debt to my colleague Martin Jönsson, who has tried valiantly to sharpen my philosophical instincts.

References

Ahn, W. K., N. S. Kim, M. E. Lassaline, and M. J. Dennis. 2000. Causal status as a determinant of feature centrality. *Cognitive Psychology* 41:361–416.

American Psychiatric Association. 1994. *Diagnostic and Statistical Manual of Mental Disorders*. 4th ed. Washington, DC: APA Publications.

Ashby, F. G., L. A. Alfonso-Reese, A. U. Turken, and E. M. Waldron. 1998. A neuropsychological theory of multiple systems in category learning. *Psychological Review* 105:442–481.

Bloom, P. 1998. Theories of artefact categorization. *Cognition* 66:87–93.

Bourne, L. E., Jr., and F. Restle. 1959. Mathematical theory of concept identification. *Psychological Review* 66:278–296.

Bruner, J. S., J. J. Goodnow, and G. A. Austin. 1956. *A Study of Thinking*. New York: Wiley.

Connolly, A., J. A. Fodor, L. R. Gleitman, and H. Gleitman. 2007. Why stereotypes don't even make good defaults. *Cognition* 103:1–22.

Dove, G. 2009. Beyond perceptual symbols: A call for representational pluralism. *Cognition* 110:412–431.

Dupré, J. 1999. Are whales fish? In *Folkbiology*, ed. D. L. Medin and S. Atran, 461–476. Cambridge, MA: MIT Press.

Endicott, T. 2000. *Vagueness in the Law*. Oxford: Oxford University Press.

Fisher, P., J. Wood, and T. Cheng. 2004. Where is Helvellyn? Fuzziness of multi-scale landscape morphometry. *Transactions of the Institute of British Geographers* (29): 106–128.

Fodor, J. A. 1998. *Concepts: Where Cognitive Science Went Wrong*. Oxford: Clarendon Press.

Gelman, S. A. 2003. *The Essential Child: Origins of Essentialism in Everyday Thought*. Oxford: Oxford University Press.

Gelman, S. A., J. D. Coley, and G. M. Gottfried. 1994. Essentialist beliefs in children: The acquisition of concepts and theories. In *Mapping the Mind: Domain Specificity in Cognition and Culture*, ed. L. A. Hirschfeld and S. A. Gelman, 341–365. Cambridge: Cambridge University Press.

Hampton, J. A. 1995. Testing the prototype theory of concepts. *Journal of Memory and Language* 34:686–708.

Hampton, J. A. 2006. Concepts as prototypes. In *The Psychology of Learning and Motivation: Advances in Research and Theory*, vol. 46. ed. B. H. Ross, 79–113. London: Academic Press.

Hampton, J. A. 2011. Concepts and natural language. In *Concepts and Fuzzy Logic*, ed. R. Belohlavek and G. J. Klir, 233–258. Cambridge, MA: MIT Press.

Hampton, J. A. 2012. Thinking intuitively: The rich (and at times illogical) world of concepts. *Current Directions in Psychological Science* 21 (6): 398–402.

Hampton, J. A., A. Passanisi, and M. L. Jönsson. 2011. The modifier effect and property mutability. *Journal of Memory and Language* 64:233–248.

Hampton, J. A., G. Storms, C. L. Simmons, and D. Heussen. 2009. Feature integration in natural language concepts. *Memory & Cognition* 37 (8): 1150–1163.

Jönsson, M. L., and J. A. Hampton. 2006. The inverse conjunction fallacy. *Journal of Memory and Language* 55:317–334.

Jönsson, M. L., and J. A. Hampton. 2012. The modifier effect in within-category induction: Default inheritance in complex noun phrases. *Language and Cognitive Processes* 27:90–116.

Kahneman, D., P. Slovic, and A. Tversky. 1982. *Judgment Under Uncertainty: Heuristics and Biases*. Cambridge: Cambridge University Press.

Keil, F. C., and N. Batterman. 1984. A characteristic-to-defining shift in the development of word meaning. *Journal of Verbal Learning and Verbal Behavior* 23:221–236.

Kuhn, T. S. 1962. *The Structure of Scientific Revolutions*. Chicago: University of Chicago Press.

Kupfer, D. J., and D. A. Regier. 2011. Neuroscience, clinical evidence, and the future of psychiatric classification in DSM-5. *American Journal of Psychiatry* 168:672–674.

Leslie, S., S. Khemlani, and S. Glucksberg. 2011. Do all ducks lay eggs? The generic overgeneralization effect. *Journal of Memory and Language* 65:15–31.

Lupyan, G. 2013. The difficulties in executing simple algorithms: Why brains make mistakes computers don't. *Cognition* 129:615–636.

Machery, E. 2009. *Doing Without Concepts*. New York: Oxford University Press.

Malt, B. C., and E. C. Johnson. 1992. Do artifact concepts have cores? *Journal of Memory and Language* 31:195–217.

Malt, B. C., and S. A. Sloman. 2003. Artifacts are not ascribed essences, nor are they treated as belonging to kinds. In *Conceptual Representation*, ed. H. E. Moss and J. A. Hampton, 563–582. Hove: Psychology Press.

Malt, B. C., S. A. Sloman, S. Gennari, M. Shi, and Y. Wang. 1999. Knowing versus naming: Similarity and the linguistic categorization of artifacts. *Journal of Memory and Language* 40:230–262.

Mayr, E. 1982. *The Growth of Biological Thought: Diversity, Evolution, and Inheritance*. Cambridge, MA: Harvard University Press.

Melville, H. 1851. *Moby-Dick; Or, The Whale*. http://www.gutenberg.org/ebooks/2701.

Messeri, L. R. 2010. The problem with Pluto: Conflicting cosmologies and the classification of planets. *Social Studies of Science* 40:187–214.

Miller, G. A., and P. N. Johnson-Laird. 1976. *Language and Perception*. Cambridge, MA: Harvard University Press.

Murphy, G. L., and D. L. Medin. 1985. The role of theories in conceptual coherence. *Psychological Review* 92:289–316.

Ogden, C. K., and I. A. Richards. 1923. *The Meaning of Meaning: A Study of the Influence of Language upon Thought and of the Science of Symbolism*. New York: Harcourt Brace Jovanovich.

Osherson, D. N., and E. E. Smith. 1981. On the adequacy of prototype theory as a theory of concepts. *Cognition* 11:35–58.

Piaget, J. 1953. *The Origin of Intelligence in the Child*. London: Routledge and Kegan Paul.

Putnam, H. 1975. The meaning of "meaning." In *Language, Mind, and Knowledge*, vol. 2, ed. K. Gunderson, 131–193. Minneapolis: University of Minnesota Press.

Rehder, B. 2003. Categorization as causal reasoning. *Cognitive Science* 27:709–748.

Rey, G. 1983. Concepts and stereotypes. *Cognition* 15:237–262.

Rips, L. J. 1989. Similarity, typicality and categorization. In *Similarity and Analogical Reasoning*, ed. S. Vosniadou and A. Ortony, 21–59. Cambridge: Cambridge University Press.

Robins, E., and S. B. Guze. 1970. Establishment of diagnostic validity in psychiatric illness: Its application to schizophrenia. *American Journal of Psychiatry* 126:983–987.

Rosch, E. R., and C. B. Mervis. 1975. Family resemblances: Studies in the internal structure of categories. *Cognitive Psychology* 7:573–605.

Rosch, E. R. 1975. Cognitive representations of semantic categories. *Journal of Experimental Psychology. General* 104:192–232.

Satlow, E., and N. Newcombe. 1998. When is a triangle not a triangle? Young children's developing concepts of geometric shape. *Cognitive Development* 13:547–559.

Smith, E. E., and D. L. Medin. 1981. *Categories and Concepts*. Cambridge, MA: Harvard University Press.

Smith, E. E., E. J. Shoben, and L. J. Rips. 1974. Structure and process in semantic Memory: A featural model for semantic decisions. *Psychological Review* 81:214–241.

Tversky, A., and D. Kahneman. 1983. Extensional versus intuitive reasoning: The conjunction fallacy in probability judgment. *Psychological Review* 90:293–315.

Wason, P. C. 1960. On the failure to eliminate hypotheses in a conceptual task. *Quarterly Journal of Experimental Psychology* 12:129–140.

Weiskopf, D. 2009. The plurality of concepts. *Synthese* 169:145–173.

Wikforss, A. M. 2005. Naming natural kinds. *Synthese* 145:65–87.

Williamson, T. 1994. *Vagueness*. London: Routledge.

24 Grounding Concepts

Frank C. Keil and Jonathan F. Kominsky

24.1 Introduction

Concepts are often described either as (1) "the smallest units of thought" (Fodor 1998) or as (2) those mental entities that enable us to identify categories and kinds and to think about those categories and their relationships to other categories. Both descriptions capture much of what cognitive scientists mean when they talk about concepts, but as the two views have matured, they have also created a tension that can make it difficult to know how concepts could actually function, especially in the minds of young children. The goal in this chapter is to illustrate the tension in more detail and then explore one way of defusing that tension and putting forth a view of concepts that is both developmentally plausible and able to account for the powerful ways in which concepts are used by adults.

24.2 Efficient Units of Thought

If concepts are truly to be the most essential units of thought, it would seem that they must be able to be used both efficiently and stably. Thus, concepts, as manifested through words, must be processed at rates compatible with both producing and understanding speech and the reading of text. When a reader seems to fully comprehend a text at three hundred words a minute, how are hundreds of concepts accessed, deployed, and interrelated each minute? Similar questions arise when individuals rapidly identify members of categories, interpret metaphors, combine concepts into larger meanings, and grasp a new concept taught by another. From this point of view, concepts should function like robust atoms in a dynamic "chemical" system that rapidly forms and re-forms compounds. One of their great virtues would seem to be their rapid deployment across a wide range of tasks.

There must be something about such an account that has merit. We can identify, refer to, and think about large numbers of individual entities and kinds in rapid succession, whether it be in a conversation, simply driving through heavy traffic, or reading a long string of emails. Yet, for concepts to work in this way, they must impose a very low cognitive load and not require much inferential machinery in real time. It would not be possible to deploy concepts so quickly and effortlessly if they required extensive processing of an elaborate web of beliefs.

One alternative is to say that we are not really using concepts as such in these speeded events. But that alternative runs counter to intuitions that when one mentions a dog in rapid conversation or thinks reflectively about a dog at length, one is working with the same mental entity. A more plausible alternative is that we somehow manage to use an abbreviated or compressed version of full-fledged concepts in daily discourse, versions that do all the work needed in real time. Perhaps just as a teenage texter conveys paragraphs in much smaller spaces, rapidly used concepts adopt similar "shorthand."

These sorts of considerations, among several others, may be related to attempts to eviscerate concepts of their content, the best known case being Fodor's *Concepts: Where Cognitive Science Went Wrong* (1998). Fodor grants that we mostly successfully "lock onto" entities using our concepts, but perhaps all the rich connotations that we associate with concepts are really ephemera that are not part of the concept itself. Because Fodor did not focus on real-time processing constraints for concepts, his views do not carry strong implications for the need to have minimalist cognitive structures in concept use; but if there were ways to use concepts rapidly in everyday tasks, a minimalist view of their internal structure would certainly be compatible with attempts to reduce the processing burdens that they impose.

24.3   Vehicles for Detecting and Reasoning about Kinds

A different tradition of scholarship on concepts comes to a starkly contrasting conclusion. It confronts a range of phenomena associated with concept use that seem to imply rich, belief-laden mental structures. Indeed, those structures often seem to have the hallmarks of coherent, theory-like, explanatory belief systems, where causal relations especially can be central. Consider in particular arguments based on categorization behavior, conceptual change, and conceptual interdependency.

At the least, our concepts are heavily influenced by the frequencies with which features occur and co-occur. These frequency-based patterns were the source of an immense literature and many debates in the early cognitive science community. There are well-trodden controversies over whether such information implicated representations that were based on prototypes, exemplars, dimensionalized representations, or some combination of all of these (Smith and Medin 1981). These debates were not clearly resolved, as refinements of each set of models led to great difficulties in deciding which view accounted for the data better and whether there might be better fits of some models with certain domains of concepts and other models with different domains. But the controversy soon became overshadowed by the *concepts-in-theories* argument.

There are several ways in which people override mere typicality or correlation in making judgments about category membership or reasoning about categories as a whole. These judgments seem to be influenced by the ways in which concepts are embedded in theory-like representations, with the differences between individual concepts being a function of how each concept is positioned in a "web of belief" (Quine and Ullian 1978). This concepts-in-theories view sees concepts as inextricable parts of large-scale explanatory systems that are typically full of causal relations, systems that heavily influence concept use. Thus, people can make category judgments that defy mere feature frequencies or correlations (Murphy and Medin 1985; Murphy and Allopenna 1994). For example, a certain child may observe more dogs that have collars than dogs that have four limbs and two ears, yet no adult or child will ever cite collars in dog categorization more than anatomical features such as legs. Moreover, people show such effects both when explicitly learning concepts and when building them up implicitly outside of awareness (Ziori and Dienes 2008); thus, the theory influence does not seem to be a conscious strategy. Similarly, if a particular correlation is expected by theoretical biases to be associated with a category, people can see illusory correlations as supporting category membership and miss other correlations that do not fit with available theories (Murphy 2002). Such theory-like infrastructures for concepts are also argued to be very early emerging, perhaps even in infancy (Gopnik and Meltzoff 1997; Gopnik and Wellman 1992).

Conceptual change is another phenomenon that seems to be intimately connected to intuitive theories. Whenever concepts change, they tend to change in terms of interconnected clusters (Carey 1985, 2009; Keil 1989; Thagard 1992). For example, in development, when a child's understanding of a particular term in a domain shifts in meaning, many others concepts in the same domain (e.g., kinship terms, cooking terms, moral terms, etc.) show comparable shifts in meaning at roughly same time (Keil 1989). Similar claims have been made for how children's concepts of weight seem to change at the same time as those of density, and heat at roughly the same time as temperature (Smith, Carey, and Wiser 1985; Wiser and Carey 1983). In the history of science, there are many other cases where a whole system of closely interrelated concepts seems to change as unit (Thagard 1992). All of these examples strongly suggest that concepts are deriving a major part of their meanings from how they are situated in larger systems of beliefs that often contain causal explanations of their properties in terms of other concepts.

In addition to empirical demonstrations of concepts shifting as interdependent clusters with other concepts, there are situations that seem to analytically make the same case, where concepts seem to be completely conceptually interdependent on other ones. For example, how can one have concepts of nut without also having a concept of a bolt? The threads on one would seem to demand an understanding of the presence of another unit with complementary threads. The same argument applies to keys and locks as well as to other concepts that seem necessarily related to others (FATHER-CHILD, BUY-SELL, TALL-SHORT, etc.). Such cases do not seem to fit with accounts of concepts as autonomous atoms each capable of existing in complete isolation from all others. Moreover, they are not necessarily just binary pairs. Thus, FATHER seems necessarily linked not just to the concept CHILD but also to that of MOTHER.

In broader terms, we seem driven to make sense of why features occur and co-occur, and much of the time, this is done through appeal to causal explanations. If two features co-occur equally often with instances of a category, we favor those that fit with what seems to be a naïve theory of why entities in a category have the properties they do (Heit 2000; Proffitt, Coley, and Medin 2000; Wisniewski and Medin 1994). Moreover, such explanation-based preferences appear very early in development (Carey 2009; Hayes and Thompson 2007). This is not to ignore substantial influences of frequency-based information as well (e.g., Hampton 2010; Hampton et al. 2009; Rogers and McClelland 2004) and the ways in which frequency-based information may be more influential in some domains (such as living kinds) than for others (such as artifacts). These considerations only serve to make concepts even more richly articulated potential hybrids of theory-like beliefs and associative complexes.

24.4   Troubles with Theories

Three classes of problems arise, however, with the idea that concepts are embedded in theories: (1) such accounts are difficult to fit with ideas of concepts as efficient units of rapid thought, (2) a closer look at the stuff of theories raises profound questions about how much work they can actually do, and (3) it may be especially hard to grasp these limitations.

The first problem arises from the tension described at the beginning of this chapter. How is it possible to deploy concepts so rapidly and efficiently if they work by interpreting a connected series of relations in an intuitive theory? When one hears the word *car* in a rapid conversation, how is it possible to access all the causal relations that categorization studies show as influencing categorization decisions about cars? Thus, to comprehend a fleeting mention of car, must one realize that cars are kinds of artifacts that serve as vehicles; that they involve engineering tradeoffs between comfort, durability, speed, and safety; or that they are organized into subtypes such as sports cars, limos, and minivans, each with coherent bodies of features? All these factors can influence categorization decisions, yet they seem to get in the way of efficient use. It isn't possible to rapidly access all this information in depth, yet it seems intrinsic to such concepts when they are considered in depth.

A natural response is that we somehow prune the complex, theory-laden structure in a manner that is just good enough to serve in rapid conversation, but there are no obvious heuristics for undertaking such pruning operations. It is tempting to employ some version of the two-systems theory so common in judgment and decision making, where fast and slow processes are in play (Kahneman 2011); but those systems usually are thought to exist as distinct modes of thought that are often in competition with each other. If the two-systems model were to work fully for concepts, there should be two different bases for concepts, which runs against intuitions that we are working with the same entity in both cases.

The second problem is that typical intuitive theories do not seem to have much content and may therefore be surprisingly different from what we might think in terms of how theories should be mentally instantiated. Thus, except for narrow areas of expertise, people tend to have extremely sparse causal explanatory accounts of category features. Ask most people to explain, for example, why dogs bark or wag their tails and they will have only minimal additional information to provide. When researchers talk about a person having a "theory" of mind, that theory often is not much more than granting that individuals have beliefs and desires, and that one's beliefs can influences one's desires and therefore one's actions. There are, of course, many more local fragments we might use in our reasoning about the minds of others (e.g., intuitive beliefs that prolonged anxiety can cause depression or that our desires can distort our beliefs), but these fragments are not connected together in a coherent theory and instead are more isolated relations that we usually cannot justify further. For a young child, the total theory of mind may be little more than three nodes and a few links between them (Wellman and Gelman 1992). Similarly, early folk biology may be little more than the beliefs that living things have vital forces, that those forces enable an organism to move, and, if there is force left over, that those forces can also enable an organism to grow (Inagaki and Hatano 2002). If such sketchy accounts are the stuff of theories, they hardly seem enough to serve as a basis for explaining the features that are associated with members of such categories as animals or personality traits. Fragments have also been extensively discussed in the case of naïve physics, where there may be a large number of such units that coexist without any of the connective tissue that would seem to be the hallmark of a theory (DiSessa 1993; DiSessa, Gillespie, and Esterly 2004).

Finally, the problem is amplified by a blindness about our own ignorance as well as about the depth of knowledge in other minds. One facet of this blindness is an "illusion of explanatory depth," in which people tend to think they have much richer and more elaborated explanatory structures of how things work than they really do (Rozenblit and Keil 2002). As a consequence, they are often unaware of the large gaps in their own understandings. This illusion is substantially larger in young children (Mills and Keil 2004) and can be found not just for explanatory understandings of devices and biological systems but also of political explanations (Alter, Oppenheimer, and Zemla

2010; Fernbach et al., 2013). People can also have illusions of insight, namely that they have gained a powerful new explanatory account of some phenomena, when in fact they have learned nothing and have only been fooled by certain lures. For example, when given explanations of behavior in which completely uninformative brain scans are mentioned, most adults will feel that they have gained more insight into the behavior than when no brain scans are mentioned (Weisberg et al. 2008).

In short, naïve theories are strikingly empty in the minds of most individuals, who are often unaware of their own theoretical shortcomings. In addition, when they do have fragments of theories, they are often full of unrecognized contradictions (Chin and Brewer 1993). For example, most adults will endorse the statement that animal species have fixed essences that define their nature while endorsing the idea of incremental evolution through natural selection (Shtulman and Schulz 2008). But these two beliefs are in fact incommensurable, as natural selection can only work if a species is understood as a distribution of traits instead of a fixed set that is common to all members of a category. Such examples are commonplace. To use another example in the moral realm, people will endorse both the idea that human behavior occurs because of causal determinism without free will and also the idea that people are morally responsible for their actions (Nahmias, Coates, and Kvaran 2007). Although some philosophers would argue that the moral "contradiction" is only an illusory contradiction arising from a philosophical mistake, it does seem clear that most laypeople will talk about moral behavior in ways that do reveal their own naïve beliefs as being contradictory.

24.5   Misplaced Meanings

It may be possible to reconcile these different facets of concepts by rethinking the nature of the explanatory component of concepts. We have argued that we need to understand how we can rapidly access concepts for daily use in discourse yet also accommodate the ways in which explanatory causal relations heavily influence category judgments, and at the same time acknowledge that people's theories are remarkably impoverished. The reconciliation relies on the now classic formulation by Hilary Putnam that meanings are not in the head (Putnam 1975). Thus, there may often in fact be well-articulated and coherent theories of the sort that could explain many of the features of kinds and clarify why two equally frequent features may nonetheless vary enormously in terms of their conceptual centrality because only one is at the heart of understanding the category. We may feel quite strongly that a cow's grazing behavior is more central to understanding what cows are than its behavior around tractors, yet be largely inarticulate as to why. The reason may be that we do, in a sense, know a good deal more about cows, but only through links to other, more expert minds. Our mistake is to assume that this knowledge in other minds is in fact in our own minds. This way of grounding concepts through deference has been systematically formulated in an account of *sustaining mechanisms* developed by Laurence and Margolis (Laurence and Margolis 2002; Margolis and Laurence 2003). They define such mechanisms as mental processes that enable concepts to lock onto specific classes of things and consider types of sustaining mechanisms: (1) Those based on an individual's theories, (2) those arising from probabilistic tabulations of features, and (3) those that work through deference to experts. Our focus here is on deference and follows the argument that sustaining mechanisms are part of the concept proper. Margolis and Laurence are careful not to equate learning sustaining mechanisms with learning concepts (Margolis and Laurence 2011). Such mechanisms, however, plus the more extended representations they lock into in other expert minds, may be thought of as essential parts of each layperson's concepts.

The special role of deference, often engaged in tacitly rather than explicitly, may be heavily underestimated, as is the cognitive apparatus that makes deference work. This discounting of deference may be a consequence of an *individualism bias,* in which we assume we are far more autonomous creators of our concepts than we really are (Gelfert 2011). Yet deference may be where the most extensive grounding of our concepts occurs. In addition, those illusions of explanatory depth and explanatory insights may in fact represent useful cues that a particular kind of knowledge is "known" in a broader sense and does ground one's concepts. The illusions may therefore conveniently spare us from actually knowing more than we really need to know. In addition, in contrast to our woefully inadequate mechanistic theories, we may be far more adept than we realize at these other cognitive processes related to grounding of our concepts through access to other minds.

Some of the ways we defer without knowing may be seen in what we call a *misplaced meaning* effect. This pattern occurs when people think that they personally know critical features that can tell apart two related concepts, when in fact they only know such features through deference. One method for exploring this is to ask people to estimate how many features they think they know that can distinguish members of category pairs. In our lab, we have done this with three kinds of pairs called *knowns, unknowns,* and *synonyms.* Knowns were pairs of closely related categories where pretesting in an unrestricted time task revealed that adults consistently knew several features that could distinguish members of these categories, for example, moth/butterfly, dog/wolf and rowboat/canoe. Unknowns were pairs of closely related categories for which pretesting through the same unrestricted time task revealed that adults knew hardly any features that could distinguish them, for example, ferret/weasel, cucumber/zucchini, and shrew/mole. Synonyms were drawn from dictionaries that classified them as having few or no feature differences. Such pairs included baby/infant, sofa/couch, and car/automobile.

In this unspeeded task, adults provided as few differences for unknown pairs as exist for synonyms (i.e., virtually none). In this sense, their knowledge of specific differences for unknown and synonym pairs is identical, while known pairs are distinct. But very different judgments emerge in a speeded task where people are asked to quickly judge how many features they know that distinguish members of such pairs. Here, they guess that they could list roughly the same number of discriminating features for the knowns and unknowns while guessing that they could list none for the synonyms (Kominsky and Keil 2014); yet when later asked to actually list the features, they performed as the pretests suggested: they could list a few features for the knowns and almost none for the unknowns. Thus, they seemed to know that there *were* differences for *unknown* pairs, but they also believed that they knew what those differences were, when in fact they did not. Young children show an even more dramatic pattern, giving higher estimates and providing fewer differences for both known and unknown items.

One way to interpret these results is simply to say that people of all ages labor under an illusion of knowing the meanings of various concepts when in fact they do not, but that may be an excessively deflationary interpretation. Instead, people may sense that there are important differences in the meaning of the unknown terms and perhaps even have hunches about the nature of the difference. By this account, people are correctly judging that there are several features, and potentially explanatory accounts, that distinguish such pairs as ferrets and weasels or shrews and moles; they have just mislocated where that information is actually stored. Indeed, the sense that a great deal of knowledge exists to be accessed seems to increase the severity of the illusion effect. In a follow-up experiment, a different set of participants were asked to estimate the number of differences between these pairs that they thought an expert would know. The difference between these estimations of expert knowledge and estimations of possessed knowledge was positively correlated with the size of the illusion effect. In other words, the illusion was strongest with items for which participants expected more information to be available overall (Kominsky and Keil 2014.).

In addition, because in many cases, they can relatively easily access that information, they do "know" the meaning through an easily available pathway to expert sources, a pathway that gets ever more effortless through Internet sources and search engine optimization techniques. However, because very young children show this effect even stronger than older children and adults, the Internet cannot be the root cause of this effect.

The misplaced meaning effect may therefore really be reflecting a useful sense of knowing meanings through deference that is masked by the individualism bias. Assuming that meaning is in one's head may be well worth the value of knowing that the concept can be grounded, or more precisely that it is plausibly the type of concept that can be grounded. That is, one may be correctly inferring that one can successfully refer to a kind, even though that act of referring must by mediated by more sophisticated knowledge in other minds. There may be special cases where this assumption is wrong (i.e., that no experts can fully explain a category contrast), but the assumption seems to grant more benefits than costs.

24.6 Grounding and the Division of Cognitive Labor

It is not yet fully clear what each individual does need to know to ground his or her concepts via expertise in other minds. There are, however, indications of a sophisticated array of cognitive skills that are present in the minds of children very early on. Many of these skills are related to knowing how to link one's own relatively shallow knowledge with more expert communities. Consider three such skills.

First, one has to have some sense of the terrain of expertise itself, that is, what are the sorts of domains that require expertise as opposed to those that are self-evident. Knowing such a distinction is not incompatible with also having an individualism bias; it simply means that the bias is not so extreme as to rule out some sense of concepts that require more expertise to master than others. By the second grade at least, and possibly earlier, children are capable of judging that there is no need for experts on categories such as "dogs with red collars," but that there may be a need for experts on categories such as "dogs that hunt" (Keil 2010). They therefore realize that there is no internal structure to some categories that would need expert support. Those categories wear their meanings on their sleeves.

In a related manner, adults and children alike also show a surprising degree of consensus on the relative complexity of both artifacts and living kinds. Thus, when asked to rate the complexity a long list of artifacts and biological parts, adults and children older than seven tend to agree very strongly on the rank orderings of complexity (Kominsky, Zamm, and Keil, in prep). They do this even when at the same time, they can say very little about the actual details of that complexity, often not being able to name more than one or two parts.

This ability to extract a sense of complexity may also help explain a curious puzzle that emerges in young children. Even preschool children seem to take a strong interest in mechanism-related information and will often ask questions about mechanisms. In addition, when adult answers do not include mechanisms, the children will continue to ask questions until they receive causal or mechanistic answers (Callanan and Oakes 1992; Frazier, Gelman, and Wellman 2009). Yet, this interest in mechanism seems at first glance to be futile since even adults, let alone children, seem to retain almost no mechanistic information at all about the kinds they query. Their behavior may make more sense, however, if asking about mechanism is understood not as entrenching mechanistic information but rather as a way to learn about a more abstract sense of complexity as well the general kinds of causal relations and property types that are involved. These senses of complexity and more schematic causal patterns may then provide valuable ways of tracking relevant expertise.

Second, one has to have a sense of the kinds of features and relations that are likely to be central to a domain even when one does not know the details. Thus, it is important to know what are plausible expert groundings versus implausible ones based on the kinds of features in play. For example, even though we do not know the difference between ferrets and weasels, we do know that it is much more plausible that the critical features will have to do with their physiology than with their rareness or expense. In a similar way, even five-year-olds prefer experts for novel artifacts who stress shape- and size-related features more than color or number of parts, while not showing such a preference for novel animals (Keil 2010). Thus, children and adults alike seem to have a strong sense of which kinds of features are likely to be causally potent in various domains and use that information to make inferences about the kinds of knowledge that experts in those domains might have.

Third, one needs to have a sense of which expert sources are likely to be good ones. This is where a now large literature shows several distinct ways in which even preschoolers evaluate the credibility of others as reliable sources. For example, preschoolers prefer experts who have not made clear mistakes in prior judgments as well as those whose statements are in agreement with others and not outlier opinions (Harris and Corriveau 2011). In elementary school, children soon come to believe that conflicts of interest are grounds for doubting experts. Thus, they assume that a person's statements might be questionable if those statements are also blatantly self-serving (Mills and Keil 2005). It appears, that from at least three years, children are constantly making judgments about source quality, or expert legitimacy, often on several different dimensions at the same time.

One source of evidence for elaborate cognitive systems that support concept grounding is the ease with which people of all ages make inferences about domains of expertise. For example, if told that a person has deep explanatory understanding of one physical mechanical phenomenon, such as why tops stay up when spinning, even preschoolers will assume that person will be a better consultant on another physical phenomenon, such as how boomerangs work, than a social phenomena, such as why people fight when they are tired (Danovitch and Keil 2004; Keil et al. 2008; Lutz and Keil 2003). Young children frequently solve the division of cognitive labor problem with surprising skill and often by referring to deep underlying causal patterns in the world that correspond to those domains. Those domains are associated with many classical areas of the natural and social sciences, such as physical mechanics, biology, chemistry, and psychology (Danovitch and Keil 2004; Keil et al. 2008; Lutz and Keil 2003). Well before they start formal schooling, children are therefore aware that all adults are not omniscient and instead have local areas of expertise and can be resources to others by virtue of having that expertise. It seems reasonable that they also know, perhaps tacitly, something about the nature of relevant experts for grounding particular concepts.

24.7   Conclusions and Future Directions

The account offered here allows for concepts to have rich cognitive structures with elaborate theory-like underpinnings, but rather than putting all that structure in the mind of a single individual, it sees concepts as usually being sparsely represented in the minds of most individuals but linked through one of Margolis's and Laurence's (2003, 2011) sustaining mechanisms to expert communities. Thus, individuals might override mere correlational information because of hunches about causal explanatory information that trumps mere correlation but largely embrace information as a matter of faith that requires access to outside experts. We all have a sense of the terrain of the division of cognitive labor that occurs in all cultures, and most of our concepts are grounded by connections to various perceived groups.

None of this, however, is infallible. Thus, one might think that a conceptual distinction is grounded when in fact it is not. One might assume that pickles and cucumbers are distinct kinds of plants and assume that difference is grounded in the testimony of relevant biologists and would involve molecular differences between the two, when in fact they are usually the same species with one having undergone additional processing. Similarly, one might assume that pneumonia is a single kind with a single pathogenic basis, when in fact it can arise from very distinct causal agents. The claim here is that people are more often right than wrong in inferring such linkages to the appropriate experts.

Another line of work suggests that people are highly adaptive in minimizing memory loads when they can outsource information (Sparrow, Liu, and Wegner 2011). In a similar manner, we may naturally try to defer and off-load cognitive work whenever we think we can reliably do so and have appropriate access when needed. This practice may be made more salient by the Internet, but it has a much more ancient history. One of the great cognitive benefits of culture is this ability to rely on knowledge in other minds; indeed the ability to do so automatically and efficiently may be a critical component of building cultures with both physical and cognitive divisions of labor.

It is not always easy to tell where the concept proper "ends" and other information associated with, but not essential to, a concept "begins." Thus, even if deference plays a far larger role than intuitions suggest in filling out details associated with concepts, what reasons are there for assuming that the deferential network is part of the concept itself? Moreover if it is, doesn't it lead to a kind of social network holism, in which full conceptual understanding requires traversing countless links in socially networked knowledge so as to fully ground deference? It seems like there must be ways of grounding our concepts through deference, and through hunches about pathways to appropriate areas of expertise, but there must also be heuristics that enable us to have a sense of such networks of support without having to fully traverse them.

If we do successfully defer to the right experts to ground our concepts, how do experts themselves use their more elaborate versions of the same concepts without falling into the lost-in-thought problem? One answer may lie in a form of *precompiling*. Experts presumably not only become experts by virtue of having a richly detailed set of theory-laden beliefs; they also become experts at answering questions based on those beliefs, a skill that could evolve into having packaged responses that have already been thought through and now can be deployed very quickly. We all have had similar experiences when someone asks us about something we have previously considered very deeply; we merely need to access the key conclusions once we are sure we know the question and know that we have thought it through completely. Only when an expert encounters a truly novel question that requires new ways of thinking about their collected body of expertise do we see them often taking much longer than novices to ground a concept.

If deference is a major part of understanding how concepts can both be used quickly but have theory-like features, important questions remain concerning the cognitive representations and processes that support this facet of concepts. In particular, even though deference may mean that we often have virtually no knowledge of specific features that distinguish ferrets from weasels (even though we think we do), we must still know a good deal that is relevant to a concept to defer successfully to the right sources. Our individual concepts cannot be completely empty or there would be no way to know in which direction to defer. How can we best characterize the knowledge that supports successful deference? We have indicated earlier that it must involve the ability to identify causal patterns that are central to a kind and to sense how those patterns are likely to be known by experts. For example, in distinguishing two species of animals that have similar appearances, we may be aware that internal essences are key to distinguishing them, and thus these essences are what experts are sensitive to. Across all the potential kinds of internal essences, we are likely to assume that only a certain subset are plausible as a basis for contrast.

In addition, we have a sense of reasonable scope of expertise, assuming that whatever experts know that helps them distinguish weasels from ferrets is of the same type that enables them to distinguish crows from ravens but is very different from what helps experts tell silver from platinum or diamonds from zirconium. Thus, we may need some abstract sense of the causal patterns that are central to a domain of expertise as well as the size of the domains that have roughly the same kinds of causal patterns as opposed to radically different ones. Spelling out the details of what we need to know and how this knowledge emerges in development is an important future line of work.

There are also questions as to what signs we use as proxies for expertise as opposed to knowing real pathways to expertise. Thus, many speakers of English may not have a sense of how the discipline of biology is organized and what it means to be an expert in terms of academic training; but they may have hunches that within the broad category of living kinds, subcategories such as plants and animals may have different kinds of experts. They may rarely if ever actually try to find out what an expert actually knows and may simply have the strong belief that there are relevant experts who do know and can be counted on. Much work needs to be done to more clearly understand how minimal the knowledge of experts and their disciplines can be and still be effective.

Finally, there are deep questions about cross-cultural variations. Assume for a moment that there are roughly similar kinds of crows in many parts of the world, including in cultures that are still highly isolated and traditional. If one lives in such a culture with no scientists, academic disciplines, or other forms of high expertise, is deference still an important part of concepts for adults in those cultures? It seems plausible that adults in those cultures might have similar concepts to ours about crows, yet if deference chains are parts of those concepts, how could concepts between highly traditional and highly technological cultures be similar? The answer at present is unclear, but one possibility is that even in those most traditional cultures, there might be beliefs in essences and that essences of living kinds are of a fundamentally different kind than those of such things as gold and silver. Perhaps those adults believe there could be experts or attribute more expertise to wise members of their cultures than they should. The finding that very young children believe in experts and map them onto causal patterns gives some reason to believe that such beliefs might even exist in cultures that don't yet really have those experts; but this can only be speculation without careful investigations of this question in diverse cultures. A related question is whether a belief that there could be experts who could tell two kinds apart, even if there aren't any now, somehow still helps to ground our concepts.

In short, the coordinated ways in which concepts change, the ways in which their meanings can be parasitic on each other, and the ways features associated with conceptual categories can be weighted heavily because of their causal explanatory roles, are all explained by the concepts-in-theories view. But if those theories are socially distributed, perhaps concepts are as well. None of this is to minimize the cognitive work done in each individual's mind, as that work involves a complex intersection of skills and knowledge to achieve successful grounding; it just may not be what we intuitively think of as the basis for our concepts.

Acknowledgments

Some of the research reported on in this article was supported by NIH grant #R37HD023922 to F. Keil.

References

Alter, A. L., D. M. Oppenheimer, and J. C. Zemla. 2010. Missing the trees for the forest: A construal level account of the illusion of explanatory depth. *Journal of Personality and Social Psychology* 99 (3): 436–451.

Callanan, M., and L. Oakes. 1992. Preschoolers' questions and parents' explanations: Causal thinking in everyday activity. *Cognitive Development* 7:213–233.

Carey, S. 1985. *Conceptual Change in Childhood*. Cambridge, MA: Bradford Books, MIT.

Carey, S. 2009. *The Origin of Concepts*. New York: Oxford University Press.

Chin, C. A., and W. F. Brewer. 1993. The role of anomalous data in knowledge acquisition: A theoretical framework and implications for science instruction. *Review of Educational Research* 63:1–49.

Danovitch, J., and F. C. Keil. 2004. Should you ask a fisherman or a biologist? Developmental shifts in ways of clustering knowledge. *Child Development* 75:918–931.

di Sessa, A. A. 1993. Toward an epistemology of physics. *Cognition and Instruction* 10:165–255.

di Sessa, A., N. Gillespie, and J. Esterly. 2004. Coherence versus fragmentation in the development of the concept of force. *Cognitive Science* 28:843–900.

Fernbach, P. M., T. Rogers, C. R. Fox, and S. A. Sloman. 2013. Political extremism is supported by an illusion of understanding. *Psychological Science* 24:939-946.

Fodor, J. A. 1998. *Concepts: Where Cognitive Science Went Wrong*. Oxford: Clarendon Press.

Frazier, B. N., S. A. Gelman, and H. M. Wellman. 2009. Preschoolers' search for explanatory information within adult-child conversation. *Child Development* 80:1592–1611.

Gelfert, A. 2011. Expertise, argumentation, and the end of inquiry. *Argumentation* 25:297–312.

Gopnik, A., and A. Meltzoff. 1997. *Words, Thoughts and Theories*. Cambridge, MA: MIT Press.

Gopnik, A., and H. M. Wellman. 1992. Why the child's theory of mind really is a theory. *Mind & Language* 7:145–171.

Hampton, J. A. 2010. Concepts in human adults. In *The Making of Human Concepts*, ed. D. Mareschal, P. Quinn, and S. E. G. Lea, 293–311. Oxford: Oxford University Press.

Hampton, J. A., G. Storms, C. L. Simmons, and D. Heussen. 2009. Feature integration in natural language concepts. *Memory & Cognition* 37:1721–1730.

Harris, P. L., and K. H. Corriveau. 2011. Young children's selective trust in informants. *Proceedings: Biological Sciences* 366:1179–1190.

Hayes, B. K., and S. P. Thompson. 2007. Causal relations and feature similarity in children's inductive reasoning. *Journal of Experimental Psychology: General* 136:470–484.

Heit, E. 2000. Properties of inductive reasoning. *Psychonomic Bulletin & Review* 7:569–592.

Inagaki, K., and G. Hatano. 2002. *Young Children's Naive Thinking about the Biological World*. New York: Psychological Press.

Kahneman, D. 2011. *Thinking, Fast and Slow*. New York: Farrar, Straus and Giroux.

Keil, F. C. 1989. *Concepts, Kinds, and Cognitive Development*. Cambridge, MA: MIT Press.

Keil, F. C. 2010. The feasibility of folk science. *Cognitive Science* 34:826–862.

Keil, F. C., C. Stein, L. Webb, V. D. Billings, and L. Rozenblit. 2008. Discerning the division of cognitive labor: An emerging understanding of how knowledge is clustered in other minds. *Cognitive Science* 38:1604–1633.

Kominsky, J. F., and F. C. Keil. 2014. Overestimation of knowledge about word meanings: The "misplaced meaning" effect. *Cognitive Science* 34:826–862.

Kominsky, J. F., A. Zamm, and F. C. Keil. In preparation. A developing sense of causal complexity.

Laurence, S., and E. Margolis. 2002. Radical concept nativism. *Cognition* 86:22–55.

Lutz, D. J., and F. C. Keil. 2003. Early understandings of the division of cognitive labor. *Child Development* 73:1073–1084.

Margolis, E., and S. Laurence. 2003. Concepts. In *The Blackwell Guide to Philosophy of Mind*, ed. S. Stich and T. Warfield, 190–213. Malden, MA: Blackwell.

Margolis, E., and S. Laurence. 2011. Learning matters: The role of learning in concept acquisition. *Mind & Language* 26:507–539.

Mills, C. M., and F. C. Keil. 2004. Knowing the limits of one's understanding: The development of an awareness of an illusion of explanatory depth. *Journal of Experimental Child Psychology* 87:1–32.

Mills, C. M., and F. C. Keil. 2005. The development of cynicism. *Psychological Science* 16:385–390.

Murphy, G. L. 2002. *The Big Book of Concepts*. Cambridge, MA: MIT Press.

Murphy, G. L., and P. D. Allopenna. 1994. The locus of knowledge effects in concept learning. *Journal of Experimental Psychology: Learning, Memory, and Cognition* 20:904–919.

Murphy, G., and D. Medin. 1985. The role of theories in conceptual coherence. *Psychological Review* 92 (3): 289–316.

Nahmias, E., J. Coates, and T. Kvaran. 2007. Free will, moral responsibility, and mechanism: Experiments on folk intuitions. *Midwest Studies in Philosophy* 31:214–242.

Proffitt, J. B., J. D. Coley, and D. L. Medin. 2000. Expertise and category-based induction. *Journal of Experimental Psychology: Learning, Memory, and Cognition* 26 (4): 811–828.

Putnam, H. 1975. The meaning of "meaning." In *Language, Mind, and Knowledge*, vol. 2, ed. K. Gunderson, 131–193. Minneapolis: University of Minnesota Press.

Quine, W. V. O., and J. S. Ullian. 1978. *The Web of Belief*. New York: Random House.

Rogers, T. T., and J. L. McClelland. 2004. *Semantic Cognition: A Parallel Distributed Processing Approach*. Cambridge, MA: MIT Press.

Rozenblit, L. R., and F. C. Keil. 2002. The misunderstood limits of folk science: An illusion of explanatory depth. *Cognitive Science* 26:521–562.

Shtulman, A., and L. Schulz. 2008. The relation between essentialist beliefs and evolutionary reasoning. *Cognitive Science* 32:1049–1062.

Smith, C., S. Carey, and M. Wiser. 1985. On differentiation: A case study of the development of the concepts of size, weight, and density. *Cognition* 21:177–237.

Smith, E. E., and D. L. Medin. 1981. *Categories and Concepts*. Cambridge, MA: Harvard University Press.

Sparrow, B., J. Liu, and D. M. Wegner. 2011. Google effects on memory: Cognitive consequences of having information at our fingertips. *Science* 333 (6043): 776–778.

Thagard, P. 1992. *Conceptual Revolutions*. Princeton, NJ: Princeton University Press.

Weisberg, D. S., F. C. Keil, J. Goodstein, E. Rawson, and J. Gray. 2008. The seductive allure of neuroscience explanations. *Journal of Cognitive Neuroscience* 20 (3): 470–477.

Wellman, H. M., and S. A. Gelman. 1992. Cognitive development: Foundational theories of core domains. *Annual Review of Psychology* 43:337–375.

Wiser, M., and S. Carey. 1983. When heat and temperature were one. In *Mental Models*, ed. D. Gentner and A. Stevens, 75–98. New York: Academic Press.

Wisniewski, E. J., and D. L. Medin. 1994. On the interaction of theory and data in concept learning. *Cognitive Science* 18:221–281.

Ziori, E., and Z. Dienes. 2008. How does prior knowledge affect implicit and explicit concept learning? *Quarterly Journal of Experimental Psychology* 61:601–624.

Index